CONSTRUCTING
NATURE

CONSTRUCTING NATURE

READINGS FROM THE AMERICAN EXPERIENCE

EDITED BY

RICHARD JENSETH
ST. LAWRENCE UNIVERSITY

EDWARD E. LOTTO
LEHIGH UNIVERSITY

A BLAIR PRESS BOOK

PRENTICE HALL, UPPER SADDLE RIVER, NJ 07458

Library of Congress Cataloging-in-Publication Data

Constructing nature: readings from the American experience / edited by Richard Jenseth,
    Edward E. Lotto.
        p.   cm.
    "A Blair Press book."
    Includes index.
    ISBN 0-13-290875-1 (pbk.)
    1. College readers.   2. Nature in literature—Problems, exercises, etc.   3. Nature—
Literary collections.   4. English language—Rhetoric.   5. American literature.
6. Readers—Nature.
    I. Jenseth, Richard.   II. Lotto, Edward E.
    PE1417.C6519   1996   95–49112
    808'.0427—dc20   CIP

Editorial/production supervision: Lauren Byrne, Editorial Services of New England
Cover director: Jayne Conte
Manufacturing buyer: Bob Anderson
Cover art: *Old Friends*, Winslow Homer, 1894, watercolor, $21\frac{1}{2}''$ X $15\frac{1}{8}''$, Worcester Art
Museum, Massachusetts.

Acknowledgments appear on pages 489–490, which constitute a continuation of the
copyright page.

A Blair Press Book

© 1996 by Prentice-Hall, Inc.
Simon & Schuster/A Viacom Company
Upper Saddle River, NJ 07458

Printed in the United States of America
10   9   8   7   6   5   4   3   2

ISBN 0-13-290875-1

Prentice-Hall International (UK) Limited, *London*
Prentice-Hall of Australia Pty. Limited, *Sydney*
Prentice-Hall Canada Inc., *Toronto*
Prentice-Hall Hispanoamericana, S.A., *Mexico*
Prentice-Hall of India Private Limited, *New Delhi*
Prentice-Hall of Japan, Inc., *Tokyo*
Simon & Schuster Asia Pte. Ltd., *Singapore*
Editora Prentice-Hall do Brasil, Ltda., *Rio de Janeiro*

PREFACE

As its title suggests, *Constructing Nature* starts from the premise that nature is more than a biological organism or a physical location. Instead, this book views nature as a cultural and social construction or concept. We construct nature not in the literal sense of changing the facts of the natural world but rather in that we shape these facts by our conceptions, values, and interpretations. As individuals and as members of a culture, a social group, or a generation, we experience and understand nature differently, and these differences have implications for what we do and what we value. No matter what the particular issue—protecting spotted owls or banning the use of pesticides—we are always debating the broader, more fundamental beliefs about what (or who) nature is and how we relate to it.

Such an approach to nature—seeing it as a socially constructed and politically contested idea, as well as a physical phenomenon—allows us to accomplish some important intellectual work. First of all, it allows us to think critically about some of the most important issues of our time. From global warming to local questions about incinerators or industrial waste disposal, environmental problems influence the quality of our lives and, in the most extreme cases, our very existence. With issues this important, it is easy to think in black-and-white terms. One side may view the other as evil industrialists who are raping the earth for profit, and the other may consider its opponents soft-headed tree huggers with no concern for the realities of modern life—jobs, living standards, economic progress. The critical thinking fostered by considering different conceptions of nature and their sources and implications allows us to move beyond the name calling.

This insistence on seeing nature as socially constructed, and therefore as a site of continuing debate and negotiation, helps explain why *Constructing Nature* presents a full range of works. In order to understand our complex and changing relations to nature, we need to look not just at the reports of scientists and naturalists, but at the argumentative essays of social critics, at poetry and fiction, at reflective essays and travel narratives. We must cast our net wide to understand fully how nature has been conceived of in our history. The forces that shape our actions and beliefs concerning nature come not just from scientific reports of hard data. We read these facts in light of our imaginative lives and our various cultural identifications. Any attempt to understand nature that ignored these issues would be, at best, incomplete and, at worst, injurious.

As would be true of any way of observing the natural world, this view of nature is inevitably limited. As the editors of *Constructing Nature,* we recognize that some of the limitations have to do with the boundaries of our own understanding and experience; others have to do with theoretical and pragmatic choices we made about what and how much to include in a book with so ambitious a title. One choice was to include fewer and therefore longer selections, which will challenge students to wrestle with ideas and make them their own. Another choice, more noticeable and debatable, was to focus primarily on the North American experience—on the American struggle to make sense of and to live in harmony with nature. We understand that Americans' experiences with nature are not finally separable from those of the rest of the world; in fact, considering nature from a larger global context strikes us as being a project of great value. On the other hand, we hope that the book has gained something important from our choice to limit the perspective. For one thing, our choice allows us to ground the readings in the real, everyday world of Americans, at least in whatever shared world Americans have at this date in history. By grounding the book in the American experience, we are able to make the questions raised by our readings important for an American audience and, to some degree, for any audience interested in understanding America. Every American lives within a local culture that has a particular conception of nature. The varied readings in *Constructing Nature* enable readers to place their local cultures within a wider context, both historically and geographically. The readings also present readers with perspectives other than their own that will help them read against the grain, as it were, of their local conceptions.

In order to acknowledge the variety of experiences within our national boundaries, we not only include the works of the founding "fathers" of our conceptions of nature, people like Thomas Jefferson and Hector St. John de Crèvecoeur. We also include works by the Spanish discoverers of our continent, by Native Americans, and by a number of women, both early and modern. Whatever shared conceptions of nature Americans may have are profoundly influenced by people of different races, cultures, and genders. Although there may be dominant conceptions of nature in our country, there is also a rich and varied history of resisting conceptions. Any construction of nature that does not take into account these resisting conceptions runs the risk of authoritarian domination.

To help place the various conceptions of nature historically, we have arranged the reading selections in *Constructing Nature* chronologically. Each conception of nature has a history, and it is important to study that history in order to understand both how we arrived at our present position and how we can work to improve our relationship with the natural world. For example, there is a long history of considering nature, or at least some places in nature, as sacred or holy. Many writers in the middle and late nineteenth century—for example, Emerson, Thoreau, Whitman, and Dickinson—make this claim fairly directly. However, the beginnings of this conception appear in earlier works, such as those by Jefferson, Crèvecoeur, and Audubon. And the debate among Roosevelt, Burroughs, Pinchot, and Leopold in the twentieth century is shaped by differing attitudes toward this same conception. Finally, modern attitudes toward nature are often shaped by the idea that nature is sacred, as can be seen in Michael Pollan's, "The Idea of a Garden," in which the author asks us to consider the complex interactions between humans and nature over the course of many centuries, so that we can decide how to act now. We can do this analysis coherently and responsibly only if we know the history of the concept of nature as a sacred place and of the causes and effects of that history.

Constructing Nature is more than a collection of readings, however. One of the most important parts of this book is the set of assignment sequences that appears at the end. We have attempted to make the individual writing assignments challenging and interesting, and we have included assignments that ask for a variety of rhetorical approaches, from close textual analyses, to arguments, to source-based writing, to creative and personal responses. And yet, we believe that each *sequence* offers more than just a collection of valuable assignments, that the sequences themselves possess an important intellectual and pedagogical potential. As writers weave their way through a series of intricately connected assignments, they are encouraged to think critically and historically about *connections* between ideas and positions. Working through a sequence invites writers to reflect on what they've read, to see events or ideas from yet another perspective, and to question previous conclusions. In other words, writers learn from their own learning and from the learning of others. The result is that the assignment sequences, combined with the completeness and complexity of the reading selections, will help students think deeply and well.

We began working on *Constructing Nature* with a lot of hope, but without a clear understanding of the difficulties of creating a book. We must thank all those who have helped us along the way with their support, criticism, and faith. First of all, we want to thank the reviewers at various colleges and universities for their helpful responses to our manuscript:

Charles M. Anderson, University of Arkansas; Nancy K. Barry, Luther College; Thomas Recchio, University of Connecticut; Sandra W. Stephan, Youngstown State University; Jeffrey M. Wallmann, University of Nevada; and Keith Woodruff, Purdue University.

In addition, we want to thank Lauren Byrne of Editorial Services of New England for her calm and thorough work. Although our conversations with her were often about the pressing and difficult matter of deadlines, her composure—and her wonderful accent—helped keep us sane and on schedule. And, of course, we must thank Nancy Perry of Blair Press for her faith in this book and her gentle insistence that we get on with it. In addition, we value greatly her sharpness, in her thinking and in her editorial pen. Without her, this book would be missing many of its virtues, and might not be at all. We also would like to thank our colleagues and students who listened to our ideas and were patient with the increased demands on their time and attention. Their first-born son would like to thank Edward W. Lotto and Evelyn Lotto for their lifelong faith in him. Finally, we would like to thank Suzanne Raffel and Christine Hofmeister for their day-to-day encouragement and for most things that make our lives seem worth living. Their ideas and beliefs can be found throughout this book and throughout our lives. If there is any immortality in this world, it is in relationships such as these.

Richard Jenseth
Edward E. Lotto

CONTENTS

CHAPTER 3
CONTESTING THE USES OF NATURE:
EARLY TO MIDDLE TWENTIETH CENTURY

CHAPTER 4
CONSTRUCTING NATURE IN WORDS:
RECENT POETRY, FICTION, AND
CREATIVE NONFICTION

CHAPTER 5
RESPONSES TO THE CURRENT
ENVIRONMENTAL CRISIS

CONTENTS

xi

ASSIGNMENT SEQUENCES

CONSTRUCTING
NATURE

1

"NEW WORLD" ENCOUNTERS

LATE FIFTEENTH TO EARLY NINETEENTH CENTURY

Thischapter opens with two dramatic narratives from what is called the *Age of Discovery*, that period between 1400 and 1700 when Spain, Portugal, France, and England literally divided up the "new" world. To call this period an age of discovery is, perhaps, just a romantic way of talking about a time of colonial expansion and colonial exploitation, as Old World powers competed for new sources of wealth and prestige. This search for territory and natural resources brought about the unrelenting westward movement that largely defines the American experience. In a complex mix of cultural myth and economic ambition, the West became a destination and a symbol of renewal, fertility, and freedom.

For discoverers like Christopher Columbus as for the explorer and settlers like William Bartram and J. Hector St. John de Crèvecoeur, the New World offered a promise as rich and vast as the land itself. Though different from one another in many ways, the writers of the seven pieces in this chapter are struggling to comprehend this vast new landscape. Each writer works diligently (sometimes desperately) to take it all in, and to bring some kind of order to his experience. Again and again, we see these writers naming, cataloging, ordering what was otherwise an incomprehensible flood of facts and objects. We also see in these accounts the struggle to find language adequate to the task of describing the strange new lands they traveled. What is Columbus to call animals or plants for which there are yet no European words? How is William Bartram to describe natural features that are so much larger, or richer, or more bountiful than anything he (or his readers) has ever seen? From the restrained letters of Columbus to the often lavish prose of Crèvecoeur or William Bartram, we see encounters that shatter Old World assumptions about nature itself.

If Columbus was such an excellent sailor—able to sail ships through terrible storms and to plot an accurate course by dead reckoning—how could he have been so wrong about what he had discovered? From the beginning, Columbus's theory of the world was shaped by his dreams and ambitions as much as by fifteenth-century geography or map making. His map put Japan where he needed it to be, and eventually the landscape and peoples he encountered became what he needed them to become: *Indians* living in the *Indies*. In each of his four voyages, Columbus transformed the physical landscape into what he expected to see: Each new body of water became a river mouth leading to a city of gold; each island became the mainland of Asia. In time, when even Columbus had to give up all hope of finding gold and gems, the labor of the native peoples themselves was transformed into an exploitable resource, no different from the harbors, forests, or wildlife.

In *The Devastation of the Indies*, Bartolomé de Las Casas exposes the darker side of the European encounter with the New World. His passionate, often terrifying, accounts of Spanish atrocities are meant to alert the Spanish court to the injustices of colonial practices. At the heart of his argument are two critical points: First, that the savage treatment of the Indians is fundamentally unchristian since it does not recognize them as part of God's wondrous creation. Second, these unchristian atrocities threaten to undermine the Spanish claims to what is clearly an earthly paradise.

In *Notes on the State of Virginia*, Thomas Jefferson presented the first effort at composing a natural history of the New World. Prompted by a series of questions asked by a European naturalist, Jefferson attempted to capture every aspect or domain of the natural world, from the size and numbers of mountains or waterfalls to the "nature" of the various races that populated this boundless new land. Jefferson, an amateur scientist and avid naturalist, was, most of all, a leading intellectual figure of the American Enlightenment, a period marked by two things: an increased faith in the powers of human reason and the rapid development of the natural sciences. Like the European naturalist whose questions prompted this work, Jefferson truly believed that the apparently chaotic and mysterious natural world could be understood through systematic study. Jefferson's *Notes* also reflects a theme common to most of the works presented in this chapter—a defense of (and a defensiveness about) the qualities of nature in the New World. In his apparently objective cataloging and describing, Jefferson is arguing that the animals and plants in Virginia are not simply inferior or degenerate versions of Old World species. The New World was, indeed, new, and its promise of inexhaustible raw materials was real.

This belief in the American landscape is very much the theme of Hector St. John de Crèvecoeur's *Letters from an American Farmer*. The perfect, simple life of Crèvecoeur's mythical farmer literally and figuratively grows out of the rich and generous soil of America. As do many writers who follow him, Crèvecoeur connects the idea of an open, unspoiled natural world with the promise of liberty. Crèvecoeur's American farmer lives free because (and only so long as) he lives in harmony with nature.

William Bartram, a scientist by training and a restless explorer by inclination, combines Jefferson's systematic observation with the eye and the voice of the artist. Like Jefferson, Bartram counts, names, and measures the complex, rich life he discovers in the swamps and forests of America. But his long lists of Latin names for species are interrupted by joyful expressions of delight or of awe. It is as if Bartram the scientific observer literally cannot believe his eyes. He is continually surprised and over-whelmed as he finds a new species of plant or animal, or as he stumbles upon yet another forest or river more beautiful, more perfect, than the last.

This combination of systematic observation and spontaneous celebra-tion is also found in the journals of John James Audubon. Audubon spent much of his adult life studying and painting birds from Pennsylvania to Louisiana. He was determined to capture on canvas every species of bird that lived in America, and he was obsessed with accurately representing those birds as he found them: alive and in their natural setting. But Audubon the Enlightenment naturalist was also a romantic adventurer, and the journals that accompanied his bird portraits are rollicking tales of encounters with nature. Often called America's most famous naturalist—and the patron saint of the modern conservation movement—the Audubon we encounter in the journals is an avid hunter, often shooting birds by the dozen or even the hundreds. What Audubon found in his travels was what travelers before him had found: a lush and complex American landscape that offered inexhaustible raw materials.

The chapter ends with two short poems by America's first nature poet, William Cullen Bryant. Bryant spent his youth in rural New England and, unable to attend college, spent his young adult life wandering the hills of New Hampshire, listening to, and recording in verse, the voice of nature. The voice that Bryant heard was one of simple honesty and quiet ele-gance, as we see in "The Yellow Violet." Bryant wrote and published most of his "nature" poetry before he was thirty, when he moved to New York City and began to work as a critic and newspaper editor. In that work, as he had in his poetry, Bryant argued that Americans should cast off Old World mythology and live instead with what he saw as the universal laws of nature. As would Henry David Thoreau and Walt Whitman more than two decades later, Bryant insisted that the American landscape was a rich and deserving subject for her artists and poets, who had for too long looked to Europe for their inspiration.

CHRISTOPHER COLUMBUS

Born in Genoa, Italy, in 1451, Christopher Columbus spent much of his adult life traveling the capitals of Europe trying to finance a daring westward expedition to Asia. After his years of research and pleading, the Spanish court offered Columbus both ships and titles—admiral, viceroy, governor-general of all the Atlantic—and on October 11, 1492, his expedition found what it thought was Japan, but was in fact an island in the Bahamas. Between 1492 and 1504 Columbus made three more voyages, each more elaborate than the previous, and each more disappointing to his investors, who had been promised cities of gold. Though a remarkable sailor, Columbus was a poor administrator and a worse politician, and by the end of the fourth voyage he returned to Spain bitter and broken, stripped of his titles and his land grants. For over two hundred years, the myth of Columbus as hero and visionary has been celebrated in worshipful biographies and epic poems. What's been forgotten, recent critics and scholars insist, is that Columbus's "discovery" began with the systematic enslavement and murder of tens of thousands of natives, and brought forth centuries of colonial domination and exploitation. The following entries from his journals of 1492–93 provide an account of Columbus's first encounter with the natural wonders of the New World, an account that sent shock waves through the capitals of Europe.

From the *Digest of Columbus's Log-Book on His First Voyage*

Sunday, 14 October. At dawn I ordered the ship's boat and the boats of the caravels to be made ready, and coasted the island in a north-easterly direction in order to see the other and eastward part and to look for villages. I saw two or three, whose people all came down to the beach calling to us and offering thanks to God. Some brought us water, others various sorts of food, and others, when they saw that I did not intend to land, jumped into the sea and swam out. We understood them to be asking us if we came from the sky. One old man got into the boat, and all the others, men and women alike, shouted, "Come and see the men who have come from the skies; and bring them food and drink." Many men and women came, each bringing something and offering thanks to God; they threw themselves on the ground and raised their hands to the sky and then called out to us, asking us to land. But I was afraid to do so, seeing a great reef of rocks which encircled the whole island. Inside there is deep water which would give sufficient anchorage for all the ships in Christendom. But the entrance is very narrow. It is true that there are some shoals within this reef, but the sea is as still as well water.

I went to view all this this morning, in order to give an account to your Majesties and to decide where a fort could be built. I saw a piece of land which is much like an island, though it is not one, on which there were six huts. It could be made into an island in two days, though I see no necessity to do so since these people are very unskilled in arms, as your Majesties will discover from seven whom I caused to be taken and brought aboard so that they may learn our language and return. However, should your Highnesses command it all the inhabitants could be taken away to Castile or held as slaves on the island, for with fifty men we could subjugate them all and make them do whatever we wish. Moreover, near the small island I have described there are groves of the loveliest trees I have seen, all green with leaves like our trees in Castile in April and May, and much water.

I examined the whole of that anchorage and then returned to the ship and set sail. I saw so many islands that I could not make up my mind which to visit first. The men I had taken told me by signs that there were so many that it was impossible to count them. They mentioned more than a hundred by name. In the end I looked for the largest and decided to go to that one, which I am doing. It is about five leagues from this island of San Salvador, and the rest are rather more or rather less. All are very flat, without mountains and very fertile. All are populated and make war with one another, although the people are very simple and do not look savage.

Wednesday, 17 October. At midday I set sail from the village off which I had anchored and where I had landed and taken water to make a circuit of this island of Fernandina. The wind was south-west and south. It was my intention to follow the coast of this island from where I was to the south-east, since it runs as a whole from north-north-west to south-south-east. I wanted to take my course to the south-south-east, because all the Indians whom I have aboard and others from whom I inquired tell me that southwards from here lies the island they call Samoet, where the gold is. Martin Alonso Pinzón, captain of the *Pinta*, in which I had placed three of these Indians, came to me and said that one of them had very explicitly given him to understand that the island could be rounded more quickly in a north-north-westerly direction.

I saw that the wind would not help me on the course I wished to steer and that it favoured the other course, so I steered north-north-west, and when I was about two leagues from the island's cape I saw a marvellous harbour with an entrance, or rather two entrances, since there is an islet in the middle. Both entrances are very narrow, but it would have been large enough to provide anchorage for a hundred ships if it had been deep and free of rocks and the entrance channels had been deep also. I thought fit to examine it closely and take soundings; therefore I anchored outside and went in with all the ships' boats and we found that it was shallow. When I first saw it I thought it was the mouth of a river, so I had ordered casks to be brought to take water. On land I saw eight or ten men who quickly came up to us and pointed to a nearby village, where I sent my men for water, which they took, some going armed and others carrying the casks. As the village was some distance away I had to remain there for two hours.

During that time I walked among the trees, which were the loveliest 6
sight I had yet seen. They were green as those of Andalusia in the month of May. But all these trees are as different from ours as day from night and so are the fruit and plants and stones, and everything else. It is true that some trees were of species that can be found in Castile, yet there was a great difference; but there are many other varieties which no one could say are like those of Castile or could compare with them. The people were all of the same kind as those already described; their condition was the same; they were naked and of the same height. They gave whatever they possessed for whatever we gave them and here I saw some ships' boys exchanging small bits of broken crockery or glass for spears.

The men who had gone for water told me that they had entered their 7
houses and that they were very clean and well swept and that their beds and blankets are like cotton nets. These houses are like large tents. They are high and have good chimneys. But of all the villages I saw none consisted of more than a dozen or fifteen houses. Here they found that married women wear cotton drawers, but girls do not, until they reach the age of eighteen. Here there were mastiffs and small dogs and here they met one man who wore in his nose a piece of gold about half the size of a *castellano* on which they saw letters. I was angry with them because they had not bargained for it and given as much as they were asked, so that we could examine it and see where the coin came from. They answered that they did not dare to bargain for it.

After taking the water I returned to the ship, raised sail and followed a 8
north-westerly course along the shore to the point where the coast turns east-west. Later all the Indians insisted that this island was smaller than Samoet and that it would be better to turn back in order to reach that island sooner. Then the wind fell and began to blow west-north-west, which was unfavourable to the course we had been following. I therefore turned back and sailed all that night in an east-south-easterly direction, sometimes due east and sometimes south-east in order to keep clear of land, because the clouds were very thick and the weather very heavy. The wind was slight and I could not make land to anchor. In the night heavy rain fell from after midnight almost till daybreak and it is still cloudy with more rain to come.

We are now at the south-east tip of the island, where I hope to anchor 9
until the weather clears, and I can see the other islands to which I am
going. It has rained practically every day since I have been in these Indies.
Your Highnesses must believe me that these islands are the most fertile,
and temperate and flat and good in the whole world.

Thursday, 18 October. When the weather cleared I followed 10
the wind and got as close to the island as I could. I anchored when I could
get no closer but did not land and at dawn I set sail.

Friday, 19 October. I raised anchor at dawn and sent the caravel 11
Pinta to the east-south-east and the *Niña* to the south-south-east and myself went south-south-east. I ordered them to follow these courses till
midday and that both should then change their courses and rejoin me, and
soon, before we had sailed three hours, we saw an island to the east, towards which we steered, and all three vessels reached its northern point
before midday. Here there is an islet and a reef of rocks, on the seaward
side to the north and another between this and the island itself, which the
Indians whom I had with me called "Samoet." I named it Isabela.

The wind was northerly and this islet lay on the course from 12
Fernandina, from which I had sailed due west. I then followed the coast
of this island westwards for twelve leagues as far as a cape which I named
Cape Hermoso (Beautiful) which is on its western coast. It is indeed
lovely, rounded and in deep water, with no shoals lying off it. At first the
shore is low and stony, but further on there is a sandy beach which continues along most of this coast. Here I anchored on this night of Friday
until morning. The whole of this coast and all of the island that I saw is
more or less beach, and, beautiful though the others are, this island is the
most beautiful I have seen. There are many trees, very green and tall, and
the land is higher than on the other islands. On it there is a hill which cannot however be called a mountain, but which makes the whole island
more beautiful. There seems to be a lot of water in the middle of the island. On this north-eastern side the coast turns sharply and is thickly covered with very large trees.

I wished to go in, anchor and land in order to see all this beauty, but 13
the water was shallow and I could only anchor some way off shore. The
wind was very favourable for sailing to this point where I am now anchored, which I named Cape Hermoso, and beautiful it is. And so I did not
anchor in that bay, seeing as I did this green and lovely cape in the distance. Everything on all these coasts is so green and lovely that I do not
know where to go first, and my eyes never weary of looking on this fine
vegetation, which is so different from that of our own lands. I think that
many trees and plants grow there which will be highly valued in Spain for
dyes and medicinal spices. But I am sorry to say that I do not recognize

them. When I reached this cape, the scent of flowers and trees blew off-shore and this was the most delightful thing in the world.

In the morning before I sail away I will land to see what is growing on this cape. There is no village, for this lies further inland, and it is there, according to the men I have with me, that the king lives who wears so much gold. Tomorrow I intend to go so far inland as to find this village and see and speak with this king, who, according to their signs, rules all the islands in this neighbourhood and wears much gold on his clothes and person. I do not attach much belief to their statements, however, because I do not understand them very well, and know that they are so poor in gold that any small amount this king may wear will seem much to them.

I have called this cape here Cape Hermoso and I believe that it is an island separate from Samoet and that there is another small island also lying between them. I did not examine this matter minutely because I could not do all this even in fifty years, being anxious to see and discover as much as I could in order to return to your Highnesses, God willing, in April. It is true that if I find any place where there is gold or spices in quantity I shall wait until I've collected as much as I can. Therefore I continue to sail on in search of such a place.

Saturday, 20 October. Today at sunrise I left the place where I was anchored off the south-west point of Samoet, which I called Cabo de la Laguna. I named the island Isabela. I intended to steer north-east and east from the southern and south-westerly end towards the place where, as I understood from the men I carried, the village with its king lay. I found the sea everywhere so shallow that I could not enter or sail to that point and I saw that to approach it from the south-west would take me far out of my course. I decided therefore to return north-north-east by the way that I had come and round the island in that direction. The winds were so light that I could only sail along this coast at night, since it is dangerous to anchor off these islands, except in daylight, when you can see where you are dropping anchor, for the bottom is very patchy, in parts rocky, in parts clean. I made up my mind to stand off under sail for the whole of Sunday night. The caravels anchored because they had reached the coast earlier and thought that when I saw them making their accustomed signals I should anchor also. But I decided not to do so.

Sunday, 21 October. At ten o'clock I reached this Cabo del Isleo and anchored, as did the caravels. After eating a meal I went ashore, but there was no village—only one house in which I found nobody. I think they had all run away from fright, for all their things were there.

I wouldn't allow anything to be touched but went with the captains and men to examine the island. Though all the others we had seen were beautiful, green and fertile, this was even more so. It has large and very green trees, and great lagoons, around which these trees stand in marvellous groves. Here and throughout the island the trees and plants are as green as in Andalusia in April. The singing of small birds is so sweet that no one could ever wish to leave this place. Flocks of parrots darken the sun and there is a marvellous variety of large and small birds very different from our own; the trees are of many kinds, each with its own fruit, and all have a marvellous scent. It grieves me extremely that I cannot identify them, for I am quite certain that they are all valuable and I am bringing samples of them and of the plants also.

As I was walking beside one of the lagoons I saw a snake, which we killed. I am bringing the skin to your Highnesses. As soon as we saw it, it swam into the lagoon and we followed it, for the water was not very deep, and we killed it with spears. It is almost five foot long and I believe there are many of them in this lagoon. Here I recognized aloe, and tomorrow I intend to have half a ton brought aboard, for they tell me it's very valuable. Also when we were looking for good water we found a village near by, half a league from where I am anchored. 19

As soon as the inhabitants saw us they ran away, leaving their houses. They hid their clothing and all that they had in the undergrowth. I allowed nothing to be taken, not even to the value of a pin. Afterwards a few of the men approached us and one of them came quite close. I gave him hawk's bells and some small glass beads, and he was very pleased and happy. In order to foster this friendship and ask for something from them, I asked them for water, and after I had returned to the ship they came down to the beach with their gourds full and gave it to us with delight. I ordered that they should be given another string of little glass beads and they said they would return the next day. 20

I decided to have all the vessels on board filled with water. Therefore if the weather allows I will presently set out to coast this island until I have speech with this king and see whether I can get the gold that I hear he wears. After this I shall set out for another large island which, according to the indications given me by the Indians whom I have aboard, must be Chipangu. They however call it Colba and say that there are many large ships and sailors there. From here I shall go to another island, which they call Bohio and say is also very large. In passing I shall see the others that lie between and according to whether I find a quantity of gold or spices I shall decide what to do next. But I am still determined to go to the city of Quinsay, to deliver your Highnesses' letters to the Grand Khan and request his answer which I shall bring back. 21

Monday, 22 October. I have waited here all night on the chance that the king of this place or other persons may bring me gold or other valuables. Many people came who were like the people in the other islands, all naked and painted white, red, black and in many different ways. 22

They carried spears and some of them brought balls of cotton to barter. These they exchanged with some of the sailors for bits of glass from broken bowls and fragments of earthenware. Some of them wore pieces of gold hanging from their noses, which they happily exchanged for little bells, for bells of the kind made for the feet of a sparrow-hawk and for glass beads, but the amount was a mere trifle. Indeed, however small the things we give them, they still consider our coming a great marvel. I think they believe that we have come from the sky. We are taking water for the ships from the lagoon which lies near Cabo del Isleo, as I named it; and there Martin Alonso Pinzón, of the *Pinta*, killed another snake about five foot long and like that of yesterday. I had as much aloe collected as was to be found.

Tuesday, 23 October. I should like to depart today for the island   23
of Colba, which I believe according to the indications of its size and riches given us by these people must be Chipangu. I shall not stay here any longer, to round this island or go to the village as I had intended, to have speech with the king or lord. I do not wish to delay long, since I see that there is no goldfield here and to round these islands one needs many changes of wind and the wind doesn't blow as one wishes. It is best to go where there is much to be done and so it is right not to stay here but to continue on our course, discovering many lands until we find one that is truly profitable. I think, however, that this place is very rich in spices. I am extremely sorry that I cannot recognize them, for I see a very great number of trees each bearing its own kind of fruit, and they are as green now as trees in Spain in the months of May and June. There are a thousand kinds of plants also, all in flower. But the only one I recognize is this aloe, which I ordered to be taken aboard yesterday and brought for your Highnesses.

I have not set out and I am not setting out for Colba, since there is no   24
wind, but dead calm and much rain. It rained heavily yesterday but was not at all cold. On the contrary the days are warm and the nights mild as in May in Andalusia.

Sunday, 28 October. They sailed on south-south-west in search   25
of the nearest point in Colba and he entered a very beautiful river very free from shoals and other dangers. And all along the coast the water was very deep up to the shore. The mouth of the river was twelve fathoms and wide enough for ships to beat about. He anchored as he says a lombard shot upstream. The Admiral says he had never seen a more beautiful country. It was covered with trees right down to the river and these were lovely and green and different from ours, and each bore its own fruit or flowers. There were many birds, large and small, which sung sweetly, and there were a great number of palms of a different kind from those of Guinea and

from ours. They were of moderate height with no bark at the foot, and the Indians cover their houses with them. The land is very flat.

The Admiral got into the boat and went ashore, where he found two 26 houses which he believed to belong to fishermen who had fled in terror. In one of these he found a dog that did not bark, and in both houses there were nets of palm fibre and lines and horn fish-hooks and bone harpoons and other fishing tackle, and there were many hearths. He believed that many people lived in each house. He gave orders that nothing should be touched in either, and his order was obeyed. The vegetation was as abundant as in April and May in Andalusia. He found much purslane and wild amaranth. He returned to the boat and went some distance up the river. He said that it was such a great joy to see the plants and trees and to hear the birds singing that he could not leave them and return. He says that this island is the most beautiful that eyes have ever seen. It has many good harbours and deep rivers, and it seems that the seas are never rough because the vegetation on the shore grows almost to the sea's edge, which is unusual where the seas are rough. So far, he had not encountered rough seas anywhere in these islands. He says that the island contains very lovely mountains, which do not form long chains but are very high. All the rest of the land is high also, like Sicily. It has plenty of water, as he gathered from the Indians from Guanahani whom he had with him, who told him by signs that it was ten large rivers and that they cannot go round it in their canoes in twenty days.

When he brought the ships close to shore, two boats or canoes came 27 out, but on seeing the sailors entering the boat and rowing about to take soundings for an anchorage, they fled. The Indians said that there are goldfields and pearls in the island and the Admiral saw that this was a likely place for pearls, since there were mussels, which are a sign of them. The Admiral understood that the Grand Khan's ships come there and that they are large and that the mainland is ten days' journey away. The Admiral called this river and harbour San Salvador....

QUESTIONS FOR DISCUSSION AND WRITING

1. "It grieves me extremely that I cannot identify them," Columbus declares as he describes a landscape "very different from our own" (par. 18). Identify and discuss several passages where Columbus attempts to help his readers see and understand this strange New World.

2. Columbus's journals serve an important administrative purpose: providing a detailed account of the human and natural features of the lands that Spain had come to rule. But Columbus also uses his journals to present an argument (or several arguments) to his sponsors back in Spain.

What argument or arguments do you see Columbus making about the value of his discoveries? What role does nature play in such arguments?

3. Columbus devotes much of his attention to the physical environment of this New World: harbors, rivers, animal and plant life, the presence or absence of gold. How does he represent the people he finds there? Try to find specific words or phrases that help to illustrate who or what Columbus imagined those natives to be. Does he consider them to be part of the natural world, or separate from it?

BARTOLOMÉ DE LAS CASAS

*Born in Seville in 1474, Bartolomé de Las Casas was the first Catholic priest or-
dained in the New World. His father and three uncles had sailed on Columbus's
second voyage, and Las Casas himself served as chaplain on a 1502 expedition to
what had become known as the* Indies. *His service was rewarded by grants of land
and slaves, but by 1514 Las Casas had freed his own slaves and had begun to
preach angry sermons about Spanish cruelty toward native peoples. For the next
forty years, Las Casas continued to protest against Spanish atrocities and to argue
for a Christian view of native peoples as virtuous individuals whose societies were
as noble as those of ancient Greece and Rome. Las Casas argued that the lush and
rich utopian garden of the New World was being defiled by Spanish barbarism,
and, not surprisingly, his attacks angered government officials and landowners.
Saved from the Inquisition only by his notoriety, Las Casas argued in* Confesionario
*(1545) that Spain's very claim to the New World was in question, since it was built
upon illegal and unjust actions. In 1552,* The Devastation of the Indies *sparked
further debates in Spain and across Europe, and Las Casas spent his remaining
years as an outspoken critic of Spanish colonial policies and an advocate for native rights.*

From *The Devastation of the Indies*

The Indies were discovered in the year one thousand four hundred and 1
ninety-two. In the following year a great many Spaniards went there with
the intention of settling the land. Thus, forty-nine years have passed since
the first settlers penetrated the land, the first so-claimed being the large
and most happy isle called Hispaniola, which is six hundred leagues in circumference. Around it in all directions are many other islands, some very
big, others very small, and all of them were, as we saw with our own eyes,
densely populated with native peoples called Indians. This large island
was perhaps the most densely populated place in the world. There must
be close to two hundred leagues of land on this island, and the seacoast
has been explored for more than ten thousand leagues, and each day
more of it is being explored. And all the land so far discovered is a bee-
hive of people; it is as though God had crowded into these lands the great
majority of mankind.

And of all the infinite universe of humanity, these people are the most 2
guileless, the most devoid of wickedness and duplicity, the most obedient
and faithful to their native masters and to the Spanish Christians whom
they serve. They are by nature the most humble, patient, and peaceable,

holding no grudges, free from embroilments, neither excitable nor quarrelsome. These people are the most devoid of rancors, hatreds, or desire for vengeance of any people in the world. And because they are so weak and complaisant, they are less able to endure heavy labor and soon die of no matter what malady. The sons of nobles among us, brought up in the enjoyments of life's refinements, are no more delicate than are these Indians, even those among them who are of the lowest rank of laborers. They are also poor people, for they not only possess little but have no desire to possess worldly goods. For this reason they are not arrogant, embittered, or greedy. Their repasts are such that the food of the holy fathers in the desert can scarcely be more parsimonious, scanty, and poor. As to their dress, they are generally naked, with only their pudenda covered somewhat. And when they cover their shoulders it is with a square cloth no more than two varas in size. They have no beds, but sleep on a kind of matting or else in a kind of suspended net called *hamacas*. They are very clean in their persons, with alert, intelligent minds, docile and open to doctrine, very apt to receive our holy Catholic faith, to be endowed with virtuous customs, and to behave in a godly fashion. And once they begin to hear the tidings of the Faith, they are so insistent on knowing more and on taking the sacraments of the Church and on observing the divine cult that, truly, the missionaries who are here need to be endowed by God with great patience in order to cope with such eagerness. Some of the secular Spaniards who have been here for many years say that the goodness of the Indians is undeniable and that if this gifted people could be brought to know the one true God they would be the most fortunate people in the world.

Yet into this sheepfold, into this land of meek outcasts there came some Spaniards who immediately behaved like ravening wild beasts, wolves, tigers, or lions that had been starved for many days. And Spaniards have behaved in no other way during the past forty years, down to the present time, for they are still acting like ravening beasts, killing, terrorizing, afflicting, torturing, and destroying the native peoples, doing all this with the strangest and most varied new methods of cruelty, never seen or heard of before, and to such a degree that this Island of Hispaniola, once so populous (having a population that I estimated to be more than three millions), has now a population of barely two hundred persons. 3

The island of Cuba is nearly as long as the distance between Valladolid and Rome; it is now almost completely depopulated. San Juan and Jamaica are two of the largest, most productive and attractive islands; both are now deserted and devastated. On the northern side of Cuba and Hispaniola lie the neighboring Lucayos comprising more than sixty islands including those called *Gigantes*, beside numerous other islands, some small some large. The least felicitous of them were more fertile and 4 beautiful than the gardens of the King of Seville. They have the healthiest lands in the world, where lived more than five hundred thousand souls; they are now deserted, inhabited by not a single living creature. All the people were slain or died after being taken into captivity and brought to the Island of Hispaniola to be sold as slaves. When the Spaniards saw that some of these had escaped, they sent a ship to find them, and it voyaged for three years among the islands searching for those who had escaped being slaughtered, for a good Christian had helped them escape, taking pity on them and had won them over to Christ; of these there were eleven persons and these I saw.

More than thirty other islands in the vicinity of San Juan are for the most   5
part and for the same reason depopulated, and the land laid waste. On these islands I estimate there are 2,100 leagues of land that have been ruined and depopulated, empty of people.

As for the vast mainland, which is ten times larger than all Spain, even   6
including Aragon and Portugal, containing more land than the distance between Seville and Jerusalem, or more than two thousand leagues, we are sure that our Spaniards, with their cruel and abominable acts, have devastated the land and exterminated the rational people who fully inhabited it. We can estimate very surely and truthfully that in the forty years that have passed, with the infernal actions of the Christians, there have been unjustly slain more than twelve million men, women, and children. In truth, I believe without trying to deceive myself that the number of the slain is more like fifteen million.

The common ways mainly employed by the Spaniards who call them-   7
selves Christian and who have gone there to extirpate those pitiful nations and wipe them off the earth is by unjustly waging cruel and bloody wars. Then, when they have slain all those who fought for their lives or to escape the tortures they would have to endure, that is to say, when they have slain all the native rulers and young men (since the Spaniards usually spare only the women and children, who are subjected to the hardest and bitterest servitude ever suffered by man or beast), they enslave any survivors. With these infernal methods of tyranny they debase and weaken countless numbers of those pitiful Indian nations.

Their reason for killing and destroying such an infinite number of souls   8
is that the Christians have an ultimate aim, which is to acquire gold, and to swell themselves with riches in a very brief time and thus rise to a high estate disproportionate to their merits. It should be kept in mind that their insatiable greed and ambition, the greatest ever seen in the world, is the cause of their villainies. And also, those lands are so rich and felicitous, the native peoples so meek and patient, so easy to subject, that our Spaniards have no more consideration for them than beasts. And I say this from my own knowledge of the acts I witnessed. But I should not say "than beasts"

for, thanks be to God, they have treated beasts with some respect; I should say instead like excrement on the public squares. And thus they have deprived the Indians of their lives and souls, for the millions I mentioned have died without the Faith and without the benefit of the sacraments. This is a well-known and proven fact which even the tyrant Governors, themselves killers, know and admit. And never have the Indians in all the Indies committed any act against the Spanish Christians, until those Christians have first and many times committed countless cruel aggressions against them or against neighboring nations. For in the beginning the Indians regarded the Spaniards as angels from Heaven. Only after the Spaniards had used violence against them, killing, robbing, torturing, did the Indians ever rise up against them.

Hispaniola

On the Island Hispaniola was where the Spaniards first landed, as I   9
have said. Here those Christians perpetrated their first ravages and oppressions against the native peoples. This was the first land in the New World to be destroyed and depopulated by the Christians, and here they began their subjection of the women and children, taking them away from the Indians to use them and ill use them, eating the food they provided with their sweat and toil. The Spaniards did not content themselves with what the Indians gave them of their own free will, according to their ability, which was always too little to satisfy enormous appetites, for a Christian eats and consumes in one day an amount of food that would suffice to feed three houses inhabited by ten Indians for one month. And they committed other acts of force and violence and oppression which made the Indians realize that these men had not come from Heaven. And some of the Indians concealed their foods while others concealed their wives and children and still others fled to the mountains to avoid the terrible transactions of the Christians.

And the Christians attacked them with buffets and beatings, until finally   10
they laid hands on the nobles of the villages. Then they behaved with such temerity and shamelessness that the most powerful ruler of the islands had to see his own wife raped by a Christian officer.

From that time onward the Indians began to seek ways to throw the   11
Christians out of their lands. They took up arms, but their weapons were very weak and of little service in offense and still less in defense. (Because of this, the wars of the Indians against each other are little more than games played by children.) And the Christians, with their horses and swords and pikes began to carry out massacres and strange cruelties

against them. They attacked the towns and spared neither the children nor the aged nor pregnant women nor women in childbed, not only stabbing them and dismembering them but cutting them to pieces as if dealing with sheep in the slaughter house. They laid bets as to who, with one stroke of the sword, could split a man in two or could cut off his head or spill out his entrails with a single stroke of the pike. They took infants from their mothers' breasts, snatching them by the legs and pitching them headfirst against the crags or snatched them by the arms and threw them into the rivers, roaring with laughter and saying as the babies fell into the water, "Boil there, you offspring of the devil!" Other infants they put to the sword along with their mothers and anyone else who happened to be nearby. They made some low wide gallows on which the hanged victim's feet almost touched the ground, stringing up their victims in lots of thirteen, in memory of Our Redeemer and His twelve Apostles, then set burning wood at their feet and thus burned them alive. To others they attached straw or wrapped their whole bodies in straw and set them afire. With still others, all those they wanted to capture alive, they cut off their hands and hung them round the victim's neck, saying, "Go now, carry the message," meaning, Take the news to the Indians who have fled to the mountains. They usually dealt with the chieftains and nobles in the following way: they made a grid of rods which they placed on forked sticks, then lashed the victims to the grid and lighted a smoldering fire underneath, so that little by little, as those captives screamed in despair and torment, their souls would leave them.

I once saw this, when there were four or five nobles lashed on grids   12 and burning; I seem even to recall that there were two or three pairs of grids where others were burning, and because they uttered such loud screams that they disturbed the captain's sleep, he ordered them to be strangled. And the constable, who was worse than an executioner, did not want to obey that order (and I know the name of that constable and know his relatives in Seville), but instead put a stick over the victims' tongues, so they could not make a sound, and he stirred up the fire, but not too much, so that they roasted slowly, as he liked. I saw all these things I have described, and countless others.

And because all the people who could do so fled to the mountains to   13 escape these inhuman, ruthless, and ferocious acts, the Spanish captains, enemies of the human race, pursued them with the fierce dogs they kept which attacked the Indians, tearing them to pieces and devouring them. And because on few and far between occasions, the Indians justifiably killed some Christians, the Spaniards made a rule among themselves that for every Christian slain by the Indians, they would slay a hundred Indians.

The Islands of San Juan and Jamaica

The Spaniards passed over to the islands of San Juan and Jamaica (both   14
of them veritable gardens and beehives of activity) in the year one thousand five hundred and nine, with the aim and purpose of making these islands a part of Hispaniola.

And on those islands the Spaniards perpetrated the same acts of ag-   15
gression against the Indians and the wicked deeds described above,
adding to them many outstanding cruelties, massacres and burnings of the
people, or executing them by flinging them to the fierce dogs, torturing
and oppressing the survivors, condemning them to the hard labor of the
mines, thus eradicating them from the earth, despoiling the land of those
unfortunate and innocent people. Before the arrival of the Spaniards there
had lived on these islands more than six hundred thousand souls, it has
been stated. I believe there were more than one million inhabitants, and
now, in each of the two islands, there are no more than two hundred persons, all the others having perished without the Faith and without the holy
sacraments.

The Island of Cuba

In the year one thousand five hundred and eleven, the Spaniards   16
passed over to the island of Cuba, which as I have said is at the same distance from Hispaniola as the distance between Valladolid and Rome, and
which was a well-populated province. They began and ended in Cuba as
they had done elsewhere, but with much greater acts of cruelty.

Among the noteworthy outrages they committed was the one they per-   17
petrated against a cacique, a very important noble, by name Hatuey, who
had come to Cuba from Hispaniola with many of his people, to flee the
calamities and inhuman acts of the Christians. When he was told by certain Indians that the Christians were now coming to Cuba, he assembled
as many of his followers as he could and said this to them: "Now you must
know that they are saying the Christians are coming here, and you know
by experience how they have put So and So and So and So, and other nobles to an end. And now they are coming from Haiti (which is Hispaniola)
to do the same here. Do you know why they do this?" The Indians replied:
"We do not know. But it may be that they are by nature wicked and cruel."
And he told them: "No, they do not act only because of that, but because
they have a God they greatly worship and they want us to worship that
God, and that is why they struggle with us and subject us and kill us."

He had a basket full of gold and jewels and he said: "You see their God   18
here, the God of the Christians. If you agree to it, let us dance for this God,

who knows, it may please the God of the Christians and then they will do us no harm." And his followers said, all together, "Yes, that is good, that is good!" And they danced round the basket of gold until they fell down exhausted. Then their chief, the cacique Hatuey, said to them: "See here, if we keep this basket of gold they will take it from us and will end up by killing us. So let us cast away the basket into the river." They all agreed to do this, and they flung the basket of gold into the river that was nearby.

This cacique, Hatuey, was constantly fleeing before the Christians from   19
the time they arrived on the island of Cuba, since he knew them and of what they were capable. Now and then they encountered him and he defended himself, but they finally killed him. And they did this for the sole reason that he had fled from those cruel and wicked Christians and had defended himself against them. And when they had captured him and as many of his followers as they could, they burned them all at the stake.

When tied to the stake, the cacique Hatuey was told by a Franciscan   20
friar who was present, an artless rascal, something about the God of the Christians and of the articles of the Faith. And he was told what he could do in the brief time that remained to him, in order to be saved and go to Heaven. The cacique, who had never heard any of this before, and was told he would go to Inferno where, if he did not adopt the Christian Faith, he would suffer eternal torment, asked the Franciscan friar if Christians all went to Heaven. When told that they did he said he would prefer to go to Hell. Such is the fame and honor that God and our Faith have earned through the Christians who have gone out to the Indies.

On one occasion when we went to claim ten leagues of a big settle-   21
ment, along with food and maintenance, we were welcomed with a bounteous quantity of fish and bread and cooked victuals. The Indians generously gave us all they could. Then suddenly, without cause and without warning, and in my presence, the devil inhabited the Christians and spurred them to attack the Indians, men, women, and children, who were sitting there before us. In the massacre that followed, the Spaniards put to the sword more than three thousand souls. I saw such terrible cruelties done there as I had never seen before nor thought to see.

A few days later, knowing that news of this massacre had spread   22
through the land, I sent messengers ahead to the chiefs of the province of Havana, knowing they had heard good things about me, telling them we were about to visit the town and telling them they should not hide but should come out to meet us, assuring them that no harm would be done to them. I did this with the full knowledge of the captain. And when we arrived in the province, there came out to welcome us twenty-one chiefs and caciques, and our captain, breaking his pledge to me and the pledge I had made to them, took all these chieftains captive, intending to burn them at the stake, telling me this would be a good thing because those

chiefs had in the past done him some harm. I had great difficulty in saving those Indians from the fire, but finally succeeded.

Afterward, when all the Indians of this island were subjected to servi- 23 tude and the same ruin had befallen there as on the island Hispaniola, the survivors began to flee to the mountains or in despair to hang themselves, and there were husbands and wives who hanged themselves together with their children, because the cruelties perpetrated by one very great Spaniard (whom I knew) were so horrifying. More than two hundred Indians hanged themselves.

• • •

The Kingdom of Yucatán

In the year one thousand five hundred and twenty-six, another wretch 24 of a Spanish tyrant was provided to govern the kingdom of Yucatán, thanks to the lies and falsehoods he told and the presents he gave to the King of Spain, as has been the case of all the other tyrants sent to govern the Indies down to this day; thus they are given charges and rank that will enable them to rob the native peoples.

The kingdom of Yucatán was filled with countless inhabitants because 25 it has a healthy climate where food is abundant and where fruits and honey abound; there is more honey and beeswax in Yucatán than in any other part of the Indies until now visited. This kingdom is three hundred leagues in circumference. The people of Yucatán were noted for their pru-dence, their good order, their lack of vices; they were very worthy to be brought to the knowledge of God. It was a kingdom where great Spanish cities could have been built, where people could have lived in an earthly Paradise, had the Spaniards been worthy. But the cities were not built, be-cause of the greed, the sinfulness, the insensitivity of the Spaniards. They were not worthy, as they were not worthy of the many other parts of the Indies, as has been shown.

This new tyrant-Governor had with him three hundred men and they 26 waged ruthless war against these good and innocent people who lived quietly in their houses, in no way offending anyone. The Spaniards mas-sacred countless numbers.

But there was no gold in this kingdom, or if there had been at one time 27 it had all been taken out of the mines. However, gold could be made of those bodies and souls for whom Jesus Christ died, and the Spaniards as-sembled all the Indians they had allowed to survive and sent them away on the many ships that came, attracted by the smell of slaves. They would be traded for wine and vinegar and pigs and clothing and for horses or anything else needed by the tyrant and his followers, or what they deemed necessary.

And the Spaniards were allowed to choose, among one hundred and 28 fifty Indian maidens the ones they liked best, paying for each one an arroba of wine or oil or vinegar or pigs, and the same for a comely boy chosen from among one or two hundred. And it sometimes happened that a boy who appeared to be the son of a noble would be traded for a whole cheese and a hundred of them for a horse.

In such actions the Spaniards were engaged from the year twenty-six to 29 the year thirty-three, which was seven years spent in despoiling and exterminating the inhabitants of this land, and they went on killing until news came of the wealth in Peru, to which the Spaniards then went, ending for a short time the infernal conditions in Yucatán.

But then the tyrant's ministers returned to perpetrate still more outrages 30 against the Indians and offenses against God, and these things they are still doing today now that they have depopulated the entire three hundred leagues of this kingdom which were, as we have said, teeming with inhabitants.

It would be hard to make anyone believe, and harder still to narrate, the 31 infamous deeds in all their details. One incident may suffice. As the Spanish wretches went about with their savage dogs trying to terrorize the Indians, men and women alike, one woman (thinking to soften the hearts of the Spaniards) tied her year-old child to her foot and hanged herself from a beam. No sooner had she done this than the dogs arrived and tore the child to pieces. It must be added that a Franciscan friar baptized the child before it died.

As the Spaniards prepared to depart from this kingdom, one of them 32 told the son of a chieftain of a certain village to come with them. The boy said No, he did not want to leave his country. The Spaniard responded: "Come with us, otherwise I will cut off your ears." The boy still said No, he did not want to leave his land. The Spaniard unsheathed his dagger and cut off the boy's ears, first one, then the other. And when the boy said again that he did not want to leave his land, the Spaniard cut off his nose, laughing as he did so, as if he had administered a punishment as trifling as to pull the boy's hair.

This Godforsaken man boasted about this act in front of a venerable 33 religious, and also said that he worked as hard as he could to get Indian women with child, for when he sold them as slaves he would be paid more if they were pregnant.

One day, and this incident happened either in the kingdom of Yucatán 34 or in New Spain, a certain Spaniard went hunting for stags or rabbits and, finding no game, and wanting to satisfy his dogs, he took a baby from its Indian mother and with his sword sliced off the child's arms and legs for the dogs to share, then after that meal on those pieces of flesh, he threw down the little body for all the dogs to share. Observe in this incident the insensitivity of the Spaniards who call themselves Christians in this land, and see how they have brought the one true God into opprobrium, *in reprobus sensus*, and in what esteem they hold these peoples created in the image of God and redeemed by the blood of the Savior. And we shall see even worse things later on.

QUESTIONS FOR DISCUSSION AND WRITING

1. How does Las Casas represent the basic nature or character of the native peoples of the Indies? By contrast, how does he characterize the nature of the Spanish (at least those in the New World)? To what does Las Casas attribute the actions of the Spanish?

2. How does Las Casas represent the land itself? How does he link the nature of the land to his sense of Spanish hopes for the New World?

3. *The Devastation of the Indies* was in part a political document, intended to shock influential readers in Spain in order to end Spanish atrocities and change unjust colonial policies. Identify and discuss specific passages that would have been effective in shocking readers. Can you think of other historical examples where descriptions of atrocities were used in this way?

THOMAS JEFFERSON

Thomas Jefferson (1743–1826) is best known as a framer of the Declaration of Independence and president of the United States, but he was also a major intellectual figure of his time. His interests were far-ranging, from architecture and scientific farming to philosophy and natural history. Just after his term as governor of Virginia, and before he was elected president, Jefferson was asked by a French nobleman and amateur naturalist to answer twenty-three questions about the social institutions and the natural geography of Virginia. The late eighteenth century was a time of great public curiosity and scientific speculation about the natural history of the New World, and Jefferson's book-length response clearly reflects his skills as a naturalist and social theorist. Notes on the State of Virginia *(1782) is still considered one of the most important scientific works produced in America; it is also a carefully crafted argument, whose meticulous detail about the great numbers and size of plants and animals was meant to refute the widely held view (represented in the following excerpt as the argument of the French naturalist Count de Buffon) that nature in the New World was somehow a degenerate version of its original Old World form.*

From *Notes on the State of Virginia*

QUERY V

Its Cascades and Caverns?

The only remarkable cascade in this country is that of the Falling Spring 1 in Augusta. It is a water of James' river where it is called Jackson's river, rising in the warm spring mountains, about twenty miles southwest of the warm spring, and flowing into that valley. About three-quarters of a mile from its source it falls over a rock two hundred feet into the valley below. The sheet of water is broken in its breadth by the rock, in two or three places, but not at all in its height. Between the sheet and the rock, at the bottom, you may walk across dry. This cataract will bear no comparison with that of Niagara as to the quantity of water composing it; the sheet being only twelve or fifteen feet wide above and somewhat more spread below; but it is half as high again, the latter being only one hundred and fifty-six feet, according to the mensuration made by order of M. Vaudreuil, Governor of Canada, and one hundred and thirty according to a more recent account.

In the lime-stone country there are many caverns of very considerable   2
extent. The most noted is called Madison's Cave, and is on the north side
of the Blue Ridge, near the intersection of the Rockingham and Augusta
line with the south fork of the southern river of Shenandoah. It is in a hill
of about two hundred feet perpendicular height, the ascent of which, on
one side, is so steep that you may pitch a biscuit from its summit into the
river which washes its base. The entrance of the cave is, in this side, about
two-thirds of the way up. It extends into the earth about three hundred
feet, branching into subordinate caverns, sometimes ascending a little, but
more generally descending, and at length terminates, in two different
places, at basins of water of unknown extent, and which I should judge to
be nearly on a level with the water of the river; however, I do not think
they are formed by refluent water from that, because they are never tur-
bid; because they do not rise and fall in correspondence with that in times
of flood or of drought; and because the water is always cool. It is probably one of the many reservoirs with which the interior parts of the earth
are supposed to abound, and yield supplies to the fountains of water, distinguished from others only by being accessible. The vault of this cave is
of solid lime-stone, from twenty to forty or fifty feet high; through which
water is continually percolating. This, trickling down the sides of the cave,
has incrusted them over in the form of elegant drapery; and dripping from
the top of the vault generates on that and on the base below, stalactites of
a conical form, some of which have met and formed massive columns.

Another of these caves is near the North Mountain, in the county of   3
Frederic, on the lands of Mr. Zane. The entrance into this is on the top of
an extensive ridge. You descend thirty or forty feet, as into a well, from
whence the cave extends, nearly horizontally, four hundred feet into the
earth, preserving a breadth of from twenty to fifty feet, and a height of
from five to twelve feet. After entering this cave a few feet, the mercury,
which in the open air was 50°, rose to 57° of Fahrenheit's thermometer,
answering to 11° of Reaumur's, and it continued at that to the remotest
parts of the cave. The uniform temperature of the cellars of the observa-
tory of Paris, which are ninety feet deep, and of all subterraneous cavities
of any depth, where no chemical agencies may be supposed to produce a
factitious heat, has been found to be 10° of Reaumur, equal to $54\frac{1}{2}$° of
Fahrenheit. The temperature of the cave above mentioned so nearly corresponds with this, that the difference may be ascribed to a difference of
instruments.

At the Panther gap, in the ridge which divides the waters of the Cow   4
and the Calf pasture, is what is called the *Blowing Cave*. It is in the side of
a hill, is of about one hundred feet diameter, and emits constantly a current of air of such force as to keep the weeds prostrate to the distance of

twenty yards before it. This current is strongest in dry, frosty weather, and in long spells of rain weakest. Regular inspirations and expirations of air, by caverns and fissures, have been probably enough accounted for by supposing them combined with intermitting fountains; as they must of course inhale air while their reservoirs are emptying themselves, and again emit it while they are filling. But a constant issue of air, only varying in its force as the weather is drier or damper, will require a new hypothesis. There is another blowing cave in the Cumberland mountain, about a mile from where it crosses the Carolina line. All we know of this is, that it is not constant, and that a fountain of water issues from it.

The *Natural Bridge*, the most sublime of nature's works, though not comprehended under the present head, must not be pretermitted. It is on the ascent of a hill, which seems to have been cloven through its length by some great convulsion. The fissure, just at the bridge, is, by some admeasurements, two hundred and seventy feet deep, by others only two hundred and five. It is about forty-five feet wide at the bottom and ninety feet at the top; this of course determines the length of the bridge, and its height from the water. Its breadth in the middle is about sixty feet, but more at the ends, and the thickness of the mass, at the summit of the arch, about forty feet. A part of this thickness is constituted by a coat of earth, which gives growth to many large trees. The residue, with the hill on both sides, is one solid rock of lime-stone. The arch approaches the semi-elliptical form; but the larger axis of the ellipsis, which would be the cord of the arch, is many times longer than the transverse. Though the sides of this bridge are provided in some parts with a parapet of fixed rocks, yet few men have resolution to walk to them, and look over into the abyss. You involuntarily fall on your hands and feet, creep to the parapet, and peep over it. Looking down from this height about a minute, gave me a violent headache. If the view from the top be painful and intolerable, that from below is delightful in an equal extreme. It is impossible for the emotions arising from the sublime to be felt beyond what they are here; so beautiful an arch, so elevated, so light, and springing as it were up to heaven! The rapture of the spectator is really indescribable! The fissure continuing narrow, deep, and straight, for a considerable distance above and below the bridge, opens a short but very pleasing view of the North mountain on one side and the Blue Ridge on the other, at the distance each of them of about five miles. This bridge is in the county of Rockbridge, to which it has given name, and affords a public and commodious passage over a valley which cannot be crossed elsewhere for a considerable distance. The stream passing under it is called Cedar creek. It is a water of James' river, and sufficient in the driest seasons to turn a grist-mill, though its fountain is not more than two miles above.

QUERY VI

A Notice of the Mines and Other Subterraneous Riches; Its Trees, Plants, Fruits, etc.

I knew a single instance of gold found in this State. It was interspersed 6
in small specks through a lump of ore of about four pounds weight, which
yielded seventeen pennyweights of gold, of extraordinary ductility. This
ore was found on the north side of Rappahanoc, about four miles below
the falls. I never heard of any other indication of gold in its neighborhood. . . .

Near the eastern foot of the North mountain are immense bodies of 7
Schist, containing impressions of shells in a variety of forms. I have received petrified shells of very different kinds from the first sources of
Kentucky, which bear no resemblance to any I have ever seen on the tide-
waters. It is said that shells are found in the Andes, in South America, fifteen thousand feet above the level of the ocean. This is considered by
many, both of the learned and unlearned, as a proof of an universal deluge. To the many considerations opposing this opinion, the following
may be added: The atmosphere, and all its contents, whether of water, air,
or other matter, gravitate to the earth; that is to say, they have weight.
Experience tells us, that the weight of all these together never exceeds that
of a column of mercury of thirty-one inches height, which is equal to one
of rain water of thirty-five feet high. If the whole contents of the atmosphere, then, were water, instead of what they are, it would cover the globe
but thirty-five feet deep; but as these waters, as they fell, would run into
the seas, the superficial measure of which is to that of the dry parts of the
globe, as two to one, the seas would be raised only fifty-two and a half feet
above their present level, and of course would overflow the lands to that
height only. In Virginia this would be a very small proportion even of the
champaign country, the banks of our tide waters being frequently, if not
generally, of a greater height. Deluges beyond this extent, then, as for instance, to the North mountain or to Kentucky, seem out of the laws of nature. But within it they may have taken place to a greater or less degree,
in proportion to the combination of natural causes which may be supposed to have produced them. History renders probably some instances
of a partial deluge in the country lying round the Mediterranean sea. It has
been often supposed, and it is not unlikely, that that sea was once a lake.
While such, let us admit an extraordinary collection of the waters of the atmosphere from the other parts of the globe to have been discharged over
that and the countries whose waters run into it. Or without supposing it a
lake, admit such an extraordinary collection of the waters of the atmosphere, and an influx from the Atlantic ocean, forced by long-continued

western winds. The lake, or that sea, may thus have been so raised as to overflow the low lands adjacent to it, as those of Egypt and Armenia, which, according to a tradition of the Egyptians and Hebrews, were overflowed about two thousand three hundred years before the Christian era; those of Attica, said to have been overflowed in the time of Ogyges, about five hundred years later; and those of Thessaly, in the time of Deucalion, still three hundred years posterior. But such deluges as these will not account for the shells found in the higher lands. A second opinion has been entertained, which is, that in times anterior to the records either of history or tradition, the bed of the ocean, the principal residence of the shelled tribe, has, by some great convulsion of nature, been heaved to the heights at which we now find shells and other marine animals. The favorers of this opinion do well to suppose the great events on which it rests to have taken place beyond all the eras of history; for within these, certainly, none such are to be found; and we may venture to say farther, that no fact has taken place, either in our own days, or in the thousands of years recorded in history, which proves the existence of any natural agents, within or without the bowels of the earth, of forces sufficient to heave, to the height of fifteen thousand feet, such masses as the Andes. The difference between the power necessary to produce such an effect, and that which shuffled together the different parts of Calabria in our days, is so immense, that from the existence of the latter, we are not authorized to infer that of the former.

M. de Voltaire has suggested a third solution of this difficulty. (Quest. Encycl. Coquilles.) He cites an instance in Touraine, where, in the space of eighty years, a particular spot of earth had been twice metamorphosed into soft stone, which had become hard when employed in building. In this stone shells of various kinds were produced, discoverable at first only with a microscope, but afterwards growing with the stone. From this fact, I suppose, he would have us infer, that, besides the usual process for generating shells by the elaboration of earth and water in animal vessels, nature may have provided an equivalent operation, by passing the same materials through the pores of calcareous earths and stones; as we see calcareous drop-stones generating every day, by the percolation of water through lime-stone, and new marble forming in the quarries from which the old has been taken out. And it might be asked, whether it is more difficult for nature to shoot the calcareous juice into the form of a shell, than other juices into the forms of crystals, plants, animals, according to the construction of the vessels through which they pass? There is a wonder somewhere. Is it greatest on this branch of the dilemma; on that which supposes the existence of a power, of which we have no evidence in any other case; or on the first, which requires us to believe the creation of a body of water and its subsequent annihilation? The establishment of the

instance, cited by M. de Voltaire, of the growth, of shells unattached to animal bodies, would have been that of his theory. But he has not established it. He has not even left it on ground so respectable as to have
rendered it an object of inquiry to the literati of his own country.
Abandoning this fact, therefore, the three hypotheses are equally unsatis-
factory; and we must be contented to acknowledge, that this great phenomenon is as yet unsolved. Ignorance is preferable to error; and he is
less remote from the truth who believes nothing, than he who believes
what is wrong.

...Our *farms* produce wheat, rye, barley, oats, buck-wheat, broom   9
corn, and Indian corn. The climate suits rice well enough, wherever the
lands do. Tobacco, hemp, flax, and cotton, are staple commodities. Indigo
yields two cuttings. The silk-worm is a native, and the mulberry, proper
for its food, grows kindly.

We cultivate, also, potatoes, both the long and the round, turnips, car-   10
rots, parsnips, pumpkins, and ground nuts (Arachis). Our grasses are
lucerne, st. foin, burnet, timothy, ray, and orchard grass; red, white, and
yellow clover; greensward, blue grass, and crab grass.

The *gardens* yield musk-melons, water-melons, tomatoes, okra, pome-   11
granates, figs, and the esculent plants of Europe.

The *orchards* produce apples, pears, cherries, quinces, peaches, nec-   12
tarines, apricots, almonds, and plums.

Our quadrupeds have been mostly described by Linnaeus and Mons.   13
de Buffon. Of these the mammoth, or big buffalo, as called by the Indians,
must certainly have been the largest. Their tradition is, that he was carnivorous, and still exists in the northern parts of America. A delegation of
warriors from the Delaware tribe having visited the Governor of Virginia,
during the revolution, on matters of business, after these had been discussed and settled in council, the Governor asked them some questions
relative to their country, and among others, what they knew or had heard
of the animal whose bones were found at the Saltlicks on the Ohio. Their
chief speaker immediately put himself into an attitude of oratory, and with
a pomp suited to what he conceived the elevation of his subject, informed
him that it was a tradition handed down from their fathers, "That in ancient times a herd of these tremendous animals came to the Big-bone
licks, and began an universal destruction of the bear, deer, elks, buffaloes,
and other animals which had been created for the use of the Indians; that
the Great Man above, looking down and seeing this, was so enraged that
he seized his lightning, descended on the earth, seated himself on a neighboring mountain, on a rock of which his seat and the print of his feet are
still to be seen, and hurled his bolts among them till the whole were
slaughtered, except the big bull, who presenting his forehead to the
shafts, shook them off as they fell; but missing one at length, it wounded

him in the side; whereon, springing round, he bounded over the Ohio, over the Wabash, the Illinois, and finally over the great lakes, where he is living at this day." It is well known, that on the Ohio, and in many parts of America further north, tusks, grinders, and skeletons of unparalleled magnitude, are found in great numbers, some lying on the surface of the earth, and some a little below it.

• • •

The opinion advanced by the Count de Buffon, is 1. That the animals common both to the old and new world are smaller in the latter. 2. That those peculiar to the new are on a smaller scale. 3. That those which have been domesticated in both have degenerated in America; and 4. That on the whole it exhibits fewer species. And the reason he thinks is, that the heats of America are less; that more waters are spread over its surface by nature, and fewer of these drained off by the hand of man. In other words, that *heat* is friendly, and *moisture* adverse to the production and development of large quadrupeds. I will not meet this hypothesis on its first doubtful ground, whether the climate of America be comparatively more humid? Because we are not furnished with observations sufficient to decide this question. And though, till it be decided, we are as free to deny as others are to affirm the fact, yet for a moment let it be supposed. The hypothesis, after this supposition, proceeds to another; that *moisture* is unfriendly to animal growth. The truth of this is inscrutable to us by reasonings a priori. Nature has hidden from us her *modus agendi*. Our only appeal on such questions is to experience; and I think that experience is against the supposition. It is by the assistance of *heat* and *moisture* that vegetables are elaborated from the elements of earth, air, water, and fire. We accordingly see the more humid climates produce the greater quantity of vegetables. Vegetables are mediately or immediately the food of every animal; and in proportion to the quantity of food, we see animals not only multiplied in their numbers, but improved in their bulk, as far as the laws of their nature will admit. Of this opinion is the Count de Buffon himself in another part of his work; "in general, it appears that rather cold countries are more suitable to our oxen than rather warm countries, and that they (the oxen) are all the larger and greater in proportion as the climate is damper and more abounding in pasturage. . . ." Here then a race of animals, and one of the largest too, has been increased in its dimensions by *cold* and *moisture*, in direct opposition to the hypothesis, which supposes that these two circumstances diminish animal bulk, and that it is their contraries *heat* and *dryness* which enlarge it. But when we appeal to experience we are not to rest satisfied with a single fact. Let us, therefore, try our question on more general ground. Let us take two portions of the earth, Europe and America for instance, sufficiently extensive to give op-

14

eration to general causes; let us consider the circumstances peculiar to each, and observe their effect on animal nature. America, running through the torrid as well as temperate zone, has more *heat* collectively taken, than Europe. But Europe, according to our hypothesis, is the *dryest*. They are equally adapted then to animal productions; each being endowed with one of those causes which befriends animal growth, and with one which opposes it. If it be thought unequal to compare Europe with America, which is so much larger, I answer, not more so than to compare America with the whole world. Besides, the purpose of the comparison is to try an hypothesis, which makes the size of animals depend on the *heat* and *moisture* of climate. If, therefore, we take a region so extensive as to comprehend a sensible distinction of climate, and so extensive, too, as that local accidents, or the intercourse of animals on its borders, may not materially affect the size of those in its interior parts, we shall comply with those conditions which the hypothesis may reasonably demand. The objection would be the weaker in the present case, because any intercourse of animals which may take place on the confines of Europe and Asia, is to the advantage of the former, Asia producing certainly larger animals than Europe. Let us then take a comparative view of the quadrupeds of Europe and America, presenting them to the eye in three different tables, in one of which shall be enumerated those found in both countries; in a second, those found in one only; in a third, those which have been domesticated in both. To facilitate the comparison, let those of each table be arranged in gradation according to their sizes, from the greatest to the smallest, so far as their sizes can be conjectured. The weights of the large animals shall be expressed in the English avoirdupois and its decimals; those of the smaller, in the same ounce and its decimals. . . . The white bear of America is as large as that of Europe. The bones of the mammoth which has been found in America, are as large as those found in the old world. It may be asked, why I insert the mammoth, as if it still existed? I ask in return, why I should omit it, as if it did not exist? Such is the economy of nature, that no instance can be produced, of her having permitted any one race of her animals to become extinct; of her having formed any link in her great work so weak as to be broken. To add to this, the traditionary testimony of the Indians, that this animal still exists in the northern and western parts of America, would be adding the light of a taper to that of the meridian sun. Those parts still remain in their aboriginal state, unexplored and undisturbed by us, or by others for us. He may as well exist there now, as he did formerly where we find his bones. If he be a carnivorous animal, as some anatomists have conjectured, and the Indians affirm, his early retirement may be accounted for from the general destruction of the wild game by the Indians, which commences in the first instant of their connection with us, for the purpose of purchasing match-coats, hatchets, and fire-locks, with their skins. There remain then the buffalo, red deer, fallow deer, wolf, roe, glutton, wild cat, monax, bison, hedgehog, marten, and water-rat, of the comparative sizes of which we have not sufficient testimony. It does not appear that Messieurs de Buffon and D'Aubenton have measured, weighed, or seen those of America. It is said of some of them, by some travellers, that they are smaller than the European. But who were these travellers? Have they not been men of a very different description from those who have laid open to us the other three quarters of the world? Was natural history the object of their travels? Did they measure or weigh the animals they speak of? or did they not judge of them by sight, or perhaps even from report only? Were they acquainted with the animals of their own country, with which they undertake to compare them? Have they not been so ignorant as often to mistake the species? A true answer to these questions would probably lighten their authority, so as to render it insufficient for the foundation of an hypothesis. How unripe we yet are, for an accurate comparison of the animals of the two countries, will appear from the work of Monsieur de Buffon. The ideas we should have formed of the sizes of some animals, from the formation he had received at his first publications concerning them, are very different from what his subsequent communications give us. And indeed his candor in this can never be too much praised. One sentence of his book must do him immortal honor. "I like a person who points out a mistake just as much as one who teaches me a truth, because, in effect, a corrected mistake is a truth.". . .

Hitherto I have considered this hypothesis as applied to brute animals only, and not in its extension to the man of America, whether aboriginal or transplanted. It is the opinion of Mons. de Buffon that the former furnishes no exception to it. . . .

An afflicting picture, indeed, which for the honor of human nature, I am glad to believe has no original. Of the Indian of South America I know nothing; for I would not honor with the appellation of knowledge, what I derive from the fables published of them. These I believe to be just as true as the fables of Aesop. This belief is founded on what I have seen of man, white, red, and black, and what has been written of him by authors, enlightened themselves, and writing among an enlightened people. The Indian of North America being more within our reach, I can speak of him somewhat from my own knowledge, but more from the information of others better acquainted with him, and on whose truth and judgment I can rely. From these sources I am able to say, in contradiction to this representation, that he is neither more defective in ardor, nor more impotent with his female, than the white reduced to the same diet and exercise; that he is brave, when an enterprise depends on bravery; education with him making the point of honor consist in the destruction of an enemy by strat-

agem, and in the preservation of his own person free from injury; or, perhaps, this is nature, while it is education which teaches us to honor force
more than finesse; that he will defend himself against a host of enemies,
always choosing to be killed, rather than to surrender, though it be to the
whites, who he knows will treat him well; that in other situations, also, he
meets death with more deliberation, and endures tortures with a firmness
unknown almost to religious enthusiasm with us; that he is affectionate to
his children, careful of them, and indulgent in the extreme; that his affections comprehend his other connections, weakening, as with us, from circle to circle, as they recede from the centre; that his friendships are strong
and faithful to the uttermost extremity; that his sensibility is keen, even the
warriors weeping most bitterly on the loss of their children, though in general they endeavor to appear superior to human events; that his vivacity
and activity of mind is equal to ours in the same situation; hence his eagerness for hunting, and for games of chance. The women are submitted
to unjust drudgery. This I believe is the case with every barbarous people.
With such, force is law. The stronger sex imposes on the weaker. It is civilization alone which replaces women in the enjoyment of their natural
equality. That first teaches us to subdue the selfish passions, and to respect those rights in others which we value in ourselves. Were we in equal
barbarism, our females would be equal drudges. The man with them is
less strong than with us, but their women stronger than ours; and both for
the same obvious reason; because our man and their woman is habituated
to labor, and formed by it. With both races the sex which is indulged with
ease is the least athletic. An Indian man is small in the hand and wrist, for
the same reason for which a sailor is large and strong in the arms and
shoulders, and a porter in the legs and thighs. They raise fewer children
than we do. The causes of this are to be found, not in a difference of nature, but of circumstance. The women very frequently attending the men
in their parties of war and of hunting, childbearing becomes extremely in-
convenient to them. It is said, therefore, that they have learned the practice of procuring abortion by the use of some vegetable; and that it even
extends to prevent conception for a considerable time after. During these
parties they are exposed to numerous hazards, to excessive exertions, to
the greatest extremities of hunger. Even at their homes the nation depends
for food, through a certain part of every year, on the gleanings of the forest; that is, they experience a famine once in every year. With all animals,
if the female be badly fed, or not fed at all, her young perish; and if both
male and female be reduced to like want, generation becomes less active,
less productive. To the obstacles, then, of want and hazard, which nature
has opposed to the multiplication of wild animals, for the purpose of restraining their numbers within certain bounds, those of labor and of voluntary abortion are added with the Indian. No wonder, then, if they

multiply less than we do. Where food is regularly supplied, a single farm will show more of cattle, than a whole country of forests can of buffaloes. The same Indian women, when married to white traders, who feed them and their children plentifully and regularly, who exempt them from excessive drudgery, who keep them stationary and unexposed to accident, produce and raise as many children as the white women. Instances are known, under these circumstances, of their rearing a dozen children. An inhuman practice once prevailed in this country, of making slaves of the Indians. It is a fact well known with us, that the Indian women so enslaved produced and raised as numerous families as either the whites or blacks among whom they lived. It has been said that Indians have less hair than the whites, except on the head. But this is a fact of which fair proof can scarcely be had. With them it is disgraceful to be hairy on the body. They say it likens them to hogs. They therefore pluck the hair as fast as it appears. But the traders who marry their women, and prevail on them to discontinue this practice, say, that nature is the same with them as with the whites. Nor, if the fact be true, is the consequence necessary which has been drawn from it. . . .

Before we condemn the Indians of this continent as wanting genius, we must consider that letters have not yet been introduced among them. Were we to compare them in their present state with the Europeans, north of the Alps, when the Roman arms and arts first crossed those mountains, the comparison would be unequal, because, at that time, those parts of Europe were swarming with numbers; because numbers produce emulation, and multiply the chances of improvement, and one improvement begets another. Yet I may safely ask, how many good poets, how many able mathematicians, how many great inventors in arts or sciences, had Europe, north of the Alps, then produced? And it was sixteen centuries after this before a Newton could be formed. I do not mean to deny that there are varieties in the race of man, distinguished by their powers both of body and mind. I believe there are, as I see to be the case in the races of other animals. I only mean to suggest a doubt, whether the bulk and faculties of animals depend on the side of the Atlantic on which their food happens to grow, or which furnishes the elements of which they are compounded? Whether nature has enlisted herself as a Cis or Trans-Atlantic partisan? I am induced to suspect there has been more eloquence than sound reasoning displayed in support of this theory; that it is one of those cases where the judgment has been seduced by a glowing pen; and whilst I render every tribute of honor and esteem to the celebrated zoologist, who has added, and is still adding, so many precious things to the treasures of science, I must doubt whether in this instance he has not cherished error also, by lending her for a moment his vivid imagination and bewitching language. . . .

17

. . .

Necessary alterations in that, and so much of the whole body of the   18
British statutes, and of acts of assembly, as were thought proper to be retained, were digested into one hundred and twenty-six new acts, in which
simplicity of style was aimed at, as far as was safe. The following are the
most remarkable alterations proposed:

To change the rules of descent, so as that the lands of any person dying   19
intestate shall be divisible equally among all his children, or other representatives, in equal degree.

To make slaves distributable among the next of kin, as other movables.   20

To have all public expenses, whether of the general treasury, or of a   21
parish or county, (as for the maintenance of the poor, building bridges,
courthouses, &c.,) supplied by assessment on the citizens, in proportion
to their property.

To hire undertakers for keeping the public roads in repair, and indem-   22
nify individuals through whose lands new roads shall be opened.

To define with precision the rules whereby aliens should become citi-   23
zens, and citizens make themselves aliens.

To establish religious freedom on the broadest bottom.   24

To emancipate all slaves born after the passing of the act. The bill re-   25
ported by the revisers does not itself contain this proposition; but an
amendment containing it was prepared, to be offered to the legislature
whenever the bill should be taken up, and farther directing, that they
should continue with their parents to a certain age, then to be brought up,
at the public expense, to tillage, arts, or sciences, according to their ge-
niuses, till the females should be eighteen, and the males twenty-one
years of age, when they should be colonized to such place as the circumstances of the time should render most proper, sending them out with
arms, implements of household and of the handicraft arts, seeds, pairs of
the useful domestic animals, &c., to declare them a free and independent
people, and extend to them our alliance and protection, till they have acquired strength; and to send vessels at the same time to other parts of the
world for an equal number of white inhabitants; to induce them to migrate
hither proper encouragements were to be proposed. It will probably be
asked, Why not retain and incorporate the blacks into the State, and thus
save the expense of supplying by importation of white settlers, the vacan-
cies they will leave? Deep-rooted prejudices entertained by the whites; ten
thousand recollections, by the blacks, of the injuries they have sustained;
new provocations; the real distinctions which nature has made; and many
other circumstances, will divide us into parties, and produce convulsions,
which will probably never end but in the extermination of the one or the
other race. To these objections, which are political, may be added others,
which are physical and moral. The first difference which strikes us is that

of color. Whether the black of the negro resides in the reticular membrane between the skin and scarf-skin, or in the scarf-skin itself; whether it proceeds from the color of the blood, the color of the bile, or from that of some other secretion, the difference is fixed in nature, and is as real as if its seat and cause were better known to us. And is this difference of no importance? Is it not the foundation of a greater or less share of beauty in the two races? Are not the fine mixtures of red and white, the expressions of every passion by greater or less suffusions of color in the one, preferable to the eternal monotony, which reigns in the countenances, that immovable veil of black which covers the emotions of the other race? Add to these, flowing hair, a more elegant symmetry of form, their own judgment in favor of the whites, declared by their preference of them, as uniformly as is the preference of the Oran-utan for the black woman over those of his own species. The circumstance of superior beauty, is thought worthy attention in the propagation of our horses, dogs, and other domestic animals; why not in that of man? Besides those of color, figure, and hair, there are other physical distinctions proving a difference of race. They have less hair on the face and body. They secrete less by the kidneys, and more by the glands of the skin, which gives them a very strong and disagreeable odor. This greater degree of transpiration, renders them more tolerant of heat, and less so of cold than the whites. Perhaps, too, a difference of structure in the pulmonary apparatus, which a late ingenious experimentalist has discovered to be the principal regulator of animal heat, may have disabled them from extricating, in the act of inspiration, so much of that fluid from the outer air, or obliged them in expiration, to part with more of it. They seem to require less sleep. A black after hard labor through the day, will be induced by the slightest amusements to sit up till midnight, or later, though knowing he must be out with first dawn of the morning. They are at least as brave, and more adventuresome. But this may perhaps proceed from a want of forethought, which prevents their seeing a danger till it be present. When present, they do not go through it with more coolness or steadiness than the whites. They are more ardent after their female; but love seems with them to be more an eager desire, than a tender delicate mixture of sentiment and sensation. Their griefs are transient. Those numberless afflictions, which render it doubtful whether heaven has given life to us in mercy or in wrath, are less felt, and sooner forgotten with them. In general, their existence appears to participate more of sensation than reflection. To this must be ascribed their disposition to sleep when abstracted from their diversions, and unemployed in labor. An animal whose body is at rest, and who does not reflect must be disposed to sleep of course. Comparing them by their faculties of memory, reason, and imagination, it appears to me that in memory they are equal to the whites; in reason much inferior, as I think one could scarcely be found capable of tracing and comprehending the investigations of Euclid; and that in imagination they are dull, tasteless, and anomalous. It would be unfair to follow them to Africa for this investigation. We will consider them here, on the same stage with the whites, and where the facts are not apocryphal on which a judgment is to be formed. It will be right to make great allowances for the difference of condition, of education, of conversation, of the sphere in which they move. Many millions of them have been brought to, and born in America. Most of them, indeed, have been confined to tillage, to their own homes, and their own society; yet many have been so situated, that they might have availed themselves of the conversation of their masters; many have been brought up to the handicraft arts, and from that circumstance have always been associated with the whites. Some have been liberally educated, and all have lived in countries where the arts and sciences are cultivated to a considerable degree, and all have had before their eyes samples of the best works from abroad. The Indians, with no advantages of this kind, will often carve figures on their pages not destitute of design and merit. They will crayon out an animal, a plant, or a country, so as to prove the existence of a germ in their minds which only wants cultivation. They astonish you with strokes of the most sublime oratory; such as prove their reason and sentiment strong, their imagination glowing and elevated. But never yet could I find that a black had uttered a thought above the level of plain narration; never saw even an elementary trait of painting or sculpture. In music they are more generally gifted than the whites with accurate ears for tune and time, and they have been found capable of imagining a small catch. Whether they will be equal to the composition of a more extensive run of melody, or of complicated harmony, is yet to be proved. Misery is often the parent of the most affecting touches in poetry. Among the blacks is misery enough, God knows, but no poetry.

• • •

Notwithstanding these considerations which must weaken their respect for the laws of property, we find among them numerous instances of the most rigid integrity, and as many as among their better instructed masters, of benevolence, gratitude, and unshaken fidelity. The opinion that they are inferior in the faculties of reason and imagination, must be hazarded with great diffidence. To justify a general conclusion, requires many observations, even where the subject may be submitted to the anatomical knife, to optical glasses, to analysis by fire or by solvents. How much more then where it is a faculty, not a substance, we are examining; where it eludes the research of all the senses; where the conditions of its existence are various and variously combined; where the effects of those which are present or absent bid defiance to calculation; let me add too, as a circumstance of great tenderness, where our conclusion would degrade a whole

26

race of men from the rank in the scale of beings which their Creator may perhaps have given them. To our reproach it must be said, that though for a century and a half we have had under our eyes the races of black and of red men, they have never yet been viewed by us as subjects of natural history. I advance it, therefore, as a suspicion only, that the blacks, whether originally a distinct race, or made distinct by time and circumstances, are inferior to the whites in the endowments both of body and mind. It is not against experience to suppose that different species of the same genus, or varieties of the same species, may possess different qualifications. Will not a lover of natural history then, one who views the gradations in all the races of animals with the eye of philosophy, excuse an effort to keep those in the department of man as distinct as nature has formed them? This unfortunate difference of color, and perhaps of faculty, is a powerful obstacle to the emancipation of these people. Many of their advocates, while they wish to vindicate the liberty of human nature, are anxious also to preserve its dignity and beauty. Some of these, embarrassed by the question, "What further is to be done with them?" join themselves in opposition with those who are actuated by sordid avarice only. Among the Romans emancipation required but one effort. The slave, when made free, might mix with, without staining the blood of his master. But with us a second is necessary, unknown to history. When freed, he is to be removed beyond the reach of mixture. . . .

QUESTIONS FOR DISCUSSION AND WRITING

1. Jefferson offers a detailed and sometimes complicated argument meant to counter the widely held view among European naturalists (like the Count de Buffon) about the quality of nature in the New World as compared with the Old. As best you can, restate Buffon's argument and Jefferson's response.

2. Jefferson devotes much of his attention to the geography and natural history of the New World, but he also analyzes and speculates about the *other* cultures that exist in Virginia. Summarize his discussion of the "nature" of blacks and their place in Virginia society. That done, offer your own reactions to Jefferson's observations and conclusions.

3. Jefferson also discusses Indian culture, especially the relative roles of men and women. How would you describe Jefferson's attitude toward Indian culture? How do his views compare with our contemporary views of Native Americans and their culture?

J. Hector St. John de Crèvecoeur

Although its author was neither American (he was a French-born aristocrat) nor much of a farmer, Letters from an American Farmer *(1782) is one of the first and most influential pieces of imaginative nature writing done in America. Born in Normandy in 1735, St. John de Crèvecoeur served with the Canadian militia at the Battle of Quebec and then emigrated to America, where he traveled the colonies as a trader and surveyor. In 1769, Crèvecoeur bought a farm in New York, married, and began his relatively brief career as an American farmer. With the start of the American Revolution, Crèvecoeur returned to France until 1783, when he was appointed French consul to New York, Connecticut, and New Jersey. Crèvecoeur began writing his letters in 1769, but* Letters from an American Farmer *was not published until 1782. As with Jefferson's* Notes on the State of Virginia, *Crèvecoeur's book caused a sensation in Europe, particularly among French readers hungry for news about America. Despite his claim that he was "but a simple farmer," Crèvecoeur's work shrewdly shows both the skills of a naturalist and the ear of a poet as it presents its readers with an America they were anxious to discover: a wild, vital land where free and honest people live in harmony with nature.*

From *Letters from an American Farmer*

LETTER II

On the Situation, Feelings, and Pleasures of an American Farmer

As you are the first enlightened European I have ever had the pleasure of being acquainted with, you will not be surprised that I should, according to your earnest desire and my promise, appear anxious of preserving your friendship and correspondence. By your accounts, I observe a material difference subsists between your husbandry, modes, and customs, and ours; everything is local; could we enjoy the advantages of the English farmer, we should be much happier, indeed, but this wish, like many others, implies a contradiction; and could the English farmer have some of those privileges we possess, they would be the first of their class in the world. Good and evil I see is to be found in all societies, and it is in vain to seek for any spot where those ingredients are not mixed. I therefore rest satisfied, and thank God that my lot is to be an American farmer, instead of a Russian boor, or an Hungarian peasant. I thank you kindly for the idea, however dreadful, which you have given me of their lot and condition; your observations have confirmed me in the justness of my ideas, and I am happier now than I thought myself before. It is strange that misery, when viewed in others, should become to us a sort of real good, though I am far from rejoicing to hear that there are in the world men so thoroughly wretched; they are no doubt as harmless, industrious, and willing to work as we are. Hard is their fate to be thus condemned to a slavery worse than that of our negroes. Yet when young I entertained some thoughts of selling my farm. I thought it afforded but a dull repetition of the same labours and pleasures. I thought the former tedious and heavy, the latter few and insipid; but when I came to consider myself as divested of my farm, I then found the world so wide, and every place so full, that I began to fear lest there would be no room for me. My farm, my house, my barn, presented to my imagination objects from which I adduced quite new ideas; they were more forcible than before. Why should not I find myself happy, said I, where my father was before? He left me no good books it is true, he gave me no other education than the art of reading and writing; but he left me a good farm, and his experience; he left me free from debts, and no kind of difficulties to struggle with.—I married, and this perfectly reconciled me to my situation; my wife rendered my house all at once cheerful and pleasing; it no longer appeared gloomy and solitary as before; when I went to work in my fields I worked with more alacrity and sprightliness; I felt that I did not work for myself alone, and this encouraged me much. My wife would often come with her knitting in her hand, and sit under the shady trees, praising the straightness of my furrows, and the docility of my horses; this swelled my heart and made everything light and pleasant, and I regretted that I had not married before.

I felt myself happy in my new situation, and where is that station which can confer a more substantial system of felicity than that of an American farmer, possessing freedom of action, freedom of thoughts, ruled by a mode of government which requires but little from us? I owe nothing, but a pepper corn to my country, a small tribute to my king, with loyalty and due respect; I know no other landlord than the lord of all land, to whom I owe the most sincere gratitude. My father left me three hundred and seventy-one acres of land, forty-seven of which are good timothy meadow, an excellent orchard, a good house, and a substantial barn. It is my duty to think how happy I am that he lived to build and to pay for all these improvements; what are the labours which I have to undergo, what are my fatigues when compared to his, who had everything to do, from the first tree he felled to the finishing of his house? Every year I kill from 1500 to 2000 weight of pork, 1200 of beef, half a dozen of good wethers in harvest: of fowls my wife has always a great stock: what can I wish more? My negroes are tolerably faithful and healthy; by a long series of industry and honest dealings, my father left behind him the name of a good man; I have but to tread his paths to be happy and a good man like him. I know enough of the law to regulate my little concerns with propriety, nor do I dread its power; these are the grand outlines of my situation, but as I can feel much more than I am able to express, I hardly know how to proceed.

When my first son was born, the whole train of my ideas were suddenly altered; never was there a charm that acted so quickly and powerfully; I ceased to ramble in imagination through the wide world; my excursions since have not exceeded the bounds of my farm, and all my principal pleasures are now centred within its scanty limits: but at the same time there is not an operation belonging to it in which I do not find some food for useful reflections. This is the reason, I suppose, that when you were here, you used, in your refined style, to denominate me the farmer of feelings; how rude must those feelings be in him who daily holds the axe or the plough, how much more refined on the contrary those of the European, whose mind is improved by education, example, books, and by every acquired advantage! Those feelings, however, I will delineate as well as I can, agreeably to your earnest request.

When I contemplate my wife, by my fire-side, while she either spins, knits, darns, or suckles our child, I cannot describe the various emotions of love, of gratitude, of conscious pride, which thrill in my heart and often overflow in involuntary tears. I feel the necessity, the sweet pleasure of acting my part, the part of an husband and father, with an attention and propriety which may entitle me to my good fortune. It is true these pleasing images vanish with the smoke of my pipe, but though they disappear from my mind, the impression they have made on my heart is indelible. When I play with the infant, my warm imagination runs forward, and eagerly anticipates his future temper and constitution. I would willingly open the book of fate, and know in which page his destiny is delineated; alas! where is the father who in those moments of paternal ecstasy can delineate one half of the thoughts which dilate his heart? I am sure I cannot; then again I fear for the health of those who are become so dear to me, and in their sicknesses I severely pay for the joys I experienced while they were well. Whenever I go abroad it is always involuntary. I never return home without feeling some pleasing emotion, which I often suppress as useless and foolish. The instant I enter on my own land, the bright idea of property, of exclusive right, of independence exalt my mind. Precious soil, I say to myself, by what singular custom of law is it that thou wast made to constitute the riches of the freeholder? What should we American farmers be without the distinct possession of that soil? It feeds, it clothes us, from it we draw even a great exuberancy, our best meat, our richest

3

4

drink, the very honey of our bees comes from this privileged spot. No wonder we should thus cherish its possession, no wonder that so many Europeans who have never been able to say that such portion of land was theirs, cross the Atlantic to realise that happiness. This formerly rude soil has been converted by my father into a pleasant farm, and in return it has established all our rights; on it is founded our rank, our freedom, our power as citizens, our importance as inhabitants of such a district. These images I must confess I always behold with pleasure, and extend them as far as my imagination can reach: for this is what may be called the true and the only philosophy of an American farmer.

Pray do not laugh in thus seeing an artless countryman tracing himself   5
through the simple modifications of his life; remember that you have required it, therefore with candour, though with diffidence, I endeavour to
follow the thread of my feelings, but I cannot tell you all. Often when I
plough my low ground, I place my little boy on a chair which screws to
the beam of the plough—its motion and that of the horses please him, he
is perfectly happy and begins to chat. As I lean over the handle, various
are the thoughts which crowd into my mind. I am now doing for him, I
say, what my father formerly did for me, may God enable him to live that
he may perform the same operations for the same purposes when I am
worn out and old! I relieve his mother of some trouble while I have him
with me, the odoriferous furrow exhilarates his spirits, and seems to do
the child a great deal of good, for he looks more blooming since I have
adopted that practice; can more pleasure, more dignity be added to that
primary occupation? The father thus ploughing with his child, and to feed
his family, is inferior only to the emperor of China ploughing as an example to his kingdom. In the evening when I return home through my low
grounds, I am astonished at the myriads of insects which I perceive dancing in the beams of the setting sun. I was before scarcely acquainted with
their existence, they are so small that it is difficult to distinguish them; they
are carefully improving this short evening space, not daring to expose
themselves to the blaze of our meridian sun. I never see an egg brought
on my table but I feel penetrated with the wonderful change it would have
undergone but for my gluttony; it might have been a gentle useful hen
leading her chickens with a care and vigilance which speaks shame to
many women. A cock perhaps, arrayed with the most majestic plumes,
tender to its mate, bold, courageous, endowed with an astonishing instinct, with thoughts, with memory, and every distinguishing characteristic of the reason of man. I never see my trees drop their leaves and their
fruit in the autumn, and bud again in the spring, without wonder; the
sagacity of those animals which have long been the tenants of my farm
astonish me: some of them seem to surpass even men in memory and
sagacity. I could tell you singular instances of that kind. What then is this

instinct which we so debase, and of which we are taught to entertain so diminutive an idea? My bees, above any other tenants of my farm, attract my attention and respect; I am astonished to see that nothing exists but what has its enemy, one species pursue and live upon the other: unfortunately our kingbirds are the destroyers of those industrious insects; but on the other hand, these birds preserve our fields from the depredation of crows which they pursue on the wing with great vigilance and astonishing dexterity.

Thus divided by two interested motives, I have long resisted the desire 6 I had to kill them, until last year, when I thought they increased too much, and my indulgence had been carried too far; it was at the time of swarming when they all came and fixed themselves on the neighbouring trees, from whence they caught those that returned loaded from the fields. This made me resolve to kill as many as I could, and I was just ready to fire, when a bunch of bees as big as my fist, issued from one of the hives, rushed on one of the birds, and probably stung him, for he instantly screamed, and flew, not as before, in an irregular manner, but in a direct line. He was followed by the same bold phalanx, at a considerable distance, which unfortunately becoming too sure of victory, quitted their military array and disbanded themselves. By this inconsiderate step they lost all that aggregate of force which had made the bird fly off. Perceiving their disorder he immediately returned and snapped as many as he wanted; nay, he had even the impudence to alight on the very twig from which the bees had drove him. I killed him and immediately opened his craw, from which I took 171 bees; I laid them all on a blanket in the sun, and to my great surprise 54 returned to life, licked themselves clean, and joyfully went back to the hive; where they probably informed their companions of such an adventure and escape, as I believe had never happened before to American bees! I draw a great fund of pleasure from the quails which inhabit my farm; they abundantly repay me, by their various notes and peculiar tameness, for the inviolable hospitality I constantly show them in the winter. Instead of perfidiously taking advantage of their great and affecting distress, when nature offers nothing but a barren universal bed of snow, when irresistible necessity forces them to my barn doors, I permit them to feed unmolested; and it is not the least agreeable spectacle which that dreary season presents, when I see those beautiful birds, tamed by hunger, intermingling with all my cattle and sheep, seeking in security for the poor scanty grain which but for them would be useless and lost. Often in the angles of the fences where the motion of the wind prevents the snow from settling, I carry them both chaff and grain; the one to feed them, the other to prevent their tender feet from freezing fast to the earth as I have frequently observed them to do.

I do not know an instance in which the singular barbarity of man is 7 so strongly delineated, as in the catching and murthering those harm-less birds, at that cruel season of the year. Mr. ———, one of the most famous and extraordinary farmers that has ever done honour to the province of Connecticut, by his timely and humane assistance in a hard winter, saved this species from being entirely destroyed. They perished all over the country, none of their delightful whistlings were heard the next spring, but upon this gentleman's farm; and to his humanity we owe the continuation of their music. When the severities of that season have dispir-ited all my cattle, no farmer ever attends them with more pleasure than I do; it is one of those duties which is sweetened with the most rational sat-isfaction. I amuse myself in beholding their different tempers, actions, and the various effects of their instinct now powerfully impelled by the force of hunger. I trace their various inclinations, and the different effects of their passions, which are exactly the same as among men; the law is to us precisely what I am in my barn yard, a bridle and check to prevent the strong and greedy from oppressing the timid and weak. Conscious of su-periority, they always strive to encroach on their neighbours; unsatisfied with their portion, they eagerly swallow it in order to have an opportunity of taking what is given to others, except they are prevented. Some I chide, others, unmindful of my admonitions, receive some blows. Could victuals thus be given to men without the assistance of any language, I am sure they would not behave better to one another, nor more philosophically than my cattle do.

The same spirit prevails in the stable; but there I have to do with more generous animals, there my well-known voice has immediate influence, and soon restores peace and tranquillity. Thus by superior knowledge I govern all my cattle as wise men are obliged to govern fools and the ig-norant. A variety of other thoughts crowd on my mind at that peculiar in-stant, but they all vanish by the time I return home. If in a cold night I swiftly travel in my sledge, carried along at the rate of twelve miles an hour, many are the reflections excited by surrounding circumstances. I ask myself what sort of an agent is that which we call frost? Our minister com-paes it to needles, the points of which enter our pores. What is become of the heat of the summer; in what part of the world is it that the N. W. keeps these grand magazines of nitre? When I see in the morning a river over which I can travel, that in the evening before was liquid, I am aston-ished indeed! What is become of those millions of insects which played in our summer fields, and in our evening meadows; they were so puny and so delicate, the period of their existence was so short, that one cannot help wondering how they could learn, in that short space, the sublime art to hide themselves and their offspring in so perfect a manner as to baffle the rigour of the season, and preserve that precious embryo of life, that small portion of ethereal heat, which if once destroyed would destroy the

8

species! Whence that irresistible propensity to sleep so common in all those who are severely attacked by the frost. Dreary as this season appears, yet it has like all others its miracles, it presents to man a variety of problems which he can never resolve; among the rest, we have here a set of small birds which never appear until the snow falls; contrary to all others, they dwell and appear to delight in that element.

It is my bees, however, which afford me the most pleasing and extensive themes; let me look at them when I will, their government, their industry, their quarrels, their passions, always present me with something new; for which reason, when weary with labour, my common place of rest is under my locust-tree, close by my bee-house. By their movements I can predict the weather, and can tell the day of their swarming; but the most difficult point is, when on the wing, to know whether they want to go to the woods or not. If they have previously pitched in some hollow trees, it is not the allurements of salt and water, of fennel, hickory leaves, etc., nor the finest box, that can induce them to stay; they will prefer those rude, rough habitations to the best polished mahogany hive. When that is the case with mine, I seldom thwart their inclinations; it is in freedom that they work: were I to confine them, they would dwindle away and quit their labour. In such excursions we only part for a while; I am generally sure to find them again the following fall. This elopement of theirs only adds to my recreations; I know how to deceive even their superlative instinct; nor do I fear losing them, though eighteen miles from my house, and lodged in the most lofty trees, in the most impervious of our forests. I once took you along with me in one of these rambles, and yet you insist on my repeating the detail of our operations: it brings back into my mind many of the useful and entertaining reflections with which you so happily beguiled our tedious hours.

After I have done sowing, by way of recreation, I prepare for a week's jaunt in the woods, not to hunt either the deer or the bears, as my neighbours do, but to catch the more harmless bees. I cannot boast that this chase is so noble, or so famous among men, but I find it less fatiguing, and full as profitable; and the last consideration is the only one that moves me. I take with me my dog, as a companion, for he is useless as to this game; my gun, for no man you know ought to enter the woods without one; my blanket, some provisions, some wax, vermilion, honey, and a small pocket compass. With these implements I proceed to such woods as are at a considerable distance from any settlements. I carefully examine whether they abound with large trees, if so, I make a small fire on some flat stones, in a convenient place; on the fire I put some wax; close by this fire, on another stone, I drop honey in distinct drops, which I surround with small quantities of vermilion, laid on the stone; and then I retire carefully to watch whether any bees appear. If there are any in that neighbourhood, I rest assured that the smell of the burnt wax will unavoidably attract them; they will soon find out the honey, for they are fond of preying on that which is not their own; and in their approach they will necessarily tinge themselves with some particles of vermilion, which will adhere long to their bodies. I next fix my compass, to find out their course, which they keep invariably straight, when they are returning home loaded. By the assistance of my watch, I observe how long those are returning which are marked with vermilion. Thus possessed of the course, and, in some measure, of the distance, which I can easily guess at, I follow the first, and seldom fail of coming to the tree where those republics are lodged. I then mark it; and thus, with patience, I have found out sometimes eleven swarms in a season; and it is inconceivable what a quantity of honey these trees will sometimes afford. It entirely depends on the size of the hollow, as the bees never rest nor swarm till it is all replenished; for like men, it is only the want of room that induces them to quit the maternal hive. Next I proceed to some of the nearest settlements, where I procure proper assistance to cut down the trees, get all my prey secured, and then return home with my prize. The first bees I ever procured were thus found in the woods, by mere accident; for at that time I had no kind of skill in this method of tracing them. The body of the tree being perfectly sound, they had lodged themselves in the hollow of one of its principal limbs, which I carefully sawed off and with a good deal of labour and industry brought it home, where I fixed it up again in the same position in which I found it growing. This was in April; I had five swarms that year, and they have been ever since very prosperous. This business generally takes up a week of my time every fall, and to me it is a week of solitary ease and relaxation.

The seed is by that time committed to the ground; there is nothing very   11
material to do at home, and this additional quantity of honey enables me to be more generous to my home bees, and my wife to make a due quantity of mead. The reason, Sir, that you found mine better than that of others is, that she puts two gallons of brandy in each barrel, which ripens it, and takes off that sweet, luscious taste, which it is apt to retain a long time. If we find anywhere in the woods (no matter on whose land) what is called a bee-tree, we must mark it; in the fall of the year when we propose to cut it down, our duty is to inform the proprietor of the land, who is entitled to half the contents; if this is not complied with we are exposed to an action of trespass, as well as he who should go and cut down a bee-tree which he had neither found out nor marked.

We have twice a year the pleasure of catching pigeons, whose numbers   12
are sometimes so astonishing as to obscure the sun in their flight. Where is it that they hatch? for such multitudes must require an immense quantity of food. I fancy they breed toward the plains of Ohio, and those about

lake Michigan, which abound in wild oats; though I have never killed any that had that grain in their craws. In one of them, last year, I found some undigested rice. Now the nearest rice fields from where I live must be at least 560 miles; and either their digestion must be suspended while they are flying, or else they must fly with the celerity of the wind. We catch them with a net extended on the ground, to which they are allured by what we call *tame wild pigeons*, made blind, and fastened to a long string; his short flights, and his repeated calls, never fail to bring them down. The greatest number I ever catched was fourteen dozen, though much larger quantities have often been trapped. I have frequently seen them at the market so cheap, that for a penny you might have as many as you could carry away; and yet from the extreme cheapness you must not conclude, that they are but an ordinary food; on the contrary, I think they are excellent. Every farmer has a tame wild pigeon in a cage at his door all the year round, in order to be ready whenever the season comes for catching them.

The pleasure I receive from the warblings of the birds in the spring, is   13
superior to my poor description, as the continual succession of their tuneful notes is for ever new to me. I generally rise from bed about that indistinct interval, which, properly speaking, is neither night or day; for this is the moment of the most universal vocal choir. Who can listen unmoved to the sweet love tales of our robins, told from tree to tree? or to the shrill cat birds? The sublime accents of the thrush from on high always retard my steps that I may listen to the delicious music. The variegated appearances of the dew drops, as they hang to the different objects, must present even to a clownish imagination, the most voluptuous ideas. The astonishing art which all birds display in the construction of their nests, ill provided as we may suppose them with proper tools, their neatness, their convenience, always make me ashamed of the slovenliness of our houses; their love to their dame, their incessant careful attention, and the peculiar songs they address to her while she tediously incubates their eggs, remind me of my duty could I ever forget it. Their affection to their helpless little ones, is a lively precept; and in short, the whole economy of what we proudly call the brute creation, is admirable in every circumstance; and vain man, though adorned with the additional gift of reason, might learn from the perfection of instinct, how to regulate the follies, and how to temper the errors which this second gift often makes him commit. This is a subject, on which I have often bestowed the most serious thoughts; I have often blushed within myself, and been greatly astonished, when I have compared the unerring path they all follow, all just, all proper, all wise, up to the necessary degree of perfection, with the coarse, the imperfect systems of men, not merely as governors and kings, but as masters, as husbands, as fathers, as citizens. But this is a sanctuary in which an ignorant farmer must not presume to enter.

If ever man was permitted to receive and enjoy some blessings that   14
might alleviate the many sorrows to which he is exposed, it is certainly in
the country, when he attentively considers those ravishing scenes with
which he is everywhere surrounded. This is the only time of the year in
which I am avaricious of every moment, I therefore lose none that can add
to this simple and inoffensive happiness. I roam early throughout all my
fields; not the least operation do I perform, which is not accompanied
with the most pleasing observations; were I to extend them as far as I have
carried them, I should become tedious; you would think me guilty of af-
fectation, and I should perhaps represent many things as pleasurable from
which you might not perhaps receive the least agreeable emotions. But,
believe me, what I write is all true and real.

Some time ago, as I sat smoking a contemplative pipe in my piazza, I   15
saw with amazement a remarkable instance of selfishness displayed in a
very small bird, which I had hitherto respected for its inoffensiveness.
Three nests were placed almost contiguous to each other in my piazza:
that of a swallow was affixed in the corner next to the house, that of a
phebe in the other, a wren possessed a little box which I had made on
purpose, and hung between. Be not surprised at their tameness, all my
family had long been taught to respect them as well as myself. The wren
had shown before signs of dislike to the box which I had given it, but I
knew not on what account; at last it resolved, small as it was, to drive the
swallow from its own habitation, and to my very great surprise it succeeded. Impudence often gets the better of modesty, and this exploit was
no sooner performed, than it removed every material to its own box with
the most admirable dexterity; the signs of triumph appeared very visible,
it fluttered its wings with uncommon velocity, an universal joy was per-
ceivable in all its movements. Where did this little bird learn that spirit of
injustice? It was not endowed with what we term reason! Here then is a
proof that both those gifts border very near on one another; for we see the
perfection of the one mixing with the errors of the other! The peaceable
swallow, like the passive Quaker, meekly sat at a small distance and never
offered the least resistance; but no sooner was the plunder carried away,
than the injured bird went to work with unabated ardour, and in a few
days the depredations were repaired. To prevent however a repetition of
the same violence, I removed the wren's box to another part of the house.

In the middle of my new parlour I have, you may remember, a curious   16
republic of industrious hornets; their nest hangs to the ceiling, by the same
twig on which it was so admirably built and contrived in the woods. Its re-
moval did not displease them, for they find in my house plenty of food;
and I have left a hole open in one of the panes of the window, which answers all their purposes. By this kind usage they are become quite harmless; they live on the flies, which are very troublesome to us throughout

the summer; they are constantly busy in catching them, even on the eye-lids of my children. It is surprising how quickly they smear them with a sort of glue, lest they might escape, and when thus prepared, they carry them to their nests, as food for their young ones. These globular nests are most ingeniously divided into many stories, all provided with cells, and proper communications. The materials with which this fabric is built, they procure from the cottony furze, with which our oak rails are covered; this substance tempered with glue, produces a sort of pasteboard, which is very strong, and resists all the inclemencies of the weather. By their assis-tance, I am but little troubled with flies. All my family are so accustomed to their strong buzzing, that no one takes any notice of them; and though they are fierce and vindictive, yet kindness and hospitality has made them useful and harmless.

We have a great variety of wasps; most of them build their nests in mud, which they fix against the shingles of our roofs, as nigh the pitch as they can. These aggregates represent nothing, at first view, but coarse and ir-regular lumps, but if you break them, you will observe, that the inside of them contains a great number of oblong cells, in which they deposit their eggs, and in which they bury themselves in the fall of the year. Thus im-mured they securely pass through the severity of that season, and on the return of the sun are enabled to perforate their cells, and to open them-selves a passage from these recesses into the sunshine. The yellow wasps, which build under ground, in our meadows, are much more to be dreaded, for when the mower unwittingly passes his scythe over their holes they immediately sally forth with a fury and velocity superior even to the strength of man. They make the boldest fly, and the only remedy is to lie down and cover our heads with hay, for it is only at the head they aim their blows; nor is there any possibility of finishing that part of the work until, by means of fire and brimstone, they are all silenced. But though I have been obliged to execute this dreadful sentence in my own defence, I have often thought it a great pity, for the sake of a little hay, to lay waste so ingenious a subterranean town, furnished with every conve-niency, and built with a most surprising mechanism. 17

I never should have done were I to recount the many objects which involuntarily strike my imagination in the midst of my work, and spon-taneously afford me the most pleasing relief. These appear insignificant trifles to a person who has travelled through Europe and America, and is acquainted with books and with many sciences; but such simple objects of contemplation suffice me, who have no time to bestow on more exten-sive observations. Happily these require no study, they are obvious, they gild the moments I dedicate to them, and enliven the severe labours which I perform. At home my happiness springs from very different objects; the gradual unfolding of my children's reason, the study of their dawning tem- 18 pers attract all my paternal attention. I have to contrive little punishments for their little faults, small encouragements for their good actions, and a variety of other expedients dictated by various occasions. But these are themes unworthy your perusal, and which ought not to be carried beyond the walls of my house, being domestic mysteries adapted only to the locality of the small sanctuary wherein my family resides. Sometimes I delight in inventing and executing machines, which simplify my wife's labour. I have been tolerably successful that way; and these, Sir, are the narrow circles within which I constantly revolve, and what can I wish for beyond them? I bless God for all the good he has given me; I envy no man's prosperity, and with no other portion of happiness than that I may live to teach the same philosophy to my children; and give each of them a farm, show them how to cultivate it, and be like their father, good substantial independent American farmers—an appellation which will be the most fortunate one a man of my class can possess, so long as our civil government continues to shed blessings on our husbandry. Adieu.

QUESTIONS FOR DISCUSSION AND WRITING

1. Crèvecoeur's writing celebrates the "great exuberancy" of the American soil as he presents what he calls "the true and the only philosophy of an American farmer" (par. 4). Outline the central premises of that philosophy, paying special attention to the connections Crèvecoeur makes between nature, the land, and liberty. Do Americans continue to believe in any of this philosophy, or does it all seem hopelessly outdated?

2. *Letters from an American Farmer* was a huge sensation with readers in Europe, and especially with French readers hungry for news about America and Americans. Beneath his exuberant details of honeybees and pigeon hunts, what powers does Crèvecoeur assign to nature in the New World that might have so excited those readers? What contrast does he make between these powers and nature in the Old World?

WILLIAM BARTRAM

Born in 1739, William Bartram literally grew up in the garden of the New World: Bartram's Botanical Garden of Philadelphia, a family business begun by his father, the famous botanist John Bartram. Like his father, William Bartram had a botanist's careful eye for detail and a love for traveling. In 1773, William began a four-year excursion through the Carolinas, Georgia, and Florida, and the diaries he kept formed the basis for The Travels of William Bartram *(1791).* Travels *is a richly detailed botanical and ethnological record, but interspersed among the exhaustive lists of flora and fauna are passionate, often poetic, celebrations of the earthly paradise he has discovered: the magnolia trees, the alligators and turtles, the honeybees and insects. When* Travels *was published in 1791, some critics objected to its overly lavish descriptions and excessive praise of the American landscape; many other readers, however, including the English poets Coleridge and Wordsworth, found inspiration in its promise of newness and renewal.*

From *The Travels of William Bartram*

I waited two or three days at this post, expecting the return of an Indian who was out hunting. This man was recommended to me as a suitable person for a protector and guide to the Indian settlements over the hills; but upon information that he would not be in shortly, and there being no other person suitable for the purpose, rather than be detained, and perhaps thereby frustrated in my purposes, I determined to set off alone and run all risks. 1

I crossed the river at a good ford just below the old fort. The river here is just one hundred yards over. After an agreeable progress for about two miles over delightful strawberry plains, and gently swelling green hills, I began to ascend more steep and rocky ridges. Having gained a very considerable elevation, looking round, I enjoyed a very comprehensive and delightful view: Keowe, which I had but just lost sight of, appeared again, and the serpentine river speeding through the lucid green plain apparently just under my feet. After observing this delightful landscape, I continued on again three or four miles, keeping the trading path, which led me over uneven rocky land, crossing rivulets and brooks, and rapidly descending over rocky precipices; when I came into a charming vale, embellished with a delightful glittering river, which meandered through it, and crossed my road. On my left hand, upon the grassy bases of the rising 2 hills, appeared the remains of a town of the ancients, as the tumuli, terraces, posts or pillars, old Peach and Plumb orchards, &c. sufficiently testify. These vales and swelling bases of the surrounding hills, afford vast crops of excellent grass and herbage fit for pasturage and hay; of the latter, Plantago Virginica, Sanguisorba, Geum, Fragaria, &c. The Panax quinquefolium, or Ginseng, now appears plentifully on the North exposure of the hill, growing out of the rich mellow humid earth amongst the stones or fragments of rocks.

Having crossed the vales, I began to ascend again the more lofty ridges of hills, then continued about eight miles over more gentle pyramidal hills, narrow vales and lawns, the soil exceedingly fertile, producing lofty forests and odoriferous groves of Calycanthus, near the banks of rivers, with Halesia, Philadelphus inodorus, Rhododendron ferrugineum, Azalea, Stewartia montana, fol. ovatis acuminatis serratis, flor. niveo, staminum corona fulgida, pericarp. pomum exsuccum, apice acuminato dehiscens, Cornus Florida, Styrax, all in full bloom, and decorated with the following sweet roving climbers, Bignonia sempervirens, Big. crucigera, Lonicera sempervirens, Rosa paniculata, &c.

Now at once the mounts divide; and disclose to view the ample Occonne vale, encircled by a wreath of uniform hills; their swelling bases clad in cheerful verdure, over which, issuing from between the mountains, plays along a glittering river, meandering through the meadows. Crossing these at the upper end of the vale, I began to ascend the Occonne mountain. On the foot of the hills are ruins of the ancient Occonne town. The first step after leaving the verdant beds of the hills, was a very high rocky chain of pointed hills, extremely well timbered with the following trees: Quercus tinctoria, Querc. alba, Querc. rubra, Fraxinus excelsior, Juglans hickory various species, Ulmus, Tilia, Acer saccharinum, Morus, Juglans nigra, Juglans alba, Annona glabra, Robinia pseudacacia, Magnolia acuminata, Aesculus sylvatica, with many more, particularly a species of Robinia new to me, though perhaps the same as figured and slightly described by Catesby in his Nat. Hist. Carol. This beautiful flowering tree grows twenty and thirty feet high, with a crooked leaning trunk; the branches spread greatly, and wreath about, some almost touching the ground; however there appears a singular pleasing wildness and freedom in its manner of growth; the slender subdivisions of the branches terminate with heavy compound panicles of rose or pink coloured flowers, amidst a wreath of beautiful pinnated leaves.

My next flight was up a very high peak, to the top of the Occonne mountain, where I rested; and turning about, found that I was now in a very elevated situation, from whence I enjoyed a view inexpressibly magnificent and comprehensive. The mountainous wilderness which I had lately traversed, down to the region of Augusta, appearing regularly undulated as the great ocean after a tempest; the undulations gradually depressing, yet perfectly regular, as the squama of fish, or imbrications of tile on a roof: the nearest ground to me of a perfect full green; next more glaucous; and lastly almost blue as the ether with which the most distant curve of the horizon seemed to be blended.

My imagination thus wholly engaged in the contemplation of this magnificent landscape, infinitely varied, and without bound, I was almost insensible or regardless of the charming objects more within my reach: a new species of Rhododendron foremost in the assembly of mountain beauties; next the flaming Azalea, Kalmia latifolia, incarnate Robinia, snowy mantled Philadelphus inodorus, perfumed Calycanthus, &c. 6

This species of Rhododendron grows six or seven feet high; many nearly erect stems arise together from the root, forming a group or coppice. The leaves are three or four inches in length, of an oblong figure, broadest toward the extremity, and terminating with an obtuse point; their upper surface of a deep green and polished; but the nether surface of a rusty iron colour, which seems to be effected by innumerable minute reddish vesicles, beneath a fine short downy pubescence; the numerous flexile branches terminate with a loose spiked raceme, or cluster of large deep rose coloured flowers, each flower being affixed in the diffused cluster of a long peduncle, which, with the whole plant, possesses an agreeable perfume. 7

After being recovered of the fatigue and labour in ascending the mountain, I began again to prosecute my task, proceeding through a shady forest; and soon after gained the most elevated crest of the Occonne mountain, and then began to descend the other side; the winding rough road carrying me over rocky hills and levels, shaded by incomparable forests, the soil exceedingly rich, and of an excellent quality for the production of every vegetable suited to the climate, and seeming peculiarly adapted for the cultivation of Vines (Vitis vinifera), Olives (Olea Europea), the Almond tree (Amygdalus communis), Fig (Ficus carica), and perhaps the Pomegranate (Punica granatum), as well as Peaches (Amyg. Persica), Prunus, Pyrus, of every variety. I passed again steep rocky ascents, and then rich levels, where grew many trees and plants common in Pennsylvania, New-York and even Canada, as Pinus strobus, Pin. sylvestris, Pin. abies, Acer saccharinum, Acer striatum, s. Pennsylvanicum, Populus tremula, Betula nigra, Juglans alba, &c.; but what seems remarkable, the yellow Jessamine (Bignonia sempervirens), which is killed by a very slight frost in the open air in Pennsylvania, here, on the summits of the Cherokee mountains associates with the Canadian vegetables, and appears roving with them in perfect bloom and gaiety; as likewise Halesia diptera, and Hal. tetraptera, mountain Stewartia, Styrax, Ptelea, Aesculus 8 pavia; but all these bear our hardest frosts in Pennsylvania. Now I enter a charming narrow vale, through which flows a rapid large creek, on whose banks are happily associated the shrubs already recited, together with the following; Staphylea, Euonimus Americana, Hamamelis, Azalea, various species, Aristolochia frutescens, s. odoratissima, which rambles over the trees and shrubs on the prolific banks of these mountain brooks. Passed through magnificent high forests, and then came upon the borders of an ample meadow on the left, embroidered by the shade of a high circular amphitheatre of hills, the circular ridges rising magnificently one over the other. On the green turfy bases of these ascents appear the ruins of a town of the ancients. The upper end of this spacious green plain is divided by a promontory or spur of the ridges before me, which projects into it: my road led me up into an opening of the ascents through which the glittering brook which watered the meadows ran rapidly down, dashing and roaring over high rocky steps. Continued yet ascending until I gained the top of an elevated rocky ridge, when appeared before me a gap or opening between other yet more lofty ascents, through which continued as the rough rocky road led me, close by the winding banks of a large rapid brook, which at length turning to the left, pouring down rocky precipices, glided off through dark groves and high forests, conveying streams of fertility and pleasure to the fields below.

The surface of the land now for three or four miles is level, yet uneven, occasioned by natural mounds or rocky knobs, but covered with a good staple of rich earth, which affords forests of timber trees and shrubs. After this, gently descending again, I travelled some miles over a varied situation of ground, exhibiting views of grand forests, dark detached groves, vales and meadows, as heretofore, and producing the like vegetable and other works of nature; the meadows, affording exuberant pasturage for cattle, and the bases of the encircling hills, flowering plants, and fruitful strawberry beds: observed frequently ruins of the habitations or villages of the ancients. Crossed a delightful river, the main branch of Tugilo, when I began to ascend again, first over swelling turfy ridges, varied with groves of stately forest trees; then ascending again more steep grassy hill sides, rested on the top of mount Magnolia, which appeared to me to be the highest ridge of the Cherokee mountains, which separate the waters of Savanna river from those of the Tanase or greater main branch of the Cherokee river. This running rapidly a North-West course through the mountains, is joined from the North-East by the Holstein; thence taking a West course yet amongst the mountains, receiving into it from either hand many large rivers, leaves the mountains immediately after being joined by a large river from the East, becomes a mighty river by the name of Hogehege, thence meanders many hundred miles through a vast country consisting of forests, meadows, groves, expansive savannas, fields and swelling hills, most fertile and delightful, flows into the beautiful Ohio, and in conjunction with its transparent waters, becomes tributary to the sovereign Mississippi.

This exalted peak I named mount Magnolia, from a new and beautiful species of that celebrated family of flowering trees, which here, at the cascades of Falling Creek, grows in a high degree of perfection: I had, indeed, noticed this curious tree several times before, particularly on the high ridges betwixt Sinica and Keowe, and on ascending the first mountain after leaving Keowe, when I observed it in flower, but here it flourishes and commands our attention. 10

This tree, or perhaps rather shrub, rises eighteen to thirty feet in height; there are usually many stems from a root or source, which lean a little, or slightly diverge from each other, in this respect imitating the Magnolia tripetala; the crooked wreathing branches arising and subdividing from the main stem without order or uniformity, their extremities turn upwards, producing a very large rosaceous, perfectly white, double or polypetalous flower, which is of a most fragrant scent; this fine flower sits in the centre of a radius of very large leaves, which are of a singular figure, somewhat lanceolate, but broad towards their extremities, terminated with an acuminated point, and backwards they attenuate and become very narrow towards their bases, terminating that way with two long narrow ears or lappets, one on each side of the insertion of the petiole; the leaves have only short footstalks, sitting very near each other, at the extremities of the floriferous branches, from whence they spread themselves after a regular order, like the spokes of a wheel, their margins touching or lightly lapping upon each other, form an expansive umbrella superbly crowned or crested with the fragrant flower, representing a white plume; the blossom is succeeded by a very large crimson cone or strobile, containing a great number of scarlet berries, which, when ripe, spring from their cells, and are for a time suspended by a white silky web or thread. The leaves of those trees which grow in a rich, light humid soil, when fully expanded and at maturity, are frequently above two feet in length, and six or eight inches where broadest. I discovered in the maritime parts of Georgia, particularly on the banks of the Alatamaha, another new species of Magnolia, whose leaves were nearly of the figure of those of this tree, but they were much less in size, not more than six or seven inches in length, and the strobile very small, oblong, sharp pointed, and of a fine deep crimson colour; but I never saw the flower. These trees grow straight and erect, thirty feet or more in height, and of a sharp conical form much resembling the Cucumber tree (Mag. acuminata) in figure. 11

The day being remarkably warm and sultry, together with the labour and fatigue of ascending the mountains, made me very thirsty and in some 12 degree sunk my spirits. Now past mid-day, I sought a cool shaded retreat, where was water for refreshment and grazing for my horse, my faithful slave and only companion. After proceeding a little farther, descending the other side of the mountain, I perceived at some distance before me, on my right hand, a level plain supporting a grand high forest and groves: the nearer I approached, my steps were the more accelerated from the flattering prospect opening to view. I now entered upon the verge of the dark forest, charming solitude! as I advanced through the animating shades, observed on the farther grassy verge a shady grove; thither I directed my steps. On approaching these shades, between the stately columns of the superb forest trees, presented to view, rushing from rocky precipices under the shade of the pensile hills, the unparalleled cascade of Falling Creek, rolling and leaping off the rocks: the waters uniting below, spread a broad glittering sheet over a vast convex elevation of plain smooth rocks, and are immediately received by a spacious bason, where trembling in the centre through hurry and agitation, they gently subside, encircling the painted still verge; from whence gliding swiftly, they soon form a delightful little river, which continuing to flow more moderately, is restrained for a moment, gently undulating in a little lake: they then pass on rapidly to a high perpendicular steep of rocks, from whence these delightful waters are hurried down with irresistible rapidity. I here seated myself on the moss-clad rocks, under the shade of spreading trees and floriferous fragrant shrubs, in full view of the cascades.

At this rural retirement were assembled a charming circle of mountain 13 vegetable beauties; Magnolia auriculata, Rhododendron ferrugineum, Kalmia latifolia, Robinia montana, Azalea flammula, Rosa paniculata, Calycanthus Floridus, Philadelphus inodorus, perfumed Convalaria majalis, Anemone thalictroides, Anemone hepatica, Erythronium maculatum, Leontice thalictroides, Trillium sessile, Trillium cesnum, Cypripedium, Arethusa, Ophrys, Sanguinaria, Viola uvularia, Epigea, Mitchella repens, Stewartia, Halesia, Styrax, Lonicera, &c. Some of these roving beauties stroll over the mossy, shelving, humid rocks, or from off the expansive wavy boughs of trees, bending over the floods, salute their delusive shade, playing on the surface; some plunge their perfumed heads and bathe their flexile limbs in the silver stream; whilst others by the mountain breezes are tossed about, their blooming tufts bespangled with pearly and chrystaline dew-drops collected from the falling mists, glistening in the rainbow arch. Having collected some valuable specimens at this friendly retreat, I continued my lonesome pilgrimage. My road for a considerable time led me winding and turning about the steep rocky hills; the descent of some of which were very rough and troublesome, by means of fragments of rocks, slippery clay and talc: but after this I entered a spacious forest, the land having gradually acquired a more level surface: a pretty grassy vale appears on my right, through which my wandering path led me, close by the banks of a delightful creek, which sometimes falling over steps of rocks, glides gently with serpentine meanders through the meadows.

After crossing this delightful brook and mead, the land rises again with 14 sublime magnificence, and I am led over hills and vales, groves and high forests, vocal with the melody of the feathered songsters; the snow-white cascades glittering on the sides of the distant hills.

It was now afternoon; I approached a charming vale, amidst sublimely 15 high forests, awful shades! Darkness gathers around; far distant thunder rolls over the trembling hills: the black clouds with august majesty and power, move slowly forwards, shading regions of towering hills, and threatening all the destruction of a thunder storm: all around is now still as death; not a whisper is heard, but a total inactivity and silence seem to pervade the earth; the birds afraid to utter a chirrup, in low tremulous voices take leave of each other, seeking covert and safety: every insect is silenced, and nothing heard but the roaring of the approaching hurricane. The mighty cloud now expands its sable wings, extending from North to South, and is driven irresistibly on by the tumultuous winds, spreading its livid wings around the gloomy concave, armed with terrors of thunder and fiery shafts of lightning. Now the lofty forests bend low beneath its fury; their limbs and wavy boughs are tossed about and catch hold of each other; the mountains tremble and seem to reel about, and the ancient hills to be shaken to their foundations: the furious storm sweeps along, smoaking through the vale and over the resounding hills: the face of the earth is obscured by the deluge descending from the firmament, and I am deafened by the din of the thunder. The tempestuous scene damps my spirits, and my horse sinks under me at the tremendous peals, as I hasten on for the plain.

The storm abating, I saw an Indian hunting cabin on the side of a hill, 16 a very agreeable prospect, especially in my present condition; I made up to it and took quiet possession, there being no one to dispute it with me except a few bats and whip-poor-wills, who had repaired thither for shelter from the violence of the hurricane.

Having turned out my horse in the sweet meadows adjoining, and 17 found some dry wood under shelter of the old cabin, I struck up a fire, dried my clothes, and comforted myself with a frugal repast of biscuit and dried beef, which was all the food my viaticum afforded me by this time, excepting a small piece of cheese which I had furnished myself with at Charleston, and kept till this time.

The night was clear, calm and cool, and I rested quietly. Next morning 18 at day-break I was awakened and summoned to resume my daily task, by the shrill cries of the social night hawk and active merry mock-bird. By the time the rising sun had gilded the tops of the towering hills, the mountains and vales rang with the harmonious shouts of the pious and cheerful tenants of the groves and meads.

I observed growing in great abundance in these mountain meadows, 19 Sanguisorba Canadensis and Heracleum maximum; the latter exhibiting a fine show, being rendered conspicuous even at a great distance, by its great height and spread, vast pennatifid leaves and expansive umbels of snow-white flowers. The swelling bases of the surrounding hills fronting the meadows presented for my acceptance the fragrant red strawberry, in painted beds of many acres surface, indeed I may safely say, many hundreds.

After passing through this meadow, the road led me over the bases of 20 a ridge of hills, which as a bold promontory dividing the fields I had just passed, form expansive green lawns. On these towering hills appeared the ruins of the ancient famous town of Sticoe. Here was a vast Indian mount or tumulus and great terrace, on which stood the council-house, with banks encompassing their circus; here were also old Peach and Plumb orchards; some of the trees appeared yet thriving and fruitful. Presently after leaving these ruins, the vale and fields are divided by means of a spur of the mountains pushing forward: here likewise the road forked; the left-hand path continued up the mountains to the Overhill towns: I followed the vale to the right hand, and soon began to ascend the hills, riding several miles over very rough, stony land, yielding the like vegetable productions as heretofore; and descending again gradually, by a dubious winding path, leading into a narrow vale and lawn, through which rolled on before me a delightful brook, water of the Tanase. I crossed it and continued a mile or two down the meadows; when the high mountains on each side suddenly receding, discovered the opening of the extensive and fruitful vale of Cowe, through which meanders the head branch of the Tanase, almost from its source, sixty miles, following its course down to Cowe.

I left for a little while, the stream passing swiftly and foaming over its 21 rocky bed, lashing the steep craggy banks, and then suddenly sunk from my sight, murmuring hollow and deep under the rocky surface of the ground. On my right hand the vale expands, receiving a pretty silvery brook of water which came hastily down from the adjacent hills, and entered the river a little distance before me. I now turn from the heights on my left, the road leading into the level lawns, to avoid the hollow rocky grounds, full of holes and cavities, arching over the river through which the waters are seen gliding along: but the river is soon liberated from these solitary and gloomy recesses, and appears waving through the green plain before me. I continued several miles, pursuing my serpentine path, though and over the meadows and green fields, and crossing the river, which is here incredibly increased in size, by the continual accession of brooks flowing in from the hills on each side, dividing their green turfy beds, forming them into parterres, vistas, and verdant swelling knolls, profusely productive of flowers and fragrant strawberries, their rich juice dying my horse's feet and ancles.

These swelling hills, the prolific beds on which the towering mountains   22
repose, seem to have been the common situations of the towns of the ancients, as appears from the remaining ruins of them yet to be seen, and the level rich vale and meadows in front, their planting grounds.

Continue yet ten or twelve miles down the vale, my road leading at   23
times close to the banks of the river, the Azalea, Kalmia, Rhododendron, Philadelphus, &c. beautifying his now elevated shores, and painting the coves with a rich and cheerful scenery, continually unfolding new prospects as I traverse the shores: towering mountains seem continually in motion as I pass along, pompously raising their superb crests towards the lofty skies, traversing the far distant horizon.

The Tanase is now greatly increased from the conflux of the multitude   24
of rivulets and brooks, descending from the hills on either side, generously contributing to establish his future fame, already a spacious river.

The mountains recede, the vale expands; two beautiful rivulets stream   25
down through lateral vales, gliding in serpentine mazes over the green turfy knolls, and enter the Tanase nearly opposite to each other. Straight forward the expansive green vale seems yet infinite: now on the right hand a lofty pyramidal hill terminates a spur of the adjacent mountain, and advances almost into the river; but immediately after doubling this promontory, an expanded wing of the vale spreads on my right, down which came precipitately a very beautiful creek, which flowed into the river just before me; but now behold, high upon the side of a distant mountain overlooking the vale, the fountain of this brisk-flowing creek; the unparalleled waterfall appears as a vast edifice with crystal front, or a field of ice lying on the bosom of the hill.

I now approach the river at the fording place, which was greatly   26
swollen by the floods of rain that fell the day before, and ran with foaming rapidity; but observing that it had fallen several feet perpendicular, and perceiving the bottom or bed of the river to be level, and covered evenly with pebbles, I ventured to cross over; however I was obliged to swim two or three yards at the deepest channel of it, and landed safely on the banks of a fine meadow, which lay on the opposite shore, where I immediately alighted and spread abroad on the turf my linen, books, and specimens of plants, &c. to dry, turned out my steed to graze, and then advanced into the strawberry plains to regale on the fragrant, delicious fruit, welcomed by communities of the splendid meleagris, the capricious roebuck, and all the free and happy tribes, which possess and inhabit those prolific fields, who appeared to invite, and joined with me in the partici-

pation of the bountiful repast presented to us from the lap of nature.

I mounted again, and followed the trading path about a quarter of a   27
mile through the fields, then gently ascended the green beds of the hills,
and entered the forests, being a point of a chain of hills projecting into the
green vale or low lands of the rivers. This forest continued about a mile,
the surface of the land level but rough, being covered with stones or fragments of rocks, and very large, smooth pebbles of various shapes and
sizes, some of ten or fifteen pounds weight: I observed on each side of the
road many vast heaps of these stones, Indian graves undoubtedly.

After I left the graves, the ample vale soon offered on my right hand,   28
through the tall forest trees, charming views, which exhibited a pleasing
contrast, immediately out of the gloomy shades and scenes of death, into
expansive, lucid, green, flowery fields, expanding between retiring hills,
and tufty eminences, the rapid Tanase gliding through, as a vast serpent
rushing after his prey.

My winding path now leads me again over the green fields into the   29
meadows, sometimes visiting the decorated banks of the river, as it meanders through the meadows, or boldly sweeps along the bases of the
mountains, its surface receiving the images reflected from the flowery
banks above.

Thus was my agreeable progress for about fifteen miles, since I came   30
upon the sources of the Tanase, at the head of this charming vale: in the
evening espying a human habitation at the foot of the sloping green hills,
beneath lofty forests of the mountains on the left hand, and at the same
time observing a man crossing the river from the opposite shore in a
canoe and coming towards me, I waited his approach, who hailing me, I
answered I was for Cowe; he entreated me very civilly to call at his house,
adding, that he would presently come to me.

I was received and entertained here until next day with the most per-   31
fect civility. After I had dined, towards evening, a company of Indian girls,
inhabitants of a village in the hills at a small distance, called, having baskets of strawberries; and this man, who kept here a trading house, being
married to a Cherokee woman of family, was indulged to keep a stock of
cattle, and his helpmate being an excellent house-wife, and a very agreeable good woman, treated us with cream and strawberries.

QUESTIONS FOR DISCUSSION AND WRITING

1. William Bartram, like his father, was a serious naturalist trained in
botany and biology, and yet even at the time of its publication *Travels* was
criticized as being too literary in its language and too excessive in its
praise of the American landscape to be considered serious "science writ-

ing." As you reread the text, look for the kinds of passages that Bartram's critics may have had in mind. If this excerpt from *Travels* were your only evidence, what conclusions would you draw about naturalists and their work?

2. Does the American landscape that Bartram travels appear to be what we today would call wilderness? Point to specific details in the text to help explain why or why not. How would you describe Bartram's feelings about the natural setting he explores? About the people he finds there?

JOHN JAMES AUDUBON

Although he is America's most famous nature artist, John James Audubon was, in fact, a Frenchman born in Haiti in 1803. He spent much of his life traveling the forests and swamps of America, sketching and painting over five hundred species of birds. Even people who don't recognize his name immediately recognize his portraits, many of which first appeared in Birds of America, *a stunning body of work laboriously published in a series of editions between 1827 and 1838. Audubon was also a prolific writer, and entries from his travel journals, like the three "episodes" included here, would appear in each edition of* Birds. *As with Jefferson's* Notes on the State of Virginia, *Audubon's meticulously detailed portraits and journals reflect his neoclassical passion for systematic study and exacting detail. So complete was this passion for getting things right that, ironically, Audubon the "naturalist" created his lifelike portraits of birds by shooting, stuffing, and painting his subjects. Still, Audubon's sketches and journals present a dramatic and complex American landscape that is very much alive. The three selections presented here were written between 1814 and 1832 but not published until 1897.*

From *Audubon and His Journals*

The Hurricane

Various portions of our country have at different periods suffered severely from the influence of violent storms of wind, some of which have been known to traverse nearly the whole extent of the United States, and to leave such deep impressions in their wake as will not easily be forgotten. Having witnessed one of these awful phenomena, in all its grandeur, I shall attempt to describe it for your sake, kind reader, and for your sake only; the recollection of that astonishing revolution of the ethereal element even now bringing with it so disagreeable a sensation that I feel as if about to be affected by a sudden stoppage of the circulation of my blood.

I had left the village of Shawanee, situated on the banks of the Ohio, on my return from Henderson, which is also situated on the banks of the same beautiful stream. The weather was pleasant, and I thought not warmer than usual at that season. My horse was jogging quietly along, and my thoughts were, for once at least in the course of my life, entirely engaged in commercial speculations. I had forded Highland Creek, and was on the eve of entering a tract of bottom land or valley that lay between it and Canoe Creek, when on a sudden I remarked a great difference in the aspect of the heavens. A hazy thickness had overspread the country, and I for some time expected an earthquake; but my horse exhibited no propensity to stop and prepare for such an occurrence. I had nearly arrived at the verge of the valley, when I thought fit to stop near a brook, and dismounted to quench the thirst which had come upon me.

I was leaning on my knees, with my lips about to touch the water,   3 when, from my proximity to the earth, I heard a distant murmuring sound of an extraordinary nature. I drank, however, and as I rose on my feet, looked towards the southwest, where I observed a yellowish oval spot, the appearance of which was quite new to me. Little time was left me for consideration, as the next moment a smart breeze began to agitate the taller trees. It increased to an unexpected height, and already the smaller branches and twigs were seen falling in a slanting direction towards the ground. Two minutes had scarcely elapsed, when the whole forest before me was in fearful motion. Here and there, where one tree pressed against another, a creaking noise was produced, similar to that occasioned by the violent gusts which sometimes sweep over the country. Turning instinctively towards the direction from which the wind blew, I saw to my great astonishment that the noblest trees of the forest bent their lofty heads for a while, and, unable to stand against the blast, were falling into pieces. First the branches were broken off with a crackling noise; then went the upper parts of the massy trunks; and in many places whole trees of gigantic size were falling entire to the ground. So rapid was the progress of the storm that before I could think of taking measures to insure my safety the hurricane was passing opposite the place where I stood. Never can I forget the scene which at that moment presented itself. The tops of the trees were seen moving in the strangest manner, in the central current of the tempest, which carried along with it a mingled mass of twigs and foliage that completely obscured the view. Some of the largest trees were seen bending and writhing under the gale; others suddenly snapped across; and many, after a momentary resistance, fell uprooted to the earth. The mass of branches, twigs, foliage, and dust that moved through the air was whirled onwards like a cloud of feathers, and on passing disclosed a wide space filled with fallen trees, naked stumps, and heaps of shapeless ruins which marked the path of the tempest. This space was about a fourth of a mile in breadth, and to my imagination resembled the dried up bed of the Mississippi, with its thousands of planters and sawyers strewed in the sand and inclined in various degrees. The horrible noise resembled that of the great cataracts of Niagara, and, as it howled along in the track of the desolating tempest, produced a feeling in my mind which it were impossible to describe.

The principal force of the hurricane was now over, although millions of   4 twigs and small branches that had been brought from a great distance were seen following the blast, as if drawn onwards by some mysterious power. They even floated in the air for some hours after, as if supported by the thick mass of dust that rose high above the ground. The sky had now a greenish lurid hue, and an extremely disagreeable sulphurous odor was diffused in the atmosphere. I waited in amazement, having sustained no material injury, until nature at length resumed her wonted aspect. For some moments I felt undetermined whether I should return to Morgantown, or attempt to force my way through the wrecks of the tempest. My business, however, being of an urgent nature, I ventured into the path of the storm, and after encountering innumerable difficulties, succeeded in crossing it. I was obliged to lead my horse by the bridle, to enable him to leap over the fallen trees, whilst I scrambled over or under them in the best way I could, at times so hemmed in by the broken tops and tangled branches as almost to become desperate. On arriving at my house, I gave an account of what I had seen, when, to my astonishment, I was told there had been very little wind in the neighborhood, although in the streets and gardens many branches and twigs had fallen in a manner which excited great surprise.

Many wondrous accounts of the devastating effects of this hurricane   5
were circulated in the country after its occurrence. Some log houses, we were told, had been overturned and their inmates destroyed. One person informed me that a wire sifter had been conveyed by the gust to a distance of many miles. Another had found a cow lodged in the fork of a large half-broken tree. But, as I am disposed to relate only what I have myself seen, I shall not lead you into the region of romance, but shall content myself with saying that much damage was done by this awful visitation. The valley is yet a desolate place, overgrown with briers and bushes, thickly entangled amidst the tops and trunks of the fallen trees, and is the resort of ravenous animals, to which they betake themselves when pursued by man, or after they have committed their depredations on the farms of the surrounding district. I have crossed the path of the storm at a distance of a hundred miles from the spot where I witnessed its fury, and again, four hundred miles farther off, in the State of Ohio. Lastly, I observed traces of its ravages on the summits of the mountains connected with the Great Pine Forest of Pennsylvania, three hundred miles beyond the place last mentioned. In all these different parts it appeared to me not to have exceeded a quarter of a mile in breadth.

St. John's River in Florida

Soon after landing at St. Augustine, in East Florida, I formed acquaintance with Dr. Simmons, Dr. Porcher, Judge Smith, the Misses Johnson, and other individuals, my intercourse with whom was as agreeable as   6 beneficial to me. Lieutenant Constantine Smith, of the United States army, I found of a congenial spirit, as was the case with my amiable but since deceased friend, Dr. Bell of Dublin. Among the planters who extended their hospitality to me, I must particularly mention General Hernandez, and my esteemed friend John Bulow, Esq. To all these estimable individuals I offer my sincere thanks.

While in this part of the peninsula I followed my usual avocation, although with little success, it then being winter. I had letters from the Secretaries of the Navy and Treasury of the United States, to the commanding officers of vessels of war of the revenue service, directing them to afford me any assistance in their power; and the schooner "Spark" having come to St. Augustine, on her way to the St. John's River, I presented my credentials to her commander Lieutenant Piercy, who readily and with politeness received me and my assistants on board. We soon after set sail with a fair breeze. The strict attention to duty on board even this small vessel of war, afforded matter of surprise to me. Everything went on with the regularity of a chronometer: orders were given, answered to, and accomplished, before they had ceased to vibrate on the ear. The neatness of the crew equalled the cleanliness of the white planks of the deck; the sails were in perfect condition; and, built as the "Spark" was, for swift sailing, on she went, gambolling from wave to wave.   7

I thought that, while thus sailing, no feeling but that of pleasure could exist in our breasts; but, alas! how fleeting are our enjoyments. When we were almost at the entrance of the river, the wind changed, the sky became clouded, and, before many minutes had elapsed, the little bark was lying to "like a Duck," as her commander expressed himself. It blew a hurricane—let it blow, reader. At break of day we were again at anchor within the bar of St. Augustine.   8

Our next attempt was successful. Not many hours after we had crossed the bar, we perceived the star-like glimmer of the light in the great lantern at the entrance of the St. John's River. This was before daylight; and, as the crossing of the sand-banks or bars, which occur at the mouths of all the streams of this peninsula is difficult, and can be accomplished only when the tide is up, one of the guns was fired as a signal for the government pilot. The good man, it seemed, was unwilling to leave his couch, but a second gun brought him in his canoe alongside. The depth of the channel was barely sufficient. My eyes, however, were not directed towards the waters, but on high, where flew some thousands of snowy Pelicans, which had fled affrighted from their resting-grounds. How beautifully they performed their broad gyrations, and how matchless, after a while, was the marshalling of their files, as they flew past us.   9

On the tide we proceeded apace. Myriads of Cormorants covered the face of the waters, and over it Fish-Crows innumerable were already ar-   10 riving from their distant roosts. We landed at one place to search for the birds whose charming melodies had engaged our attention, and here and there some young Eagles we shot, to add to our store of fresh provisions. The river did not seem to me equal in beauty to the fair Ohio; the shores were in many places low and swampy, to the great delight of the numberless Herons that moved along in gracefulness, and the grim Alligators that swam in sluggish sullenness. In going up a bayou, we caught a great number of the young of the latter for the purpose of making experiments upon them.

After sailing a considerable way, during which our commander and officers took the soundings, as well as the angles and bearings of every nook and crook of the sinuous stream, we anchored one evening at a distance of fully one hundred miles from the mouth of the river. The weather, although it was the 12th of February, was quite warm, the thermometer on board standing at 75°, and on shore at 90°. The fog was so thick that neither of the shores could be seen, and yet the river was not a mile in breadth. The "blind mosquitoes" covered every object, even in the cabin, and so wonderfully abundant were these tormentors that they more than once fairly extinguished the candles whilst I was writing my journal, which I closed in despair, crushing between the leaves more than a hundred of the little wretches. Bad as they are, however, these blind mosquitoes do not bite. As if purposely to render our situation doubly uncomfortable, there was an establishment for jerking beef on the nearer shores, to the windward of our vessel, from which the breeze came laden with no sweet odors.

In the morning when I arose, the country was still covered with thick fogs, so that although I could plainly hear the notes of the birds on shore, not an object could I see beyond the bowsprit, and the air was as close and sultry as on the previous evening. Guided by the scent of the jerkers' works we went on shore, where we found the vegetation already far advanced. The blossoms of the jessamine, ever pleasing, lay steeped in dew, the humming bee was collecting her winter's store from the snowy flowers of the native orange; and the little warblers frisked along the twigs of the smilax. Now, amid the tall pines of the forest, the sun's rays began to force their way, and as the dense mists dissolved in the atmosphere, the bright luminary at length shone forth. We explored the woods around, guided by some friendly live-oakers who had pitched their camp in the vicinity. After a while the "Spark" again displayed her sails, and as she silently glided along, we spied a Seminole Indian approaching us in his canoe. The poor, dejected son of the woods, endowed with talents of the highest order, although rarely acknowledged by the proud usurpers of his native soil, has spent the night in fishing, and the morning in procuring the superb feathered game of the swampy thickets; and with both he comes

11

12

to offer them for our acceptance. Alas! thou fallen one, descendant of an ancient line of freeborn hunters, would that I could restore to thee thy birthright, thy natural independence, the generous feelings that were once fostered in thy brave bosom. But the irrevocable deed is done, and I can merely admire the perfect symmetry of his frame, as he dexterously throws on our deck the Trout and Turkeys which he has captured. He receives a recompense, and without smile or bow, or acknowledgment of any kind, off he starts with the speed of an arrow from his own bow.

Alligators were extremely abundant, and the heads of the fishes which they had snapped off, lay floating around on the dark waters. A rifle bullet was now and then sent through the eye of one of the largest, which, with a tremendous splash of its tail, expired. One morning we saw a monstrous fellow lying on the shore. I was desirous of obtaining him to make an accurate drawing of his head, and accompanied by my assistant and two of the sailors, proceeded cautiously towards him. When within a few yards, one of us fired, and sent through his side an ounce ball which tore open a hole large enough to receive a man's hand. He slowly raised his head, bent himself upwards, opened his huge jaws, swung his tail to and fro, rose on his legs, blew in a frightful manner, and fell to the earth. My assistant leaped on shore, and, contrary to my injunctions, caught hold of the animal's tail, when the alligator, awakening from its trance, with a last effort crawled slowly towards the water, and plunged heavily into it. Had he thought of once flourishing his tremendous weapon, there might have been an end of his assailant's life, but he fortunately went in peace to his grave, where we left him, as the water was too deep. The same morning, another of equal size was observed swimming directly for the bows of our vessel, attracted by the gentle rippling of the water there. One of the officers, who had watched him, fired, and scattered his brain through the air, when he tumbled and rolled at a fearful rate, blowing all the while most furiously. The river was bloody for yards around, but although the monster passed close by the vessel, we could not secure him, and after a while he sunk to the bottom. 13

Early one morning, I hired a boat and two men, with the view of returning to St. Augustine by a short-cut. Our baggage being placed on board, I bade adieu to the officers, and off we started. About four in the afternoon we arrived at the short-cut, forty miles distant from our point of departure, and where we had expected to procure a wagon, but were disappointed. So we laid our things on the bank, and leaving one of my assistants to look after them, I set out accompanied by the other and my Newfoundland dog. We had eighteen miles to go; and as the sun was only two hours high, we struck off at a good rate. Presently we entered a pine-barren. The country was as level as a floor; our path, although narrow, was well-beaten, having been used by the Seminole Indians for ages, and 14 the weather was calm and beautiful. Now and then a rivulet occurred, from which we quenched our thirst, while the magnolias and other flowering plants on its banks relieved the dull uniformity of the woods. When the path separated into two branches, both seemingly leading the same way, I would follow one, while my companion took the other, and unless we met again in a short time, one of us would go across the intervening forest.

The sun went down behind a cloud, and the southeast breeze that   15
sprung up at this moment, sounded dolefully among the tall pines. Along the eastern horizon lay a bed of black vapor, which gradually rose, and soon covered the heavens. The air felt hot and oppressive, and we knew that a tempest was approaching. Plato was now our guide, the white spots on his coat being the only objects that we could discern amid the darkness, and as if aware of his utility in this respect, he kept a short way before us on the trail. Had we imagined ourselves more than a few miles from the town, we should have made a camp, and remained under its shelter for the night; but conceiving that the distance could not be great, we resolved to trudge along.

Large drops began to fall from the murky mass overhead; thick impen-   16
etrable darkness surrounded us, and to my dismay, the dog refused to proceed. Groping with my hands on the ground, I discovered that several trails branched out at the spot where he lay down; and when I had selected one, he went on. Vivid flashes of lightning streamed across the heavens, the wind increased to a gale, and the rain poured down upon us like a torrent. The water soon rose on the level ground so as almost to cover our feet, and we slowly advanced, fronting the tempest. Here and there a tall pine on fire presented a magnificent spectacle, illumining the trees around it, and surrounding them with a halo of dim light, abruptly bordered with the deep black of the night. At one time we passed through a tangled thicket of low trees, at another crossed a stream flushed by the heavy rain, and again proceeded over the open barrens.

How long we thus, half lost, groped our way is more than I can tell you;   17
but at length the tempest passed over, and suddenly the clear sky became spangled with stars. Soon after, we smelt the salt marshes, and walking directly towards them, like pointers advancing on a covey of partridges, we at last to our great joy descried the light of the beacon near St. Augustine. My dog began to run briskly around, having met with ground on which he had hunted before, and taking a direct course, led us to the great causeway that crosses the marshes at the back of the town. We refreshed ourselves with the produce of the first orange-tree that we met with, and in half an hour more arrived at our hotel. Drenched with rain, steaming with perspiration, and covered to the knees with mud, you may imagine what figures we cut in the eyes of the good people whom we found snugly en-

joying themselves in the sitting-room. Next morning, Major Gates, who had received me with much kindness, sent a wagon with mules and two trusty soldiers for my companion and luggage.

The Florida Keys

As the "Marion" neared the Inlet called "Indian Key," which is situated on the eastern coast of the peninsula of Florida, my heart swelled with uncontrollable delight. Our vessel once over the coral reef that everywhere stretches along the shore like a great wall reared by an army of giants, we found ourselves in safe anchoring grounds, within a few furlongs of the land. The next moment saw the oars of a boat propelling us towards the shore, and in brief time we stood on the desired beach. With what delightful feelings did we gaze on the objects around us!—the gorgeous flowers, the singular and beautiful plants, the luxuriant trees. The balmy air which we breathed filled us with animation, so pure and salubrious did it seem to be. The birds which we saw were almost all new to us; their lovely forms appeared to be arrayed in more brilliant apparel than I had ever seen before, and as they fluttered in happy playfulness among the bushes, or glided over the light green waters, we longed to form a more intimate acquaintance with them. [18]

Students of nature spend little time in introductions, especially when they present themselves to persons who feel an interest in their pursuits. This was the case with Mr. Thruston, the deputy collector of the island, who shook us all heartily by the hand, and in a trice had a boat manned, and at our service. Accompanied by him, his pilot and fishermen, off we went, and after a short pull landed on a large key. Few minutes had elapsed when shot after shot might be heard, and down came whirling through the air the objects of our desire. One thrust himself into the tangled groves that covered all but the beautiful coral beach that in a continued line bordered the island, while others gazed on the glowing and diversified hues of the curious inhabitants of the deep. I saw one of my party rush into the limpid element to seize on a crab, that, with claws extended upward, awaited his approach, as if determined not to give way. A loud voice called him back to the land, for sharks are as abundant along these shores as pebbles, and the hungry prowlers could not have found a more savory dinner. [19]

The pilot, besides being a first-rate shot, possessed a most intimate acquaintance with the country. He had been a "conch diver," and no matter what number of fathoms measured the distance between the surface of the water and its craggy bottom, to seek for curious shells in their retreat seemed to him more pastime than toil. Not a Cormorant or Pelican, a [20]

Flamingo, an Ibis, or Heron had ever in his days formed its nest without his having marked the spot; and as to the Keys to which the Doves are wont to resort, he was better acquainted with them than many fops are with the contents of their pockets. In a word, he positively knew every channel that led to these islands, and every cranny along their shores. For years his employment had been to hunt those singular animals called Sea-cows or Manatees, and he had conquered hundreds of them, "merely," as he said, because the flesh and hide bring "a fair price" at Havana. He never went anywhere to land without "Long Tom," which proved indeed to be a wonderful gun, and which made smart havoc when charged with "gro-ceries" a term by which he designated the large shot he used. In like man-ner, he never paddled his light canoe without having by his side the trusty javelin with which he unerringly transfixed such fishes as he thought fit ei-ther for market or for his own use. In attacking Turtles, netting, or over-turning them, I doubt if his equal ever lived on the Florida coast. No sooner was he made acquainted with my errand, than he freely offered his best services, and from that moment until I left Key West he was seldom out of my hearing.

While the young gentlemen who accompanied us were engaged in procuring plants, shells, and small birds, he tapped me on the shoulder, and with a smile said to me, "Come along, I'll show you something better worth your while." To the boat we betook ourselves, with the captain and only a pair of tars, for more he said would not answer. The yawl for a while was urged at a great rate, but as we approached a point, the oars were taken in, and the pilot alone sculling desired us to make ready, for in a few minutes we should have "rare sport." As we advanced, the more slowly did we move, and the most profound silence was maintained, until suddenly coming almost in contact with a thick shrubbery of mangroves, we beheld, right before us, a multitude of Pelicans. A discharge of artillery seldom produced more effect; the dead, the dying, and the wounded, fell from the trees upon the water, while those unscathed flew screaming through the air in terror and dismay. "There," said he, "did not I tell you so; is it not rare sport?" The birds, one after another, were lodged under the gunwales, when the pilot desired the captain to order the lads to pull away. Within about half a mile we reached the extremity of the Key. "Pull away," cried the pilot, "never mind them on the wing, for those black ras-cals don't mind a little firing—now, boys, lay her close under the nests." And there we were with four hundred Cormorant's nests over our heads. The birds were sitting, and when we fired, the number that dropped as if dead, and plunged into the water was such, that I thought by some unac-countable means or other we had killed the whole colony. You would have smiled at the loud laugh and curious gestures of the pilot. "Gen-tlemen," said he, "almost a blank shot!" And so it was, for, on following the birds as one after another peeped up from the water, we found only a few unable to take to wing. "Now," said the pilot, "had you waited until *I had spoken* to the black villains, you might have killed a score or more of them." On inspection, we found that our shots had lodged in the tough dry twigs of which these birds form their nests, and that we had lost the more favorable opportunity of hitting them, by not waiting until they rose. "Never mind," said the pilot, "if you wish it, you may load *The Lady of the Green Mantle* with them in less than a week. Stand still, my lads; and now, gentlemen, in ten minutes you and I will bring down a score of them." And so we did. As we rounded the island, a beautiful bird of the species called Peale's Egret came up, and was shot. We now landed, took in the rest of our party, and returned to Indian Key, where we arrived three hours before sunset.

The sailors and other individuals to whom my name and pursuits had become known, carried our birds to the pilot's house. His good wife had a room ready for me to draw in, and my assistant might have been seen busily engaged in skinning, while George Lehman was making a sketch of the lovely isle. 22

Time is ever precious to the student of nature. I placed several birds in their natural attitudes, and began to outline them. A dance had been prepared also, and no sooner was the sun lost to our eye, than males and females, including our captain and others from the vessel, were seen advancing gayly towards the house in full apparel. The birds were skinned, the sketch was on paper, and I told my young men to amuse themselves. As to myself, I could not join in the merriment, for, full of the remembrance of you, reader, and of the patrons of my work both in America and in Europe, I went on "grinding"—not on an organ, like the Lady of Bras d'Or, but on paper, to the finishing not merely of my outlines, but of my notes respecting the objects seen this day. 23

The room adjoining that in which I worked was soon filled. Two miserable fiddlers screwed their screeching, silken strings,—not an inch of catgut graced their instruments,—and the bouncing of brave lads and fair lasses shook the premises to the foundation. One with a slip came down heavily on the floor, and the burst of laughter that followed echoed over the isle. Diluted claret was handed round to cool the ladies, while a beverage of more potent energies warmed their partners. After supper our captain returned to the "Marion," and I, with my young men, slept in light swinging hammocks under the eaves of the piazza. 24

It was the end of April, when the nights were short, and the days therefore long. Anxious to turn every moment to account, we were on board Mr. Thruston's boat at three next morning. Pursuing our way through the deep and tortuous channels that everywhere traverse the immense muddy soap-like flats that stretch from the outward Keys to the Main, we pro- 25 ceeded on our voyage of discovery. Here and there we met with great beds of floating seaweeds, which showed us that Turtles were abundant there, these masses being the refuse of their feeding. On talking to Mr. Thruston of the nature of these muddy flats, he mentioned that he had once been lost amongst their narrow channels for several days and nights, when in pursuit of some smugglers' boat, the owners of which were better acquainted with the place than the men who were along with him. Although in full sight of several of the Keys, as well as of the main land, he was unable to reach either until a heavy gale raised the water, when he sailed directly over the flats, and returned home almost exhausted with fatigue and hunger. His present pilot often alluded to the circumstance afterwards, ending with a great laugh, and asserting that had he "been there, the rascals would not have escaped."

Coming under a Key on which multitudes of Frigate Pelicans had begun to form their nests, we shot a good number of them, and observed their habits. The boastings of our pilot were here confirmed by the exploits which he performed with his long gun, and on several occasions he brought down a bird from a height of fully a hundred yards. The poor bird, unaware of the range of our artillery, sailed calmly along, so that it was not difficult for "Long Tom," or rather for his owner, to furnish us with as many as we required. The day was spent in this manner, and towards night we returned, laden with booty, to the hospitable home of the pilot. 26

The next morning was delightful. The gentle sea-breeze glided over the flowery isle, the horizon was clear, and all was silent, save the long breakers that rushed over the distant reefs. As we were proceeding towards some Keys seldom visited by men, the sun rose from the bosom of the waters with a burst of glory that flashed on my soul the idea of that power which called into existence so magnificent an object. The moon, thin and pale, as if ashamed to show her feeble light, concealed herself in the dim west. The surface of the waters shone in its tremulous smoothness, and the deep blue of the clear heavens was pure as the world that lies beyond them. The Heron heavily flew towards the land, like a glutton retiring at daybreak, with well lined paunch, from the house of some wealthy patron of good cheer. The Night Heron and the Owl, fearful of day, with hurried flight sought safety in the recesses of the deepest swamps; while the Gulls and Terns, ever cheerful, gambolled over the water, exulting in the prospect of abundance. I also exulted in hope, my whole frame seemed to expand; and our sturdy crew showed by their merry faces that nature had charms for them too. How much of beauty and joy is lost to them who never view the rising sun, and of whose waking existence, the best half is nocturnal. 27

Twenty miles our men had to row before we reached "Sandy Island," and as on its level shores we all leaped, we plainly saw the southernmost 28 cape of the Foridas. The flocks of birds that covered the shelly beaches, and those hovering overhead, so astonished us that we could for a while scarcely believe our eyes. The first volley procured a supply of food sufficient for two days' consumption. Such tales, you have already been told, are well enough at a distance from the place to which they refer; but you will doubtless be still more surprised when I tell you that our first fire among a crowd of the Great Godwits laid prostrate sixty-five of these birds. Rose-colored Curlews stalked gracefully beneath the mangroves. Purple Herons rose at almost every step we took, and each cactus supported the nest of a White Ibis. The air was darkened by whistling wings, while, on the waters, floated Gallinules and other interesting birds. We formed a kind of shed with sticks and grass, the sailor cook commenced his labors, and ere long we supplied the deficiencies of our fatigued frames. The business of the day over, we secured ourselves from insects by means of mosquito-nets, and were lulled to rest by the cacklings of the beautiful Purple Gallinules!

QUESTIONS FOR DISCUSSION AND WRITING

1. If you begin with contemporary assumptions about naturalists and environmentalists, you may be startled by Audubon's accounts of shooting birds and animals. As you reread these descriptions of hunting, study the details of how Audubon and his companions hunt and look for explanations of why they do it. That done, characterize Audubon's attitude toward the animals or birds that he and his companions shoot. Do you find indifference? Pity? Respect?

2. In these journal entries, Audubon calls himself a "student of nature" (par. 23). As you read his accounts of his encounters with nature, what do you think he meant? How would you compare Audubon's "study" of nature with that of the other naturalists represented in this chapter, Jefferson and Bartram? How would you compare it with our contemporary expectations for studying nature?

3. Maria Audubon, John James Audubon's granddaughter, published his complete journals in 1897, in part because she wanted Americans to know more fully the personality behind the famous but somewhat technical nature paintings. Compose a brief but detailed portrait of the person you meet. Speculate about where among today's disparate political, animal rights, and land-use movements he would feel most at home.

WILLIAM CULLEN BRYANT

*William Cullen Bryant (1794–1878) was born just after the American Revolution
and lived until well past the Civil War. After a brief career in law, Bryant spent most
of his professional life as the editor and owner of a newspaper, the* New York
Evening Post. *He was also an influential figure in the cultural and political life of
his still-young country, participating in the antislavery movement and becoming
an early supporter of Lincoln. Bryant traveled extensively in America and abroad,
publishing three popular volumes of travel letters. Bryant's reputation as an important American nature poet is based on a relatively modest collection of work,
much of it written early in his life. Still, his poetry was enormously popular with
American readers, who appreciated its celebration of American landscapes and
American scenes, even if rendered in decidedly Old World forms such as the sonnet. The two poems reprinted here represent Bryant's early and later poetic work;
"The Yellow Violet" was written in 1814 and "Sonnet—to an American Painter
Departing for Europe" in 1832.*

"Sonnet—to an American Painter Departing for Europe"

Thine eyes shall see the light of distant skies:
    Yet, Cole! they heart shall bear to Europe's strand
    A living image of thy native land,
Such as on thy own glorious canvass lies.
Lone lakes—savannahs where the bison roves—   5
    Rocks rich with summer garlands—solemn streams—
    Skies, where the desert eagle wheels and screams—
Spring bloom and autumn blaze of boundless groves.

Fair scenes shall greet thee where thou goest—fair,
    But different—every where the trace of men,   10
    Paths, homes, graves, ruins, from the lowest glen
To where life shrinks from the fierce Alpine air.
    Gaze on them, till the tears shall dim thy sight,
    But keep that earlier, wilder image bright.

"The Yellow Violet"

When beechen buds begin to swell,
 And woods the blue-bird's warble know,
The yellow violet's modest bell
 Peeps from the last year's leaves below.

Ere russet fields their green resume,   5
 Sweet flower! I love in forest bare,
To meet thee, when thy faint perfume
 Alone is in the virgin air.

Of all her train, the hands of Spring
 First plant thee in the watery mould;   10
And I have seen thee blossoming
 Beside the snow-bank's edges cold.

Thy Parent Sun, who bade thee view
 Pale skies, and chilling moisture sip,
Has bathed thee in his own bright hue,   15
 And streak'd with jet thy glowing lip.

Yet slight thy form, and low thy seat,
 And earthward bent thy gentle eye,
Unapt the passing view to meet,
 When loftier flowers are flaunting nigh.   20

Oft, in the sunless April day,
 Thy early smile has staid my walk;
But midst the gorgeous blooms of May
 I pass'd thee on thy humble stalk.

So they, who climb to wealth, forget   25
 The friends in darker fortunes tried;
I copied them—but I regret
 That I should ape the ways of pride.

And when again the genial hour
 Awakes the painted tribes of light,   30
I'll not o'erlook the modest flower
 That made the woods of April bright.

QUESTIONS FOR DISCUSSION AND WRITING

1. Bryant was a popular poet, but he was also an active newspaper editor and editorialist who took on the important political and social issues of his day. In a sense, "Sonnet—to an American Painter Departing for Europe" can be said to make an argument or take an editorial position. Summarize the poem's argument or editorial position. Against what is it reacting? To whom is Bryant making his argument?

2. As is true of much of Bryant's poetry, "The Yellow Violet" is often said to present the reader with a lesson or a message. One clue about a possible lesson is the opposition Bryant creates between other "loftier" flowers and the violet, a "modest flower" with a "humble stalk." Find other places where Bryant creates this kind of contrast, or where he assigns specific qualities to the yellow violet. That done, use what you have found to explore the poem's lessons about nature and human nature.

2

NATURE,
SELF,
AND SPIRIT

MIDDLE AND LATE
NINETEENTH CENTURY

The middle and late nineteenth century were times of great change in America. The country moved from a rural and agricultural economy to become an industrial nation with desires for an overseas empire. During this time the railroad, telegraph, electricity, telephone, and automobile were developed, and at the end of the century the airplane was almost a reality. It was also during this time that our concept of nature started to change. At the midpoint of the century, people could still conceive of nature as an endless resource to be developed and used in any way that would produce profit; by the end of the century, however, there was a growing sense that we would deplete our natural resources unless we worked to conserve and use wisely what we had left.

Another important development of this period was the transcendental tradition, a philosophy that sought spiritual redemption in nature. Transcendentalists believe that God is everywhere in the world. Thus, one way of finding spiritual meaning is to look carefully at nature because truth and beauty reside there as part of God's presence. The authentic experience of every individual is also important because God is present in all of us. This faith in God's presence in every human being leads to a mystical stance that asks each of us to clear our souls of the confusion brought by civilization so that we can sense God's light in us.

Ralph Waldo Emerson was at the center of the transcendental movement. He read widely and brought a variety of sources to bear in his work, including the ideas of Kant, Coleridge, Plato, and various writers about Eastern religion. But he also grounded much of his thought in his own experience with nature, in keeping with his more general concern that human beings rely on their own experiences and intuition to understand the world. Emerson believed in an almost mystical connection among humans, nature, and God.

If Emerson gave us an optimistic view of the connections among humans, nature, and God, Nathaniel Hawthorne gave us a much more pessimistic vision tinged with the guilt he felt over the harsh actions of his Puritan ancestors. For Hawthorne, nature could be a terrifying place where the sins of humans could find full expression, although it also could offer the hope of a new beginning. Hawthorne's nature is a complex, almost literary, place full of allegorical and symbolic meaning rather than a closely observed world full of concrete, specific details.

Probably the most important statement of the transcendental movement's conception of nature can be found in Henry David Thoreau's *Walden*. Thoreau neither imbues nature with allegorical meanings nor uses it as a manifestation of the connections between humans and God. Rather, he looks closely at nature and uses it as a way to understand the deep roots of his own thought. Out of this thought he forges a strongly individualistic vision of nature as a place to put aside the corruptions and petty demands of civilization in order to understand our true place in the world.

Much the same lesson can be drawn from the poetry of Walt Whitman and Emily Dickinson, although the two poets go about teaching us in very different ways. Whitman pulls us into a grand vision of the entire earth, one that is open to all types of experience and all sorts of people. Although Whitman's vision is grounded in nature, it also includes much of the world humans have created. Dickinson, on the other hand, looks to small things yet finds in them a whole world. Of course Whitman will also look at small things, the most famous example being a blade of summer grass, but he moves outward from these moments to the wider world whereas Dickinson stays with the small moments and makes them reverberate with the rest of the world. Together these two poets offer a complementary vision of nature, sharing an intensity but differing in perspective.

A Lady's Life in the Rocky Mountains was written from a very different perspective from that of the New England transcendentalists and at a somewhat later date. Instead of staying at home and cultivating her own piece of nature, Isabella L. Bird traveled widely and wrote about the exotic things she saw. In 1873 the American West was still a wild and uncivilized place; Bird writes of its great beauty and the spiritual feeling it inspires in her, passing rather lightly over the very real dangers it poses. When she writes in 1880 that the American West is becoming settled, she does so with a hint of nostalgia for the adventure possible in nature at its wildest.

This contrast between civilization and nature is central in Sarah Orne Jewett's story "A White Heron." Civilization, in the form of the young hunter, intrudes on the pastoral pleasures of an isolated farm, a place that itself is partly of nature and partly of the civilized world. Although the farm has no resources to be exploited, its neighbor is a beautiful white heron, a rare bird the hunter covets for his collection. As the story reveals through the main character, a young girl who is torn between the spiritual rewards of nature and the financial rewards of society, nature for Jewett is no longer a simple place to find pleasure but rather a place where conflicting desires and needs are worked out.

RALPH WALDO EMERSON

Ralph Waldo Emerson (1803–82) was one of the most influential writers and thinkers in nineteenth-century America. He was at the center of the transcendental movement in New England and knew many of the greatest writers in Victorian England, including Tennyson, Wordsworth, Dickens, and Carlisle. His work has helped shape American literature, philosophy, and religion. Most of his works were presented orally in the great debates of his day on topics ranging from the slavery question to the role of the intellectual life in America.

In Nature *(1836), Emerson starts to bring together the ideas that will be important in his transcendental philosophy. An early work, it shows Emerson's enthusiasm and skill for striking uses of language and difficult thought. The entire essay consists of an introduction and eight chapters, with the introduction, first chapter, which has no title, and the chapters on commodity, beauty, language, and spirit reprinted here. Together, these selections give an indication of Emerson's developing sense of the role of nature in human affairs.*

From *Nature*

A subtle chain of countless rings
The next unto the farthest brings;
The eye reads omens where it goes,
And speaks all languages the rose;
And, striving to be man, the worm
Mounts through all the spires of form.

INTRODUCTION

Our age is retrospective. It builds the sepulchres of the fathers. It writes biographies, histories, and criticism. The foregoing generations beheld God and nature face to face; we, through their eyes. Why should not we also enjoy an original relation to the universe? Why should not we have a poetry and philosophy of insight and not of tradition, and a religion by revelation to us, and not the history of theirs? Embosomed for a season in nature, whose floods of life stream around and through us, and invite us by the powers they supply, to action proportioned to nature, why should we grope among the dry bones of the past, or put the living generation into masquerade out of its faded wardrobe? The sun shines to-day also.

1

There is more wool and flax in the fields. There are new lands, new men, new thoughts. Let us demand our own works and laws and worship.

Undoubtedly we have no questions to ask which are unanswerable. We must trust the perfection of the creation so far, as to believe that whatever curiosity the order of things has awakened in our minds, the order of things can satisfy. Every man's condition is a solution in hieroglyphic to those inquiries he would put. He acts it as life, before he apprehends it as truth. In like manner, nature is already, in its forms and tendencies, describing its own design. Let us interrogate the great apparition, that shines so peacefully around us. Let us inquire, to what end is nature? 2

All science has one aim, namely, to find a theory of nature. We have theories of races and of functions, but scarcely yet a remote approach to an idea of creation. We are now so far from the road to truth, that religious teachers dispute and hate each other, and speculative men are esteemed unsound and frivolous. But to a sound judgment, the most abstract truth is the most practical. Whenever a true theory appears, it will be its own evidence. Its test is, that it will explain all phenomena. Now many are thought not only unexplained but inexplicable; as language, sleep, madness, dreams, beasts, sex. 3

Philosophically considered, the universe is composed of Nature and the Soul. Strictly speaking, therefore, all that is separate from us, all which Philosophy distinguishes as the NOT ME, that is, both nature and art, all other men and my own body, must be ranked under this name, NATURE. In enumerating the values of nature and casting up their sum, I shall use the word in both senses,—in its common and in its philosophical import. In inquiries so general as our present one, the inaccuracy is not material; no confusion of thought will occur. *Nature*, in the common sense, refers to essences unchanged by man; space, the air, the river, the leaf. *Art* is applied to the mixture of his will with the same things, as in a house, a canal, a statue, a picture. But his operations taken together are so insignificant, a little chipping, baking, patching, and washing, that in an impression so grand as that of the world on the human mind, they do not vary the result. 4

CHAPTER I

To go into solitude, a man needs to retire as much from his chamber as from society. I am not solitary whilst I read and write, though nobody is with me. But if a man would be alone, let him look at the stars. The rays that come from those heavenly worlds will separate between him and what he touches. One might think the atmosphere was made transparent 5 with this design, to give man, in the heavenly bodies, the perpetual presence of the sublime. Seen in the streets of cities, how great they are! If the stars should appear one night in a thousand years, how would men believe and adore; and preserve for many generations the remembrance of the city of God which had been shown! But every night come out these envoys of beauty, and light the universe with their admonishing smile.

The stars awaken a certain reverence, because though always present, they are inaccessible; but all natural objects make a kindred impression, when the mind is open to their influence. Nature never wears a mean appearance. Neither does the wisest man extort her secret, and lose his curiosity by finding out all her perfection. Nature never became a toy to a wise spirit. The flowers, the animals, the mountains, reflected the wisdom of his best hour, as much as they had delighted the simplicity of his childhood. 6

When we speak of nature in this manner, we have a distinct but most poetical sense in the mind. We mean the integrity of impression made by manifold natural objects. It is this which distinguishes the stick of timber of the woodcutter, from the tree of the poet. The charming landscape which I saw this morning is indubitably made up of some twenty or thirty farms. Miller owns this field, Locke that, and Manning the woodland beyond. But none of them owns the landscape. There is a property in the horizon which no man has but he whose eye can integrate all the parts, that is, the poet. This is the best part of these men's farms, yet to this their warranty-deeds give no title. 7

To speak truly, few adult persons can see nature. Most persons do not see the sun. At least they have a very superficial seeing. The sun illuminates only the eye of the man, but shines into the eye and the heart of the child. The lover of nature is he whose inward and outward senses are still truly adjusted to each other; who has retained the spirit of infancy even into the era of manhood. His intercourse with heaven and earth, becomes part of his daily food. In the presence of nature, a wild delight runs through the man, in spite of real sorrows. Nature says,—he is my creature, and maugre all his impertinent griefs, he shall be glad with me. Not the sun or the summer alone, but every hour and season yields its tribute of delight; for every hour and season yields its tribute of delight; for every hour and change corresponds to and authorizes a different state of the mind, from breathless noon to grimmest midnight. Nature is a setting that fits equally well a comic or a mourning piece. In good health, the air is a cordial of incredible virtue. Crossing a bare common, in snow puddles, at twilight, under a clouded sky, without having in my thoughts any occurrence of special good fortune, I have enjoyed a perfect exhilaration. I am glad to the brink of fear. In the woods too, a man casts off his years, as the 8 snake his slough, and at what period soever of life, is always a child. In the woods, is perpetual youth. Within these plantations of God, a decorum and sanctity reign, a perennial festival is dressed, and the guest sees not how he should tire of them in a thousand years. In the woods, we return to reason and faith. There I feel that nothing can befall me in life,—no disgrace, no calamity (leaving me my eyes), which nature cannot repair. Standing on the bare ground,—my head bathed by the blithe air, and uplifted into infinite space,—all mean egotism vanishes. I become a transparent eyeball; I am nothing; I see all; the currents of the Universal Being circulate through me; I am part or particle of God. The name of the nearest friend sounds then foreign and accidental: to be brothers, to be acquaintances,—master or servant, is then a trifle and a disturbance. I am the lover of uncontained and immortal beauty. In the wilderness, I find something more dear and connate than in streets or villages. In the tranquil landscape, and especially in the distant line of the horizon, man beholds somewhat as beautiful as his own nature.

The greatest delight which the fields and woods minister, is the suggestion of an occult relation between man and the vegetable. I am not alone and unacknowledged. They nod to me, and I to them. The waving of the boughs in the storm, is new to me and old. It takes me by surprise, and yet is not unknown. Its effect is like that of a higher thought or a better emotion coming over me, when I deemed I was thinking justly or doing right. 9

Yet it is certain that the power to produce this delight does not reside in nature, but in man, or in a harmony of both. It is necessary to use these pleasures with great temperance. For, nature is not always tricked in holiday attire, but the same scene which yesterday breathed perfume and glittered as for the frolic of the nymphs, is overspread with melancholy today. Nature always wears the colors of the spirit. To a man laboring under calamity, the heat of his own fire hath sadness in it. Then, there is a kind of contempt of the landscape felt by him who has just lost by death a dear friend. The sky is less grand as it shuts down over less worth in the population. 10

CHAPTER II

Commodity

Whoever considers the final cause of the world, will discern a multitude of uses that enter as parts into that result. They all admit of being thrown into one of the following classes: Commodity; Beauty; Language; and Discipline. 11

Under the general name of Commodity, I rank all those advantages   12
which our senses owe to nature. This, of course, is a benefit which is temporary and mediate, not ultimate, like its service to the soul. Yet although
low, it is perfect in its kind, and is the only use of nature which all men ap-
prehend. The misery of man appears like childish petulance, when we explore the steady and prodigal provision that has been made for his
support and delight on this green ball which floats him through the heavens. What angels invented these splendid ornaments, these rich conve-
niencies, this ocean of air above, this ocean of water beneath, this firmament of earth between? this zodiac of lights, this tent of dropping clouds,
this striped coat of climates, this fourfold year? Beasts, fire, water, stones,
and corn serve him. The field is at once his floor, his workyard, his playground, his garden, and his bed.

> "More servants wait on man
> Than he'll take notice of."

Nature, in its ministry to man, is not only the material, but is also the   13
process and the result. All the parts incessantly work into each other's
hands for the profit of man. The wind sows the seed; the sun evaporates
the sea; the wind blows the vapor to the field; the ice, on the other side of
the planet, condenses rain on this; the rain feeds the plant; the plant feeds
the animal; and thus the endless circulations of the divine charity nourish
man.

The useful arts are reproductions or new combinations by the wit of   14
man, of the same natural benefactors. He no longer waits for favoring
gales, but by means of steam, he realizes the fable of Aeolus's bag, and
carries the two-and-thirty winds in the boiler of his boat. To diminish friction, he paves the road with iron bars, and, mounting a coach with a ship-
load of men, animals, and merchandise behind him, he darts through the
country from town to town, like an eagle or a swallow through the air. By
the aggregate of these aids, how is the face of the world changed, from the
era of Noah to that of Napoleon! The private poor man hath cities, ships,
canals, bridges, built for him. He goes to the post-office, and the human
race run on his errands; to the book-shop, and the human race read and
write of all that happens, for him; to the court-house, and nations repair
his wrongs. He sets his house upon the road, and the human race go forth
every morning, and shovel out the snow, and cut a path for him.

But there is no need of specifying particulars in this class of uses. The   15
catalogue is endless, and the examples so obvious, that I shall leave them
to the reader's reflection, with the general remark, that this mercenary
benefit is one which has respect to a further good. A man is fed, not that
he may be fed, but that he may work.

CHAPTER III

Beauty

A nobler want of man is served by nature, namely, the love of beauty.   16

The ancient Greeks called the world κοσμος, beauty. Such is the con-   17
stitution of all things, or such the plastic power of the human eye, that the
primary forms, as the sky, the mountain, the tree, the animal, give us a delight *in and for themselves;* a pleasure arising from outline, color, motion,
and grouping. This seems partly owing to the eye itself. The eye is the best
of artists. By the mutual action of its structure and of the laws of light, perspective is produced, which integrates every mass of objects, of what
character soever, into a well-colored and shaded globe, so that where the
particular objects are mean and unaffecting, the landscape which they
compose is round and symmetrical. And as the eye is the best composer,
so light is the first of painters. There is no object so foul that intense light
will not make beautiful. And the stimulus it affords to the sense, and a sort
of infinitude which it hath, like space and time, make all matter gay. Even
the corpse has its own beauty. But besides this general grace diffused over
nature, almost all the individual forms are agreeable to the eye, as is
proved by our endless imitations of some of them, as the acorn, the grape,
the pine-cone, the wheat-ear, the egg, the wings and forms of most birds,
the lion's claw, the serpent, the butterfly, sea-shells, flames, clouds, buds,
leaves, and the forms of many trees, as the palm.

For better consideration, we may distribute the aspects of Beauty in a   18
threefold manner.

1. First, the simple perception of natural forms is a delight. The influ-   19
ence of the forms and actions in nature is so needful to man, that, in its
lowest functions, it seems to lie on the confines of commodity and beauty.
To the body and mind which have been cramped by noxious work or
company, nature is medicinal and restores their tone. The tradesman, the
attorney comes out of the din and craft of the street, and sees the sky and
the woods, and is a man again. In their eternal calm, he finds himself. The
health of the eye seems to demand a horizon. We are never tired, so long
as we can see far enough.

But in other hours, Nature satisfies by its loveliness, and without any   20
mixture of corporeal benefit. I see the spectacle of morning from the hilltop over against my house, from day-break to sunrise, with emotions
which an angel might share. The long slender bars of cloud float like
fishes in the sea of crimson light. From the earth, as a shore, I look out into
that silent sea. I seem to partake its rapid transformations: the active enchantment reaches my dust, and I dilate and conspire with the morning
wind. How does Nature deify us with a few and cheap elements! Give me

health and a day, and I will make the pomp of emperors ridiculous. The dawn is my Assyria; the sunset and moonrise my Paphos, and unimaginable realms of faerie; broad noon shall be my England of the senses and the understanding; the night shall be my Germany of mystic philosophy and dreams.

Not less excellent, except for our less susceptibility in the afternoon, 21 was the charm, last evening, of a January sunset. The western clouds divided and subdivided themselves into pink flakes modulated with tints of unspeakable softness; and the air had so much life and sweetness, that it was a pain to come within doors. What was it that nature would say? Was there no meaning in the live repose of the valley behind the mill, and which Homer or Shakespeare could not re-form for me in words? The leafless trees become spires of flame in the sunset, with the blue east for their background, and the stars of the dead calices of flowers, and every withered stem and stubble rimed with frost, contribute something to the mute music.

The inhabitants of cities suppose that the country landscape is pleasant 22 only half the year. I please myself with the graces of the winter scenery, and believe that we are as much touched by it as by the genial influences of summer. To the attentive eye, each moment of the year has its own beauty, and in the same field, it beholds, every hour, a picture which was never seen before, and which shall never be seen again. The heavens change every moment, and reflect their glory or gloom on the plains beneath. The state of the crop in the surrounding farms alters the expression of the earth from week to week. The succession of native plants in the pastures and roadsides, which makes the silent clock by which time tells the summer hours, will make even the divisions of the day sensible to a keen observer. The tribes of birds and insects, like the plants punctual to their time, follow each other, and the year has room for all. By watercourses, the variety is greater. In July, the blue pontederia or pickerel-weed blooms in large beds in the shallow parts of our pleasant river, and swarms with yellow butterflies in continual motion. Art cannot rival this pomp of purple and gold. Indeed the river is a perpetual gala, and boasts each month a new ornament.

But this beauty of Nature which is seen and felt as beauty, is the least 23 part. The shows of day, the dewy morning, the rainbow, mountains, orchards in blossom, stars, moonlight, shadows in still water, and the like, if too eagerly hunted, become shows merely, and mock us with their unreality. Go out of the house to see the moon, and 't is mere tinsel; it will not please as when its light shines upon your necessary journey. The beauty that shimmers in the yellow afternoons of October, who ever could clutch it? Go forth to find it, and it is gone: 'tis only a mirage as you look from the windows of diligence.

2. The presence of a higher, namely, of the spiritual element is essen-   24
tial to its perfection. The high and divine beauty which can be loved without effeminacy, is that which is found in combination with the human will.
Beauty is the mark God sets upon virtue. Every natural action is graceful.
Every heroic act is also decent, and causes the place and the bystanders to
shine. We are taught by great actions that the universe is the property of
every individual in it. Every rational creature has all nature for his dowry
and estate. It is his, if he will. He may divest himself of it; he may creep
into a corner, and abdicate his kingdom, as most men do, but he is entitled to the world by his constitution. In proportion to the energy of his
thought and will, he takes up the world into himself. "All those things for
which men plough, build, or sail, obey virtue," said Sallust. "The winds
and waves," said Gibbon, "are always on the side of the ablest navigators."
So are the sun and moon and all the stars of heaven. When a noble act is
done,—perchance in a scene of great natural beauty; when Leonidas and
his three hundred martyrs consume one day in dying, and the sun and
moon come each and look at them once in the steep defile of Ther-
mopylae; when Arnold Winkelried, in the high Alps, under the shadow of
the avalanche, gathers in his side a sheaf of Austrian spears to break the
line for his comrades; are not these heroes entitled to add the beauty of
the scene to the beauty of the deed? When the bark of Columbus nears the
shore of America;—before it, the beach lined with savages, fleeing out of
all their huts of cane; the sea behind; and the purple mountains of the
Indian Archipelago around, can we separate the man from the living picture? Does not the New World clothe his form with her palm-groves and
savannahs as fit drapery? Ever does natural beauty steal in like air, and en-
velope great actions. When Sir Harry Vane was dragged up the Tower-hill,
sitting on a sled to suffer death, as the champion of the English laws, one
of the multitude cried out to him, "You never sat on so glorious a seat."
Charles II., to intimidate the citizens of London, caused the patriot Lord
Russell to be drawn in an open coach, through the principal streets of the
city, on his way to the scaffold. "But," his biographer says, "the multitude
imagined they saw liberty and virtue sitting by his side." In private places,
among sordid objects, an act of truth or heroism seems at once to draw to
itself the sky as its temple, the sun as its candle. Nature stretcheth out her
arms to embrace man, only let his thoughts be of equal greatness.
Willingly does she follow his steps with the rose and the violet, and bend
her lines of grandeur and grace to the decoration of her darling child. Only
let his thoughts be of equal scope, and the frame will suit the picture. A
virtuous man is in unison with her works, and makes the central figure of
the visible sphere. Homer, Pindar, Socrates, Phocion, associate themselves
fitly in our memory with the geography and climate of Greece. The visible
heavens and earth sympathize with Jesus. And in common life, whosoever

has seen a person of powerful character and happy genius will have re-marked how easily he took all things along with him,—the persons, the opinions, and the day, and nature became ancillary to a man.

3. There is still another aspect under which the beauty of the world may   25
be viewed, namely, as it becomes an object of the intellect. Beside the re-lation of things to virtue, they have a relation to thought. The intellect searches out the absolute order of things as they stand in the mind of God, and without the colors of affection. The intellectual and the active powers seem to succeed each other, and the exclusive activity of the one gener-ates the exclusive activity of the other. There is something unfriendly in each to the other, but they are like the alternate periods of feeding and working in animals; each prepares and will be followed by the other. Therefore does beauty, which, in relation to actions, as we have seen, comes unsought, and comes because it is unsought, remain for the ap-prehension and pursuit of the intellect; and then again, in its turn, of the active power. Nothing divine dies. All good is eternally reproductive. The beauty of nature re-forms itself in the mind, and not for barren contem-plation, but for new creation.

All men are in some degree impressed by the face of the world; some   26
men even to delight. This love of beauty is Taste. Others have the same love in such excess, that, not content with admiring, they seek to embody it in new forms. The creation of beauty is Art.

The production of a work of art throws a light upon the mystery of hu-   27
manity. A work of art is an abstract or epitome of the world. It is the result or expression of nature, in miniature. For, although the works of nature are innumerable and all different, the result or the expression of them all is similar and single. Nature is a sea of forms radically alike and even unique. A leaf, a sunbeam, a landscape, the ocean, make an analogous im-pression on the mind. What is common to them all,—that perfectness and harmony, is beauty. The standard of beauty is the entire circuit of natural forms,—the totality of nature; which the Italians expressed by defining beauty "il più nell' uno." Nothing is quite beautiful alone; nothing but is beautiful in the whole. A single object is only so far beautiful as it suggests this universal grace. The poet, the painter, the sculptor, the musician, the architect, seek each to concentrate this radiance of the world on one point, and each in his several work to satisfy the love of beauty which stimulates him to produce. Thus is Art, a nature passed through the alem-bic of man. Thus in art, does nature work through the will of a man filled with the beauty of her first works.

The world thus exists to the soul to satisfy the desire of beauty. This   28
element I call an ultimate end. No reason can be asked or given why the soul seeks beauty. Beauty, in its largest and profoundest sense, is one ex-pression for the universe. God is the all-fair. Truth and goodness and

beauty are but different faces of the same All. But beauty in nature is not ultimate. It is the herald of inward and internal beauty, and is not alone a solid and satisfactory good. It must stand as a part, and not as yet the last or highest expression of the final cause of Nature.

CHAPTER IV

Language

Language is a third use which Nature subserves to man. Nature is the vehicle of thought, and in a simple, double, and threefold degree. 29

1. Words are signs of natural facts.
2. Particular natural facts are symbols of particular spiritual facts.
3. Nature is the symbol of spirit.

1. Words are signs of natural facts. The use of natural history is to give us aid in supernatural history: the use of the outer creation, to give us language for the beings and changes of the inward creation. Every word which is used to express a moral or intellectual fact, if traced to its root, is found to be borrowed from some material appearance. *Right* means *straight; wrong* means *twisted. Spirit* primarily means *wind; transgression,* the crossing of a *line; supercilious,* the *raising of the eyebrow.* We say the *heart* to express emotion, the *head* to denote thought; and *thought* and *emotion* are words borrowed from sensible things, and now appropriated to spiritual nature. Most of the process by which this transformation is made is hidden from us in the remote time when language was framed; but the same tendency may be daily observed in children. Children and savages use only nouns or names of things, which they convert into verbs, and apply to analogous mental acts. 30

2. But this origin of all words that convey a spiritual import—so conspicuous a fact in the history of language—is our least debt to nature. It is not words only that are emblematic; it is things which are emblematic. Every natural fact is a symbol of some spiritual fact. Every appearance in nature corresponds to some state of the mind, and that state of the mind can only be described by presenting that natural appearance as its picture. An enraged man is a lion, a cunning man is a fox, a firm man is a rock, a learned man is a torch. A lamb is innocence; a snake is subtle spite; flowers express to us the delicate affections. Light and darkness are our familiar expression for knowledge and ignorance; and heat for love. Visible distance behind and before us is respectively our image of memory and hope. 31

Who looks upon a river in a meditative hour, and is not reminded of 32 the flux of all things? Throw a stone into the stream, and the circles that propagate themselves are the beautiful type of all influence. Man is conscious of a universal soul within or behind his individual life, wherein, as in a firmament, the natures of Justice, Truth, Love, Freedom, arise and shine. This universal soul, he calls Reason: it is not mine or thine, or his, but we are its; we are its property and men. And the blue sky in which the private earth is buried, the sky with its eternal calm, and full of everlasting orbs, is the type of Reason. That which, intellectually considered, we call Reason, considered in relation to nature, we call Spirit. Spirit is the Creator. Spirit hath life in itself. And man in all ages and countries embodies it in his language, as the FATHER.

It is easily seen that there is nothing lucky or capricious in these analogies, but that they are constant, and pervade nature. These are not the dreams of a few poets, here and there, but man is an analogist, and studies relations in all objects. He is placed in the centre of beings, and a ray of relation passes from every other being to him. And neither can man be understood without these objects, nor these objects without man. All the facts in natural history taken by themselves have no value, but are barren like a single sex. But marry it to human history, and it is full of life. Whole Floras, all Linnaeus's and Buffon's volumes, are dry catalogues of facts; but the most trivial of these facts, the habit of a plant, the organs, or work, or noise of an insect, applied to the illustration of a fact in intellectual philosophy, or, in any way, associated to human nature, affects us in the most lively and agreeable manner. The seed of a plant,—to what affecting analogies in the nature of man is that little fruit made use of, in all discourse, up to the voice of Paul, who calls the human corpse a seed,—"It is sown a natural body; it is raised a spiritual body." The motion of the earth round its axis, and round the sun, makes the day, and the year. These are certain amounts of brute light and heat. But is there no intent of an analogy between man's life and the seasons? And do the seasons gain no grandeur or pathos from that analogy? The instincts of the ant are very unimportant, considered as the ant's; but the moment a ray of relation is seen to extend from it to man, and the little drudge is seen to be a monitor, a little body with a mighty heart, then all its habits, even that said to be recently observed, that it never sleeps, become sublime.

Because of this radical correspondence between visible things and human thoughts, savages, who have only what is necessary, converse in figures. As we go back in history, language becomes more picturesque, until its infancy, when it is all poetry; or all spiritual facts are represented by natural symbols. The same symbols are found to make the original elements of all languages. It has moreover been observed, that the idioms of all languages approach each other in passages of the greatest eloquence and power. And as this is the first language, so is it the last. This

33

34

immediate dependence of language upon nature, this conversion of an outward phenomenon into a type of somewhat in human life, never loses its power to affect us. It is this which gives that piquancy to the conversation of a strong-natured farmer or backwoodsman, which all men relish.

A man's power to connect his thought with its proper symbol, and so   35
to utter it, depends on the simplicity of his character, that is, upon his love of truth, and his desire to communicate it without loss. The corruption of man is followed by the corruption of language. When simplicity of character and the sovereignty of ideas is broken up by the prevalence of secondary desires, the desire of riches, of pleasure, of power, and of praise,—and duplicity and falsehood take place of simplicity and truth, the power over nature as an interpreter of the will is in a degree lost; new imagery ceases to be created, and old words are perverted to stand for things which are not; a paper currency is employed, when there is no bullion in the vaults. In due time, the fraud is manifest, and words lose all power to stimulate the understanding or the affections. Hundreds of writers may be found in every long-civilized nation, who for a short time believe, and make others believe, that they see and utter truths, who do not of themselves clothe one thought in its natural garment, but who feed unconsciously on the language created by the primary writers of the country, those, namely, who hold primarily on nature.

But wise men pierce this rotten diction and fasten words again to visi-   36
ble things; so that picturesque language is at once a commanding certificate that he who employs it is a man in alliance with truth and God. The moment our discourse rises above the ground line of familiar facts, and is inflamed with passion or exalted by thought, it clothes itself in images. A man conversing in earnest, if he watch his intellectual processes, will find that a material image, more or less luminous, arises in his mind, cotemporaneous with every thought, which furnishes the vestment of the thought. Hence, good writing and brilliant discourse are perpetual allegories. This imagery is spontaneous. It is the blending of experience with the present action of the mind. It is proper creation. It is the working of the Original Cause through the instruments he has already made.

These facts may suggest the advantage which the country life possesses   37
for a powerful mind, over the artificial and curtailed life of cities. We know more from nature than we can at will communicate. Its light flows into the mind evermore, and we forget its presence. The poet, the orator, bred in the woods, whose senses have been nourished by their fair and appeasing changes, year after year, without design and without heed,—shall not lose their lesson altogether, in the roar of cities or the broil of politics. Long hereafter, amidst agitation and terror in national councils,—in the hour of revolution,—these solid images shall reappear in their morning lustre, as fit symbols and words of the thoughts which the passing events shall

awaken. At the call of a noble sentiment, again the woods wave, the pines murmur, the river rolls and shines, and the cattle low upon the mountains, as he saw and heard them in his infancy. And with these forms, the spells of persuasion, the keys of power are put into his hands.

3. We are thus assisted by natural objects in the expression of particu- 38 lar meanings. But how great a language to convey such pepper-corn informations! Did it need such noble races of creatures, this profusion of forms, this host of orbs in heaven, to furnish man with the dictionary and grammar of his municipal speech? Whilst we use this grand cipher to expedite the affairs of our pot and kettle, we feel that we have not yet put it to its use, neither are able. We are like travellers using the cinders of a volcano to roast their eggs. Whilst we see that it always stands ready to clothe what we would say, we cannot avoid the question, whether the characters are not significant of themselves. Have mountains, and waves, and skies, no significance but what we consciously give them, when we employ them as emblems of our thoughts? The word is emblematic. Parts of speech are metaphors, because the whole of nature is a metaphor of the human mind. The laws of moral nature answer to those of matter as face to face in a glass. "The visible world and the relation of its parts, is the dial-plate of the invisible." The axioms of physics translate the laws of ethics. Thus, "the whole is greater than its part"; "reaction is equal to action"; "the smallest weight may be made to lift the greatest, the difference of weight being compensated by time"; and many the like propositions, which have an ethical as well as physical sense. These propositions have a much more extensive and universal sense when applied to human life, than when confined to technical use.

In like manner, the memorable words of history, and the proverbs of 39 nations, consist usually of a natural fact, selected as a picture or parable of a moral truth. Thus; A rolling stone gathers no moss; A bird in the hand is worth two in the bush; A cripple in the right way will beat a racer in the wrong; Make hay while the sun shines; 'Tis hard to carry a full cup even; Vinegar is the son of wine; The last ounce broke the camel's back; Long-lived trees make roots first; and the like. In their primary sense these are trivial facts, but we repeat them for the value of their analogical import. What is true of proverbs is true of all fables, parables, and allegories.

This relation between the mind and matter is not fancied by some poet, 40 but stands in the will of God, and so is free to be known by all men. It appears to men, or it does not appear. When in fortunate hours we ponder this miracle, the wise man doubts, if, at all other times, he is not blind and deaf;

> "Can these things be,
> And overcome us like a summer's cloud,
> Without our special wonder?"

for the universe becomes transparent, and the light of higher laws than its own shines through it. It is the standing problem which has exercised the wonder and the study of every fine genius since the world began; from the era of the Egyptians and the Brahmins, to that of Pythagoras, of Plato, of Bacon, of Leibnitz, of Swedenborg. There sits the Sphinx at the roadside, and from age to age, as each prophet comes by, he tries his fortune at reading her riddle. There seems to be a necessity in spirit to manifest itself in material forms; and day and night, river and storm, beast and bird, acid and alkali, pre-exist in necessary Ideas in the mind of God, and are what they are by virtue of preceding affections, in the world of spirit. A Fact is the end or last issue of spirit. The visible creation is the terminus or the circumference of the invisible world. "Material objects," said a French philosopher, "are necessarily kinds of *scoriae* of the substantial thoughts of the Creator, which must always preserve an exact relation to their first origin; in other words, visible nature must have a spiritual and moral side."

This doctrine is abstruse, and though the images of "garment," "sco-   41
riae," "mirror," &c., may stimulate the fancy, we must summon the aid of subtler and more vital expositors to make it plain. "Every scripture is to be interpreted by the same spirit which gave it forth," is the fundamental law of criticism. A life in harmony with nature, the love of truth and of virtue, will purge the eyes to understand her text. By degrees we may come to know the primitive sense of the permanent objects of nature, so that the world shall be to us an open book, and every form significant of its hidden life and final cause.

A new interest surprises us, whilst, under the view now suggested, we   42
contemplate the fearful extent and multitude of objects; since "every object rightly seen unlocks a new faculty of the soul." That which was unconscious truth becomes, when interpreted and defined in an object, a part of the domain of knowledge,—a new weapon in the magazine of power.

CHAPTER VII

Spirit

It is essential to a true theory of nature and of man, that it should con-   43
tain somewhat progressive. Uses that are exhausted or that may be, and facts that end in the statement, cannot be all that is true of this brave lodging wherein man is harbored, and wherein all his faculties find appropriate and endless exercise. And all the uses of nature admit of being summed in one, which yields the activity of man an infinite scope.

Through all its kingdoms, to the suburbs and outskirts of things, it is faithful to the cause whence it had its origin. It always speaks of Spirit. It suggests the absolute. It is a perpetual effect. It is a great shadow pointing always to the sun behind us.

The aspect of nature is devout. Like the figure of Jesus, she stands with 44
bended head, and hands folded upon the breast. The happiest man is he who learns from nature the lesson of worship.

Of that ineffable essence which we call Spirit, he that thinks most, will 45
say least. We can foresee God in the coarse, as it were, distant phenomena of matter; but when we try to define and describe himself, both language and thought desert us, and we are as helpless as fools and savages. That essence refuses to be recorded in propositions, but when man has worshipped him intellectually, the noblest ministry of nature is to stand as the apparition of God. It is the organ through which the universal spirit speaks to the individual, and strives to lead back the individual to it.

When we consider Spirit, we see that the views already presented do 46
not include the whole circumference of man. We must add some related thoughts.

Three problems are put by nature to the mind; What is matter? Whence 47
is it? and Whereto? The first of these questions only, the ideal theory answers. Idealism saith: matter is a phenomenon, not a substance. Idealism acquaints us with the total disparity between the evidence of our own being, and the evidence of the world's being. The one is perfect; the other, incapable of any assurance; the mind is a part of the nature of things; the world is a divine dream, from which we may presently awake to the glories and certainties of the day. Idealism is a hypothesis to account for nature by other principles than those of carpentry and chemistry. Yet, if it only deny the existence of matter, it does not satisfy the demands of the spirit. It leaves God out of me. It leaves me in the splendid labyrinth of my perceptions, to wander without end. Then the heart resists it, because it balks the affections in denying substantive being to men and women. Nature is so pervaded with human life, that there is something of humanity in all, and in every particular. But this theory makes nature foreign to me, and does not account for that consanguinity which we acknowledge to it.

Let it stand, then, in the present state of our knowledge, merely as a 48
useful introductory hypothesis, serving to apprise us of the eternal distinction between the soul and the world.

But when, following the invisible steps of thought, we come to inquire, 49
Whence is matter? and Whereto? many truths arise to us out of the recesses of consciousness. We learn that the highest is present to the soul of man, that the dread universal essence, which is not wisdom, or love, or beauty, or power, but all in one, and each entirely, is that for which all

things exist, and that by which they are; that spirit creates; that behind nature, throughout nature, spirit is present; one and not compound, it does
not act upon us from without, that is, in space and time, but spiritually, or
through ourselves: therefore, that spirit, that is, the Supreme Being, does
not build up nature around us, but puts it forth through us, as the life of
the tree puts forth new branches and leaves through the pores of the old.
As a plant upon the earth, so a man rests upon the bosom of God; he is
nourished by unfailing fountains, and draws, at his need, inexhaustible
power. Who can set bounds to the possibilities of man? Once inhale the
upper air, being admitted to behold the absolute natures of justice and
truth, and we learn that man has access to the entire mind of the Creator,
is himself the creator in the finite. This view, which admonishes me where
the sources of wisdom and power lie, and points to virtue as to

> "The golden key
> Which opes the palace of eternity,"

carries upon its face the highest certificate of truth, because it animates me
to create my own world through the purification of my soul.

The world proceeds from the same spirit as the body of man. It is a
remoter and inferior incarnation of God, a projection of God in the unconscious. But it differs from the body in one important respect. It is not,
like that, now subjected to the human will. Its serene order is inviolable by
us. It is, therefore, to us, the present expositor of the divine mind. It is a
fixed point whereby we may measure our departure. As we degenerate,
the contrast between us and our house is more evident. We are as much
strangers in nature, as we are aliens from God. We do not understand the
notes of birds. The fox and the deer run away from us; the bear and tiger
rend us. We do not know the uses of more than a few plants, as corn and
the apple, the potato and the vine. Is not the landscape, every glimpse of
which hath a grandeur, a face of him? Yet this may show us what discord
is between man and nature, for you cannot freely admire a noble landscape, if laborers are digging in the field hard by. The poet finds something ridiculous in his delight, until he is out of the sight of men.

50

QUESTIONS FOR DISCUSSION AND WRITING

1. After separating nature from the soul in his introduction, Emerson
spends a lot of time in the rest of his essay bringing them back together
and discussing their relationship to God or spirit. Read back through the
selection here, looking for places where Emerson ties humans and their
souls to nature. How does he do this within each of the sections on com-

modity, beauty, language, and spirit? What is the relationship among the four sections? Which does Emerson seem to value most and which least?

2. What position would Emerson take in the current environmental debates? Think of a particular debate over clean water, or logging, or freeing wolves in our western parks, for example. Then search this essay for sections that seem to address the debate you have chosen. Organize the sections you find into a coherent argument and then discuss what insights you have gained about this debate from reading Emerson.

3. In *Nature* Emerson clearly values nature greatly. Do you find his reasons for valuing nature convincing? Why or why not? In your discussion try to get at the ways in which this essay has helped you to think about nature more carefully.

NATHANIEL HAWTHORNE

Nathaniel Hawthorne (1804–64) is remembered primarily for his gripping and strange, almost surreal, stories about New England. His work chronicles a harsh land and a hard people who are often tortured by guilt and a strong sense of duty. Although this "Puritan" strain may seem to have disappeared from modern America, it was a powerful force in shaping much of our history and remains influential in many aspects of American life.

The Scarlet Letter (1850), set in seventeenth-century Boston, tells the story of Hester Prynne, who commits adultery with a minister, Arthur Dimmesdale, and has a child, Pearl, from the union. The two keep their sin a secret, but when Hester bears Pearl and refuses to name the father, she is punished with imprisonment and then made to wear a scarlet A on her bosom. In the scene from the novel reprinted here, Arthur happens upon Hester and Pearl in the forest, and they contemplate running away to Europe to avoid the vengeance of Roger Chillingworth, who was Hester's husband.

From *The Scarlet Letter*

XVIII

A Flood of Sunshine

Arthur Dimmesdale gazed into Hester's face with a look in which hope and joy shone out, indeed, but with fear betwixt them, and a kind of horror at her boldness, who had spoken what he vaguely hinted at, but dared not speak. 1

But Hester Prynne, with a mind of native courage and activity, and for so long a period not merely estranged, but outlawed, from society, had habituated herself to such latitude of speculation as was altogether foreign to the clergyman. She had wandered, without rule or guidance, in a moral wilderness; as vast, as intricate and shadowy, as the untamed forest, amid the gloom of which they were now holding a colloquy that was to decide their fate. Her intellect and heart had their home, as it were, in desert places, where she roamed as freely as the wild Indian in his woods. For years past she had looked from this estranged point of view at human institutions, and whatever priests or legislators had established; criticizing all with hardly more reverence than the Indian would feel for the clerical band, the judicial robe, the pillory, the gallows, the fireside, or the church. 2

The tendency of her fate and fortunes had been to set her free. The scarlet letter was her passport into regions where other women dared not tread. Shame, Despair, Solitude! These had been her teachers,—stern and wild ones,—and they had made her strong, but taught her much amiss.

The minister, on the other hand, had never gone through an experience calculated to lead him beyond the scope of generally received laws; although, in a single instance, he had so fearfully transgressed one of the most sacred of them. But this had been a sin of passion, not of principle, nor even purpose. Since that wretched epoch, he had watched, with morbid zeal and minuteness, not his acts,—for those it was easy to arrange,—but each breath of emotion, and his every thought. At the head of the social system, as the clergymen of that day stood, he was only the more trammelled by its regulations, its principles, and even its prejudices. As a priest, the framework of his order inevitably hemmed him in. As a man who had once sinned, but who kept his conscience all alive and painfully sensitive by the fretting of an unhealed wound, he might have been supposed safer within the line of virtue than if he had never sinned at all.

Thus, we seem to see that, as regarded Hester Prynne, the whole seven years of outlaw and ignominy had been little other than a preparation for this very hour. But Arthur Dimmesdale! Were such a man once more to fall, what plea could be urged in extenuation of his crime? None; unless it avail him somewhat, that he was broken down by long and exquisite suffering; that his mind was darkened and confused by the very remorse which harrowed it; that, between fleeing as an avowed criminal, and remaining as a hypocrite, conscience might find it hard to strike the balance; that it was human to avoid the peril of death and infamy, and the inscrutable machinations of an enemy; that, finally, to this poor pilgrim, on his dreary and desert path, faint, sick, miserable, there appeared a glimpse of human affection and sympathy, a new life, and a true one, in exchange for the heavy doom which he was now expiating. And be the stern and sad truth spoken, that the breach which guilt has once made into the human soul is never, in this mortal state, repaired. It may be watched and guarded; so that the enemy shall not force his way again into the citadel, and might even, in his subsequent assaults, select some other avenue, in preference to that where he had formerly succeeded. But there is still the ruined wall, and, near it, the stealthy tread of the foe that would win over again his unforgotten triumph.

The struggle, if there were one, need not be described. Let it suffice, that the clergyman resolved to flee, and not alone.

"If, in all these past seven years," thought he, "I could recall one instant of peace or hope, I would yet endure, for the sake of that earnest of Heaven's mercy. But now,—since I am irrevocably doomed,—wherefore should I not snatch the solace allowed to the condemned culprit before

3

4

5

6

his execution? Or, if this be the path to a better life, as Hester would persuade me, I surely give up no fairer prospect by pursuing it! Neither can I
any longer live without her companionship; so powerful is she to sustain,—so tender to soothe! O Thou to whom I dare not lift mine eyes, wilt
Thou yet pardon me!"

"Thou wilt go!" said Hester, calmly, as he met her glance.   7

The decision once made, a glow of strange enjoyment threw its flicker-   8
ing brightness over the trouble of his breast. It was the exhilarating
effect—upon a prisoner just escaped from the dungeon of his own
heart—of breathing the wild, free atmosphere of an unredeemed, un-
christianized, lawless region. His spirit rose, as it were, with a bound, and
attained a nearer prospect of the sky, than throughout all the misery which
had kept him grovelling on the earth. Of a deeply religious temperament,
there was inevitably a tinge of the devotional in his mood.

"Do I feel joy again?" cried he, wondering at himself. "Methought the   9
germ of it was dead in me! O Hester, thou art my better angel! I seem to
have flung myself—sick, sin-stained, and sorrow-blackened—down
upon these forest-leaves, and to have risen up all made anew, and with
new powers to glorify Him that hath been merciful! This is already the better life! Why did we not find it sooner?"

"Let us not look back," answered Hester Prynne. "The past is gone!   10
Wherefore should we linger upon it now? See! With this symbol, I undo it
all, and make it as it had never been!"

So speaking, she undid the clasp that fastened the scarlet letter, and,   11
taking it from her bosom, threw it to a distance among the withered
leaves. The mystic token alighted on the hither verge of the stream. With
a hand's breadth further flight it would have fallen into the water, and
have given the little brook another woe to carry onward, besides the un-
intelligible tale which it still kept murmuring about. But there lay the embroidered letter, glittering like a lost jewel, which some ill-fated wanderer
might pick up, and thenceforth be haunted by strange phantoms of guilt,
sinkings of the heart, and unaccountable misfortune.

The stigma gone, Hester heaved a long, deep sigh, in which the burden   12
of shame and anguish departed from her spirit. O exquisite relief! She had
not known the weight, until she felt the freedom! By another impulse, she
took off the formal cap that confined her hair; and down it fell upon her
shoulders, dark and rich, with at once a shadow and a light in its abundance, and imparting the charm of softness to her features. There played
around her mouth, and beamed out of her eyes, a radiant and tender
smile, that seemed gushing from the very heart of womanhood. A crimson
flush was glowing on her cheek, that had been long so pale. Her sex, her
youth, and the whole richness of her beauty, came back from what men
call the irrevocable past, and clustered themselves, with her maiden hope,

and a happiness before unknown, within the magic circle of this hour. And, as if the gloom of the earth and sky had been but the effluence of these two mortal hearts, it vanished with their sorrow. All at once, as with a sudden smile of heaven, forth burst the sunshine, pouring a very flood into the obscure forest, gladdening each green leaf, transmuting the yellow fallen ones to gold, and gleaming adown the gray trunks of the solemn trees. The objects that had made a shadow hitherto, embodied the brightness now. The course of the little brook might be traced by its merry gleam afar into the wood's heart of mystery, which had become a mystery of joy.

Such was the sympathy of Nature—that wild, heathen Nature of the   13
forest, never subjugated by human law, nor illumined by higher truth— with the bliss of these two spirits! Love, whether newly born, or aroused from a death-like slumber, must always create a sunshine, filling the heart so full of radiance, that it overflows upon the outward world. Had the forest still kept its gloom, it would have been bright in Hester's eyes, and bright in Arthur Dimmesdale's!

Hester looked at him with the thrill of another joy.   14

"Thou must know Pearl!" said she. "Our little Pearl! Thou has seen   15
her,—yes, I know it!—but thou wilt see her now with other eyes. She is a strange child! I hardly comprehend her! But thou wilt love her dearly, as I do, and wilt advise me how to deal with her."

"Dost thou think the child will be glad to know me?" asked the minis-   16
ter, somewhat uneasily. "I have long shrunk from children, because they often show a distrust,—a backwardness to be familiar with me. I have even been afraid of little Pearl!"

"Ah, that was sad!" answered the mother. "But she will love thee dearly,   17
and thou her. She is not far off. I will call her! Pearl! Pearl!"

"I see the child," observed the minister. "Yonder she is, standing in a   18
streak of sunshine, a good way off, on the other side of the brook. So thou thinkest the child will love me?"

Hester smiled, and again called to Pearl, who was visible, at some dis-   19
tance, as the minister had described her, like a bright-apparelled vision, in a sunbeam, which fell down upon her through an arch of boughs. The ray quivered to and fro, making her figure dim or distinct,—now like a real child, now like a child's spirit,—as the splendor went and came again. She heard her mother's voice, and approached slowly through the forest.

Pearl had not found the hour pass wearisomely, while her mother sat   20
talking with the clergyman. The great black forest—stern as it showed itself to those who brought the guilt and troubles of the world into its bosom—became the playmate of the lonely infant, as well as it knew how. Sombre as it was, it put on the kindest of its moods to welcome her. It offered her the partridge-berries, the growth of the preceding autumn,

but ripening only in the spring, and now red as drops of blood upon the withered leaves. These Pearl gathered, and was pleased with their wild flavor. The small denizens of the wilderness hardly took pains to move out of her path. A partridge, indeed, with a brood of ten behind her, ran forward threateningly, but soon repented of her fierceness, and clucked to her young ones not to be afraid. A pigeon, alone on a low branch, allowed Pearl to come beneath, and uttered a sound as much of greeting as alarm. A squirrel, from the lofty depths of his domestic tree, chattered either in anger or merriment,—for a squirrel is such a choleric and humorous little personage, that it is hard to distinguish between his moods,—so he chattered at the child, and flung down a nut upon her head. It was a last year's nut, and already gnawed by his sharp tooth. A fox, startled from his sleep by her light footstep on the leaves, looked inquisitively at Pearl, as doubting whether it were better to steal off, or renew his nap on the same spot. A wolf, it is said,—but here the tale has surely lapsed into the improbable,—came up, and smelt of Pearl's robe, and offered his savage head to be patted by her hand. The truth seems to be, however, that the mother-forest, and these wild things which it nourished, all recognized a kindred wildness in the human child.

And she was gentler here than in the grassy-margined streets of the settlement, or in her mother's cottage. The flowers appeared to know it; and one and another whispered as she passed, "Adorn thyself with me, thou beautiful child, adorn thyself with me!"—and, to please them, Pearl gathered the violets, and anemones, and columbines, and some twigs of the freshest green, which the old trees held down before her eyes. With these she decorated her hair, and her young waist, and became a nymph-child, or an infant dryad, or whatever else was in closest sympathy with the antique wood. In such guise had Pearl adorned herself, when she heard her mother's voice, and came slowly back. 21

Slowly; for she saw the clergyman! 22

XIX

The Child at the Brook-Side

"Thou wilt love her dearly," repeated Hester Prynne, as she and the minister sat watching little Pearl. "Dost thou not think her beautiful? And see with what natural skill she has made those simple flowers adorn her! Had she gathered pearls, and diamonds, and rubies, in the wood, they could not have become her better. She is a splendid child! But I know whose brow she has!" 23

"Dost thou know, Hester," said Arthur Dimmesdale, with an unquiet 24
smile, "that this dear child, tripping about always at thy side, hath caused
me many an alarm? Methought—O Hester, what a thought is that, and
how terrible to dread it!—that my own features were partly repeated in
her face, and so strikingly that the world might see them! But she is mostly
thine!"

"No, no! Not mostly!" answered the mother, with a tender smile. "A 25
little longer, and thou needest not to be afraid to trace whose child she is.
But how strangely beautiful she looks, with those wild flowers in her hair!
It is as if one of the fairies, whom we left in our dear old England, had
decked her out to meet us."

It was with a feeling which neither of them had ever before experi- 26
enced, that they sat and watched Pearl's slow advance. In her was visible
the tie that united them. She had been offered to the world, these seven
years past, as the living hieroglyphic, in which was revealed the secret
they so darkly sought to hide,—all written in this symbol,—all plainly
manifest,—had there been a prophet or magician skilled to read the character of flame! And Pearl was the oneness of their being. Be the foregone
evil what it might, how could they doubt that their earthly lives and future
destinies were conjoined, when they beheld at once the material union,
and the spiritual idea, in whom they met, and were to dwell immortally together? Thoughts like these—and perhaps other thoughts, which they did
not acknowledge or define—threw an awe about the child, as she came
onward.

"Let her see nothing strange—no passion nor eagerness—in thy way 27
of accosting her," whispered Hester. "Our Pearl is a fitful and fantastic little elf, sometimes. Especially, she is seldom tolerant of emotion, when she
does not fully comprehend the why and wherefore. But the child hath
strong affections! She loves me, and will love thee!"

"Thou canst not think," said the minister, glancing aside at Hester 28
Prynne, "how my heart dreads this interview, and yearns for it! But, in
truth, as I already told thee, children are not readily won to be familiar
with me. They will not climb my knee, nor prattle in my ear, nor answer
to my smile; but stand apart, and eye me strangely. Even little babes, when
I take them in my arms, weep bitterly. Yet Pearl, twice in her little lifetime,
hath been kind to me! The first time,—thou knowest it well! The last was
when thou ledst her with thee to the house of yonder stern old Governor."

"And thou didst plead so bravely in her behalf and mine!" answered the 29
mother. "I remember it; and so shall little Pearl. Fear nothing! She may be
strange and shy at first, but will soon learn to love thee!"

By this time Pearl had reached the margin of the brook, and stood on 30
the further side, gazing silently at Hester and the clergyman, who still sat
together on the mossy tree-trunk, waiting to receive her. Just where she

had paused, the brook chanced to form a pool, so smooth and quiet that it reflected a perfect image of her little figure, with all the brilliant picturesqueness of her beauty, in its adornment of flowers and wreathed foliage, but more refined and spiritualized than the reality. This image, so nearly identical with the living Pearl, seemed to communicate somewhat of its own shadowy and intangible quality to the child herself. It was strange, the way in which Pearl stood, looking so steadfastly at them through the dim medium of the forest-gloom; herself, meanwhile, all glorified with a ray of sunshine, that was attracted thitherward as by a certain sympathy. In the brook beneath stood another child,—another and the same,—with likewise its ray of golden light. Hester felt herself, in some indistinct and tantalizing manner, estranged from Pearl; as if the child, in her lonely ramble through the forest, had strayed out of the sphere in which she and her mother dwelt together, and was now vainly seeking to return to it.

There was both truth and error in the impression; the child and mother were estranged, but through Hester's fault, not Pearl's. Since the latter rambled from her side, another inmate had been admitted within the circle of the mother's feelings, and so modified the aspect of them all, that Pearl, the returning wanderer, could not find her wonted place, and hardly knew where she was.   31

"I have a strange fancy," observed the sensitive minister, "that this brook is the boundary between two worlds, and that thou canst never meet thy Pearl again. Or is she an elfish spirit, who, as the legends of our childhood taught us, is forbidden to cross a running stream? Pray hasten her; for this delay has already imparted a tremor to my nerves."   32

"Come, dearest child!" said Hester, encouragingly, and stretching out both her arms. "How slow thou art! When hast thou been so sluggish before now? Here is a friend of mine, who must be thy friend also. Thou wilt have twice as much love, henceforward, as thy mother alone could give thee! Leap across the brook, and come to us. Thou canst leap like a young deer!"   33

Pearl, without responding in any manner to these honey-sweet expressions, remained on the other side of the brook. Now she fixed her bright, wild eyes on her mother, now on the minister, and now included them both in the same glance; as if to detect and explain to herself the relation which they bore to one another. For some unaccountable reason, as Arthur Dimmesdale felt the child's eyes upon himself, his hand—with that gesture so habitual as to have become involuntary—stole over his heart. At length, assuming a singular air of authority, Pearl stretched out her hand, with the small forefinger extended, and pointing evidently towards her mother's breast. And beneath, in the mirror of the brook, there was the flower-girdled and sunny image of little Pearl, pointing her small forefinger too.   34

"Thou strange child, why dost thou not come to me?" exclaimed Hester.   35

Pearl still pointed with her forefinger; and a frown gathered on her   36
brow; the more impressive from the childish, the almost baby-like aspect
of the features that conveyed it. As her mother still kept beckoning to her,
and arraying her face in a holiday suit of unaccustomed smiles, the child
stamped her foot with a yet more imperious look and gesture. In the
brook, again, was the fantastic beauty of the image, with its reflected
frown, its pointed finger, and imperious gesture, giving emphasis to the
aspect of little Pearl.

"Hasten, Pearl; or I shall be angry with thee!" cried Hester Prynne, who,   37
however inured to such behavior on the elf-child's part at other seasons,
was naturally anxious for a more seemly deportment now. "Leap across
the brook, naughty child, and run hither! Else I must come to thee!"

But Pearl, not a whit startled at her mother's threats, any more than   38
mollified by her entreaties, now suddenly burst into a fit of passion, gesticulating violently, and throwing her small figure into the most extrava-
gant contortions. She accompanied this wild outbreak with piercing
shrieks, which the woods reverberated on all sides; so that, alone as she
was in her childish and unreasonable wrath, it seemed as if a hidden multitude were lending her their sympathy and encouragement. Seen in the
brook, once more, was the shadowy wrath of Pearl's image, crowned and
girdled with flowers, but stamping its foot, wildly gesticulating, and, in the
midst of all, still pointing its small forefinger at Hester's bosom!

"I see what ails the child," whispered Hester to the clergyman, and   39
turning pale in spite of a strong effort to conceal her trouble and annoyance. "Children will not abide any, the slightest, change in the accustomed
aspect of things that are daily before their eyes. Pearl misses something
which she has always seen me wear!"

"I pray you," answered the minister, "if thou hast any means of pacify-   40
ing the child, do it forthwith! Save it were the cankered wrath of an old
witch, like Mistress Hibbins," added he, attempting to smile, "I know
nothing that I would not sooner encounter than this passion in a child. In
Pearl's young beauty, as in the wrinkled witch, it has a preternatural effect.
Pacify her, if thou lovest me!"

Hester turned again towards Pearl, with a crimson blush upon her   41
cheek, a conscious glance aside at the clergyman, and then a heavy sigh;
while, even before she had time to speak, the blush yielded to a deadly
pallor.

"Pearl," said she, sadly, "look down at thy feet! There!—before thee!   42
—on the hither side of the brook!"

The child turned her eyes to the point indicated; and there lay the scar-   43
let letter, so close upon the margin of the stream, that the gold embroidery
was reflected in it.

"Bring it hither!" said Hester.   44

"Come thou and take it up!" answered Pearl.   45

"Was ever such a child!" observed Hester, aside to the minister. "O, I   46
have much to tell thee about her! But, in very truth, she is right as regards
this hateful token. I must bear its torture yet a little longer,—only a few
days longer,—until we shall have left this region, and look back hither as
to a land which we have dreamed of. The forest cannot hide it! The mid-
ocean shall take it from my hand, and swallow it up forever!"

With these words, she advanced to the margin of the brook, took up   47
the scarlet letter, and fastened it again into her bosom. Hopefully, but a
moment ago, as Hester had spoken of drowning it in the deep sea, there
was a sense of inevitable doom upon her, as she thus received back this
deadly symbol from the hand of fate. She had flung it into infinite space!—
she had drawn an hour's free breath!—and here again was the scarlet misery, glittering on the old spot! So it ever is, whether thus typified or no,
that an evil deed invests itself with the character of doom. Hester next
gathered up the heavy tresses of her hair, and confined them beneath her
cap. As if there were a withering spell in the sad letter, her beauty, the
warmth and richness of her womanhood, departed, like fading sunshine;
and a gray shadow seemed to fall across her.

When the dreary change was wrought, she extended her hand to Pearl.   48

"Dost thou know thy mother now, child?" asked she, reproachfully,   49
but with a subdued tone. "Wilt thou come across the brook, and own thy
mother, now that she has her shame upon her,—now that she is sad?"

"Yes; now I will!" answered the child, bounding across the brook, and   50
clasping Hester in her arms. "Now thou art my mother indeed! And I am
thy little Pearl!"

In a mood of tenderness that was not usual with her, she drew down   51
her mother's head, and kissed her brow and both her cheeks. But then—
by a kind of necessity that always impelled this child to alloy whatever
comfort she might chance to give with a throb of anguish—Pearl put up
her mouth, and kissed the scarlet letter too!

"That was not kind!" said Hester. "When thou hast shown me a little   52
love, thou mockest me!"

"Why doth the minister sit yonder?" asked Pearl.   53

"He waits to welcome thee," replied her mother. "Come thou, and en-   54
treat his blessing! He loves thee, my little Pearl, and loves thy mother too.
Wilt thou not love him? Come! he longs to greet thee!"

"Doth he love us?" said Pearl, looking up, with acute intelligence, into   55
her mother's face. "Will he go back with us, hand in hand, we three together, into the town?"

"Not now, dear child," answered Hester. "But in days to come he will   56
walk hand in hand with us. We will have a home and fireside of our own;
and thou shalt sit upon his knee; and he will teach thee many things, and
love thee dearly. Thou wilt love him; wilt thou not?"

"And will he always keep his hand over his heart?" inquired Pearl.   57

"Foolish child, what a question is that!" exclaimed her mother. "Come   58
and ask his blessing!"

But, whether influenced by the jealousy that seems instinctive with   59
every petted child towards a dangerous rival, or from whatever caprice of
her freakish nature, Pearl would show no favor to the clergyman. It was
only by an exertion of force that her mother brought her up to him, hanging back, and manifesting her reluctance by odd grimaces; of which, ever
since her babyhood, she had possessed a singular variety, and could
transform her mobile physiognomy into a series of different aspects, with
a new mischief in them, each and all. The minister—painfully embarrassed, but hoping that a kiss might prove a talisman to admit him into the
child's kindlier regards—bent forward, and impressed one on her brow.
Hereupon, Pearl broke away from her mother, and, running to the brook,
stooped over it, and bathed her forehead, until the unwelcome kiss was
quite washed off, and diffused through a long lapse of the gliding water.
She then remained apart, silently watching Hester and the clergyman;
while they talked together, and made such arrangements as were suggested by their new position, and the purposes soon to be fulfilled.

And now this fateful interview had come to a close. The dell was to be   60
left a solitude among its dark, old trees, which, with their multitudinous
tongues, would whisper long of what had passed there, and no mortal be
the wiser. And the melancholy brook would add this other tale to the mystery with which its little heart was already overburdened, and whereof it
still kept up a murmuring babble, with not a whit more cheerfulness of
tone than for ages heretofore.

QUESTIONS FOR DISCUSSION AND WRITING

1. The weather and even nature itself seem to change dramatically in the
course of this selection. Read through it again, carefully noting these
changes. What particular people, animals, plants, or general conditions
change? What patterns can you detect in the changes? Use this analysis to
explain how Hawthorne manipulates his image of nature to convey the
meaning of the story.

2. Hawthorne writes that Hester has wandered in a moral wilderness "as
vast, as intricate and shadowy, as the untamed forest" (par. 2). What effect
has this wandering had on Hester, and on Pearl? Look throughout this selection for signs of the effect the wilderness, both literal and figurative, has
had on mother and daughter.

3. In this selection Hawthorne contrasts nature with the civilized world.
By acknowledging her sin, Hester has stepped outside of society, and "her
intellect and heart had their home, as it were, in desert places" (par. 2).

Arthur, on the other hand, is tied to society through his silence. Hester is the one who argues strongly for their escape from society, and she starts this escape by removing her scarlet letter and letting down her hair. But then Pearl, "nature's child," forces Hester to put her letter back on and gather her hair up under her cap. Considering these events, do you think that Arthur and Hester will be able to run away from their confining society? Why or why not?

HENRY DAVID THOREAU

Henry David Thoreau (1817–62) valued his privacy greatly, as can be seen in this chapter on solitude from Walden *(1854) Much of Thoreau's writing seems intensely personal and inward looking, taking the form of poetry, essays, lectures, descriptions of nature, and accounts of his travels throughout New England. Although he never had a regular job, he was able to support himself and his simple needs through odd jobs and surveying. His real job was to live life fully and think deeply; he looked to himself and to nature to answer the question of how to live well. Thoreau's writing was never popular while he was still alive, but it has come to have great influence today on our thinking about nature and our sense of the value of the individual conscience in society.*

In Walden *Thoreau writes of his experiences living in a tiny one-room cabin, which cost him 28.12\frac{1}{2}$ to build, near Walden Pond in Concord, Massachusetts. He moved in on the Fourth of July, 1845, and stayed two years. Although he was not quite as isolated as he would have us believe, he did find sufficient solitude to learn much from nature and his own thoughts.*

Solitude

This is a delicious evening, when the whole body is one sense, and imbibes delight through every pore. I go and come with a strange liberty in Nature, a part of herself. As I walk along the stony shore of the pond in my shirt sleeves, though it is cool as well as cloudy and windy, and I see nothing special to attract me, all the elements are unusually congenial to me. The bullfrogs trump to usher in the night, and the note of the whippoorwill is borne on the rippling wind from over the water. Sympathy with the fluttering alder and poplar leaves almost takes away my breath; yet, like the lake, my serenity is rippled but not ruffled. These small waves raised by the evening wind are as remote from storm as the smooth reflecting surface. Though it is now dark, the wind still blows and roars in the wood, the waves still dash, and some creatures lull the rest with their notes. The repose is never complete. The wildest animals do not repose, but seek their prey now; the fox, and skunk, and rabbit, now roam the fields and woods without fear. They are Nature's watchmen,—links which connect the days of animated life. 1

When I return to my house I find that visitors have been there and left 2 their cards, either a bunch of flowers, or a wreath of evergreen, or a name in pencil on a yellow walnut leaf or a chip. They who come rarely to the woods take some little piece of the forest into their hands to play with by the way, which they leave, either intentionally or accidentally. One has peeled a willow wand, woven it into a ring, and dropped it on my table. I could always tell if visitors had called in my absence, either by the bended twigs or grass, or the print of their shoes, and generally of what sex or age or quality they were by some slight trace left, as a flower dropped, or a bunch of grass plucked and thrown away, even as far off as the railroad, half a mile distant, or by the lingering odor of a cigar or pipe. Nay, I was frequently notified of the passage of a traveller along the highway sixty rods off by the scent of his pipe.

There is commonly sufficient space about us. Our horizon is never quite at our elbows. The thick wood is not just at our door, nor the pond, but somewhat is always clearing, familiar and worn by us, appropriated and fenced in some way, and reclaimed from Nature. For what reason have I this vast range and circuit, some square miles of unfrequented forest, for my privacy, abandoned to me by men? My nearest neighbor is a mile distant, and no house is visible from any place but the hill-tops within half a mile of my own. I have my horizon bounded by woods all to myself; a distant view of the railroad where it touches the pond on the one hand, and of the fence which skirts the woodland road on the other. But for the most part it is as solitary where I live as on the prairies. It is as much Asia or Africa as New England. I have, as it were, my own sun and moon and stars, and a little world all to myself. At night there was never a traveller passed my house, or knocked at my door, more than if I were the first or last man; unless it were in the spring, when at long intervals some came from the village to fish for pouts,—they plainly fished much more in the Walden Pond of their own natures, and baited their hooks with darkness,—but they soon retreated, usually with light baskets, and left "the world to darkness and to me," and the black kernel of the night was never profaned by any human neighborhood. I believe that men are generally still a little afraid of the dark, though the witches are all hung, and Christianity and candles have been introduced.

Yet I experienced sometimes that the most sweet and tender, the most innocent and encouraging society may be found in any natural object, even for the poor misanthrope and most melancholy man. There can be no very black melancholy to him who lives in the midst of Nature and has his senses still. There was never yet such a storm but it was Aeolian music to a healthy and innocent ear. Nothing can rightly compel a simple and brave man to a vulgar sadness. While I enjoy the friendship of the seasons I trust that nothing can make life a burden to me. The gentle rain which waters my beans and keeps me in the house to-day is not drear and melancholy, but good for me too. Though it prevents my hoeing them, it is of far more worth than my hoeing. If it should continue so long as to cause the seeds to rot in the ground and destroy the potatoes in the low lands, it would still be good for the grass on the uplands, and, being good for the grass, it would be good for me. Sometimes, when I compare myself with other men, it seems as if I were more favored by the gods than they, beyond any deserts that I am conscious of; as if I had a warrant and surety at their hands which my fellows have not, and were especially guided and guarded. I do not flatter myself, but if it be possible they flatter me. I have never felt lonesome, or in the least oppressed by a sense of solitude, but once, and that was a few weeks after I came to the woods, when, for an hour, I doubted if the near neighborhood of man was not essential to a serene and healthy life. To be alone was something unpleasant. But I was at the same time conscious of a slight insanity in my mood, and seemed to foresee my recovery. In the midst of a gentle rain while these thoughts prevailed, I was suddenly sensible of such sweet and beneficent society in Nature, in the very pattering of the drops, and in every sound and sight around my house, an infinite and unaccountable friendliness all at once like an atmosphere sustaining me, as made the fancied advantages of human neighborhood insignificant, and I have never thought of them since. Every little pine needle expanded and swelled with sympathy and befriended me. I was so distinctly made aware of the presence of something kindred to me, even in scenes which we are accustomed to call wild and dreary, and also that the nearest of blood to me and humanest was not a person nor a villager, that I thought no place could ever be strange to me again.—

> "Mourning untimely consumes the sad;
> Few are their days in the land of the living,
> Beautiful daughter of Toscar."

Some of my pleasantest hours were during the long rain storms in the   5
spring or fall, which confined me to the house for the afternoon as well as the forenoon, soothed by their ceaseless roar and pelting; when an early twilight ushered in a long evening in which many thoughts had time to take root and unfold themselves. In those driving northeast rains which tried the village houses so, when the maids stood ready with mop and pail in front entries to keep the deluge out, I sat behind my door in my little house, which was all entry, and thoroughly enjoyed its protection. In one heavy thunder shower the lightning struck a large pitch-pine across the pond, making a very conspicuous and perfectly regular spiral groove from top to bottom, an inch or more deep, and four or five inches wide, as you would groove a walking-stick. I passed it again the other day, and was struck with awe on looking up and beholding that mark, now more dis-

tinct than ever, where a terrific and resistless bolt came down out of the harmless sky eight years ago. Men frequently say to me, "I should think you would feel lonesome down there, and want to be nearer to folks, rainy and snowy days and nights especially." I am tempted to reply to such,—This whole earth which we inhabit is but a point in space. How far apart, think you, dwell the two most distant inhabitants of yonder star, the breadth of whose disk cannot be appreciated by our instruments? Why should I feel lonely? is not our planet in the Milky Way? This which you put seems to me not to be the most important question. What sort of space is that which separates a man from his fellows and makes him solitary? I have found that no exertion of the legs can bring two minds much nearer to one another. What do we want most to dwell near to? Not to many men surely, the depot, the post-office, the bar-room, the meeting-house, the school-house, the grocery, Beacon Hill, or the Five Points, where men most congregate, but to the perennial source of our life, whence in all our experience we have found that to issue, as the willow stands near the water and sends out its roots in that direction. This will vary with different natures, but this is the place where a wise man will dig his cellar . . . . I one evening overtook one of my townsmen, who has accumulated what is called "a handsome property,"—though I never got a *fair* view of it,—on the Walden road, driving a pair of cattle to market, who inquired to me how I could bring my mind to give up so many of the comforts of life. I answered that I was very sure I liked it passably well; I was not joking. And so I went home to my bed, and left him to pick his way through the darkness and the mud to Brighton,—or Bright-town,—which place he would reach some time in the morning.

Any prospect of awakening or coming to life to a dead man makes in-   6
different all times and places. The place where that may occur is always the same, and indescribably pleasant to all our senses. For the most part we allow only outlying and transient circumstances to make our occasions. They are, in fact, the cause of our distraction. Nearest to all things is that power which fashions their being. *Next* to us the grandest laws are continually being executed. *Next* to us is not the workman whom we have hired, with whom we love so well to talk, but the workman whose work we are.

"How vast and profound is the influence of the subtile powers of   7
Heaven and of Earth!"

"We seek to perceive them, and we do not see them; we seek to hear   8
them, and we do not hear them; identified with the substance of things, they cannot be separated from them."

"They cause that in all the universe men purify and sanctify their hearts,   9
and clothe themselves in their holiday garments to offer sacrifices and oblations to their ancestors. It is an ocean of subtile intelligences. They are

everywhere, above us, on our left, on our right; they environ us on all sides."

We are the subjects of an experiment which is not a little interesting to me. Can we not do without the society of our gossips a little while under these circumstances,—have our own thoughts to cheer us? Confucius says truly, "Virtue does not remain as an abandoned orphan; it must of necessity have neighbors." 10

With thinking we may be beside ourselves in a sane sense. By a conscious effort of the mind we can stand aloof from actions and their consequences; and all things, good and bad, go by us like a torrent. We are not wholly involved in Nature. I may be either the drift-wood in the stream, or Indra in the sky looking down on it. I *may* be affected by a theatrical exhibition; on the other hand, I *may not* be affected by an actual event which appears to concern me much more. I only know myself as a human entity; the scene, so to speak, of thoughts and affections; and am sensible of a certain doubleness by which I can stand as remote from myself as from another. However intense my experience, I am conscious of the presence and criticism of a part of me, which, as it were, is not a part of me, but spectator, sharing no experience, but taking note of it; and that is no more I than it is you. When the play, it may be the tragedy, of life is over, the spectator goes his way. It was a kind of fiction, a work of the imagination only, so far as he was concerned. This doubleness may easily make us poor neighbors and friends sometimes. 11

I find it wholesome to be alone the greater part of the time. To be in company, even with the best, is soon wearisome and dissipating. I love to be alone. I never found the companion that was so companionable as solitude. We are for the most part more lonely when we go abroad among men than when we stay in our chambers. A man thinking or working is always alone, let him be where he will. Solitude is not measured by the miles of space that intervene between a man and his fellows. The really diligent student in one of the crowded hives of Cambridge College is as solitary as a dervis in the desert. The farmer can work alone in the field or the woods all day, hoeing or chopping, and not feel lonesome, because he is employed; but when he comes home at night he cannot sit down in a room alone, at the mercy of his thoughts, but must be where he can "see the folks," and recreate, and as he thinks remunerate, himself for his day's solitude; and hence he wonders how the student can sit alone in the house all night and most of the day without ennui and "the blues"; but he does not realize that the student, though in the house, is still at work in *his* field, and chopping in *his* woods, as the farmer in his, and in turn seeks the same recreation and society that the latter does, though it may be a more condensed form of it. 12

Society is commonly too cheap. We meet at very short intervals, not 13

In vain the speeding or shyness,
In vain the plutonic rocks send their old heat against my approach,
In vain the mastodon retreats beneath its own powdered bones,   675
In vain objects stand leagues off and assume manifold shapes,
In vain the ocean settling in hollows and the great monsters lying
      low,
In vain the buzzard houses herself with the sky,
In vain the snake slides through the creepers and logs,   680
In vain the elk takes to the inner passes of the woods,
In vain the razorbilled auk sails far north to Labrador,
I follow quickly . . . . I ascend to the nest in the fissure of the cliff.

[33]

Swift wind! Space! My Soul! Now I know it is true what I guessed at;
What I guessed when I loafed on the grass,   710
What I guessed while I lay alone in my bed . . . . and again as I
      walked the beach under the paling stars of the morning.

My ties and ballasts leave me . . . . I travel . . . . I sail . . . . my elbows
      rest in the sea-gaps,
I skirt the sierras . . . . my palms cover continents,
I am afoot with my vision.

By the city's quadrangular houses . . . . in log-huts, or camping with
      lumbermen,   715
Along the ruts of the turnpike . . . . along the dry gulch and rivulet
      bed,
Hoeing my onion-patch, and rows of carrots and parsnips . . . .
      crossing savannas . . . . trailing in forests,
Prospecting . . . . gold-digging . . . . girdling the trees of a new
      purchase,
Scorched ankle-deep by the hot sand . . . . hauling my boat down
      the shallow river;
Where the panther walks to and fro on a limb overhead . . . . where
      the buck turns furiously at the hunter,   720
Where the rattlesnake suns his flabby length on a rock . . . . where
      the otter is feeding on fish,
Where the alligator in his tough pimples sleeps by the bayou,
Where the black bear is searching for roots or honey . . . . where the
      beaver pats the mud with his paddle-tail;
Over the growing sugar . . . . over the cottonplant . . . . over the rice in
      its low moist field;
Over the sharp-peaked farmhouse with its scalloped scum and
      slender shoots from the gutters;   725

Over the western persimmon . . . . over the longleaved corn and the
    delicate blue-flowered flax;
Over the white and brown buckwheat, a hummer and a buzzer
    there with the rest,
Over the dusky green of the rye as it ripples and shades in the
    breeze;
Scaling mountains . . . . pulling myself cautiously up . . . . holding on
    by low scragged limbs,
Walking the path worn in the grass and beat through the leaves of
    the brush; 730
Where the quail is whistling betwixt the woods and the wheatlot,
Where the bat flies in the July eve . . . . where the great goldbug
    drops through the dark;
Where the flails keep time on the barn floor,
Where the brook puts out of the roots of the old tree and flows to
    the meadow,
Where cattle stand and shake away flies with the tremulous
    shuddering of their hides, 735
Where the cheese-cloth hangs in the kitchen, and andirons
    straddle the hearth-slab, and cobwebs fall in festoons from the
    rafters;
Where triphammers crash . . . . where the press is whirling its
    cylinders;
Wherever the human heart beats with terrible throes out of its ribs;
Where the pear-shaped balloon is floating aloft . . . . floating in it
    myself and looking composedly down;
Where the life-car is drawn on the slipnoose . . . . where the heat
    hatches pale-green eggs in the dented sand, 740
Where the she-whale swims with her calves and never forsakes
    them,
Where the steamship trails hindways its long pennant of smoke,
Where the ground-shark's fin cuts like a black chip out of the water,
Where the half-burned brig is riding on unknown currents,
Where shells grow to her slimy deck, and the dead are corrupting
    below; 745
Where the striped and starred flag is borne at the head of the
    regiments;
Approaching Manhattan, up by the long-stretching island,
Under Niagara, the cataract falling like a veil over my countenance;
Upon a door-step . . . . upon the horse-block of hard wood outside,
Upon the race-course, or enjoying pic-nics or jigs or a good game of
    base-ball, 750
At he-festivals with blackguard jibes and ironical license and
    bull-dances and drinking and laughter,

At the cider-mill, tasting the sweet of the brown sqush . . . . sucking
the juice through a straw,
At apple-peelings, wanting kisses for all the red fruit I find,
At musters and beach-parties and friendly bees and huskings and
house-raisings;
Where the mockingbird sounds his delicious gurgles, and cackles
and screams and weeps,   755
Where the hay-rick stands in the barnyard, and the dry-stalks are
scattered, and the brood cow waits in the hovel,
Where the bull advances to do his masculine work, and the stud to
the mare, and the cock is treading the hen,
Where the heifers browse, and the geese nip their food with short
jerks;
Where the sundown shadows lengthen over the limitless and
lonesome prairie,
Where the herds of buffalo make a crawling spread of the square
miles far and near;   760
Where the hummingbird shimmers . . . . where the neck of the
longlived swan is curving and winding;
Where the laughing-gull scoots by the slappy shore and laughs her
near-human laugh;
Where beehives range on a gray bench in the garden half-hid by
the high weeds;
Where the band-necked partridges roost in a ring on the ground
with their heads out;
Where burial coaches enter the arched gates of a cemetery;   765
Where winter wolves bark amid wastes of snow and icicled trees;
Where the yellow-crowned heron comes to the edge of the marsh
at night and feeds upon small crabs;
Where the splash of swimmers and divers cools the warm noon;
Where the katydid works her chromatic reed on the walnut-tree
over the well;
Through patches of citrons and cucumbers with silver-wired leaves,   770
Through the salt-lick or orange glade . . . . or under conical firs;
Through the gymnasium . . . . through the curtained saloon . . .
through the office or public hall;
Pleased with the native and pleased with the foreign . . . . pleased
with the new and old,
Pleased with women, the homely as well as the handsome,
Pleased with the quakeress as she puts off her bonnet and talks
melodiously,   775
Pleased with the primitive tunes of the choir of the whitewashed
church,

Pleased with the earnest words of the sweating Methodist preacher,
  or any preacher . . . . looking seriously at the camp-meeting;
Looking in at the shop-windows in Broadway the whole
  forenoon . . . . pressing the flesh of my nose to the thick
  plate-glass,
Wandering the same afternoon with my face turned up to the
  clouds;
My right and left arms round the sides of two friends and I in the
  middle;   780
Coming home with the bearded and dark-cheeked bush-boy . . . .
  riding behind him at the drape of the day;
Far from the settlements studying the print of animals' feet, or the
  moccasin print;
By the cot in the hospital reaching lemonade to a feverish patient,
By the coffined corpse when all is still, examining with a candle;
Voyaging to every port to dicker and adventure;   785
Hurrying with the modern crowd, as eager and fickle as any,
Hot toward one I hate, ready in my madness to knife him;
Solitary at midnight in my back yard, my thoughts gone from me a
  long while,
Walking the old hills of Judea with the beautiful gentle god by my
  side;
Speeding through space . . . . speeding through heaven and the stars, 790
Speeding amid the seven satellites and the broad ring and the
  diameter of eighty thousand miles,
Speeding with tailed meteors . . . . throwing fire-balls like the rest,
Carrying the crescent child that carries its own full mother in its
  belly:
Storming enjoying planning loving cautioning,
Backing and filling, appearing and disappearing,   795
I tread day and night such roads.

I visit the orchards of God and look at the spheric product,
And look at quintillions ripened, and look at quintillions green.

I fly the flight of the fluid and swallowing soul,
My course runs below the soundings of plummets.   800

I help myself to material and immaterial,
No guard can shut me off, no law can prevent me.

I anchor my ship for a little while only,
My messengers continually cruise away or bring their returns to me.

I go hunting polar furs and the seal . . . . leaping chasms with a pike-
    pointed staff . . . . clinging to topples of brittle and blue.   805

I ascend to the foretruck . . . . I take my place late at night in the
    crow's nest . . . . we sail through the arctic sea . . . . it is plenty light
    enough,
Through the clear atmosphere I stretch around on the wonderful
    beauty,
The enormous masses of ice pass me and I pass them . . . . the
    scenery is plain in all directions,
The white-topped mountains point up in the distance . . . . I fling
    out my fancies toward them;
We are about approaching some great battlefield in which we are
    soon to be engaged,   810
We pass the colossal outposts of the encampment . . . . we pass with
    still feet and caution;
Or we are entering by the suburbs some vast and ruined city . . . .
    the blocks and fallen architecture more than all the living cities
    of the globe.

I am a free companion . . . . I bivouac by invading watchfires.

QUESTIONS FOR DISCUSSION AND WRITING

1. In terms of its structure, this selection consists of brief statements of beliefs or actions followed by long lists of parallel clauses that modify the brief statements. Why do you think Whitman uses this structure? What does he gain from it, and what is its effect on the reader? In thinking about these questions, you might look at the different things Whitman describes in the parallel clauses. Which ones are part of nature and which are part of the civilized world? Which ones seem inviting and which seem disturbing?

2. In this selection the poet seems to merge with nature; he is "stucco'd with quadrupeds and birds" (line 671) and says, "I help myself to material and immaterial, / No guard can shut me off, no law can prevent me" (lines 801 and 802). How do all the things that are part of him work to make him something different? What is the relationship of the "shop windows in Broadway" to the moccasin print "far from the settlements"? And what is the role of God in all this? In working on these questions, you might want to consider the ending of the selection, which passes from the arctic sea to a great battlefield to a vast and ruined city.

EMILY DICKINSON

Emily Dickinson (1830–86) spent almost her entire life in the New England village of Amherst, Massachusetts, never marrying, and living in the house of her father, a lawyer and member of Congress. Although legend pictures her as a recluse, Dickinson in fact had strong intellectual attachments to several men and kept up some social interactions throughout her life. And during her life she must have thought and observed and felt keenly, for she left more than a thousand short lyric poems marked by intense, compressed feeling. These she kept from almost everybody; she showed a few to her closest friends and published only seven during her lifetime.

In her poems Dickinson writes of death and God or of small events in nature or the home, often using striking metaphors or insightful images. In "There's a certain Slant of light" (c. 1861), Dickinson describes the quality of light on winter afternoons; in "The Brain is wider than the Sky" (c. 1862), she makes some rather astounding claims for the brain. Both poems show her intense meditations on nature; for Dickinson, nature is intimately tied to what we know and feel as human beings.

There's a certain Slant of light

There's a certain Slant of light,
Winter Afternoons—
That oppresses, like the Heft
Of Cathedral Tunes—

Heavenly Hurt, it gives us—   5
We can find no scar,
But internal difference,
Where the Meanings, are—

None may teach it—Any—
'Tis the Seal Despair—   10
An imperial affliction
Sent us of the Air—

When it comes, the Landscape listens—
Shadows—hold their breath—
When it goes, 'tis like the Distance   15
On the look of Death—

The Brain is wider than the Sky

The Brain—is wider than the Sky—
For—put them side by side—
The one the other will contain
With ease—and You—beside—

The Brain is deeper than the sea—   5
For—hold them—Blue to Blue—
The one the other will absorb—
As Sponges—Buckets—do—

The Brain is just the weight of God—
For—Heft them—Pound for Pound—   10
And they will differ—if they do—
As Syllable from Sound—

QUESTIONS FOR DISCUSSION AND WRITING

1. In "There's a certain Slant of light" Dickinson associates winter light with heavenly hurt, despair, and death. Although it is not unusual to think of winter as a time for dark thoughts, Dickinson enriches her poem with particular images from nature and human culture that resonate with emotion. For example, the slant of light calls to mind sunlight slanting in a window late in the afternoon, weakly illuminating the world before sunset. What other images does Dickinson use, and how do they affect you?

2. What is Dickinson saying about the relationship between human beings and nature in "The Brain is wider than the Sky"? In your response, pay close attention to the particular wording Dickinson uses. For example, when she says, "The one the other will contain" (line 3), what does she gain by the ambiguous use of the words "one" and "other"? "One" might refer to the brain or the sky, and so might the word "other." Why does she use the phrase "if they do" (line 11)? And how does a syllable differ from a sound?

Isabella L. Bird

Isabella Bird (1832–1904) was born in Yorkshire, England, the daughter of a cu-rate. She started her extensive traveling career in 1854 with a trip to America, and her book about that trip made her name as a travel writer. Eventually she visited most of the inhabited world, including Canada, Australia, Hawaii, Japan, Southeast Asia, India, the Middle East, Tibet, central Asia, and China. In addition to her travel writing, Bird wrote on the need for social reform, studied nursing, and built a hospital in the Middle East and another in India.

Bird wrote A Lady's Life in the Rocky Mountains *during her travels through the American West in the fall of 1873; she wrote originally in the form of letters to her sister. In the section reprinted here, Bird recounts her trip to Breckenridge Pass and the crest of the Continental Divide. As she describes her journey, Bird emerges as a woman of great courage, strength, and good humor. Before starting this section of the journey, she has to endure the conversation of four men who live in the area and who make it clear that they believe the journey will be very difficult, if not im-possible, especially for a woman. In spite of this, she sets out, as she puts it, "ready to enjoy the fatigues of another day."*

From *A Lady's Life in the Rocky Mountains*

LETTER XI

Tarryall Creek—The Red Range—Excelsior—Importunate pedlars—Snow and heat—A bison calf—Deep drifts—South Park—The Great Divide—Comanche Bill—Difficulties—Hall's Gulch—A Lord Dundreary—Ridiculous fears.

Hall's Gulch, Colorado, November 6.

It was another cloudless morning, one of the many here on which one awakes early, refreshed, and ready to enjoy the fatigues of another day. In our sunless, misty climate you do not know the influence which persistent fine weather exercises on the spirits. I have been ten months in almost perpetual sunshine, and now a single cloudy day makes me feel quite de-pressed. I did not leave till 9:30, because of the slipperiness, and shortly after starting turned off into the wilderness on a very dim trail. Soon seeing a man riding a mile ahead, I rode on and overtook him, and we rode eight miles together, which was convenient to me, as without him I should several times have lost the trail altogether. Then his fine American horse, on which he had only ridden two days, broke down, while my "mad, bad *bronco,*" on which I had been traveling for a fortnight, cantered lightly over the snow. He was the only traveler I saw in a day of nearly twelve hours. I thoroughly enjoyed every minute of that ride. I concentrated all my faculties of admiration and of locality, for truly the track was a difficult one. I sometimes thought it deserved the bad name given to it at Link's. For the most part it keeps in sight of Tarryall Creek, one of the large affluents of the Platte, and is walled in on both sides by mountains, which are sometimes so close together as to leave only the narrowest canyon between them, at others breaking wide apart, till, after winding and climbing up and down for twenty-five miles, it lands one on a barren rock-girdled park, watered by a rapid fordable stream as broad as the Ouse at Huntingdon, snow fed and ice fringed, the park bordered by fantastic rocky hills, snow covered and brightened only by a dwarf growth of the beautiful silver spruce. I have not seen anything hitherto so thoroughly wild and unlike the rest of these parts.

I rode up one great ascent where hills were tumbled about confusedly; and suddenly across the broad ravine, rising above the sunny grass and the deep green pines, rose in glowing and shaded red against the glittering blue heaven a magnificent and unearthly range of mountains, as shapely as could be seen, rising into colossal points, cleft by deep blue ravines, broken up into sharks' teeth, with gigantic knobs and pinnacles rising from their inaccessible sides, very fair to look upon—a glowing, heavenly, unforgettable sight, and only four miles off. Mountains they looked not of this earth, but such as one sees in dreams alone, the blessed ranges of "the land which is very far off." They were more brilliant than those incredible colors in which painters array the fiery hills of Moab and the Desert, and one could not believe them for ever uninhabited, for on them rose, as in the East, the similitude of stately fortresses, not the gray castellated towers of feudal Europe, but gay, massive, Saracenic architecture, the outgrowth of the solid rock. They were vast ranges, apparently of enormous height, their color indescribable, deepest and reddest near the pine-draped bases, then gradually softening into wonderful tenderness, till the highest summits rose all flushed, and with an illusion of transparency, so that one might believe that they were taking on the hue of sunset. Below them lay broken ravines of fantastic rocks, cleft and canyoned by the river, with a tender unearthly light over all, the apparent warmth of a glowing clime, while I on the north side was in the shadow among the pure unsullied snow.

With us the damp, the chill, the gloom;
With them the sunset's rosy bloom.

The dimness of earth with me, the light of heaven with them. Here, again, worship seemed the only attitude for a human spirit, and the question was ever present, "Lord, what is man, that Thou art mindful of him; or the son of man, that Thou visitest him?" I rode up and down hills laboriously in snow-drifts, getting off often to ease my faithful Birdie by walking down ice-clad slopes, stopping constantly to feast my eyes upon that changeless glory, always seeing some new ravine, with its depths of color or miraculous brilliancy of red, or phantasy of form. Then below, where the trail was locked into a deep canyon where there was scarcely room for it and the river, there was a beauty of another kind in solemn gloom. There the stream curved and twisted marvellously, widening into shallows, narrowing into deep boiling eddies, with pyramidal firs and the beautiful silver spruce fringing its banks, and often falling across it in artistic grace, the gloom chill and deep, with only now and then a light trickling through the pines upon the cold snow, when suddenly turning round I saw behind, as if in the glory of an eternal sunset, those flaming and fantastic peaks. The effect of the combination of winter and summer was singular. The trail ran on the north side the whole time, and the snow lay deep and pure white, while not a wreath of it lay on the south side, where abundant lawns basked in the warm sun.

The pitch pine, with its monotonous and somewhat rigid form, had disappeared; the white pine became scarce, both being displayed by the slim spires and silvery green of the miniature silver spruce. Valley and canyon were passed, the flaming ranges were left behind, the upper altitudes became grim and mysterious. I crossed a lake on the ice, and then came on a park surrounded by barren contorted hills, overtopped by snow mountains. There, in some brushwood, we crossed a deepish stream on the ice, which gave way, and the fearful cold of the water stiffened my limbs for the rest of the ride. All these streams become bigger as you draw nearer to their source, and shortly the trail disappeared in a broad rapid river, which we forded twice. The trail was very difficult to recover. It ascended ever in frost and snow, amidst scanty timber dwarfed by cold and twisted by storms, amidst solitudes such as one reads of in the High Alps; there were no sounds to be heard but the crackle of ice and snow, the pitiful howling of wolves, and the hoot of owls. The sun to me had long set; the peaks which had blushed were pale and sad; the twilight deepened into green; but still "Excelsior!" There were no happy homes with light of household fires; above, the spectral mountains lifted their cold summits. As darkness came on I began to fear that I had confused the cabin to which I had been directed with the rocks. To confess the truth, I was cold, for my boots and stockings had frozen on my feet, and I was hungry too, having eaten nothing but raisins for fourteen hours. After riding thirty miles I saw a light a little way from the track, and found it to be the cabin of the daughter of the pleasant people with whom I had spent the previous night. Her husband had gone to the Plains, yet she, with two infant children, was living there in perfect security. Two pedlars, who were peddling their way down from the mines, came in for a night's shelter soon after I arrived—ill-looking fellows enough. They admired Birdie in a suspicious fashion, and offered to "swop" their pack horse for her. I went out the last thing at night and the first thing in the morning to see that "the powny" was safe, for they were very importunate on the subject of the "swop." I had before been offered 150 dollars for her. I was obliged to sleep with the mother and children, and the pedlars occupied a room within ours. It was hot and airless. The cabin was papered with the *Phrenological Journal*, and in the morning I opened my eyes on the very best portrait of Dr. Candlish I ever saw, and grieved truly that I should never see that massive brow and fantastic face again.

Mrs. Link was an educated and very intelligent young woman. The pedlars were Irish Yankees, and the way in which they "traded" was as amusing as "Sam Slick." They not only wanted to "swop" my pony, but to "trade" my watch. They trade their souls, I know. They displayed their wares for an hour with much dexterous flattery and persuasiveness, but Mrs. Link was untemptable, and I was only tempted into buying a handkerchief to keep the sun off. There was another dispute about my route. It was the most critical day of my journey. If a snowstorm came on, I might be detained in the mountains for many weeks; but if I got through the snow and reached the Denver wagon road, no detention would signify much. The pedlars insisted that I could not get through, for the road was not broken. Mrs. L. thought I could, and advised me to try, so I saddled Birdie and rode away.

More than half of the day was far from enjoyable. The morning was magnificent, but the light too dazzling, the sun too fierce. As soon as I got out I felt as if I should drop off the horse. My large handkerchief kept the sun from my neck, but the fierce heat caused soul and sense, brain and eye, to reel. I never saw or felt the like of it. I was at a height of 12,000 feet, where, of course, the air was highly rarefied, and the snow was so pure and dazzling that I was obliged to keep my eyes shut as much as possible to avoid snow blindness. The sky was a different and terribly fierce color; and when I caught a glimpse of the sun, he was white and unwinking like a lime-ball light, yet threw off wicked scintillations. I suffered so from nausea, exhaustion, and pains from head to foot, that I felt as if I must lie down in the snow. It may have been partly the early stage of *soroche*, or mountain sickness. We plodded on for four hours, snow all round, and nothing else to be seen but an ocean of glistening peaks against that sky of infuriated blue. How I found my way I shall never know, for the only marks on the snow were occasional footprints of a man, and I had no means of knowing whether they led in the direction I ought to take. Earlier, before the snow became so deep, I passed the last great haunt of the magnificent mountain bison, but, unfortunately, saw nothing but horns and bones. Two months ago Mr. Link succeeded in separating a calf from the herd, and has partially domesticated it. It is a very ugly thing at seven months old, with a thick beard, and a short, thick, dark mane on its heavy shoulders. It makes a loud grunt like a pig. It can outrun their fastest horse, and it sometimes leaps over the high fence of the corral, and takes all the milk of five cows.

The snow grew seriously deep. Birdie fell thirty times, I am sure. She 7 seemed unable to keep up at all, so I was obliged to get off and stumble along in her foot-marks. By that time my spirit for overcoming difficulties had somewhat returned, for I saw a lie of country which I knew must contain South Park, and we had got under cover of a hill which kept off the sun. The trail had ceased; it was only one of those hunter's tracks which continually mislead one. The getting through the snow was awful work. I think we accomplished a mile in something over two hours. The snow was two feet eight inches deep, and once we went down in a drift the surface of which was rippled like sea sand, Birdie up to her back, and I up to my shoulders!

At last we got through, and I beheld, with some sadness, the goal of my 8 journey, "The Great Divide," the Snowy Range, and between me and it South Park, a rolling prairie seventy-five miles long and over 10,000 feet high, treeless, bounded by mountains, and so rich in sun-cured hay that one might fancy that all the herds of Colorado could find pasture there. Its chief center is the rough mining town of Fairplay, but there are rumors of great mineral wealth in various quarters. The region has been "rushed," and mining camps have risen at Alma and elsewhere, so lawless and brutal that vigilance committees are forming as a matter of necessity. South Park is closed, or nearly so, by snow during an ordinary winter; and just now the great freight wagons are carrying up the last supplies of the season, and taking down women and other temporary inhabitants. A great many people come up here in the summer. The rarefied air produces great oppression on the lungs, accompanied with bleeding. It is said that you can tell a new arrival by seeing him go about holding a blood-stained handkerchief to his mouth. But I came down upon it from regions of ice and snow; and as the snow which had fallen on it had all disappeared by evaporation and drifting, it looked to me quite lowland and livable, though lonely and indescribably mournful, "a silent sea," suggestive of "the muffled oar." I cantered across the narrow end of it, delighted to have got through the snow; and when I struck the "Denver stage road" I supposed that all the difficulties of mountain travel were at an end, but this has not turned out to be exactly the case.

A horseman shortly joined me and rode with me, got me a fresh horse, and accompanied me for ten miles. He was a picturesque figure and rode a very good horse. He wore a big slouch hat, from under which a number of fair curls hung nearly to his waist. His beard was fair, his eyes blue, and his complexion ruddy. There was nothing sinister in his expression, and his manner was respectful and frank. He was dressed in a hunter's buckskin suit ornamented with beads, and wore a pair of exceptionally big brass spurs. His saddle was very highly ornamented. What was unusual was the number of weapons he carried. Besides a rifle laid across his saddle and a pair of pistols in the holsters, he carried two revolvers and a knife in his belt, and a carbine slung behind him. I found him what is termed "good company." He told me a great deal about the country and its wild animals, with some hunting adventures, and a great deal about Indians and their cruelty and treachery. All this time, having crossed South Park, we were ascending the Continental Divide by what I think is termed the Breckenridge Pass, on a fairly good wagon road. We stopped at a cabin, where the woman seemed to know my companion, and, in addition to bread and milk, produced some venison steaks. We rode on again, and reached the crest of the Divide, and saw snow-born streams starting within a quarter of a mile from each other, one for the Colorado and the Pacific, the other for the Platte and the Atlantic. Here I wished the hunter good-bye, and reluctantly turned north-east. It was not wise to go up the Divide at all, and it was necessary to do it in haste. On my way down I spoke to the woman at whose cabin I had dined, and she said, "I am sure you found Comanche Bill a real gentleman"; and I then knew that, if she gave me correct information, my intelligent, courteous companion was one of the most notorious desperadoes of the Rocky Mountains, and the greatest Indian exterminator on the frontier—a man whose father and family fell in a massacre at Spirit Lake by the hands of Indians, who carried away his sister, then a child of eleven. His life has since been mainly devoted to a search for this child, and to killing Indians wherever he can find them.

After riding twenty miles, which made the distance for that day fifty, I remounted Birdie to ride six miles farther, to a house which had been mentioned to me as a stopping place. The road ascended to a height of 11,000 feet, and from thence I looked my last at the lonely, uplifted prairie sea. "Denver stage road!" The worst, rudest, dismallest, darkest road I have yet traveled on, nothing but a winding ravine, the Platte canyon, pine crowded and pine darkened, walled in on both sides for six miles by pine-skirted mountains 12,000 feet high! Along this abyss for fifty miles there are said to be only five houses, and were it not for miners going down, and freight wagons going up, the solitude would be awful. As it was, I did not see a creature. It was four when I left South Park, and between those mountain walls and under the pines it soon became quite dark, a darkness which could be felt. The snow which had melted in the sun had refrozen, and was one sheet of smooth ice. Birdie slipped so alarmingly that I got off and walked, but then neither of us could keep our feet, and in the darkness she seemed so likely to fall upon me, that I took out of my pack the man's socks which had been given me at Perry's Park, and drew them on over her fore-feet—an expedient which for a time succeeded admirably, and which I commend to all travelers similarly circumstanced. It was unutterably dark, and all these operations had to be performed by the sense of touch only. I remounted, allowed her to take her own way, as I could not see even her ears, and though her hind legs slipped badly, we contrived to get along through the narrowest part of the canyon, with a tumbling river close to the road. The pines were very dense, and sighed and creaked mournfully in the severe frost, and there were other eerie noises not easy to explain. At last, when the socks were nearly worn out, I saw the blaze of a camp-fire, with two hunters sitting by it, on the hill side, and at the mouth of a gulch something which looked like buildings. We got across the river partly on ice and partly by fording, and I found that this was the place where, in spite of its somewhat dubious reputation, I had been told that I could put up.

A man came out in the sapient and good-natured stage of intoxication, 11 and, the door being opened, I was confronted by a rough bar and a smoking, blazing kerosene lamp without a chimney. This is the worst place I have put up at as to food, lodging, and general character; an old and very dirty log cabin, not chinked, with one dingy room used for cooking and feeding, in which a miner was lying very ill of fever; then a large roofless shed with a canvas side, which is to be an addition, and then the bar. They accounted for the disorder by the building operations. They asked me if I were the English lady written of in the *Denver News,* and for once I was glad that my fame had preceded me, as it seemed to secure me against being quietly "put out of the way." A horrible meal was served—dirty, greasy, disgusting. A celebrated hunter, Bob Craik, came in to supper with a young man in tow, whom, in spite of his rough hunter's or miner's dress, I at once recognized as an English gentleman. It was their camp-fire which I had seen on the hill side. This gentleman was lording it in true caricature fashion, with a Lord Dundreary drawl and a general execration of everything; while I sat in the chimney corner, speculating on the reason why many of the upper class of my countrymen—"High Toners," as they are called out here—make themselves so ludicrously absurd. They neither know how to hold their tongues or to carry their personal pretensions. An

American is nationally assumptive, an Englishman personally so. He took no notice of me till something passed which showed him I was English, when his manner at once changed into courtesy, and his drawl was shortened by a half. He took pains to let me know that he was an officer in the Guards, of good family, on four months' leave, which he was spending in slaying buffalo and elk, and also that he had a profound contempt for everything American. I cannot think why Englishmen put on these broad, mouthing tones, and give so many personal details. They retired to their camp, and the landlord having passed into the sodden, sleepy stage of drunkenness, his wife asked if I should be afraid to sleep in the large canvas-sided, unceiled, doorless shed, as they could not move the sick miner. So, I slept there on a shake-down, with the stars winking overhead through the roof, and the mercury showing 30° of frost.

I never told you that I once gave an unwary promise that I would not travel alone in Colorado unarmed, and that in consequence I left Estes Park with a Sharp's revolver loaded with ball cartridge in my pocket, which has been the plague of my life. Its bright ominous barrel peeped out in quiet Denver shops, children pulled it out to play with, or when my riding dress hung up with it in the pocket, pulled the whole from the peg to the floor; and I cannot conceive of any circumstances in which I could feel it right to make any use of it, or in which it could do me any possible good. Last night, however, I took it out, cleaned and oiled it, and laid it under my pillow, resolving to keep awake all night. I slept as soon as I lay down, and never woke till the bright morning sun shone through the roof, making me ridicule my own fears and abjure pistols for ever! 12

QUESTIONS FOR DISCUSSION AND WRITING

1. Bird sees some spectacular scenery and meets some interesting people during her journey. Sometimes the country she travels through exhilarates her, and sometimes it is frightening; sometimes the people she meets are friendly and helpful, and sometimes they are menacing. What similarities can you find among the people and places she enjoys or among those she does not? In answering this question, think about the relationship between the people she meets and nature.

2. Later in her book, as she is leaving the Rocky Mountains, Bird writes, "Never again shall I hear that strange talk of Nature and her doings which is the speech of those who live with her and her alone. Already the dismalness of a level land comes over me." Given what you have read in the section here, what do you think she means by "the dismalness of a level land"?

3. In a note to the third edition of her book, printed in 1880, Bird writes that already the American West is rapidly changing, frame houses are replacing log cabins, and "footprints of elk and bighorn may be searched for in vain on the dewy slopes of Estes Park." Why do you think she feels the need to claim that the things she saw a mere seven years earlier can no longer be seen? Have you ever made the same sort of claim? If so, why?

SARAH ORNE JEWETT

Sarah Orne Jewett (1849–1909) was born and died in the small town of South Berwick in southern Maine. Although she lived there for at least part of every year, she also spent long periods of time living in Boston and traveling in Europe with her close friend Annie Fields. Her family was well off, and she moved easily in the literary circles of New England and Europe, but she always had a strong attachment to small-town life and nature. Jewett's masterpiece, The Country of the Pointed Firs *(1896), is a series of vignettes and character sketches of people living close to nature in her native Maine, people whose emotional lives are shaped by the natural landscape around them.*

"A White Heron" (1886) is part of a collection of stories published near the middle of Jewett's career. Unlike many of Jewett's stories, it is set not in a small town but rather on an isolated farm. The value of a life close to nature is strong here. The main character, a young girl born in a "crowded manufacturing town" but now living on the rural farm, is tempted by a young man she meets to betray the white heron. Her reaction to this temptation is complex and important, telling us much about the connections between humans and nature.

A White Heron

I

The woods were already filled with shadows one June evening, just before eight o'clock, though a bright sunset still glimmered faintly among the trunks of the trees. A little girl was driving home her cow, a plodding, dilatory, provoking creature in her behavior, but a valued companion for all that. They were going away from the western light, and striking deep into the dark woods, but their feet were familiar with the path, and it was no matter whether their eyes could see it or not.

There was hardly a night the summer through when the old cow could be found waiting at the pasture bars; on the contrary, it was her greatest pleasure to hide herself away among the high huckleberry bushes, and though she wore a loud bell she had made the discovery that if one stood perfectly still it would not ring. So Sylvia had to hunt for her until she

found her and call Co'! Co'! with never an answering Moo, until her childish patience was quite spent. If the creature had not given good milk and
plenty of it, the case would have seemed very different to her owners.
Besides, Sylvia had all the time there was, and very little use to make of it.
Sometimes in pleasant weather it was a consolation to look upon the
cow's pranks as an intelligent attempt to play hide and seek, and as the
child had no playmates she lent herself to this amusement with a good
deal of zest. Though this chase had been so long that the wary animal herself had given an unusual signal of her whereabouts, Sylvia had only
laughed when she came upon Mistress Moolly at the swamp-side, and
urged her affectionately homeward with a twig of birch leaves. The old
cow was not inclined to wander farther, she even turned in the right direction for once as they left the pasture, and stepped along the road at a
good pace. She was quite ready to be milked now, and seldom stopped to
browse. Sylvia wondered what her grandmother would say because they
were so late. It was a great while since she had left home at half past five
o'clock, but everybody knew the difficulty of making this errand a short
one. Mrs. Tilley had chased the horned torment too many summer
evenings herself to blame any one else for lingering, and was only thank-
ful as she waited that she had Sylvia, nowadays, to give such valuable assistance. The good woman suspected that Sylvia loitered occasionally on
her own account; there never was such a child for straying about out-of-
doors since the world was made! Everybody said that it was a good
change for a little maid who had tried to grow for eight years in a crowded
manufacturing town, but, as for Sylvia herself, it seemed as if she never
had been alive at all before she came to live at the farm. She thought often
with wistful compassion of a wretched dry geranium that belonged to a
town neighbor.

"'Afraid of folks,'" old Mrs. Tilley said to herself, with a smile, after she   3
had made the unlikely choice of Sylvia from her daughter's houseful of
children, and was returning to the farm. "'Afraid of folks,' they said! I
guess she won't be troubled no great with 'em up to the old place!" When
they reached the door of the lonely house and stopped to unlock it, and
the cat came to purr loudly, and rub against them, a deserted pussy, indeed, but fat with young robins, Sylvia whispered that this was a beautiful
place to live in, and she never should wish to go home.

The companions followed the shady wood-road, the cow taking slow   4
steps, and the child very fast ones. The cow stopped long at the brook to
drink, as if the pasture were not half a swamp, and Sylvia stood still and
waited, letting her bare feet cool themselves in the shoal water, while the
great twilight moths struck softly against her. She waded on through the
brook as the cow moved away, and listened to the thrushes with a heart

that beat fast with pleasure. There was a stirring in the great boughs over-head. They were full of little birds and beasts that seemed to be wide-awake, and going about their world, or else saying good-night to each other in sleepy twitters. Sylvia herself felt sleepy as she walked along. However, it was not much farther to the house, and the air was soft and sweet. She was not often in the woods so late as this, and it made her feel as if she were a part of the gray shadows and the moving leaves. She was just thinking how long it seemed since she first came to the farm a year ago, and wondering if everything went on in the noisy town just the same as when she was there; the thought of the great red-faced boy who used to chase and frighten her made her hurry along the path to escape from the shadow of the trees.

Suddenly this little woods-girl is horror-stricken to hear a clear whistle   5
not very far away. Not a bird's whistle, which would have a sort of friend-liness, but a boy's whistle, determined, and somewhat aggressive. Sylvia left the cow to whatever sad fate might await her, and stepped discreetly aside into the bushes, but she was just too late. The enemy had discovered her, and called out in a very cheerful and persuasive tone, "Halloa, little girl, how far is it to the road?" and trembling Sylvia answered almost in-audibly, "A good ways."

She did not dare to look boldly at the tall young man, who carried a gun   6
over his shoulder, but she came out of her bush and again followed the cow, while he walked alongside.

"I have been hunting for some birds," the stranger said kindly, "and I   7
have lost my way, and need a friend very much. Don't be afraid," he added gallantly. "Speak up and tell me what your name is, and whether you think I can spend the night at your house, and go out gunning early in the morning."

Sylvia was more alarmed than before. Would not her grandmother con-   8
sider her much to blame? But who could have foreseen such an accident as this? It did not appear to be her fault, and she hung her head as if the stem of it were broken, but managed to answer, "Sylvy," with much effort when her companion again asked her name.

Mrs. Tilley was standing in the doorway when the trio came into view.   9
The cow gave a loud moo by way of explanation.

"Yes, you'd better speak up for yourself, you old trial! Where'd she   10
tucked herself away this time, Sylvy?" Sylvia kept an awed silence; she knew by instinct that her grandmother did not comprehend the gravity of the situation. She must be mistaking the stranger for one of the farmer-lads of the region.

The young man stood his gun beside the door, and dropped a heavy   11
game-bag beside it; then he bade Mrs. Tilley good-evening, and repeated his wayfarer's story, and asked if he could have a night's lodging.

"Put me anywhere you like," he said. "I must be off early in the morn-   12
ing, before day; but I am very hungry, indeed. You can give me some milk
at any rate, that's plain."

"Dear sakes, yes," responded the hostess, whose long slumbering hos-   13
pitality seemed to be easily awakened. "You might fare better if you went
out on the main road a mile or so, but you're welcome to what we've got.
I'll milk right off, and you make yourself at home. You can sleep on husks
or feathers," she proffered graciously. "I raised them all myself. There's
good pasturing for geese just below here towards the ma'sh. Now step
round and set a plate for the gentleman, Sylvy!" And Sylvia promptly
stepped. She was glad to have something to do, and she was hungry herself.

It was a surprise to find so clean and comfortable a little dwelling in this   14
New England wilderness. The young man had known the horrors of its
most primitive housekeeping, and the dreary squalor of that level of society which does not rebel at the companionship of hens. This was the best
thrift of an old-fashioned farmstead, though on such a small scale that it
seemed like a hermitage. He listened eagerly to the old woman's quaint
talk, he watched Sylvia's pale face and shining gray eyes with ever growing enthusiasm, and insisted that this was the best supper he had eaten for
a month; then, afterward, the new-made friends sat down in the doorway
together while the moon came up.

Soon it would be berry-time, and Sylvia was a great help at picking. The   15
cow was a good milker, though a plaguy thing to keep track of, the hostess gossiped frankly, adding presently that she had buried four children,
so that Sylvia's mother, and a son (who might be dead) in California were
all the children she had left. "Dan, my boy, was a great hand to go gunning," she explained sadly. "I never wanted for pa'tridges or gray squer'ls
while he was to home. He's been a great wand'rer, I expect, and he's no
hand to write letters. There, I don't blame him, I'd ha' seen the world myself if it had been so I could.

"Sylvia takes after him," the grandmother continued affectionately,   16
after a minute's pause. "There ain't a foot o' ground she don't know her
way over, and the wild creatur's counts her one o' themselves. Squer'ls
she'll tame to come an' feed right out o' her hands, and all sorts o' birds.
Last winter she got the jay-birds to bangeing here, and I believe she'd 'a'
scanted herself of her own meals to have plenty to throw out amongst 'em,
if I hadn't kep' watch. Anything but crows, I tell her, I'm willin' to help
support,—though Dan he went an' tamed one o' them that did seem to
have reason same as folks. It was round here a good spell after he went
away. Dan an' his father they didn't hitch,—but he never held up his head
ag'in after Dan had dared him an' gone off."

The guest did not notice this hint of family sorrows in his eager interest   17 in something else.

"So Sylvy knows all about birds, does she?" he exclaimed, as he looked   18
round at the little girl who sat, very demure but increasingly sleepy, in the
moonlight. "I am making a collection of birds myself. I have been at it ever
since I was a boy." (Mrs. Tilley smiled.) "There are two or three very rare
ones I have been hunting for these five years. I mean to get them on my
own ground if they can be found."

"Do you cage 'em up?" asked Mrs. Tilley doubtfully, in response to this   19
enthusiastic announcement.

"Oh, no, they're stuffed and preserved, dozens and dozens of them,"   20
said the ornithologist, "and I have shot or snared every one myself. I
caught a glimpse of a white heron three miles from here on Saturday, and
I have followed it in this direction. They have never been found in this district at all. The little white heron, it is," and he turned again to look at
Sylvia with the hope of discovering that the rare bird was one of her acquaintances.

But Sylvia was watching a hop-toad in the narrow footpath.   21

"You would know the heron if you saw it," the stranger continued   22
eagerly. "A queer tall white bird with soft feathers and long thin legs. And
it would have a nest perhaps in the top of a high tree, made of sticks,
something like a hawk's nest."

Sylvia's heart gave a wild beat; she knew that strange white bird, and   23
had once stolen softly near where it stood in some bright green swamp
grass, away over at the other side of the woods. There was an open place
where the sunshine always seemed strangely yellow and hot, where tall,
nodding rushes grew, and her grandmother had warned her that she
might sink in the soft black mud underneath and never be heard of more.
Not far beyond were the salt marshes and beyond those was the sea, the
sea which Sylvia wondered and dreamed about, but never had looked
upon, though its great voice could often be heard above the noise of the
woods on stormy nights.

"I can't think of anything I should like so much as to find that heron's   24
nest," the handsome stranger was saying. "I would give ten dollars to anybody who could show it to me," he added desperately, "and I mean to
spend my whole vacation hunting for it if need be. Perhaps it was only migrating, or had been chased out of its own region by some bird of prey."

Mrs. Tilley gave amazed attention to all this, but Sylvia still watched the   25
toad, not divining, as she might have done at some calmer time, that the
creature wished to get to its hole under the doorstep, and was much hin-
dered by the unusual spectators at that hour of the evening. No amount of
thought, that night, could decide how many wished-for treasures the ten
dollars, so lightly spoken of, would buy.

The next day the young sportsman hovered about the woods, and   26
Sylvia kept him company, having lost her first fear of the friendly lad, who
proved to be most kind and sympathetic. He told her many things about
the birds and what they knew and where they lived and what they did
with themselves. And he gave her a jack-knife, which she thought as great
a treasure as if she were a desert-islander. All day long he did not once
make her troubled or afraid except when he brought down some unsus-
pecting singing creature from its bough. Sylvia would have liked him
vastly better without his gun; she could not understand why he killed the
very birds he seemed to like so much. But as the day waned, Sylvia still
watched the young man with loving admiration. She had never seen anybody so charming and delightful; the woman's heart, asleep in the child,
was vaguely thrilled by a dream of love. Some premonition of that great
power stirred and swayed these young foresters who traversed the solemn
woodlands with soft-footed silent care. They stopped to listen to a bird's
song; they pressed forward again eagerly, parting the branches—speaking
to each other rarely and in whispers; the young man going first and Sylvia
following, fascinated, a few steps behind, with her gray eyes dark with
excitement.

She grieved because the longed-for white heron was elusive, but she   27
did not lead the guest, she only followed, and there was no such thing as
speaking first. The sound of her own unquestioned voice would have terrified her—it was hard enough to answer yes or no when there was need
of that. At last evening began to fall, and they drove the cow home together, and Sylvia smiled with pleasure when they came to the place
where she heard the whistle and was afraid only the night before.

II

Half a mile from home, at the farther edge of the woods, where the land   28
was highest, a great pine-tree stood, the last of its generation. Whether it
was left for a boundary mark, or for what reason, no one could say; the
woodchoppers who had felled its mates were dead and gone long ago,
and a whole forest of sturdy trees, pines and oaks and maples, had grown
again. But the stately head of this old pine towered above them all and
made a landmark for sea and shore miles and miles away. Sylvia knew it
well. She had always believed that whoever climbed to the top of it could
see the ocean; and the little girl had often laid her hand on the great rough
trunk and looked up wistfully at those dark boughs that the wind always
stirred, no matter how hot and still the air might be below. Now she

thought of the tree with a new excitement, for why, if one climbed it at break of day, could not one see all the world, and easily discover whence the white heron flew, and mark the place, and find the hidden nest?

What a spirit of adventure, what wild ambition! What fancied triumph   29
and delight and glory for the later morning when she could make known the secret! It was almost too real and too great for the childish heart to bear.

All night the door of the little house stood open, and the whippoorwills   30
came and sang upon the very step. The young sportsman and his old hostess were sound asleep, but Sylvia's great design kept her broad awake and watching. She forgot to think of sleep. The short summer night seemed as long as the winter darkness, and at last when the whippoorwills ceased, and she was afraid the morning would after all come too soon, she stole out of the house and followed the pasture path through the woods, hastening toward the open ground beyond, listening with a sense of comfort and companionship to the drowsy twitter of a half-awakened bird, whose perch she had jarred in passing. Alas, if the great wave of human interest which flooded for the first time this dull little life should sweep away the satisfactions of an existence heart to heart with nature and the dumb life of the forest!

There was the huge tree asleep yet in the paling moonlight, and small   31
and hopeful Sylvia began with utmost bravery to mount to the top of it, with tingling, eager blood coursing the channels of her whole frame, with her bare feet and fingers, that pinched and held like bird's claws to the monstrous ladder reaching up, up, almost to the sky itself. First she must mount the white oak tree that grew alongside, where she was almost lost among the dark branches and the green leaves heavy and wet with dew; a bird fluttered off its nest, and a red squirrel ran to and fro and scolded pettishly at the harmless housebreaker. Sylvia felt her way easily. She had often climbed there, and knew that higher still one of the oak's upper branches chafed against the pine trunk, just where its lower boughs were set close together. There, when she made the dangerous pass from one tree to the other, the great enterprise would really begin.

She crept out along the swaying oak limb at last, and took the daring   32
step across into the old pine-tree. The way was harder than she thought; she must reach far and hold fast, the sharp dry twigs caught and held her and scratched her like angry talons, the pitch made her thin little fingers clumsy and stiff as she went round and round the tree's great stem, higher and higher upward. The sparrows and robins in the woods below were beginning to wake and twitter to the dawn, yet it seemed much lighter there aloft in the pine-tree, and the child knew that she must hurry if her project were to be of any use.

The tree seemed to lengthen itself out as she went up, and to reach   33 farther and farther upward. It was like a great main-mast to the voyaging earth; it must truly have been amazed that morning through all its ponderous frame as it felt this determined spark of human spirit creeping and climbing from higher branch to branch. Who knows how steadily the least twigs held themselves to advantage this light, weak creature on her way! The old pine must have loved his new dependent. More than all the hawks, and bats, and moths, and even the sweet-voiced thrushes, was the brave, beating heart of the solitary gray-eyed child. And the tree stood still and held away the winds that June morning while the dawn grew bright in the east.

Sylvia's face was like a pale star, if one had seen it from the ground,   34 when the last thorny bough was past, and she stood trembling and tired but wholly triumphant, high in the tree-top. Yes, there was the sea with the dawning sun making a golden dazzle over it, and toward that glorious east flew two hawks with slow-moving pinions. How low they looked in the air from that height when before one had only seen them far up, and dark against the blue sky. Their gray feathers were as soft as moths; they seemed only a little way from the tree, and Sylvia felt as if she too could go flying away among the clouds. Westward, the woodlands and farms reached miles and miles into the distance; here and there were church steeples, and white villages; truly it was a vast and awesome world.

The birds sang louder and louder. At last the sun came up bewil-   35 deringly bright. Sylvia could see the white sails of ships out at sea, and the clouds that were purple and rose-colored and yellow at first began to fade away. Where was the white heron's nest in the sea of green branches, and was this wonderful sight and pageant of the world the only reward for having climbed to such a giddy height? Now look down again, Sylvia, where the green marsh is set among the shining birches and dark hemlocks; there where you saw the white heron once you will see him again; look, look! a white spot of him like a single floating feather comes up from the dead hemlock and grows larger, and rises, and comes close at last, and goes by the landmark pine with steady sweep of wing and outstretched slender neck and crested head. And wait! wait! do not move a foot or a finger, little girl, do not send an arrow of light and consciousness from your two eager eyes, for the heron has perched on a pine bough not far beyond yours, and cries back to his mate on the nest, and plumes his feathers for the new day!

The child gives a long sigh a minute later when a company of shouting   36 cat-birds comes also to the tree, and vexed by their fluttering and lawlessness the solemn heron goes away. She knows his secret now, the wild, light, slender bird that floats and wavers, and goes back like an arrow presently to his home in the green world beneath. Then Sylvia, well satisfied, makes her perilous way down again, not daring to look far below the branch she stands on, ready to cry sometimes because her fingers ache and her lamed feet slip. Wondering over and over again what the stranger would say to her, and what he would think when she told him how to find his way straight to the heron's nest.

"Sylvy, Sylvy!" called the busy old grandmother again and again, but nobody answered, and the small husk bed was empty, and Sylvia had disappeared. 37

The guest waked from a dream, and remembering his day's pleasure hurried to dress himself that it might sooner begin. He was sure from the way the shy little girl looked once or twice yesterday that she had at least seen the white heron, and now she must really be persuaded to tell. Here she comes now, paler than ever, and her worn old frock is torn and tattered, and smeared with pine pitch. The grandmother and the sportsman stand in the door together and question her, and the splendid moment had come to speak of the dead hemlock-tree by the green marsh. 38

But Sylvia does not speak after all, though the old grandmother fretfully rebukes her, and the young man's kind appealing eyes are looking straight in her own. He can make them rich with money; he has promised it, and they are poor now. He is so well worth making happy, and he waits to hear the story she can tell. 39

No, she must keep silence! What is it that suddenly forbids her and makes her dumb? Has she been nine years growing, and now, when the great world for the first time puts out a hand to her, must she thrust it aside for a bird's sake? The murmur of the pine's green branches is in her ears, she remembers how the white heron came flying through the golden air and how they watched the sea and the morning together, and Sylvia cannot speak; she cannot tell the heron's secret and give its life away. 40

Dear loyalty, that suffered a sharp pang as the guest went away disappointed later in the day, that could have served and followed him and loved him as a dog loves! Many a night Sylvia heard the echo of his whistle haunting the pasture path as she came home with the loitering cow. She forgot even her sorrow at the sharp report of his gun and the piteous sight of thrushes and sparrows dropping silent to the ground, their songs hushed and their pretty feathers stained and wet with blood. Were the birds better friends than their hunter might have been,—who can tell? Whatever treasures were lost to her, woodlands and summer-time, remember! Bring your gifts and graces and tell your secrets to this lonely country child! 41

QUESTIONS FOR DISCUSSION AND WRITING

1. Sylvia is a child who seems very much in harmony with nature. Reread the story, looking for all the ways that Jewett ties Sylvia to animals and the natural landscape. What are the particular characteristics that Sylvia shares with nature? Are there any situations in which Sylvia and nature seem not to be in harmony, situations in which she is frightened or impeded by nature? If so, how do you account for the lack of harmony?

2. Toward the end of the story the narrator asks, "Were the birds better friends than their hunter might have been,—who can tell?" (par. 41). What do you think the answer to this question is? In responding you might consider what Sylvia gets from the birds and what she might get from the hunter.

3. Sylvia lives in a world that is almost exclusively female. Even though all the major female characters have names—including the cow, Mistress Moolly—the young man does not. He is simply a hunter or the handsome stranger. Of course, nature itself is often considered female, we speak of Mother Nature and Mother Earth. How are the implications of this female world played out in the story? What is the relationship between the thrift of Mrs. Tilley's "old-fashioned farmstead" and the horrors the young man has known in New England's "most primitive housekeeping" (par. 14)? Which type of housekeeping seems more natural?

3

CONTESTING
THE USES
OF NATURE

EARLY TO MIDDLE
TWENTIETH CENTURY

To fully understand the construction of nature in this period, we need to look back to one of the most dramatic intellectual events of the previous century, the publication of Charles Darwin's *On the Origin of Species* in 1859. When they first appeared, Darwin's claims about the origins of life created a great stir among scientists, philosophers, and theologians. By the early twentieth century, however, his theory of evolution and selection had brought about a fundamental change in the way most people understood nature. All forms of life, Darwin had demonstrated, from the lowly worm to the human being, adapt themselves to their surroundings and evolve through a process of "natural selection." This meant that nature was not just an unfathomable, capricious force but a logical, systematic *process* that could be studied, comprehended, and perhaps even controlled. Darwin's ideas also had the effect of reducing human beings from their special status in nature, since the evolutionary process applied equally to *all* animals.

A second critical event that influenced the construction of nature during this period was the expansion of industrial and urban America and the accompanying loss of open lands and wilderness. As early as 1893, Frederick Jackson Turner had declared the American frontier "closed" and speculated about what the loss of this "vast unoccupied domain that stretched … to the Pacific Ocean" might mean to our national character and to the very idea of democracy. This "closing" of the frontier was, of course, a symbolic and not a literal one, since great numbers of people continued to move west well into the 1960s. What had changed, however, was the assurance of *wildness*—the promise of unlimited amounts of unspoiled territory always waiting to the west. It was a promise that had helped to define the New World experience since the first voyage of Christopher Columbus, or William Bradford's 1620 expedition to Plymouth or Thomas Jefferson's sponsorship of Lewis and Clark.

Quite simply, the country was filling up with people, machines, highways, and cities. In the time between Jefferson's presidency and Theodore Roosevelt's, America's population had grown from four million to over sixty. The accompanying economic and physical expansion was equally dramatic. None of this had mattered much to a young nation convinced that its natural resources were inexhaustible; but by the early twentieth century many Americans feared that all the vast open spaces had already been explored, charted, and settled. What had once been a struggle simply to make sense out of a vast, unexplored landscape became a struggle to save whatever land was left.

Increasingly, adventurers like Theodore Roosevelt began expressing concerns about the loss of rugged open spaces where people could test themselves in "raw" nature. Professional conservationists like Gifford Pinchot warned about the rapid depletion of natural resources, and naturalists like John Burroughs and John Muir illustrated how the continent was being stripped of wild places and wildlife. In a land where birds had once been so plentiful that Audubon and his companions could unthinkingly shoot hundreds at a time, entire species had become scare, or had disappeared altogether: the Labrador duck in 1878, the Carolina parakeet in 1904, the passenger pigeon in 1914.

By the time Aldo Leopold took his first job with the Forest Service in 1909, the shift in consciousness was almost complete. Nature could no longer be unself-consciously assumed and consumed. It had become, instead, a subject of concern and a site of social and economic conflict. Some saw nature as a vital spiritual force connected to our humanity and our freedom; others saw nature as a valuable commodity to be preserved and regulated for the better use of humans. Naturally, all of this regulation and conservation required trained experts working for newly formed government agencies: the Bureau of Fisheries (1871), the Bureau of Biological Survey (1885), and the Forest Service (1906). Both the federal government and groups of concerned citizens began to use the political system in order to identify and set aside huge tracts of land like Yellowstone Park, America's first and largest national park.

In their very different ways, the writers in this chapter helped to shape these changing views of nature, and often they helped to reshape the American landscape itself. In the tradition of literary naturalists like Thoreau and Muir, John Burroughs recorded his quiet and careful observations of nature; Theodore Roosevelt continued the tradition of the outdoor enthusiast and hunter, although unlike earlier enthusiasts (Audubon, for example), Roosevelt could no longer just assume that his precious "rugged outdoors" would be there for future generations. With a growing sense of urgency, Roosevelt and a new breed of activists, professional environmentalists, and wildlife managers took on the political and economic task of protecting nature from its most dangerous and persistent threat: human progress. Although they had quite different views of nature, Gifford Pinchot, Aldo Leopold, and Rachel Carson, were all college-educated scientists who at some point in their careers worked for government agencies charged with managing the land and regulating natural resources. In time, and in their very different ways, all three became influential advocates for the environment.

In "Wilderness Reserves: Yellowstone Park," we meet one of the most complicated and controversial figures in American political and environmental history, Theodore Roosevelt. As president, Roosevelt helped preserve thousands of acres of land in the West, most notably Yellowstone Park. On the other hand, Roosevelt's interests in nature focused on its usefulness to humans. Typically, "Yellowstone Park" opens not with a celebration of natural beauty but with a melancholy discussion of the disappearance of big game. Later in the essay, Roosevelt recounts his 1903 tour of the park with John Burroughs, though here again Roosevelt's eyes stay fixed on the game.

John Burroughs's "The Spell of Yosemite," is an account of his 1909 excursion west, with the naturalist John Muir as his guide. Muir was a rugged mountain climber and environmental activist, while Burroughs had spent most of his life quietly hiking and bird-watching in the Catskill Mountains. Burroughs is dazzled by the majesty and rugged beauty of the landscape but, typically, begins his account by quietly observing a single robin "singing from a tree top in the old familiar way."

Gifford Pinchot was yet another complex and controversial figure in the American experience with nature. With his formal education in science and forest management, Pinchot represents the shift to professional rather than amateur advocates in the modern environmental movement. As chief of the U.S. Forest Service and Roosevelt's closest adviser on land use, Pinchot put into effect the "wise use" philosophy he outlines in *The Fight for Conservation*. Aldo Leopold was also trained in the natural sciences and worked for a federal agency, the same U.S. Forest Service founded by Pinchot. Leopold eventually resigned his position and became chair of a newly formed Department of Wildlife Management at the University of Wisconsin. Throughout his career, Leopold used the short essay to criticize the utilitarian views of Pinchot and other conservationists, and to stake out his positions on issues of land use and forest management. In time, though, Leopold began to develop a more fully realized philosophy of nature, represented here by his two most important essays, "The Land Ethic" and "The River of the Mother of God."

This chapter closes with a writer most responsible for making environmental concerns part of America's conscience and its political agenda. Rachel Carson was yet another trained scientist, an aquatic biologist, who worked both in academia and for a government agency, the Bureau of Fisheries. Her first several books used her scientific research on oceans and fisheries to help Americans understand nature as a complex ecological system. Her most famous book, *Silent Spring*, shocked the American public into realizing how newly developed pesticides were poisoning the earth.

THEODORE ROOSEVELT

Perhaps more than any other figure in this book, Theodore Roosevelt (1858–1919) stands as a symbol of America at the beginning of the twentieth century: good-hearted and confident (perhaps even overbearing at times); physically impressive; tireless in his enthusiasms. Roosevelt was a prominent political figure who served as president of the United States (from 1901 to 1909) and as governor of New York, but he was also a world adventurer, a soldier, an avid big-game hunter, and an amateur naturalist in the tradition of Thomas Jefferson and John Audubon. Throughout his adult life, Roosevelt pursued adventure from the Amazon to Africa; much of his time, however, was spent riding and hunting in the open spaces of the American West. Roosevelt chronicled his outdoor adventures in a series of popular books, including Ranch Life and the Hunting-Trail *(1888),* African Game Trails *(1910), and* Through the Brazilian Wilderness *(1914). In* The Strenuous Life *(1900), Roosevelt outlined his common-sense philosophy (almost a religion, really) of "manly virtues" and what one critic has called "muscular Christianity." For this, and for his influence on the modern preservation movement, Roosevelt has always been a source of both admiration and controversy. On the one hand, while other naturalists courted public opinion through their writing, the presidency allowed Roosevelt to protect huge tracts of undeveloped lands, like Yellowstone Park. On the other hand, Roosevelt's attitudes toward nature were seen by his critics as largely utilitarian and paternalistic. In "Wilderness Reserves: Yellowstone Park" (1905), he writes of nature primarily as a worthy foe against which to test oneself, or as an increasingly scarce resource whose primary value is its usefulness to humans.*

Wilderness Reserves: Yellowstone Park

The most striking and melancholy feature in connection with American big game is the rapidity with which it has vanished. When, just before the outbreak of the Revolutionary War, the rifle-bearing hunters of the backwoods first penetrated the great forests west of the Alleghanies, deer, elk, black bear, and even buffalo, swarmed in what are now the States of Kentucky and Tennessee and the country north of the Ohio was a great and almost virgin hunting-ground. From that day to this the shrinkage has gone on, only partially checked here and there, and never arrested as a whole. As a matter of historical accuracy, however, it is well to bear in mind that many writers, in lamenting this extinction of the game, have from time to time anticipated or overstated the facts. Thus as good an author as Colonel Richard Irving Dodge spoke of the buffalo as practically

1

extinct, while the great Northern herd still existed in countless thousands. As early as 1880 sporting authorities spoke not only of the buffalo but of the elk, deer, and antelope as no longer to be found in plenty; and recently one of the greatest of living hunters has stated that it is no longer possible to find any American wapiti bearing heads comparable with the red deer of Hungary. As a matter of fact, in the early eighties there were still large regions where every species of game that had ever been known within historic times on our continent was still to be found as plentifully as ever. In the early nineties there were still big tracts of wilderness in which this was true of all game except the buffalo; for instance, it was true of the elk in portions of northwestern Wyoming, of the blacktail in northwestern Colorado, of the whitetail here and there in the Indian Territory, and of the antelope in parts of New Mexico. Even at the present day there are smaller, but still considerable, regions where these four animals are yet found in abundance; and I have seen antlers of wapiti shot since 1900 far surpassing any of which there is record from Hungary. In New England and New York, as well as New Brunswick and Nova Scotia, the whitetail deer is more plentiful than it was thirty years ago, and in Maine (and to an even greater extent in New Brunswick) the moose, and here and there the caribou, have, on the whole, increased during the same period. There is yet ample opportunity for the big-game hunter in the United States, Canada, and Alaska.

While it is necessary to give this word of warning to those who, in praising time past, always forget the opportunities of the present, it is a thousandfold more necessary to remember that these opportunities are, nevertheless, vanishing; and if we are a sensible people, we will make it our business to see that the process of extinction is arrested. At the present moment the great herds of caribou are being butchered, as in the past the great herds of bison and wapiti have been butchered. Every believer in manliness and therefore in manly sport, and every lover of nature, every man who appreciates the majesty and beauty of the wilderness and of wild life, should strike hands with the farsighted men who wish to preserve our material resources, in the effort to keep our forests and our game beasts, game-birds, and game-fish,—indeed, all the living creatures of prairie and woodland and seashore—from wanton destruction. 2

Above all, we should realize that the effort toward this end is essentially a democratic movement. It is entirely in our power as a nation to preserve large tracts of wilderness, which are valueless for agricultural purposes and unfit for settlement, as playgrounds for rich and poor alike, and to preserve the game so that it shall continue to exist for the benefit of all lovers of nature, and to give reasonable opportunities for the exercise of the skill of the hunter, whether he is or is not a man of means. But this end can only be achieved by wise laws and by a resolute enforcement of the 3 laws. Lack of such legislation and administration will result in harm to all of us, but most of all in harm to the nature-lover who does not possess vast wealth. Already there have sprung up here and there through the country, as in New Hampshire and the Adirondacks, large private preserves. These preserves often serve a useful purpose, and should be encouraged within reasonable limits; but it would be a misfortune if they increased beyond a certain extent or if they took the place of great tracts of wild land, which continue as such either because of their very nature, or because of the protection of the State exerted in the form of making them State or national parks or reserves. It is foolish to regard proper game-laws as un-democratic, unrepublican. On the contrary, they are essentially in the interests of the people as a whole, because it is only through their enact-ment and enforcement that the people as a whole can preserve the game and can prevent its becoming purely the property of the rich, who are able to create and maintain extensive private preserves. The wealthy man can get hunting anyhow, but the man of small means is dependent solely upon wise and well-executed game-laws for his enjoyment of the sturdy pleasure of the chase. In Maine, in Vermont, in the Adirondacks, even in parts of Massachusetts and on Long Island, people have waked up to this fact, particularly so far as the common whitetail deer is concerned, and in Maine also as regards the moose and caribou. The effect is shown in the increase in these animals. Such game protection results, in the first place, in securing to the people who live in the neighborhood permanent op-portunities for hunting; and in the next place, it provides no small source of wealth to the locality because of the visitors which it attracts. A deer wild in the woods is worth to the people of the neighborhood many times the value of its carcass, because of the way it attracts sportsmen, who give employment and leave money behind them.

True sportsmen, worthy of the name, men who shoot only in season and in moderation, do no harm whatever to game. The most objectionable of all game-destroyers is, of course, the kind of game-butcher who simply kills for the sake of the record of slaughter, who leaves deer and ducks and prairie-chickens to rot after he has slain them. Such a man is wholly obnoxious; and, indeed, so is any man who shoots for the purpose of es-tablishing a record of the amount of game killed. To my mind this is one very unfortunate feature of what is otherwise the admirably sportsmanlike English spirit in these matters. The custom of shooting great bags of deer, grouse, partridges, and pheasants, the keen rivalry in making such bags, and their publication in sporting journals, are symptoms of a spirit which is most unhealthy from every standpoint. It is to be earnestly hoped that every American hunting or fishing club will strive to inculcate among its own members, and in the minds of the general public, that anything like an excessive bag, any destruction for the sake of making a record, is to be severely reprobated.

But, after all, this kind of perverted sportsman, unworthy though he be, is not the chief actor in the destruction of our game. The professional skin or market hunter is the real offender. Yet he is of all others the man who would ultimately be most benefited by the preservation of the game. The frontier settler, in a thoroughly wild country, is certain to kill game for his own use. As long as he does no more than this, it is hard to blame him; although if he is awake to his own interests he will soon realize that to him, too, the live deer is worth far more than the dead deer, because of the way in which it brings money into the wilderness. The professional market-hunter who kills game for the hide or for the feathers or for the meat or to sell antlers and other trophies; the marketmen who put game in cold storage; and the rich people, who are content to buy what they have not the skill to get by their own exertions—these are the men who are the real enemies of game. Where there is no law which checks the market-hunters, the inevitable result of their butchery is that the game is completely destroyed, and with it their own means of livelihood. If, on the other hand, they were willing to preserve it, they could make much more money by acting as guides. In northwestern Colorado, at the present moment, there are still blacktail deer in abundance, and some elk are left. Colorado has fairly good game-laws, but they are indifferently enforced. The country in which the game is found can probably never support any but a very sparse population, and a large portion of the summer range is practically useless for settlement. If the people of Colorado generally, and above all the people of the counties in which the game is located, would resolutely co-operate with those of their own number who are already alive to the importance of preserving the game, it could, without difficulty, be kept always as abundant as it now is, and this beautiful region would be a permanent health resort and playground for the people of a large part of the Union. Such action would be a benefit to every one, but it would be a benefit most of all to the people of the immediate locality.

The practical common sense of the American people has been in no way made more evident during the last few years than by the creation and use of a series of large land reserves—situated for the most part on great plains and among the mountains of the West—intended to keep the forests from destruction, and therefore to conserve the water-supply. These reserves are, and should be, created primarily for economic purposes. The semiarid regions can only support a reasonable population under conditions of the strictest economy and wisdom in the use of the water-supply, and in addition to their other economic uses the forests are indispensably necessary for the preservation of the water-supply and for rendering possible its useful distribution throughout the proper seasons. In addition, however, to this economic use of the wilderness, selected portions of it have been kept here and there in a state of nature, not merely for the sake of preserving the forests and the water but for the sake of preserving all its beauties and wonders unspoiled by greedy and short-sighted vandalism. What has been actually accomplished in the Yellowstone Park affords the best possible object-lesson as to the desirability and practicability of establishing such wilderness reserves. This reserve is a natural breeding-ground and nursery for those stately and beautiful haunters of the wilds which have now vanished from so many of the great forests, the vast lonely plains, and the high mountain ranges, where they once abounded.

On April 8, 1903, John Burroughs and I reached the Yellowstone Park, and were met by Major John Pitcher of the regular army, the superintendent of the Park. The major and I forthwith took horses; he telling me that he could show me a good deal of game while riding up to his house at the Mammoth Hot Springs. Hardly had we left the little town of Gardiner and gotten within the limits of the Park before we saw prongbuck. There was a band of at least a hundred feeding some distance from the road. We rode leisurely toward them. They were tame compared to their kindred in unprotected places; that is, it was easy to ride within fair rifle-range of them; and though they were not familiar in the sense that we afterward found the bighorn and the deer to be familiar, it was extraordinary to find them showing such familiarity almost literally in the streets of a frontier town. It spoke volumes for the good sense and law-abiding spirit of the people of the town. During the two hours following my entry into the Park we rode around the plains and lower slopes of the foot-hills in the neighborhood of the mouth of the Gardiner and we saw several hundred—probably a thousand all told—of these antelopes. Major Pitcher informed me that all the pronghorns in the Park wintered in this neighborhood. Toward the end of April or the first of May they migrate back to their summering homes in the open valleys along the Yellowstone and in the plains south of the Golden Gate. While migrating they go over the mountains through forests if occasion demands. Although there are plenty of coyotes in the Park, there are no big wolves, and save for very infrequent poachers, the only enemy of the antelope, as indeed the only enemy of all the game, is the cougar.

Cougars, known in the Park, as elsewhere through the West, as "mountain-lions," are plentiful, having increased in numbers of recent years. Except in the neighborhood of the Gardiner River—that is within a few miles of Mammoth Hot Springs—I found them feeding on elk, which in the Park far outnumber all other game put together, being so numerous that the ravages of the cougars are of no real damage to the herds. But in the neighborhood of the Mammoth Hot Springs the cougars are noxious because of the antelope, mountain-sheep, and deer which they kill; and the superintendent has imported some hounds with which to hunt them. These hounds are managed by Buffalo Jones, a famous old plainsman, who is now in the Park taking care of the buffalo. On this first day of my visit to the Park I came across the carcass of a deer and of an antelope which the cougars had killed. On the great plains cougars rarely get antelope, but here the country is broken so that the big cats can make their stalks under favorable circumstances. To deer and mountain-sheep the cougar is a most dangerous enemy—much more so than the wolf.

The antelope we saw were usually in bands of from twenty to one hundred and fifty, and they traveled strung out almost in single file, though those in the rear would sometimes bunch up. I did not try to stalk them, but got as near them as I could on horseback. The closest approach I was able to make was to within about eighty yards of two which were by themselves—I think, a doe and a last year's fawn. As I was riding up to them, although they looked suspiciously at me, one actually lay down. When I was passing them at about eighty yards' distance the big one became nervous, gave a sudden jump, and away the two went at full speed. 9

Why the prongbucks were so comparatively shy I do not know, for right on the ground with them we came upon deer, and, in the immediate neighborhood, mountain-sheep, which were absurdly tame. The mountain-sheep were nineteen in number—for the most part does and yearlings with a couple of three-year-old rams—but not a single big fellow, for the big fellows at this season are off by themselves, singly or in little bunches, high up in the mountains. The band I saw was tame to a degree matched by but few domestic animals. 10

They were feeding on the brink of a steep washout at the upper edge of one of the benches on the mountainside just below where the abrupt slope began. They were alongside a little gully with sheer walls. I rode my horse to within forty yards of them, one of them occasionally looking up and at once continuing to feed. Then they moved slowly off, and leisurely crossed the gully to the other side. I dismounted, walked around the head of the gully, and moving cautiously, but in plain sight, came closer and closer until I was within twenty yards, when I sat down on a stone and spent certainly twenty minutes looking at them. They paid hardly any attention to my presence—certainly no more than well-treated domestic creatures would pay. 11

• • •

On the last day of my stay it was arranged that I should ride down from Mammoth Hot Springs to the town of Gardiner, just outside the Park limits, and there make an address at the laying of the corner-stone of the arch 12 by which the main road is to enter the Park. Some three thousand people had gathered to attend the ceremonies. A little over a mile from Gardiner we came down out of the hills to the flat plain; from the hills we could see the crowd gathered around the arch, waiting for me to come. We put spurs to our horses and cantered rapidly toward the appointed place, and on the way we passed within forty yards of a score of blacktails, which merely moved to one side and looked at us, and within almost as short a distance of half a dozen antelope. To any lover of nature it could not help being a delightful thing to see the wild and timid creatures of the wilderness rendered so tame; and their tameness in the immediate neighborhood of Gardiner, on the very edge of the Park, spoke volumes for the patriotic good sense of the citizens of Montana. At times the antelope actually cross the Park line to Gardiner, which is just outside, and feed unmolested in the very streets of the town; a fact which shows how very far advanced the citizens of Gardiner are in right feeling on this subject; for of course the Federal laws cease to protect the antelope as soon as they are out of the Park. Major Pitcher informed me that both the Montana and Wyoming people were co-operating with him in zealous fashion to preserve the game and put a stop to poaching. For their attitude in this regard they deserve the cordial thanks of all Americans interested in these great popular playgrounds, where bits of the old wilderness scenery and old wilderness life are to be kept unspoiled for the benefit of our children's children. Eastern people and especially Eastern sportsmen, need to keep steadily in mind the fact that the Westerners who live in the neighborhood of the forest preserves are the men who in the last resort will determine whether or not these preserves are to be permanent. They cannot in the long run be kept as forest and game reservations unless the settlers round about believe in them and heartily support them; and the rights of these settlers must be carefully safeguarded, and they must be shown that the movement is really in their interest. The Eastern sportsman who fails to recognize these facts can do little but harm by advocacy of forest reserves.

It was in the interior of the Park, at the hotels beside the lake, the falls, 13 and the various geyser basins, that we would have seen the bears had the season been late enough; but unfortunately the bears were still for the most part hibernating. We saw two or three tracks, but the animals themselves had not yet begun to come about the hotels. Nor were the hotels open. No visitors had previously entered the Park in the winter or early spring, the scouts and other employees being the only ones who occasionally traverse it. I was sorry not to see the bears, for the effect of protection upon bear life in the Yellowstone has been one of the phenomena of natural history. Not only have they grown to realize that they are safe, but, being natural scavengers and foul feeders, they have come to recognize the garbage heaps of the hotels as their special sources of food-supply. Throughout the summer months they come to all the hotels in numbers, usually appearing in the late afternoon or evening, and they have become as indifferent to the presence of men as the deer themselves—some of them very much more indifferent. They have now taken their place among the recognized sights of the Park, and the tourists are nearly as much interested in them as in the geysers. In mussing over the garbage heaps they sometimes get tin cans stuck on their paws, and the result is painful. Buffalo Jones and some of the other scouts in extreme cases rope the bear, tie him up, cut the tin can off his paw, and let him go again. It is not an easy feat, but the astonishing thing is that it should be performed at all.

It was amusing to read the proclamations addressed to the tourists by the Park management, in which they were solemnly warned that the bears were really wild animals, and that they must on no account be either fed or teased. It is curious to think that the descendants of the great grizzlies which were the dread of the early explorers and hunters should now be semidomesticated creatures, boldly hanging around crowded hotels for the sake of what they can pick up, and quite harmless so long as any reasonable precaution is exercised. They are much safer, for instance, than any ordinary bull or stallion, or even ram, and, in fact, there is no danger from them at all unless they are encouraged to grow too familiar or are in some way molested. Of course among the thousands of tourists there is a percentage of fools; and when fools go out in the afternoon to look at the bears feeding they occasionally bring themselves into jeopardy by some senseless act. The black bears and the cubs of the bigger bears can readily be driven up trees, and some of the tourists occasionally do this. Most of the animals never think of resenting it; but now and then one is run across which has its feelings ruffled by the performance. In the summer of 1902 the result proved disastrous to a too inquisitive tourist. He was traveling with his wife, and at one of the hotels they went out toward the garbage pile to see the bears feeding. The only bear in sight was a large she, which, as it turned out, was in a bad temper because another party of tourists a few minutes before had been chasing her cubs up a tree. The man left his wife and walked toward the bear to see how close he could get. When he was some distance off she charged him, whereupon he bolted back toward his wife. The bear overtook him, knocked him down, and bit him severely. But the man's wife, without hesitation, attacked the bear with that thoroughly feminine weapon, an umbrella, and frightened her off. The man spent several weeks in the Park hospital before he recovered. Perhaps the following telegram sent by the manager of the Lake Hotel to Major Pitcher illustrates with sufficient clearness the mutual relations of the bears, the tourists, the guardians of the public weal in the Park. The original was sent me by Major Pitcher. It runs:

"Lake. 7–27–'03. Major Pitcher, Yellowstone: As many as seventeen   15
bears in an evening appear on my garbage dump. To-night eight or ten.
Campers and people not of my hotel throw things at them to make them
run away. I cannot, unless there personally, control this. Do you think you
could detail a trooper to be there every evening from say six o'clock until
dark and make people remain behind danger line laid out by Warden
Jones? Otherwise I fear some accident. The arrest of one or two of these
campers might help. My own guests do pretty well as they are told. James
Barton Key. 9 A. M."

Major Pitcher issued the order as requested.   16

At times the bears get so bold that they take to making inroads on the   17
kitchen. One completely terrorized a Chinese cook. It would drive him off
and then feast upon whatever was left behind. When a bear begins to act
in this way or to show surliness it is sometimes necessary to shoot it. Other
bears are tamed until they will feed out of the hand, and will come at once
if called. Not only have some of the soldiers and scouts tamed bears in this
fashion, but occasionally a chambermaid or waiter girl at one of the hotels
has thus developed a bear as a pet.

This whole episode of bear life in the Yellowstone is so extraordinary   18
that it will be well worth while for any man who has the right powers and
enough time to make a complete study of the life and history of the
Yellowstone bears. Indeed, nothing better could be done by some of our
outdoor faunal naturalists than to spend at least a year in the Yellowstone,
and to study the life habits of all the wild creatures therein. A man able to
do this, and to write down accurately and interestingly what he has seen,
would make a contribution of permanent value to our nature literature.

QUESTIONS FOR DISCUSSION AND WRITING

1.   As he argues for "wise laws" (par. 3) in the management of natural resources, Roosevelt presents his views of wilderness conservation in terms
of "patriotic good sense" (par. 12) and "democratic movement" (par. 3).
Explain and discuss his argument about the need for protecting more
wilderness and creating more game laws. Are Roosevelt's concerns about
elitism and land use still valid today? Are his solutions?

2.   Based upon what you have read here, how would you characterize
Roosevelt's attitude toward nature? What did he see as a proper and useful relationship between humans and the natural world? It may help to
look at specific passages in the reading, as when Roosevelt discusses the
cougars who attack game and farm animals in the West, or his account of
the "tame" bears in Yellowstone.

3. These days we tend to think of hunting and a love of nature as contradictory, but Roosevelt was a self-proclaimed nature lover and an avid hunter. Though he had killed everything from tapir in Brazil to buffalo in Colorado, in this essay we see that even Roosevelt is critical of some forms of hunting and some kinds of hunters. Discuss the hierarchy of hunting and hunters he creates. According to what principles does he defend some hunters and attack others? How might such a hierarchy of hunting (or fishing) look today?

GIFFORD PINCHOT

Unlike many of the writers in this book, Gifford Pinchot (1865–1946) was not an amateur naturalist or a literary traveler; instead, he was a professional public official and an academic trained in the natural sciences. After completing his education at Yale, Pinchot studied forestry in Europe. In 1898, working with Theodore Roosevelt, Pinchot founded and then served as chief of what is now called the U.S. Forest Service. Pinchot recognized that America's natural resources were threatened by economic development and overuse. He believed that the systematic study of nature could lead to practical solutions. Pinchot was fired as chief of the Forest Service in 1910 for insubordination, after suing President Taft's Department of the Interior for failing to enforce the conservation laws established by the Roosevelt administration. From 1903 until 1936, Pinchot held the position of professor of forestry at Yale's newly formed Pinchot School of Forestry. In addition to A Primer of Forestry *(1899), Pinchot published two influential and controversial books,* The Fight for Conservation *(1909) and* Breaking New Ground *(1947). Ironically, though he was fired for speaking out about the failures of government officials, Pinchot was frequently under attack by critics who charged that the Forest Service was dominated by the forest industry, and that its primary goal was not to protect the nation's forests but to supply much-needed lumber to an expanding American economy. In fact, Pinchot's "wise use" philosophy was intended to recognize the needs of all parties, including the timber industry and those who would preserve areas of wilderness. Obviously, such issues remain a source of controversy, as do judgments of Pinchot's contributions to the environmental health of America.*

From *The Fight for Conservation*

The first principle of conservation is development, the use of the natural now existing on this continent for the benefit of the people who live here now. There may be just as much waste in neglecting the development and use of certain natural resources as there is in their destruction. We have a limited supply of coal, and only a limited supply. Whether it is to last for a hundred or a hundred and fifty or a thousand years, the coal is limited in amount, unless through geological changes which we shall not live to see, there will never be any more of it than there is now. But coal is in a sense the vital essence of our civilization. If it can be preserved, if the life of the mines can be extended, if by preventing waste there can be more coal left in this country after we of this generation have made every needed use of this source of power, then we shall have deserved well of our descendants.

Conservation stands emphatically for the development and use of water-power now, without delay. It stands for the immediate construction of navigable waterways under a broad and comprehensive plan as assistants to the railroads. More coal and more iron are required to move a ton of freight by rail than by water, three to one. In every case and in every direction the conservation movement has development for its first principle, and at the very beginning of its work, The development of our natural resources and the fullest use of them for the present generation is the first duty of this generation. So much for development.

In the second place conservation stands for the prevention of waste. There has come gradually in this country an understanding that waste is not a good thing and that the attack on waste is an industrial necessity. I recall very well indeed how, in the early days of forest fires, they were considered simply and solely as acts of God, against which any opposition was hopeless and any attempt to control them not merely hopeless but childish. It was assumed that they came in the natural order of things, as inevitably as the seasons or the rising and setting of the sun. To-day we understand that forest fires are wholly within the control of men. So we are coming in like manner to understand that the prevention of waste in all other directions is a simple matter of good business. The first duty of the human race is to control the earth it lives upon.

We are in a position more and more completely to say how far the waste and destruction of natural resources are to be allowed to go on and where they are to stop. It is curious that the effort to stop waste, like the effort to stop forest fires, has often been considered as a matter controlled wholly by economic law. I think there could be no greater mistake. Forest fires were allowed to burn long after the people had means to stop them. The idea that men were helpless in the face of them held long after the time had passed when the means of control were fully within our reach. It was the old story that "as a man thinketh, so is he"; we came to see that we could stop forest fires, and we found that the means had long been at hand. When at length we came to see that the control of logging in certain directions was profitable, we found it had long been possible. In all these matters of waste of natural resources, the education of the people to understand that they can stop the leakage comes before the actual stopping and after the means of stopping it have long been ready at our hands.

In addition to the principles of development and preservation of our resources there is a third principle. It is this: The natural resources must be developed and preserved for the benefit of the many, and not merely for the profit of a few. We are coming to understand in this country that public action for public benefit has a very much wider field to cover and a much larger part to play than was the case when there were resources enough for every one, and before certain constitutional provisions had given so tremendously strong a position to vested rights and property in general. . . .

The people of the United States are on the verge of one of the great 6
quiet decisions which determine national destinies. Crises happen in
peace as well as in war, and a peaceful crisis may be as vital and controlling as any that comes with national uprising and the clash of arms. Such
a crisis, at first uneventful and almost unperceived, is upon us now, and
we are engaged in making the decision that is thus forced upon us. And,
so far as it has gone, our decision is largely wrong. Fortunately it is not yet
final.

The question we are deciding with so little consciousness of what it 7
involves is this: What shall we do with our natural resources? Upon the
final answer that we shall make to it hangs the success or failure of this
Nation in accomplishing its manifest destiny.

Few Americans will deny that it is the manifest destiny of the United 8
States to demonstrate that a democratic republic is the best form of government yet devised, and that the ideals and institutions of the great republic taken together must and do work out in a prosperous, contented,
peaceful, and righteous people; and also to exercise, through precept and
example, an influence for good among the nations of the world. That destiny seems to us brighter and more certain of realization to-day than ever
before. It is true that in population, in wealth, in knowledge, in national
efficiency generally, we have reached a place far beyond the farthest
hopes of the founders of the Republic. Are the causes which have led to
our marvellous development likely to be repeated indefinitely in the future, or is there a reasonable possibility, or even a probability, that conditions may arise which check our growth?

Danger to a nation comes either from without or from within. In the 9
first great crisis of our history, the Revolution, another people attempted
from without to halt the march of our destiny by refusing to us liberty.
With reasonable prudence and preparedness we need never fear another
such attempt. If there be danger, it is not from an external source. In the
second great crisis, the Civil War, a part of our own people strove for an
end which would have checked the progress of development. Another
such attempt has become forever impossible. If there be danger, it is not
from a division of our people.

In the third great crisis of our history, which has now come squarely 10
upon us, the special interests and the thoughtless citizens seem to have
united together to deprive the Nation of the great natural resources without which it cannot endure. This is the pressing danger now, and it is not
the least to which our National life has been exposed. A nation deprived
of liberty may win it, a nation divided may reunite, but a nation whose nat-

ural resources are destroyed must inevitably pay the penalty of poverty, degradation, and decay.

At first blush this may seem like an unpardonable misconception and over-statement, and if it is not true it certainly is unpardonable. Let us consider the facts. Some of them are well known, and the salient ones can be put very briefly. 11

The five indispensably essential materials in our civilization are wood, water, coal, iron, and agricultural products. 12

We have timber for less than thirty years at the present rate of cutting. The figures indicate that our demands upon the forest have increased twice as fast as our population. 13

We have anthracite coal for but fifty years, and bituminous coal for less than two hundred. 14

Our supplies of iron ore, mineral oil, and natural gas are being rapidly depleted, and many of the great fields are already exhausted. Mineral resources such as these when once gone are gone forever. 15

We have allowed erosion, that great enemy of agriculture, to impoverish and, over thousands of square miles, to destroy our farms. The Mississippi alone carries yearly to the sea more than 400,000,000 tons of the richest soil within its drainage basin. If this soil is worth a dollar a ton, it is probable that the total loss of fertility from soil-wash to the farmers and forest-owners of the United States is not far from a billion dollars a year. Our streams, in spite of the millions of dollars spent upon them, are less navigable now than they were fifty years ago, and the soil lost by erosion from the farms and the deforested mountain sides, is the chief reason. The great cattle and sheep ranges of the West, because of overgrazing, are capable, in an average year, of carrying but half the stock they once could support and should still. Their condition affects the price of meat in practically every city of the United States. 16

These are but a few of the more striking examples. The diversion of great areas of our public lands from the home-maker to the landlord and the speculator; the national neglect of great water powers, which might well relieve, being perennially renewed, the drain upon our non-renewable coal; the fact that but half the coal has been taken from the mines which have already been abandoned as worked out and by caving-in have made the rest forever inaccessible; the disuse of the cheaper transportation of our waterways, which involves comparatively slight demand upon our non-renewable supplies of iron ore, and the use of the rail instead—these are other items in the huge bill of particulars of national waste. 17

We have a well-marked national tendency to disregard the future, and it has led us to look upon all our natural resources as inexhaustible. Even 18 now that the actual exhaustion of some of them is forcing itself upon us in higher prices and the greater cost of living, we are still asserting, if not always in words, yet in the far stronger language of action, that nevertheless and in spite of it all, they still are inexhaustible.

It is this national attitude of exclusive attention to the present, this absence of foresight from among the springs of national action, which is directly responsible for the present condition of our natural resources. It was precisely the same attitude which brought Palestine, once rich and populous, to its present desert condition, and which destroyed the fertility and habitability of vast areas in northern Africa and elsewhere in so many of the older regions of the world. 19

The conservation of our natural resources is a question of primary importance on the economic side. It pays better to conserve our natural resources than to destroy them, and this is especially true when the national interest is considered. But the business reason, weighty and worthy though it be, is not the fundamental reason. In such matters, business is a poor master but a good servant. The law of self-preservation is higher than the law of business, and the duty of preserving the Nation is still higher than either. 20

The American Revolution had its origin in part in economic causes, and it produced economic results of tremendous reach and weight. The Civil War also arose in large part from economic conditions, and it has had the largest economic consequences. But in each case there was a higher and more compelling reason. So with the third great crisis of our history. It has an economic aspect of the largest and most permanent importance, and the motive for action along that line, once it is recognized, should be more than sufficient. But that is not all. In this case, too, there is a higher and more compelling reason. The question of the conservation of natural resources, or national resources, does not stop with being a question of profit. It is a vital question of profit, but what is still more vital, it is a question of national safety and patriotism also. 21

We have passed the inevitable stage of pioneer pillage of natural resources. The natural wealth we found upon this continent has made us rich. We have used it, as we had a right to do, but we have not stopped there. We have abused, and wasted, and exhausted it also, so that there is the gravest danger that our prosperity to-day will have been bought at the price of the suffering and poverty of our descendants. We may now fairly ask of ourselves a reasonable care for the future and a natural interest in those who are to come after us. No patriotic citizen expects this Nation to run its course and perish in a hundred or two hundred, or five hundred years; but, on the contrary, we expect it to grow in influence and power and, what is of vastly greater importance, in the happiness and prosperity of our people. But we have as little reason to expect that all this will hap- 22 pen of itself as there would have been for the men who established this Nation to expect that a United States would grow of itself without their efforts and sacrifices. It was their duty to found this Nation, and they did it. It is our duty to provide for its continuance in well-being and honor. That duty it seems as though we might neglect—not in, not in any lack of patriotic devotion, when once our patriotism is aroused, but in mere thoughtlessness and inability or unwillingness to drop the interests of the moment long enough to realize that what we do now will decide the future of the Nation. For, if we do not take action to conserve the Nation's natural resources, and that soon, our descendants will suffer the penalty of our neglect.

Let me use a homely illustration: We have all known fathers and mothers, devoted to their children, whose attention was fixed and limited by the household routine of daily life. Such parents were actively concerned with the common needs and precautions and remedies entailed in bringing up a family, but blind to every threat that was at all unusual. Fathers and mothers such as these often remain serenely unaware while some dangerous malady or injurious habit is fastening itself upon a favorite child. Once the evil is discovered, there is no sacrifice too great to repair the damage which their unwitting neglect may have allowed to become irreparable. So it is, I think, with the people of the United States. Capable of every devotion in a recognized crisis, we have yet carelessly allowed the habit of improvidence and waste of resources to find lodgment. It is our great good fortune that the harm is not yet altogether beyond repair. 23

The profoundest duty that lies upon any father is to leave his son with a reasonable equipment for the struggle of life and an untarnished name. So the noblest task that confronts us all to-day is to leave this country unspotted in honor, and unexhausted in resources, to our descendants, who will be, not less than we, the children of the Founders of the Republic. I conceive this task to partake of the highest spirit of patriotism. 24

QUESTIONS FOR DISCUSSION AND WRITING

1. Pinchot's primary purpose in this often dramatic essay was to persuade the American public that the problem of conserving natural resources was far more serious than they had imagined. Identify and discuss some of the strategies Pinchot uses to accomplish this. What analogies or metaphors does he use to characterize the situation? What "red-flag" or emotional terms does he use, especially in the opening section? Do you imagine that such strategies were effective with Pinchot's readers in 1906? Would they be effective today?

2. Pinchot is the founder of the modern conservation movement, and this essay is one of best-known statements of the "wise use" philosophy. As you reread the essay, collect the five or six statements that you feel best capture the essence of this philosophy. That done, write a brief essay in which you respond to the ideas of the "wise use" movement. Do you agree or disagree with its view of nature and how humans relate to the natural world?

3. Like Roosevelt, Pinchot was a government official as well as a naturalist, and, like Roosevelt, he used his high position to shape national land-management policy and influence the actions of business and government. Finally, Pinchot argued that the preservation of natural resources was a matter of "the highest spirit of patriotism" (par. 24) not just economic expediency. For Pinchot, in what sense is the proper management of nature a patriotic duty?

JOHN BURROUGHS

*John Burroughs (1837–1921) was one of the most popular and influential nature
writers in late nineteenth- and early twentieth-century America. His two dozen
books have sold well over a million copies, and many are still in print today. Born
in upstate New York, Burroughs spent much of his life hiking and bird-watching in
the Catskill Mountains, and living quietly on a small farm on the Hudson River.
After a brief attempt at teaching, Burroughs spent ten years working for the
Treasury Department in Washington, D.C. From an early age, though, what he
wanted most was to be a nature writer, and beginning in the 1860s he published
natural history essays in major national magazines. He also published a study of
the American poet Walt Whitman, whom Burroughs befriended while in
Washington. Wake-Robin, Burroughs first essay collection, was published in 1871.
For the next forty years, Burroughs explored and wrote about the American outdoors. As is true of most American nature writers, he was influenced greatly by
the writing and the philosophy of Emerson and Thoreau. He was also influenced
by the work of Audubon, and in Field and Study (1919) produced his own careful
study of American birds. Burroughs's style of writing is seldom didactic or overtly
philosophical but instead quietly observes the small details of nature, and in those
small details finds delight and wonder. Burroughs wrote "The Spell of Yosemite"
(1912) after a 1909 excursion in which he, with John Muir as his guide, explored
the Grand Canyon and the Yosemite Valley. As the essay suggests, Burroughs was
deeply moved by the grand size and rugged beauty of what he saw but was happy,
nonetheless, to return to his beloved Catskills.*

The Spell of Yosemite

I

Yosemite won my heart at once, as it seems to win the hearts of all who   1
visit it. In my case many things helped to do it, but I am sure a robin, the
first I had seen since leaving home, did his part. He struck the right note,
he brought the scene home to me, he supplied the link of association.
There he was, running over the grass or perching on the fence, or singing
from a tree-top in the old familiar way. Where the robin is at home, there
at home am I. But many other things helped to win my heart to the
Yosemite—the whole character of the scene, not only its beauty and sublimity, but the air of peace and protection, and of homelike seclusion that
pervades it; the charm of a nook, a retreat, combined with the power and
grandeur of nature in her sternest moods.

169

After passing from the hotel at El Portal along the foaming and roaring   2
Merced River, and amid the tumbled confusion of enormous granite boulders shaken down from the cliffs above, you cross the threshold of the
great valley as into some vast house or hall carved out of the mountains,
and at once feel the spell of the brooding calm and sheltered seclusion
that pervades it. You pass suddenly from the tumultuous, the chaotic, into
the ordered, the tranquil, the restful, which seems enhanced by the power
and grandeur that encompass them about. You can hardly be prepared for
the hush that suddenly falls upon the river and for the gentle rural and sylvan character of much that surrounds you; the peace of the fields, the
seclusion of the woods, the privacy of sunny glades, the enchantment of
falls and lucid waters, with a touch of human occupancy here and there—
all this, set in that enormous granite frame, three or four thousand feet
high, ornamented with domes and spires and peaks still higher—it is all
this that wins your heart and fills your imagination in the Yosemite.

As you ride or walk along the winding road up the level valley amid   3
thenoble pines and spruces and oaks, and past the groves and bits of
meadow and the camps of many tents, and the huge mossy granite boulders here and there reposing in the shade of the trees, with the full, clear,
silent river winding through the plain near you, you are all the time aware
of those huge vertical walls, their faces scarred and niched, streaked with
color, or glistening with moisture, and animated with waterfalls, rising up
on either hand, thousands of feet high, not architectural, or like something
builded, but like the sides and the four corners of the globe itself. What an
impression of mass and of power and of grandeur in repose filters into
you as you walk along! El Capitan stands there showing its simple sweeping lines through the trees as you approach, like one of the veritable pillars of the firmament. How long we are nearing it and passing it! It is so
colossal that it seems near while it is yet far off. It is so simple that the eye
takes in its naked grandeur at a glance. It demands of you a new standard
of size which you cannot at once produce. It is as clean and smooth as the
flank of a horse, and as poised and calm as a Greek statue. It curves out
toward the base as if planted there to resist the pressure of worlds—probably the most majestic single granite column or mountain buttress on the
earth. Its summit is over three thousand feet above you. Across the valley,
nearly opposite, rise the Cathedral Rocks to nearly the same height, while
farther along, beyond El Capitan, the Three Brothers shoulder the sky at
about the same dizzy height. Near the head of the great valley, North
Dome, perfect in outline as if turned in a lathe, and its brother, the Half
Dome (or shall we say half-brother?) across the valley, look down upon
Mirror Lake from an altitude of over four thousand feet. These domes suggest enormous granite bubbles if such were possible pushed up from
below and retaining their forms through the vast geologic ages. Of course

they must have weathered enormously, but as the rock seems to peel off in concentric sheets, their forms are preserved.

II

One warm, bright Sunday near the end of April, six of us walked up 4 from the hotel to Vernal and Nevada Falls, or as near to them as we could get, and took our fill of the tumult of foaming waters struggling with the wreck of huge granite cliffs: so impassive and immobile the rocks, so impetuous and reckless and determined the onset of the waters, till the falls are reached, when the obstructed river seems to find the escape and the freedom it was so eagerly seeking. Better to be completely changed into foam and spray by one single leap of six hundred feet into empty space, the river seems to say, than be forever baffled and tortured and torn on this rack of merciless boulders.

We followed the zigzagging trail up the steep side of the valley, touch- 5 ing melting snow-banks in its upper courses, passing huge granite rocks also melting in the slow heat of the geologic ages, pausing to take in the rugged, shaggy spruces and pines that sentineled the mountain-sides here and there, or resting our eyes upon Liberty Cap, which carries its suggestive form a thousand feet or more above the Nevada Fall. What beauty, what grandeur attended us that day! the wild tumult of waters, the snow-white falls, the motionless avalanches of granite rocks, and the naked granite shaft, Liberty Cap, dominating all!

And that night, too, when we sat around a big camp-fire near our tents 6 in the valley, and saw the full moon come up and look down upon us from behind Sentinel Rock, and heard the intermittent booming of Yosemite Falls sifting through the spruce trees that towered around us, and felt the tender, brooding spirit of the great valley, itself touched to lyric intensity by the grandeurs on every hand, steal in upon us, and possess our souls—surely that was a night none of us can ever forget. As Yosemite can stand the broad, searching light of midday and not be cheapened, so its enchantments can stand the light of the moon and the stars and not be rendered too vague and impalpable.

III

Going from the Grand Cañon to Yosemite is going from one sublimity 7 to another of a different order. The cañon is the more strange, unearthly, apocryphal, appeals more to the imagination, and is the more overwhelming in its size, its wealth of color, and its multitude of suggestive forms. But for quiet majesty and beauty, with a touch of the sylvan and pastoral, too, Yosemite stands alone. One could live with Yosemite, camp in it, tramp in it, winter and summer in it, and find nature in her tender and human, almost domestic moods, as well as in her grand and austere. But I do not think one could ever feel at home in or near the Grand Cañon; it is too unlike anything we have ever known upon the earth; it is like a vision of some strange colossal city uncovered from the depth of geologic time. You may have come to it, as we did, from the Petrified Forests, where you saw the silicified trunks of thousands of gigantic trees or tree ferns, that grew millions of years ago, most of them uncovered, but many of them protruding from banks of clay and gravel, and in their interiors rich in all the colors of the rainbow, and you wonder if you may not now be gazing upon some petrified antediluvian city of temples and holy places exhumed by mysterious hands and opened up to the vulgar gaze of to-day. You look into it from above and from another world and you descend into it at your peril. Yosemite you enter as into a gigantic hall and make your own; the cañon you gaze down upon, and are an alien, whether you enter it or not. Yosemite is carved out of the most majestic and enduring of all rocks, granite; the Grand Cañon is carved out of one of the most beautiful, but perishable, red Carboniferous sandstone and limestone. There is a maze of beautiful and intricate lines in the latter, a wilderness of temple-like forms and monumental remains, and noble architectural profiles that delight while they bewilder the eye. Yosemite has much greater simplicity, and is much nearer the classic standard of beauty. Its grand and austere features predominate, of course, but underneath these and adorning them are many touches of the idyllic and the picturesque. Its many waterfalls fluttering like white lace against its vertical granite walls, its smooth, level floor, its noble pines and oaks, its open glades, its sheltering groves, its bright, clear, winding river, its soft voice of many waters, its flowers, its birds, its grass, its verdure, even its orchards of blooming apple trees, all inclosed in this tremendous granite frame— what an unforgettable picture it all makes, what a blending of the sublime and the homelike and familiar it all is! It is the waterfalls that make the granite alive, and bursting into bloom as it were. What a touch they give! how they enliven the scene! What music they evoke from these harps of stone!

The first leap of Yosemite Falls is sixteen hundred feet—sixteen hundred feet of a compact mass of snowy rockets shooting downward and bursting into spray around which rainbows flit and hover. The next leap is four hundred feet, and the last six hundred. We tried to get near the foot and inspect the hidden recess in which this airy spirit again took on a

8

more tangible form of still, running water, but the spray over a large area fell like a summer shower, drenching the trees and the rocks, and holding the inquisitive tourist off at a safe distance. We had to beat a retreat with dripping garments before we had got within fifty yards of the foot of the fall. At first I was surprised at the volume of water that came hurrying out of the hidden recess of dripping rocks and trees—a swiftly flowing stream, thirty or forty feet wide, and four or five feet deep. How could that comparatively narrow curtain of white spray up there give birth to such a full robust stream? But I saw that in making the tremendous leap from the top of the precipice, the stream was suddenly drawn out, as we stretch a rubber band in our hands, and that the solid and massive current below was like the rubber again relaxed. The strain was over, and the united waters deepened and slowed up over their rocky bed.

Yosemite for a home or a camp, the Grand Cañon for a spectacle. I have spoken of the robin I saw in Yosemite Valley. Think how forlorn and out of place a robin would seem in the Grand Cañon! What would he do there? There is no turf for him to inspect, and there are no trees for him to perch on. I should as soon expect to find him amid the pyramids of Egypt, or amid the ruins of Karnak. The bluebird was in the Yosemite also, and the water-ouzel haunted the lucid waters.   9

I noticed a peculiarity of the oak in Yosemite that I never saw elsewhere[1]—a fluid or outflowing condition of the growth aboveground, such as one usually sees in the roots of trees—so that it tended to envelop and swallow, as it were, any solid object with which it came in contact. If its trunk touched a point of rock, it would put out great oaken lips several inches in extent as if to draw the rock into its maw. If a dry limb was cut or broken off, a foot from the trunk, these thin oaken lips would slowly creep out and envelop it—a sort of Western omnivorous trait appearing in the trees.   10

Whitman refers to "the slumbering and liquid trees." These Yosemite oaks recall his expression more surely than any of our Eastern trees.   11

The reader may create for himself a good image of Yosemite by thinking of a section of seven or eight miles of the Hudson River, midway of its course, as emptied of its water and deepened three thousand feet or more, having the sides nearly vertical, with snow-white waterfalls fluttering against them here and there, the famous spires and domes planted along the rim, and the landscape of groves and glades, with its still, clear winding river, occupying the bottom.   12

---

[1] I have since observed the same trait in the oaks in Georgia—probably a characteristic of this tree in southern latitudes.

IV

One cannot look upon Yosemite or walk beneath its towering walls   13
without the question arising in his mind, How did all this happen? What
were the agents that brought it about? There has been a great geologic
drama enacted here; who or what were the star actors? There are two
other valleys in this part of the Sierra, Hetch-Hetchy and King's River, that
are almost identical in their main features, though the Merced Yosemite is
the widest of the three. Each of them is a tremendous chasm in the granite rock, with nearly vertical walls, domes, El Capitans, and Sentinel and
Cathedral Rocks, and waterfalls—all modeled on the same general plan. I
believe there is nothing just like this trio of Yosemites anywhere else on
the globe.

Guided by one's ordinary sense or judgment alone, one's judgment as   14
developed and disciplined by the everyday affairs of life and the everyday
course of nature, one would say on beholding Yosemite that here is the
work of exceptional and extraordinary agents or world-building forces. It
is as surprising and exceptional as would be a cathedral in a village street,
or a gigantic sequoia in a grove of our balsam firs. The approach to it up
the Merced River does not prepare one for any such astonishing spectacle
as awaits one. The rushing, foaming water amid the tumbled confusion of
huge granite rocks and the open V-shaped valley, are nothing very remarkable or unusual. Then suddenly you are on the threshold of this hall
of the elder gods. Demons and furies might lurk in the valley below, but
here is the abode of the serene, beneficent Olympian deities. All is so
calm, so hushed, so friendly, yet so towering, so stupendous, so unspeak-
ably beautiful. You are in a mansion carved out of the granite foundations
of the earth, with walls two or three thousand feet high, hung here and
there with snowwhite waterfalls, and supporting the blue sky on domes
and pinnacles still higher. Oh, the calmness and majesty of the scene! the
evidence of such tremendous activity of some force, some agent, and now
so tranquil, so sheltering, so beneficent!

That there should be two or three Yosemites in the Sierra not very far   15
apart, all with the main features singularly alike, is very significant—as if
this kind of valley was latent in the granite of that region—some peculiarity of rock structure that lends itself readily to these formations. The
Sierra lies beyond the southern limit of the great continental ice-sheet of
late Tertiary times, but it nursed and reared many local glaciers, and to the
eroding power of these its Yosemites are partly due. But water was at
work here long before the ice—eating down into the granite and laying
open the mountain for the ice to begin its work. Ice may come, and ice
may go, says the river, but I go on forever. Water tends to make a V-shaped
valley, ice a U-shaped one, though in the Hawaiian Islands, where water

erosion alone has taken place, the prevailing form of the valleys is that of the U-shaped. Yosemite approximates to this shape, and ice has certainly played a part in its formation. But the glacier seems to have stopped at the outlet of the great valley; it did not travel beyond the gigantic hall it had helped to excavate. The valley of the Merced from the mouth of Yosemite downward is an open valley strewn with huge angular granite rocks and shows no signs of glaciation whatever. The reason of this abruptness is quite beyond my ken. It is to me a plausible theory that when the granite that forms the Sierra was lifted or squeezed up by the shrinking of the earth, large fissures and crevasses may have occurred, and that Yosemite and kindred valleys may be the result of the action of water and ice in enlarging these original chasms. Little wonder that the earlier geologists, such as Whitney, were led to attribute the exceptional character of these valleys to exceptional and extraordinary agents—to sudden faulting or dislocation of the earth's crust. But geologists are becoming more and more loath to call in the cataclysmal to explain any feature of the topography of the land. Not to the thunder or the lightning, to earthquake or volcano, to the forces of upheaval or dislocation, but to the still, small voice of the rain and the winds, of the frost and the snow,—the gentle forces now and here active all about us, carving the valleys and reducing the mountains, and changing the courses of rivers,—to these, as Lyell taught us, we are to look in nine cases out of ten, yes, in ninety-nine out of a hundred, to account for the configuration of the continents.

The geologists of our day, while not agreeing as to the amount of work   16 done respectively by ice and water, yet agree that to the latter the larger proportion of the excavation is to be ascribed. At any rate between them both they have turned out one of the most beautiful and stupendous pieces of mountain carving to be found upon the earth.

QUESTIONS FOR DISCUSSION AND WRITING

1. After touring both Yosemite and the Grand Canyon on his expedition with Muir, how does Burroughs represent the character and quality of nature in each of the two parks? What are the key distinctions he makes between the two places? Which place does he prefer and why?

2. At one point Burroughs wonders what kind of force or "agent" (par. 14) could have created two places of such power and grandeur. Burroughs appears not to answer his own question, at least not directly. What answer are we to infer from his accounts of this experience?

ALDO LEOPOLD

Like Pinchot, Aldo Leopold (1886–1948) was not an amateur naturalist but a professional environmentalist and a government official. Leopold studied forestry and wildlife management at Yale's Pinchot School of Forestry (founded by Pinchot, whose utilitarian views of nature Leopold would later reject). After graduating, Leopold worked as a forest ranger in Arizona and New Mexico. In his early years, Leopold accepted the "wise use" doctrine, but by 1933, the year he delivered a speech called "The Land Ethic," he had begun to see that the land was, in fact, a complex living organism. Through the 1930s Leopold worked in a number of government and private positions, most having to do with preserving or managing wildlife. In 1936 he helped to form what would become the Wilderness Society, and in 1939 he became chairman of the new Department of Wildlife Management at the University of Wisconsin. Throughout his career, Leopold had been writing short essays on conservation issues and policies. In 1948 Oxford University Press accepted A Sand County Almanac, *including "The Land Ethic," which begins on page 181. In* Sand County, *which was not published until after his death in 1948, Leopold was able to fully develop the environmental philosophy. A second collection of his essays,* The River of the Mother of God, *appeared in 1991. Leopold believed that it is ethically wrong, not just unwise, for humans to dominate the land. We are not mere managers of a resource but citizens of a community of interdependent parts—water, soil, plants, animals. Probably no single idea has had a greater effect on the modern environmental movement.*

The River of the Mother of God

The *Yale Review,* a literary magazine, turned down this most poignant of Leopold's wilderness essays. It remained in his desk as a yellowed, slightly edited typescript evoking the mystery of unknown places.

I am conscious of a considerable personal debt to the continent of South America. 1

It has given me, for instance, rubber for motor tires, which have carried me to lonely places on the face of Mother Earth where all her ways are pleasantness, and all her paths are peace. 2

It has given me coffee, and to brew it, many a memorable campfire with dawn-wind rustling in autumnal trees. 3

It has given me rare woods, pleasant fruits, leather, medicines, nitrates to make my garden bloom, and books about strange beasts and ancient peoples. I am not unmindful of my obligation for these things. But more 4 than all of these, it has given me the River of the Mother of God.

The river has been in my mind so long that I cannot recall just when   5
or how I first heard of it. All that I remember is that long ago a Spanish
Captain, wandering in some far Andean height, sent back word that he
had found where a mighty river falls into the trackless Amazonian forest,
and disappears. He had named it el Rio Madre de Dios. The Spanish
Captain never came back. Like the river, he disappeared. But ever since
some maps of South America have shown a short heavy line running eastward beyond the Andes, a river without beginning and without end, and
labelled it the River of the Mother of God.

That short heavy line flung down upon the blank vastness of tropical   6
wilderness has always seemed the perfect symbol of the Unknown Places
of the earth. And its name, resonant of the clank of silver armor and the
cruel progress of the Cross, yet carrying a hush of reverence and a murmur of the prows of galleons on the seven seas, has always seemed the
symbol of Conquest, the Conquest that has reduced those Unknown
Places, one by one, until now there are none left.

And when I read that MacMillan has planted the Radio among the   7
Eskimos of the furthest polar seas, and that Everest is all but climbed, and
that Russia is founding fisheries in Wrangel Land, I know the time is not
far off when there will no more be a short line on the map, without beginning and without end, no mighty river to fall from far Andean heights
into the Amazonian wilderness, and disappear. Motor boats will sputter
through those trackless forests, the clank of steam hoists will be heard in
the Mountain of the Sun, and there will be phonographs and chewing
gum upon the River of the Mother of God.

No doubt it was "for this the earth lay preparing quintillions of years,   8
for this the revolving centuries truly and steadily rolled." But it marks a
new epoch in the history of mankind, an epoch in which Unknown Places
disappear as a dominant fact in human life.

Ever since paleolithic man became conscious that his own home hunt-   9
ing ground was only part of a greater world, Unknown Places have been
a seemingly fixed fact in human environment, and usually a major influence in human lives. Sumerian tribes, venturing the Unknown Places,
found the valley of the Euphrates and an imperial destiny. Phoenician
sailors, venturing the unknown seas, found Carthage and Cornwall and
established commerce upon the earth. Hanno, Ulysses, Eric, Columbus—
history is but a succession of adventures into the Unknown. For unnum-
bered centuries the test of men and nations has been whether they "chose
rather to live miserably in this realm, pestered with inhabitants, or to venture forth, as becometh men, into those remote lands."

And now, speaking geographically, the end of the Unknown is at hand.   10
This fact in our environment, seemingly as fixed as the wind and the sun-

set, has at last reached the vanishing point. Is it to be expected that it shall be lost from human experience without something likewise being lost from human character?

I think not. In fact, there is an instinctive human reaction against the loss of fundamental environmental influences, of which history records many examples. The chase, for instance, was a fundamental fact in the life of all nomadic tribes. Again and again, when these tribes conquered and took possession of agricultural regions, where they settled down and became civilized and had no further need of hunting, they nevertheless continued it as a sport, and as such it persists to this day, with ten million devotees in America alone.

It is this same reaction against the loss of adventure into the unknown which causes the hundreds of thousands to sally forth each year upon little expeditions, afoot, by pack train, or by canoe, into the odd bits of wilderness which commerce and "development" have regretfully and temporarily left us here and there. Modest adventurers to be sure, compared with Hanno, or Lewis and Clark. But so is the sportsman, with his setter dog in pursuit of partridges, a modest adventurer compared with his Neolithic ancestor in single combat with the Auroch bull. The point is that along with the necessity for expression of racial instincts there happily goes that capacity for illusion which enables little boys to fish happily in wash-tubs. That capacity is a precious thing, if not overworked.

But there is a basic difference between the adventures of the chase and the adventures of wilderness travel. Production of game for the chase can, with proper skill, be superimposed upon agriculture and forestry and can thus be indefinitely perpetuated. But the wilderness cannot be superimposed upon anything. The wilderness and economics are, in every ordinary sense, mutually exclusive. If the wilderness is to be perpetuated at all, it must be in areas exclusively dedicated to that purpose.

We come now to the question: Is it possible to preserve the element of Unknown Places in our national life? Is it practicable to do so, without undue loss in economic values? I say "yes" to both questions. But we must act vigorously and quickly, before the remaining bits of wilderness have disappeared.

Like parks and playgrounds and other "useless" things, any system of wilderness areas would have to be owned and held for public use by the Government. The fortunate thing is that the Government already owns enough of them, scattered here and there in the poorer and rougher parts of the National Forests and National Parks, to make a very good start. The one thing needful is for the Government to draw a line around each one and say: "This is wilderness, and wilderness it shall remain." A place where Americans may "venture forth, as becometh men, into remote lands."

Such a policy would not subtract even a fraction of one per cent from   16
our economic wealth, but would preserve a fraction of what has, since
first the flight of years began, been wealth to the human spirit.

There is a current advertisement of Wells' Outline of History which   17
says "The unforgivable sin is standing still. In all Nature, to cease to grow
is to perish." I suppose this pretty accurately summarizes the rebuttal
which the Economic American would make to the proposal of a national
system of wilderness playgrounds. But what is standing still? And what
constitutes growth? The Economic American has shown very plainly that
he thinks growth is the number of ciphers added yearly to the national
population and the national bank-roll. But the Gigantosaurus tried out
that definition of growth for several million years. He was a quantitative
economist of the first water. He added two ciphers to his stature, and a
staggering row of them to his numbers. But he perished, the blind victim
of natural and "economic" laws. They made him, and they destroyed him.

There has been just one really new thing since the Gigantosaurus. That   18
new thing is Man, the first creature in all the immensities of time and space
whose evolution is self-directed. The first creature, in any spiritual sense,
to create his own environment. Is it not in that fact, rather than in mere ciphers of dollars or population, that we have grown?

The question of wilderness playgrounds is a question in self-control   19
of environment. If we had not exercised that control in other ways,
we would already be in the process of destruction by our own ciphers.
Wilderness playgrounds simply represent a new need for exercising it in
a new direction. Have we grown enough to realize that before it is too
late?

I say "too late" because wilderness is the one thing we can not build to   29
order. When our ciphers result in slums, we can tear down enough of
them to re-establish parks and playgrounds. When they choke traffic, we
can tear down enough of them to build highways and subways. But when
our ciphers have choked out the last vestige of the Unknown Places, we
cannot build new ones. To artificially create wilderness areas would over-
work the capacity for illusion of even little boys with wash-tubs.

Just what is it that is choking out our last vestiges of wilderness? Is it   21
real economic need for farmlands? Go out and see them—they contain no
farmlands worthy of the name. Is it real economic need for timber? They
contain timber to be sure, much of it better to look at than to saw, but until
we start growing timber on the eighty million acres of fire-gutted wastes
created by our "economic" system we have small call to begrudge what
timber they contain. The thing that is choking out the wilderness is not
true economics at all, but rather that Frankenstein which our boosters
have builded, the "Good Roads Movement."

This movement, entirely sound and beneficial in its inception, has been   22 boosted until it resembles a gold-rush, with about the same regard for ethics and good craftsmanship. The spilled treasures of Nature and of the Government seem to incite about the same kind of stampede in the human mind.

In this case the yellow lure is the Motor Tourist. Like Mammon, he must   23 now be spelled with a capital, and as with Mammon, we grovel at his feet, and he rules us with the insolence characteristic of a new god. We offer up our groves and our greenswards for him to camp upon, and he litters them with cans and with rubbish. We hand him our wild life and our wild flowers, and humbly continue the gesture after there are none left to hand. But of all offerings foolish roads are to him the most pleasing of sacrifice.

(Since they are mostly to be paid for by a distant treasury or by a dis-   24 tant posterity, they are likewise pleasing to us.)

And of all foolish roads, the most pleasing is the one that "opens up"   25 some last little vestige of virgin wilderness. With the unholy zeal of fanatics we hunt them out and pile them upon his altar, while from the throats of a thousand luncheon clubs and Chambers of Commerce and Greater Gopher Prairie Associations rises the solemn chant "There is No God but Gasoline and Motor is his Prophet!"

The more benignant aspects of the Great God Motor and the really   26 sound elements of the Good Roads Movement need no defense from me. They are cried from every housetop, and we all know them. What I am trying to picture is the tragic absurdity of trying to whip the March of Empire into a gallop.

Very specifically, I am pointing out that in this headlong stampede for   27 speed and ciphers we are crushing the last remnants of something that ought to be preserved for the spiritual and physical welfare of future Americans, even at the cost of acquiring a few less millions of wealth or population in the long run. Something that has helped build the race for such innumerable centuries that we may logically suppose it will help preserve it in the centuries to come.

Failing this, it seems to me we fail in the ultimate test of our vaunted   28 superiority—the self-control of environment. We fall back into the biological category of the potato bug which exterminated the potato, and thereby exterminated itself.

QUESTIONS FOR DISCUSSION AND WRITING

1.   Leopold begins by insisting on the importance of untouched wilderness to the American character. "And now," Leopold argues, "the end of the Unknown is at hand" (par. 10). With this dramatic historical change, it is to be expected that something will "be lost from human character" (par. 10). What exactly did Leopold argue would be lost? This essay was written in 1924; reading it today, how accurate do you feel Leopold was about what would be lost?

2. Leopold creates an assortment of symbolic characters in order to make his points about the crisis facing modern industrial America in 1924: "Motor Tourist" (par. 23), "Gigantosaurus," "Economic American" (par. 17). Take a moment to identify and define these and other such characters. Which, if any, seem out of date? Which are still familiar in contemporary America?

The Land Ethic

When god-like Odysseus returned from the wars in Troy, he hanged all   1
on one rope a dozen slave-girls of his household whom he suspected of misbehavior during his absence.

This hanging involved no question of propriety. The girls were prop-   2
erty. The disposal of property was then, as now, a matter of expediency, not of right and wrong.

Concepts of right and wrong were not lacking from Odysseus' Greece;   3
witness the fidelity of his wife through the long years before at last his black-prowed galleys clove the wine-dark seas for home. The ethical structure of that day covered wives, but had not yet been extended to human chattels. During the three thousand years which have since elapsed, ethical criteria have been extended to many fields of conduct, with corresponding shrinkages in those judged by expediency only.

The Ethical Sequence

This extension of ethics, so far studied only by philosophers, is actually   4
a process in ecological evolution. Its sequences may be described in ecological as well as in philosophical terms. An ethic, ecologically, is a limitation on freedom of action in the struggle for existence. An ethic, philosophically, is a differentiation of social from anti-social conduct. These are two definitions of one thing. The thing has its origin in the tendency of interdependent individuals or groups to evolve modes of cooperation. The ecologist calls these symbioses. Politics and economics

are advanced symbioses in which the original free-for-all competition has been replaced, in part, by co-operative mechanisms with an ethical content.

The complexity of co-operative mechanisms has increased with popu-   5 lation density, and with the efficiency of tools. It was simpler, for example, to define the anti-social uses of sticks and stones in the days of the mastodons than of bullets and billboards in the age of motors.

The first ethics dealt with the relation between individuals; the Mosaic   6 Decalogue is an example. Later accretions dealt with the relation between the individual and society. The Golden Rule tries to integrate the individual to society; democracy to integrate social organization to the individual.

There is as yet no ethic dealing with man's relation to land and to the   7 animals and plants which grow upon it. Land, like Odysseus' slave-girls, is still property. The land-relation is still strictly economic, entailing privileges but not obligations.

The extension of ethics to this third element in human environment is,   8 if I read the evidence correctly, an evolutionary possibility and an ecological necessity. It is the third step in a sequence. The first two have already been taken. Individual thinkers since the days of Ezekiel and Isaiah have asserted that the despoliation of land is not only inexpedient but wrong. Society, however, has not yet affirmed their belief. I regard the present conservation movement as the embryo of such an affirmation.

An ethic may be regarded as a mode of guidance for meeting ecologi-   9 cal situations so new or intricate, or involving such deferred reactions, that the path of social expediency is not discernible to the average individual. Animal instincts are modes of guidance for the individual in meeting such situations. Ethics are possibly a kind of community instinct in-the-making.

The Community Concept

All ethics so far evolved rest upon a single premise: that the individual   10 is a member of a community of interdependent parts. His instincts prompt him to compete for his place in that community, but his ethics prompt him also to co-operate (perhaps in order that there may be a place to compete for).

The land ethic simply enlarges the boundaries of the community to   11 include soils, waters, plants, and animals, or collectively: the land.

This sounds simple: do we not already sing our love for and obligation   12 to the land of the free and the home of the brave? Yes, but just what and whom do we love? Certainly not the soil, which we are sending helterskelter downriver. Certainly not the waters, which we assume have no function except to turn turbines, float barges, and carry off sewage. Certainly not the plants, of which we exterminate whole communities without batting an eye. Certainly not the animals, of which we have already extirpated many of the largest and most beautiful species. A land ethic of course cannot prevent the alteration, management, and use of these "resources," but it does affirm their right to continued existence, and, at least in spots, their continued existence in a natural state.

In short, a land ethic changes the role of Homo sapiens from conqueror of the land-community to plain member and citizen of it. It implies respect for his fellow-members, and also respect for the community as such.   13

In human history, we have learned (I hope) that the conqueror role is eventually self-defeating. Why? Because it is implicit in such a role that the conqueror knows, ex cathedra, just what makes the community clock tick, and just what and who is valuable, and what and who is worthless, in community life. It always turns out that he knows neither, and this is why his conquests eventually defeat themselves.   14

In the biotic community, a parallel situation exists. Abraham knew exactly what the land was for: it was to drip milk and honey into Abraham's mouth. At the present moment, the assurance with which we regard this assumption is inverse to the degree of our education.   15

The ordinary citizen today assumes that science knows what makes the community clock tick; the scientist is equally sure that he does not. He knows that the biotic mechanism is so complex that its workings may never be fully understood.   16

That man is, in fact, only a member of a biotic team is shown by an ecological interpretation of history. Many historical events, hitherto explained solely in terms of human enterprise, were actually biotic interactions between people and land. The characteristics of the land determined the facts quite as potently as the characteristics of the men who lived on it.   17

Consider, for example, the settlement of the Mississippi valley. In the years following the Revolution, three groups were contending for its control: the native Indian, the French and English traders, and the American settlers. Historians wonder what would have happened if the English at Detroit had thrown a little more weight into the Indian side of those tipsy scales which decided the outcome of the colonial migration into the cane-lands of Kentucky. It is time now to ponder the fact that the cane-lands, when subjected to the particular mixture of forces represented by the cow, plow, fire, and axe of the pioneer, became bluegrass. What if the plant succession inherent in this dark and bloody ground had, under the impact of these forces, given us some worthless sedge, shrub, or weed? Would Boone and Kenton have held out? Would there have been any overflow into Ohio, Indiana, Illinois, and Missouri? Any Louisiana Purchase? Any transcontinental union of new states? Any Civil War?   18

Kentucky was one sentence in the drama of history. We are commonly   19
told what the human actors in this drama tried to do, but we are seldom
told that their success, or the lack of it, hung in large degree on the reaction of particular soils to the impact of the particular forces exerted by
their occupancy. In the case of Kentucky, we do not even know where
the bluegrass came from—whether it is a native species, or a stowaway
from Europe.

Contrast the cane-lands with what hindsight tells us about the   20
Southwest, where the pioneers were equally brave, resourceful, and per-
severing. The impact of occupancy here brought no bluegrass, or other
plant fitted to withstand the bumps and buffetings of hard use. This region, when grazed by livestock, reverted through a series of more and
more worthless grasses, shrubs, and weeds to a condition of unstable
equilibrium. Each recession of plant types bred erosion; each increment to
erosion bred a further recession of plants. The result today is a progressive
and mutual deterioration, not only of plants and soils, but of the animal
community subsisting thereon. The early settlers did not expect this: on
the ciénegas of New Mexico some even cut ditches to hasten it. So subtle
has been its progress that few residents of the region are aware of it. It is
quite invisible to the tourist who finds this wrecked landscape colorful
and charming (as indeed it is, but it bears scant resemblance to what it was
in 1848).

This same landscape was "developed" once before, but with quite dif-   21
ferent results. The Pueblo Indians settled the Southwest in pre-Columbian
times, but they happened *not* to be equipped with range livestock. Their
civilization expired, but not because their land expired.

In India, regions devoid of any sod-forming grass have been settled,   22
apparently without wrecking the land, by the simple expedient of carrying the grass to the cow, rather than vice versa. (Was this the result of
some deep wisdom, or was it just good luck? I do not know.)

In short, the plant succession steered the course of history; the pioneer   23
simply demonstrated, for good or ill, what successions inhered in the land.
Is history taught in this spirit? It will be, once the concept of land as a community really penetrates our intellectual life.

The Ecological Conscience

Conservation is a state of harmony between men and land. Despite   24
nearly a century of propaganda, conservation still proceeds at a snail's
pace; progress still consists largely of letterhead pieties and convention oratory. On the back forty we still slip two steps backward for each forward
stride.

The usual answer to this dilemma is "more conservation education." No   25
one will debate this, but is it certain that only the *volume* of education
needs stepping up? Is something lacking in the *content* as well?

It is difficult to give a fair summary of its content in brief form, but, as I   26
understand it, the content is substantially this: obey the law, vote right,
join some organizations, and practice what conservation is profitable on
your own land; the government will do the rest.

Is not this formula too easy to accomplish anything worth-while? It   27
defines no right or wrong, assigns no obligation, calls for no sacrifice,
implies no change in the current philosophy of values, In respect of
land-use, it urges only enlightened self-interest. Just how far will such
education take us? An example will perhaps yield a partial answer.

By 1930 it had become clear to all except the ecologically blind that   28
Southwestern Wisconsin's topsoil was slipping seaward. In 1933 the farmers were told that if they would adopt certain remedial practices for five
years, the public would donate CCC labor to install them, plus the necessary machinery and materials. The offer was widely accepted, but the
practices were widely forgotten when the five-year contract period was
up. The farmers continued only those practices that yielded an immediate
and visible economic gain for themselves.

This led to the idea that maybe farmers would learn more quickly if   29
they themselves wrote the rules. Accordingly the Wisconsin Legislature in
1937 passed the Soil Conservation District Law. This said to farmers, in
effect: *We, the public, will furnish you free technical service and loan
you specialized machinery, if you will write your own rules for land-use.
Each county may write its own rules, and these will have the force of law.*
Nearly all the counties promptly organized to accept the proffered help,
but after a decade of operation, *no county has yet written a single rule.*
There has been visible progress in such practices as strip-cropping, pasture renovation, and soil liming, but none in fencing woodlots against
grazing, and none in excluding plow and cow from steep slopes. The
farmers, in short, have selected those remedial practices which were profitable anyhow, and ignored those which were profitable to the community, but not clearly profitable to themselves.

When one asks why no rules have been written, one is told that the   30
community is not yet ready to support them; education must precede
rules. But the education actually in progress makes no mention of obligations to land over and above those dictated by self-interest. The net result
is that we have more education but less soil, fewer healthy woods, and as
many floods as in 1937.

The puzzling aspect of such situations is that the existence of obliga-   31
tions over and above self-interest is taken for granted in such rural community enterprises as the betterment of roads, schools, churches, and

baseball teams. Their existence is not taken for granted, nor as yet seriously discussed, in bettering the behavior of the water that falls on the land, or in the preserving of the beauty or diversity of the farm landscape. Land-use ethics are still governed wholly by economic self-interest, just as social ethics were a century ago.

To sum up: we asked the farmer to do what he conveniently could to 32 save his soil, and he has done just that, and only that. The farmer who clears the woods off a 75 per cent slope, turns his cows into the clearing, and dumps its rainfall, rocks, and soil into the community creek, is still (if otherwise decent) a respected member of society. If he puts lime on his fields and plants his crops on contour, he is still entitled to all the privileges and emoluments of his Soil Conservation District. The District is a beautiful piece of social machinery, but it is coughing along on two cylinders because we have been too timid, and too anxious for quick success, to tell the farmer the true magnitude of his obligations. Obligations have no meaning without conscience, and the problem we face is the extension of the social conscience from people to land.

No important change in ethics was ever accomplished without an 33 internal change in our intellectual emphasis, loyalties, affections, and convictions. The proof that conservation has not yet touched these foundations of conduct lies in the fact that philosophy and religion have not yet heard of it. In our attempt to make conservation easy, we have made it trivial.

Substitutes for a Land Ethic

When the logic of history hungers for bread and we hand out a stone, 34 we are at pains to explain how much the stone resembles bread. I now describe some of the stones which serve in lieu of a land ethic.

One basic weakness in a conservation system based wholly on eco- 35 nomic motives is that most members of the land community have no economic value. Wildflowers and songbirds are examples. Of the 22,000 higher plants and animals native to Wisconsin, it is doubtful whether more than 5 per cent can be sold, fed, eaten, or otherwise put to economic use. Yet these creatures are members of the biotic community, and if (as I believe) its stability depends on its integrity, they are entitled to continuance.

When one of these non-economic categories is threatened, and if we 36 happen to love it, we invent subterfuges to give it economic importance. At the beginning of the century songbirds were supposed to be disappearing. Ornithologists jumped to the rescue with some distinctly shaky evidence to the effect that insects would eat us up if birds failed to control them. The evidence had to be economic in order to be valid.

It is painful to read these circumlocutions today. We have no land ethic   37
yet, but we have at least drawn nearer the point of admitting that birds
should continue as a matter of biotic right, regardless of the presence or
absence of economic advantage to us.

A parallel situation exists in respect of predatory mammals, raptorial   38
birds, and fish-eating birds. Time was when biologists somewhat overworked the evidence that these creatures preserve the health of game by
killing weaklings, or that they control rodents for the farmer, or that they
prey only on "worthless" species. Here again, the evidence bad to be economic in order to be valid. It is only in recent years that we hear the more
honest argument that predators are members of the community, and that
no special interest has the right to exterminate them for the sake of a benefit, real or fancied, to itself. Unfortunately this enlightened view is still in
the talk stage. In the field the extermination of predators goes merrily on:
witness the impending erasure of the timber wolf by fiat of Congress, the
Conservation Bureaus, and many state legislatures.

Some species of trees have been "read out of the party" by economics-   39
minded foresters because they grow too slowly, or have too low a sale
value to pay as timber crops: white cedar, tamarack, cypress, beech, and
hemlock are examples. In Europe, where forestry is ecologically more advanced, the non-commercial tree species are recognized as members of
the native forest community, to be preserved as such, within reason.
Moreover some (like beech) have been found to have a valuable function
in building up soil fertility. The interdependence of the forest and its constituent tree species, ground flora, and fauna is taken for granted.

Lack of economic value is sometimes a character not only of species   40
or groups, but of entire biotic communities: marshes, bogs, dunes, and
"deserts" are examples. Our formula in such cases is to relegate their conservation to government as refuges, monuments, or parks. The difficulty
is that these communities are usually interspersed with more valuable private lands; the government cannot possibly own or control such scattered
parcels. The net effect is that we have relegated some of them to ultimate
extinction over large areas. If the private owner were ecologically minded,
he would be proud to be the custodian of a reasonable proportion of such
areas, which add diversity and beauty to his farm and to his community.

In some instances, the assumed lack of profit in these "waste" areas has   41
proved to be wrong, but only after most of them had been done away
with. The present scramble to reflood muskrat marshes is a case in point.

There is a clear tendency in American conservation to relegate to   42
government all necessary jobs that private landowners fail to perform.
Government ownership, operation, subsidy, or regulation is now widely
prevalent in forestry, range management, soil and watershed management, park and wilderness conservation, fisheries management, and mi-

gratory bird management, with more to come. Most of this growth in governmental conservation is proper and logical, some of it is inevitable. That I imply no disapproval of it is implicit in the fact that I have spent most of my life working for it. Nevertheless the question arises: What is the ultimate magnitude of the enterprise? Will the tax base carry its eventual ramifications? At what point will governmental conservation, like the mastodon, become handicapped by its own dimensions? The answer, if there is any, seems to be in a land ethic, or some other force which assigns more obligation to the private landowner.

Industrial landowners and users, especially lumbermen and stockmen, are inclined to wail long and loudly about the extension of government ownership and regulation to land, but (with notable exceptions) they show little disposition to develop the only visible alternative: the voluntary practice of conservation on their own lands.   43

When the private landowner is asked to perform some unprofitable act for the good of the community, he today assents only with outstretched palm. If the act costs him cash this is fair and proper, but when it costs only forethought, open-mindedness, or time, the issue is at least debatable. The overwhelming growth of land-use subsidies in recent years must be ascribed, in large part, to the government's own agencies for conservation education: the land bureaus, the agricultural colleges, and the extension services. As far as I can detect, no ethical obligation toward land is taught in these institutions.   44

To sum up: a system of conservation based solely on economic self-interest is hopelessly lopsided. It tends to ignore, and thus eventually to eliminate, many elements in the land community that lack commercial value, but that are (as far as we know) essential to its healthy functioning. It assumes, falsely, I think, that the economic parts of the biotic clock will function without the uneconomic parts. It tends to relegate to government many functions eventually too large, too complex, or too widely dispersed to be performed by government.   45

An ethical obligation on the part of the private owner is the only visible remedy for these situations.   46

The Land Pyramid

An ethic to supplement and guide the economic relation to land presupposes the existence of some mental image of land as a biotic mechanism. We can be ethical only in relation to something we can see, feel, understand, love, or otherwise have faith in.   47

The image commonly employed in conservation education is "the balance of nature." For reasons too lengthy to detail here, this figure of   48 speech fails to describe accurately what little we know about the land mechanism. A much truer image is the one employed in ecology: the biotic pyramid. I shall first sketch the pyramid as a symbol of land, and later develop some of its implications in terms of land-use.

Plants absorb energy from the sun. This energy flows through a circuit called the biota, which may be represented by a pyramid consisting of layers. The bottom layer is the soil. A plant layer rests on the soil, an insect layer on the plants, a bird and rodent layer on the insects, and so on up through various animal groups to the apex layer, which consists of the larger carnivores.

The species of a layer are alike not in where they came from, or in what they look like, but rather in what they eat. Each successive layer depends on those below it for food and often for other services, and each in turn furnishes food and services to those above. Proceeding upward, each successive layer decreases in numerical abundance. Thus, for every carnivore there are hundreds of his prey, thousands of their prey, millions of insects, uncountable plants. The pyramidal form of the system reflects this numerical progression from apex to base. Man shares an intermediate layer with the bears, raccoons, and squirrels which eat both meat and vegetables.

The lines of dependency for food and other services are called food chains. Thus soil-oak-deer-Indian is a chain that has now been largely converted to soil-corn-cow-farmer. Each species, including ourselves, is a link in many chains. The deer eats a hundred plants other than oak, and the cow a hundred plants other than corn. Both, then, are links in a hundred chains. The pyramid is a tangle of chains so complex as to seem disorderly, yet the stability of the system proves it to be a highly organized structure. Its functioning depends on the co-operation and competition of its diverse parts.

In the beginning, the pyramid of life was low and squat; the food chains short and simple. Evolution has added layer after layer, link after link. Man is one of thousands of accretions to the height and complexity of the pyramid. Science has given us many doubts, but it has given us at least one certainty: the trend of evolution is to elaborate and diversify the biota.

Land, then, is not merely soil; it is a fountain of energy flowing through a circuit of soils, plants, and animals. Food chains are the living channels which conduct energy upward; death and decay return it to the soil. The circuit is not closed; some energy is dissipated in decay, some is added by absorption from the air, some is stored in soils, peats, and long-lived forests; but it is a sustained circuit, like a slowly augmented revolving fund of life. There is always a net loss by downhill wash, but this is normally small and offset by the decay of rocks. It is deposited in the ocean and, in the course of geological time, raised to form new lands and new pyramids.

The velocity and character of the upward flow of energy depend on the   54
complex structure of the plant and animal community, much as the upward flow of sap in a tree depends on its complex cellular organization.
Without this complexity, normal circulation would presumably not occur.
Structure means the characteristic numbers, as well as the characteristic
kinds and functions, of the component species. This interdependence between the complex structure of the land and its smooth functioning as an
energy unit is one of its basic attributes.

When a change occurs in one part of the circuit, many other parts must   55
adjust themselves to it. Change does not necessarily obstruct or divert the
flow of energy; evolution is a long series of self-induced changes, the net
result of which has been to elaborate the flow mechanism and to lengthen
the circuit. Evolutionary changes, however, are usually slow and local.
Man's invention of tools has enabled him to make changes of unprecedented violence, rapidity, and scope.

One change is in the composition of floras and faunas. The larger   56
predators are lopped off the apex of the pyramid; food chains, for the first
time in history, become shorter rather than longer. Domesticated species
from other lands are substituted for wild ones, and wild ones are moved
to new habitats. In this world-wide pooling of faunas and floras, some
species get out of bounds as pests and diseases, others are extinguished.
Such effects are seldom intended or foreseen; they represent unpredicted
and often untraceable readjustments in the structure. Agricultural science
is largely a race between the emergence of new pests and the emergence
of new techniques for their control.

Another change touches the flow of energy through plants and animals   57
and its return to the soil. Fertility is the ability of soil to receive, store, and
release energy. Agriculture, by overdrafts on the soil, or by too radical a
substitution of domestic for native species in the superstructure, may de-
range the channels of flow or deplete storage. Soils depleted of their storage, or of the organic matter which anchors it, wash away faster than they
form. This is erosion.

Waters, like soil, are part of the energy circuit. Industry, by polluting   58
waters or obstructing them with dams, may exclude the plants and animals necessary to keep energy in circulation.

Transportation brings about another basic change: the plants or ani-   59
mals grown in one region are now consumed and returned to the soil in another. Transportation taps the energy stored in rocks, and in the air, and uses
it elsewhere; thus we fertilize the garden with nitrogen gleaned by the guano
birds from the fishes of seas on the other side of the Equator. Thus the formerly localized and self-contained circuits are pooled on a world-wide scale.

The process of altering the pyramid for human occupation releases   60
stored energy, and this often gives rise, during the pioneering period, to a

deceptive exuberance of plant and animal life, both wild and tame. These releases of biotic capital tend to becloud or postpone the penalties of violence.

This thumbnail sketch of land as an energy circuit conveys three basic   61
ideas:

1. That land is not merely soil.
2. That the native plants and animals kept the energy circuit open; others may or may not.
3. That the man-made changes are of a different order than evolutionary changes, and have effects more comprehensive than is intended or foreseen.

These ideas, collectively, raise two basic issues: Can the land adjust   62
to the new order? Can the desired alterations be accomplished with less violence?

Biotas seem to differ in their capacity to sustain violent conversion.   63
Western Europe, for example, carries a far different pyramid than Caesar found there. Some large animals are lost; swampy forests have become meadows or plow-land; many new plants and animals are introduced, some of which escape as pests; the remaining natives are greatly changed in distribution and abundance. Yet the soil is still there and, with the help of imported nutrients, still fertile; the waters flow normally; the new structure seems to function and to persist. There is no visible stoppage or derangement of the circuit.

Western Europe, then, has a resistant biota. Its inner processes are   64
tough, elastic, resistant to strain. No matter how violent the alterations, the pyramid, so far, has developed some new modus vivendi which preserves its habitability for man, and for most of the other natives.

Japan seems to present another instance of radical conversion without   65
disorganization.

Most other civilized regions, and some as yet barely touched by civi-   66
lization, display various stages of disorganization, varying from initial symptoms to advanced wastage. In Asia Minor and North Africa diagnosis is confused by climatic changes, which may have been either the cause or the effect of advanced wastage. In the United States the degree of disorganization varies locally; it is worst in the Southwest, the Ozarks, and parts of the South, and least in New England and the Northwest. Better land-uses may still arrest it in the less advanced regions. In parts of Mexico, South America, South Africa, and Australia a violent and accelerating wastage is in progress, but I cannot assess the prospects.

This almost world-wide display of disorganization in the land seems to   67
be similar to disease in an animal, except that it never culminates in com-

plete disorganization or death. The land recovers, but at some reduced level of complexity, and with a reduced carrying capacity for people, plants, and animals. Many biotas currently regarded as "lands of opportunity" are in fact already subsisting on exploitative agriculture, i.e. they have already exceeded their sustained carrying capacity. Most of South America is overpopulated in this sense.

In arid regions we attempt to offset the process of wastage by reclamation, but it is only too evident that the prospective longevity of reclamation projects is often short. In our own West, the best of them may not last a century.   68

The combined evidence of history and ecology seems to support one general deduction: the less violent the man-made changes, the greater the probability of successful readjustment in the pyramid. Violence, in turn, varies with human population density; a dense population requires a more violent conversion. In this respect, North America has a better chance for permanence than Europe, if she can contrive to limit her density.   69

This deduction runs counter to our current philosophy, which assumes that because a small increase in density enriched human life, that an indefinite increase will enrich it indefinitely. Ecology knows of no density relationship that holds for indefinitely wide limits. All gains from density are subject to a law of diminishing returns.   70

Whatever may be the equation for men and land, it is improbable that we as yet know all its terms. Recent discoveries in mineral and vitamin nutrition reveal unsuspected dependencies in the up-circuit: incredibly minute quantities of certain substances determine the value of soils to plants, of plants to animals. What of the down-circuit? What of the vanishing species, the preservation of which we now regard as an esthetic luxury? They helped build the soil; in what unsuspected ways may they be essential to its maintenance? Professor Weaver proposes that we use prairie flowers to reflocculate the wasting soils of the dust bowl; who knows for what purpose cranes and condors, otters and grizzlies may some day be used?   71

Land Health and the A-B Cleavage

A land ethic, then, reflects the existence of an ecological conscience, and this in turn reflects a conviction of individual responsibility for the health of the land. Health is the capacity of the land for self-renewal. Conservation is our effort to understand and preserve this capacity.   72

Conservationists are notorious for their dissensions. Superficially these   73 seem to add up to mere confusion, but a more careful scrutiny reveals a single plane of cleavage common to many specialized fields. In each field one group (A) regards the land as soil, and its function as commodity-production; another group (B) regards the land as a biota, and its function as something broader. How much broader is admittedly in a state of doubt and confusion.

In my own field, forestry, group A is quite content to grow trees like cabbages, with cellulose as the basic forest commodity. It feels no inhibition against violence; its ideology is agronomic. Group B, on the other hand, sees forestry as fundamentally different from agronomy because it employs natural species, and manages a natural environment rather than creating an artificial one. Group B prefers natural reproduction on principle. It worries on biotic as well as economic grounds about the loss of species like chestnut, and the threatened loss of the white pines. It worries about a whole series of secondary forest functions: wildlife, recreation, watersheds, wilderness areas. To my mind, Group B feels the stirrings of an ecological conscience. 74

In the wildlife field, a parallel cleavage exists. For Group A the basic commodities are sport and meat; the yardsticks of production are ciphers of take in pheasants and trout. Artificial propagation is acceptable as a permanent as well as a temporary recourse—if its unit costs permit. Group B, on the other hand, worries about whole series of biotic side-issues. What is the cost in predators of producing a game crop? Should we have further recourse to exotics? How can management restore the shrinking species, like prairie grouse, already hopeless as shootable game? How can management restore the threatened rarities, like trumpeter swan and whooping crane? Can management principles be extended to wildflowers? Here again it is clear to me that we have the same A-B cleavage as in forestry. 75

In the larger field of agriculture I am less competent to speak, but there seem to be somewhat parallel cleavages. Scientific agriculture was actively developing before ecology was born, hence a slower penetration of ecological concepts might be expected. Moreover the farmer, by the very nature of his techniques, must modify the biota more radically than the forester or the wildlife manager. Nevertheless, there are many discontents in agriculture which seem to add up to a new vision of "biotic farming." 76

Perhaps the most important of these is the new evidence that poundage or tonnage is no measure of the food-value of farm crops; the products of fertile soil may be qualitatively as well as quantitatively superior. We can bolster poundage from depleted soils by pouring on imported fertility, but we are not necessarily bolstering food-value. The possible ultimate ramifications of this idea are so immense that I must leave their exposition to abler pens. 77

The discontent that labels itself "organic farming," while bearing some 78
of the earmarks of a cult, is nevertheless biotic in its direction, particularly
in its insistence on the importance of soil flora and fauna.

The ecological fundamentals of agriculture are just as poorly known to 79
the public as in other fields of land-use. For example, few educated people realize that the marvelous advances in technique made during recent
decades are improvements in the pump, rather than the well. Acre for
acre, they have barely sufficed to offset the sinking level of fertility.

In all of these cleavages, we see repeated the same basic paradoxes: 80
man the conqueror versus man the biotic citizen; science the sharpener
of his sword versus science the searchlight on his universe; land the slave
and servant versus land the collective organism. Robinson's injunction to
Tristram may well be applied, at this juncture, to Homo sapiens as a
species in geological time:

> Whether you will or not
> You are a King, Tristram, for you are one
> Of the time-tested few that leave the world,
> When they are gone, not the same place it was.
> Mark what you leave.

The Outlook

It is inconceivable to me that an ethical relation to land can exist with- 81
out love, respect, and admiration for land, and a high regard for its value.
By value, I of course mean something far broader than mere economic
value; I mean value in the philosophical sense.

Perhaps the most serious obstacle impeding the evolution of a land 82
ethic is the fact that our educational and economic system is headed away
from, rather than toward, an intense consciousness of land. Your true
modem is separated from the land by many middlemen, and by innumerable physical gadgets. He has no vital relation to it; to him it is the space
between cities on which crops grow. Turn him loose for a day on the land,
and if the spot does not happen to be a golf links or a "scenic" area, he is
bored stiff. If crops could be raised by hydroponics instead of farming, it
would suit him very well. Synthetic substitutes for wood, leather, wool,
and other natural land products suit him better than the originals. In short,
land is something he has "outgrown."

Almost equally serious as an obstacle to a land ethic is the attitude of 83
the farmer for whom the land is still an adversary, or a taskmaster that
keeps him in slavery. Theoretically, the mechanization of farming ought
to cut the farmer's chains, but whether it really does is debatable.

One of the requisites for an ecological comprehension of land is an 84 understanding of ecology, and this is by no means co-extensive with "education"; in fact, much higher education seems deliberately to avoid ecological concepts. An understanding of ecology does not necessarily originate in courses bearing ecological labels; it is quite as likely to be labeled geography, botany, agronomy, history, or economics. This is as it should be, but whatever the label, ecological training is scarce.

The case for a land ethic would appear hopeless but for the minority   85
which is in obvious revolt against these "modern" trends.

The "key-log" which must be moved to release the evolutionary proc-   86
ess for an ethic is simply this: quit thinking about decent land-use as solely an economic problem. Examine each question in terms of what is ethically and esthetically right, as well as what is economically expedient. A thing is right when it tends to preserve the integrity, stability, and beauty of the biotic community. It is wrong when it tends otherwise.

It of course goes without saying that economic feasibility limits the   87
tether of what can or cannot be done for land. It always has and it always will. The fallacy the economic determinists have tied around our collective neck, and which we now need to cast off, is the belief that economics determines *all* land-use. This is simply not true. An innumerable host of actions and attitudes, comprising perhaps the bulk of all land relations, is determined by the land-users' tastes and predilections, rather than by his purse. The bulk of all land relations hinges on investments of time, forethought, skill, and faith rather than on investments of cash. As a land-user thinketh, so is he.

I have purposely presented the land ethic as a product of social evo-   88
lution because nothing so important as an ethic is ever "written." Only the most superficial student of history supposes that Moses "wrote" the Decalogue; it evolved in the minds of a thinking community, and Moses wrote a tentative summary of it for a "seminar." I say tentative because evolution never stops.

The evolution of a land ethic is an intellectual as well as emotional   89
process. Conservation is paved with good intentions which prove to be futile, or even dangerous, because they are devoid of critical understanding either of the land, or of economic land-use. I think it is a truism that as the ethical frontier advances from the individual to the community, its intellectual content increases.

The mechanism of operation is the same for any ethic: social approba-   90
tion for right actions: social disapproval for wrong actions.

By and large, our present problem is one of attitudes and implements.   91
We are remodeling the Alhambra with a steam-shovel, and we are proud of our yardage. We shall hardly relinquish the shovel, which after all has many good points, but we are in need of gentler and more objective criteria for its successful use.

QUESTIONS FOR DISCUSSION AND WRITING

1. Explain what Leopold means by an "evolution" in our understanding of nature and humanity, and his notion of a "third element" (par. 8) in traditional ethics. How do these ideas relate to other key concepts in his essay, like community, citizenship, and conscience?

2. Leopold insisted, "In our attempt to make conservation easy, we have made it trivial" (par. 33) What evidence does he offer to explain or support this claim? What evidence would you offer to show that the same is or is not true today? Have we made conservation (or environmentalism) so easy that we have made it trivial?

3. Leopold argues that a serious response to our destruction of nature would require an internal change in our intellectual emphasis, loyalties, affections, and convictions" (par. 33). What proof does he offer that such changes had not yet happened in 1948, the year this essay was revised for publication? What proof would you offer that such changes have or have not happened since then?

RACHEL CARSON

Rachel Carson (1907–64) was educated as a marine biologist at the Pennsylvania College for Women and at John Hopkins University. She taught zoology at the University of Maryland from 1931 to 1936 and then worked as an aquatic biologist for the Bureau of Fisheries, later to become the Fish and Wildlife Service. In 1952 Carson resigned from her position in order to write full-time. By the time Silent Spring *was published in 1962, Carson had established herself as a respected research scientist and as a writer who could explain complex issues in clear and honest prose. Her earlier books,* Under the Sea Wind *(1941),* The Sea Around Us *(1951), and* Edge of the Sea *(1955), had been best-sellers and award winners. Her scientific reputation and her public acceptance would serve her well as the publication of* Silent Spring *threw Carson into a firestorm of controversy and public attacks. In a remarkable combination of good science and powerful prose, Carson had called out a warning: Whatever else they promised, pesticides were an invisible poison that threatened our water, our soil, our food, our children. Carson's warning came, of course, just as the chemical industry was promising safety and prosperity through better and stronger pesticides, like DDT. Threatened and embarrassed, the powerful business establishment responded quickly and viciously, attacking both Carson and her science. In the end, the attacks on her did not matter, and* Silent Spring *captured the attention of America in a way that few public documents ever have: It changed our politics and our laws, as even timid politicians were forced to act. More than that, however, it helped to change the way that people understood nature—as a complex and fragile living system.*

From *Silent Spring*

17. THE OTHER ROAD

We stand now where two roads diverge. But unlike the roads in Robert Frost's familiar poem, they are not equally fair. The road we have long been traveling is deceptively easy, a smooth superhighway on which we progress with great speed, but at its end lies disaster. The other fork of the road—the one "less traveled by"—offers our last, our only chance to reach a destination that assures the preservation of our earth. 1

The choice, after all, is ours to make. If, having endured much, we have at last asserted our "right to know," and if, knowing, we have concluded that we are being asked to take senseless and frightening risks, then we should no longer accept the counsel of those who tell us that we must fill 2 our world with poisonous chemicals; we should look about and see what other course is open to us.

A truly extraordinary variety of alternatives to the chemical control of insects is available. Some are already in use and have achieved brilliant success. Others are in the stage of laboratory testing. Still others are little more than ideas in the minds of imaginative scientists, waiting for the opportunity to put them to the test. All have this in common: they are *biological* solutions, based on understanding of the living organisms they seek to control, and of the whole fabric of life to which these organisms belong. Specialists representing various areas of the vast field of biology are contributing—entomologists, pathologists, geneticists, physiologists, biochemists, ecologists—all pouring their knowledge and their creative inspirations into the formation of a new science of biotic controls.

"Any science may be likened to a river," says a Johns Hopkins biologist, Professor Carl P. Swanson. "It has its obscure and unpretentious beginning; its quiet stretches as well as its rapids; its periods of drought as well as of fullness. It gathers momentum with the work of many investigators and as it is fed by other streams of thought; it is deepened and broadened by the concepts and generalizations that are gradually evolved."

So it is with the science of biological control in its modern sense. In America it had its obscure beginnings a century ago with the first attempts to introduce natural enemies of insects that were proving troublesome to farmers, an effort that sometimes moved slowly or not at all, but now and again gathered speed and momentum under the impetus of an outstanding success. It had its period of drought when workers in applied entomology, dazzled by the spectacular new insecticides of the 1940's, turned their backs on all biological methods and set foot on "the treadmill of chemical control." But the goal of an insect-free world continued to recede. Now at last, as it has become apparent that the heedless and unrestrained use of chemicals is a greater menace to ourselves than to the targets, the river which is the science of biotic control flows again, fed by new streams of thought.

Some of the most fascinating of the new methods are those that seek to turn the strength of a species against itself—to use the drive of an insect's life forces to destroy it. The most spectacular of these approaches is the "male sterilization" technique developed by the chief of the United States Department of Agriculture's Entomology Research Branch, Dr. Edward Knipling, and his associates.

About a quarter of a century ago Dr. Knipling startled his colleagues by proposing a unique method of insect control. If it were possible to sterilize and release large numbers of insects, he theorized, the sterilized males would, under certain conditions, compete with the normal wild males so successfully that, after repeated releases, only infertile eggs would be produced and the population would die out.

The proposal was met with bureaucratic inertia and with skepticism 8
from scientists, but the idea persisted in Dr. Knipling's mind. One major problem remained to be solved before it could be put to the test—a practical method of insect sterilization had to be found. Academically, the fact that insects could be sterilized by exposure to X-ray had been known since 1916, when an entomologist by the name of G. A. Runner reported such sterilization of cigarette beetles. Hermann Muller's pioneering work on the production of mutations by X-ray opened up vast new areas of thought in the late 1920's, and by the middle of the century various workers had reported the sterilization by X-rays or gamma rays of at least a dozen species of insects.

But these were laboratory experiments, still a long way from practical 9
application. About 1950, Dr. Knipling launched a serious effort to turn insect sterilization into a weapon that would wipe out a major insect enemy of livestock in the South, the screw-worm fly. The females of this species lay their eggs in any open wound of a warm-blooded animal. The hatching larvae are parasitic, feeding on the flesh of the host. A full-grown steer may succumb to a heavy infestation in 10 days, and livestock losses in the United States have been estimated at $40,000,000 a year. The toll of wildlife is harder to measure, but it must be great. Scarcity of deer in some areas of Texas is attributed to the screw-worm. This is a tropical or subtropical insect, inhabiting South and Central America and Mexico, and in the United States normally restricted to the Southwest. About 1933, however, it was accidentally introduced into Florida, where the climate allowed it to survive over winter and to establish populations. It even pushed into southern Alabama and Georgia, and soon the livestock industry of the southeastern states was faced with annual losses running to $20,000,000.

A vast amount of information on the biology of the screw-worm had 10
been accumulated over the years by Agriculture Department scientists in Texas. By 1954, after some preliminary field trials on Florida islands, Dr. Knipling was ready for a full-scale test of his theory. For this, by arrangement with the Dutch Government, he went to the island of Curaçao in the Caribbean, cut off from the mainland by at least 50 miles of sea.

Beginning in August 1954, screw-worms reared and sterilized in an 11
Agriculture Department laboratory in Florida were flown to Curaçao and released from airplanes at the rate of about 400 per square mile per week. Almost at once the number of egg masses deposited on experimental goats began to decrease, as did their fertility. Only seven weeks after the releases were started, all eggs were infertile. Soon it was impossible to find

a single egg mass, sterile or otherwise. The screw-worm had indeed been eradicated on Curaçao.

The resounding success of the Curaçao experiment whetted the appetites of Florida livestock raisers for a similar feat that would relieve them of the scourge of screw-worms. Although the difficulties here were relatively enormous—an area 300 times as large as the small Caribbean island—in 1957 the United States Department of Agriculture and the State of Florida joined in providing funds for an eradication effort. The project involved the weekly production of about 50 million screw-worms at a specially constructed "fly factory," the use of 20 light airplanes to fly prearranged flight patterns, five to six hours daily, each plane carrying a thousand paper cartons, each carton containing 200 to 400 irradiated flies. 12

The cold winter of 1957–58, when freezing temperatures gripped northern Florida, gave an unexpected opportunity to start the program while the screw-worm populations were reduced and confined to a small area. By the time the program was considered complete at the end of 17 months, $3\frac{1}{2}$ billion artificially reared, sterilized flies had been released over Florida and sections of Georgia and Alabama. The last-known animal wound infestation that could be attributed to screw-worms occurred in February 1959. In the next few weeks several adults were taken in traps. Thereafter no trace of the screw-worm could be discovered. Its extinction in the Southeast had been accomplished—a triumphant demonstration of the worth of scientific creativity, aided by thorough basic research, persistence; and determination. 13

Now a quarantine barrier in Mississippi seeks to prevent the reentrance of the screw-worm from the Southwest, where it is firmly entrenched. Eradication there would be a formidable undertaking, considering the vast areas involved and the probability of re-invasion from Mexico. Nevertheless, the stakes are high and the thinking in the Department seems to be that some sort of program, designed at least to hold the screw-worm populations at very low levels, may soon be attempted in Texas and other infested areas of the Southwest. 14

The brilliant success of the screw-worm campaign has stimulated tremendous interest in applying the same methods to other insects. Not all, of course, are suitable subjects for this technique, much depending on details of the life history, population density, and reactions to radiation. 15

Experiments have been undertaken by the British in the hope that the method could be used against the tsetse fly in Rhodesia. This insect infests about a third of Africa, posing a menace to human health and preventing the keeping of livestock in an area of some $4\frac{1}{2}$ million square miles of wooded grasslands. The habits of the tsetse differ considerably from those of the screw-worm fly, and although it can be sterilized by radiation some 16 technical difficulties remain to be worked out before the method can be applied.

The British have already tested a large number of other species for sus-   17
ceptibility to radiation. United States scientists have had some encouraging early results with the melon fly and the oriental and Mediterranean
fruit flies in laboratory tests in Hawaii and field tests on the remote island
of Rota. The corn borer and the sugarcane borer are also being tested.
There are possibilities, too, that insects of medical importance might be
controlled by sterilization. A Chilean scientist has pointed out that malaria-
carrying mosquitoes persist in his country in spite of insecticide treatment;
the release of sterile males might then provide the final blow needed to
eliminate this population.

The obvious difficulties of sterilizing by radiation have led to the search   18
for an easier method of accomplishing similar results, and there is now a
strongly running tide of interest in chemical sterilants.

Scientists at the Department of Agriculture laboratory in Orlando,   19
Florida, are new sterilizing the housefly in laboratory experiments and
even in some field trials, using chemicals incorporated in suitable foods.
In a test on an island in the Florida Keys in 1961, a population of flies was
nearly wiped out within a period of only five weeks. Repopulation of
course followed from nearby islands, but as a pilot project the test was
successful. The Department's excitement about the promise of this
method is easily understood. In the first place, as we have seen, the
housefly has now become virtually uncontrollable by insecticides. A completely new method of control is undoubtedly needed. One of the problems of sterilization by radiation is that this requires not only artificial
rearing but the release of sterile males in larger number than are present
in the wild population. This could be done with the screw-worm, which
is actually not an abundant insect. With the housefly, however, more than
doubling the population through releases could be highly objectionable,
even though the increase would be only temporary. A chemical sterilant,
on the other hand, could be combined with a bait substance and introduced into the natural environment of the fly; insects feeding on it would
become sterile and in the course of time the sterile flies would predominate and the insects would breed themselves out of existence.

The testing of chemicals for a sterilizing effect is much more difficult   20
than the testing of chemical poisons. It takes 30 days to evaluate one
chemical—although, of course, a number of tests can be run concur-
rently. Yet between April 1958 and December 1961 several hundred
chemicals were screened at the Orlando laboratory for a possible sterilizing effect. The Department of Agriculture seems happy to have found
among these even a handful of chemicals that show promise.

Now other laboratories of the Department are taking up the problem, 21
testing chemicals against stable flies, mosquitoes, boll weevils, and an assortment of fruit flies. All this is presently experimental but in the few
years since work began on chemosterilants the project has grown enormously. In theory it has many attractive features. Dr. Knipling has pointed
out that effective chemical insect sterilization "might easily outdo some of
the best of known insecticides." Take an imaginary situation in which a
population of a million insects is multiplying five times in each generation.
An insecticide might kill 90 per cent of each generation, leaving 125,000
insects alive after the third generation. In contrast, a chemical that would
produce 90 percent sterility would leave only 125 insects alive.

On the other side of the coin is the fact that some extremely potent 22
chemicals are involved. It is fortunate that at least during these early stages
most of the men working with chemosterilants seem mindful of the need
to find safe chemicals and safe methods of application. Nonetheless, sug-
gestions are heard here and there that these sterilizing chemicals might
be applied as aerial sprays—for example, to coat the foliage chewed by
gypsy moth larvae. To attempt any such procedure without thorough advance research on the hazards involved would be the height of irrespon-
sibility. If the potential hazards of the chemosterilants are not constantly
borne in mind we could easily find ourselves in even worse trouble than
that now created by the insecticides.

The sterilants currently being tested fall generally into two groups, both 23
of which are extremely interesting in their mode of action. The first are intimately related to the life processes, or metabolism, of the cell; i.e., they
so closely resemble a substance the cell or tissue needs that the organism
"mistakes" them for the true metabolite and tries to incorporate them in its
normal building processes. But the fit is wrong in some detail and the
process comes to a halt. Such chemicals are called antimetabolites.

The second group consists of chemicals that act on the chromosomes, 24
probably affecting the gene chemicals and causing the chromosomes to
break up. The chemosterilants of this group are alkylating agents, which
are extremely reactive chemicals, capable of intense cell destruction, damage to chromosomes, and production of mutations. It is the view of Dr.
Peter Alexander of the Chester Beatty Research Institute in London that
"any alkylating agent which is effective in sterilizing insects would also be
a powerful mutagen and carcinogen." Dr. Alexander feels that any conceivable use of such chemicals in insect control would be "open to the
most severe objections." It is to be hoped, therefore, that the present experiments will lead not to actual use of these particular chemicals but to
the discovery of others that will be safe and also highly specific in their action on the target insect.

Some of the most interesting of the recent work is concerned with still 25 other ways of forging weapons from the insect's own life processes. Insects produce a variety of venoms, attractants, repellents. What is the chemical nature of these secretions? Could we make use of them as, perhaps, very selective insecticides? Scientists at Cornell University and elsewhere are trying to find answers to some of these questions, studying the defense mechanisms by which many insects protect themselves from attack by predators, working out the chemical structure of insect secretions. Other scientists are working on the so-called "juvenile hormone," a powerful substance which prevents metamorphosis of the larval insect until the proper stage of growth has been reached.

Perhaps the most immediately useful result of this exploration of insect secretion is the development of lures, or attractants. Here again, nature has pointed the way. The gypsy moth is an especially intriguing example. The female moth is too heavy-bodied to fly. She lives on or near the ground, fluttering about among low vegetation or creeping up tree trunks. The male, on the contrary, is a strong flier and is attracted even from considerable distances by a scent released by the female from special glands. Entomologists have taken advantage of this fact for a good many years, laboriously preparing this sex attractant from the bodies of the female moths. It was then used in traps set for the males in census operations along the fringe of the insect's range. But this was an extremely expensive procedure. Despite the much publicized infestations in the northeastern states, there were not enough gypsy moths to provide the material, and hand-collected female pupae had to be imported from Europe, sometimes at a cost of half a dollar per tip. It was a tremendous breakthrough, therefore, when, after years of effort, chemists of the Agriculture Department recently succeeded in isolating the attractant. Following upon this discovery was the successful preparation of a closely related synthetic material from a constituent of castor oil; this not only deceives the male moths but is apparently fully as attractive as the natural substance. As little as one microgram (1/1000 gram) in a trap is an effective lure.

26

All this is of much more than academic interest, for the new and economical "gyplure" might be used not merely in census operations but in control work. Several of the more attractive possibilities are now being tested. In what might be termed an experiment in psychological warfare, the attractant is combined with a granular material and distributed by planes. The aim is to confuse the male moth and alter the normal behavior so that, in the welter of attractive scents, he cannot find the true scent trail leading to the female. This line of attack is being carried even further in experiments aimed at deceiving the male into attempting to mate with a spurious female. In the laboratory, male gypsy moths have attempted copulation with chips of wood, vermiculite, and other small, inanimate objects, so long as they were suitably impregnated with gyplure. Whether

27

such diversion of the mating instinct into nonproductive channels would actually serve to reduce the population remains to be tested, but it is an interesting possibility.

The gypsy moth lure was the first insect sex attractant to be synthe- 28 sized, but probably there will soon be others. A number of agricultural insects are being studied for possible attractants that man could imitate. Encouraging results have been obtained with the Hessian fly and the tobacco hornworm.

Combinations of attractants and poisons are being tried against several 29 insect species. Government scientists have developed an attractant called methyl-eugenol, which males of the oriental fruit fly and the melon fly find irresistible. This has been combined with a poison in tests in the Bonin Islands 450 miles south of Japan. Small pieces of fiberboard were impregnated with the two chemicals and were distributed by air over the entire island chain to attract and kill the male flies. This program of "male annihilation" was begun in 1960: a year later the Agriculture Department estimated that more than 99 percent of the population had been eliminated. The method as here applied seems to have marked advantages over the conventional broadcasting of insecticides. The poison, an organic phosphorus chemical, is confined to squares of fiberboard which are unlikely to be eaten by wildlife; its residues, moreover, are quickly dissipated and so are not potential contaminants of soil or water.

But not all communication in the insect world is by scents that lure or 30 repel. Sound also may be a warning or an attraction. The constant stream of ultrasonic sound that issues from a bat in flight (serving as a radar system to guide it through darkness) is heard by certain moths, enabling them to avoid capture. The wing sounds of approaching parasitic flies warn the larvae of some sawflies to herd together for protection. On the other hand, the sounds made by certain wood-boring insects enable their parasites to find them, and to the male mosquito the wing-beat of the female is a siren song.

What use, if any, can be made of this ability of the insect to detect and 31 react to sound? As yet in the experimental stage, but nonetheless interesting, is the initial success in attracting male mosquitoes to playback recordings of the flight sound of the female. The males were lured to a charged grid and so killed. The repellent effect of bursts of ultrasonic sound is being tested in Canada against corn borer and cutworm moths. Two authorities on animal sound, Professors Hubert and Mable Frings of the University of Hawaii, believe that a field method of influencing the behavior of insects with sound only awaits discovery of the proper key to unlock and apply the vast existing knowledge of insect sound production and reception. Repellent sounds may offer greater possibilities than attractants. The Fringses are known for their discovery that starlings scatter in alarm before a recording of the distress cry of one of their fellows; perhaps somewhere in this fact is a central truth that may be applied to insects. To practical men of industry the possibilities seem real enough so that at least one major electronic corporation is preparing to set up a laboratory to test them.

Sound is also being tested as an agent of direct destruction. Ultrasonic   32
sound will kill all mosquito larvae in a laboratory tank; however, it kills the aquatic organisms as well. In other experiments, blowflies, mealworms, and yellow fever mosquitoes have been killed by airborne ultrasonic sound in a matter of seconds. All such experiments are first steps toward wholly new concepts of insect control which the miracles of electronics may some day make a reality.

The new biotic control of insects is not wholly a matter of electronics   33
and gamma radiation and other products of man's inventive mind. Some of its methods have ancient roots, based on the knowledge that, like ourselves, insects are subject to disease. Bacterial infections sweep through their populations like the plagues of old; under the onset of a virus their hordes sicken and die. The occurrence of disease in insects was known before the time of Aristotle; the maladies of the silkworm were celebrated in medieval poetry; and through study of the diseases of this same insect the first understanding of the principles of infectious disease came to Pasteur.

Insects are beset not only by viruses and bacteria but also by fungi, pro-   34
tozoa, microscopic worms, and other beings from all that unseen world of minute life that, by and large, befriends mankind. For the microbes include not only disease organisms but those that destroy waste matter, make soils fertile, and enter into countless biological processes like fermentation and nitrification. Why should they not also aid us in the control of insects?

One of the first to envision such use of microorganisms was the 19th-   35
century zoologist Elie Metchnikoff. During the concluding decades of the 19th and the first half of the 20h centuries the idea of microbial control was slowly taking form. The first conclusive proof that an insect could be brought under control by introducing a disease into its environment came in the late 1930's with the discovery and use of milky disease for the Japanese beetle, which is caused by the spores of a bacterium belonging to the genus *Bacillus*. This classic example of bacterial control has a long history of use in the eastern part of the United States.

High hopes now attend tests of another bacterium of this genus—   36
Bacillus thuringiensis—originally discovered in Germany in 1911 in the province of Thuringia, where it was found to cause a fatal septicemia in the larvae of the flour moth. This bacterium actually kills by poisoning

rather than by disease. Within its vegetative rods there are formed, along with spores, peculiar crystals composed of a protein substance highly toxic to certain insects, especially to the larvae of the mothlike lepidopteras. Shortly after eating foliage coated with this toxin the larva suffers paralysis, stops feeding, and soon dies. For practical purposes, the fact that feeding is interrupted promptly is of course an enormous advantage, for crop damage stops almost as soon as the pathogen is applied. Compounds containing spores of *Bacillus thuringiensis* are now being manufactured by several firms in the United States under various trade names. Field tests are being made in several countries in France and Germany against larvae of the cabbage butterfly, in Yugoslavia against the fall webworm, in the Soviet Union against a tent caterpillar. In Panama, where tests were begun in 1961, this bacterial insecticide may be the answer to one or more of the serious problems confronting banana growers. There the root borer is a serious pest of the banana, so weakening its roots that the trees are easily toppled by wind. Dieldrin has been the only chemical effective against the borer, but it has now set in motion a chain of disaster. The borers are becoming resistant. The chemical has also destroyed some important insect predators and so has caused an increase in the tortricids—small, stout-bodied moths whose larvae scar the surface of the bananas. There is reason to hope the new microbial insecticide will eliminate both the tortricids and the borers and that it will do so without upsetting natural controls.

In eastern forests of Canada and the United States bacterial insecticides 37 may be one important answer to the problems of such forest insects as the budworms and the gypsy moth. In 1960 both countries began field tests with a commercial preparation of *Bacillus thuringiensis*. Some of the early results have been encouraging. In Vermont, for example, the end results of bacterial control were as good as those obtained with DDT. The main technical problem now is to find a carrying solution that will stick the bacterial spores to the needless of the evergreens. On crops this is not a problem—even a dust can be used. Bacterial insecticides have already been tried on a wide variety of vegetables, especially in California.

Meanwhile, other perhaps less spectacular work is concerned with 38 viruses. Here and there in California fields of young alfalfa are being sprayed with a substance as deadly as any insecticide for the destructive alfalfa caterpillar—a solution containing a virus obtained from the bodies of caterpillars that have died because of infection with this exceedingly virulent disease. The bodies of only five diseased caterpillars provide enough virus to eat an acre of alfalfa. In some Canadian forests a virus that affects pine sawflies has proved so effective in control that it has replaced insecticides.

Scientists in Czechoslovakia are experimenting with protozoa against 39 webworms and other insect pests, and in the United States a protozoan parasite has been found to reduce the egg-laying potential of the corn borer.

To some the term microbial insecticide may conjure up pictures of bac-   40
terial warfare that would endanger other forms of life. This is not true. In contrast to chemicals, insect pathogens are harmless to all but their intended targets. Dr. Edward Steinhaus, an outstanding authority on insect pathology, has stated emphatically that there is "no authenticated recorded instance of a true insect pathogen having caused an infectious disease in a vertebrate animal either experimentally or in nature." The insect pathogens are so specific that they infect only a small group of insects— sometimes a single species. Biologically they do not belong to the type of organisms that cause disease in higher animals or in plants. Also, as Dr. Steinhaus points out, outbreaks of insect disease in nature always remain confined to insects, affecting neither the host plants nor animals feeding on them.

Insects have many natural enemies—not only microbes of many kinds   41
but other insects. The first suggestion that an insect might be controlled by encouraging its enemies is generally credited to Erasmus Darwin about 1800. Probably because it was the first generally practiced method of biological control, this setting of one insect against another is widely but erroneously thought to be the only alternative to chemicals.

In the United States the true beginnings of conventional biological con-   42
trol date from 1888 when Albert Koebele, the first of a growing army of entomologist explorers, went to Australia to search for natural enemies of the cottony cushion scale that threatened the California citrus industry with destruction. The mission was crowned with spectacular success, and in the century that followed the world has been combed for natural enemies to control the insects that have come uninvited to our shores. In all, about 100 species of imported predators and parasites have become established. Besides the vedalia beetles brought in by Koebele, other importations have been highly successful. A wasp imported from Japan established complete control of an insect attacking eastern apple orchards. Several natural enemies of the spotted alfalfa aphid, an accidental import from the Middle East, are credited with saving the California alfalfa industry. Parasites and predators of the gypsy moth achieved good control, as did the *Tiphia* wasp against the Japanese beetle. Biological control of scales and mealy bugs is estimated to save California several millions of dollars a year—indeed, one of the leading entomologists of that state, Dr. Paul DeBach, has estimated that for an investment of $4,000,000 in biological control work California has received a return of $100,000,000.

Examples of successful biological control of serious pests by importing   43
their natural enemies are to be found in some 40 countries distributed

over much of the world. The advantages of such control over chemicals are obvious: it is relatively inexpensive, it is permanent, it leaves no poisonous residues. Yet biological control has suffered from lack of support. California is virtually alone among the states in having a formal program in biological control, and many states have not even one entomologist who devotes full time to it. Perhaps for want of support biological control through insect enemies has not always been carried out with the scientific thoroughness it requires—exacting studies of its impact on the populations of insect prey have seldom been made, and releases have not always been made with the precision that might spell the difference between success and failure.

The predator and the preyed upon exist not alone, but as a part of a   44
vast web of life, all of which needs to be taken into account. Perhaps the opportunities for the more conventional types of biological control are greatest in the forests. The farmlands of modern agriculture are highly artificial, unlike anything nature ever conceived. But the forests are a different world, much closer to natural environments. Here, with a minimum of help and a maximum of noninterference from man, Nature can have her way, setting up all that wonderful and intricate system of checks and balances that protects the forest from undue damage by insects.

In the United States our foresters seem to have thought of biological   45
control chiefly in terms of introducing insect parasites and predators. The Canadians take a broader view, and some of the Europeans have gone farthest of all to develop the science of "forest hygiene" to an amazing extent. Birds, ants, forest spiders, and soil bacteria are as much a part of a forest as the trees, in the view of European foresters, who take care to inoculate a new forest with these protective factors. The encouragement of birds is one of the first steps. In the modern era of intensive forestry the old hollow trees are gone and with them homes for woodpeckers and other tree-nesting birds. This lack is met by nesting boxes, which draw the birds back into the forest. Other boxes are specially designed for owls and for bats, so that these creatures may take over in the dark hours the work of insect hunting performed in daylight by the small birds.

But this is only the beginning. Some of the most fascinating control   46
work in European forests employs the forest red ant as an aggressive insect predator—a species which, unfortunately, does not occur in North America. About 25 years ago Professor Karl Gösswald of the University of Würzburg developed a method of cultivating this ant and establishing colonies. Under his direction more than 10,000 colonies of the red ant have been established in about 90 test areas in the German Federal Republic. Dr. Gösswald's method has been adopted in Italy and other countries, where ant farms have been established to supply colonies for

distribution in the forests. In the Apennines, for example, several hundred nests have been set out to protect reforested areas.

"Where you can obtain in your forest a combination of birds' and ants' protection together with some bats and owls, the biological equilibrium has already been essentially improved," says Dr. Heinz Ruppertshofen, a forestry officer in Mölln, Germany, who believes that a single introduced predator or parasite is less effective than an array of the "natural companions" of the trees.   47

New ant colonies in the forests at Mölln are protected from woodpeckers by wire netting to reduce the toll. In this way the woodpeckers, which have increased by 400 per cent in 10 years in some of the test areas, do not seriously reduce the ant colonies, and pay handsomely for what they take by picking harmful caterpillars off the trees. Much of the work of caring for the ant colonies (and the birds' nesting boxes as well) is assumed by a youth corps from the local school, children 10 to 14 years old. The costs are exceedingly low; the benefits amount to permanent protection of forests.   48

Another extremely interesting feature of Dr. Ruppertshofen's work is his use of spiders, in which he appears to be a pioneer. Although there is a large literature on the classification and natural history of spiders, it is scattered and fragmentary and deals not at all with their value as an agent of biological control. Of the 22,000 known kinds of spiders, 760 are native to Germany (and about 2000 to the United States). Twenty-nine families of spiders inhabit German forests.   49

To a forester the most important fact about a spider is the kind of net it builds. The wheel-net spiders are most important, for the webs of some of them are so narrow-meshed that they can catch all flying insects. A large web (up to 16 inches in diameter) of the cross spider bears some 120,000 adhesive modules on its strands. A single spider may destroy in her life of 18 months an average of 2000 insects. A biologically sound forest has 50 to 150 spiders to the square meter (a little more than a square yard). Where there are fewer, the deficiency may be remedied by collecting and distributing the baglike cocoons containing the eggs. "Three cocoons of the wasp spider [which occurs also in America] yield a thousand spiders, which can catch 200,000 flying insects," says Dr. Ruppertshofen. The tiny and delicate young of the wheel-net spiders that emerge in the spring are especially important, he says, "as they spin in a teamwork a net umbrella above the top shoots of the trees and thus protect the young shoots against the flying insects." As the spiders molt and grow, the net is enlarged.   50

Canadian biologists have pursued rather similar lines of investigation, although with differences dictated by the fact that North American forests   51 are largely natural rather than planted, and that the species available as aids in maintaining a healthy forest are somewhat different. The emphasis in Canada is on small mammals, which are amazingly effective in the control of certain insects, especially those that live within the spongy soil of the forest floor. Among such insects are the sawflies, so-called because the female has a saw-shaped ovipositor with which she slits open the needles of evergreen trees in order to deposit her eggs. The larvae eventually drop to the ground and form cocoons in the peat of tamarack bogs or the duff under spruce or pines. But beneath the forest floor is a world honeycombed with the tunnels and runways of small mammals—whitefooted mice, voles, and shrews of various species. Of all these small burrowers, the voracious shrews find and consume the largest number of sawfly cocoons. They feed by placing a forefoot on the cocoon and biting off the end, showing an extraordinary ability to discriminate between sound and empty cocoons. And for their insatiable appetite the shrews have no rivals. Whereas a vole can consume about 200 cocoons a day, a shrew, depending on the species, may devour up to 800! This may result, according to laboratory tests, in destruction of 75 to 98 per cent of the cocoons present.

It is not surprising that the island of Newfoundland, which has no 52 native shrews but is beset with sawflies, so eagerly desired some of these small, efficient mammals that in 1958 the introduction of the masked shrew—the most efficient sawfly predator—was attempted. Canadian officials report in 1962 that the attempt has been successful. The shrews are multiplying and are spreading out over the island, some marked individuals have been recovered as much as ten miles from the point of release.

There is, then, a whole battery of armaments available to the forester 53 who is willing to look for permanent solutions that preserve and strengthen the natural relations in the forest. Chemical pest control in the forest is at best a stopgap measure bringing no real solution, at worst killing the fishes in the forest streams, bringing on plagues of insects, and destroying the natural controls and those we may be trying to introduce. By such violent measures, says Dr. Ruppertshofen, "the partnership for life of the forest is entirely being unbalanced, and the catastrophes caused by parasites repeat in shorter and shorter periods.... We, therefore, have to put an end to these unnatural manipulations brought into the most important and almost last natural living space which has been left for us."

Through all these new, imaginative, and creative approaches to the 54 problem of sharing our earth with other creatures there runs a constant theme, the awareness that we are dealing with life—with living populations and all their pressures and counterpressures, their surges and recessions. Only by taking account of such life forces and by cautiously seeking to guide them into channels favorable to ourselves can we hope to achieve a reasonable accommodation between the insect hordes and ourselves.

The current vogue for poisons has failed utterly to take into account   55
these most fundamental considerations. As crude a weapon as the cave man's club, the chemical barrage has been hurled against the fabric of life—a fabric on the one hand delicate and destructible, on the other miraculously tough and resilient, and capable of striking back in unexpected ways. These extraordinary capacities of life have been ignored by the practitioners of chemical control who have brought to their task no "high-minded orientation," no humility before the vast forces with which they tamper.

The "control of nature" is a phrase conceived in arrogance, born of the   56
Neanderthal age of biology and philosophy, when it was supposed that nature exists for the convenience of man. The concepts and practices of applied entomology for the most part date from that Stone Age of science. It is our alarming misfortune that so primitive a science has armed itself with the most modern and terrible weapons, and that in turning them against the insects it has also turned them against the earth.

QUESTIONS FOR DISCUSSION AND WRITING

1. *Silent Spring* was intended to shock and outrage the American public as it showed how modern society had come to threaten the natural world. But Carson also offered a hopeful alternative, what she calls here "The Other Road." What are the key ideas of this "other road"? Does Carson suggest what cost or sacrifice this alternative road would require? How hopeful was Carson that modern society would choose this other road? How hopeful are you?

2. Carson clearly demonstrates that modern science created the chemical poisons that threaten the natural world, but is this reading an attack on science? What is Carson's attitude toward science and scientists? What role does science have to play in solving the very problems it helped to create? How would you characterize our contemporary attitudes about science? What role do we imagine for science in solving our environmental problems?

3. Chemical poisons are, Carson argues, "as crude a weapon as the cave man's club" (par. 53). She offers instead what she calls a "partnership for life" (par. 55) in the forests and fields. Use some of Carson's examples to explain and illustrate the nature of this partnership.

4

CONSTRUCTING
NATURE
IN WORDS

———◆———

RECENT POETRY, FICTION, AND CREATIVE NONFICTION

THEODORE ROOSEVELT

Perhaps more than any other figure in this book, Theodore Roosevelt (1858–1919) stands as a symbol of America at the beginning of the twentieth century: good-hearted and confident (perhaps even overbearing at times); physically impressive; tireless in his enthusiasms. Roosevelt was a prominent political figure who served as president of the United States (from 1901 to 1909) and as governor of New York, but he was also a world adventurer, a soldier, an avid big-game hunter, and an amateur naturalist in the tradition of Thomas Jefferson and John Audubon. Throughout his adult life, Roosevelt pursued adventure from the Amazon to Africa; much of his time, however, was spent riding and hunting in the open spaces of the American West. Roosevelt chronicled his outdoor adventures in a series of popular books, including Ranch Life and the Hunting-Trail *(1888),* African Game Trails *(1910), and* Through the Brazilian Wilderness *(1914). In* The Strenuous Life *(1900), Roosevelt outlined his common-sense philosophy (almost a religion, really) of "manly virtues" and what one critic has called "muscular Christianity." For this, and for his influence on the modern preservation movement, Roosevelt has always been a source of both admiration and controversy. On the one hand, while other naturalists courted public opinion through their writing, the presidency allowed Roosevelt to protect huge tracts of undeveloped lands, like Yellowstone Park. On the other hand, Roosevelt's attitudes toward nature were seen by his critics as largely utilitarian and paternalistic. In "Wilderness Reserves: Yellowstone Park" (1905), he writes of nature primarily as a worthy foe against which to test oneself, or as an increasingly scarce resource whose primary value is its usefulness to humans.*

Wilderness Reserves: Yellowstone Park

The most striking and melancholy feature in connection with American   1
big game is the rapidity with which it has vanished. When, just before the
outbreak of the Revolutionary War, the rifle-bearing hunters of the backwoods first penetrated the great forests west of the Alleghanies, deer, elk,
black bear, and even buffalo, swarmed in what are now the States of
Kentucky and Tennessee and the country north of the Ohio was a great
and almost virgin hunting-ground. From that day to this the shrinkage has
gone on, only partially checked here and there, and never arrested as a
whole. As a matter of historical accuracy, however, it is well to bear in
mind that many writers, in lamenting this extinction of the game, have
from time to time anticipated or overstated the facts. Thus as good an author as Colonel Richard Irving Dodge spoke of the buffalo as practically

T he last half of the twentieth century has seen the increasing incursion of civilization on nature. Within the last fifty years, we have developed the ability not only to destroy the earth with nuclear weapons but also to alter its climate and pollute the entire planet, as well as parts of space. Along with, and perhaps partly as a result of, this incursion, America has also seen a tremendous growth in its natural wealth. But in spite of this wealth, many people who write about nature find the culture we have created empty, mercenary, and alienating. For them, the endless pursuit of consumer goods at whatever cost destroys any deeper meaning in life. Living for the moment and taking whatever they can get right away leaves them feeling disconnected from the world and the people around them, drifting with a vague sense of uneasiness and unhappiness.

These writers try to find something in nature that will relieve the modern sense of alienation and give a foundation to our experience. In a world where everything seems relative, nature can provide a place to find certainties. In many ways, these writers are the descendants of the early writers on nature and the human spirit even though they are writing today within a drastically changed context. These modern nature writers are still concerned with nature as a place of spiritual redemption, but their concerns are shaped by other issues in our society, issues such as the counterculture of the 1960s and 1970s, the struggle of Native Americans to find a place in our society, the conflict between our national government and the rights of states, and a host of other struggles and conflicts in our culture. They look to nature for lessons on how to deal with the difficulties before us. Nature serves as a refuge and a source of wisdom and strength.

Jack Kerouac was one of the first writers to struggle with the alienation of our time. Although the late 1950s and early 1960s were for many people times of financial growth, security, and happiness, Kerouac sensed the growing purposelessness in the culture, and he reacted against it. His usual method of escaping the pressures for conformity around him was to travel around America by the least expensive means possible, staying in cheap hotels and talking with everybody he met, but he also could find spiritual guidance in an isolated natural setting. His escape to the top of Desolation Mountain let him shake off the confusing noise of our culture.

Instead of trying to escape modern culture, N. Scott Momaday seeks an alternative view of the world in Native American ways. Like his mother, who was not a Native American, he consciously chooses this way of looking at the world because of the vision it provides. He was among the first in modern times to look toward Native American poetry, myth, and history in order to combine them with his personal experience. From this mixture he creates a perspective that allows him to overcome the modern division between humans and the natural world.

Like Momaday, who writes about Oklahoma, Edward Abbey was drawn to the open landscape of the American interior. He chose to honor and protect our great southwestern deserts, fighting with a fierce anger against anybody who threatened to destroy or even change their natural beauty. Abbey's *Monkey Wrench Gang* helped convince radical environmentalists, such as the members of Earth First!, that it is impossible to stop the destruction of the earth through normal political channels. In order to preserve what is left of the natural world, the members of the Monkey Wrench Gang engage in *egotage,* the illegal destruction of the machinery used to harm the earth.

Norman Maclean writes not out of a fierce anger but instead out of his great love for the Montana wilderness as it existed in the early twentieth century. He describes a way of life that is gone, showing us both the strict religious beliefs he grew up with and the discipline necessary to survive in that time and place. "A River Runs Through It" argues passionately for the connections to be found in nature, connections among trout fishing, religion, the rocks under the river, and eternity.

Although Annie Dillard also loves nature greatly, she doesn't look back in time but rather looks closely at a shallow suburban pond to find a bit of the wildness left there. In the tenacity of a weasel she sees an image of something lacking in our lives. She writes, "A weasel lives as he's meant to, yielding at every moment to the perfect freedom of single necessity." The desire to yield to a single necessity can be especially strong when we feel pulled in a variety of directions by the demands of home, school or work, friends, and the numerous other interests many of us have.

Leslie Marmon Silko, writing almost twenty years after Momaday published *The Way to Rainy Mountain,* also looks to Native American culture for a way to live in harmony with nature. Instead of combining poetry, myth, history, and personal reminiscences, she takes a long and hard look at the Pueblo imagination, finding it very different from the typical Western imagination. The Pueblo people, Silko shows, never make the distinction between the self and the world around it, a distinction that is crucial in Western thought and philosophy. She also shows that within the Pueblo imagination stories serve an important function, giving meaning and resonance to the land while conveying practical information.

The landscape and the lessons to be learned from it are the focus of Gretel Ehrlich's work. In the seasonal changes of the Wyoming countryside, she finds resolutions to some of the difficulties in her life. Ehrlich starts her essay in autumn, when she sees "this rain and snow bending green branches, this turning of light to shadow in my throat, these bird-notes going flat." She then returns to the spring preceding this autumn and works her way back to the snows of winter. By following this progression of the seasons, she comes to terms with death and loneliness. Nature becomes for her a place where she can go to find both understanding and solace.

This chapter ends by turning from the broad strokes of fiction and the essay to the fine lines that poetry paints so well. Three of the four poems, "Approaching August," "Rough Country," and "Sleeping in the Forest," look to nature for renewal and harmony. Moving beyond the logic of prose, they reach for knowledge that is difficult to put into words, drawing us into moments when we are close to nature. The fourth poem, "Names," is a partly ironic, partly serious elegy for the species we have destroyed. The listening of the names of these species inscribes in our minds the consequences of our acts.

JACK KEROUAC

Jack Kerouac (1922–1969) was one of the most prominent members of the "Beat generation," a group of poets and writers working during the 1950s in America. The members of the Beat generation struggled against what they saw as the stifling conformity around them, writing about their experiences with drugs, alcohol, sex, and music. As the title of his most famous work would have it, Kerouac spent much of his life "on the road," traveling by car, train, or bus; staying with friends or in the cheapest accommodations possible; meeting people from all walks of life; and always living life to the fullest.

Kerouac can be seen as a descendant of Thoreau, Emerson, and Whitman, and as an ancestor of the hippies of the 1960s and 1970s. Unlike Thoreau, Kerouac did not spend much time in nature, but he did spend the summer of 1956 as a fire lookout on Desolation Mountain in Washington State. "Alone on a Mountaintop" (1960), which is from Lonesome Traveler, *describes his experiences there. As a self-professed city boy, Kerouac had some trouble getting used to the isolation, but when he did, he came to see the beauty of the place. Like the nineteenth-century transcendentalists, Kerouac was influenced by Eastern religions, and under this influence he came to see the close connections between human beings and nature.*

Alone on a Mountaintop

After all this kind of fanfare, and even more, I came to a point where I needed solitude and just stop the machine of "thinking" and "enjoying" what they call "living," I just wanted to lie in the grass and look at the clouds— 1

They say, too, in ancient scripture:—"Wisdom can only be obtained from the viewpoint of solitude." 2

And anyway I was sick and tired of all the ships and railroads and Times Squares of all time— 3

I applied with the U.S. Agriculture Department for a job as a fire lookout in the Mount Baker National Forest in the High Cascades of the Great Northwest. 4

Just to look at these words made me shiver to think of cool pine trees by a morning lake. 5

I beat my way out to Seattle three thousand miles from the heat and dust of eastern cities in June. 6

Anybody who's been to Seattle and missed Alaskan Way, the old water front, has missed the point—here the totem-pole stores, the waters of 7

Puget Sound washing under old piers, the dark gloomy look of ancient warehouses and pier sheds, and the most antique locomotives in America switching boxcars up and down the water front, give a hint, under the pure cloud-mopped sparkling skies of the Northwest, of great country to come. Driving north from Seattle on Highway 99 is an exciting experience because suddenly you see the Cascade Mountains rising on the northeast horizon, truly *Komo Kulshan* under their uncountable snows.—The great peaks covered with trackless white, worlds of huge rock twisted and heaped and sometimes almost spiraled into fantastic unbelievable shapes.

All this is seen far above the dreaming fields of the Stilaquamish and   8
Skagit valleys, agricultural flats of peaceful green, the soil so rich and dark it is proudly referred to by inhabitants as second only to the Nile in fertility. At Milltown Washington your car rolls over the bridge across the Skagit River.—To the left—seaward, westward—the Skagit flows into Skagit Bay and the Pacific Ocean.—At Burlington you turn right and head for the heart of the mountains along a rural valley road through sleepy little towns and one bustling agricultural market center known as Sedro-Woolley with hundreds of cars parked aslant on a typical country-town Main Street of hardware stores, grain-and-feed stores and five-and-tens.—On deeper into the deepening valley, cliffs rich with timber appearing by the side of the road, the narrowing river rushing more swiftly now, a pure translucent green like the green of the ocean on a cloudy day but a saltless rush of melted snow from the High Cascades—almost good enough to drink north of Marblemount.—The road curves more and more till you reach Concrete, the last town in Skagit Valley with a bank and a five-and-ten— after that the mountains rising secretly behind foothills are so close that now you don't see them but begin to feel them more and more.

At Marblemount the river is a swift torrent, the work of the quiet moun-   9
tains.—Fallen logs beside the water provide good seats to enjoy a river wonderland, leaves jiggling in the good clean northwest wind seem to re- joice, the topmost trees on nearby timbered peaks swept and dimmed by low-flying clouds seem contented.—The clouds assume the faces of her- mits or of nuns, or sometimes look like sad dog acts hurrying off into the wings over the horizon.—Snags struggle and gurgle in the heaving bulk of the river.—Logs rush by at twenty miles an hour. The air smells of pine and sawdust and bark and mud and twigs—birds flash over the water looking for secret fish.

As you drive north across the bridge at Marblemount and on to   10
Newhalem the road narrows and twists until finally the Skagit is seen pouring over rocks, frothing, and small creeks come tumbling from steep hillsides and pile right in.—The mountains rise on all sides, only their shoulders and ribs visible, their heads out of sight and now snowcapped.

At Newhalem extensive road construction raises a cloud of dust over   11 shacks and cats and rigs, the dam there is the first in a series that create the Skagit watershed which provides all the power for Seattle.

The road ends at Diablo, a peaceful company settlement of neat cot- 12 tages and green lawns surrounded by close packed peaks named Pyramid and Colonial and Davis.—Here a huge lift takes you one thousand feet up to the level of Diablo Lake and Diablo Dam.—Over the dam pours a jet roar of water through which a stray log could go shooting out like a tooth-pick in a one-thousand-foot arc.—Here for the first time you're high enough really to begin to see the Cascades. Dazzles of light to the north show where Ross Lake sweeps back all the way to Canada, opening a view of the Mt. Baker National Forest as spectacular as any vista in the Colorado Rockies.

The Seattle City Light and Power boat leaves on regular schedule from 13 a little pier near Diablo Dam and heads north between steep timbered rocky cliffs toward Ross Dam, about half an hour's ride. The passengers are power employees, hunters and fishermen and forestry workers. Below Ross Dam the footwork begins—you must climb a rocky trail one thou-sand feet to the level of the dam. Here the vast lake opens out, disclosing small resort floats offering rooms and boats for vacationists, and just be-yond, the floats of the U.S. Forestry Service. From this point on, if you're lucky enough to be a rich man or a forest-fire lookout, you can get packed into the North Cascade Primitive Area by horse and mule and spend a summer of complete solitude.

I was a fire lookout and after two nights of trying to sleep in the boom 14 and slap of the Forest Service flats, they came for me one rainy morning— a powerful tugboat lashed to a large corral float bearing four mules and three horses, my own groceries, feed, batteries and equipment.—The muleskinner's name was Andy and he wore the same old floppy cowboy hat he'd worn in Wyoming twenty years ago. "Well, boy, now we're gonna put you away where we cant reach ya—you better get ready."

"It's just what I want, Andy, be alone for three solid months nobody to 15 bother me."

"It's what you're sayin' now but you'll change your tune after a week." 16

I didn't believe him.—I was looking forward to an experience men sel- 17 dom earn in this modern world: complete and comfortable solitude in the wilderness, day and night, sixty-three days and nights to be exact. We had no idea how much snow had fallen on my mountain during the winter and Andy said: "If there didnt it means you gotta hike two miles down that hard trail every day or every other day with two buckets, boy. I aint en-vyin' you—I been back there. And one day it's gonna be hot and you're about ready to broil, and bugs you cant even count 'em, and next day a li'l' ole summer blizzard come hit you around the corner of Hozomeen which sits right there near Canada in your back yard and you wont be able to stick logs fast enough in that potbelly stove of yours."—But I had a full rucksack loaded with turtleneck sweaters and warm shirts and pants and long wool socks bought on the Seattle water front, and gloves and an earmuff cap, and lots of instant soup and coffee in my grub list.

"Shoulda brought yourself a quart of brandy, boy," says Andy shaking his head as the tug pushed our corral float up Ross Lake through the log gate and around to the left dead north underneath the immense rain shroud of Sourdough Mountain and Ruby Mountain. [18]

"Where's Desolation Peak?" I asked, meaning my own mountain (*A mountain to be kept forever,* I'd dreamed all that spring) (O lonesome traveler!) [19]

"You aint gonna see it today till we're practically on top it and by that time you'll be so soakin' wet you wont care." [20]

Assistant Ranger Marty Gohlke of Marblemount Ranger Station was with us too, also giving me tips and instructions. Nobody seemed to envy Desolation Peak except me. After two hours pushing through the storming waves of the long rainy lake with dreary misty timber rising steeply on both sides and the mules and horses chomping on their feedbags patient in the downpour, we arrived at the foot of Desolation Trail and the tugman (who'd been providing us with good hot coffee in the pilot cabin) eased her over and settled the float against a steep muddy slope full of bushes and fallen trees.—The muleskinner whacked the first mule and she lurched ahead with her double-sided pack of batteries and canned goods, hit the mud with forehoofs, scrambled, slipped, almost fell back in the lake and finally gave one mighty heave and went skittering out of sight in the fog to wait on the trail for the other mules and her master.—We all got off, cut the barge loose, waved to the tug man, mounted our horses and started up a sad and dripping party in heavy rain. [21]

At first the trail, always steeply rising, was so dense with shrubbery we kept getting shower after shower from overhead and against our out-saddled knees.—The trail was deep with round rocks that kept causing the animals to slip.—At one point a great fallen tree made it impossible to go on until Old Andy and Marty went ahead with axes and cleared a short cut around the tree, sweating and cursing and hacking as I watched the animals.—By-and-by they were ready but the mules were afraid of the rough steepness of the short cut and had to be prodded through with sticks.—Soon the trail reached alpine meadows powdered with blue lupine everywhere in the drenching mists, and with little red poppies, tiny-budded flowers as delicate as designs on a small Japanese teacup.—Now the trail zigzagged widely back and forth up the high [22] meadow.—Soon we saw the vast foggy heap of a rock-cliff face above and Andy yelled "Soon's we get up high as that we're almost there but that's another two thousand feet though you think you could reach up and touch it!"

I unfolded my nylon poncho and draped it over my head, and, drying a little, or, rather, ceasing to drip, I walked alongside the horse to warm my blood and began to feel better. But the other boys just rode along with their heads bowed in the rain. As for altitude all I could tell was from some occasional frightening spots on the trail where we could look down on distant treetops.   23

The alpine meadow reached to timber line and suddenly a great wind blew shafts of sleet on us.—"Gettin' near the top now!" yelled Andy—and suddenly there was snow on the trail, the horses were chumping through a foot of slush and mud, and to the left and right everything was blinding white in the gray fog.—"About five and a half thousand feet right now" said Andy rolling a cigarette as he rode in the rain.—   24

We went down, then up another spell, down again, a slow gradual climb, and then Andy yelled "There she is!" and up ahead in the mountaintop gloom I saw a little shadowy peaked shack standing alone on the top of the world and gulped with fear: 25

"This my home all summer? And *this* is summer?"   26

The inside of the shack was even more miserable, damp and dirty, left-over groceries and magazines torn to shreds by rats and mice, the floor muddy, the windows impenetrable.—But hardy Old Andy who'd been through this kind of thing all his life got a roaring fire crackling in the pot-belly stove and had me lay out a pot of water with almost half a can of cof-fee in it saying "Coffee aint no good 'less it's *strong!*" and pretty soon the coffee was boiling a nice brown aromatic foam and we got our cups out and drank deep.—   27

Meanwhile I'd gone out on the roof with Marty and removed the bucket from the chimney and put up the weather pole with the anemometer and done a few other chores—when we came back in Andy was frying Spam and eggs in a huge pan and it was almost like a party.—Outside, the pa-tient animals chomped on their supper bags and were glad to rest by the old corral fence built of logs by some Desolation lookout of the Thirties.   28

Darkness came, incomprehensible.   29

In the gray morning after they'd slept in sleeping bags on the floor and I on the only bunk in my mummy bag, Andy and Marty left, laughing, say-ing, "Well, whatayou think now hey? We been here twelve hours and you still aint been able to see more than twelve feet!"   30

By gosh that's right, what am I going to do for watching fires?"   31

"Dont worry boy, these clouds'll roll away and you'll be able to see a hunnerd miles in every direction."   32

I didn't believe it and I felt miserable and spent the day trying to clean   33
up the shack or pacing twenty careful feet each way in my "yard" (the
ends of which appeared to be sheer drops into silent gorges), and I went
to bed early.—About bedtime I saw my first star, briefly, then giant phan-
tom clouds billowed all around me and the star was gone.—But in that instant I thought I'd seen a mile-down maw of grayblack lake where Andy
and Marty were back in the Forest Service boat which had met them at
noon.

In the middle of the night I woke up suddenly and my hair was stand-   34
ing on end—I saw a huge black shadow in my window.—Then I saw that
it had a star above it, and realized that this was Mt. Hozomeen (8080 feet)
looking in my window from miles away near Canada.—I got up from the
forlorn bunk with the mice scattering underneath and went outside and
gasped to see black mountain shapes gianting all around, and not only
that but the billowing curtains of the northern lights shifting behind the
clouds.—It was a little too much for a city boy—the fear that the
Abominable Snowman might be breathing behind me in the dark sent
me back to bed where I buried my head inside my sleeping bag.—

But in the morning—Sunday, July sixth—I was amazed and overjoyed   35
to see a clear blue sunny sky and down below, like a radiant pure snow
sea, the clouds making a marshmallow cover for all the world and all the
lake while I abided in warm sunshine among hundreds of miles of snow-
white peaks.—I brewed coffee and sang and drank a cup on my drowsy
warm doorstep.

At noon the clouds vanished and the lake appeared below, beautiful   36
beyond belief, a perfect blue pool twenty five miles long and more, and
the creeks like toy creeks and the timber green and fresh everywhere
below and even the joyous little unfolding liquid tracks of vacationists'
fishingboats on the lake and in the lagoons.—A perfect afternoon of sun,
and behind the shack I discovered a snowfield big enough to provide me
with buckets of cold water till late September.

My job was to watch for fires. One night a terrific lightning storm made   37
a dry run across the Mt. Baker National Forest without any rainfall.—
When I saw that ominous black cloud flashing wrathfully toward me I shut
off the radio and laid the aerial on the ground and waited for the worst.—
Hiss! hiss! said the wind, bringing dust and lightning nearer.—Tick! said
the lightning rod, receiving a strand of electricity from a strike on nearby
Skagit Peak.—Hiss! tick! and in my bed I felt the earth move.—Fifteen
miles to the south, just east of Ruby Peak and somewhere near Panther
Creek, a large fire raged, a huge orange spot.—At ten o'clock lightning hit
it again and it flared up dangerously.—

I was supposed to note the general area of lightning strikes.—By mid-   38
night I'd been staring so intently out the dark window I got hallucinations

of fires everywhere, three of them right in Lightning Creek, phosphorescent orange verticals of ghost fire that seemed to come and go.

In the morning, there at 177° 16′ where I'd seen the big fire was a 39 strange brown patch in the snowy rock showing where the fire had raged and sputtered out in the all-night rain that followed the lightning. But the result of this storm was disastrous fifteen miles away at McAllister Creek where a great blaze had outlasted the rain and exploded the following afternoon in a cloud that could be seen from Seattle. I felt sorry for the fellows who had to fight these fires, the smokejumpers who parachuted down on them out of planes and the trail crews who hiked to them, climbing and scrambling over slippery rocks and scree slopes, arriving sweaty and exhausted only to face the wall of heat when they got there. As a lookout I had it pretty easy and only had to concentrate on reporting the exact location (by instrument findings) of every blaze I detected.

Most days, though, it was the routine that occupied me.—Up at seven 40 or so every day, a pot of coffee brought to a boil over a handful of burning twigs, I'd go out in the alpine yard with a cup of coffee hooked in my thumb and leisurely make my wind speed and wind direction and temperature and moisture readings—then, after chopping wood, I'd use the two-way radio and report to the relay station on Sourdough.—At 10 A.M. I usually got hungry for breakfast, and I'd make delicious pancakes, eating them at my little table that was decorated with bouquets of mountain lupine and sprigs of fir.

Early in the afternoon was the usual time for my kick of the day, instant 41 chocolate pudding with hot coffee.—Around two or three I'd lie on my back on the meadowside and watch the clouds float by, or pick blueberries and eat them right there. The radio was on loud enough to hear any calls for Desolation.

Then at sunset I'd roust up my supper out of cans of yams and Spam 42 and peas, or sometimes just pea soup with corn muffins baked on top of the wood stove in aluminum foil.—Then I'd go out to that precipitous snow slope and shovel my two pails of snow for the water tub and gather an armful of fallen firewood from the hillside like the proverbial Old Woman of Japan.—For the chipmunks and conies I put pans of leftovers under the shack, in the middle of the night I could hear them clanking around. The rat would scramble down from the attic and eat some too.

Sometimes I'd yell questions at the rocks and trees, and across gorges, 43 or yodel—"What is the meaning of the void?" The answer was perfect silence, so I knew.—

Before bedtime I'd read by kerosene lamp whatever books were in the 44 shack.—It's amazing how people in solitary hunger after books.—After poring over every word of a medical tome, and the synopsized versions of

Shakespeare's plays by Charles and Mary Lamb, I climbed up in the little attic and put together torn cowboy pocket books and magazines the mice had ravaged—I also played stud poker with three imaginary players.

Around bedtime I'd bring a cup of milk almost to a boil with a table- 45
spoon of honey in it, and drink that for my lamby nightcap, then I'd curl up in my sleeping bag.

No man should go through life without once experiencing healthy, 46
even bored solitude in the wilderness, finding himself depending solely on himself and thereby learning his true and hidden strength.—Learning, for instance, to eat when he's hungry and sleep when he's sleepy.

Also around bedtime was my singing time. I'd pace up and down the 47
well-worn path in the dust of my rock singing all the show tunes I could remember, at the top of my voice too, with nobody to hear except the deer and the bear.

In the red dusk, the mountains were symphonies in pink snow—Jack 48
Mountain, Three Fools Peak, Freezeout Peak, Golden Horn, Mt. Terror, Mt. Fury, Mt. Despair, Crooked Thumb Peak, Mt. Challenger and the incomparable Mt. Baker bigger than the world in the distance—and my own little Jackass Ridge that completed the Ridge of Desolation.—Pink snow and the clouds all distant and frilly like ancient remote cities of Buddhaland splendor, and the wind working incessantly—whish, whish—booming, at times rattling my shack.

For supper I made chop suey and baked some biscuits and put the left- 49
overs in a pan for deer that came in the moonlit night and nibbled like big strange cows of peace—long-antlered buck and does and babies too—as I meditated in the alpine grass facing the magic moon-laned lake.—And I could see firs reflected in the moonlit lake five thousand feet below, up-side down, pointing to infinity.—

And all the insects ceased in honor of the moon. 50

Sixty-three sunsets I saw revolve on that perpendicular hill—mad rag- 51
ing sunsets pouring in sea foams of cloud through unimaginable crags like the crags you grayly drew in pencil as a child, with every rose-tint of hope beyond, making you feel just like them, brilliant and bleak beyond words.—

Cold mornings with clouds billowing out of Lightning Gorge like 52
smoke from a giant fire but the lake cerulean as ever.

August comes in with a blast that shakes your house and augurs little 53
Augusticity—then that snowy-air and woodsmoke feeling—then the snow comes sweeping your way from Canada, and the wind rises and dark low clouds rush up as out of a forge. Suddenly a green-rose rainbow appears right on your ridge with steamy clouds all around and an orange sun turmoiling . . .

What is a rainbow,
Lord?—a hoop
For the lowly

. . . and you go out and suddenly your shadow is ringed by the rainbow as you walk on the hilltop, a lovely-haloed mystery making you want to pray.—

A blade of grass jiggling in the winds of infinity, anchored to a rock, and for your own poor gentle flesh no answer.   54

Your oil lamp burning in infinity.   55

One morning I found bear stool and signs of where the monster had taken a can of frozen milk and squeezed it in his paws and bit into it with one sharp tooth trying to suck out the paste.—In the foggy dawn I looked down the mysterious Ridge of Starvation with its fog-lost firs and its hills humping into invisibility, and the wind blowing the fog by like a faint blizzard and I realized that somewhere in the fog stalked the bear.   56

And it seemed as I sat there that this was the Primordial Bear, and that he owned all the Northwest and all the snow and commanded all the mountains.—He was King Bear, who could crush my head in his paws and crack my spine like a stick and this was his house, his yard, his domain.—Though I looked all day, he would not show himself in the mystery of those silent foggy slopes—he prowled at night among unknown lakes, and in the early morning the pearl-pure light that shadowed mountainsides of fir made him blink with respect.—He had millenniums of prowling here behind him, he had seen the Indians and Redcoats come and go, and would see much more.—He continuously heard the reassuring rapturous rush of silence, except when near creeks, he was aware of the light material the world is made of, yet he never discoursed, nor communicated by signs, nor wasted a breath complaining—he just nibbled and pawed and lumbered along snags paying no attention to things inanimate or animate.—His big mouth chew-chewed in the night, I could hear it across the mountain in the starlight.—Soon he would come out of the fog, huge, and come and stare in my window with big burning eyes.—He was Avalokitesvara the Bear, and his sign was the gray wind of autumn.—   57

I was waiting for him. He never came.   58

Finally the autumn rains, all-night gales of soaking rain as I lie warm as toast in my sleeping bag and the mornings open cold wild fall days with high wind, racing fogs, racing clouds, sudden bright sun, pristine light on hill patches and my fire crackling as I exult and sing at the top of my voice.—Outside my window a wind-swept chipmunk sits up straight on a rock, hands clasped he nibbles an oat between his paws—the little nutty lord of all he surveys.   59

Thinking of the stars night after night I begin to realize "The stars are   60
words" and all the innumerable worlds in the Milky Way are words, and
so is this world too. And I realize that no matter where I am, whether in a
little room full of thought, or in this endless universe of stars and mountains, it's all in my mind. There's no need for solitude. So love life for what
it is, and form no preconceptions whatever in your mind.

What strange sweet thoughts come to you in the mountain solitudes!   61
—One night I realized that when you give people understanding and encouragement a funny little meek childish look abashes their eyes, no matter what they've been doing they weren't sure it was right—lambies all
over the world.

For when you realize that God is Everything you know that you've got   62
to love everything no matter how bad it is, in the ultimate sense it was neither good nor bad (consider the dust), it was just *what was,* that is, what
was made to appear.—Some kind of drama to teach something to something, some "despiséd substance of divinest show."

And I realized I didnt have to hide myself in desolation but could ac-   63
cept society for better or for worse, like a wife—I saw that if it wasnt for
the six senses, of seeing, hearing, smelling, touching, tasting and thinking,
the self of that, which is non-existent, there would be no phenomena to
perceive at all, in fact no six senses or self.—The fear of extinction is much
worse than extinction (death) itself.—To chase after extinction in the old
Nirvanic sense of Buddhism is ultimately silly, as the dead indicate in the
silence of their blissful sleep in Mother Earth which is an Angel hanging in
orbit in Heaven anyway.—

I just lay on the mountain meadowside in the moonlight, head to grass,   64
and heard the silent recognition of my temporary woes.—Yes, so try to *attain* to Nirvana when you're already there, to attain to the top of a mountain when you're already there and only have to stay—thus to *stay* in the
Nirvana Bliss, is all I have to do, you have to do, no effort, no path really,
no discipline but just to know that all is empty and awake, a Vision and a
Movie in God's Universal Mind *(Alaya-Vijnana)* and to stay more or less
wisely in that.—Because silence itself is the sound of diamonds which can
cut through anything, the sound of Holy Emptiness, the sound of extinction and bliss, that graveyard silence which is like the silence of an infant's
smile, the sound of eternity, of the blessedness surely to be believed, the
sound of nothing-ever-happened-except-God (which I'd soon hear in a
noisy Atlantic temptest).—What exists is God in His Emanation, what
does not exist is God in His peaceful Neutrality, what neither exists nor
does not exist is God's immortal primordial dawn of Father Sky (this
world this very minute).—So I said:—"Stay in that, no dimensions here to
any of the mountains or mosquitos and whole milky ways of worlds—"

Because sensation is emptiness, old age is emptiness.—'T's only the Golden Eternity of God's Mind so practise kindness and sympathy, remember that men are *not responsible in themselves as men* for their ignorance and unkindness, they should be pitied, God does pity it, because who says anything about anything since everything is just what it is, free of interpretations.—God is not the "attainer," he is the "farer" in that which everything is, the "abider"—one caterpillar, a thousand hairs of God.—So know constantly that this is only you, God, empty and awake and eternally free as the unnumerable atoms of emptiness everywhere.

I decided that when I would go back to the world down there I'd try to keep my mind clear in the midst of murky human ideas smoking like factories on the horizon through which I would walk, forward . . .   65

When I came down in September a cool old golden look had come into the forest, auguring cold snaps and frost and the eventual howling blizzard that would cover my shack completely, unless those winds at the top of the world would keep her bald. As I reached the bend in the trail where the shack would disappear and I would plunge down to the lake to meet the boat that would take me out and home, I turned and blessed Desolation Peak and the little pagoda on top and thanked them for the shelter and the lesson I'd been taught.   66

QUESTIONS FOR DISCUSSION AND WRITING

1.   Kerouac writes of his experiences on the mountaintop as a kind of journey. He starts in the heat and dust of the eastern cities in June and ends as he walks away from the peak in the fall, blessing Desolation Peak and its pagoda. Outline the various stages of this journey and characterize each one. What is each stage like, what does Kerouac experience at each stage, and what does he learn?

2.   When Kerouac tells the muleskinner, Andy, that he wants to be alone for three months, Andy replies, "[Y]ou'll change your tune after a week" (par. 16). Why does Andy think Kerouac will change his tune, and how does Kerouac confound Andy's expectation? In answering this question, think of what Kerouac does by himself for three months. What does he do on a regular basis, and what surprises does he find? As part of your response, think of how you would respond to the isolation in Kerouac's situation.

3.   Toward the end of his narrative, Kerouac realizes that " 'The stars are worlds' " (par. 60). What does this mean, and what do the words in the stars, and in the worlds of the Milky Way, and in this world, too, tell Kerouac? Do the King Bear and the "little nutty lord" of a chipmunk speak words, too? If so, what is their connection to the words of the stars?

N. Scott Momaday

N. Scott Momaday (b. 1934) writes from his Kiowa roots. Although his mother is Anglo, Momaday has chosen to identify with his father's tribe. In grounding himself in his Kiowa heritage, he seeks a deep understanding of the Native American relationship with the land. He believes that "the Indian has an understanding of the physical world and of the earth as a spiritual entity that is his, very much his own." Through this vision of human beings in harmony with nature, Momaday strives to overcome the modern, Western sense of alienation.

Momaday has won prizes for his poetry and fiction, but his most influential work is probably The Way to Rainy Mountain *(1969). In it he blends poetry, history, myth, and personal reminiscences to bring the reader into the world of the Kiowa people, who moved from Yellowstone to the Great Plains of our continent three hundred years ago. With the acquisition of horses they became hunters, fighters, and worshipers of the sun and buffalo. When they were defeated by the U.S. Cavalry in the mid–nineteenth century, they lost their source of spiritual strength with the destruction of the great herds of buffalo.* The Way to Rainy Mountain *consists of a prologue, introduction, three chapters (called "The Setting Out," "The Going On," and "The Closing In"), and an epilogue; all but "The Setting Out" are included here. Momaday divides his chapters into numbered sections consisting of three parts, usually concerning myth, history, and personal reminiscences, with the three parts set in different type fonts.*

From *The Way to Rainy Mountain*

Headwaters

Noon in the intermountain plain:
There is scant telling of the marsh—
A log, hollow and weather-stained,
An insect at the mouth, and moss—
Yet waters rise against the roots,   5
Stand brimming to the stalks. What moves?
What moves on this archaic force
Was wild and welling at the source.

Prologue

The journey began one day long ago on the edge of the northern 1
Plains. It was carried on over a course of many generations and many hundreds of miles. In the end there were many things to remember, to dwell
upon and talk about.

"You know, everything had to begin. . . ." For the Kiowas the beginning 2
was a struggle for existence in the bleak northern mountains. It was there,
they say, that they entered the world through a hollow log. The end, too,
was a struggle, and it was lost. The young Plains culture of the Kiowas
withered and died like grass that is burned in the prairie wind. There came
a day like destiny; in every direction, as far as the eye could see, carrion
lay out in the land. The buffalo was the animal representation of the sun,
the essential and sacrificial victim of the Sun Dance. When the wild herds
were destroyed, so too was the will of the Kiowa people; there was nothing to sustain them in spirit. But these are idle recollections, the mean and
ordinary agonies of human history. The interim was a time of great adventure and nobility and fulfillment.

Tai-me came to the Kiowas in a vision born of suffering and despair. 3
"Take me with you," Tai-me said, "and I will give you whatever you
want." And it was so. The great adventure of the Kiowas was a going forth
into the heart of the continent. They began a long migration from the
headwaters of the Yellowstone River eastward to the Black Hills and south
to the Wichita Mountains. Along the way they acquired horses, the religion of the Plains, a love and possession of the open land. Their nomadic
soul was set free. In alliance with the Comanches they held dominion in
the southern Plains for a hundred years. In the course of that long migration they had come of age as a people. They had conceived a good idea
of themselves; they had dared to imagine and determine who they were.

In one sense, then, the way to Rainy Mountain is preeminently the his- 4
tory of an idea, man's idea of himself, and it has old and essential being in
language. The verbal tradition by which it has been preserved has suffered a deterioration in time. What remains is fragmentary: mythology,
legend, lore, and hearsay—and of course the idea itself, as crucial and
complete as it ever was. That is the miracle.

The journey herein recalled continues to be made anew each time the 5
miracle comes to mind, for that is peculiarly the right and responsibility of
the imagination. It is a whole journey, intricate with motion and meaning;
and it is made with the whole memory, that experience of the mind which
is legendary as well as historical, personal as well as cultural. And the
journey is an evocation of three things in particular: a landscape that
is incomparable, a time that is gone forever, and the human spirit, which
endures. The imaginative experience and the historical express equally

the traditions of man's reality. Finally, then, the journey recalled is among other things the revelation of one way in which these traditions are conceived, developed, and interfused in the human mind. There are on the way to Rainy Mountain many landmarks, many journeys in the one. From the beginning the migration of the Kiowas was an expression of the human spirit, and that expression is most truly made in terms of wonder and delight: "There were many people, and oh, it was beautiful. That was the beginning of the Sun Dance. It was all for Tai-me, you know, and it was a long time ago."

Introduction

A single knoll rises out of the plain in Oklahoma, north and west of the   6 Wichita Range. For my people, the Kiowas, it is an old landmark, and they gave it the name Rainy Mountain. The hardest weather in the world is there. Winter brings blizzards, hot tornadic winds arise in the spring, and in summer the prairie is an anvil's edge. The grass turns brittle and brown, and it cracks beneath your feet. There are green belts along the rivers and creeks, linear groves of hickory and pecan, willow and witch hazel. At a distance in July or August the steaming foliage seems almost to writhe in fire. Great green and yellow grasshoppers are everywhere in the tall grass, popping up like corn to sting the flesh, and tortoises crawl about on the red earth, going nowhere in the plenty of time. Loneliness is an aspect of the land. All things in the plain are isolate; there is no confusion of objects in the eye, but *one* hill or *one* tree or *one* man. To look upon that landscape in the early morning, with the sun at your back, is to lose the sense of proportion. Your imagination comes to life, and this, you think, is where Creation was begun.

I returned to Rainy Mountain in July. My grandmother had died in the   7 spring, and I wanted to be at her grave. She had lived to be very old and at last infirm. Her only living daughter was with her when she died, and I was told that in death her face was that of a child.

I like to think of her as a child. When she was born, the Kiowas were   8 living the last great moment of their history. For more than a hundred years they had controlled the open range from the Smoky Hill River to the Red, from the headwaters of the Canadian to the fork of the Arkansas and Cimarron. In alliance with the Comanches, they had ruled the whole of the southern Plains. War was their sacred business, and they were among the finest horsemen the world has ever known. But warfare for the Kiowas was preeminently a matter of disposition rather than of survival; and they never understood the grim, unrelenting advance of the U.S. Cavalry. When at last, divided and ill-provisioned, they were driven onto the

Staked Plains in the cold rains of autumn, they fell into panic. In Palo Duro Canyon they abandoned their crucial stores to pillage and had nothing then but their lives. In order to save themselves, they surrendered to the soldiers at Fort Sill and were imprisoned in the old stone corral that now stands as a military museum. My grandmother was spared the humiliation of those high gray walls by eight or ten years, but she must have known from birth the affliction of defeat, the dark brooding of old warriors.

Her name was Aho, and she belonged to the last culture to evolve in 9 North America. Her forebears came down from the high country in western Montana nearly three centuries ago. They were a mountain people, a mysterious tribe of hunters whose language has never been positively classified in any major group. In the late seventeenth century they began a long migration to the south and east. It was a journey toward the dawn, and it led to a golden age. Along the way the Kiowas were befriended by the Crows, who gave them the culture and religion of the Plains. They acquired horses, and their ancient nomadic spirit was suddenly free of the ground. They acquired Tai-me, the sacred Sun Dance doll, from that moment the object and symbol of their worship, and so shared in the divinity of the sun. Not least, they acquired the sense of destiny, therefore courage and pride. When they entered upon the southern Plains they had been transformed. No longer were they slaves to the simple necessity of survival; they were a lordly and dangerous society of fighters and thieves, hunters and priests of the sun. According to their origin myth, they entered the world through a hollow log. From one point of view, their migration was the fruit of an old prophecy, for indeed they emerged from a sunless world.

Although my grandmother lived out her long life in the shadow of 10 Rainy Mountain, the immense landscape of the continental interior lay like memory in her blood. She could tell of the Crows, whom she had never seen, and of the Black Hills, where she had never been. I wanted to see in reality what she had seen more perfectly in the mind's eye, and traveled fifteen hundred miles to begin my pilgrimage.

Yellowstone, it seemed to me, was the top of the world, a region of 11 deep lakes and dark timber, canyons and waterfalls. But, beautiful as it is, one might have the sense of confinement there. The skyline in all directions is close at hand, the high wall of the woods and deep cleavages of shade. There is a perfect freedom in the mountains, but it belongs to the eagle and the elk, the badger and the bear. The Kiowas reckoned their stature by the distance they could see, and they were bent and blind in the wilderness.

Descending eastward, the highland meadows are a stairway to the 12 plain. In July the inland slope of the Rockies is luxuriant with flax and buckwheat, stonecrop and larkspur. The earth unfolds and the limit of the land recedes. Clusters of trees, and animals grazing far in the distance, cause the vision to reach away and wonder to build upon the mind. The sun follows a longer course in the day, and the sky is immense beyond all comparison. The great billowing clouds that sail upon it are shadows that move upon the grain like water, dividing light. Farther down, in the land of the Crows and Blackfeet, the plain is yellow. Sweet clover takes hold of the hills and bends upon itself to cover and seal the soil. There the Kiowas paused on their way; they had come to the place where they must change their lives. The sun is at home on the plains. Precisely there does it have the certain character of a god. When the Kiowas came to the land of the Crows, they could see the dark lees of the hills at dawn across the Bighorn River, the profusion of light on the grain shelves, the oldest deity ranging after the solstices. Not yet would they veer southward to the caldron of the land that lay below; they must wean their blood from the northern winter and hold the mountains a while longer in their view. They bore Tai-me in procession to the east.

A dark mist lay over the Black Hills, and the land was like iron. At the top of a ridge I caught sight of Devil's Tower upthrust against the gray sky as if in the birth of time the core of the earth had broken through its crust and the motion of the world was begun. There are things in nature that engender an awful quiet in the heart of man; Devil's Tower is one of them. Two centuries ago, because they could not do otherwise, the Kiowas made a legend at the base of the rock. My grandmother said: 13

> Eight children were there at play, seven sisters and their brother. Suddenly the boy was struck dumb; he trembled and began to run upon his hands and feet. His fingers became claws, and his body was covered with fur. Directly there was a bear where the boy had been. The sisters were terrified; they ran, and the bear after them. They came to the stump of a great tree, and the tree spoke to them. It bade then climb upon it, and as they did so it began to rise into the air. The bear came to kill them, but they were just beyond its reach. It reared against the tree and scored the bark all around with its claws. The seven sisters were borne into the sky, and they became the stars of the Big Dipper.

From that moment, and so long as the legend lives, the Kiowas have kinsmen in the night sky. Whatever they were in the mountains, they could be no more. However tenuous their well-being, however much they had suffered and would suffer again, they had found a way out of the wilderness.

My grandmother had a reverence for the sun, a holy regard that now is all but gone out of mankind. There was a wariness in her, and an ancient awe. She was a Christian in her later years, but she had come a long way about, and she never forgot her birthright. As a child she had been to the Sun Dances; she had taken part in those annual rites, and by them she had   14 learned the restoration of her people in the presence of Tai-me. She was about seven when the last Kiowa Sun Dance was held in 1887 on the Washita River above Rainy Mountain Creek. The buffalo were gone. In order to consummate the ancient sacrifice—to impale the head of a buffalo bull upon the medicine tree—a delegation of old men journeyed into Texas, there to beg and barter for an animal from the Goodnight herd. She was ten when the Kiowas came together for the last time as a living Sun Dance culture. They could find no buffalo; they had to hang an old hide from the sacred tree. Before the dance could begin, a company of soldiers rode out from Fort Sill under orders to disperse the tribe. Forbidden without cause the essential act of their faith, having seen the wild herds slaughtered and left to rot upon the ground, the Kiowas backed away forever from the medicine tree. That was July 20, 1890, at the great bend of the Washita. My grandmother was there. Without bitterness, and for as long as she lived, she bore a vision of deicide.

Now that I can have her only in memory, I see my grandmother in the 15 several postures that were peculiar to her: standing at the wood stove on a winter morning and turning meat in a great iron skillet; sitting at the south window, bent above her beadwork, and afterwards, when her vision failed, looking down for a long time into the fold of her hands; going out upon a cane, very slowly as she did when the weight of age came upon her; praying. I remember her most often at prayer. She made long, rambling prayers out of suffering and hope, having seen many things. I was never sure that I had the right to hear, so exclusive were they of all mere custom and company. The last time I saw her she prayed standing by the side of her bed at night, naked to the waist, the light of a kerosene lamp moving upon her dark skin. Her long, black hair, always drawn and braided in the day, lay upon her shoulders and against her breasts like a shawl. I do not speak Kiowa, and I never understood her prayers, but there was something inherently sad in the sound, some merest hesitation upon the syllables of sorrow. She began in a high and descending pitch, exhausting her breath to silence; then again and again—and always the same intensity of effort, of something that is, and is not, like urgency in the human voice. Transported so in the dancing light among the shadows of her room, she seemed beyond the reach of time. But that was illusion; I think I knew then that I should not see her again.

Houses are like sentinels in the plain, old keepers of the weather 16 watch. There, in a very little while, wood takes on the appearance of great age. All colors wear soon away in the wind and rain, and then the wood is burned gray and the grain appears and the nails turn red with rust. The windowpanes are black and opaque; you imagine there is nothing within, and indeed there are many ghosts, bones given up to the land. They stand here and there against the sky, and you approach them for a longer time than you expect. They belong in the distance; it is their domain.

Once there was a lot of sound in my grandmother's house, a lot of com-   17
ing and going, feasting and talk. The summers there were full of excitement and reunion. The Kiowas are a summer people; they abide the cold
and keep to themselves, but when the season turns and the land becomes
warm and vital they cannot hold still; an old love of going returns upon
them. The aged visitors who came to my grandmother's house when I was
a child were made of lean and leather, and they bore themselves upright.
They wore great black hats and bright ample shirts that shook in the wind.
They rubbed fat upon their hair and wound their braids with strips of colored cloth. Some of them painted their faces and carried the scars of old
and cherished enmities. They were an old council of warlords, come to
remind and be reminded of who they were. Their wives and daughters
served them well. The woman might indulge themselves; gossip was at
once the mark and compensation of their servitude. They made loud and
elaborate talk among themselves, full of jest and gesture, fright and false
alarm. They went abroad in fringed and flowered shawls, bright beadwork and German silver. They were at home in the kitchen, and they prepared meals that were banquets.

There were frequent prayer meetings, and great nocturnal feasts. When   18
I was a child I played with my cousins outside, where the lamplight fell
upon the ground and the singing of the old people rose up around us and
carried away into the darkness. There were a lot of good things to eat, a
lot of laughter and surprise. And afterwards, when the quiet returned, I lay
down with my grandmother and could hear the frogs away by the river
and feel the motion of the air.

Now there is a funeral silence in the rooms, the endless wake of some   19
final word. The walls have closed in upon my grandmother's house. When
I returned to it in mourning, I saw for the first time in my life how small it
was. It was late at night, and there was a white moon, nearly full. I sat for
a long time on the stone steps by the kitchen door. From there I could see
out across the land; I could see the long row of trees by the creek, the low
light upon the rolling plains, and the stars of the Big Dipper. Once I
looked at the moon and caught sight of a strange thing. A cricket had
perched upon the handrail, only a few inches away from me. My line of
vision was such that the creature filled the moon like a fossil. It had gone
there, I thought, to live and die, for there, of all places, was its small definition made whole and eternal. A warm wind rose up and purled like the
longing within me.

The next morning I awoke at dawn and went out on the dirt road to   20
Rainy Mountain. It was already hot, and the grasshoppers began to fill the
air. Still, it was early in the morning, and the birds sang out of the shadows. The long yellow grass on the mountain shone in the bright light, and
a scissortail hied above the land. There, were it ought to be, at the end of
a long and legendary way, was my grandmother's grave. Here and there

on the dark stones were ancestral names. Looking back once, I saw the mountain and came away.

THE GOING ON

XII

An old man there was who lived with his wife and child. One night the woman was pounding meat, and her little son wanted to taste it. She gave him a ball of meat and he went outside to eat it. Then he returned and wanted more. She gave him another ball of meat, and again he went outside. A third time he came and asked for meat. The old man began to be afraid. He told his wife to give the child a large ball of meat and to act as if these things were all right. When the little boy came in again, there was an enemy with him. The enemy said: "There are many of us and we are all around. We came to kill you, but your son has given me food. If you will feed us all, we will not harm you." But the old man did not believe his enemy, and while his wife cooked fat upon the fire he crept out and led their horses upstream. When he was well away, he called out in the voice of a bird. Then the woman knew that it was time to go. She set fire to the fat and threw it all around upon the enemies, who were sitting there; then she took up the little boy in her arms and ran upstream. That is how the old man and the woman and their child got away. From a safe distance they could see the fire and hear the screams of their enemies.

In the winter of 1872–73, a fine heraldic tipi was accidentally destroyed by fire. Known as the Do-giagya guat, *"tipi with battle pictures," it was ornamented with fine pictures of fighting men and arms on one side and wide, horizontal bands of black and yellow on the other. The* Do-giagya guat *belonged to the family of the great chief Dohasan and occupied the second place in the tribal circle on ceremonial occasions.*

There are meadowlarks and quail in the open land. One day late in the afternoon I walked about among the headstones at Rainy Mountain Cemetery. The shadows were very long; there was a deep blush on the sky, and the dark red earth seemed to glow with the setting sun. For a few moments, at that particular time of the day, there is deep silence. Nothing moves, and it does not occur to you to make any sound. Something is going on there in the shadows. Everything has slowed to a stop in order that the sun might take leave of the land. And then there is the sudden, piercing call of a bobwhite. The whole world is startled by it.

XIII

If an arrow is well made, it will have tooth marks upon it. That is how   24
you know. The Kiowas made fine arrows and straightened them in their
teeth. Then they drew them to the bow to see if they were straight. Once
there was a man and his wife. They were alone at night in their tipi. By the
light of the fire the man was making arrows. After a while he caught sight
of something. There was a small opening in the tipi where two hides were
sewn together. Someone was there on the outside, looking in. The man
went on with his work, but he said to his wife: "Someone is standing outside. Do not be afraid. Let us talk easily, as of ordinary things." He took up
an arrow and straightened it in his teeth; then, as it was right for him to do,
he drew it to the bow and took aim, first in this direction and then in that.
And all the while he was talking, as if to his wife. But this is how he spoke:
"I know that you are there on the outside, for I can feel your eyes upon
me. If you are a Kiowa, you will understand what I am saying, and you
will speak your name." But there was no answer, and the man went on in
the same way, pointing the arrow all around. At last his aim fell upon the
place where his enemy stood, and he let go of the string. The arrow went
straight to the enemy's heart.

The old men were the best arrowmakers, for they could bring time and   25
patience to their craft. The young men—the fighters and hunters—were
willing to pay a high price for arrows that were well made.

When my father was a boy, an old man used to come to Mammedaty's   26
house and pay his respects. He was a lean old man in braids and was im-
pressive in his age and bearing. His name was Cheney, and he was an ar-
rowmaker. Every morning, my father tells me, Cheney would paint his
wrinkled face, go out, and pray aloud to the rising sun. In my mind I can
see that man as if he were there now. I like to watch him as he makes his
prayer. I know where he stands and where his voice goes on the rolling
grasses and where the sun comes up on the land. There, at dawn, you can
feel the silence. It is cold and clear and deep like water. It takes hold of you
and will not let you go.

XIV

The Kiowa language is hard to understand, but, you know, the storm   27
spirit understands it. This is how it was: Long ago the Kiowas decided to
make a horse; they decided to make it out of clay, and so they began to
shape the clay with their hands. Well, the horse began to be. But it was a

terrible, terrible thing. It began to writhe, slowly at first, then faster and faster until there was a great commotion everywhere. The wind grew up and carried everything away; great trees were uprooted, and even the buffalo were thrown up into the sky. The Kiowas were afraid of that awful thing, and they went running about, talking to it. And at last it was calm. Even now, when they see the storm clouds gathering, the Kiowas know what it is: that a strange wild animal roams on the sky. It has the head of a horse and the tail of a great fish. Lightning comes from its mouth, and the tail, whipping and thrashing on the air, makes the high, hot wind of the tornado. But they speak to it, saying "Pass over me." They are not afraid of *Man-ka-ih,* for it understands their language.

At times the plains are bright and calm and quiet; at times they are   28
black with the sudden violence of weather. Always there are winds.

A few feet from the southwest corner of my grandmother's house, there   29
is a storm cellar. It will be there, I think, when the house and the arbor and
the barn have disappeared. There are many of those crude shelters in that
part of the world. They conform to the shape of the land and are scarcely
remarkable: low earthen mounds with heavy wooden trapdoors that ap-
pear to open upon the underworld. I have seen the wind drive the rain so
hard that a grown man could not open the door against it, and once, de-
scending into that place, I saw the whole land at night become visible and
blue and phosphorescent in the flash of lightning.

XV

Quoetotai was a good-looking young man and a great warrior besides.   30
One of Many Bears' wives fell in love with him, and they carried on. After that, Quoetotai went out one day. As he was crossing the river, Many Bears came out of a hiding place on the bank and shot him with an arrow; then he ran away. Quoetotai went back to the camp and someone pulled the arrow out of him. He was very sick, and he had lost a lot of blood. The medicine man worked over him for a long time, and the next day Quoetotai was all right. You know, he made up his mind to take Many Bears' wife away. After that, some of the men wanted to raid in Mexico. It was the custom to have a dance on the night before the men went away. There was a lot of singing, and now and then someone got up to say brave things. Many Bears' wife got up and called attention to herself. She said: "All of you, listen to my song. Something will happen tonight." Then she sang, and, you know, the old people still remember her song.

> I am going to leave my belongings,
> I am going to leave my home.
> Again I say it, I am going to leave my son.

Quoetotai took that woman away, and they roamed with the Comanches for fifteen years. When at last they returned to their own people, Many Bears was the first man to welcome them. "Quoetotai," he said, "from this time on you and I will be brothers. Now I give you six horses."

The artist George Catlin traveled among the Kiowas in 1834. He observes that they are superior to the Comanches and Wichitas in appearance. They are tall and straight, relaxed and graceful. They have fine, classical features, and in this respect they resemble more closely the tribes of the north than those of the south. 31

Catlin's portrait of Kotsatoah is the striking figure of a man, tall and lean, yet powerful and fully developed. He is lithe, and he knows beyond any doubt of his great strength and vigor. He stands perfectly at ease, the long drape of his robe flowing with the lines of his body. His left hand rests upon his shield and holds a bow and arrows. His head is set firmly, and there is a look of bemused and infinite tolerance in his eyes. He is said to have been nearly seven feet tall and able to run down and kill a buffalo on foot. I should like to have seen that man, as Catlin saw him, walking toward me, or away in the distance, perhaps, alone and against the sky. 32

XVI

There was a strange thing, a buffalo with horns of steel. One day a 33
man came upon it in the plain, just there where once upon a time four trees stood close together. The man and the buffalo began to fight. The man's hunting horse was killed right away, and the man climbed one of the trees. The great bull lowered its head and began to strike the tree with its black metal horns, and soon the tree fell. But the man was quick, and he leaped to the safety of the second tree. Again the bull struck with its unnatural horns, and the tree soon splintered and fell. The man leaped to the third tree and all the while he shot arrows at the beast; but the arrows glanced away like sparks from its dark hide. At last there remained only one tree and the man had only one arrow. He believed then that he would surely die. But something spoke to him and said: "Each time the buffalo prepares to charge, it spreads its cloven hooves and strikes the ground.

Only there in the cleft of the hoof is it vulnerable; it is there you must aim." The buffalo went away and turned, spreading its hooves, and the man drew the arrow to his bow. His aim was true and the arrow struck deep into the soft flesh of the hoof. The great bull shuddered and fell, and its steel horns flashed once in the sun.

Forty years ago the townspeople of Carnegie, Oklahoma, gathered   34
about two old Kiowa men who were mounted on work horses and armed with bows and arrows. Someone had got a buffalo, a poor broken beast in which there was no trace left of the wild strain. The old men waited silently amid the laughter and talk; then, at a signal, the buffalo was let go. It balked at first, more confused, perhaps, than afraid, and the horses had to be urged and then brought up short. The people shouted, and at last the buffalo wheeled and ran. The old men gave chase, and in the distance they were lost to view in a great, red cloud of dust. But they ran that animal down and killed it with arrows.

One morning my father and I walked in Medicine Park, on the edge   35
of a small herd of buffalo. It was late in the spring, and many of the cows had newborn calves. Nearby a calf lay in the tall grass; it was red-orange in color, delicately beautiful with new life. We approached, but suddenly the cow was there in our way, her great dark head low and fearful-looking. Then she came at us, and we turned and ran as hard as we could. She gave up after a short run, and I think we had not been in any real danger. But the spring morning was deep and beautiful and our hearts were beating fast and we knew just then what it was to be alive.

XVII

Bad women are thrown away. Once there was a handsome young   36
man. He was wild and reckless, and the chief talked to the wind about him. After that, the man went hunting. A great whirlwind passed by, and he was blind. The Kiowas have no need of a blind man; they left him alone with his wife and child. The winter was coming on and food was scarce. In four days the man's wife grew tired of caring for him. A herd of buffalo came near, and the man knew the sound. He asked his wife to hand him a bow and an arrow. "You must tell me," he said, "when the buffalo are directly in front of me." And in that way he killed a bull, but his wife said that he had missed. He asked for another arrow and killed another bull, but again his wife said that he had missed. Now the man was a hunter, and he knew the sound an arrow makes when it strikes home, but he said nothing. Then his wife helped herself to the meat and ran away with her child.

The man was blind; he ate grass and kept himself alive. In seven days a band of Kiowas found him and took him to their camp. There in the firelight a woman was telling a story. She told of how her husband had been killed by enemy warriors. The blind man listened, and he knew her voice. That was a bad woman. At sunrise they threw her away.

In the Kiowa calendars there is graphic proof that the lives of women 37 *were hard, whether they were "bad women" or not. Only the captives, who were slaves, held lower status. During the Sun Dance of 1843, a man stabbed his wife in the breast because she accepted Chief Dohasan's invitation to ride with him in the ceremonial procession. And in the winter of 1851–52, Big Bow stole the wife of a man who was away on a raiding expedition. He brought her to his father's camp and made her wait outside in the bitter cold while he went to collect his things. But his father knew what was going on, and he held Big Bow and would not let him go. The woman was made to wait in the snow until her feet were frozen.*

Mammedaty's grandmother, Kau-au-ointy, was a Mexican captive, 38 taken from her homeland when she was a child of eight or ten years. I never knew her, but I have been to her grave at Rainy Mountain.

KAU-AU-OINTY

BORN 1834

DIED 1929

AT REST

She raised a lot of eyebrows, they say, for she would not play the part of a Kiowa woman. From slavery she rose up to become a figure in the tribe. She owned a great herd of cattle, and she could ride as well as any man. She had blue eyes.

XVIII

You know, the Kiowas are a summer people. Once upon a time a 39 group of young men sat down in a circle and spoke of mighty things. This is what they said: "When the fall of the year comes around, where does the summer go? Where does it live?" They decided to follow the sun southward to its home, and so they set out on horseback. They rode for days and weeks and months, farther to the south than any Kiowa had ever gone before, and they saw many strange and wonderful things. At last they came to the place where they saw the strangest thing of all. Night was coming on, and they were very tired of riding; they made camp in a great thicket. All but one of them went right to sleep. He was a good hunter, and he could see well in the moonlight. He caught sight of something: men were all about in the trees, moving silently from limb to limb. They darted across the face of the full moon, *and he saw that they were small and had tails!* He could not believe his eyes, but the next morning he told the others of what he had seen. They only laughed at him and told him not to eat such a large supper again. But later, as they were breaking camp, a certain feeling came over them all at once: they felt that they were being watched. And when they looked up, the small men with tails began to race about in the limbs overhead. That is when the Kiowas turned around and came away; they had had quite enough of that place. They had found the sun's home after all, they reasoned, and they were hungry for the good buffalo meat of their homeland.

> *It is unnecessary to dilate on the revolution made in the life of the In-* 40
> *dian by the possession of the horse. Without it he was a half-starved skulker*
> *in the timber, creeping up on foot toward the unwary deer or building a*
> *brush corral with infinite labor to surround a herd of antelope, and sel-*
> *dom venturing more than a few days' journey from home. With the horse*
> *he was transformed into the daring buffalo hunter, able to procure in a*
> *single day enough food to supply his family for a year, leaving him free*
> *then to sweep the plains with his war parties along a range of a thousand*
> *miles.—Mooney*

> *Some of my earliest memories are of the summers on Rainy Mountain* 41
> *Creek, when we lived in the arbor, on the north side of my grandmother's*
> *house. From there you could see downhill to the pecan grove, the dense,*
> *dark growth along the water, and beyond, the long sweep of the earth it-*
> *self, curving out on the sky. The arbor was open on all sides to the light and*
> *the air and the sounds of the land. You could see far and wide even at night,*
> *by the light of the moon; there was nothing to stand in your way. And when*
> *the season turned and it was necessary to move back into the house, there*
> *was a sense of confinement and depression for a time. Now and then in*
> *winter, when I passed by the arbor on my way to draw water at the well, I*
> *looked inside and thought of the summer. The hard dirt floor was dark red*
> *in color—the color of pipestone.*

The Closing In

XIX

On a raid against the Utes, one of two brothers was captured. The 42
other, alone and of his own will, stole into the Ute camp and tried to set
his brother free, but he too was captured. The chief of the Utes had re-

spect for the man's bravery, and he made a bargain with him. If he could carry his brother on his back and walk upon a row of greased buffalo heads without falling to the ground, both brothers would be given horses and allowed to return in safety to their home. The man bore his brother on his back and walked upon the heads of the buffalo and kept his footing. The Ute chief was true to his word, and the brothers returned to their own people on horseback.

After the fight at Palo Duro Canyon, the Kiowas came in, a few at a   43
time, to surrender at Fort Sill. Their horses and weapons were confiscated,
and they were imprisoned. In a field just west of the post, the Indian ponies
were destroyed. Nearly 800 horses were killed outright; two thousand more
were sold, stolen, given away.

Summer 1879

Tsen-pia Kado, "Horse-eating sun dance." It is indicated on the Set-tan   44
calendar by the figure of a horse's head above the medicine lodge. This
dance was held on Elm Fork of Red River, and was so called because the
buffalo had now become so scarce that the Kiowa, who had gone on their
regular hunt the preceding winter had found so few that they were obliged
to kill and eat their ponies during the summer to save themselves from
starving. This may be recorded as the date of the disappearance of the buf-
falo from the Kiowa country. Thenceforth the appearance of even a single
animal was a rare event.— Mooney

In New Mexico the land is made of many colors. When I was a boy I   45
rode out over the red and yellow and purple earth to the west of Jemez
Pueblo. My horse was a small red roan, fast and easy-riding. I rode among
the dunes, along the bases of mesas and cliffs, into canyons and arroyos. I
came to know that country, not in the way a traveler knows the landmarks
he sees in the distance, but more truly and intimately, in every season, from
a thousand points of view. I know the living motion of a horse and the
sound of hooves. I know what it is, on a hot day in August or September, to
ride into a bank of cold, fresh rain.

XX

Once there was a man who owned a fine hunting horse. It was black   46
and fast and afraid of nothing. When it was turned upon an enemy it charged in a straight line and struck at full speed; the man need have no hand upon the rein. But, you know, that man knew fear. Once during a

charge he turned that animal from its course. That was a bad thing. The hunting horse died of shame.

In 1861 a Sun Dance was held near the Arkansas River in Kansas. As 47 *an offering to Tai-me, a spotted horse was left tied to a pole in the medicine lodge, where it starved to death. Later in that year an epidemic of smallpox broke out in the tribe, and the old man Gaapiatan sacrificed one of his best horses, a fine black-eared animal, that he and his family might be spared.*

I like to think of old man Gaapiatan and his horse. I think I know how 48 *much he loved that animal; I think I know what was going on in his mind: If you will give me my life and the lives of my family, I will give you the life of this black-eared horse.*

XXI

Mammedaty was the grandson of Guipahgo, and he was well-known 49 on that account. Now and then Mammedaty drove a team and wagon out over the plain. Once, in the early morning, he was on the way to Rainy Mountain. It was summer and the grass was high and meadowlarks were calling all around. You know, the top of the plain is smooth and you can see a long way. There was nothing but the early morning and the land around. Then Mammedaty heard something. Someone whistled to him. He looked up and saw the head of a little boy nearby above the grass. He stopped the horses and got down from the wagon and went to see who was there. There was no one; there was nothing there. He looked for a long time, but there was nothing there.

There is a single photograph of Mammedaty. He is looking past the 50 *camera and a little to one side. In his face there is calm and good will, strength and intelligence. His hair is drawn close to the scalp, and his braids are long and wrapped with fur. He wears a kilt, fringed leggings, and beaded moccasins. In his right hand there is a peyote fan. A family characteristic: the veins stand out in his hand, and his hands are small and rather long.*

Mammedaty saw four things that were truly remarkable. This head of 51 *the child was one, and the tracks of the water beast another. Once, when he walked near the pecan grove, he saw three small alligators on a log. No one had ever seen them before and no one ever saw them again. Finally, there was this: something had always bothered Mammedaty, a small ag-gravation that was never quite out of mind, like a name on the tip of the tongue. He had always wondered how it is that the mound of earth which a mole makes around the opening of its burrow is so fine. It is nearly as fine as powder, and it seems almost to have been sifted. One day Mammedaty was sitting quietly when a mole came out of the earth. Its cheeks were puffed out as if it had been a squirrel packing nuts. It looked all around for a moment, then blew the fine dark earth out of its mouth. And this it did again and again, until there was a ring of black, powdery earth on the ground. That was a strange and meaningful thing to see. It meant that Mammedaty had got possession of a powerful medicine.*

XXII

Mammedaty was the grandson of Guipahgo, and he got on well most of the time. But, you know, one time he lost his temper. This is how it was: There were several horses in a pasture, and Mammedaty wanted to get them out. A fence ran all the way around and there was just one gate. There was a lot of ground inside. He could not get those horses out. One of them led the others; every time they were driven up to the gate, that one wheeled and ran as fast as it could to the other side. Well, that went on for a long time, and Mammedaty burned up. He ran to the house and got his bow and arrows. The horses were running in single file, and he shot at the one that was causing all that trouble. He missed, though, and the arrow went deep into the neck of the second horse. 52

In the winter of 1852–53, a Pawnee boy who had been held as a captive among the Kiowas succeeded in running away. He took with him an espe-cially fine hunting horse, known far and wide as Guadal-tseyu, "Little Red." That was the most important event of the winter. The loss of that horse was a hard thing to bear. 53

Years ago there was a box of bones in the barn, and I used to go there to look at them. Later someone stole them, I believe. They were the bones of a horse which Mammedaty called by the name "Little Red." It was a small bay, nothing much to look at, I have heard, but it was the fastest runner in that whole corner of the world. White men and Indians alike came from far and near to match their best animals against it, but it never lost a race. I have often thought about that red horse. There have been times when I thought I understood how it was that a man might be moved to preserve the bones of a horse—and another to steal them away. 54

XXII

Aho remembered something, a strange thing. This is how it was: You 55
know, the Tai-me bundle is not very big, but it is full of power. Once Aho
went to see the Tai-me keeper's wife. The two of them were sitting together, passing the time of day, when they heard an awful noise, as if a
tree or some other very heavy object had fallen down. It frightened them,
and they went to see what on earth it was. It was Tai-me—Tai-me had
fallen to the floor. No one knows how it was that Tai-me fell; nothing
caused it, as far as anyone could see.

For a time Mammedaty wore one of the grandmother bundles. This he 56
did for his mother Keahdinekeah; he wore it on a string tied around his
neck. Aho remembered this: that if anyone who wore a medicine bundle
failed to show it the proper respect, it grew extremely heavy around his
neck.

There was a great iron kettle which stood outside of my grandmother's 57
house next to the south porch. It was huge and immovable, or so I thought
when I was a child; I could not imagine that anyone had strength enough
to lift it up. I don't know where it came from; it was always there. It rang
like a bell when you struck it, and with the tips of your fingers you could
feel the black metal sing for a long time afterward. It was used to catch the
rainwater with which we washed our hair.

XXIV

East of my grandmother's house, south of the pecan grove, there is 58
buried a woman in a beautiful dress. Mammedaty used to know where she
is buried, but now no one knows. If you stand on the front porch of the
house and look eastward towards Carnegie, you know that the woman is
buried somewhere within the range of your vision. But her grave is un-
marked. She was buried in a cabinet, and she wore a beautiful dress. How
beautiful it was! It was one of those fine buckskin dresses, and it was decorated with elk's teeth and beadwork. That dress is still there, under the
ground.

Aho's high moccasins are made of softest, cream-colored skins. On each 59
instep there is a bright disc of beadwork—an eight-pointed star, red and
pale blue on a white field—and there are bands of beadwork at the soles
and ankles. The flaps of the leggings are wide and richly ornamented with
blue and red and green and white and lavender beads.

East of my grandmother's house the sun rises out of the plain. Once in 60
his life a man ought to concentrate his mind upon the remembered earth,
I believe. He ought to give himself up to a particular landscape in his ex-
perience, to look at it from as many angles as he can, to wonder about it,
to dwell upon it. He ought to imagine that he touches it with his hands at
every season and listens to the sounds that are made upon it. He ought to
imagine the creatures there and all the faintest motions of the wind. He
ought to recollect the glare of noon and all the colors of the dawn and
dusk.

Epilogue

During the first hours after midnight on the morning of November 13, 61
1833, it seemed that the world was coming to an end. Suddenly the stillness of the night was broken; there were brilliant flashes of light in the
sky, light of such intensity that people were awakened by it. With the
speed and density of a driving rain, stars were falling in the universe.
Some were brighter than Venus; one was said to be as large as the moon.

That most brilliant shower of Leonid meteors has a special place in the 62
memory of the Kiowa people. It is among the earliest entries in the Kiowa
calendars, and it marks the beginning as it were of the historical period
in the tribal mind. In the preceding year Tai-me had been stolen by a band
of Osages, and although it was later returned, the loss was an almost
unimaginable tragedy; and in 1837 the Kiowas made the first of their
treaties with the United States. The falling stars seemed to image the sudden and violent disintegration of an old order.

But indeed the golden age of the Kiowas had been short-lived, ninety 63
or a hundred years, say, from about 1740. The culture would persist for a
while in decline, until about 1875, but then it would be gone, and there
would be very little material evidence that it had ever been. Yet it is within
the reach of memory still, though tenuously now, and moreover it is even
defined in a remarkably rich and living verbal tradition which demands to
be preserved for its own sake. The living memory and the verbal tradition
which transcends it were brought together for me once and for all in the
person of Ko-sahn.

A hundred-year-old woman came to my grandmother's house one 64
afternoon in July. Aho was dead; Mammedaty had died before I was born.
There were very few Kiowas left who could remember the Sun Dances;
Ko-sahn was one of them; she was a grown woman when my grandpar-
ents came into the world. Her body was twisted and her face deeply lined
with age. Her thin white hair was held in place by a cap of black netting,
though she wore braids as well, and she had but one eye. She was dressed

in the manner of a Kiowa matron, a dark, full-cut dress that reached nearly to the ankles, full, flowing sleeves, and a wide, apron-like sash. She sat on a bench in the arbor so concentrated in her great age that she seemed extraordinarily small. She was quiet for a time—she might almost have been asleep—and then she began to speak and to sing. She spoke of many things, and once she spoke of the Sun Dance:

My sisters and I were very young; that was a long time ago. Early one 65
morning they came to wake us up. They had brought a great buffalo in from the plain. Everyone went out to see and to pray. We heard a great many voices. One man said that the lodge was almost ready. We were told to go there, and someone gave me a piece of cloth. It was very beautiful. Then I asked what I ought to do with it, and they said that I must tie it to the Taime tree. There were other pieces of cloth on the tree, and so I put mine there as well.
When the lodge frame was finished, a woman—sometimes a man—began to sing. It was like this:

> Everything is ready.
> Now the four societies must go out.
> They must go out and get the leaves,
>> the branches for the lodge.

And when the branches were tied in place, again there was singing:

> Let the boys go out.
> Come on, boys, now we must get the earth.

The boys began to shout. Now they were not just ordinary boys, not all of them; they were those for whom prayers had been made, and they were dressed in different ways. There was an old, old, woman. She had something on her back. The boys went out to see. The old woman had a bag full of earth on her back. It was a certain kind of sandy earth. That is what they must have in the lodge. The dancers must dance upon the sandy earth. The old woman held a digging tool in her hand. She turned towards the south and pointed with her lips. It was like a kiss, and she began to sing:

> We have brought the earth.
> Now it is time to play;
> As old as I am, I still have the feeling of play.

That was the beginning of the Sun Dance. The dancers treated themselves with buffalo medicine, and slowly they began to take their steps . . . And all the people were around, and they wore splendid things—beautiful buck-skin and beads. The chiefs wore necklaces, and their pendants shone like the sun. There were many people, and oh, it was beautiful! That was the beginning of the Sun Dance. It was all for Tai-me, you know, and it was a long time ago.

It was—all of this and more—a quest, a going forth upon the way to 66
Rainy Mountain. Probably Ko-sahn too is dead now. At times, in the quiet of evening. I think she must have wondered, dreaming, who she was. Was she become in her sleep that old purveyor of the sacred earth, perhaps, the ancient one who, old as she was, still had the feeling of play? And in her mind, at times, did she see the falling stars?

Rainy Mountain Cemetery

Most is your name the name of this dark stone.
Deranged in death, the mind to be inheres
Forever in the nominal unknown,
The wake of nothing audible he hears
Who listens here and now to hear your name.   5

The early sun, red as a hunter's moon,
Runs in the plain. The mountain burns and shines;
And silence is the long approach of noon
Upon the shadow that your name defines—
And death this cold, black density of stone.   10

QUESTIONS FOR DISCUSSION AND WRITING

1. The organization of *The Way to Rainy Mountain* is extremely complex and important since Momaday uses it to help convey his meaning. This organization brings together myth, history, and Momaday's own experiences with little concern for a strict chronological order. Outline and describe the organization of this piece as carefully as you can, making note of when events occur chronologically as compared with where they occur within the essay. Look at the framing sections—the prologue, introduction, and epilogue—and also analyze the use of the three sections within each numbered part.

2. Using your analysis of the organization of this selection, discuss the meanings Momaday conveys through the structure of his essay. What can he say about nature with this structure that he couldn't say with any other?

3. Momaday writes that his grandmother "bore a vision of deicide," by which he means she saw the last time the Kiowas came together as "a living Sun Dance Culture" (par. 14). In 1890 they were "[f]orbidden without cause the essential act of their faith, having seen the wild herds [of buffalo] slaughtered and left to rot upon the ground" (par. 14). How does Momaday try to resurrect the spirituality of that Sun Dance culture? How well does he succeed?

EDWARD ABBEY

*Edward Abbey (1927–1989) was an angry, sometimes bitter man who found little
of worth in modern civilization. Instead he loved the wild deserts and mountains
of the American Southwest and fought to keep them untouched by corporations,
ranchers, and casual tourists who did not feel the proper reverence for their beauty.
He lived in the desert, worked for the Forest Service and the National Park Service
there, and now is buried somewhere in the desert. He had a tremendous hatred for
fences, roads, bridges, or any other intrusion of humans on the natural beauty of
the West. This hatred is the major theme running through* The Monkey Wrench
Gang *(1975), an underground cult classic.*

*One of the epigraphs in the book is from Walt Whitman—"Resist Much. Obey
Little"—and this is certainly the motto of the four people who make up the monkey
wrench gang: Seldom Seen Smith, a river man; George Hayduke, a Vietnam vet
who was in Special Forces; and Doc Sarvis and Bonnie Abbzug, a couple in a
rather unorthodox way. With a common love of the wild and hatred for those who
would destroy it, their ultimate goal is to blow up the Glen Canyon Dam and free
the canyon once again. In this excerpt they throw a "monkey wrench" into the
plans of some road builders.*

From *The Monkey Wrench Gang*

One fine day in early June, bearing west from Blanding, Utah, on their   1
way to cache more goods, the gang paused at the summit of Comb Ridge
for a look at the world below. They were riding four abreast in the wide
cab of Seldom Seen Smith's truck. It was lunchtime. He pulled off the
dusty road—Utah State Road 95—and turned south on a jeep track that
followed close to the rim. Comb Ridge is a great monocline, rising gradually on the east side, dropping off at an angle close to 90 degrees on the
west side. The drop-off from the rim is about five hundred feet straight
down, with another three hundred feet or more of steeply sloping talus
below the cliff. Like many other canyons, mesas and monoclines in south-
east Utah, Comb Ridge forms a serious barrier to east-west land travel. Or
it used to. God meant it to.

Smith pulled the truck up onto a shelf of slickrock within twenty feet of   2
the rim and stopped. Everybody got out, gratefully, and walked close to
the edge. The sun stood high in the clouds; the air was still and warm.
Flowers grew from cracks in the rock—globe mallow, crownbeard, gilia,

rock cress—and flowering shrubs—cliff rose, Apache plume, chamisa, others. Doc was delighted.

"Look," he said, *"Arabis pulchra. Fallugia paradoxa. Cowania mexi-*   3
cana, by God."

"What's this?" Bonnie said, pointing to little purplish things in the   4
shade of a pinyon pine.

"Pedicularis centranthera."   5

"Yeah, okay, but what is it?"   6

"What is it?" Doc paused. "What it is, no man knows, but men call it ...   7
wood betony."

"Don't be a wise-ass."   8

"Also known as lousewort. A child came to me saying, 'What is the   9
lousewort?' And I said, 'Perhaps it is the handkerchief of the lord.'"

"Nobody loves a wise-ass."   10

"I know," he admitted.   11

Smith and Hayduke stood on the brink of five hundred feet of naked   12
gravity. That yawning abyss which calls men to sleep. But they were looking not down at death but southward at life, or at least at a turmoil of dust
and activity. Whine of motors, snort and growl of distant diesels.

"The new road," Smith explained.   13

"Uh huh." Hayduke raised his field glasses and studied the scene, some   14
three miles off. "Big operation," he mumbled. "Euclids, D-Nines, haulers,
scrapers, loaders, backhoes, drills, tankers. What a beautiful fucking layout."

Doc and Bonnie came up, flowers in their hair. Far off south in the dust,   15
sunlight flashed on glass, on bright steel.

"What's going on down there?" Doc said.   16

"That's the new road they're working on," Smith said.   17

"What's wrong with the old road?"   18

"The old road is too old," Smith explained. "It crawls up and down   19
hills and goes in and out of draws and works around the head of canyons and it ain't paved and it generally takes too long to get anywhere.
This new road will save folks ten minutes from Blanding to Natural
Bridges."

"It's a county road?" Doc asked.   20

"It's built for the benefit of certain companies that operate in this   21
county, but it's not a county road, it's a state road. It's to help out the poor
fellas that own the uranium mines and the truck fleets and the marinas on
Lake Powell, that's what it's for. They gotta eat too."

"I see," said Doc. "Let me have a look, George."   22

Hayduke passed the field glasses to the doctor, who took a long look,   23
puffing on his Marsh-Wheeling.

"Busy busy busy," he said. He returned the glasses to Hayduke. "Men,   24
we have work to do tonight."

"Me too," Bonnie said.   25

"You too."   26

One thin scream came floating down, like a feather, from the silver-   27
clouded sky. Hawk. Redtail, solitaire, one hawk passing far above the red
reef, above the waves of Triassic sandstone, with a live snake clutched in
its talons. The snake wriggled, casually, as it was borne away to a different world. Lunchtime.

After a little something themselves the gang got back in Smith's truck   28
and drove two miles closer, over the rock and through the brush, in low
range and four-wheel drive, to a high point overlooking the project more
directly. Smith parked the truck in the shade of the largest pinyon pine
available, which was not big enough to effectively conceal it.

Netting, Hayduke thought; we need camouflage netting. He made a   29
note in his notebook.

Now the three men and the girl worked their way to the rim again, to   30
the edge of the big drop-off. Out of habit Hayduke led the way, crawling
forward on hands and knees, then on his belly the last few yards to their
observation point. Were such precautions necessary? Probably not, so
early in their game; the Enemy, after all, was not aware yet that Hayduke
& Co. existed. The Enemy, in fact, still fondly imagined that he enjoyed the
favor of the American public, with no exceptions.

Incorrect. They lay on their stomachs on the warm sandstone, under   31
the soft and pearly sky, and peered down seven hundred vertical feet and
half a mile by line of sight to where the iron dinosaurs romped and roared
in their pit of sand. There was love in neither head nor heart of Abbzug,
Hayduke, Smith and Sarvis. No sympathy. But considerable involuntary
admiration for all that power, all that controlled and directed superhuman
force.

Their vantage point gave them a view of the heart, not the whole, of the   32
project. The surveying crews, far ahead of the big machines, had finished
weeks earlier, but evidence of their work remained: the Day-Glo ribbon,
shocking pink, that waved from the boughs of juniper trees, the berib-
boned stakes planted in the earth marking center line and shoulder of the
coming road, the steel pins hammered into the ground as reference
points.

What Hayduke and friends could and did see were several of the many   33
phases of a road-building project that follow the survey. To the far west,
on the rise beyond Comb Wash, they saw bulldozers clearing the right-of-
way. In forested areas the clearing job would require a crew of loggers
with chain saws, but here in southeast Utah, on the plateau, the little
pinyon pines and junipers offered no resistance to the bulldozers. The

crawler-tractors pushed them all over with nonchalant ease and shoved them aside, smashed and bleeding, into heaps of brush, where they would be left to die and decompose. No one knows precisely how sentient is a pinyon pine, for example, or to what degree such woody organisms can feel pain or fear, and in any case the road builders had more important things to worry about, but this much is clearly established as scientific fact: a living tree, once uprooted, takes many days to wholly die.

Behind the first wave of bulldozers came a second, blading off the soil   34
and ripping up loose stone down to the bedrock. Since this was a cut-and-fill operation it was necessary to blast away the bedrock down to the grade level specified by the highway engineers. Watching from their comfortable grandstand bleachers, the four onlookers saw drill rigs crawl on self-propelled tracks to the blasting site, followed by tractors towing air compressors. Locked in position and linked to the compressors, the drill steel bit into the rock with screaming teconite bits, star-shaped and carbide-tipped. Powdered stone floated on the air as the engines roared. Resonant vibrations shuddered through the bone structure of the earth. More mute suffering. The drill rigs moved on over the hill to the next site.

The demolition team arrived. Charges were lowered into the bore   35
holes, gently tamped and stemmed, and wired to an electrical circuit. The watchers on the rim heard the chief blaster's warning whistle, saw the crew move off to a safe distance, saw the spout of smoke and heard the thunder as the blaster fired his shot. More bulldozers, loaders and giant trucks moved in to shovel up and haul away the debris.

Down in the center of the wash below the ridge the scrapers, the earth-   36
movers and the dump trucks with eighty-ton beds unloaded their loads, building up the fill as the machines beyond were deepening the cut. Cut and fill, cut and fill, all afternoon the work went on. The object in mind was a modern high-speed highway for the convenience of the trucking industry, with grades no greater than 8 percent. That was the immediate object. The ideal lay still farther on. The engineer's dream is a model of perfect sphericity, the planet Earth with all irregularities removed, highways merely painted on a surface smooth as glass. Of course the engineers still have a long way to go but they are patient tireless little fellows; they keep hustling on, like termites in a termitorium. It's steady work, and their only natural enemies, they believe, are mechanical breakdown or "down time" for the equipment, and labor troubles, and bad weather, and sometimes faulty preparation by the geologists and surveyors.

The one enemy the contractor would not and did not think of was the   37
band of four idealists stretched out on their stomachs on a rock under the desert sky.

Down below the metal monsters roared, bouncing on rubber through   38 the cut in the ridge, dumping their loads and thundering up the hill for more. The green beasts of Bucyrus, the yellow brutes of Caterpillar, snorting like dragons, puffing black smoke into the yellow dust.

The sun slipped three degrees westward, beyond the clouds, beyond   39
the silver sky. The watchers on the ridge munched on jerky, sipped from their canteens. The heat began to slacken off. There was talk of supper, but no one had much appetite. There was talk of getting ready for the evening program. The iron machines still rolled in the wash below, but it seemed to be getting close to quitting time.

"The main thing we have to watch for," Hayduke said, "is a night   40
watchman. They just might keep some fucker out here at night. Maybe with a dog. Then we'll have problems."

"There won't be any watchman," Smith said. "Not all night, anyhow."   41

"What makes you so sure?"   42

"It's the way they do things around here; we're out in the country.   43
Nobody lives out here. It's fifteen miles from Blanding. This here project is three miles off the old road, which hardly nobody drives at night anyhow. They don't expect any trouble."

"Maybe some of them are camping out here," Hayduke said.   44

"Naw," Smith said. "They don't do that kind of thing either. These   45
boys work like dogs all day long; they wanta get back to town in the evening. They like their civilized comforts. They ain't campers. These here construction workers don't think nothing of driving fifty miles to work every morning. They're all crazy as bedbugs. I worked in these outfits myself."

Doc and Hayduke, armed with the field glasses, kept watch. Smith and   46
Bonnie crawled down from the ridge, keeping out of sight, until they were below the skyline. Then they walked to the truck, set up the campstove and began preparing a meal for the crew. The doctor and Hayduke, poor cocks, made good dishwashers. All four were qualified eaters, but only Bonnie and Smith cared enough about food to cook it with decency.

Smith was right; the construction workers departed all together long   47
before sundown. Leaving their equipment lined up along the right-of-way, nose to tail, like a herd of iron elephants, or simply in situ, where quitting time found them, the operators straggled back in small groups to their transport vehicles. Far above, Doc and Hayduke could hear their voices, the laughter, the rattle of lunch buckets. The carryalls and pickups driven by men at the eastern end of the job came down through the big notch to meet the equipment operators. The men climbed in; the trucks turned and ground uphill through the dust, into the notch again and out of sight. For some time there was the fading sound of motors, a cloud of dust rising above the pinyon and juniper; then that too was gone. A tanker truck appeared, full of diesel fuel, groaning down the grade toward the

machines, and proceeded from one to the next, the driver and his helper filling the fuel tanks of each, topping them off. Finished, the tanker turned and followed the others back through the evening toward the distant glow of town, somewhere beyond the eastward bulge of the plateau.

Now the stillness was complete. The watchers on the rim, eating their suppers from tin plates, heard the croon of a mourning dove far down the wash. They heard the hoot of an owl, the cries of little birds retiring to sleep in the dusty cottonwoods. The great golden light of the setting sun streamed across the sky, glowing upon the clouds and the mountains. Almost all the country within their view was roadless, uninhabited, a wilderness. They meant to keep it that way. They sure meant to try. *Keep it like it was.* 48

The sun went down. 49

Tactics, materials, tools, gear. 50

Hayduke was reading off his checklist. "Gloves! Everybody got his gloves? Put 'em on now. Anybody goes fucking around down there without gloves I'll chop his hands off." 51

"You haven't washed the dishes yet," Bonnie said. 52

"Hard hat! Everybody got his hard hat?" He looked around at the crew. "You—put that thing on your head." 53

"It doesn't fit," she said. 54

"Make it fit. Somebody show her how to adjust the headband. Jesus Christ." Looking back at his list. "Bolt cutters!" Hayduke brandished his own, a 24-inch pair of cross-levered steel jaws for cutting bolts, rods, wire, most anything up to half an inch in diameter. The rest of the party were equipped with fencing pliers, good enough for most purposes. 55

"Now, you lookouts," he went on, addressing Bonnie and Doc. "Do you know your signals?" 56

"One short and a long for warning, take cover," Doc said, holding up his metal whistle. "One short and two longs for all clear, resume operations. Three longs for distress, come help. Four longs for . . . what are four longs for?" 57

"Four longs mean work completed, am returning to camp," Bonnie said. "And one long means acknowledgment, message received." 58

"Don't much like them tin whistles," Smith said. "We need something more natural. More eco-logical. Owl hoots, maybe. Anybody hears them tin whistles will know there's two-legged animals slinkin' around. Lemme show you how to hoot like a owl." 59

Training time. Hands cupped and close, one little opening between thumbs, shape the lips, blow. Blow from the belly, down deep; the call will float through canyons, across mountainsides, all the way down in the valley. Hayduke showed Dr. Sarvis; Smith showed Abbzug, personally, holding her hands in the necessary way, blowing into them, letting her 60

blow into his. She picked it up quickly, the doctor not so fast. They rehearsed the signals. For a while the twilight seemed full of great horned
owls, talking. Finally they were ready. Hayduke returned to his checklist.

"Okay, gloves, hats, wire cutters, signals, Now: Karo syrup, four quarts   61
each. Matches. Flashlights—be careful with those: keep the light close to
your work, don't swing it around, shut it off when you're moving. Maybe
we should work out light signals? Naw, later. Water. Jerky. Hammer,
screwdriver, cold chisel—okay, I got them. What else?"

"We're all set," Smith said. "Let's get a move on."   62

They shouldered their packs. Hayduke's pack, with most of the hard-   63
ware in it, weighed twice as much as anyone else's. He didn't care. Seldom
Seen Smith led the way through the sundown gloom. The others followed
in single file, Hayduke at the rear. There was no trail, no path. Smith
picked the most economic route among the scrubby trees, around the
bayonet leaves of the yucca and the very hairy prickly pear, across the little sandy washes below the crest of the ridge. As much as possible he led
them on the rock, leaving no tracks.

They were headed south by the stars, south by the evening breeze,   64
toward a rising Scorpio sprawled out fourteen galactic worlds wide across
the southern sky. Owls hooted from the pygmy forest. The saboteurs
hooted back.

Smith circumvented an anthill, a huge symmetric arcologium of sand   65
surrounded by a circular area denuded of any vestige of vegetation. The
dome home of the harvester ants. Smith went around and so did Bonnie
but Doc stumbled straight into it, stirring up the formicary. The big red
ants swarmed out looking for trouble; one of them bit Doc on the calf. He
stopped, turned and dismantled the anthill with a series of vigorous kicks.

"Thus I refute R. Buckminster Fuller," he growled. "Thus do I refute   66
Paolo Soleri, B. F. Skinner and the late Walter Gropius."

'How late was he?" Smith asked.   67

"Doc hates ants," Bonnie explained. "And they hate him."   68

' The anthill," said Doc, "is sign, symbol and symptom of what we are   69
about out here, stumbling through the gloaming like so many stumble-
bums. I mean it is the model in microcosm of what we must find a way to
oppose and halt. The anthill, like the Fullerian foam fungus, is the mark of
social disease. Anthills abound where over-grazing prevails. The plastic
dome follows the plague of runaway industrialism, prefigures technological tyranny and reveals the true quality of our lives, which sinks in inverse
ratio to the growth of the Gross National Product. End of mini-lecture by
Dr. Sarvis."

"Good," Bonnie said.   70

"Amen," said Smith.   71

The evening gave way to night, a dense violet solution of starlight and   72

darkness mixed with energy, each rock and shrub and tree and scarp outlined by an aura of silent radiation. Smith led the conspirators along the
contour of the terrain until they came to the brink of something, an edge,
a verge, beyond which stood nothing tangible. This was not the rim of the
monocline, however, but the edge of the big man-made cut *through* the
monocline. Below in the gloom those with sufficient night vision could
see the broad new roadway and the dark forms of machines, two hundred
feet down.

Smith and friends proceeded along this new drop-off until they reached   73
a point where it was possible to scramble down to the crushed rock and
heavy dust of the roadbed. Looking northeast, toward Blanding, they saw
this pale raw freeway leading straight across the desert, through the scrub
forest and out of sight in the darkness. No lights were visible, only the faint
glow of the town fifteen miles away. In the opposite direction the roadbed
curved down between the walls of the cut, sinking out of view toward the
wash. They walked into the cut.

The first thing they encountered, on the shoulder of the roadbed, were   74
survey stakes. Hayduke pulled them up and tossed them into the brush.

"Always pull up survey stakes," he said. "Anywhere you find them.   75
Always. That's the first goddamned general order in the monkey wrench
business. Always pull up survey stakes."

They walked deeper into the cut to where it was possible, looking   76
down and west, to make out though dimly the bottom of Comb Wash, the
fill area, the scattered earth-moving equipment. Here they stopped for further consultation.

"We want our first lookout here," Hayduke said.   77

"Doc or Bonnie?"   78

"I want to wreck something," Bonnie said. "I don't want to sit here in   79
the dark making owl noises."

"I'll stay here," Doc said.   80

Once more they rehearsed signals. All in order. Doc made himself com-   81
fortable on the operator's seat of a giant compactor machine. He toyed
with the controls. "Stiff," he said, "but it's transportation."

"Why don't we start with this fucker right here?" Hayduke said, mean-   82
ing Doc's machine. "Just for the practice."

Why not? Packs were opened, tools and flashlights brought out. While   83
Doc stood watch above them his three comrades entertained themselves
cutting up the wiring, fuel lines, control link rods and hydraulic hoses
of the machine, a beautiful new 27-ton tandem-drummed yellow Hyster
C-450A, Caterpillar 330 HP diesel engine, sheepsfoot rollers, manufac-
turer's suggested retail price only $29,500 FOB Saginaw, Michigan. One of
the best. A dreamboat.

They worked happily. Hard hats clinked and clanked against the steel.   84

Lines and rods snapped apart with the rich *spang!* and solid *clunk!* of metal severed under tension. Doc lit another stogie. Smith wiped a drop of oil from his eyelid. The sharp smell of hydraulic fluid floated on the air, mixing uneasily with the aroma of Doc's smoke. Running oil pattered on the dust. There was another sound, far away, as of a motor. They paused. Doc stared into the dark. Nothing. The noise faded.

"All's clear," he said. "Carry on, lads." 85

When everything was cut which they could reach and cut, Hayduke 86 pulled the dipstick from the engine block—to check the oil? not exactly —and poured a handful of fine sand into the crankcase. Too slow. He unscrewed the oil-filler cap, took chisel and hammer and punched a hole through the oil strainer and poured in more sand. Smith removed the fueltank cap and emptied four quart bottles of sweet Karo syrup into the fuel tank. Injected into the cylinders, that sugar would form a solid coat of carbon on cylinder walls and piston rings. The engine should seize up like a block of iron, when they got it running. If they could get it running.

What else? Abbzug, Smith and Hayduke stood back a little and stared 87 at the quiet hulk of the machine. All were impressed by what they had done. The murder of a machine. Decide. All of them, even Hayduke, a little awed by the enormity of their crime. By the sacrilege of it.

"Let's slash the seat," said Bonnie. 88

"That's vandalism," Doc said. "I'm against vandalism. Slashing seats is 89 petty-bourgeois."

"So okay, okay," Bonnie said. "Let's get on to the next item." 90

"Then we'll all meet back here?" Doc said. 91

"It's the only way back up on the ridge," Smith said. 92

"But if there's any shit," Hayduke said, "don't wait for us. We'll meet at 93 the truck."

"I couldn't find my way back there if my life depended on it," Doc said. 94 "Not in the dark."

Smith scratched his long jaw. "Well, Doc," he said, "if there's any kind 95 of trouble maybe you better just hightail it up on the bank there, above the road, and wait for us. Don't forget the hoot owl. We'll find you that way."

They left him there in the dark, perched on the seat of the maimed and 96 poisoned compactor. The one red eye of his cigar watched them depart. The plan was for Bonnie to stand watch at the far west end of the project, alone, while Hayduke and Smith worked on the equipment down in the wash. She murmured against them.

"You ain't afraid of the dark, are you?" Smith asked. 97

"Of course I'm afraid of the dark." 98

"You afraid to be alone?" 99

"Of course I'm afraid to be alone." 100

"You mean you don't want to be lookout?" 101

"I'll be lookout." 102

"No place for women," Hayduke muttered. 103

"You shut up," she said. "Am I complaining? I'll be lookout. So shut up 104
before I take your jaw off."

The dark seemed warm, comfortable, secure to Hayduke. He liked it. 105
The Enemy, if he appeared, would come loudly announced with roar of
engines, blaze of flares, an Operation Rolling Thunder of shells and
bombs, just as in Vietnam. So Hayduke assumed. For the night and the
wilderness belong to *us*. This is Indian country. Our country. Or so he
assumed.

Downhill, maybe a mile, in one great switchback, the roadway de- 106
scended through the gap to the built-up fill across the floor of Comb Wash.
They soon reached the first group of machines—the earthmovers, the big
trucks, the landscape architects.

Bonnie was about to go on by herself. Smith took her arm for a mo- 107
ment. "You stay close, honey," he told her, "only concentrate on looking
and listening; let me and George do the hard work. Take the hard hat off
so you can hear better. Okay?"

"Well," she agreed, "for the moment." But she wanted a bigger share of 108
the action later. He agreed. Share and share alike. He showed her where
to find the steps that led to the open cab of an 85-ton Euclid mountain
mover. She sat up there, like a lookout in a crow's nest, while he and
Hayduke went to work.

Busywork. Cutting and snipping, snapping and wrenching. They 109
crawled all over a Caterpillar D-9A, world's greatest bulldozer, the idol
of all highwaymen. Put so much sand in the crankcase that Hayduke
couldn't get the dipstick reinserted all the way. He trimmed it short with
the rod-and-bolt cutter. Made it fit. Sand in the oil intake. He climbed into
the cab, tried to turn the fuel-tank cap. Wouldn't turn. Taking hammer and
chisel he broke it loose, unscrewed it, poured four quarts of good high-
energy Karo into the diesel fuel. Replaced the cap. Sat in the driver's seat
and played for a minute with the switches and levers.

"You know what would be fun?" he said to Smith, who was down 110
below hacking through a hydraulic hose.

"What's that, George?" 111

"Get this fucker started, take it up to the top of the ridge and run it over 112
the rim."

"That there'd take us near half the night, George." 113

"Sure would be fun." 114

"We can't get it started anyhow." 115

"Why not?" 116

"There ain't no rotor arm in the magneto. I looked. They usually take 117
out the rotor arm when they leave these beasts out on the road."

"Yeah?" Hayduke takes notebook and pencil from his shirt pocket, turns on his flashlight, makes notation: *Rotor arms.* "You know something else that would be fun?" 118

Smith, busy nullifying all physical bond between cylinder heads and fuel injection lines, says, "What?" 119

"We could knock a pin out of each tread. Then when the thing moved it would run right off its own fucking tracks. That would really piss them." 120

"George, this here tractor ain't gonna move at all for a spell. It ain't-a-goin' *nowheres.*" 121

"For a spell." 122

"That's what I said." 123

"That's the trouble." 124

Hayduke climbed down from the cab and came close to Smith, there in the black light of the stars, doing his humble chores, the pinpoint of his flashlight beam fixed on a set screw in an engine block the weight of three Volkswagen buses. The yellow Caterpillar, enormous in the dark, looms over the two men with the indifference of a god, submitting without a twitch of its enameled skin to their malicious ministrations. The down payment on this piece of equipment comes to around $30,000. What were the men worth? In any rational chemico-psycho-physical analysis? In a nation of two hundred and ten million (210,000,000) bodies? Getting cheaper by the day, as mass production lowers the unit cost? 125

"That's the trouble," he said again. "All this wire cutting is only going to slow them down, not stop them. God-fuckingdammit, Seldom, we're wasting our time." 126

"What's the matter, George?" 127

"We're wasting our time." 128

"What do you mean?" 129

"I mean we ought to really blast this motherfucker. This one and all the others. I mean set them on fire. Burn them up." 130

"That there's arson." 131

"For chrissake, what's the difference? You think what we're doing now is much nicer? You know damn well if old Morrison-Knudsen was out here now with his goons he'd be happy to see us all shot dead." 132

"They ain't gonna be too happy about this, you're right there. They ain't gonna understand us too good." 133

"They'll understand us. They'll hate our fucking guts." 134

"They won't understand why we're doin' this, George. That's what I mean. I mean we're gonna be misunderstood." 135

"No, we're not gonna be misunderstood. We're gonna be hated." 136

"Maybe we should explain." 137

"Maybe we should do it right. None of this petty fucking around." 138

Smith was silent. 139

"Let's *destroy* this fucker."   140

"I don't know," Smith said.   141

"I mean roast it in its own grease. I just happen to have a little siphon   142
hose here in my pack. Like I just happen to have some matches. I mean
we just siphon some of that fuel out of the tank and we just sort of slosh it
around over the engine and cab and then we just sort of toss a match at it.
Let God do the rest."

"Yeah, I guess He would," Smith agreed. "If God meant this here bull-   143
dozer to live He wouldn't of filled its tank with diesel fuel. Now would He
of? But George, what about Doc?"

"What about him? Since when is he the boss?"   144

"He's the one bankrolling this here operation. We need him."   145

"We need his money."   146

"Well, all right, put it this way: I like old Doc. And I like that little old   147
lady of his too. And I think all four of us got to stick together. And I think
we can't do anything that all four of us ain't agreed to do beforehand.
Think about it that way, George."

"Is that the end of the sermon?"   148

"That's the end of the sermon."   149

Now Hayduke was silent for a while. They worked. Hayduke thought.   150
After a minute he said, "You know something, Seldom? I guess you're
right."

"I thought I was wrong once," Seldom said, "but I found out later I was   151
mistaken."

They finished with the D-9A. The siphon hose and the matches re-   152
mained inside Hayduke's pack. For the time being. Having done all they
could to sand, jam, gum, mutilate and humiliate the first bulldozer, they
went on to the next, the girl with them. Smith put his arm around her.

"Miss Bonnie," he says, "how do you like the night shift?"   153

"Too peaceful. When's my turn to wreck something?"   154

"We need you to look out."   155

"I'm bored."   156

"Don't you worry about that none, honey. We're gonna have enough   157
excitement pretty soon to last you and me for the rest of our lives. If we
live that long. How do you think old Doc is doing back there all by his
lonesome?"

"He's all right. He lives inside his head most of the time anyway."   158

Another giant machine looms out of the darkness before them. A   159
hauler; they chop it up. Then the next. Bonnie watches from her post in
the cab of a nearby earthmover. Next! The men go on.

"If only we could start up the motors on these som-bitches," Hayduke   160
said. "We could drain the oil out, let the motors run and walk away.
They'd take care of themselves and we'd be finished a lot faster."

"That'd do it," Smith allowed. "Drain the oil and let the engines run. 161
They'd seize up tighter'n a bull's asshole in fly time. They never would get
them buggers prised open."

"We could give each one a try anyhow." And acting on his words, 162
Hayduke climbed to the controls of a big bulldozer. "How do you start this
mother?"

"I'll show you if we find one ready to go." 163

"How about a hot wire? Maybe we could start it that way. Bypass the 164
ignition."

"Not a caterpillar tractor. This ain't no car, George, you know. This is 165
a D-Eight. This here's heavy-duty industrial equipment; this ain't the old
Farmall back home."

"Well, I'm ready for driving lessons anytime." 166

Hayduke climbed down from the operator's seat. They worked on the 167
patient, sifting handfuls of fine Triassic sand into the crankcase, cutting up
the wiring, the fuel lines, the hydraulic hoses to fore and aft attachments,
dumping Karo into the fuel tanks. Why Karo instead of plain sugar? Smith
wanted to know. Pours better, Hayduke explained; mixes easier with the
diesel, doesn't jam up in strainers. You sure about that? No.

Hayduke crawled under the bulldozer to find the drain plug in the oil 168
pan. He found it, through an opening in the armored skid plate, but
needed a big wrench to crack it loose. They tried the toolbox in the cab.
Locked. Hayduke broke the lock with his cold chisel and hammer. Inside
they found a few simple and massive instruments: an iron spanner three
feet long; a variety of giant end wrenches; a sledgehammer; a wooden-
handled monkey wrench; nuts, bolts, friction tape, wire.

Hayduke took the spanner, which looked like the right size, and 169
crawled again underneath the tractor. He struggled for a while with the
plug, finally broke it loose and let out the oil. The great machine began to
bleed; its lifeblood drained out with pulsing throbs, onto the dust and
sand. When it was all gone he replaced the plug. Why? Force of habit—
thought he was changing the oil in his jeep.

Hayduke surfaced, smeared with dust, grease, oil, rubbing a bruised 170
knuckle, "Shit," he said, "I don't know."

"What's the matter?" 171

"Are we doing this job right? That's what I don't know. Now the opera- 172
tor gets on this thing in the morning, tries to start it up, nothing happens.
So the first thing he sees is all the wiring cut, all the fuel lines cut. So
putting sand in the crankcase, draining the oil, isn't going to do any good
till they get the motor to run. But when they fix all the wiring and lines
they're gonna be checking other things too. Like the oil level, naturally.
Then they find the sand. Then they see somebody's drained the oil. I'm
thinking if we really want to do this monkey wrench business right,

maybe we should hide our work. I mean keep it simple and sophisticated."

"Well, George, you was the one wanted to set these things on fire about   173
a minute ago."

"Yeah. Now I'm thinking the other way."   174

"Well, it's too late. We already showed our hand here. We might as   175
well go on like we started."

"Now think about it a minute, Seldom. They'll all get here about the   176
same time tomorrow morning. Everybody starts up the engine on his
piece of equipment, or tries to. Some'll discover right away that we cut up
the wiring. I mean on the machines we already cut. But look, on the others, if we let the wiring alone, let the fuel lines alone, so they can start the
engines, then the sand and the Karo will really do some good. I mean
they'll have a chance to do the work we want them to do: ruin the engines.
What do you think about that?"

They leaned side by side against the steel track of the Cat, gazing at   177
each other through the soft starlight.

"I kind of wish we had figured all this out before," Smith said. "We   178
ain't got all night."

"Why don't we have all night?"   179

"Because I reckon we ought to be fifty miles away from here come   180
morning. That's why."

"Not me," Hayduke said. "I'm going to hang around and watch what   181
happens. I want that personal fucking satisfaction."

A hoot owl hooted from the earthmover up ahead. "What's going on   182
back there?" Bonnie called. "You think this is a picnic or something?"

"Okay," Smith said, "let's keep it kinda simple. Let's put these here   183
cutters away for a while and just work on the oil and fuel systems. God
knows we got plenty of sand here. About ten thousand square miles of it."
Agreed.

They went on, quickly and methodically now, from machine to ma-   184
chine, pouring sand into each crankcase and down every opening which
led to moving parts. When they had used up all their Karo syrup, they
dumped sand into the fuel tanks, as an extra measure.

All the way, into the night, Hayduke, Smith, they worked their way to   185
the end of the line. Now one, now the other, would relieve Bonnie at the
lookout post so that she could participate fully in field operations.
Teamwork, that's what made America great: teamwork and initiative,
that's what made America what it is today. They worked over the Cats,
they operated on the earthmovers, they gave the treatment to the
Schramm air compressors the Hyster compactors the Massey crawler-
loaders the Joy Ram track drills the Dart D-600 wheel loaders not overlooking one lone John Deere 690-A excavator backhoe, and that was

about all for the night; that was about enough; old Morrison-Knudsen had plenty of equipment all right but somebody was due for headaches in the morning when the sun came up and engines were fired up and all those little particles of sand, corrosive as powdered emery, began to wreak earth's vengeance on the cylinder walls of the despoilers of the desert.

When they reached the terminus of the cut-and-fill site, high on the 186 folded earth across the wash from Comb Ridge, and had thoroughly sand-packed the last piece of road-building equipment, they sat down on a ju-niper log to rest. Seldom Seen, reckoning by the stars, estimated the time at 2 A.M. Hayduke guessed it was only 11:30. He wanted to go on, follow-ing the surveyors, and remove all the stakes, pins and flagging that he knew was waiting out there, in the dark, in the semi-virgin wilds beyond. But Abbzug had a better idea; instead of destroying the survey crew's signs, she suggested, why not relocate them all in such a manner as to lead the right-of-way in a grand loop back to the starting point? Or lead it to the brink of, say, Muley Point, where the contractors would confront a twelve-hundred-foot vertical drop-off down to the goosenecks of the San Juan River.

"Don't give them any ideas," Hayduke said. "They'd just want to 187 build another goddamned bridge."

"Them survey markings go on west for twenty miles," Smith said. He 188 was against both plans.

"So what do we do?" says Bonnie. 189

"I'd like to crawl into the sack," Smith said. "Get some sleep." 190

"I like that idea myself." 191

"But the night is young," Hayduke said. 192

"George," says Smith, "we can't do everything in one night. We got 193 to get Doc and get back to the truck and haul ass. We don't want to be around here in the morning."

"They can't prove a thing." 194

"That's what Pretty-Boy Floyd said. That's what Baby-Face Nelson said 195 and John Dillinger and Butch Cassidy and that other fella, what's his name—?"

"Jesus," Hayduke growls. 196

"Yeah, Jesus Christ. That's what they all said and look what happened 197 to them. Nailed."

"This is our first big night," Hayduke said. "We ought to do as much 198 work as we can. We're not likely to get more easy operations like this. Next time they'll have locks on everything. Maybe booby traps. And watchmen with guns, shortwave radios, dogs."

Poor Hayduke: won all his arguments but lost his immortal soul. He 199 had to yield.

They marched back the way they'd come, past the quiet, spayed, med- 200 icated machinery. Those doomed dinosaurs of iron, waiting patiently through the remainder of the night for buggering morning's rosy-fingered denouement. The agony of cylinder rings, jammed by a swollen piston, may be like other modes of sodomy a crime against nature in the eyes of deus ex machina; who can say?

A hoot owl called from what seemed far away, east in the pitchblack shadows of the dynamite notch. One short and a long, then a pause, one short and a long repeated. Warning cry. 201

"Doc's on the job," Smith said. "That there's Doc a-talkin' to us." 202

The men and the girl stood in the dark, listening hard, trying to see. The warning call was repeated, twice more. The lonesome hoot owl, speaking. 203

Listening. Nervous crickets chirred in the dry grass under the cottonwoods. A few doves stirred in the boughs. 204

They heard, faint but growing, the mutter of a motor. Then they saw, beyond the notch, the swing of headlight beams. A vehicle appeared, two blazing eyes, grinding down the grade in low gear. 205

"Okay," says Hayduke, "off the roadway. Watch out for a spotlight. And if there's any shit we scatter." 206

Understood. Caught in the middle of the big fill, there was nowhere to go but over the side. They slid down the loose rock to the jumble of boulders at the bottom. There, nursing abrasions, they took cover. 207

The truck came down the roadway, moved slowly by, went as far as it could and stopped among the machines huddled at the far end of the fill. There it paused for five minutes, engine still, lights turned off. The man inside the truck, sitting with windows open, sipped coffee from a thermos jug and listened to the night. He switched on his left-hand spotlight and played the beam over the roadbed and the machinery. So far as he could see, all was well. He started the engine, turned back the way he had come, passed the listeners fifty feet below, drove on up the grade through the notch and disappeared. 208

Hayduke slipped his revolver back into his rucksack, blew his nose through his fingers and scrambled up the talus to the top of the roadway. Smith and Abbzug emerged from the dark. 209

"Next time dogs," says Hayduke. "Then gunners in helicopters. Then the napalm. Then the B-52s." 210

They walked through the dark, up the long grade into the eastern cut. Listening for the bearded goggled great bald owl to sound. 211

"I don't think it's quite like that," Smith was saying. "They're people too, like us. We got to remember that, George. If we forget we'll get just like them and then where are we?" 212

"They're not like us," Hayduke said. "They're different. They come from the moon. They'll spend a million dollars to burn one gook to death." 213

"Well, I got a brother-in-law in the U.S. Air Force. And he's a sergeant.   214
I took a general's family down the river once. Them folks are more or less
human, George, just like us."

"Did you meet the general?"   215

"No, but his wife, she was sweet as country pie."   216

Hayduke was silent, smiling grimly in the dark. The heavy pack on his   217
back, overloaded with water and weapons and hardware, felt good, solid,
real, meant business. He felt potent as a pistol, dangerous as dynamite,
tough and mean and hard and full of love for his fellowman. And for his
fellow woman too, e.g., Abbzug there, goddamn her, in her goddamned
tight jeans and that shaggy baggy sweater which failed nevertheless to
quite fully conceal the rhythmic swing, back and forth, of her uncon-
strained fucking mammaries. Christ, he thought, I need work. Work!

They found Doc sitting on a rock at the edge of the cutbank, smoking   218
the apparently inextinguishable and interminable stogie. "Well?" he says.

"Well now," Smith says, "I'd say I reckon we done our best."   219

"The war has begun," says Hayduke.   220

The stars looked down. Preliminary premonitions of the old moon   221
already modifying the eastern reaches. There was no wind, no sound but
the vast transpiration, thinned to a whisper by distance, of the mountain
forest, of sagebrush and juniper and pinyon pine spread out over a hundred miles of semi-arid plateau. The world hesitated, waiting for something. At the rising of the moon.

QUESTIONS FOR DISCUSSION AND WRITING

1.   The members of the Monkey Wrench Gang have varied backgrounds,
but they all feel the need to take violent action against what they see as the
destruction of nature. Given what is revealed about the characters—
Sarvis, Abbzug, Smith, and Hayduke—what can you tell about the motivation of each one? How are their motivations alike and how are they
different? How does each view nature?

2.   How does this excerpt characterize the activity of building the road?
You might want to consider the descriptions of the road-building machines, of the workers, or simply of the scale of the project. As you think
about this question, you might compare the descriptions of road building
with the descriptions of nature.

3.   Is the Monkey Wrench Gang justified in its actions? In answering this
question, you might want to compare the motives of the gang with the
motives of the road builders. Is there any other way the gang could have
stopped the road? How much harm does the road do? How much good?

NORMAN MACLEAN

Norman Maclean (1902–90) began writing fiction at the age of seventy, after he had retired as an English professor at the University of Chicago. Maclean says he wrote "A River Runs Through It" (1976) at the urging of his children, "who wanted me to put down in writing some of the stories I had told them when they were young." The story takes place in the western Rocky Mountains, where Maclean grew up. In his introduction to the book in which "A River Runs Through It" first appeared, Maclean notes that as he wrote he consulted "experts"—a rancher from the Helena Valley, a woodsman from the Forest Service, an expert fly fisherman "who tied flies for my brother and me over forty years ago."

"A River Runs Through It" is the story of two brothers who grew up "at the junction of great trout rivers in western Montana" in a family where "there was no clear line between religion and fly fishing." Trained by their father in the art of fishing with a dry fly, the two brothers respond differently both to that teaching and to their natural environment.

From "A River Runs Through It"

I was at the wheel, and I knew before we started just where we were going. It couldn't be far up the Blackfoot, because we were starting late, and it had to be a stretch of water of two or three deep holes for Paul and me and one good hole with no bank too steep for Father to crawl down. Also, since he couldn't wade, the good fishing water had to be on his side of the river. They argued while I drove, although they knew just as well as I did where we had to go, but each one in our family considered himself the leading authority on how to fish the Blackfoot River. When we came to the side road going to the river above the mouth of Belmont Creek, they spoke in unison for the first time. "Turn here," they said, and, as if I were following their directions, I turned to where I was going anyway.

The side road brought us down to a flat covered with ground boulders and cheat grass. No livestock grazed on it, and grasshoppers took off like birds and flew great distances, because on this flat it is a long way between feeding grounds, even for grasshoppers. The flat itself and its crop of boulders are the roughly ground remains of one of geology's great disasters. The flat may well have been the end of the ice age lake, half as big as Lake Michigan, that in places was two thousand feet deep until the glacial dam broke and this hydraulic monster of the hills charged out on

1

2

to the plains of eastern Washington. High on the mountains above where we stopped to fish are horizontal scars slashed by passing icebergs.

I had to be careful driving toward the river so I wouldn't high-center the   3
car on a boulder and break the crankcase. The flat ended suddenly and the river was down a steep bank, blinking silver through the trees and then turning to blue by comparing itself to a red and green cliff. It was another world to see and feel, and another world of rocks. The boulders on the flat were shaped by the last ice age only eighteen or twenty thousand years ago, but the red and green precambrian rocks beside the blue water were almost from the basement of the world and time.

We stopped and peered down the bank. I asked my father, "Do you   4
remember when we picked a lot of red and green rocks down there to build our fireplace? Some were red mudstones with ripples on them."

"Some had raindrops on them," he said. His imagination was always   5
stirred by the thought that he was standing in ancient rain spattering on mud before it became rocks.

"Nearly a billion years ago," I said, knowing what he was thinking.   6

He paused. He had given up the belief that God had created all there   7
was, including the Blackfoot River, on a six-day work schedule, but he didn't believe that the job so taxed God's powers that it took Him forever to complete.

"Nearly half a billion years ago," he said as his contribution to recon-   8
ciling science and religion. He hurried on, not wishing to waste any part of old age in debate, except over fishing. "We carried those big rocks up the bank," he said, "but now I can't crawl down it. Two holes below, though, the river comes out in the open and there is almost no bank. I'll walk down there and fish, and you fish the first two holes. I'll wait in the sun. Don't hurry."

Paul said, "You'll get 'em," and all of a sudden Father was confident in   9
himself again. Then he was gone.

We could catch glimpses of him walking along the bank of the river   10
which had been the bottom of the great glacial lake. He held his rod straight in front of him and every now and then he lunged forward with it, perhaps reenacting some glacial race memory in which he speared a hairy ice age mastodon and ate him for breakfast.

Paul said, "Let's fish together today." I knew then that he was still tak-   11
ing care of me, because we almost always split up when we fished. "That's fine," I said. "I'll wade across and fish the other side," he said. I said, "Fine," again, and was doubly touched. On the other side you were backed against cliffs and trees, so it was mostly a roll-casting job, never my specialty. Besides, the river was powerful here with no good place to wade, and next to fishing Paul liked swimming rivers with his rod in his hand. It turned out he didn't have to swim here, but as he waded some-

times the wall of water rose to his upstream shoulder while it would be no higher than his hip behind him. He stumbled to shore from the weight of water in his clothes, and gave me a big wave.

I came down the bank to catch fish. Cool wind had blown in from   12
Canada without causing any electric storms, so the fish should be off the bottom and feeding again. When a deer comes to water, his head shoots in and out of his shoulders to see what's ahead, and I was looking all around to see what fly to put on. But I didn't have to look further than my neck or my nose. Big clumsy flies bumped into my face, swarmed on my neck and wiggled in my underwear. Blundering and soft-bellied, they had been born before they had brains. They had spent a year under water on legs, had crawled out on a rock, had become flies and copulated with the ninth and tenth segments of their abdomens, and then had died as the first light wind blew them into the water where the fish circled excitedly. They were a fish's dream come true—stupid, succulent, and exhausted from copulation. Still, it would be hard to know what gigantic portion of human life is spent in this same ratio of years under water on legs to one premature, exhausted moment on wings.

I sat on a log and opened my fly box. I knew I had to get a fly that   13
would match these flies exactly, because when a big hatch like this or the salmon fly is out, the fish won't touch anything else. As proof, Paul hadn't had a strike yet, so far as I could see.

I figured he wouldn't have the right fly, and I knew I had it. As I ex-   14
plained earlier, he carried all his flies in his hat-band. He thought that with four or five generals in different sizes he could imitate the action of nearly any aquatic or terrestrial insect in any stage from larval to winged. He was always kidding me because I carried so many flies. "My, my," he would say, peering into my fly box, "wouldn't it be wonderful if a guy knew how to use ten of all those flies." But I've already told you about the Bee, and I'm still sure that there are times when a general won't turn a fish over. The fly that would work now had to be a big fly, it had to have a yellow, black-banded body, and it had to ride high in the water with extended wings, something like a butterfly that has had an accident and can't dry its wings by fluttering in the water.

It was so big and flashy it was the first fly I saw when I opened my box.   15
It was called a Bunyan Bug, tied by a fly tyer in Missoula named Normal Means, who ties a line of big flashy flies all called Bunyan Bugs. They are tied on big hooks, No. 2's and No. 4's, have cork bodies with stiff horse-hair tied crosswise so they ride high in the water like dragonflies on their backs. The cork bodies are painted different colors and then are shel-lacked. Probably the biggest and flashiest of the hundred flies my brother made fun of was the Bunyan Bug No. 2 Yellow Stone Fly.

I took one look at it and felt perfect. My wife, my mother-in-law, and   16

my sister-in-law, each in her somewhat obscure style, had recently rede-
clared their love for me. I, in my somewhat obscure style, had returned
their love. I might never see my brother-in-law again. My mother had
found my father's old tackle and once more he was fishing with us. My
brother was taking tender care of me, and not catching any fish. I was
about to make a killing.

It is hard to cast Bunyan Bugs into the wind because the cork and   17
horsehair make them light for their bulk. But, though the wind shortens
the cast, it acts at the same time to lower the fly slowly and almost vertically to the water with no telltale splash. My Stone Fly was still hanging
over the water when what seemed like a speedboat went by it, knocked
it high into the air, circled, opened the throttle wide on the returning
straight away, and roared over the spot marked X where the Stone Fly had
settled. Then the speedboat turned into a submarine, disappearing with all
on board including my fly, and headed for deep water. I couldn't throw
line into the rod fast enough to keep up with what was disappearing and
I couldn't change its course. Not being as fast as what was under water, I
literally forced it into the air. From where I was I suppose I couldn't see
what happened, but my heart was at the end of the line and telegraphed
back its impressions as it went by. My general impression was that marine
life had turned into a rodeo. My particular information was that a large
Rainbow had gone sun-fishing, turning over twice in the air, hitting my
line each time and tearing loose from the fly which went sailing out into
space. My distinct information was that it never looked around to see. My
only close-at-hand information was that when the line was reeled in, there
was nothing on the end of it but some cork and some hairs from a horse's
tail.

The stone flies were just as thick as ever, fish still swirled in quiet water,   18
and I was a little smarter. I don't care much about taking instructions, even
from myself, but before I made the next cast I underlined the fact that big
Rainbows sometimes come into quiet waters because aquatic insects
hatch in or near quiet waters. "Be prepared," I said to myself, remembering an old war song. I also accepted my own advice to have some extra
coils of line in my left hand to take some of the tension off the first run of
the next big Rainbow swirling in quiet water.

So on this wonderful afternoon when all things came together it took   19
me one cast, one fish, and some reluctantly accepted advice to attain perfection. I did not miss another.

From then on I let them run so far that sometimes they surged clear   20
across the river and jumped right in front of Paul.

When I was young, a teacher had forbidden me to say "more perfect"   21
because she said if a thing is perfect it can't be more so. But by now I had
seen enough of life to have regained my confidence in it. Twenty minutes

ago I had felt perfect, but by now my brother was taking off his hat and changing flies every few casts. I knew he didn't carry any such special as a Bunyan Bug No. 2 Yellow Stone Fly. I had five or six big Rainbows in my basket which began to hurt my shoulder so I left it behind on shore. Once in a while I looked back and smiled at the basket. I could hear it thumping on the rocks and falling on its side. However I may have violated grammar, I was feeling more perfect with every Rainbow.

Just after my basket gave an extra large thump there was an enormous 22 splash in the water to the left of where I was casting. "My God," I thought before I could look, "there's nothing that big that swims in the Blackfoot," and, when I dared look, there was nothing but a large circle that got bigger and bigger. Finally the first wave went by my knees. "It must be a beaver," I thought. I was waiting for him to surface when something splashed behind me. "My God," I said again, "I would have seen a beaver swim by me under water." While I was wrenching my neck backwards, the thing splashed right in front of me, too close for comfort but close enough so I could watch what was happening under water. The silt was rising from the bottom like smoke from the spot where lightning had struck. A fair-sized rock was sitting in the spot where the smoke was rising.

While I was relating my past to the present rock, there was another 23 big splash in front of me, but this time I didn't bother to jump.

Beaver, hell! Without looking, I knew it was my brother. It didn't hap- 24 pen often in this life, only when his fishing partner was catching fish and he couldn't. It was a sight, however rare, that he could not bear to watch. So he would spoil his partner's hole, even if it was his brother's. I looked up just in time to see a fair-sized boulder come out of the sky and I ducked too late to keep it from splashing all over me.

He had his hat off and he shook his fist at me. I knew he had fished 25 around his hat band before he threw the rocks. I shook my fist back at him, and waded to shore, where my basket was still thumping. In all my life, I had got the rock treatment only a couple of times before. I was feeling more perfect than ever.

I didn't mind that he spoiled the hole before I had filled my basket, be- 26 cause there was another big hole between us and father. It was a beautiful stretch of water, against cliffs and in shadows. The hole I had just fished was mostly in sunlight—the weather had become cooler, but was still warm enough so that the hole ahead in shadows should be even better than the one in sunlight and I should have no trouble finishing off my basket with a Bunyan Bug No. 2 Yellow Stone Fly.

Paul and I walked nearly the length of the first hole before we could 27 hear each other yell across the river. I knew he hated to be heard yelling,

"What were they biting on?" The last two words, "biting on," kept echoing across the water and pleased me.

When the echoes ceased, I yelled back, "Yellow stone flies." These words kept saying themselves until they subsided into sounds of the river. He kept turning his hat round and round in his hands.

28

I possibly began to get a little ashamed of myself. "I caught them on a Bunyan Bug," I yelled. "Do you want one?"

29

"No," he yelled before "want one" had time to echo. Then "want one" and "no" passed each other on the back turns.

30

"I'll wade across with one," I said through the cup of my hands. That's a lot to say across a river, and the first part of it returning met the last part of it just starting. I didn't know whether he had understood what I had said, but the river still answered, "No."

31

While I was standing in quiet, shady water, I half noticed that no stone flies were hatching, and I should have thought longer about what I saw but instead I found myself thinking about character. It seems somehow natural to start thinking about character when you get ahead of somebody, especially about the character of the one who is behind. I was thinking of how, when things got tough, my brother looked to himself to get himself out of trouble. He never looked for any flies from me. I had a whole round of thoughts on this subject before I returned to reality and yellow stone flies. I started by thinking that, though he was my brother, he was sometimes knot-headed. I pursued this line of thought back to the Greeks who believed that not wanting any help might even get you killed. Then I suddenly remembered that my brother was almost always a winner and often because he didn't borrow flies. So I decided that the response we make to character on any given day depends largely on the response fish are making to character on the same day. And thinking of the response of fish, I shifted rapidly back to reality, and said to myself, "I still have one more hole to go."

32

I didn't get a strike and I didn't see a stone fly and it was the same river as the one above, where I could have caught my limit a few minutes before if my brother hadn't thrown rocks in it. My prize Bunyan Bug began to look like a fake to me as well as to the fish. To me, it looked like a floating mattress. I cast it upstream and let it drift down naturally as if it had died. Then I popped it into the water as if it had been blown there. Then I made it zigzag while retrieving it, as if it were trying to launch itself into flight. But it evidently retained the appearance of a floating mattress. I took it off, and tried several other flies. There were no flies in the water for me to match, and by the same token there were no fish jumping.

33

I began to cast glances across the river under my hat brim. Paul wasn't doing much either. I saw him catch one, and he just turned and walked to

34

shore with it, so it couldn't have been much of a fish. I was feeling a little less than more perfect.

Then Paul started doing something he practically never did, at least not since he had been old enough to be cocky. He suddenly started fishing upstream, back over the water he had just fished. That's more like me when I feel I haven't fished the hole right or from the right angle, but, when my brother fished a hole, he assumed nothing was left behind that could be induced to change its mind. 35

I was so startled I leaned against a big rock to watch. 36

Almost immediately he started hauling them in. Big ones, and he didn't spend much time landing them either. I thought he gave them too little line and took them in too fast, but I knew what he was up to. He expected to make a killing in this hole, and he wasn't going to let any one fish thrash around in the water until it scared the rest off. He had one on now and he held the line on it so tight he was forcing it high in the air. When it jumped, he leaned back on his rod and knocked the fish into the water again. Full of air now, it streaked across the top of the water with its tail like the propeller of a seaplane until it could get its submarine chambers adjusted and submerge again. 37

He lost a couple but he must have had ten by the time he got back to the head of the hole. 38

Then he looked across the river and saw me sitting beside my rod. He started fishing again, stopped, and took another look. He cupped his hands and yelled, "Do you have George's No. 2 Yellow Hackle with a feather not a horsehair wing?" It was fast water and I didn't get all the words immediately. "No. 2" I caught first, because it is a hell of a big hook, and then "George," because he was our fishing pal, and then "Yellow." With that much information I started to look in my box, and let the other words settle into a sentence later. 39

One bad thing about carrying a box loaded with flies, as I do, is that nearly half the time I still don't have the right one. 40

"No," I admitted across the water, and water keeps repeating your admissions. 41

"I'll be there," he called back and waded upstream. 42

"No," I yelled after him, meaning don't stop fishing on my account. You can't convey an implied meaning across a river, or, if you can, it is easy to ignore. My brother walked to the lower end of the first hole where the water was shallow and waded across. 43

By the time he got to me, I had recovered most of the pieces he must have used to figure out what the fish were biting. From the moment he had started fishing upstream his rod was at such a slant and there was so much slack in his line that he must have been fishing with a wet fly and 44 letting it sink. In fact, the slack was such that he must have been letting the fly sink five or six inches. So when I was fishing this hole as I did the last one—with a cork-body fly that rides on top of the water—I was fighting the last war. "No. 2" hook told me of course it was a hell of a big insect, but "yellow" could mean a lot of things. My big question by the time he got to me was, "Are they biting on some aquatic insect in a larval or nymph stage or are they biting on a drowned fly?"

He gave me a pat on the back and one of George's No. 2 Yellow 45
Hackles with a feather wing. He said, "They are feeding on drowned yellow stone flies."

I asked him, "How did you think that out?" 46

He thought back on what had happened like a reporter. He started to 47
answer, shook his head when he found he was wrong, and then started out again. "All there is to thinking," he said, "is seeing something noticeable which makes you see something you weren't noticing which makes you see something that isn't even visible."

I said to my brother, "Give me a cigarette and say what you mean." 48

"Well," he said, "the first thing I noticed about this hole was that my 49
brother wasn't catching any. There's nothing more noticeable to a fisherman than that his partner isn't catching any.

"This made me see that I hadn't seen any stone flies flying around this 50
hole."

Then he asked me, "What's more obvious on earth than sunshine and 51
shadow, but until I really saw that there were no stone flies hatching here I didn't notice that the upper hole where they were hatching was mostly in sunshine and this hole was in shadow."

I was thirsty to start with, and the cigarette made my mouth drier so I 52
flipped the cigarette into the water.

"Then I knew," he said, "if there were flies in this hole they had come 53
from the hole above that's in the sunlight where there's enough heat to make them hatch.

"After that, I should have seen them dead in the water. Since I couldn't 54
see them dead in the water, I knew they had to be at least six or seven inches under the water where I couldn't see them. So that's where I fished."

He leaned against a big rock with his hands behind his head to make 55
the rock soft. "Wade out there and try George's No. 2," he said, pointing at the fly he had given me.

I didn't catch one right away, and I didn't expect to. My side of the river 56
was the quiet water, the right side to be on in the hole above where the stone flies were hatching, but the drowned stone flies were washed down in the powerful water on the other side of this hole. After seven or eight

casts, though, a small ring appeared on the surface. A small ring usually means that a small fish has risen to the surface, but it can also mean a big fish has rolled under water. If it is a big fish under water, he won't look so much like a fish as an arch of a rainbow that has appeared and disappeared.

Paul didn't even wait to see if I landed him. He waded out to talk to me. 57 He went on talking as if I had time to listen to him and land a big fish. He said, "I'm going to wade back again and fish the rest of the hole." Sometimes I said, "Yes," and when the fish went out of the water, speech failed me, and when the fish made a long run I said at the end of it, "You'll have to say that over again."

Finally, we understood each other. He was going to wade the river 58 again and fish the other side. We both should fish fairly fast, because Father probably was already waiting for us. Paul threw his cigarette in the water and was gone without seeing whether I landed the fish.

Not only was I on the wrong side of the river to fish with drowned 59 stone flies, but Paul was a good enough roll caster to have already fished most of my side from his own. But I caught two more. They also started as little circles that looked like little fish feeding on the surface but were broken arches of big rainbows under water. After I caught these two, I quit. They made ten, and the last three were the finest fish I ever caught. They weren't the biggest or most spectacular fish I ever caught, but they were three fish I caught because my brother waded across the river to give me the fly that would catch them and because they were the last fish I ever caught fishing with him.

After cleaning my fish, I set these three apart with a layer of grass and 60 wild mint.

Then I lifted the heavy basket, shook myself into the shoulder strap 61 until it didn't cut any more, and thought, "I'm through for the day. I'll go down and sit on the bank by my father and talk." Then I added, "If he doesn't feel like talking, I'll just sit."

I could see the sun ahead. The coming burst of light made it look from 62 the shadows that I and a river inside the earth were about to appear on earth. Although I could as yet see only the sunlight and not anything in it, I knew my father was sitting somewhere on the bank. I knew partly because he and I shared many of the same impulses, even to quitting at about the same time. I was sure without as yet being able to see into what was in front of me that he was sitting somewhere in the sunshine reading the New Testament in Greek. I knew this both from instinct and experience.

Old age had brought him moments of complete peace. Even when we 63 went duck hunting and the roar of the early morning shooting was over, he would sit in the blind wrapped in an old army blanket with his Greek

New Testament in one hand and his shotgun in the other. When a stray duck happened by, he would drop the book and raise the gun, and, after the shooting was over, he would raise the book again, occasionally interrupting his reading to thank his dog for retrieving the duck.

The voices of the subterranean river in the shadows were different from the voices of the sunlit river ahead. In the shadows against the cliff the river was deep and engaged in profundities, circling back on itself now and then to say things over to be sure it had understood itself. But the river ahead came out into the sunny world like a chatterbox, doing its best to be friendly. It bowed to one shore and then to the other so nothing would feel neglected. 64

By now I could see inside the sunshine and had located my father. He was sitting high on the bank. He wore no hat. Inside the sunlight, his faded red hair was once again ablaze and again in glory. He was reading, although evidently only by sentences because he often looked away from the book. He did not close the book until some time after he saw me. 65

I scrambled up the bank and asked him, "How many did you get?" He said, "I got all I want." I said, "But how many did you get?" He said, "I got four or five." I asked, "Are they any good?" He said, "They are beautiful." 66

He was about the only man I ever knew who used the word "beautiful" as a natural form of speech, and I guess I picked up the habit from hanging around him when I was little. 67

"How many did you catch?" he asked. "I also caught all I want," I told him. He omitted asking me just how many that was, but he did ask me, "Are they any good?" "They are beautiful," I told him, and sat down beside him. 68

"What have you been reading?" I asked. "A book," he said. It was on the ground on the other side of him. So I would not have to bother to look over his knees to see it, he said, "A good book." 69

Then he told me, "In the part I was reading it says the Word was in the beginning, and that's right. I used to think water was first, but if you listen carefully you will hear that the words are underneath the water." 70

"That's because you are a preacher first and then a fisherman," I told him. "If you ask Paul, he will tell you that the words are formed out of water." 71

"No," my father said, "you are not listening carefully. The water runs over the words. Paul will tell you the same thing. Where is Paul anyway?" 72

I told him he had gone back to fish the first hole over again. "But he promised to be here soon," I assured him. "He'll be here when he catches his limit," he said. "He'll be here soon," I reassured him, partly because I could already see him in the subterranean shadows. 73

My father went back to reading and I tried to check what we had said 74 by listening. Paul was fishing fast, picking up one here and there and wasting no time in walking them to shore. When he got directly across from us, he held up a finger on each hand and my father said, "He needs two more for his limit."

I looked to see where the book was left open and knew just enough   75
Greek to recognize λόγος as the Word. I guessed from it and the argument that I was looking at the first verse of John. While I was looking, Father said, "He has one on."

It was hard to believe, because he was fishing in front of us on the other   76
side of the hole that Father had just fished. Father slowly rose, found a good-sized rock and held it behind his back. Paul landed the fish, and waded out again for number twenty and his limit. Just as he was making the first cast, Father threw the rock. He was old enough so that he threw awkwardly and afterward had to rub his shoulder, but the rock landed in the river about where Paul's fly landed and at about the same time, so you can see where my brother learned to throw rocks into his partner's fishing water when he couldn't bear to see his partner catch any more fish.

Paul was startled for only a moment. Then he spotted Father on the   77
bank rubbing his shoulder, and Paul laughed, shook his fist at him, backed to shore and went downstream until he was out of rock range. From there he waded into the water and began to cast again, but now he was far enough away so we couldn't see his line or loops. He was a man with a wand in a river, and whatever happened we had to guess from what the man and the wand and the river did.

As he waded out, his big right arm swung back and forth. Each circle of   78
his arm inflated his chest. Each circle was faster and higher and longer until his arm became defiant and his chest breasted the sky. On shore we were sure, although we could see no line, that the air above him was singing with loops of line that never touched the water but got bigger and bigger each time they passed and sang. And we knew what was in his mind from the lengthening defiance of his arm. He was not going to let his fly touch any water close to shore where the small and middle-sized fish were. We knew from his arm and chest that all parts of him were saying, "No small one for the last one." Everything was going into one big cast for one last big fish.

From our angle high on the bank, my father and I could see where in   79
the distance the wand was going to let the fly first touch water. In the middle of the river was a rock iceberg, just its tip exposed above water and underneath it a rock house. It met all the residential requirements for big fish—powerful water carrying food to the front and back doors, and rest and shade behind them.

My father said, "There has to be a big one out there."   80

I said, "A little one couldn't live out there." 81

My father said, "The big one wouldn't let it." 82

My father could tell by the width of Paul's chest that he was going to let 83
the next loop sail. It couldn't get any wider. "I wanted to fish out there,"
he said, "but I couldn't cast that far."

Paul's body pivoted as if he were going to drive a golf ball three hun- 84
dred yards, and his arm went high into the great arc and the tip of his
wand bent like a spring, and then everything sprang and sang.

Suddenly, there was an end of action. The man was immobile. There 85
was no bend, no power in the wand. It pointed at ten o'clock and ten
o'clock pointed at the rock. For a moment the man looked like a teacher
with a pointer illustrating something about a rock to a rock. Only water
moved. Somewhere above the top of the rock house a fly was swept in
water so powerful only a big fish could be there to see it.

Then the universe stepped on its third rail. The wand jumped convul- 86
sively as it made contact with the magic current of the world. The wand
tried to jump out of the man's right hand. His left hand seemed to be frantically waving good-bye to a fish, but actually was trying to throw enough
line into the rod to reduce the voltage and ease the shock of what had
struck.

Everything seemed electrically charged but electrically unconnected. 87
Electrical sparks appeared here and there on the river. A fish jumped so
far downstream that it seemed outside the man's electrical field, but, when
the fish had jumped, the man had leaned back on the rod and it was then
that the fish had toppled back into the water not guided in its reentry by
itself. The connections between the convulsions and the sparks became
clearer by repetition. When the man leaned back on the wand and the fish
reentered the water not altogether under its own power, the wand
recharged with convulsions, the man's hand waved frantically at another
departure, and much farther below a fish jumped again. Because of the
connections, it became the same fish.

The fish made three such long runs before another act in the perform- 88
ance began. Although the act involved a big man and a big fish, it looked
more like children playing. The man's left hand sneakily began recaptur-
ing line, and then, as if caught in the act, threw it all back into the rod as
the fish got wise and made still another run.

"He'll get him," I assured my father. 89

"Beyond doubt," my father said. The line going out became shorter 90
than what the left hand took in.

When Paul peered into the water behind him, we knew he was going 91
to start working the fish to shore and didn't want to back into a hole or
rock. We could tell he had worked the fish into shallow water because he

held the rod higher and higher to keep the fish from bumping into anything on the bottom. Just when we thought the performance was over, the
wand convulsed and the man thrashed through the water after some unseen power departing for the deep.

"The son of a bitch still has fight in him," I thought I said to myself,   92
but unmistakably I said it out loud, and was embarrassed for having said
it out loud in front of my father. He said nothing.

Two or three more times Paul worked him close to shore, only to have   93
him swirl and return to the deep, but even at that distance my father and
I could feel the ebbing of the underwater power. The rod went high in the
air, and the man moved backwards swiftly but evenly, motions which
when translated into events meant the fish had tried to rest for a moment
on top of the water and the man had quickly raised the rod high and skidded him to shore before the fish thought of getting under water again. He
skidded him across the rocks clear back to a sandbar before the shocked
fish gasped and discovered he could not live in oxygen. In belated despair, he rose in the sand and consumed the rest of momentary life dancing the Dance of Death on his tail.

The man put the wand down, got on his hands and knees in the sand,   94
and, like an animal, circled another animal and waited. Then the shoulder
shot straight out, and my brother stood up, faced us, and, with uplifted
arm proclaimed himself the victor. Something giant dangled from his fist.
Had Romans been watching they would have thought that what was dangling had a helmet on it.

"That's his limit," I said to my father.   95

"He is beautiful," my father said, although my brother had just finished   96
catching his limit in the hole my father had already fished.

This was the last fish we were ever to see Paul catch. My father and I   97
talked about this moment several times later, and whatever our other feelings, we always felt it fitting that, when we saw him catch his last fish, we
never saw the fish but only the artistry of the fisherman.

While my father was watching my brother, he reached over to pat me,   98
but he missed, so he had to turn his eyes and look for my knee and try
again. He must have thought that I felt neglected and that he should tell
me he was proud of me also but for other reasons.

It was a little too deep and fast where Paul was trying to wade the river,   99
and he knew it. He was crouched over the water and his arms were spread
wide for balance. If you were a wader of big rivers you could have felt
with him even at a distance the power of the water making his legs weak
and wavy and ready to swim out from under him. He looked downstream
to estimate how far it was to an easier place to wade.

My father said, "He won't take the trouble to walk downstream. He'll   100 swim it." At the same time Paul thought the same thing, and put his cigarettes and matches in his hat.

My father and I sat on the bank and laughed at each other. It never occurred to either of us to hurry to the shore in case he needed help with a rod in his right hand and a basket loaded with fish on his left shoulder. In our family it was no great thing for a fisherman to swim a river with matches in his hair. We laughed at each other because we knew he was getting damn good and wet, and we lived in him, and were swept over the rocks with him and held his rod high in one of our hands.   101

As he moved to shore he caught himself on his feet and then was washed off them, and, when he stood again, more of him showed and he staggered to shore. He never stopped to shake himself. He came charging up the bank showering molecules of water and images of himself to show what was sticking out of his basket, and he dripped all over us, like a young duck dog that in its joy forgets to shake itself before getting close.   102

"Let's put them all out on the grass and take a picture of them," he said. So we emptied our baskets and arranged them by size and took turns photographing each other admiring them and ourselves. The photographs turned out to be like most amateur snapshots of fishing catches—the fish were white from overexposure and didn't look as big as they actually were and the fishermen looked self-conscious as if some guide had to catch the fish for them.   103

However, one closeup picture of him at the end of this day remains in my mind, as if fixed by some chemical bath. Usually, just after he finished fishing he had little to say unless he saw he could have fished better. Otherwise, he merely smiled. Now flies danced around his hatband. Large drops of water ran from under his hat on to his face and then into his lips when he smiled.   104

At the end of this day, then, I remember him both as a distant abstraction in artistry and as a closeup in water and laughter.   105

My father always felt shy when compelled to praise one of his family, and his family always felt shy when he praised them. My father said, "You are a fine fisherman."   106

My brother said, "I'm pretty good with a rod, but I need three more years before I can think like a fish."   107

Remembering that he had caught his limit by switching to George's No. 2 Yellow Hackle with a feather wing, I said without knowing how much I said, "You already know how to think like a dead stone fly."   108

We sat on the bank and the river went by. As always, it was making sounds to itself, and now it made sounds to us. It would be hard to find three men sitting side by side who knew better what a river was saying.   109

On the Big Blackfoot River above the mouth of Belmont Creek the 110
banks are fringed by large Ponderosa pines. In the slanting sun of late
afternoon the shadows of great branches reached from across the river,
and the trees took the river in their arms. The shadows continued up the
bank, until they included us.

A river, though, has so many things to say that it is hard to know what 111
it says to each of us. As we were packing our tackle and fish in the car,
Paul repeated, "Just give me three more years." At the time, I was surprised at the repetition, but later I realized that the river somewhere,
sometime, must have told me, too, that he would receive no such gift. For,
when the police sergeant early next May wakened me before daybreak, I
rose and asked no questions. Together we drove across the Continental
Divide and down the length of the Big Blackfoot River over forest floors
yellow and sometimes white with glacier lilies to tell my father and mother
that my brother had been beaten to death by the butt of a revolver and his
body dumped in an alley.

My mother turned and went to her bedroom where, in a house full of 112
men and rods and rifles, she had faced most of her great problems alone.
She was never to ask me a question about the man she loved most and understood least. Perhaps she knew enough to know that for her it was
enough to have loved him. He was probably the only man in the world
who had held her in his arms and leaned back and laughed.

When I finished talking to my father, he asked, "Is there anything else 113
you can tell me?"

Finally, I said, "Nearly all the bones in his hand were broken." 114

He almost reached the door and then turned back for reassurance. "Are 115
you sure that the bones in his hand were broken?" he asked. I repeated,
"Nearly all the bones in his hand were broken." "In which hand?" he
asked. "In his right hand," I answered.

After my brother's death, my father never walked very well again. He 116
had to struggle to lift his feet, and, when he did get them up, they came
down slightly out of control. From time to time Paul's right hand had to be
reaffirmed; then my father would shuffle away again. He could not shuffle in a straight line from trying to lift his feet. Like many Scottish ministers
before him, he had to derive what comfort he could from the faith that his
son had died fighting.

For some time, though, he struggled for more to hold on to. "Are you 117
sure you have told me everything you know about his death?" he asked.
I said, "Everything." "It's not much, is it?" "No," I replied, "but you can
love completely without complete understanding." "That I have known
and preached," my father said.

Once my father came back with another question. "Do you think I 118 could have helped him?" he asked. Even if I might have thought longer, I would have made the same answer. "Do you think I could have helped him?" I answered. We stood waiting in deference to each other. How can a question be answered that asks a lifetime of questions?

After a long time he came with something he must have wanted to ask   119
from the first. "Do you think it was just a stick-up and foolishly he tried to fight his way out? You know what I mean—that it wasn't connected with anything in his past."

"The police don't know," I said.   120

"But do you?" he asked, and I felt the implication.   121

"I've said I've told you all I know. If you push me far enough, all I re-   122
ally know is that he was a fine fisherman."

"You know more than that," my father said. "He was beautiful."   123

"Yes," I said, "he was beautiful. He should have been—you taught   124
him."

My father looked at me for a long time—he just looked at me. So this   125
was the last he and I ever said to each other about Paul's death.

Indirectly, though, he was present in many of our conversations. Once,   126
for instance, my father asked me a series of questions that suddenly made me wonder whether I understood even my father whom I felt closer to than any man I have ever known. "You like to tell true stories, don't you?" he asked, and I answered, "Yes, I like to tell stories that are true."

Then he asked, "After you have finished your true stories sometime,   127
why don't you make up a story and the people to go with it?

"Only then will you understand what happened and why.   128

"It is those we live with and love and should know who elude us."   129

Now nearly all those I loved and did not understand when I was young   130
are dead, but I still reach out to them.

Of course, now I am too old to be much of a fisherman, and now of   131
course I usually fish the big waters alone, although some friends think I shouldn't. Like many fly fishermen in western Montana where the summer days are almost Arctic in length, I often do not start fishing until the cool of the evening. Then in the Arctic half-light of the canyon, all existence fades to a being with my soul and memories and the sounds of the Big Blackfoot River and a four-count rhythm and the hope that a fish will rise.

Eventually, all things merge into one, and a river runs through it. The   132
river was cut by the world's great flood and runs over rocks from the basement of time. On some of the rocks are timeless raindrops. Under the rocks are the words, and some of the words are theirs.

I am haunted by waters.   133

QUESTIONS FOR DISCUSSION AND WRITING

1. Reread the story, paying attention to how the fish are represented. What attitudes do the various characters in the story take toward them? Do the characters treat them with reverence, indifference, or some other attitude? What role do the fish play in the story and the rituals it describes? What do the various attitudes toward the fish tell us about the relationship between human beings and nature?

2. Though clearly autobiographical, "A River Runs Through It" is a work of fiction, and one way to talk about a work of fiction is to focus on its narrator. What can you say about the teller of this story? Who is telling it, and from what perspective? Why is he telling it? What does the narrator find in nature that is important to him?

3. As the narrator and his father watch Paul fish, the father says, "He is beautiful" (par. 96), and the narrator says they "lived in him, and were swept over the rocks with him and held his rod high in one of our hands" (par. 101). Yet in spite of this empathy, the two brothers are different, especially in their attitudes toward nature. How are they different? Which brother's attitude do you find more satisfying?

ANNIE DILLARD

Annie Dillard (b. 1945) wrote Pilgrim at Tinker Creek, *one of the most popular and influential recent books on nature, when she was only twenty-nine years old. As the title of this book implies, Dillard writes as a pilgrim seeking knowledge of God in the natural world: in particular, the woods and natural places in the Roanoke valley in southwestern Virginia. This book was greeted with tremendous critical acclaim, winning the Pulitzer Prize and moving many people to write Dillard to tell her how the book changed their lives. In addition to several books of nonfiction, Dillard has written poetry and a recent novel,* The Living *(1992).*

"Living Like Weasels" (1982) is from Teaching a Stone to Talk, *a collection of essays. The setting is the same as in* Pilgrim at Tinker Creek, *yet here she puts aside the illusion that Tinker Creek is in the wilderness and reminds us, "This is, mind you, suburbia." Dillard lavishes all her skill on this short essay about weasels and a pond that is "a remarkable piece of shallowness." The comparisons and analogies reach toward a meaning that is both mystical and profoundly practical.*

———•◦•———

Living Like Weasels

A weasel is wild. Who knows what he thinks? He sleeps in his underground den, his tail draped over his nose. Sometimes he lives in his den for two days without leaving. Outside, he stalks rabbits, mice, muskrats, and birds, killing more bodies than he can eat warm, and often dragging the carcasses home. Obedient to instinct, he bites his prey at the neck, either splitting the jugular vein at the throat or crunching the brain at the base of the skull, and he does not let go. One naturalist refused to kill a weasel who was socketed into his hand deeply as a rattlesnake. The man could in no way pry the tiny weasel off, and he had to walk half a mile to water, the weasel dangling from his palm, and soak him off like a stubborn label.

And once, says Ernest Thompson Seton—once, a man shot an eagle out of the sky. He examined the eagle and found the dry skull of a weasel fixed by the jaws to his throat. The supposition is that the eagle had pounced on the weasel and the weasel swiveled and bit as instinct taught him, tooth to neck, and nearly won. I would like to have seen that eagle from the air a few weeks or months before he was shot: was the whole weasel still attached to his feathered throat, a fur pendant? Or did the eagle eat what he could reach, gutting the living weasel with his talons before his breast, bending his beak, cleaning the beautiful airborne bones?

I have been reading about weasels because I saw one last week. I star- 3
tled a weasel who startled me, and we exchanged a long glance.

Twenty minutes from my house, through the woods by the quarry and 4
across the highway, is Hollins Pond, a remarkable piece of shallowness,
where I like to go at sunset and sit on a tree trunk. Hollins Pond is also
called Murray's Pond; it covers two acres of bottomland near Tinker Creek
with six inches of water and six thousand lily pads. In winter, brown-and-
white steers stand in the middle of it, merely dampening their hooves;
from the distant shore they look like miracle itself, complete with miracle's
nonchalance. Now, in summer, the steers are gone. The water lilies have
blossomed and spread to a green horizontal plane that is terra firma to
plodding blackbirds, and tremulous ceiling to black leeches, crayfish, and
carp.

This is, mind you, suburbia. It is a five-minute walk in three directions 5
to rows of houses, though none is visible here. There's a 55 mph highway
at one end of the pond, and a nesting pair of wood ducks at the other.
Under every bush is a muskrat hole or a beer can. The far end is an alternating series of fields and woods, fields and woods, threaded everywhere
with motorcycle tracks—in whose bare clay wild turtles lay eggs.

So. I had crossed the highway, stepped over two low barbed-wire 6
fences, and traced the motorcycle path in all gratitude through the wild
rose and poison ivy of the pond's shoreline up into high grassy fields.
Then I cut down through the woods to the mossy fallen tree where I sit.
This tree is excellent. It makes a dry, upholstered bench at the upper,
marshy end of the pond, a plush jetty raised from the thorny shore between a shallow blue body of water and a deep blue body of sky.

The sun had just set. I was relaxed on the tree trunk, ensconced in the 7
lap of lichen, watching the lily pads at my feet tremble and part dreamily
over the thrusting path of a carp. A yellow bird appeared to my right and
flew behind me. It caught my eye; I swiveled around—and the next instant, inexplicably, I was looking down at a weasel, who was looking up
at me.

Weasel! I'd never seen one wild before. He was ten inches long, thin as 8
a curve, a muscled ribbon, brown as fruitwood, soft-furred, alert. His face
was fierce, small and pointed as a lizard's; he would have made a good ar-
rowhead. There was just a dot of chin, maybe two brown hairs' worth, and
then the pure white fur began that spread down his underside. He had
two black eyes I didn't see, any more than you see a window.

The weasel was stunned into stillness as he was emerging from beneath 9
an enormous shaggy wild rose bush four feet away. I was stunned into
stillness twisted backward on the tree trunk. Our eyes locked, and someone threw away the key.

Our look was as if two lovers, or deadly enemies, met unexpectedly on   10
an overgrown path when each had been thinking of something else: a
clearing blow to the gut. It was also a bright blow to the brain, or a sudden beating of brains, with all the charge and intimate grate of rubbed bal-
loons. It emptied our lungs. It felled the forest, moved the fields, and
drained the pond; the world dismantled and tumbled into that black hole
of eyes. If you and I looked at each other that way, our skulls would split
and drop to our shoulders. But we don't. We keep our skulls. So.

He disappeared. This was only last week, and already I don't remem-   11
ber what shattered the enchantment. I think I blinked, I think I retrieved
my brain from the weasel's brain, and tried to memorize what I was seeing, and the weasel felt the yank of separation, the careening splashdown
into real life and the urgent current of instinct. He vanished under the wild
rose. I waited motionless, my mind suddenly full of data and my spirit
with pleadings, but he didn't return.

Please do not tell me about "approach-avoidance conflicts." I tell you   12
I've been in that weasel's brain for sixty seconds, and he was in mine.
Brains are private places, muttering through unique and secret tapes—
but the weasel and I both plugged into another tape simultaneously, for a
sweet and shocking time. Can I help it if it was a blank?

What goes on in his brain the rest of the time? What does a weasel think   13
about? He won't say. His journal is tracks in clay, a spray of feathers,
mouse blood and bone: uncollected, unconnected, loose-leaf, and blown.

I would like to learn, or remember, how to live. I come to Hollins Pond   14
not so much to learn how to live as, frankly, to forget about it. That is, I
don't think I can learn from a wild animal how to live in particular—shall
I suck warm blood, hold my tail high, walk with my footprints precisely
over the prints of my hands?—but I might learn something of mindless-
ness, something of the purity of living in the physical senses and the dignity of living without bias or motive. The weasel lives in necessity and we
live in choice, hating necessity and dying at the last ignobly in its talons. I
would like to live as I should, as the weasel lives as he should. And I suspect that for me the way is like the weasel's: open to time and death painlessly, noticing everything, remembering nothing, choosing the given
with a fierce and pointed will.

I missed my chance. I should have gone for the throat. I should have   15
lunged for that streak of white under the weasel's chin and held on, held
on through mud and into the wild rose, held on for a dearer life. We could
live under the wild rose wild as weasels, mute and uncomprehending. I
could very calmly go wild. I could live two days in the den, curled, leaning on mouse fur, sniffing bird bones, blinking, licking, breathing musk,

my hair tangled in the roots of grasses. Down is a good place to go, where the mind is single. Down is out, out of your ever-loving mind and back to your careless senses. I remember muteness as a prolonged and giddy fast, where every moment is a feast of utterance received. Time and events are merely poured, unremarked, and ingested directly, like blood pulsed into my gut through a jugular vein. Could two live that way? Could two live under the wild rose, and explore by the pond, so that the smooth mind of each is as everywhere present to the other, and as received and as unchallenged, as falling snow?

We could, you know. We can live any way we want. People take vows 16
of poverty, chastity, and obedience—even of silence—by choice. The thing is to stalk your calling in a certain skilled and supple way, to locate the most tender and live spot and plug into that pulse. This is yielding, not fighting. A weasel doesn't "attack" anything; a weasel lives as he's meant to, yielding at every moment to the perfect freedom of single necessity.

I think it would be well, and proper, and obedient, and pure, to grasp 17
your own necessity and not let it go, to dangle from it limp wherever it takes you. Then even death, where you're going no matter how you live, cannot you part. Seize it and let it seize you up aloft even, till your eyes burn out and drop; let your musky flesh fall off in shreds, and let your very bones unhinge and scatter, loosened over fields, over fields and woods, lightly, thoughtless, from any height at all, from as high as eagles.

QUESTIONS FOR DISCUSSION AND WRITING

1. In this essay Dillard juxtaposes natural images with images of civilization. For example, at one point she talks about "motorcycle tracks—in whose bare clay wild turtles lay eggs" (par. 5). Reread the essay to find other such juxtapositions. Why does she bring together images from such different sources?

2. In describing the look between her and the weasel, Dillard says, "If you and I looked at each other that way, our skulls would split and drop to our shoulders" (par. 10). Why would this happen? What keeps this from happening to Dillard and the weasel?

3. In the end, this essay argues for the value of living like weasels. As Dillard says, "I think it would be well, and proper, and obedient, and pure, to grasp your one necessity and not let it go, to dangle from it limp wherever it takes you" (par. 17). What images from nature does Dillard use to support this point? Do you find her argument convincing?

LESLIE MARMON SILKO

Growing up on the Laguna Pueblo Reservation in New Mexico, Leslie Marmon Silko (b. 1948) learned the stories and ways of the Laguna people from early in her life. She is of mixed ancestry—Laguna, Anglo, Mexican, and other Native American tribes—but writes out of the five-hundred-year-old tradition of the Laguna Pueblo. Silko graduated magna cum laude from the University of New Mexico and attended law school before going to graduate school in English and devoting her time to writing. Her poetry, fiction, and nonfiction have won a number of awards, and her first novel, Ceremony, *has been called "powerfully conceived" and "a magnificent novel." It tells the story of a veteran of World War II who returns to the Indian reservation and learns about the need for ceremony to find harmony in the universe.*

In "Landscape, History, and the Pueblo Imagination" (1986), Silko writes of the way the people of the Pueblo conceive of their world. Referring to the French Enlightenment philosopher René Descartes, she notes that the Pueblo people "never deteriorated into Cartesian duality, cutting off the human from the natural world." This unity allows them to live in a "high arid plateau," a place of great hardship and beauty.

Landscape, History, and the Pueblo Imagination

From a High Arid Plateau in New Mexico

You see that after a thing is dead, it dries up. It might take weeks or years, but eventually if you touch the thing, it crumbles under your fingers. It goes back to dust. The soul of the thing has long since departed. With the plants and wild game the soul may have already been borne back into bones and blood or thick green stalk and leaves. Nothing is wasted. What cannot be eaten by people or in some way used must then be left where other living creatures may benefit. What domestic animals or wild scavengers can't eat will be fed to the plants. The plants feed on the dust of these few remains. 1

The ancient Pueblo people buried the dead in vacant rooms or partially collapsed rooms adjacent to the main living quarters. Sand and clay used to construct the roof make layers many inches deep once the roof has collapsed. The layers of sand and clay make for easy gravedigging. The vacant room fills with cast-off objects and debris. When a vacant room has 2

289

filled deep enough, a shallow but adequate grave can be scooped in a far corner. Archaeologists have remarked over formal burials complete with elaborate funerary objects excavated in trash middens of abandoned rooms. But the rocks and adobe mortar of collapsed walls were valued by the ancient people. Because each rock had been carefully selected for size and shape, then chiseled to an even face. Even the pink clay adobe melting with each rainstorm had to be prayed over, then dug and carried some distance. Corn cobs and husks, the rinds and stalks and animal bones were not regarded by the ancient people as filth or garbage. The remains were merely resting at a mid-point in their journey back to dust. Human remains are not so different. They should rest with the bones and rinds where they all may benefit living creatures—small rodents and insects— until their return is completed. The remains of things—animals and plants, the clay and the stones—were treated with respect. Because for the ancient people all these things had spirit and being. The antelope merely consents to return home with the hunter. All phases of the hunt are conducted with love. The love the hunter and the people have for the Antelope People. And the love of the antelope who agree to give up their meat and blood so that human beings will not starve. Waste of meat or even the thoughtless handling of bones cooked bare will offend the antelope spirits. Next year the hunters will vainly search the dry plains for antelope. Thus it is necessary to return carefully the bones and hair, and the stalks and leaves to the earth who first created them. The spirits remain close by. They do not leave us.

The dead become dust, and in this becoming they are once more 3 joined with the Mother. The ancient Pueblo People called the earth the Mother Creator of all things in this world. Her sister, the Corn Mother, occasionally merges with her because all succulent green life rises out of the depths of the earth.

Rocks and clay are part of the Mother. They emerge in various forms, 4 but at some time before, they were smaller particles or great boulders. At a later time they may again become what they once were. Dust.

A rock shares this fate with us and with animals and plants as well. A 5 rock has being or spirit, although we may not understand it. The spirit may differ from the spirit we know in animals or plants or in ourselves. In the end we all originate from the depths of the earth. Perhaps this is how all beings share in the spirit of the Creator. We do not know.

From the Emergence Place

Pueblo potters, the creators of petroglyphs and oral narratives, never 6 conceived of removing themselves from the earth and sky. So long as the human consciousness remains within the hills, canyons, cliffs, and the plants, clouds, and sky, the term landscape, as it has entered the English language, is misleading. "A portion of territory the eye can comprehend in a single view" does not correctly describe the relationship between the human being and his or her surroundings. This assumes the viewer is somehow outside or separate from the territory he or she surveys. Viewers are as much a part of the landscape as the boulders they stand on. There is no high mesa edge or mountain peak where one can stand and not immediately be part of all that surrounds. Human identity is linked with all the elements of Creation through the clan: you might belong to the Sun Clan or the Lizard Clan or the Corn Clan or the Clay Clan.[1] Standing deep within the natural world, the ancient Pueblo understood the thing as it was—the squash blossom, grasshopper, or rabbit itself could never be created by the human hand. Ancient Pueblos took the modest view that the thing itself (the landscape) could not be improved upon. The ancients did not presume to tamper with what had already been created. Thus *realism*, as we now recognize it in painting and sculpture, did not catch the imaginations of Pueblo people until recently.

The squash blossom is *one thing:* itself. So the ancient Pueblo potter abstracted what she saw to be the key elements of the squash blossom—the four symmetrical petals, with four symmetrical stamens in the center. These key elements, while suggesting the squash flower, also link it with the four cardinal directions. By representing only its intrinsic form, the squash flower is released from a limited meaning or restricted identity. Even in the most sophisticated abstract form, a squash flower or a cloud or a lightning bolt became intricately connected with a complex system of relationships which the ancient Pueblo people maintained with each other, and with the populous natural world they lived within. A bolt of lightning is itself, but at the same time it may mean much more. It may be a messenger of good fortune when summer rains are needed. It may deliver death, perhaps the result of manipulations by the Gunnadeyahs, destructive necromancers. Lightning may strike down an evil-doer. Or lightning may strike a person of good will. If the person survives, lightning endows him or her with heightened power. 7

Pictographs and petroglyphs of constellations or elk or antelope draw their magic in part from the process wherein the focus of all prayer and concentration is upon the thing itself, which, in its turn, guides the hunter's hand. Connection with the spirit dimensions requires a figure or form which is all-inclusive. A "lifelike" rendering of an elk is too restrictive. Only the elk *is* itself. A *realistic* rendering of an elk would be only 8

---

[1] *Clan*—A social unit composed of families sharing common ancestors who trace their lineage back to the Emergence where their ancestors allied themselves with certain plants or animals or elements. [*Silko's note*]

one particular elk anyway. The purpose of the hunt rituals and magic is to make contact with *all* the spirits of the Elk.

The land, the sky, and all that is within them—the landscape—   9
includes human beings. Interrelationships in the Pueblo landscape are complex and fragile. The unpredictability of the weather, the aridity and harshness of much of the terrain in the high plateau country explain in large part the relentless attention the ancient Pueblo people gave the sky and the earth around them. Survival depended upon harmony and cooperation not only among human beings, but among all things—the animate and the less animate, since rocks and mountains were known to move, to travel occasionally.

The ancient Pueblos believed the Earth and the Sky were sisters (or sis-   10
ter and brother in the post-Christian version). As long as good family relations are maintained, then the Sky will continue to bless her sister, the Earth, with rain, and the Earth's children will continue to survive. But the old stories recall incidents in which troublesome spirits or beings threaten the earth. In one story, a malicious ka'tsina, called the Gambler, seizes the Shiwana, or Rainclouds, the Sun's beloved children.[2] The Shiwana are snared in magical power late one afternoon on a high mountain top. The Gambler takes the Rainclouds to his mountain stronghold where he locks them in the north room of his house. What was his idea? The Shiwana were beyond value. They brought life to all things on earth. The Gambler wanted a big stake to wager in his games of chance. But such greed, even on the part of only one being, had the effect of threatening the survival of all life on earth. Sun Youth, aided by old Grandmother Spider, outsmarts the Gambler and the rigged game, and the Rainclouds are set free. The drought ends, and once more life thrives on earth.

Through the Stories We Hear Who We Are

All summer the people watch the west horizon, scanning the sky from   11
south to north for rain clouds. Corn must have moisture at the time the tassels form. Otherwise pollination will be incomplete, and the ears will be stunted and shriveled. An inadequate harvest may bring disaster. Stories told at Hopi, Zuni, and at Acoma and Laguna describe drought and starvation as recently as 1900. Precipitation in west-central New Mexico averages fourteen inches annually. The western pueblos are located at altitudes over 5,600 feet above sea level, where winter temperatures at night fall below freezing. Yet evidence of their presence in the high desert

---

[2] *Ka'tsina*—Ka'tsinas are spirit beings who roam the earth and who inhabit kachina masks worn in Pueblo ceremonial dances. *[Silko's note]*

plateau country goes back ten thousand years. The ancient Pueblo people not only survived in this environment, but many years they thrived. In A.D. 1100 the people at Chaco Canyon had built cities with apartment buildings of stone five stories high. Their sophistication as sky-watchers was surpassed only by Mayan and Inca astronomers. Yet this vast complex of knowledge and belief, amassed for thousands of years, was never recorded in writing.

Instead, the ancient Pueblo people depended upon collective memory   12
through successive generations to maintain and transmit an entire culture, a world view complete with proven strategies for survival. The oral narrative, or "story," became the medium in which the complex of Pueblo knowledge and belief was maintained. Whatever the event or the subject, the ancient people perceived the world and themselves within that world as part of an ancient continuous story composed of innumerable bundles of other stories.

The ancient Pueblo vision of the world was inclusive. The impulse was   13
to leave nothing out. Pueblo oral tradition necessarily embraced all levels of human experience. Otherwise, the collective knowledge and beliefs comprising ancient Pueblo culture would have been incomplete. Thus stories about the Creation and Emergence of human beings and animals into this World continue to be retold each year for four days and four nights during the winter solstice. The "humma-hah" stories related events from the time long ago when human beings were still able to communicate with animals and other living things. But, beyond these two preceding categories, the Pueblo oral tradition knew no boundaries. Accounts of the appearance of the first Europeans in Pueblo country or of the tragic encounters between Pueblo people and Apache raiders were no more and no less important than stories about the biggest mule deer ever taken or adulterous couples surprised in cornfields and chicken coops. Whatever happened, the ancient people instinctively sorted events and details into a loose narrative structure. Everything became a story.

Traditionally everyone, from the youngest child to the oldest person,   14
was expected to listen and to be able to recall or tell a portion, if only a small detail, from a narrative account or story. Thus the remembering and retelling were a communal process. Even if a key figure, an elder who knew much more than others, were to die unexpectedly, the system would remain intact. Through the efforts of a great many people, the community was able to piece together valuable accounts and crucial information that might otherwise have died with an individual.

Communal storytelling was a self-correcting process in which listeners   15
were encouraged to speak up if they noted an important fact or detail omitted. The people were happy to listen to two or three different ver-

sions of the same event or the same humma-hah story. Even conflicting versions of an incident were welcomed for the entertainment they provided. Defenders of each version might joke and tease one another, but seldom were there any direct confrontations. Implicit in the Pueblo oral tradition was the awareness that loyalties, grudges, and kinship must always influence the narrator's choices as she emphasizes to listeners this is the way *she* has always heard the story told. The ancient Pueblo people sought a communal truth, not an absolute. For them this truth lived somewhere within the web of differing versions, disputes over minor points, outright contradictions tangling with old feuds and village rivalries.

A dinner-table conversation, recalling a deer hunt forty years ago when the largest mule deer ever was taken, inevitably stimulates similar memories in listeners. But hunting stories were not merely after-dinner entertainment. These accounts contained information of critical importance about behavior and migration patterns of mule deer. Hunting stories carefully described key landmarks and locations of fresh water. Thus a deer-hunt story might also serve as a "map." Lost travelers, and lost piñon-nut gathers, have been saved by sighting a rock formation they recognize only because they once heard a hunting story describing this rock formation.   16

The importance of cliff formations and water holes does not end with hunting stories. As offspring of the Mother Earth, the ancient Pueblo people could not conceive of themselves within a specific landscape. Location, or "place," nearly always plays a central role in the Pueblo oral narratives. Indeed, stories are most frequently recalled as people are passing by a specific geographical feature or the exact place where a story takes place. The precise date of the incident often is less important than the place or location of the happening. "Long, long ago," "a long time ago," "not too long ago," and "recently" are usually how stories are classified in terms of time. But the places where the stories occur are precisely located, and prominent geographical details recalled, even if the landscape is well-known to listeners. Often because the turning point in the narrative involved a peculiarity or special quality of a rock or tree or plant found only at that place. Thus, in the case of many of the Pueblo narratives, it is impossible to determine which came first: the incident or the geographical feature which begs to be brought alive in a story that features some unusual aspect of this location.   17

There is a giant sandstone boulder about a mile north of Old Laguna, on the road to Paguate. It is ten feet tall and twenty feet in circumference. When I was a child, and we would pass this boulder driving to Paguate village, someone usually made reference to the story about Kochininako, Yellow Woman, and the Estrucuyo, a monstrous giant who nearly ate her. The Twin Hero Brothers saved Kochininako, who had been out hunting rabbits to take home to feed her mother and sisters. The Hero Brothers   18 had heard her cries just in time. The Estrucuyo had cornered her in a cave too small to fit its monstrous head. Kochininako had already thrown to the Estrucuyo all her rabbits, as well as her moccasins and most of her clothing. Still the creature had not been satisfied. After killing the Estrucuyo with their bows and arrows, the Twin Hero Brothers slit open the Estrucuyo and cut out its heart. They threw the heart as far as they could. The monster's heart landed there, beside the old trail to Paguate village, where the sandstone boulder rests now.

It may be argued that the existence of the boulder precipitated the cre- 19
ation of a story to explain it. But sandstone boulders and sandstone formations of strange shapes abound in the Laguna Pueblo area. Yet most of them do not have stories. Often the crucial element in a narrative is the terrain—some specific detail of the setting.

A high dark mesa rises dramatically from a grassy plain fifteen miles 20
southeast of Laguna, in an area known as Swanee. On the grassy plain one hundred and forty years ago, my great-grandmother's uncle and his brother-in-law were grazing their herd of sheep. Because visibility on the plain extends for over twenty miles, it wasn't until the two sheepherders came near the high dark mesa that the Apaches were able to stalk them. Using the mesa to obscure their approach, the raiders swept around from both ends of the mesa. My great-grandmother's relatives were killed, and the herd lost. The high dark mesa played a critical role: the mesa had compromised the safety which the openness of the plains had seemed to assure. Pueblo and Apache alike relied upon the terrain, the very earth herself, to give them protection and aid. Human activities or needs were maneuvered to fit the existing surroundings and conditions. I imagine the last afternoon of my distant ancestors as warm and sunny for late September. They might have been traveling slowly, bringing the sheep closer to Laguna in preparation for the approach of colder weather. The grass was tall and only beginning to change from green to a yellow which matched the late-afternoon sun shining off it. There might have been comfort in the warmth and the sight of the sheep fattening on good pasture which lulled my ancestors into their fatal inattention. They might have had a rifle whereas the Apaches had only bows and arrows. But there would have been four or five Apache raiders, and the surprise attack would have canceled any advantage the rifles gave them.

Survival in any landscape comes down to making the best use of all 21
available resources. On that particular September afternoon, the raiders made better use of the Swantee terrain than my poor ancestors did. Thus the high dark mesa and the story of the two lost Laguna herders became inextricably linked. The memory of them and their story resides in part with the high black mesa. For as long as the mesa stands, people within the family and clan will be reminded of the story of that afternoon long

ago. Thus the continuity and accuracy of the oral narratives are reinforced by the landscape—and the Pueblo interpretation of that landscape is *maintained*.

The Migration Story: An Interior Journey

The Laguna Pueblo migration stories refer to specific places—mesas, springs, or cottonwood trees—not only locations which can be visited still, but also locations which lie directly on the state highway route linking Paguate village with Laguna village. In traveling this road as a child with older Laguna people I first heard a few of the stories from that much larger body of stories linked with the Emergence and Migration.[3] It may be coincidental that Laguna people continue to follow the same route which, according to the Migration story, the ancestors followed south from the Emergence Place. It may be that the route is merely the shortest and best route for car, horse, or foot traffic between Laguna and Paguate villages. But if the stories about boulders, springs, and hills are actually remnants from a ritual that retraces the creation and emergence of the Laguna Pueblo people as a culture, as the people they became, then continued use of that route creates a unique relationship between the ritual-mythic world and the actual, everyday world. A journey from Paguate to Laguna down the long incline of Paguate Hill retraces the original journey from the Emergence Place, which is located slightly north of the Paguate village. Thus the landscape between Paguate and Laguna takes on a deeper significance: the landscape resonates the spiritual or mythic dimension of the Pueblo world even today.

Although each Pueblo culture designates a specific Emergence Place— usually a small natural spring edged with mossy sandstone and full of cattails and wild watercress—it is clear that they do not agree on any single location or natural spring as the one and only true Emergence Place. Each Pueblo group recounts its own stories about Creation, Emergence, and Migration, although they all believe that all human beings, with all the animals and plants, emerged at the same place and at the same time.[4]

---

[3] *The Emergence*—All the human beings, animals, and life which had been created emerged from the four worlds below when the earth became habitable.

The Migration—The Pueblo people emerged into the Fifth World, but they had already been warned they would have to travel and search before they found the place they were meant to live. [*Silko's note*]

[4] *Creation*—Tse'itsi'nako, Thought Woman, the Spider, thought about it, and everything she thought came into being. First she thought of three sisters for herself, and they helped her think of the rest of the Universe, including the Fifth World and the Four worlds below. *The Fifth World* is the world we are living in today. There are four previous words below this world. [*Silko's note*]

Natural springs are crucial sources of water for all life in the high desert   24
plateau country. So the small spring near Paguate village is literally the
source and continuance of life for the people in the area. The spring also
functions on a spiritual level, recalling the original Emergence Place and
linking the people and the spring water to all other people and to that moment when the Pueblo people became aware of themselves as they are
even now. The Emergence was an emergence into a precise cultural identity. Thus the Pueblo stories about the Emergence and Migration are not to
be taken as literally as the anthropologists might wish. Prominent geographical features and landmarks which are mentioned in the narratives
exist for ritual purposes, not because the Laguna people actually journeyed south for hundreds of years from Chaco Canyon or Mesa Verde, as
the archaeologists say, or eight miles from the site of the natural springs at
Paguate to the sandstone hilltop at Laguna.

The eight miles, marked with boulders, mesas, springs, and river cross-   25
ings, are actually a ritual circuit or path which marks the interior journey
the Laguna people made: a journey of awareness and imagination in
which they emerged from being within the earth and from everything included in earth to the culture and people they became, differentiating
themselves for the first time from all that had surrounded them, always
aware that interior distances cannot be reckoned in physical miles or in
calendar years.

The narratives linked with prominent features of the landscape be-   26
tween Paguate and Laguna delineate the complexities of the relationship
which human beings must maintain with the surrounding natural world if
they hope to survive in this place. Thus the journey was an interior
process of the imagination, a growing awareness that being human is
somehow different from all other life—animal, plant, and inanimate. Yet
we are all from the same source: the awareness never deteriorated into
Cartesian duality, cutting off the human from the natural world.

The people found the opening into the Fifth World too small to allow   27
them or any of the animals to escape. They had sent a fly out through the
small hole to tell them if it was the world which the Mother Creator had
promised. It was, but there was the problem of getting out. The antelope
tried to butt the opening to enlarge it, but the antelope enlarged it only a
little. It was necessary for the badger with her long claws to assist the antelope, and at last the opening was enlarged enough so that all the people
and animals were able to emerge up into the Fifth World. The human beings could not have emerged without the aid of antelope and badger. The
human beings depended upon the aid and charity of the animals. Only
through interdependence could the human beings survive. Families belonged to clans, and it was by clan that the human being joined with the
animal and plant world. Life on the high arid plateau became viable when

the human beings were able to imagine themselves as sisters and brothers to the badger, antelope, clay, yucca, and sun. Not until they could find a viable relationship to the terrain, the landscape they found themselves in, could they *emerge*. Only at the moment the requisite balance between human and *other* was realized could the Pueblo people become a culture, a distinct group whose population and survival remained stable despite the vicissitudes of climate and terrain.

Landscape thus has similarities with dreams. Both have the power to   28
seize terrifying feelings and deep instincts and translate them into images—visual, aural, tactile—into the concrete where human beings may more readily confront and channel the terrifying instincts or powerful emotions into rituals and narratives which reassure the individual while reaffirming cherished values of the group. The identity of the individual as a part of the group and the greater Whole is strengthened, and the terror of facing the world alone is extinguished.

Even now, the people at Laguna Pueblo spend the greater portion of   29
social occasions recounting recent incidents or events which have occurred in the Laguna area. Nearly always, the discussion will precipitate the retelling of older stories about similar incidents or other stories connected with a specific place. The stories often contain disturbing or provocative material, but are nonetheless told in the presence of children and women. The effect of these inter-family or inter-clan exchanges is the reassurance for each person that she or he will never be separated or apart from the clan, no matter what might happen. Neither the worst blunders or disasters nor the greatest financial prosperity and joy will ever be permitted to isolate anyone from the rest of the group. In the ancient times, cohesiveness was all that stood between extinction and survival, and, while the individual certainly was recognized, it was always as an individual simultaneously bonded to family and clan by a complex bundle of custom and ritual. You are never the first to suffer a grave loss or profound humiliation. You are never the first, and you understand that you will probably not be the last to commit or be victimized by a repugnant act. Your family and clan are able to go on at length about others now passed on, others older or more experienced than you who suffered similar losses.

The wide deep arroyo near the Kings Bar (located across the reserva-   30
tion borderline) has over the years claimed many vehicles. A few years ago, when a Viet Nam veteran's new red Volkswagen rolled backwards into the arroyo while he was inside buying a six-pack of beer, the story of his loss joined the lively and large collection of stories already connected with that big arroyo. I do not know whether the Viet Nam veteran was consoled when he was told the stories about the other cars claimed by the

ravenous arroyo. All his savings of combat pay had gone for the red Volkswagen. But this man could not have felt any worse than the man who, some years before, had left his children and mother-in-law in his station wagon with the engine running. When he came out of the liquor store his station wagon was gone. He found it and its passengers upside down in the big arroyo. Broken bones, cuts and bruises, and a total wreck of the car. The big arroyo has a wide mouth. Its existence needs no explanation. People in the area regard the arroyo much as they might regard a living being, which has a certain character and personality. I seldom drive past that wide deep arroyo without feeling a familiarity with and even a strange affection for this arroyo. Because as treacherous as it may be, the arroyo maintains a strong connection between human beings and the earth. The arroyo demands from us the caution and attention that constitute respect. It is this sort of respect the old believers have in mind when they tell us we must respect and love the earth.

Hopi Pueblo elders have said that the austere and, to some eyes, bar- 31
ren plains and hills surrounding their mesa-top villages actually help to nurture the spirituality of the Hopi *way.* The Hopi elders say the Hopi people might have settled in locations far more lush where daily life would not have been so grueling. But there on the high silent sandstone mesas that overlook the sandy arid expanses stretching to all horizons, the Hopi elders say the Hopi people must "live by their prayers" if they are to survive. The Hopi way cherishes the intangible: the riches realized from interaction and interrelationships with all beings above all else. Great abundances of material things, even food, the Hopi elders believe, tend to lure human attention away from what is most valuable and important. The views of the Hopi elders are not much different from those elders in all the Pueblos.

The bare vastness of the Hopi landscape emphasizes the visual impact 32
of every plant, every rock, every arroyo. Nothing is overlooked or taken for granted. Each ant, each lizard, each lark is imbued with great value simply because the creature is there, simply because the creature is alive in a place where any life at all is precious. Stand on the mesa edge at Walpai and look west over the bare distances toward the pale blue outlines of the San Francisco peaks where the ka'tsina spirits reside. So little lies between you and the sky. So little lies between you and the earth. One look and you know that simply to survive is a great triumph, that every possible resource is needed, every possibly ally—even the most humble insect or reptile. You realize you will be speaking with all of them if you intend to last out the year. Thus it is that the Hopi elders are grateful to the landscape for aiding them in their quest as spiritual people.

QUESTIONS FOR DISCUSSION AND WRITING

1.   Toward the middle of this essay Silko writes of "a growing awareness that being human is somehow different from all other life. . . . Yet we are all from the same source" (par. 26). How is the delicate balance between being different from all other life yet being from the same source worked out in the stories told in this essay? Which stories stress the similarities between human and other life, and which stress the differences?

2.   The first section of this essay is called "From a High Arid Plateau in New Mexico." Why is the aridity of this place important in the Pueblo imagination? How does the lack of water shape the particular forms taken by various stories and legends as well as the whole structure of the imagination?

3.   Silko writes that the term *landscape* is misleading for the Pueblo imagination because it implies that the viewer is separate from the territory being observed. One reason the Pueblo people see themselves as part of the land is that this perspective allows them to survive in a difficult place; they come to understand the interconnectedness of all things to ensure their place in this world. To what degree do you think of yourself as being part of the natural landscape? What value do you find in your position in relationship to the landscape?

GRETEL EHRLICH

Gretel Ehrlich (b. 1946) was working for the Public Broadcasting System in 1976 on a documentary film about Wyoming sheepherders when she learned her partner, David, had died. In an attempt to come to terms with her feelings, she traveled for two years before settling in northern Wyoming, where she hoped to find happiness in the natural world. In Wyoming she met and married a rancher, and she kept a journal of her experiences that became an award-winning book of essays, The Solace of Open Spaces. *In these essays Ehrlich describes life on a ranch in a state characterized by wild scenery and brutal weather. She also describes the people she meets there with warmth and understanding.*

    Ehrlich has continued to write essays, and she has also written poetry, stories, and a novel, Heart Mountain, *about an interment camp in Wyoming for Japanese Americans during World War II. "This Autumn Morning" (1990) continues many of the themes found in* The Solace of Open Spaces. *In it Ehrlich writes of the Wyoming land, weather, and animals, always exploring the landscape of her heart through the descriptions of nature.*

— • —

This Autumn Morning

    When did all this happen, this rain and snow bending green branches, this turning of light to shadow in my throat, these birdnotes going flat, and how did these sawtooth willow leaves unscrew themselves from the twig, and the hard, bright paths trampled into the hills loosen themselves to mud? When did the wind begin churning inside trees, and why did the sixty-million-year-old mountains start looking like two uplifted hands holding and releasing the gargled, whistling, echoing grunts of bull elk, and when did the loose fires inside me begin *not* to burn?   1

    Wasn't it only last week, in August, that I saw the stained glass of a monarch butterfly clasping a purple thistle flower, then rising as if a whole cathedral had taken flight?   2

    Now what looks like smoke is only mare's tails—clouds streaming— and as the season changes, my young dog and I wonder if raindrops might not be shattered lightning.   3

    It's September. At this time of year light is on the wane. There is no fresh green breast of earth to embrace. None of that. Just to breathe is a kind of violence against death. To long for love, to have experienced passion's deep pleasure, even once, is to understand the mercilessness of   4

301

having a human body whose memory rides desire's back unanchored from season to season.

Last night while driving to town I hit a deer. She jumped into my path 5 from behind bushes so close I could not stop. A piece of red flesh flew up and hit the windshield. I watched as she ran off limping. There was nothing I could do. Much later, on the way home, I looked for her again. I could see where a deer had bedded down beside a tree, but there was no sign of a wounded animal, so I continued on.

Halfway up our mountain road a falling star burned a red line across 6 the sky—a meteorite, a pristine piece of galactic debris that came into existence billions of years before our solar system was made. The tail stretched out gold and slid. I stopped the truck, then realized I was at the exact place where, years ago, I declared love to a friend as a meteor shower burst over us. At dawn, a belted kingfisher peered down into water as if reading a message to us about how to live, about what would suffice.

Tonight on the same road in a different year I see only the zigzagging 7 of foxes whose red tails are long floats that give their small bodies buoyancy. No friends meet me to view the stars. The nights have turned cold. The crickets' summer mating songs have hardened into drumbeats and dark rays of light pole out from under clouds as if steadying the flapping tent of the sky.

Even when the air is still I keep hearing a breeze, the way it shinnies up 8 the bones of things, up the bark of trees. A hard frost pales the hayfields. Tucked into the flickering universe of a cottonwood tree, yellow leaves shaped like gloved hands reach across the green umbrella for autumn.

It's said that after fruition nothing will suffice, there is no more, but who 9 can know the answer? I've decided to begin at the end, where the earth is black and barren. I want to see how death is mixed in, how the final plurals are taken back to single things—if they are; how and where life stirs out of ash.

On May 5, the first day the roads opened, my husband and I drove to 10 Yellowstone Park. Twenty miles before the east entrance, we were greeted by buffalo: four mother cows, one yearling, and a newly born calf. At Sylvan Pass a young couple were skiing down a precipitous snow-covered landslide, then trudging up the nearly vertical slope carrying their skis. Just before we reached Yellowstone Lake, a pair of blue grouse, in the midst of a courting display, could not be moved from the center of the road. Neck and tail feathers plumed and fanned out; we waited. The lake was all ice. Far out, a logjam—upended, splintered, frozen in place—was the eye's only resting place in all that white.

Around the next bend I came on a primordial scene: north of Mary's 11

Bay, wide, ice-covered meadows were full of dead buffalo, and searching for grass in among the carcasses were the barely live bison who had survived a rigorous winter, so thin they looked like cardboard cutouts, a deep hollow between their withers and ribs.

We drove on. More dead bison, and dead elk. The park biologists were saying that roughly 28 percent of both herds wintered-killed this year, not only because the fires diminished some of their forage but also because the drought had brought us five years of mild winters, thus allowing the old and sick animals to survive. 12

Between Madison Junction and the Firehold River we stood in the charred ruins of a lodgepole pine forest. The hollow trunks of burned-out trees looked as if they had been picked up and dropped, coming to rest at every possible angle. The ground was black. Where the fire had burned underground, smoldering root systems upended trees; where there had once been a pond or a bog with ducks and swans was now a waterless depression. Way back in the trees, a geyser hissed, its plume of white steam a ghost of last year's hundred-mile-long streamer of smoke. 13

Later we returned to the lake and sat on the end of a long spit of land that angles out into water. From there it's difficult to tell there was a fire. Lodgepole pines fringe the shore. A cloud that had moved off Mount Sheridan to the south rolled toward us, its front edge buffeted by a north wind. In ancient Greece it's said that Boreas, god of the north wind, became jealous of his lover, Pitys, who had been flirting with Pan, and threw her against a rocky ledge. In that moment she turned into a pine tree. The amber drops of sap at the breaks of limbs are her tears. 14

Boreas shattered the cloud above me and blew it over the lake, and the trees at the edge took on wild shapes. The Buriats in eastern Siberia considered groves of pines sacred and always rode through them in silence. A trumpeter swan glided by, then a tribe of golden-eye ducks headed for a sheltered inlet. 15

Pines are such ancient trees, first appearing 170 million years ago. But what does Boreas care? He cut through the cloud and sent a bulbous chunk toward me until it broke off that fragile tail of land as if it had been a tree. 16

That was May, and now it's September and already frost is breaking down the green in leaves, then clotting like blood as tannin, anthocyanin, carotene, and xanthophyll. If pines represent continuance then cottonwood leaves show me how the illusion of time punctuates space, how we fill those dusty, gaseous voids with escapades of life and death, dropping the tiny spans of human days into them. 17

This morning I found a yearling heifer, bred by a fence-jumping bull out of season, trying to calve. I saw her high up on a sage-covered slope, 18 lying down, flicking her tail, and thought she must have colic. But I was wrong. The calf's front feet and head had already pushed out, who knows how many hours before, and it was dead.

I walked her down the mountain to the calving shed, where a friend,   19 Ben, and I winched the dead calf out. We doctored the heifer for uterine infections, and I made a bed of straw, brought fresh creek water and hay. The heifer ate and rested. By evening she had revived, but by the next morning she seemed to have contracted pneumonia. Immediately I gave her a huge shot of penicillin. She worsened. The antibiotics didn't kick in.

That night she lay on her straw bed emitting grunts and high-pitched   20 squeals. The vet came at midnight. We considered every possibility—infection, pneumonia, poisoning—what else could it be? Another day and her condition worsened. Not any one symptom, but a steady decline. I emptied more medicine into her, knowing it was doing no good, but my conscience forbade me to do less. The vet came again and left. He suggested it might be "hardware disease," a euphemism for an ingested piece of metal, a nail or barbed wire, cutting into her throat or stomach or heart. I put a magnet down her throat. Strange as it seems, it sometimes picks up the metal, taking it all the way through the digestive tract. No response. I sat with her. I played music, Merle Haggard and Mozart, wondering if my presence consoled or irritated her. This was not a cow we had raised, and she seemed unsure of me. Could a calf-puller, a shot-giver, *not* mean harm?

In the morning I found she had not eaten or taken any water. Her   21 breathing was worse. I lay on the straw beside her and slept. Before coming to the barn I had smelled something acrid—an old, familiar smell of death's presence, although she was still alive. Yet the sounds she made now had changed from grunting to a low moan, the kind of sound one makes when giving in to something. By nightfall she was dead.

Today yellow is combed all through the trees, and the heart-shaped   22 cottonwood leaves spin downward to nothingness. I know how death is made—not why—but where in the body it begins, its lurking presence before the fact, its strangled music as if the neck of a violin were being choked; I know how breathing begins to catch on each rib, how the look of the eye flattens, gives up its depth, no longer sees past itself; I know how easily existence is squandered, how noiselessly love is dropped to the ground.

When I go to town I notice the feed store calendar: a cornucopia burst-   23 ing with the produce of the season—nuts, apples, wheat, corn, pumpkins, beans. I've seen death eat away at the edges of plenty. Now I want to watch life fill in the fractal geometries of what exists no more.

Now I walk to the ranch graveyard. On a ranch, death is as much a con-   24 stant as birth. The heifer is there with her calf, legs stretched out straight, belly bloated ... but the white droppings of ravens, who are making a meal of her, cascade down her ribcage like a waterfall.

I wander through the scattered bones of other animals who have died. 25 Two carcasses are still intact: Blue and Lawyer, saddle horses who put in many good years. Manes, tails, hair gone, their skin has hardened to rawhide, dried to a tautness, peeling back just slightly from ribs, noses, and hooves, revealing a hollow interior as if letting me see that the souls are really gone.

After fruition, after death, after black ash, perhaps there is something 26 more, even if it is only the droppings of a scavenger, or bones pointing every which way as if to say, "Touch here, touch here," and the velocity of the abyss when a loved one goes his way, and the way wind stirs hard over fresh graves, and the emptying out of souls into rooms and the mischief they get into, flipping switches, opening windows, knocking candles out of silver holders, and after, shimmering on water like leaked gas ready to explode.

Mid-September. Afternoons I paddle my blue canoe across our nine- 27 acre lake, letting water take me where it will. The canoe was a gift: eight dollars at the local thrift store.

As I drift aimlessly, ducks move out from the reeds, all mallards. 28 Adaptable, omnivorous, and hardy, they nest here every year on the two tiny islands in the lake. After communal courtship and mating, the extra male ducks are chased away, but this year one stayed behind. Perhaps he fathered a clutch on the sly or was too young to know where else to go. When the ducklings hatched and began swimming, he often tagged along, keeping them loosely together until the official father sent him away. Then he'd swim the whole circumference of the lake alone, too bewildered and dignified to show defeat.

A green net of aquatic weeds knots the water, holding and releasing me 29 as if I were weightless, as if I were loose change. Raised on the Pacific, I can row a boat, but I hardly know how to paddle. The water is either ink or a clear, bloodless liquid, and the black water snakes that writhe as I plunge my paddle are trying to write words.

Evening. In Kyoto I was taken to a moon-viewing room atop an ancient 30 house on temple grounds. The room was square and the windows on four sides were rice-paper cutouts framed by bamboo, rounds split down the center, allowing the viewer to recreate the moon's phase. To view the moon, one had to look through the moon of the window.

Tonight the lake is a mirror. The moon swims across. Every now and 31 then I slide my paddle into its face. Last week I saw the moon rise twice in one night: once, heavy and orange—a harvest moon—heaving over the valley, and later, in the mountains, it rose small, tight, and bright. But in August the moon went blind. I sat outside with a bottle of wine and watched a shade pull across its difficult, cratered solitude. Earlier, while thumbing through a book of late Tang poets, I came on this: "But this night, the fifteenth of the eighth month, was not like other nights; for now we saw a strange thing: the rim was as though a strong man hacked off pieces with an axe," and "Darkness smeared the whole sky like soot, and then it seemed for thousands of ages the sky would never open." That was 810. Over a thousand years later, a lunar eclipse happened again: same day, same month.

Now a half-moon slants down light, and shadows move desolation all over the place. At dawn a flicker knocks. The hollow sound of his labor makes leaves drop in yellow skirts around the trunks of trees. Water bends daylight. Thoughts shift like whitecaps, wild and bitter. My gut is a harp. Its strings get plucked in advance of any two-way communication by people I love, so that I know when attentions wane or bloom, when someone dear goes from me. From the same battered book I read this by Meng Chiao: "The danger of the road is not in the distance, ten yards is far enough to break a wheel. The peril of love is not in loving too often. A single evening can leave its wound in the soul."   32

Tonight thin spines of boreal light pin down thoughts as if skewered on the ends of thrown quills. I'm trying to understand how an empty tube behind a flower swells to fruit, how leaves twisting from trees are pieces of last year's fire spoiling to humus. Now trees are orange globes, their brightness billowing into cumulus clouds. As the sun rises, the barometer drops. Wind swings around, blasting me from the east, and every tin roof shudders to a new tune.   33

Stripped of leaves, stripped of love, I run my hands over my single wound and remember how one man was like a light going up inside me, not flesh. Wind comes like horn blasts: the whole mountain range is gathered in one sucking breath. Leaves keep coming off trees as if circulating through a fountain; aspens growing in steep groves glow.   34

I search for the possible in the impossible. Nothing. Then I try for the opposite, but the yellow leaves in trees—shaped like mouths—just laugh. Tell me, how can I shut out the longing to comprehend?   35

Wind slices off pondswells, laying them sharp and flat. I paddle and paddle. Rain fires into the water all around me, denting the mirror. The pond goes colorless. It is blue or gray or black. Where the warm spring feeds in, a narrow lane has been cut through aquatic flowers to the deep end. I slide my canoe into the channel. Tendrils of duckweed wave green arms. Are they saying hello or goodbye?   36

Willows, clouds, and mountains lie in the lake's mirror, although they look as if they're standing. I dip my paddle and glide—I think I'm getting the hang of it now—and slide over great folds of time, through lapping   37 depositions of memory, over Precambrian rock, then move inward, up a narrow gorge where a hidden waterfall gleams. After fruition, water mirrors water.

The canoe slides to shore and I get out. The way a cloud tears, letting   38
sun through, then closes again, I know that every truth flies. I get down on my hands and knees and touch my tongue to water: the lake divides. Its body is only chasm after chasm. Like water I have no skin, only surface tension. How exposed I feel. Where a duck tips down to feed, one small ripple causes random turbidity, ceaseless chaos, and the lake won't stop breaking . . . I can punch my finger through anything . . .

Much later, in the night, in the dark, I shine a flashlight down: my sin-   39
gle wound is a bright scar that gives off hooked light like a new moon.

I try to cut things out of my heart, but the pack rat who has invaded my   40
study won't let me. He has made himself the curator of my effects, my despair, my questioning, my memory. Every day a new show is installed. As if courting, he brings me bouquets of purple aster and sage gone to seed, cottonwood twigs whose leaves are the color of pumpkins. His scat is scattered like black rain: books, photographs, and manuscripts are covered. The small offering I set out years ago when I began using this room—a fistful of magpie feathers and the orange husks of two tangerines—has been gnawed into. Only the carved stone figure of a monk my mother gave me during tumultuous teenage years stands solid. The top of the narrow French desk where I write is strewn with torn-off cactus paddles, all lined up end to end, as if to remind me of how prickly the practice of vandalizing one's consciousness can be, how what seems inexpressible is like a thorn torn off under the skin.

The pack rat keeps me honest and this is how: he reminds me that I've   41
left something out. Last August I returned to Yellowstone Park. I wanted to begin again in barrenness, I wanted to understand ash. This time the carcasses were gone—some eaten by bears, coyotes, eagles, and ravens; others taken away by the park. Those charnel grounds where only a green haze of vegetation showed had become tall stands of grass. And the bison—those who survived—were fat.

In a grassland at the northern end of the park I stood in fairy rings of   42
ash where sagebrush had burned hot, and saw how mauve lupine seeds had been thrown by twisted pods into those bare spots. At the edges were thumbnail-size sage seedlings. Under a stand of charred Douglas firs was a carpet of purple asters and knee-high pine grass in bloom for the first time in two hundred years—its inflorescence had been stimulated by fire. I saw a low-lying wild geranium that appears only after a fire, then goes into dormancy again, exhibiting a kind of patience I know nothing of. In another blackened stand of trees it was possible to follow the exact course

of the fire by stepping only where pine grass was in flower; I could see how groundfire had moved like rivulets of water. In places where the fire burned hottest there was no grass, because the organic matter in the soil had burned away, but there were hundreds of lodgepole pine seedlings; the black hills were covered with dark pink fireweed.

Just when all is black ash, something new happens. Ash, of course, is a 43 natural fertilizer, and it's now thought to have a water-holding capacity: black ground is self-irrigating in a self-regulating universe. How quickly "barrenness becomes a thousand things and so exists no more."

Now it's October. I'm on the pond again, that dumping ground for 44 thought. Water clanks against the patched hull. It is my favorite music, like that made by halyards against aluminum masts. It is the music emptiness would compose if emptiness could change into something. The seat of my pants is wet because the broken seat in the canoe is a sponge holding last week's rainwater. All around me sun-parched meadows are green again.

In the evening the face of the mountain looks like a ruined city. 45 Branches stripped bare of leaves are skeletons hung from a gray sky and next to them are tall buildings of trees still on fire. Bands and bars of color are like layers of thought, moving the way stream water does, bending at point bars, eroding cutbanks. I lay my paddle down, letting the canoe drift. I can't help wondering how many ways water shapes the body, how the body shapes desire, how desire moves water, how water stirs color, how thought rises from land, how wind polishes thought, how spirit shapes matter, how a stream that carves through rock is shaped by rock.

Now the lake is flat but the boat's wake—such as it is—pushes water 46 into a confusion of changing patterns, new creations: black ink shifting to silver, and tiny riptides breaking forward-moving swells.

I glide across rolling clouds and ponder what my astronomer friend 47 told me: that in those mysterious moments before the big bang there was no beginning, no tuning up of the orchestra, only a featureless simplicity, a stretch of emptiness more vast than a hundred billion Wyoming skies. By chance this quantum vacuum blipped or burped as if a bar towel had been snapped, and resulted in a cosmic plasma that fluctuated into and out of existence, finally moving in the direction of life.

"But where did the bar towel come from?" I asked my friend in a small 48 voice. No answer. Somehow life proceeded from artlessness and instability, burping into a wild diversity that follows no linear rules. Yet, in all this indeterminacy, life keeps opting for life. Galactic clouds show a propensity to become organic, not inorganic, matter; carbon-rich meteorites have seeded our earthly oasis with rich carbon-based compounds; sea vents let out juvenile water warm enough to make things grow, and sea meadows brew up a marine plasma—matter that is a thousandth of a millimeter wide—and thus give rise to all plant life and the fish, insects, and animals with which it coevolved.

I dip my paddle. The canoe pivots around. Somewhere out there in the cosmos, shock waves collapsed gas and dust into a swirl of matter made of star-grains so delicate as to resemble smoke, slowly aggregating, gradually sweeping up and colliding with enough material to become a planet like ours.   49

Dusk. A bubble of cloud rises over the mountains. It looks like the moon, then a rock tooth pierces it and wind burnishes the pieces into soft puffs of mist. Forms dissolve into other forms: a horse head becomes a frog; the frog becomes stick figures scrawled across the sky. I watch our single sun drop. Beyond the water, a tree's yellow leaves are hung like butterlamps high up near the trunk. As the sun sinks, the tree appears to be lit from the inside.   50

Another day. Listen, it's nothing fancy. Just a man-made pond in the center of the ranch, which is at the northern, mountainous edge of a desolate state. And it's fall, not too much different from the last fourteen autumns I've lived through here, maybe warmer at times, maybe windier, maybe rainier. I've always wondered why people sit at the edge of water and throw rocks. Better to toss stones at the car that brought you, then sit quietly.   51

This lake is a knowing eye that keeps tabs on me. I try to behave. Last summer I swam in its stream of white blossoms contemplating "the floating life." Now I lie on its undulant surface. For a moment the lake is a boat sliding hard to the bottom of a deep trough, then it is a lover's body reshaping me. Whenever I try to splice discipline into my heart, the lake throws diamonds at me, but I persist, staring into its dangerous light as if into the sun. On its silvered surface I finally locate desire deep in the eye, to use Wallace Stevens's words, "behind all actual seeing."   52

Now wind pinches water into peaked roofs as if this were a distant city at my feet. I slide my canoe onto one of the tiny, humpbacked islands. The rind of earth at water's edge shows me where deer have come to drink and ducks have found shelter. It's not shelter I seek but a way of going to the end of thought.   53

I sit the way a monk taught me: legs crossed, hands cupped, thumbs touching, palms upward. The posture has a purpose—it helps transform breathing into energy—but the pose, as it must appear to the onlooker, is a ruse. There is no such thing as stillness, of course, since life progresses by vibration—the constant flexing and releasing of muscles, the liquid pulse, the chemical storms in the brain. I use this island only to make my body stop, this posture to lower the mind's high-decibel racket.   54

The ground is cold. All week blasts of Arctic air have braided into lin-   55 gering warmth. Sometimes a lip of ice grows outward from shore, but afternoon sun burns it back. Water rubs against earth as if trying to make a spark. Nothing. The fountain of leaves in trees has stopped. But how weightless everything appears without the burden of leaves.

At last light, my friend the bachelor duck makes a last spin around the 56 lake's perimeter. When the breeze that sweeps up from the south turns on itself, he swims against the current, dipping out of sight behind a gold-tinged swell. Fruition comes to this, then: not barrenness but lambency.

November 1. The ducks are gone. A lip of ice grew grotesquely fast 57 during the night and now stretches across the water. I *can't* sit. Even the desire to be still, to take refuge from despair in the extremes of diversity, to bow down to light, is a mockery. Nothing moves. Looking out across the lake is like viewing a corpse: no resemblance to the living body. I go to the house despondent. When news of the California earthquake came I thought about stillness and movement, how their juxtaposition creates an equilibrium, how their constant rubbing sparks life and imposes death. But now I don't know. Now the island is like a wobbly tooth, hung by a fine thread to the earth's mantle, and the lake is a solid thing, a pane of glass that falls vertically, cutting autumn off.

A week later. It has snowed and I'm sitting on the white hump of the is- 58 land. My thrift-store canoe is hopelessly locked in ice. Today the frozen lake is the color of my mother's eyes, slate blue but without the sparkle. Snow under me, ice at my feet, no mesmerizing continuum of ripples forwarding memory, no moving lines in which to write music. And yet ...

I put my nose to ice. It's the only way I'll know what I'm facing. At first 59 it looks flat and featureless, like an unborn cosmos, but closer I see its surface is dented and pocked, and across the middle, where the water is deepest, there are white splotches radiating arms like starfish. It's like looking up the spiral arm of a galaxy.

At midday the barometer drops and the radio carries stockmen's warn- 60 ings: high winds, snow and blowing snow in the northern mountains. That's us. Sure enough the wind comes, but it's a warm chinook. Instead of snow, rain undulates across the face of the mountains. Then the storm blows east.

In the morning I go to the lake. Drifts of snow dapple the white surface 61 like sand dunes, and between, dead leaves scud across the ones trapped under ice. But at the north end, where the warm spring feeds in, there is open water—a tiny oval cut like a gem. Something catches my eye: a duck swims out from the reeds, all alone. Is it my bachelor duck? Around and around he goes, then climbs onto the lip of ice and faces the warm sun.

How fragile death is, how easily it opens back into life. Inside the oval, 62 water ripples, then lies flat. The mirror it creates is so small I can see only a strip of mountains and the duck's fat chest bulging. I want to call out to him: "Look this way, I'm here too this autumn morning," but I'm afraid I'll scare him.

He goes anyway, first sliding into the water, then swimming anxious laps. When he takes off, his head is like a green flame. He circles so close I can hear the wing-creak and rasp of feathers. Over the lake he flies, crossing the spillway and dam bank, then up through a snowy saddle, not south as I would have expected, but northwest, in the direction of on-coming storms. 63

QUESTIONS FOR DISCUSSION AND WRITING

1. "This Autumn Morning" goes back and forth in time, from autumn, to spring, and finally to the edge of winter. Trace carefully the chronological sequence Ehrlich uses and explain why you think she chooses to arrange her essay in this way. What ideas and images is she able to bring together and stress through this chronological arrangement?

2. Ehrlich writes near the beginning of this essay, "It's said that after fruition nothing will suffice, there is no more, but who can know the answer?" (par. 9). Later in the essay, however, she writes, "After fruition, after death, after black ash, perhaps there is something more" (par. 26); near the end she says, "How fragile death is, how easily it opens back into life" (par 62). How does Ehrlich use her descriptions of nature to find the hope she has at the end of the essay? What is the connection between her descriptions of nature and the sections of the essay about the men Ehrlich has loved?

3. In this essay Ehrlich writes of water, in the form of lakes, rain, and snow; the moon; and death, both of animals and of plants. What is the connection among these topics? How does Ehrlich use the images and descriptions she creates to say something beyond them?

Recent Poems

A number of contemporary poets have written about nature. These poets often attempt to reestablish their connections with the natural world while acknowledging the growing pressures from civilization that draw them away. They find something akin to spiritual peace in connections with nature.

Sandra Alcosser (b. 1944), who lives in Montana, frequently writes about the place of women in the wilderness. She is particularly concerned with wildlife rehabilitation and environmental issues. In "Approaching August" she compares the elegance of the wilderness with the civilization of France. Dana Gioia (b. 1950), a self-described "working-class kid," grew up in California. In "Rough Country" he seeks a "landscape made of obstacles," one that will reveal that not everything in nature is owned by somebody.

William Matthews (b. 1942) has taught poetry at a number of colleges and universities. In "Names" he lists a wide variety of extinct species, tying the names to their biblical source, Adam and Eve. Mary Oliver (b. 1935) often writes about nature, bringing together humans and the natural world. In "Sleeping in the Forest," the earth seems to remember her and welcome her back.

Approaching August

Night takes on its own elegance.
The catenary curve of snakes,
the breathing, pentagonal-shaped
flowers, the shadblow pliant
and black with berries. Orion   5
rises in the east, over
fat green gardens, and all meanness
is forgiven.

We canoe the river
in the amethyst hour before dark.   10
Twenty-five billion beats to each heart.
Two passengers fish, two paddle
past the chalk caves, the banks
of aster, the flood plains dense
with white tail and beaver.   15

We are lost near midnight, a moonless
summer evening, midseason in our senses,
midlife. The sky overhead like glitter ice.
The water round swollen cottonwoods
pulls like tresses and torn paper.   20

Today I had a letter from France.
"What a truly civilized nation," my friend wrote
as she drank her morning coffee with thick cream
in a country cafe near Avignon. "To my right
a man in a black tuxedo sips raspberry liqueur   25
and soda."

And here on the same latitude we lie back at dawn
on the caving bank of the Bitterroot.
A shadow slips through the silver grasses.
And then a moth.
And then the moon.   30

                              SANDRA ALCOSSER

Rough Country

Give me a landscape made of obstacles,
of steep hills and jutting glacial rock,
where the low-running streams are quick to flood
the grassy fields and bottomlands.
                              A place   5
no engineers can master—where the roads
must twist like tendrils up the mountainside
on narrow cliffs where boulders block the way.

Where tall black trunks of lightning-scalded pine
push through the tangled woods to make a roost   10
for hawks and swarming crows.
                              And sharp inclines
where twisting through the thorn-thick underbrush,
scratched and exhausted, one turns suddenly

to find an unexpected waterfall,   15
not half a mile from the nearest road,
a spot so hard to reach that no one comes—

a hiding place, a shrine for dragonflies
and nesting jays, a sign that there is still
one piece of property that won't be owned.   20

DANA GIOIA

Names

Ten kinds of wolf are gone and twelve of rat
and not a single insect species.
Three sorts of skink are history and two
of minnow, two of pupfish, ten of owl.
Seventeen kinds of rail are out of here   5
and five of finch. It comforts us to think
the dinosaurs bought their farms all at once,
but they died at a rate of one species
per thousand years. Life in a faster lane
erased the speckled dace, the thicktail chub,   10
two kinds of thrush and six of wren, the heath
hen and Ash Meadows killfish. There are four
kinds of sucker not born any minute
anymore. The Christmas Island musk shrew
is defunct. Some places molt and peel so fast   15
it's a wonder they have any name:
the Chatham Island bellbird flew the coop
as did the Chatham Island fernbird, the
Lord Howe Island fantail and the Lord Howe
Island blackbird. The Utah Lake sculpin,   20
Arizona jaguar and Puerto
Rican caviomorph, the Vegas Valley
leopard frog and New Caledonian lorikeet?
They've hit the road for which there is no name
a mouth surrounds so well as it did theirs.   25
The sea mink's crossed the bar and the great auk's
ground time here was brief. Four forms the macaw
took are cancelled checks. Sad Adam fills his lungs
with haunted air, and so does angry Eve:
they meant no name they made up for farewell.   30
They were just a couple starting out,
a place they could afford, a few laughs,
no champagne but a bottle of rosé.
In fact Adam and Eve are not their names.

WILLIAM MATTHEWS

Sleeping in the Forest

    I thought the earth
remembered me, she
took me back so tenderly, arranging,
   her dark skirts, her pockets
full of lichens and seeds. I slept   5
   as never before, a stone
   on the riverbed, nothing
between me and the white fire of the stars
  but my thoughts, and they floated
light as moths among the branches   10
  of the perfect trees. All night
I heard the small kingdoms breathing
around me, the insects, and the birds
who do their work in the darkness. All night
I rose and fell, as if in water, grappling   15
with a luminous doom. By morning
I had vanished at least a dozen times
   into something better.

MARY OLIVER

QUESTIONS FOR DISCUSSION AND WRITING

1. Both "Approaching August" and "Rough Country" describe places that are untouched by civilization. Alcosser talks about canoeing on the Bitterroot River, setting this scene against a man in a tuxedo sipping raspberry liqueur, and Gioia looks for a hidden waterfall, "a place / no engineers can master" (lines 4 and 5). How are the man sipping raspberry liqueur and an engineer alike? How are they different? How do the differences affect the sense of the natural world presented in the two poems?

2. In "Names" Matthews combines rather technical names for species (the thicktail chub, the Christmas Island musk shrew) with a rather informal diction—"sucker not born any minute" (line 13), "they've hit the road," (line 24), "a place they could afford, a few laughs" (line 32). Why does he do this? What is he saying about nature by using this technique?

3. In "Sleeping in the Forest," how does Oliver blur the line between herself and the earth? In what ways does she make the earth human, and in what ways does she make herself seem part of the natural world? Why does she do this, and how convincing do you find her attempt?

5

RESPONSES TO THE CURRENT ENVIRONMENTAL CRISIS

In the second half of the twentieth century, most of the competing concepts of nature that had long shaped the American experience—nature as a healing force, as a source of identity, as a source of raw materials—were still at issue. What had changed was the economic and cultural context. In the two decades after World War II, America had become the strongest, most economically potent nation in the world, perhaps in history. What had once been an agrarian and then an industrial culture had become an expanding consumer culture. Accompanying the rise of consumer culture was rise of modern technology—chemicals, plastics, genetic engineering, all of which helped to create better and less expensive products, but which often brought serious ecological consequences.

By the late 1970s, America's long-term concern for the environment had become an ecological "crisis" as the litany of threats to our planet had become a part of our everyday vocabulary: global warming, toxic waste, the greenhouse effect, acid rain. At the same time social critics and industry representatives were insisting there was no crisis, other people began to suspect that industry could not be trusted to police itself, and that the government agencies responsible for enforcing environmental laws had become part of the problem. Despite years of talk and political posturing, species were still being lost, rivers and lakes were still being poisoned, and, as Roosevelt, Pinchot, and Leopold had warned, forests and wetlands were rapidly disappearing. Suddenly, Americans faced what in Roosevelt's time had seemed a remote prospect: the loss of everything wild in America.

As America entered the post-Vietnam, post-Watergate era, this combination of urgency and frustration with government inaction began to produce a series of grassroots responses to specific environmental disasters: Love Canal in 1978, Three-Mile Island in 1979. As the list of ecological problems grew, however, many people began to suspect that such local responses were unlikely to stop the degradation of the planet. Gradually, concerned individuals began to join the established environmental groups, some of which had been around since the turn of the century. By the early 1980s, when Ronald Reagan began what many saw as a systematic attack on the environment, nature had become a *cause*, and environmentalism had become a massive social and political movement.

Organizations like the Sierra Club and the Wilderness Society soon were large corporate entities themselves, actively involved in political lobbying high-profile lawsuits, publishing books and magazines, and raising millions of dollars through mass mailings. In time, some members of these mainstream environmental groups, disgruntled with the tactics of compromise and suspicious of the corporate trappings, began to form smaller, more radical, "direct-action groups." The Sea Shepherds, who had broken away from Greenpeace, chose to ram whaling ships on the high seas, or sink them at their docks, as described in Rik Scarce's "Raid on Reykjavik." Radical groups like Earth First! (whose motto is "No Compromise in Defense of Mother Earth!") chose to spike trees and burn bulldozers in order to stop the logging of old-growth forests. The effectiveness of such radical actions is the subject of debate, as are the ethics, but clearly the modern environmental movement had developed a complex and diverse set of responses to a common threat.

Another important aspect of this contemporary response to America's ecological crisis has been a call for philosophical and spiritual renewal. In the spirit of Emerson, Thoreau, and Whitman, Americans were asking fundamental questions about our relationship with nature: Can and should human beings attempt to control nature? Does nature exist primarily for the convenience of human civilization, or does it have a value and purpose beyond our needs? For contemporary writers like the ones represented in this chapter, the root causes of our current environmental crisis are as much spiritual and philosophical as they are scientific or economic. And so are the solutions. Creating a livable planet will require much more than establishing new regulations or recycling cans and bottles. We must change the way we live, and the way we relate to the natural world.

While such views of nature had great appeal for many Americans, they also had their critics. As the influence of environmentalism grew, these critics questioned both the arguments and the tactics used by what they called "eco-doomsters." Are we really so close to ecological Armageddon? Is it really sensible, or even possible, to stop economic progress in order to protect every species and every wilderness area? Shouldn't we consider the human costs of environmental decisions: unemployment, disrupted communities, lower standards of living?

This chapter's exploration of these diverse responses opens with Ernest Callenbach's fictional account of life in "Ecotopia," an alternative community set somewhere in the not-too-distant future. What Callenbach shows is what happens to the lives of people who live in closer harmony with natural systems, and with one another. In "Environmentalism of the Spirit," Al Gore argues that the causes and the solutions to our ecological crisis are as much spiritual as they are economic or scientific. Gore looks to the spiritual beliefs of diverse cultures—Native American, Islamic, Judeo-Christian—in order to illustrate how each religion identifies the earth as sacred. Paula DiPerna's "Truth vs. 'Facts'" also looks to our rela-

tionships with nature for the solut...
particular, she demonstrates how wo...
"special connection" to the earth, since th...
effects of pollution and dwindling resource...
gues DiPerna, means that women hold the ke...
problems. In "Renegotiating the Contracts," Bar...
modern urban life has left us isolated from nature; if...
nature, and thereby our selves, we must renegotiate o...
tracts" with animals, contracts that begin in "a sense of mut...
and courtesy."

Both Carolyn Merchant's "Global Ecological Crisis" and Rik...
"Raid on Reykjavik" offer the perspective of radical ecology. Mercha...
gins with a stark and uncompromising description of the crisis we fac...
then points to the philosophical and economic traditions of consumer
capitalism as root causes. The search for a livable planet, says Merchant,
will demand fundamental changes in our social and economic relationships. Rik Scarce provides a sympathetic account of a raid by two eco-
warriors who snuck into Iceland in order to sink whaling ships. Scarce
helps us to understand the philosophy behind such extreme actions:
"They live by—and were willing to risk death for—ecocentric principles."

By contrast, both P. J. O'Rourke's essay "The Greenhouse Affect" and
Michael Pollan's essay "The Idea of a Garden" offer cautions against the
many forms of philosophical and political extremism they see in the modern environmental movement. O'Rourke uses satire and sharp wit to tease
the "eco-doomster's" for their "eco-Armageddon" vision of our future, and
to ask quite serious questions about the tyranny implicit in all "mass
movements." Michael Pollan uses a local environmental disaster—the destruction of a old-growth forest by a storm—to explore our obsession for
a pristine "original" nature that no longer exists, and perhaps never did.
Pollan would have us replace our outdated "wilderness ethic" with what
he calls a "garden ethic" in order to develop a more realistic relationship
with nature as it is, not as we imagine it to be.

ions to serious ecological problems. In
men around the world live with a
hey are usually the first to feel the
This special connection, ar-
to solving our ecological
Lopez contends that
we are to rediscover
ur "original con-
nal obligation

Scarce's
be-

sed the issue of how
ving "lightly on the
sue, was rejected by
anyan Tree Books, to
s validated when the
id was translated into
itten Living Poor *with*
topia Emerging, a his-
nich take up topics im-
el can teach us a great

reated some time in the
Oregon broke with the
lieve that we should live
earth everything that we
mpletely eliminated. The
tates for twenty years at
rm of newspaper stories
ent to tell the rest of the

and private journal of a ... *United States what this strange place is like. The newspaper reports are in regular type, and the private journal is in italics.*

From *Ecotopia*

Food, Sewage, and "Stable States"

San Francisco, May 6. When I arrived at the Ministry of Food for my interview with the Minister, I was unhappy to find that she was too busy to see me. I was introduced instead to an Assistant Minister, a man in his early thirties, who recieved me in a work overalls outfit. His office was also surprisingly unimpressive for a person of importance. It had no desk, no conference table, no soft chairs. Along one wall was a cluttered series of wooden filing cases, bookshelves, and tables covered with papers in utter disorder. Against another wall was a kind of laboratory set-up, with testing equipment of various kinds.

The Assistant Minister is, like many Ecotopians, unnervingly relaxed, with a deep, slow voice. He sprawled on woven cushions in a sunny corner of the floor, under a skylight with some kind of ivy hanging near it,

1

2

and his lab assistant produced hot water for tea on a Bunsen burner. I squatted awkwardly, and began by asking my carefully prepared questions about Ecotopian agricultural output. These were ignored. Instead the Assistant Minister insisted on giving me "a little background." He then began to discuss, not agriculture at all, but sewage. The first major project of his ministry after Independence, he said, had been to put the country's food cycle on a stable-state basis: all food wastes, sewage and garbage were to be turned into organic fertilizer and applied to the land, where it would again enter into the food production cycle. Every Ecotopian household, thus, is required to compulsively sort all its garbage into compostable and recyclable categories, at what must be an enormous expenditure of personal effort; and expanded fleets of garbage trucks are also needed.

The sewage system inherited from the past, according to the Assistant Minister, could only be called a "disposal" system. In it a sewage and industrial wastes had not been productively recycled but merely dumped, in a more or less toxic condition, into rivers, bays and oceans. This, he maintained, was not only dangerous to the public health and the life of water creatures, but its very objective was wasteful and unnatural. With a smile, he added that some of the sewage practices of earlier days would even be considered criminal if carried out today.

"In my papers over there," he said, "you can find historical reports of great sums being spent on incinerators to burn up sewage sludge. Their designers boasted of relatively smog-free stacks. We were of course accused of 'sewer socialism,' like our Milwaukee predecessors. Nonetheless, we constructed a national system of sludge drying and natural fertilizer production. After seven years we were able to dispense with chemical fertilizers entirely. This was partly through sewage recycling, partly through garbage composting, partly through reliance on some novel nitrogen-fixing crops and crop rotation, and partly through methods of utilizing animal manure. You may have seen from the train that our farm animals are not kept in close confinement like yours. We like them to live in conditions approaching the natural. But not only for sentimental reasons. It also avoids the gigantic accumulation of manure which is such a problem in your feedlots and poultry factories."

Naturally, this smug account roused all my skepticism, and I questioned him about the economic drawbacks of such a system. My questions, however, met a flat denial. "On the contrary," he replied, "our system is considerably cheaper than yours, if we add in *all* the costs. Many of your costs are ignored, or passed on through subterfuge to posterity or the general public. We on the other hand must acknowledge all costs. Otherwise we could not hope to achieve the stable-state life systems which are our fundamental ecological and political goal. If, for instance, we had continued your practice of 'free' disposal of wastes in watercourses, sooner or later somebody else would have had to calculate (and bear) the costs of the resulting dead rivers and lakes. We prefer to do it ourselves. It is obviously not easy to quantify certain of these costs. But we have been able to approximate them in workable political terms—especially since our country is relatively sensible in scale."

I obtained the detailed analyses on which his assertions are based, and have studied them at leisure. Extensive objective research would be necessary to confirm or disprove them. They do appear to be surprisingly hard-nosed. Of course the Ecotopian situation has allowed their government to take actions that would be impossible under the checks and balances of our kind of democracy.

6

Next I asked the Assistant Minister about Ecotopian food production and processing. I knew he must be aware of the great achievements of our food industry in recent decades, not only in the introduction of synthetic meat and other protein foods, but also in pre-cooking and packaging generally. I was curious to see how he would justify the regressive practices that, according to many rumors, had returned western agriculture to the dark ages, and cooks to their chopping blocks and hot stoves (microwave ovens being illegal in Ecotopia). Again I quote his reply at length. It is, I am discovering, characteristic of the way in which Ecotopians justify extremist policies.

7

"You must remember," he began, "that Ecotopia at the beginning was faced with a stupendous surplus of food production capacity. California alone had produced about a third of the food eaten in the United States. Oregon and Washington had enormous fruit and grain production. We could produce, therefore, something like five times the amount of food needed by our own population. With food export to the U.S. ended because of the political crisis, our problem was how to shrink our agricultural output drastically. At the same time we wanted to end extractive and polluting practices in farming. Luckily, the new employment policies, which reduced the normal work week to about 20 hours, helped a lot. Also we were able to absorb some surplus farm labor in construction work required by our recycling systems. Along with simplification in food processing, we also achieved many economies in food distribution. As your grocery executives know, a store handling a thousand items is far less difficult and expensive to operate than one handling five thousand or more, as yours do. But probably our greatest economies were obtained simply by stopping production of many processed and packaged foods. These had either been outlawed on health grounds or put on Bad Practice lists."

8

This sounded like a loophole that might house a large and rather totalitarian rat. "What are these lists and how are they enforced?" I asked.

9

"Acutally, they aren't enforced at all. They're a mechanism of moral   10
persuasion, you might say. But they're purely informal. They're issued by
study groups from consumer co-ops. Usually, when a product goes onto
such a list, demand for it drops sharply. The company making it then ordinarily has to stop production, or finds it possible to sell only in specialized stores."

"But surely these committees are not allowed to act simply on their   11
own say-so, without scientific backing or government authorization?"

The Assistant Minister smiled rather wanly. "In Ecotopia," he said,   12
"you will find many many things happening without government authorization. But the study committees do operate with scientific advice, of
the most sophisticated and independent type imaginable. Scientists in
Ecotopia are forbidden to accept payments or favors from either state or
private enterprises for any consultation or advice they offer. They speak,
therefore, on the same uncorrupted footing as any citizen. Thus we avoid
the unfortunate situation where all your oil experts are in the pay of the
oil companies, all the agricultural experts in the pay of agribusiness, and
so on."

This was too much. "No doubt," I said, "it is scientists of this type   13
who have frittered away the great industrial heritage you possessed at
Independence, and wrecked your marvelous street and highway system,
and dissolved your fine medical centers. What benefits of civilization are
they prepared to undermine next?"

"I will not speak to any but food questions," he replied. "I can provide   14
you with whatever evidence you require to prove that Ecotopians eat better food than any nation on earth, because we grow it to be nutritious and
taste good, not look good or pack efficiently. Our food supplies are un-
contaminated with herbicides and insecticides, because we use cultivation
for weeds and biological controls for insects. Our food preparation practices are sound, avoiding the processing that destroys food values. Most
important of all, our agriculture has reached an almost totally stable state,
with more than 99 percent of our wastes being recycled. In short, we have
achieved a food system that can endure indefinitely. That is, if the level of
foreign poisons dumped on our lands by rain and wind doesn't rise above
the present inexcusable figures."

The Assistant Minister scrambled to his feet, went to his shelves, and   15
pulled down a half dozen pamphlets. "You will find some relevant information summarized here," he said. "Let me recommend that, after you
have digested it, you follow Ecotopian ways in not wasting it."

This bad joke took me by surprise, but it did break the tension, and I   16
laughed. He led me to the door. "You may phone if you develop further
questions," he said gravely.

I returned to my hotel and read the pamphlets. One was a highly tech-   17 nical discussion of the relations between sewage sludge, mineral fertilizer requirements, groundwater levels and run-off, farm manure, and various disease organisms. Another, which struck me as particularly depressing because of its moralizing tone, surveyed food habits that had been common before Independence, analyzing the health hazards involved. Its humorless approach seemed to imply that soda drinks had been some kind of plot against mankind. Apparently, over a 30-year period, American soda manufacturers should have been held personally accountable for some 10 billion tooth cavities! This relentless tendency to fix responsibility on producers is, I begin to see, widespread in Ecotopian life—to the complete neglect of the responsibility, in this case, of the soda consumers.

My room boasts a trio of recycle chutes, and I have now, like a proper 18 Ecotopian, carefully disposed of the pamphlets in the one marked P. It is a good thing Ecotopians do not have chewing gum—which chute would that belong in?

(May 7) The stable-state concept may seem innocuous enough, until 19 *you stop to grasp its implications for every aspect of life, from the most personal to the most general. Shoes cannot have composition soles beause they will not decay. New types of glass and pottery have had to be developed, which will decompose into sand when broken into small pieces. Aluminum and other nonferrous metals largely abandoned, except for a few applications where nothing else will serve—only iron, which rusts away in time, seems a "natural" metal to the Ecotopians. Belt buckles are made of bone or very hard woods. Cooking pots have no stick-free plastic lining, and are usually heavy iron. Almost nothing is painted since paints must be based either on lead or rubber or on plastics, which do not decompose. And people seem to accumulate few goods like books; they read quite a bit compared to Americans, but they then pass the copies on to friends, or recycle them. Of course there are aspects of life which have escaped the stable-state criterion: vehicles are rubber-tired, tooth fillings are made of silver, some structures are built of concrete, and so on. But it is still an amazing process, and people clearly take great delight in pushing it further and further.*

(I was wrong to think more garbage trucks needed: actually Ecotopians 20 *generate very little of what we would call garbage—material that simply has to be disposed of in a dump somewhere. But of course they do need more trucks to haul away material from the recycle bins.)*

These people are horribly over-emotional. Last night after supper I was 21 *sitting in my hotel room writing when loud screams began in the corridor. A man and a woman, threatening each other with what sounded like murder. At first I thought I'd better keep out of it. They went off down the hall and I figured were probably going out or returning to their room. But they drifted back, yelling and screaming, until they were right outside my door. I finally stuck my head out, and found three or four other hotel guests standing around watching, placidly, and doing absolutely nothing to interfere. It seemed to be a matter of a passionate affair coming to a bitter ending. The woman, hair half-covering her teary but beautiful face, screamed at the man and kicked at him viciously—still no action from the onlookers, some of whom in fact actually smiled faintly. The man, his own face red with anger, took the woman by the shoulders as if he was about to bash her head against the wall—and at this, finally, two of the Ecotopians present stepped forward and put restraining hands on his shoulders. Instead of knocking her brains out, therefore, the man was reduced to spitting in her face—whereupon she unleashed a horrible stream of curses and insults, things more personally wounding than I have ever heard (much less said) in private, not to mention with a bunch of strangers looking on. But the man did not seem humiliated or surprised—and indeed gave back insults just as dreadful as he got. The scene had gone on for perhaps 15 minutes, with more spectators gathering. It was more theatrical than anything I've seen in Italy. Finally the man and woman evidently ran out of fury. They stood limply, looking at each other, and then fell into each other's arms, crying and nuzzling each other wetly, and staggered off down the corridor to their room. At this the spectators began exchanging lively observations, making the kind of appreciative and comparative remarks we make after a particularly vicious round in a boxing match. Nobody seemed to care what it had all been about, but they sure got a kick out of the expression of intense feeling! Evidently restraints on interpersonal behavior have been very much relaxed here, and extreme hostility can be accepted as normal behavior.*

Maybe I'm not as good a traveler these days. Don't have much appetite for the sugarless Ecotopian food, despite their pride in their "natural" cuisine. Find myself worrying about what I'll do if I get sick or have an accident. The Ecotopians have probably turned medical science back fifty years. I have visions of being bled, *like in the middle ages.* 22

Even began thinking almost fondly, last night, of my years with Pat and the kids. Maybe I'm beginning to miss the comfort of just lying around at home. (Why should this particular jaunt make me so confused and tired? It's an exciting story, an unusual opportunity—all my colleagues envy me. I just can't quite seem to get my hands on it.) Kids used to come into bed with us Sunday mornings, and play Bear Comes Over the Mountain—giggly and floppy and lovable. Afterwards, when they'd gone out, Pat would infallibly ask when I was going away again. No man can live with reproaches before breakfast. But I loved her in my fashion. 23

The Ecotopian work schedule and the intermixture of work and play   24
can make the simplest things practically impossible to accomplish here.
Went to the wire office to file my story yesterday. It has to go via Seattle and
Vancouver, since there have been no direct transcontinental connections
since secession. Different clerk in the office, picked up the copy, started
reading it, laughed, tried to argue with me about the way I quoted the food
guy. "Look," I said, "I'm just doing my job—how about you just doing
yours? Put it on the fucking wire!"

    He looked at me with real hurt, as if I'd just told him his office smelled.   25
"I didn't realize you were in such a hurry," he said, "We don't get
American reporters in here every day, you know, and what you're writing
is really interesting. I wasn't trying to be boorish."

    You can't argue with these people. "Go ahead, read it," I said, figuring   26
to shame him into quick action. But he gave me an appeased glance, said
"Thanks," and settled down to read. I drummed on the counter with my
fingers for a while, but Ecotopian leisure time had clearly set in. Finally he
finished, went over to the machine, sat down, turned and said, "Well, it's
okay for a beginning. I'll send it real fast for you." Then he zapped the
thing out at about 80 words a minute! And came back to hand me the copy
with a broad, pleased smile. "My name's Jerry, by the way. I went to school
with George (the Assistant Minister) and you got him down very well." I
suppose I believe him. Anyway, couldn't help smiling back. "Thanks,
Jerry," I said. "See you tomorrow."

Car-less Living in Ecotopia's New Towns

    San Francisco, May 7. Under the new regime, the established cities of   27
Ecotopia have to some extent been broken up into neighborhoods or
communities, but they are still considered to be somewhat outside the
ideal long-term line of development of Ecotopian living patterns. I have
just had the opportunity to visit one of the strange new minicities that
are arising to carry out the more extreme urban vision of this decentral-
ized society. Once a sleepy village, it is called Alviso, and is located on the
southern shores of San Francisco Bay. You get there on the interurban
train, which drops you off in the basement of a large complex of buildings. The main structure, it turns out, is not the city hall or courthouse, but
a factory. It produces the electric traction units—they hardly qualify as
cars or trucks in our terms—that are used for transporting people and
goods in Ecotopian cities and for general transportation in the countryside. (Individually owned vehicles were prohibited in "car-free" zones
soon after Independence. These zones at first covered only downtown
areas where pollution and congestion were most severe. As minibus serv-

ice was extended, these zones expanded, and now cover all densely settled city areas.)

Around the factory, where we would have a huge parking lot, Alviso 28
has a cluttered collection of buildings, with trees everywhere. There are
restaurants, a library, bakeries, a "core store" selling groceries and clothes,
small shops, even factories and workshops—all jumbled amid apartment
buildings. These are generally of three or four stories, arranged around a
central courtyard of the type that used to be common in Paris. They are
built almost entirely of wood, which has become the predominant building material in Ecotopia, due to the reforestation program. Though these
structures are old-fashioned looking, they have pleasant small balconies,
roof gardens, and verandas—often covered with plants, or even small
trees. The apartments themselves are very large by our standards—with
10 or 15 rooms, to accommodate their communal living groups.

Alviso streets are named, not numbered, and they are almost as narrow 29
and winding as those of medieval cities—not easy for a stranger to get
around in. They are hardly wide enough for two cars to pass; but then of
course there *are* no cars, so that is no problem. Pedestrians and bicyclists
meander along. Once in a while you see a delivery truck hauling a piece
of furniture or some other large object, but the Ecotopians bring their
groceries home in string bags or large bicycle baskets. Supplies for the
shops, like most goods in Ecotopia, are moved in containers. These are
much smaller than our cargo containers, and proportioned to fit into
Ecotopian frieght cars and onto their electric trucks. Farm produce, for instance, is loaded into such containers either at the farms or at the container
terminal located on the edge of each minicity. From the terminal an underground conveyor belt system connects to all the shops and factories in
the minicity, each of which has a kind of siding where the containers are
shunted off. This idea was probably lifted from our automated warehouses, but turned backwards. It seems to work very well, though there
must be a terrible mess if there is some kind of jam-up underground.

My guides on this expedition were two young students who have just 30
finished an apprenticeship year in the factory. They're full of information
and observations. It seems that the entire population of Alviso, about
9,000 people, lives within a radius of a half mile from the transit station.
But even this density allows for many small park-like places: sometimes
merely widenings of the streets, sometimes planted gardens. Trees are
everywhere—there are no large paved areas exposed to the sun. Around
the edges of town are the schools and various recreation grounds. At the
northeast corner of town you meet the marshes and sloughs and saltflats
of the Bay. A harbor has been dredged for small craft; this opens onto the
ship channel through which a freighter can move right up to the factory
dock. My informants admitted rather uncomfortably than there is a mod-

est export trade in electric vehicles—the Ecotopians allow themselves to import just enough metal to replace what is used in the exported electric motors and other metal parts.

Kids fish off the factory dock; the water is clear. Ecotopians love the water, and the boats in the harbor are a beautiful collection of both traditional and highly unorthodox designs. From this harbor, my enthusiastic guides tell me, they often sail up the Bay and into the Delta, and even out to sea through the Golden Gate, then down the coast to Monterey. Their boat is a lovely though heavy-looking craft, and they proudly offered to take me out on it if I have time. 31

We toured the factory, which is a confusing place. Like other Ecotopian workplaces, I am told, it is not organized on the assembly-line principles generally thought essential to really efficient mass production. Certain aspects are automated: the production of the electric motors, suspension frames, and other major elements. However, the assembly of these items is done by groups of workers who actually fasten the parts together one by one, taking them from supply bins kept full by the automated machines. The plant is quiet and pleasant compared to the crashing racket of a Detroit plant, and the workers do not seem to be under Detroit's high output pressures. Of course the extreme simplification of Ecotopian vehicles must make the manufacturing process much easier to plan and manage— indeed there seems little reason why it could not be automated entirely. 32

Also, I discovered, much of the factory's output does not consist of finished vehicles at all. Following the mania for "doing it yourself" which is such a basic part of Ecotopian life, this plant chiefly turns out "front ends," "rear ends," and battery units. Individuals and organizations then connect these to bodies of their own design. Many of them are weird enough to make San Francisco minibuses look quite ordinary. I have seen, for instance, a truck built of driftwood, almost every square foot of it decorated with abalone shells—it belonged to a fishery commune along the coast. 33

The "front end" consists of two wheels, each driven by an electric motor and supplied with a brake. A frame attaches them to are steering and suspension unit, together with a simple steering wheel, accelerator, brake, instrument panel, and a pair of headlights. The motor drives are capable of no more than 30 miles per hour (on the level!) so their engineering requirements must be modest—though my guides told me the suspension is innovative, using a clever hydraulic load-leveling device which in addition needs very little metal. The "rear end" is even simpler, since it doesn't have to steer. The battery units, which seem to be smaller and lighter than even our best Japanese imports, are designed for use in vehicles of various configurations. Each comes with a long reel-in extension cord to plug into recharging outlets. 34

The factory does produce several types of standard bodies, to which 35 the propulsion units can be attached with only four bolts at each end. (They are always removed for repair.) The smallest and commonest body is a shrunken version of our pick-up truck. It has a tiny cab that seats only two people, and a low, square, open box in back. The rear of the cab can be swung upward to make a roof, and sometimes canvas sides are rigged to close in the box entirely.

A taxi-type body is still manufactured in small numbers. Many of these 36 were used in the cities after Independence as a stop-gap measure while minibus and transit systems were developing. These bodies are molded from heavy plastic in one huge mold.

These primitive and underpowered vehicles obviously cannot satisfy 37 the urge for speed and freedom which has been so well met by the American auto industry and our aggressive highway program. My guides and I got into a hot debate on this question, in which I must admit they proved uncomfortably knowledgeable about the conditions that sometimes prevail on our urban throughways—where movement at *any* speed can become impossible. When I asked, however, why Ecotopia did not build speedy cars for its thousands of miles of rural highways—which are now totally uncongested even if their rights of way have partly been taken over for trains—they were left speechless. I attempted to sow a few seeds of doubt in their minds: no one can be utterly insensitive to the pleasures of the open road, I told them, and I related how it feels to roll along in one of our powerful, comfortable cars, a girl's hair blowing in the wind....

We had lunch in one of the restaurants near the factory, amid a cheery, 38 noisy crowd of citizens and workers. I noticed that they drank a fair amount of the excellent local wine with their soups and sandwiches. Afterward we visited the town hall, a modest wood structure indistinguishable from the apartment buildings. There I was shown a map on which adjacent new towns are drawn, each centered on its own rapid-transit stop. It appears that a ring of such new towns is being built to surround the Bay, each one a self-contained community, but linked to its neighbors by train so that the entire necklace of towns will constitute one city. It is promised that you can, for instance, walk five minutes to your transit station, take a train within five minutes to a town ten stops away, and then walk another five minutes to your destination. My informants are convinced that this represents a halving of the time we would spend on a similar trip, not to mention problems of parking, traffic, and of course the pollution.

What will be the fate of the existing cities as these new minicities come 39 into existence? They will gradually be razed, although a few districts will be preserved as living museum displays (of "our barbarian past," as the boys jokingly phrased it). The land will be returned to grassland, forest, orchards, or gardens—often, it appears, groups from the city own plots of land outside in the country, where they probably have a small shack and perhaps grow vegetables, or just go for a change of scene.

After leaving Alviso we took the train to Redwood City, where the reversion process can be seen in action. Three new towns have sprung up there along the Bay, separated by a half mile or so of open country, and two more are under construction as part of another string several miles back from the Bay, in the foothills. In between, part of the former suburban residential area has already been turned into alternating woods and grassland. The scene reminded me a little of my boyhood country summers in Pennsylvania. Wooded strips follow the winding lines of creeks. Hawks circle lazily. Boys out hunting with bows and arrows wave to the train as it zips by. The signs of a once busy civilization—streets, cars, service stations, supermarkets—have been entirely obliterated, as if they never existed. The scene was sobering, and made me wonder what a Carthaginian might have felt after ancient Carthage was destroyed and plowed under by the conquering Romans.

(May 8) Something peculiar is going on in this place. Can't yet exactly locate the source of the feeling. It's like waking up after a dream and not being quite able to remember what it was about. The way people deal with each other—and with me—keeps reminding me of something—but I don't know what. Always takes me off guard, makes me feel I was confronted with some fine personal opportunity—a friendship, learning something's important, love—which by then has just passed.... And they often seem to be surprised, a little disappointed maybe—as if I was a child who was not proving a very fast learner. (But what am I supposed to be learning?)

Then sometimes life here seems like a throwback to a past I might have known through old photographs. Or a skip ahead in time: these people, who are so American despite their weird social practices, might be what we will become. (They miss no chance, of course, to tell me we should get on with it.) Also keep feeling I have gotten stuck on vacation in the country. Partly it's all the trees, and maybe the dark nights (which still make me feel a power blackout must have struck), and also it's hard to get used to the quiet. Must be doing something to my New York paranoia system, geared to respond to honking, screeching, buzzing, bangs, knocks, not to mention a shot or a scream now and then. You expect silence in the country. But here I am in a metropolitan area of several million, constantly surrounded by people—and the only really loud noises are human shouts or babies crying. There's no "New Man" bullshit in Ecotopia, but how do they stand the quiet?

Or for that matter, how do they stand their isolation from us? Has bred a brash kind of self-sufficiency. They seem to be in surprisingly good touch

40

41

42

43

with the rest of the world, but as far as we're concerned, they're strictly on their own—like adolescent children who have rejected their parents' ways. They'll probably get over it.

Ecotopians a little vague about time, I notice—few wear watches, and they pay more attention to things like sunrise and sunset or the tides than to actual hour time. They will accede to the demands of industrial civilization to some extent, but grudgingly. "You'd never catch an Indian wearing a watch." Many Ecotopians sentimental about Indians, and there's some sense in which they envy the Indians their lost natural place in the American wilderness. Indeed this probably a major Ecotopian myth; keep hearing references to what Indians would or wouldn't do in a given situation. Some Ecotopian articles—clothing and baskets and personal ornamentation—perhaps directly Indian in inspiration. But what matters most is the aspiration to live in balance with nature, "walk lightly on the land," treat the earth as a mother. No surprise that to such a morality most industrial processes, work schedules, and products are suspect! Who would use an earth-mover on his own mother? 44

Hotel was okay for a while, but has gotten kind of boring. Have taken to spending a good bit of time a few blocks away, down near the waterfront, at "Franklin's Cove," a sort of press commune, where maybe 40 Ecotopian journalists and writers and TV people live. They've been extremely hospitable—really make me feel welcome. The place must have once been a warehouse, and is now broken up into rooms. They cook collectively, have work rooms (no electric typewriters, I notice, but lots of handy light video recorders), even a kind of gym. Beautiful wild garden in back where people spend a lot of time lying around on sunny days—part of it in crumbling ruins of one wing of the warehouse, which nobody has bothered to wreck and haul away. ("Time is taking its course, and we just let it," replied one of the residents when I asked why this unsightly condition was tolerated.) Center of things is a lounge-library filled with soft chairs and sofas. I've been there so much I even have a favorite chair. 45

Ecotopians, both male and female, have a secure sense of themselves as animals. At the Cove they lie about utterly relaxed, curled up on couches or floor, flopped down in sunny spots on little rugs or mats, almost like a bunch of cats. They stretch, rearrange themselves, do mysterious yoga-like exercises, and just seem to enjoy their bodies tremendously. Nor do they keep this to themselves, particularly—I've several times walked in on people making love, who didn't seem much embarrassed or annoyed—it was hardly different from walking in on somebody taking a bath. I find myself envying them this comfortableness in their biological beings. They seem to breathe better, move more loosely. I'm experimenting, trying to imitate them. . . . 46

Especially in the evenings, though of course they have a lot of free time   47
during the day as well, people gather round and talk—the kind of lei-
surely talk I associate with college days. Jumps around from topic to topic,
and people kid a lot, and cheer each other up when need be, but there's
some thread to it usually. Last evening spent quite a while talking to an in-
teresting guy I've met at the Cove—Bert Luckman (that seems to be his real
name). He was studying at Berkeley at the time of Independence—bright
Jewish kid from New York. Had gone through Maoist phase, then got into
secessionist movement. Politics and science writer (not an odd combina-
tion here) for the S. F. Times. Has written a book on cosmology, has a mys-
tic streak, but still a reporter's reporter: tough, wry, well-organized writing.
Is surprisingly skeptical about U.S. science, which he regards as bureau-
cratically constipated and wasteful. "You made the dreadful mistake," he
said, "of turning your science establishment over to established scientists,
who could be trusted. But it's mainly young and untrustworthy scientists
who get important new ideas.—You still have a few things happening, but
it's lost the momentum you need." (I wonder. Check when get back.)

After some drinks the conversation got livelier and more personal.   48
Thought I'd do some probing. "Doesn't this stable-state business get aw-
fully static? I'd think it would drive you crazy after a certain point!"

Bert looked at me with amusement, and batted the ball back. "Well,   49
don't forget that we don't have to be stable. The system provides the stabil-
ity, and we can be erratic within it. I mean we don't try to be perfect, we
just try to be okay on the average—which means adding up a bunch of
ups and downs." "But it means giving up any notions of progress. You
just want to get to that stable point and stay there, like a lump."

"It may sound that way, but in practice there's no stable point. We're   50
always striving to approximate it, but we never get there. And you know
how much we disagree on exactly what is to be done—we only agree on
the root essentials, everything else is in dispute." I grinned. "I've noticed
that—you're a quarrelsome lot!" "We can afford to be, because of that
root agreement. Besides, that's half the fun of relating to each other—try-
ing to work through different perspectives, seeing how other people feel
about things."

"It's still flying in the face of reality, this striving for stability." Bert took   51
this more seriously: "Is it? But we've actually achieved something like
stability. Our system meanders on its peaceful way, while yours has con-
stant convulsions. I think of ours as like a meadow in the sun. There's a lot
of change going on—plants growing, other plants dying, bacteria decom-
posing them, mice eating seeds, hawks eating mice, a tree or two begin-
ning to grow up and shade the grasses. But the meadow sustains itself on
a steady-state basis—unless men come along and mess it up."

"I begin to see what you mean. It may not look so static to the mouse."   52

After his student years Bert traveled a lot—in Canada, Latin America, 53
Europe, Asia. Even thought of going to the U.S. sub rosa—but didn't do it
(or says he didn't). Attached to a charming giddy woman named Clara,
some years older and also a journalist—they have separate rooms at the
Cove. Bert seems to be a wanderer—has also worked on papers in Seattle,
Vancouver, and a little California coast resort town called Mendocino. We
exchanged life histories, and he pumped me for inside intrigues on my
travels, my relations with sources in our government, and so on. Caught
me in a couple of prevarications, but seems to take their measure quickly
and understand them. We went on talking in a frank and almost brotherly
way, so I tried harder to be candid and scrupulous. Told him about
Francine; he wanted to know precisely the nature of my relationship with
her, and seemed surprised that it is so tentative, even though its gone on
for three years now. "It seems contradictory to me," he said. "You live
in separate apartments, see each other a couple of times a week, spend
weeks on end away from each other altogether. At the same time you
don't have a group of people to live with, to support you emotionally, to
keep your collective life going on actively and strongly while you're apart.
I'd think that during one of these absences you'd have split up long ago—
one of you would have taken up seriously with someone else, and then
there'd be two other little separate worlds, instead of the two you have now.
I'd find that very scary."

"It is very scary," I said, "and once or twice we have gotten involved 54
with someone else. But we have always come back to each other." "It still
sounds frivolous to me," he said, frowning. "It gives too much power to
loneliness. Here we try to arrange it so we are not lonely very often. That
keeps us from making a lot of emotional mistakes. We don't think commit-
ment is something you go off and do by yourselves, just two of you. It has to
have a structure, social surroundings you can rely on. Human beings are
tribal animals, you know. They need lots of contact."

"You might be right," I said doubtfully. "I never thought of myself that 55
way particularly. Though at one point I remember wondering if having
lots and lots of children might not be a good thing." "Well, there are other
kinds of families, you know," he said gently and with a slight smile. "I'll
take you to visit some."

Have also had some good talks with Tom, a writer for a major magazine 56
called Flow. He's maybe 35 but has a face that already shows lines; also a
temper, and he was swearing at somebody who had challenged his view of
recent American strategy in Brazil. I kept quiet at first, but it happened I
knew Tom was right: we had set up a system of electronically fenced en-
claves in São Paulo as a means of controlling guerrilla movements, though
it had been portrayed as an urban-redevelopment measure. "Look," said
Tom finally, "we have a goddamn American reporter right here, why

*don't we ask him?" "All right," said the other guy to me, "do you know
anything about it?"*

"Yeah," I said, "I do. Tom's got it straight. There are sensor fields all 57
*over São Paulo. Anything that moves, the army knows about." "How did
you get your information? Are you sure?"*

"Sure I'm sure. I heard the President give the order—and I also heard 58
*him tell the press that he'd deny it if we reported it." Tom burst out laugh-
ing. He and his opponent didn't speak for several days after that, but Tom
and I made up for it. Talked not only about Brazil—also about functions
of journalists, and the changes in man-woman relationships that have occurred in Ecotopia. According to him, women in Ecotopia have totally escaped the dependent roles they still tend to play with us. Not that they
domineer over men—but they exercise power in work and in relationships
just as men do. Above all, they don't have to manipulate men: the
Survivalist Party, and social developments generally, have arranged the
society so that women's objective situation is equal to men's. Thus people
can be just people, without our symbolic loading on sex roles. (I notice,
however, that Ecotopian women still seem to me feminine, with a relaxed
air of their biological attractiveness, even fertility, though I don't see how
they combine this with their heavy responsibilities and hard work. And
men, though they express feelings more openly than American men—even
feelings of weakness—still seem masculine.)*

Tom's bright, and cynical as any good newspaperman is, yet strangely 59
*optimistic about the future. Believes that the nature of political power is
changing, that the technology and social structure can be put at the service of mankind, instead of the other way round. Skeptical but not, I notice,
bitter. Must be comfortable to think like that.*

Am missing Francine's reliably amiable "attentions." (Whenever I'm 60
*away I realize anew what a faithful playmate she is; despite our having
deliberately resolved never to be faithful to each other.) Have the awful suspicion that every woman around me is secretly, constantly fucking and
that I could have them if I only knew the password—but I don't. I must be
missing something—can the women journalists at the Cove simply find me
unattractive in some mysterious way? They are friendly enough, direct,
open; they even touch me sometimes, which of course feels good and gives
me a warm rush. But again, it's sisterly: if I touch them back, they seem to
feel I'm making an improper advance, and back off. There must be some
move, when a woman here comes close to you, that I don't know how to
make? Yet I watch the Ecotopian men, and they don't seem to do anything,
except maybe smile a little; and then things go on from there, or sometimes
don't—it's all very casual and nobody seems to worry about it. Very confusing all around; makes me feel hung up on my own patterns. Many*

Ecotopian women are beautiful in a simple, unadorned way. They're not dependent for their attractiveness on cosmetics or dress—they give the impression of being strong, secure, pleasure-loving people, very honest and straightforward emotionally. They seem to like me: in the Cove as on the streets they meet my eyes openly, are glad to talk, even quite personally. Yet I can't get past that stage to any real action. Have to think about that some more. Maybe I'll learn something.

Ecotopian Television and Its Wares

San Francisco, May 10. Ecotopians claim to have sifted through modern technology and rejected huge tracts of it, because of its ecological harmfulness. However, despite this general technological austerity, they employ video devices even more extensively than we do. Feeling that they should transport their bodies only when it's a pleasure, they seldom travel "on business" in our manner. Instead, they tend to transact business by using their picturephones. These employ the same cables that provide television connections; the whole country, except for a few isolated rural spots, is wired with cable. (There is no ordinary broadcasting.) Video sets are everywhere, but strangely enough I have seldom seen people sitting before them blotted out in the American manner. Whether this is because of some mysterious national traits, or because of the programming being markedly different, or both, I cannot yet tell. But Ecotopians seem to use TV, rather than letting it use them. 61

Some channels are apparently literal parts of the government structure—something like a council chamber with a PA system would be. People watch these when the doings of local governments or the national legislature are being transmitted. (Virtually no government proceedings are closed to press and public anyway.) Viewers not only watch—they expect to participate. They phone in with questions and comments, sometimes for the officials present, sometimes for the TV staffs. Thus TV doesn't only provide news—much of the time it *is* the news. The routine governmental fare includes debates that involve public figures, or aspirants to public office; many court proceedings and executive meetings; and meetings of the legislatures and especially of their committees. Running comment is interspersed from a variety of sources, ranging from the narrators to vehemently partisan analysts. There is no rule of objectivity, as with our newscasters; Ecotopians in general scorn the idea as a "bourgeois fetish," and profess to believe that truth is best served by giving some label indicating your general position, and then letting fly. 62

Other channels present films and various entertainment programs, but the commercials are awkwardly bunched entirely *between* shows, rather 63 than scattered throughout. Not only does this destroy the rhythm we're used to on TV—commercials giving us timely respites from the drama— but it increases the tendency for the commercials to fight each other. And this is bad enough anyway, because they are limited to mere announcements, without impersonated housewives or other consumers, and virtually without adjectives. (Some prohibition must exist for all the media, since ads in magazines and newspapers are similarly bland.) It's hard to get excited about a product's specifications-list, but Ecotopian viewers do manage to watch them. Sometimes, I suspect, they watch merely in hopes of a counter-ad to follow—an announcement of a competing product, in which the announcer sneeringly compares the two.

Also, the commercials may seem watchable because they are islands of   64 sanity in the welter of viewpoints, personnel, and visual image quality that make up "normal" Ecotopian TV fare. Some channels even change managments entirely—at noon, or 6 P.M., a channel that has been programming political events or news will suddenly switch over to household advice, loud rock music, or weird surrealistic films bringing your worst nightmares to garish life. (Ecotopians don't seem to believe overmuch in color tuning. The station engineers sometimes joke around and transmit signals in which people deliberately come out green or fuchsia, with orange skies.) Then again you may come upon a super-serious program imported from Canada or England. And there are a few people who tune in American satellite signals and watch our reruns, or laugh it up at our commercials. But this seems to be an acquired, minority taste—and it also requires an expensive special adapter to pick up the signals directly.

Television, incidentally, may be an important reason for Ecotopians'   65 odd attitudes toward material goods. Of course many consumer items are considered ecologically offensive and are simply not available, so nobody has them: thus electric can openers, hair curlers, frying pans, and carving knives are unknown. And to curb industrial proliferation the variety which is so delightful in our department stores is much restricted here. Many basic necessities are utterly standardized. Bath towels, for instance, can be bought in only one color, white—so people have to dye their own in attractive patterns (using gentle natural hues from plant and mineral sources, I am told). Ecotopians generally seem to travel light, with few possessions, though each household, naturally, has a full component of necessary utensils. As far as personal goods are concerned Ecotopians possess or at least care about mainly things like knives and other tools, clothing, brushes, musical instruments, which they are concerned to have of the highest possible quality. These are handmade and prized by their owners as works of art—which I must admit they sometimes are.

Objects that *are* available in stores seem rather old-fashioned. I have   66 seen few Ecotopian-made appliances that would not look pretty primitive on American TV. One excuse I've heard is that they are designed for easy repair by users. At any rate they lack the streamlining we're used to—parts stick out at odd angles, bolts and other fasteners are plainly visible, and sometimes parts are even made of wood.

I have, however, observed that Ecotopians do repair their own things. 67 In fact there are no repair shops on the streets. A curious corollary is that guarantees don't seem to exist at all. People take it for granted that manufactured items will be sturdy, durable, and self-fixable—which of course means they are also relatively unsophisticated compared to ours. This state of affairs has not been achieved easily: I have heard many funny stories about ridiculous designs produced in the early days, lawsuits against their manufacturers, and other tribulations. One law now in effect requires that pilot models of new devices must be given to a public panel of ten ordinary people ("consumers" is not a term used in polite conversation here). Only if they all find they can fix likely breakdowns with ordinary tools is manufacture permitted.

An exception of sorts is made for video and other electronic items. 68 These are required to be built of standard modularized parts and shops must stock component modules as well as test equipment, so users can isolate and replace defective components. And of course much electronic gear is now so small that it must simply be recycled if it stops working. The Ecotopians, indeed, have produced some remarkably miniaturized electronic devices, such as stereo sets no larger than a plate, ingeniously responsive controls for solar heat systems and industrial processes, and short-range radiotelephones built into a tiny earphone. These evidently satisfy a national urge for compactness, lightness, and low power requirements.

The Ecotopian Economy: Fruit of Crisis

San Francisco, May 12. It is widely believed among Americans that the 69 Ecotopians have become a shiftless and lazy people. This was the natural conclusion drawn after Independence, when the Ecotopians adopted a 20-hour work week. Yet even so no one in America, I think, has yet fully grasped the immense break this represented with our way of life—and even now it is astonishing that the Ecotopian legislature, in the first flush of power, was able to carry through such a revolutionary measure.

What was at stake, informed Ecotopians insist, was nothing less than 70 the revision of the Protestant work ethic upon which America had been built. The consequences were plainly severe. In economic terms, Ecotopia was forced to isolate its economy from the competition of harder-working peoples. Serious dislocations plagued their industries for years. There was a drop in Gross National Product by more than a third. But the profoundest implications of the decreased work week were philosophical and ecological: mankind, the Ecotopians assumed, was not meant for production, as the 19th and early 20th centuries had believed. Instead, humans were meant to take their modest place in a seamless, stable-state web of living organisms, disturbing that web as little as possible. This would mean sacrifice of present consumption, but it would ensure future survival—which became an almost religious objective, perhaps akin to earlier doctrines of "salvation." People were to be happy not to the extent they dominated their fellow creatures on the earth, but to the extent they lived in balance with them.

This philosophical change may have seemed innocent on the surface. 71 Its grave implications were soon spelled out, however. Ecotopian economists, who included some of the most highly regarded in the American nation, were well aware that the standard of living could only be sustained and increased by relentless pressure on work hours and worker productivity. Workers might call this "speed-up," yet without a slow but steady rise in labor output, capital could not be attracted or even held; financial collapse would quickly ensue.

The deadly novelty introduced into this accepted train of thought by a 72 few Ecotopian militants was to spread the point of view that economic disaster was not identical with survival disaster for persons—and that, in particular, a financial panic could be turned to advantage if the new nation could be organized to devote its real resources of energy, knowledge, skills, and materials to the basic necessities of survival. If that were done, even a catastrophic decline in the GNP (which was, in their opinion, largely composed of wasteful activity anyway) might prove politically useful.

In short, financial chaos was to be not endured but deliberately engineered. With the ensuing flight of capital, most factories, farms and other productive facilities would fall into Ecotopian hands like ripe plums.

And in reality it took only a few crucial measures to set this dismal series of events in motion: the nationalization of agriculture; the announcement of an impending moratorium on oil-industry activities; the forced consolidation of the basic retail network constituted by Sears, Penney's, Safeway, and a few other chains; and the passage of stringent conservation laws that threatened the profits of the lumber interests.

These moves, of course, set off an enormous clamor in Washington. 75 Lobbyists for the various interests affected tried to commit the federal government to intervene militarily. This was, however, several months after Independence. The Ecotopians had established and intensively trained a nationwide militia, and airlifted arms for it from France and Czechoslovakia. It was also believed that at the time of secession they had mined major eastern cities with atomic weapons, which they had constructed in secret or seized from weapons research laboratories. Washington, therefore, although it initiated a ferocious campaign of economic and political pressure against the Ecotopians, and mined their harbors, finally decided against an invasion.

This news set in motion a wave of closures and forced sales of businesses—reminiscent, I was told, of what happened to the Japanese-Americans who were interned in World War II. Members of distinguished old San Francisco families were forced to bargain on most unfavorable terms with representatives of the new regime. Properties going back to Spanish land-grant claims were hastily disposed of. Huge corporations, used to dictating policy in city halls and statehouses, found themselves begging for compensation and squirming to explain that their properties were actually worth far more than their declared tax value. 76

Tens of thousands of employees were put out of work as a consequence, and the new government made two responses to this. One was to absorb the unemployed in construction of the train network and of the sewage and other recycling facilities necessary to establish stable-state life systems. Some were also put to work dismantling allegedly hazardous or unpleasant relics of the old order, like gas stations. The other move was to adopt 20 hours as the basic work week—which, in effect, doubled the number of jobs but virtually halved individual income. (There were, for several years, rigid price controls on all basic foods and other absolute necessities.) 77

Naturally, the transition period that ensued was hectic—though many people also remember it as exciting. It is alleged by many who lived through those times that no one suffered seriously from lack of food, shelter, clothing, or medical treatment—though some discomfort was widespread, and there were gross dislocations in the automobile and related industries, in the schools, and in some other social functions. Certainly many citizens were deprived of hard-earned comforts they had been used to: their cars, their prepared and luxury foods, their habitual new clothes and appliances, their many efficient service industries. These disruptions were especially severe on middle-aged people—though one now elderly man told me that he had been a boy in Warsaw during World War II, had lived on rats and moldy potatoes, and found the Ecotopian experience relatively painless. To the young, the disruptions seem to have had a kind of wartime excitement—and indeed sacrifices may have been made more palatable by the fear of attack from the United States. It is said by some, however, that the orientation of the new government toward basic biological survival was a unifying and reassuring force. Panic food hoarding, it is said, was rare. (The generosity with food which is such a feature of Ecotopian life today may have arisen at that time.) 78

Of course the region that comprises Ecotopia had natural advantages   79
that made the transition easier. Its states had more doctors per capita, a
higher educational level, a higher percentage of skilled workers, a greater
number of engineers and other technicians, than most other parts of the
Union. Its major cities, without exception, were broadly based manufacturing and trade complexes that produced virtually all the necessities of
life. Its universities were excellent, and its resources for scientific research
included a number of the topnotch facilities in the United States. Its temperate climate encouraged an outdoor style of life, and made fuel short-
ages caused by ecological policies an annoyance rather than the matter of
life or death they would have been in the severe eastern winters. The people were unusually well versed in nature and conservation lore, and experienced in camping and survival skills.

We cannot, however, ignore the political context in which the transition   80
took place. As Ecotopian militants see the situation, by the last decade of
the old century American control over the underdeveloped world had
crumbled. American troops had failed to hold Vietnam, and the impoverished peoples of many other satellite countries were rebelling too.
Evading Congressional controls, the U.S. administration continued secret
wars against these uprisings, and the burden of outlays for an enromous
arms establishment caused a profound long-term decline in the world
competitiveness of American civilian industry. A slow drop in per capita
income led to widespread misery, increased tension between rich and
poor, and ended citizen confidence in economic gains; for a time, wildcat
strikes and seizures of plants by workers required the almost constant mo-
bilization of the National Guard. After the abortive antipollution efforts of
the early seventies, the toll of death and destruction had resumed its
climb. Energy crises had bred economic disruption and price gouging.
And chronic Washington scandals had greatly reduced faith in central
government.

"All this," one Ecotopian told me, "convinced us that if we wished to   81
survive we had to take matters into our own hands." I pointed out that this
had always been the claim of conspiratorial revolutionaries, who presume
to act in the name of the majority, but take care not to allow the majority
to have any real power. "Well," he replied, "things were clearly not getting
any better—so people really were ready for change. They were literally
sick of bad air, chemicalized foods, lunatic advertising. They turned to
politics because it was finally the only route to self-preservation."

"So," I replied, "in order to follow an extremist ecological program,   82
millions of people were willing to jeopardize their whole welfare, economic and social?"

"Their welfare wasn't doing so well, at that point," he said. "Something   83
had to be done. And nobody else was doing it. Also"—he shrugged, and

grinned—"we were very lucky." This gallows humor, which reminds me of the Israelis or Viennese, is common in Ecotopia. Perhaps it helps explain how the whole thing happened.

(May 13) Mysteriously, the Ecotopians do not feel "separate" from their 84 *technology. They evidently feel a little as the Indians must have felt: that the horse and the teepee and the bow and arrow all sprang, like the human bring, from the womb of nature, organically. Of course the Ecotopians work on natural materials far more extensively and complexly than the Indians worked stone into arrowpoint, or hide into teepee. But they treat materials in the same spirit of respect, comradeship. The other day I stopped to watch some carpenters working on a building. They marked and sawed the wood lovingly (using their own muscle power, not our saws). Their nail patterns, I noticed, were beautifully placed and their rhythm of hammering seemed patient, almost placid. When they raised wood pieces into place, they held them carefully, fitted them (they make many joints by notching as well as nailing). They seemed almost to be collaborating with the wood rather than forcing it into the shape of a building....*

Ecotopian Education's Surprises

San Francisco, June 4. Schools are perhaps the most antiquated aspect 85 of Ecotopian society. Our computer-controlled individual home instruction has no parallels here. Pupils are still assembled physically all day for their lessons. (Indeed few electronic teaching aids are used at all, in the belief that simply being in the presence of teachers and fellow pupils has an educational effect.) In fact if Crick School, which I visited, is any example, Ecotopian schools look more like farms than anything else. An Ecotopian teacher replied to this observation, "Well, that's because we've crossed over into the age of biology. Your school system is still physics-dominated. That's the reason for all the prison atmosphere. You can't allow things to *grow* there."

Crick School is situated on the outskirts of the minicity of Reliez and 86 its 125 students trudge *out* to the country every day. (About a dozen such schools ring the city.) The school owns eight acres, including a woodlot and a creek. The name is in honor of Francis Crick, co-discoverer of the structure of DNA. There is not a single permanent building of any significance; instead, classes take place either outdoors or in small, temporary-seeming wood buildings barely big enough to hold a teacher and 10 pupils, which are scattered here and there on the school grounds. I was unable to locate the school office, and when I inquired, I was told the school has none—its records consist of a single drawerful of cards! With only a half dozen teachers, my informants said, the coordination and decision-making for the school is simply part of everyday life. Since class periods fluctuate wildly (there are no hour bells) the teachers can always get together if they feel like it, and they also eat supper together once a week for more extended discussions.

Incredibly enough, the children spend only an hour or so a day in actual class work. When I asked how they are kept from destroying the school during the times they are not under teacher control, I was told that they are usually busy attending to their "projects." I could see evidence of such projects on every hand, so perhaps the explanation, optimistic though it may seem to us, is accurate.   87

The woodlot is a main focus of activity, especially for the boys, who tend to gang up into tribal units of six or eight. They build tree houses and underground hide-outs, make bows and arrows, attempt to trap the gophers that permeate the hillside, and generally carry on like happy savages—though I notice their conversation is laced with biological terminology and they seem to have an astonishing scientific sophistication. (One six-year-old, examining a creepy-looking bug: "Oh, yes, that's the larval stage.") There are some projects, such as a large garden and a weaving shed, which seem to be dominated by girl children, though some of the girls are members of chiefly male gangs. Most of the children's study and work time, however, is spent in mixed groups.   88

By "work," I mean that children in Ecotopian schools literally spend at least two hours a day actually *working*. The school gardens count in this, since they supply food for the midday meals. But apparently most schools also have small factories. In the Crick workshop I found about 20 boys and girls busily making two kinds of small wooden articles—which turned out to be birdhouses and flats for seedlings. (The flats, mercifully, are uniform in dimensions and style. The birdhouses assume fanciful shapes and many different sizes. This double standard is not by accident.) The system is intended to teach children that work is a normal part of every person's life, and to inculcate Ecotopian ideas about how work places are controlled: there are no "bosses" in the shop, and the children seem to discuss and agree among themselves about how the work is to be done. The shop contains a lot of other projects in one stage or another of development. In working these out together, as I watched them do for a half hour or so, the children need to use concepts in geometry and physics, do complex calculations, and bring to bear considerable skills in carpentry. They marshal the necessary information with a verve that is altogether different from the way our children absorb prepackaged formal learning. The children also, I am told, dispose of the workshop profits as they please. Though some of the money seems to be distributed (equally) among the individual chil-   89 dren, some is used to buy things for the school: I was shown a particularly fine archery set that was recently bought in this way.

It was sunny during my visit, but Crick School must be appallingly muddy in the rainy winters. To provide some protection, and also to give a place for meetings, parties, films and video shows, the school possesses a giant teepee-like tent. The white canvas covering is no longer new and carries many charming decorative patches. Usually the lower rim of fabric is rolled up to head height, making the teepee into a kind of pavilion. Here the children sometimes play when it is raining heavily. (They are never forbidden to go out in the wet, and learn to take care of drying themselves off.) A large pit in the center is the site of occasional barbecues, when a deer (or one of the school pigs) is roasted and eaten; and a kitchen at one side of the teepee is often used by groups of children making themselves lunches or treats.

Does this extremely unregulated atmosphere lead to wild conduct among the children? So far as I could tell, not at all; in fact, the school is curiously quiet. Small bands of children roam here and there on mysterious but obviously engrossing errands. A few groups play ball games, but the school as a whole has little of that hectic, noisy quality we associate with our schoolgrounds. Indeed at first I could not believe that more than 30 or 40 children were present, considering the lack of babble. The tribal play groups, incidentally, are not all of an age; each contains some older kids who exercise leadership but do not seem to be tyrannical. This is perhaps encouraged by the teachers, or at least not discouraged, for they work with groups at one general level of development but do not object if an older or younger child wishes to join in or just watch one of the class sessions.

Some of the teachers, especially those occupied mainly with the younger children, apparently teach everything. But other teachers specialize to some extent—one teaches music, another math, another "mechanics"—by which he means not only that branch of physics, but also the construction, design and repair of phyiscal objects. In this way they feel free to indulge their own interests, which they assume will have an educational effect on the children. Certainly it seems to keep their own minds lively. All the teachers teach a lot of biology, of course. The emphases and teaching loads are flexible, and set by discussion among the teachers themselves.

This, like the general operation of the school, is possible because of the most remarkable fact of all about Ecotopian schools: they are private enterprises. Or rather, just as most factories and shops in Ecotopia are owned by the people who work in them, so the schools are enterprises collectively but personally owned by the teachers who run them. Crick School is legally a corporation; its teacher members own the land, buildings and reputation (such as it is) of their school. They are free to operate it however they wish, follow whatever educational philosophy they wish, and parents are free to send their children to Crick School or to another school as *they* wish.

The only controls on the schools, aside from a maximum-fee rule and matters of plumbing and safe buildings, stem from the national examinations which each child takes at ages 12 and 18. Apparently, although no direct administrative controls exist, the indirect pressure from parents to prepare children for these exams—as well as for life—is such that the schools make a strong effort to educate their students effectively. The exams are made up yearly by a prestigious committee, comprising some educators, some political figures, and some parents—a partly elected and partly appointed body whose members have tenure for seven years and are thus somewhat insulated, like our senators or judges, from short-term political pressures. 94

Indeed there seems to be a brisk competition among schools, and children switch around a good deal. On the secondary level the situation is apparently a little like ours; one school near San Francisco, which has produced a large number of scientists and political leaders, consequently has a long waiting list. 95

It is hard to tell how the children themselves react to the competitiveness that exists, on some levels, along with the laxity of Ecotopian life. I often saw older children helping younger ones with school work, and there seems to be an easy working recognition that some people know more than others and can aid them. But greater ability doesn't seem so invidious as with us, where it is really valued because it brings rewards of money and power; the Ecotopians seem to regard their abilities more as gifts which they share with each other. Certainly I never saw happen at Crick School what I have seen in my daughter's American school: one child calling another "stupid" because he did not grasp something as fast as the first child did. Ecotopians prize excellence, but they seem to have an intuitive feeling for the fact that people excel in different things, and that they can give to each other on many different levels. 96

Do Ecotopians accept the idea that poorer parents might not be willing or able, given the tuition costs, to send their children to school at all? In this crucial area, Ecotopians have not allowed their thinking to revert to that of harsher ages. Rather than a scholarship system, however, they give outright sliding grants to families with incomes below a certain level, and one component of these is marked for tuition. Thus the Ecotopian state, while not willing to lift the burden of education entirely off the parents' backs (thus perhaps encouraging larger families!) is still willing to force citizens to educate their children in *some* manner. The possibilities of "kickback schools," such as arose in the U.S. when tuition vouchers were 97

erally r
their ov

Judg
does n
arithme
also le;
year-ol
though
food; h
animal
backp;
seem i
crowd
ize the
irregul
be doi

AL GORE

Al Gore (b. 1948) was born into a prominen
father was an influential congressman an
the political tumult of Washington, D.C
Gore served as an army reporter in
porter for the Nashville Tennessee
Gore went on to graduate fron
House of Representatives in
was active in the environ
vironmental causes, i
1987 Gore unsucce
to "elevate the i
1993 Gore w
has contin
(1992),
finall
a

1. Co
does h
can assume the journal records his real thoughts, how do you explain the
differences between it and the public stories? How does his attitude in
each change as he spends time in Ecotopia? What effect does Callenbach
achieve by giving us these two different versions of Ecotopia?

2. Weston writes a great deal about the strong and public display of
emotions among Ecotopians. What is the connection between these emotions and the values important in Ecotopia, values such as existing in harmony with others, being strongly connected with other human beings and
the world about us, and living life fully? How does a strong display of
emotions bring people together when it seems to give rise to lots of anger?
And what is the connection between the desire for a stable-state way of
life and these emotions?

3. Leaving aside the question of whether or not a place like Ecotopia
could never exist, would you like to live in such a place? What parts of life
there would you enjoy, and what parts would you hate? You might want
to talk about the schools, transportation, entertainment, consumer goods,
or work habits. If there are parts of the Ecotopian life you would enjoy, is
there any way to incorporate these parts in your own life?

Environmentalism of the Spirit

Twenty years ago, E. F. Schumacher defined an important new issue 1
arising from the relationship between a technology and the context—social, cultural, political, and ecological—in which it is used. For example,
a nuclear power plant can certainly generate a lot of electricity, but it may
not be an "appropriate" technology for an underdeveloped nation with an
unstable government, a shortage of trained engineers, an absence of any
power grid to distribute the electricity generated, and a megalomaniacal
ruler anxious to acquire fissionable material with which to construct nuclear weapons. The appropriateness of a technology becomes increasingly important as its power grows and its potential for destroying the
environment expands.

It is time we asked a similar question about ourselves and our relation- 2
ship to the global environment: When giving us dominion over the earth,
did God choose an appropriate technology?

Knowing what we do about our new power as a species to interfere 3

348

with and even overwhelm the earth's natural systems and recognizing that we are now doing so with reckless abandon, one is tempted to answer, the jury is still out.

Whether we believe that our dominion derives from God or from our own ambition, there is little doubt that the way we currently relate to the environment is wildly inappropriate. But in order to change, we have to address some fundamental questions about our purpose in life, our capacity to direct the powerful inner forces that have created this crisis, and who we are. These questions go beyond any discussion of whether the human species is an appropriate technology; these questions are not for the mind or the body but the spirit. 4

A change in our essential character is not possible without a realistic hope that we can make change happen. But hope itself is threatened by the realization that we are now capable of destroying ourselves and the earth's environment. Moreover, the stress of coping with the complicated artificial patterns of our lives and the flood of manufactured information creates a pervasive feeling of exhaustion just when we have an urgent need for creativity. Our economy is described as post-industrial; our architecture is called post-modern; our geopolitics are labeled post–Cold War. We know what we are not, but we don't seem to know what we are. The forces that shape and reshape our lives seem to have an immutable logic of their own; they seem so powerful that any effort to define ourselves creatively will probably be wasted, its results quickly erased by successive tidal waves of change. Inevitably, we resign ourselves to whatever fate these powerful forces are propelling us toward, a fate we have little role in choosing. 5

Perhaps because it is unprecedented, the environmental crisis seems completely beyond our understanding and outside of what we call common sense. We consign it to some seldom visited attic in our minds where we place ideas that we vaguely understand but rarely explore. We tag it with the same mental labels we might use for Antarctica: remote, alien, hopelessly distorted by the maps of the world we inhabit, too hard to get to and too unforgiving to stay very long. When we do visit this attic, when we learn about how intricately the causes of the crisis are woven into the fabric of industrial civilization, our hope of solving it seems chimerical. It seems so forbidding that we resist taking even the first steps toward positive change. 6

We turn by default to an imprudent hope that we can adapt to whatever changes are in store. We have grown accustomed to adapting; we are good at it. After all, we have long since adapted, with the help of technology, to every climate extreme on the surface of the earth, at the bottom of the sea and even in the vacuum of space. It is by adapting, in fact, that we 7 have extended our dominion into every corner of the earth. And so it is tempting to conclude that this familiar strategy is the obvious response to our rapidly emerging dilemma.

But the magnitude of the change to which we now consider adapting is so large that the proposals quickly trend toward the absurd. A study sponsored by the National Academy of Sciences, for example, suggested that as the earth warms, we might create huge corridors of wilderness as pathways to accommodate all of the species trying to migrate from south to north in search of a familiar climate. (Meanwhile, of course, we are laying siege to many of the wilderness areas that already exist—in the Pacific Northwest, for example—in search of timber and other resources.) Some even imagine that genetic engineering will soon magnify our power to adapt even our physical form. We might decide to extend our dominion of nature into the human gene pool, not just to cure terrible diseases, but to take from God and nature the selection of genetic variety and robustness that gives our species its resilience and aligns us with the natural rhythms in the web of life. Once again, we might dare to exercise godlike powers unaccompanied by godlike wisdom.   8

But our willingness to adapt is an important part of the underlying problem. Do we have so much faith in our own adaptability that we will risk destroying the integrity of the entire global ecological system? If we try to adapt to the changes we are causing rather than prevent them in the first place, have we made an appropriate choice? Can we understand how much destruction this choice might finally cause?   9

Believing that we can adapt to just about anything is ultimately a kind of laziness, an arrogant faith in our ability to react in time to save our skin. But in my view this confidence in our quick reflexes is badly misplaced; indeed, a laziness in our spirit has estranged us from our true selves and from the quickness and vitality of the world at large. We have been so seduced by industrial civilization's promise to make our lives comfortable that we allow the synthetic routines of modern life to soothe us in an inauthentic world of our own making. Life can be easy, we assure ourselves. We need not suffer the heat or the cold; we need not sow or reap or hunt and gather. We can heal the sick, fly through the air, light up the darkness, and be entertained in our living rooms by orchestras and clowns whenever we like. And as our needs and whims are sated, we watch electronic images of nature's destruction, distant famine, and apocalyptic warnings. all with the bone-weariness of the damned. "What can we do?" we ask ourselves, already convinced that the realistic answer is nothing.   10

With the future so open to doubt, we routinely choose to indulge our own generation at the expense of all who will follow. We enshrine the self as the unit of ethical account, separate and distinct not just from the natural world but even from a sense of obligation to others—not just others   11 in future generations, but increasingly even to others in the same generation; and not just those in distant lands, but increasingly even in our own communities. We do this not because we don't care but because we don't really live in our lives. We are monumentally distracted by a pervasive technological culture that appears to have a life of its own, one that insists on our full attention, continually seducing us and pulling us away from the opportunity to experience directly the true meaning of our own lives.

How can we shake loose this distraction? How can we direct our attention to more important matters when our attention has become a commodity to be bought and sold? Whenever a new source of human interest and desire is found, prospectors flock to stake their claim. Using every available tool—newspapers, movies, television, magazines, billboards, blimps, buttons, designer labels, junk faxes—they assault our attention from every side. Advertisers strip-mine it; politicians covet it; pollsters measure it; terrorists steal it as a weapon of war. As the amounts close to the surface are exhausted, the search for fresh supplies leads onto primal paths that run deep into our being, back through our evolutionary heritage, past thought and beyond emotion, to instinct—and a rich vein of primal fears and passions that are also now exploited as raw material in the colossal enterprise of mass distraction. The prospectors of attention fragment our experience of the world, carry away the spoils, and then, in an ultimate irony, accuse us of having short attention spans.   12

The way we experience the world is governed by a kind of inner ecology that relates perception, emotions, thinking, and choices to forces outside ourselves. We interpret our experience through multiple lenses that focus—and distort—the information we receive through our senses. But this ecology now threatens to fall badly out of balance because the cumulative impact of the changes brought by the scientific and technological revolution are potentially devastating to our sense of who we are and what our purpose in life might be. Indeed, it may now be necessary to foster a new "environmentalism of the spirit." How do we, for example, conserve hope and minimize the quantity of corrosive fear we spill into our lives? How do we recycle the sense of wonder we felt as children, when the world was new? How do we use the power of technology without adapting to it so completely that we ourselves behave like machines, lost in the levers and cogs, lonesome for the love of life, hungry for the thrill of directly experiencing the vivid intensity of the ever-changing moment?   13

No wonder we have become disconnected from the natural world—indeed, it's remarkable we feel any connection to ourselves. And no wonder we have become resigned to the idea of a world without a future. The engines of distraction are gradually destroying the inner ecology of the human experience. Essential to that ecology is the balance between respect for the past and faith in the future, between a belief in the individ-   14 ual and a commitment to the community, between our love for the world and our fear of losing it—the balance, in other words, on which an environmentalism of the spirit depends.

To some, this global environmental crisis is primarily a crisis of values. 15 In this view, the basic cause of the problem is that we as a civilization base our decisions about how to relate to the environment on premises that are fundamentally unethical. And since religion has traditionally been the most powerful source of ethical guidance for our civilization, the search for villains has led to the doorstep of the major religious systems.

Here in the West, some have charged—inaccurately, I believe—that 16 the Judeo-Christian tradition chartered the relentless march of civilization to dominate nature, beginning with the creation story of Genesis, in which humankind is granted "dominion" over the earth. In its basic form, the charge is that our tradition assigns divine purpose to our exercise of virtually complete power to work our will over nature. It is alleged that by endowing human beings with a completely unique relationship to God and then delegating God's authority over nature to human beings, the tradition sanctions as ethical all choices that put a higher priority on human needs and desires that on the rest of nature. Simply put, according to this view, it is "ethical" to make sure that whenever nature gets in the way of what we want, nature loses.

But this is a cartoon version of the Judeo-Christian tradition, one that 17 bears little resemblance to the reality. Critics attack religion for inspiring an arrogant and reckless attitude toward nature, but they have not always read the relevant texts carefully enough. Although it is certainly true that our civilization is built on the premise that it is certainly true that our civilization is built on the premise that we can use nature for our own ends without regard to the impact we have on it, it is not fair to charge any of the major world religions with promoting this dangerous attitude. Indeed, all of them mandate an ethical responsibility to protect and care for the well-being of the natural world.

In the Judeo-Christian tradition, the biblical concept of dominion is 18 quite different from the concept of domination, and the difference is crucial. Specifically, followers of this tradition are charged with the duty of stewardship, because the same biblical passage that grants them "dominion" also requires them to "care for" the earth even as they "work" it. The requirement of stewardship and its grant of dominion are not in conflict; in recognizing the sacredness of creation, believers are called upon to remember that even as they "till" the earth they must also "keep" it.

This has long been clear to those who have dedicated their lives 19 to these duties. Richard Cartwright Austin, for example, a Presbyterian minister working among the poor in Appalachia, reports on his experience in trying to stop irresponsible strip mining: "I learned early on from my years as a pastor in Appalachia and from the days when I started fighting strip mining in southwest Virginia that the only defense those mountains have from exploitation by the energy conglomerates' bulldozers is the poor, isolated people who live in those hollows, who care so deeply that they would fight for that land. Take those people away and the mountains are totally defenseless.... From the biblical point of view, nature is only safe from pollution and brought into a secure moral relationship when it is united with people who love it and care for it."

All around the world, the efforts to stop the destruction of the environ- 20
ment have come mainly from people who recognize the damage being done in that part of the world in which they themselves have "dominion." Lois Gibbs and the other homeowners at Love Canal, Christine and Woodrow Sterling and their family, whose well water was poisoned in West Tennessee, "Harrison" Gnau and the indigenous peoples of the Sarawak rain forest in East Malaysia, Chico Mendes and his rubber tappers in the Amazon, the unemployed fishermen of the Aral Sea—all began their battles to save the environment becauseof the marriage of dominion and stewardship in their hearts. This is precisely the relationship between humankind and the earth called for in the Judeo-Christian ethic.

In my own religious experience and training—I am a Baptist—the 21
duty to care for the earth is rooted in the fundamental relationship between God, creation, and humankind. In the Book of Genesis, Judaism first taught that after God created the earth, He "saw that it was good." In the Twenty-fourth Psalm, we learn that "the earth is the Lord's and the fullness thereof." In other words, God is pleased with his creation, and "dominion" does not mean that the earth belongs to humankind; on the contrary, whatever is done to the earth must be done with an awareness that it belongs to God.

My tradition also teaches that the purpose of life is "to glorify God." 22
And there is a shared conviction within the Judeo-Christian tradition that believers are expected to "do justice, love mercy, and walk humbly with your God." But whatever verses are selected in an effort to lend precision to the Judeo-Christian definition of life's purpose, that purpose is clearly inconsistent with the reckless destruction of that which belongs to God and which God has seen as "good." How can one glorify the Creator while heaping contempt on the creation? How can one walk humbly with nature's God while wreaking havoc on nature?

The story of Noah and the ark offers further evidence of Judaism's con- 23
cern for stewardship. Noah is commanded by God to take into his ark at least two of every living species in order to save them from the Flood—a commandment that might appear in modern form as: Thou shalt preserve biodiversity. Indeed, does God's instruction have new relevance for those

who share Noah's faith in this time of another worldwide catastrophe, this time one of our own creation? Noah heeded this commandment, and after he and his family and a remnant of every living species on earth survived the Flood, God made a new covenant with him which affirmed His commitment to humankind. Often overlooked, however, is the second half of God's convenant, made not only with Noah but with "all living creatures," again affirming the sacredness of creation, which He pledged to safeguard in "seed time and harvest, cold and heat, summer and winter." It was the promise never again to destroy the earth by floods, which, according to Genesis, is the symbolic message of every rainbow.

In spite of the clear message from a careful reading of these and other 24 Scriptures, critics have gained currency in part because of the prevailing silence with which most denominations have reacted to the growing evidence of an ecological holocaust. Nor does it help that some religious leaders have seemed to encourage environmental recklessness. I remember listening with closed eyes and bowed head to the invocation at the groundbreaking for a new construction project as the minister cited our "dominion over the earth" and then immediately went on to list with great relish every instrument of environmental mayhem he could name, from bulldozers and backhoes to chain saws and steamrollers, as though they were divinely furnished tools we should use with abandon in reshaping the earth for the sheer joy of doing so. Both behaviors—silence in the face of disaster and unthinking enthusiasm for further degradation—do nothing to counter the cartoon image of a faith bent on the domination of nature.

Happily, it has recently become clear that a great movement to protect 25 the earth is stirring deeply within the faith, and many religious leaders are now sounding the alarm. But until now they have seemed reluctant to lend their moral authority to the effort to rescue the earth. Why?

In their defense, it should be said that religious leaders have faced the 26 same difficulties as the rest of us in recognizing this unprecedented pattern of destruction, in comprehending the strategic nature of the threat, and in realizing the profound and sudden change in the relationship between the human species and the rest of the environment. But their failure to act is especially disturbing because the Christian Scriptures carry such a strong activist message. To me, it is best expressed in one of Jesus' parables, recounted in three of the four gospels, the Parable of the Unfaithful Servant. The master of a house, preparing to depart on a journey, leaves his servant in charge of the home and gives him strict instructions to remain alert in case vandals or thieves attempt to ransack the house while the master is away. The servant is explicitly warned that if the vandals come while he is asleep, he still has a duty to protect the house against them—and the fact that he was asleep will not be an acceptable excuse. A question raised by the parable is clear: If the earth is the Lord's and His servants are given the responsibility to care for it, then how are we to respond to the global vandalism now wreaking such unprecedented destruction on the earth? Are we asleep? Is that now an acceptable excuse?

But there is something else at work in organized religion as well. Many   27
of those who might otherwise find themselves in the vanguard of the resistance to this onslaught are preoccupied with other serious matters. For example, Christian theologians and clergy who have traditionally supported a liberal political agenda have inherited a specific set of concerns defined early in this century as the Social Gospel. According to this humane view of the Church's role, follwers of Christ should assign priority to the needs of the poor, the powerless, the sick and frail, the victims of discrimination and hatred, the forgotten human fodder chewed up by the cogs of industrial civilization. The moral imperative attached to this set of priorities leads many advocates of the Social Gospel to vigorously resist the introduction of competing concerns which they see as distractions from their appointed task, diluting their already overtaxed resources of money, time, moral authority, and emotional labor. After all, as an issue, "the environment" sometimes seems far from the more palpable sins of social injustice.

On the other hand, politically conservative theologians and clergy   28
have inherited a different agenda, also defined early in this century. The 'atheistic communism" against which they have properly inveighed for decades is, for them, only the most extreme manifestation of a statist impulse to divert precious resources—money, time, moral authority, and emotional labor—away from the mission of spiritual redemption and toward an idolatrous alternative: the search for salvation through a grand reordering of the material world. As a result, they are deeply suspicious of any effort to focus their moral attention on a crisis in the material world that might require as part of its remedy a new exercise of something resembling moral authority by the state. And the prospect of coordinated action by governments all over the world understandably heightens their fears and suspicions.

Thus, with activists of both the left and the right resisting the inclusion   29
of the environment on their list of concerns, the issue has not received the attention from religious leaders one may have expected. This is unfortunate, because the underlying concern is theologically consistent with the perspectives of both sides; equally important, the issue provides a rare opportunity for them to meet on common ground.

As it happens, the idea of social justice is inextricably linked in the   30
Scriptures with ecology. In passage after passage, environmental degradation and social injustice go hand in hand. Indeed, the first instance of "pollution" in the Bible occurs when Cain slays Abel and his blood falls on the ground, rendering it fallow. According to Genesis, after the murder,

when Cain asks, "Am I my brother's keeper?" the Lord replies, "Your brother's blood calls out to me from the ground. What have you done?" God then tells Cain that his brother's blood has defiled the ground and that as a result, "no longer will it yield crops for you, even if you toil on it forever!"

In today's world, the links between social injustice and environmental 31 degradation can be seen everywhere: the placement of toxic waste dumps in poor neighborhoods, the devastation of indigenous peoples and the extinction of their cultures when the rain forests are destroyed, disproportionate levels of lead and toxic air pollution in inner-city ghettos, the corruption of many government officials by people who seek to profit from the unsustainable exploitation of resources.

Meanwhile, religious conservatives might be surprised to find that 32 many deeply committed environmentalists have become, if anything, even more hostile to overreaching statism than they are. The most serious examples of environmental degradation in the world today are tragedies that were created or actively encouraged by governments—usually in pursuit of some notion that a dramatic reordering of the material world would enhance the greater good. And it is no accident that the very worst environmental tragedies were created by communist governments, in which the power of the state completely overwhelms the capabilities of the individual steward. Chernobyl, the Aral Sea, the Yangtze River, the "black town" of Copsa Mica in Romania—these and many other disasters testify to the severe environmental threats posed by statist governments.

Both conservative and liberal theologians have every reason, scriptural 33 as well as ideological, to define their spiritual mission in a way that prominently includes the defense of God's creation. Slowly and haltingly, both camps are beginning to do so. But most clergy are still reluctant to consider this cause worthy of their sustained attention; in my opinion, an important source of this reluctance is a philosophical assumption that humankind is separate from the rest of nature, an assumption shared by both liberals and conservatives. The basis for it deserves further attention, especially since the tendency to see human needs as essentially detached from the well-being of the earth's natural systems is not fundamentally Christian in origin. Even so, this tendency reflects a view of the world that was absorbed into the Christian tradition early on; specifically, it was part of the heritage of Greek philosophy, a heritage that had a powerful influence on early Christian thinking and behavior.

A little more than three hundred years before the birth of Christ, 34 Greek culture and philosophy were introduced throughout the lands conquered by Alexander the Great. The inherent power of Greek philosophy as an analytic tool ensured its continued popularity, even as it was adapted to scores of different religious and cultural traditions. It served, of course, as the foundation for the fiercely logical and systematic way of thinking that enabled Rome to conquer all of the "known world," including not only Palestine, where Christianity originated, but also every city in which Christ's disciples preached. It was natural, then, for early Christians to use some of the dominant language and concepts as they spread the Word.

As the world discovered, the greatest Greek philosophers were, first, 35 Plato and, second, Aristotle. The most significant difference between them concerned the relationship between the intellect and physical reality or, in other words, between humankind and nature. Plato believed that the soul exists in a realm quite apart from the body and that the thinker is separate from the world he thinks about. But Aristotle felt that everything in our intellect comes from the senses, and thus the thinker is powerfully connected to the world he thinks about. This dispute began in ancient Greece and continued throughout the early history of Christian thought, through the Middle Ages, and up to the seventeenth century.

One of the most influential thinkers in the early Church, Saint 36 Augustine, recounts how attracted he was, early in the fifth century, to Plato's view of the physical world and how he struggled to overcome his love of Platonic theory before he could "rationalize" his acceptance of Christ's true message. Indeed, this tension—which still exists—has been described by the theologian Michael Novak as the "great temptation of the West." For example, throughout the first five centuries of Christianity, the heresy of Gnosticism—which portrayed physical reality as an illusion—drew powerfully upon Plato's conception of a disembodied spiritual intellect hovering above the material world. But even after the Gnostic view was formally rejected, it periodically resurfaced in various guises, and the Platonic assumption upon which it was based—that man is separate from the world of nature—continued to flourish as a major strain of Christian thought. It may have been overemphasized because of early struggles with paganism.

The heritage of Aristotle's thought, on the other hand, was kept alive 37 principally in the Arabic-speaking world. Alexander, who was tutored by Aristotle, established his thought throughout the lands he conquered, and the city he chose as his capital, Alexandria, became the greatest center of learning in the ancient world. But for many centuries the West was isolated from this intellectual tradition; only after the returning crusaders brought new ideas back to Europe did the West rediscover the other half of its Greek heritage. As the thirteenth century began, Europeans impressed with the intellectual achievements of Arab civilization discovered and translated several works by Aristotle—*Ethics, Politics, Logic,* among others—which had disappeared from Western thought but had been preserved in Arabic. Influenced by the powerful work of Maimonides, the Jewish scholar writing in Arabic (in Alexandria) who reinterpreted Judaism in Aristotelian terms, Saint Thomas Aquinas undertook the same reinterpretation of Christian thought and antagonized the Church establishment with his assertions of an Aristotelian view of the relationship between the spirit and the flesh, between humankind and the world. He saw a philosophical closeness between the soul and physical reality that discomfited the Church. Although his books were banned, burned, and not widely read until almost three centuries later, his powerful thinking eventually played a role in the Church's acquiescence to the impulses that led to the Renaissance, including the impulse to reconnect with the earth. A classic painting by Raphael in 1510 portrays this same philosophical tension at the beginning of the Renaissance: Plato appears with one finger pointing toward the heavens; next to him, Aristotle is gesturing toward the earth.

But just a century later, the reemerging Aristotelian view was dealt a severe blow. On November 10, 1619, René Descartes, soon to become one of the founders of modern philosophy, was a twenty-three-year-old mathematician lying on the banks of the Danube. That day he had a startling vision of a mechanistic world filled with inanimate matter, moving predictably in mathematically determined patterns—patterns that could be discerned and mastered by analytical minds through sustained inquiry and detached observation. In a real sense, Descartes' vision initiated the scientific revolution. It is often said that "all Western philosophy is a footnote to Plato," and much of the credit for this should go to the work of Descartes, who broke through the tension in the seventeenth century between the ideas of Aristotle and Plato with his famous dictum, *Cogito ergo sum,* "I think therefore I am." 38

By the time Descartes had finished his life's work, Raphael's picture was obsolete as a representation of Western thought. The new modern person pointed decisively upward—away from nature, away from the earth—toward an ethereal realm from which the detached human intellect could observe the movement of matter everywhere in the universe. Floating somewhere above it all, this new disembodied mind could systematically and relentlessly decipher the scientific laws that would eventually enable us to understand nature—and control it. This strange relationship between spirit and nature would later be called that of the "ghost in the machine." 39

The Church, meanwhile, was supposed to be on guard against any Faustian effort of the people to gain unseemly power to alter God's world, but it fell victim once again to the Platonic vision by reducing its spiritual mission to an effort to guide the inner life of the mind while discounting the moral significance of humankind's manipulations of the natural world. Sir Francis Bacon, lord chancellor of England, author of *The New Atlantis* (1624) and one of the principal founders of the scientific method, under- 40 took to ease any doubts the Church might have about allowing humankind to acquire and exercise the vast new powers of science. Taking "Cartesian dualism" one step further, Bacon argued that not only were humans separate from nature; science, he said, could safely be regarded as separate from religion. In his view, "facts" derived through the scientific method had no moral significance in and of themselves; only "moral knowledge" of matters concerning the distinction between good and evil had religious significance. This facile distinction carried a profound implication: the new power derived from scientific knowledge could be used to dominate nature with moral impunity.

Thus began the long, 350-year separation of science and religion. The 41 astronomical discoveries of Copernicus and Galileo had earlier upset the Church's peaceful coexistence with science, but neither man had intentionally challenged the primacy of the Church's moral teachings as the basis for interpreting the new facts discovered from observing the universe. However, Bacon suggested a moral detour: facts need not be considered in light of their implications. Not long afterward, the Church came to consider science as an adversary, as it posed challenge after challenge to the Church's authority to explain the meaning of existence.

This fundamental shift in Western thinking—which in a very real sense 42 marks the beginning of modern history—gave humankind increasing dominance in the world, as a flood of scientific discoveries began unlocking the secrets of God's blueprint for the universe. But how could this new power be used wisely? Descartes and Bacon ensured the gradual abandonment of the philosophy that humankind is one vibrant strand in an elaborate web of life, matter, and meaning. And ironically, major scientific discoveries have often undermined the Church's tendency to exaggerate our uniqueness as a species and defend our separation from the rest of nature. Charles Darwin's *Origin of Species* claimed jurisdiction for science over the human physical form by placing our evolution in the context of the animal world. Half a century later, Sigmund Freud's explanation of the unconscious claimed part of the mind for nature as well. Thanks to the revolution in thinking they helped to start, it seemed to many that the rational portion of the intellect—that part that created science—became the only remaining province for the moral authority of the Church.

Yet science itself offers a new way to understand—and perhaps begin 43 healing—the long schism between science and religion. Earlier in this century, the Heisenberg Principle established that the very act of observing a natural phenomenon can change what is being observed. Although the initial theory was limited in practice to special cases in subatomic physics, the philosophical implications were and are staggering. It is now apparent that since Descartes reestablished the Platonic notion and began the scientific revolution, human civilization has been experiencing a kind of Heisenberg Principle writ large. The very act of intellectually separating oneself from the world in order to observe it changes the world that is being observed—simply because it is no longer connected to the observer in the same way. This is not a mere word game; the consequences are all too real. The detached observer feels free to engage in a range of experiments and manipulations that might never spring to mind except for the intellectual separation. In the final analysis, all discussions of morality and ethics in science are practically pointless as long as the world of the intellect is assumed to be separate from the physical world. That first separation led inevitably to the separation of mind and body, thinking and feeling, power and wisdom; as a consequence, the scientific method changed our relationship to nature and is now, perhaps irrevocably, changing nature itself.

Although many scientists resist the notion that science can ever be re-   44
united with religion, there is now a powerful impulse in some parts of the scientific community to heal the breach. While Plato tended to emphasize the eternity of existence rather than the concept of creation, and while Descartes' mechanistic explanation also implied an eternal world, many scientists who have had no use for religion in the past now believe that the evidence from recent breakthroughs in astronomy and cosmology points toward a definite beginning for the universe. Some have, as a result, softened their resistance to the notion that the universe, and humankind as a part of it, were "created." Arno Penzias, for example, who shared a Nobel Prize for his discovery of the measurable echo of the Big Bang that accompanied the beginning of time, was asked on a radio call-in show what existed *before* the Big Bang. He said he didn't know but that the answer most consistent with the mathematical evidence was "nothing." When the next caller, infuriated by his answer, accused him of being an atheist, he replied, "Ma'am, I don't think you listened carefully to the implications of what I just said." Those implications—including the notion that some kind of Creator might be responsible for making "something" where there was once only "nothing"—suggest a potential for healing the hostility of science toward religion. And if science and religion are one day reunited, we may recapture a deeper curiosity about not only the nature of existence but its meaning as well, a deeper understanding of not only the universe but of our role and purpose as part of it.

Indeed, there is even, in this emerging scientific view, a palpable   45
"physical" role for human thought in the shaping of reality. Erwin Schrodinger, a pioneer in quantum physics, first offered the astounding view that consciousness is one of the building blocks of the physical universe and that a shift in the "attention" of an observer can have tangible consequences in the location and physical properties of subatomic parti-

cles. When he tried to explain one of the enduring puzzles of biology, how a pattern of life can emerge from a formless cluster of molecules, Schrodinger speculated that living organisms are endowed with "an astonishing gift of concentrating a 'stream of order' on [themselves] and thus escaping the decay into atomic chaos." If the mental activity necessary to focus one's "attention" turns out to have tangible consequences of the kind we now associate with a form of physical energy, then, ironically, science may one day definitively disprove Bacon's assertion that there can be a separation between facts and values, between the thoughts of a scientist and the moral duties of a human being.

My own curiosity leads me to this speculation: that the original 46
scientific impulse—before Descartes and before Plato—was made possible by the conception (or revelation) of a single Creator. When Akhnaton first conceptualized a single God and when Judaism introduced the idea of monotheism, it became possible for humankind to develop a new understanding of the nature of all the things they beheld in the world around them. For those who came to believe in a single Creator, there was no longer any reason to imagine that each object and living thing had a unique spiritual force and that each was imbued with mysterious meaning and motivated by unknown powers. Monotheism was a profoundly empowering idea: just as a navigator can—through the technique of triangulation—locate his position anywhere at sea by identifying any other two points with known locations, like familiar stars or constellations, those who came to believe in a single God gained the intellectual power to navigate skillfully through the ocean of superstition and bewilderment that engulfed the ancient world. Whatever these monotheists beheld could be philosophically located with reference to two known points: the Creator, philosophically equidistant from everything He had created, and themselves.

This process of spiritual triangulation identified the natural world as 47
sacred, not because each rock and tree was animated by a mysterious spirit, but because each rock and tree was created by God. Moreover, the physical world was understood, investigated, and ordered in terms of its relationship to the one God who had created it. And the very process by which this inquiry into the nature of the world took place reinforced the assumption that humankind is part of the world, because each inquiry relied on an understanding of our relationship to both God and the physical world in which we live. All three elements—God, human beings, and nature—were understood in relation to one another and were essential to this process of triangulation.

Many centuries after Akhnaton, Plato's intellectual inquiry followed an 48
entirely different path. Although he searched for a single cause behind all

things, he attempted to discern their nature by locating them in relation to only one point of reference—human intellect—rather than through a process of philosophical triangulation, which would have relied on two points, humankind and the Creator (or what could also be called a single cause). By assuming that the human intellect is not anchored in a context of meaningful relationships, with both the physical world and the Creator, Plato assured that later explanations of the workings of the world would become progressively more abstract.

Francis Bacon is a case in point. His moral confusion—the confusion at the heart of much of modern science—came from his assumption, echoing Plato, that human intellect could safely analyze and understand the natural world without reference to any moral principles defining our relationship and duties to both God and God's creation. Bacon, for example, was able to enthusiastically advocate vivisection for the pure joy of learning without reference to any moral purpose, such as saving human lives, as justification for the act. 49

And tragically, since the onset of the scientific and technological revolution, it has seemingly become all too easy for ultrarational minds to create an elaborate edifice of clockwork efficiency capable of nightmarish cruelty on an industrial scale. The atrocities of Hilter and Stalin, and the mechanical sins of all who helped them, might have been inconceivable except for the separation of facts from values and knowledge from morality. In her study of Adolf Eichmann, who organized the death camp bureaucracy, Hannah Arendt coined the memorable phrase "the banality of evil" to describe the bizarre contrast between the humdrum and ordinary quality of the acts themselves—the thousands of small, routine tasks committed by workaday bureaucrats—and the horrific and satanic quality of their proximate consequences. It was precisely the machinelike efficiency of the system that carried out the genocide which seemed to make it possible for its functionaries to separate the thinking required in their daily work from the moral sensibility for which, because they were human beings, they must have had some capacity. This mysterious, vacant space in their souls, between thinking and feeling, is the suspected site of the inner crime. This barren of the spirit, rendered fallow by the blood of unkept brothers, is the precinct of the disembodied intellect, which knows the way things work but not the way they are. 50

It is my view that the underlying moral schism that contributed to these extreme manifestations of evil has also conditioned our civilization to insulate its conscience from any responsibility for the collective endeavors that invisibly link millions of small, silent, banal acts and omissions together in a pattern of terrible cause and effect. Today, we enthusiastically participate in what is in essence a massive and unprecedented experiment with the natural systems of the global environment, with little regard for 51 the moral consequences. But for the separation of science and religion, we might not be pumping so much gaseous chemical waste into the atmosphere and threatening the destruction of the earth's climate balance. But for the separation of useful technological know-how and the moral judgments to guide its use, we might not be slashing and burning one football field's worth of rain forest every second. But for the assumed separation of humankind from nature, we might not be destroying half the living species on earth in the space of a single lifetime. But for the separation of thinking and feeling, we might not tolerate the deaths every day of 37,000 children under the age of five from starvation and preventable diseases made worse by failures of crops and politics.

But we do tolerate—and collectively perpetrate—all these things. 52 They are going on right now. When future generations wonder how we could go along with our daily routines in silent complicity with the collective destruction of the earth, will we, like the Unfaithful Servant, claim that we did not notice these things because we were morally asleep? Or will we try to explain that we were not so much asleep as living in a waking trance, a strange Cartesian spell under whose influence we felt no connection between our routine, banal acts and the moral consequences of what we did, as long as they were far away at the other end of the massive machine of civilization?

And what would future generations say in response to such a pitiful 53 plea? They might remember the ancient words of the psalmist, who condemned a people who, in their fascination with the works of their own civilization, lost their awareness of the sacred and came to resemble the idolatrous artifacts with which they were fatally enchanted: "They have a mouth but they will not speak, they have eyes but they will not see, they have nostrils but they will not smell, they have hands but they will not feel."

Modern philosophy has gone so far in its absurd pretensions about 54 the separateness of human beings from nature as to ask the famous question: "If a tree falls in the forest and no person is there to hear it, does it make a sound?" If robotic chain saws finally destroy all the rain forests on earth, and if the people who set them in motion are far enough away so that they don't hear the crash of the trees on the naked forest floor, does it matter? This rational, detached, scientific intellect, observing a world of which it is no longer a part, is too often arrogant, unfeeling, uncaring. And its consequences can be monstrous.

The strange absence of emotion, the banal face of evil so often mani- 55 fested by mass technological assaults on the global environment, is surely a consequence of the belief in an underlying separation of intellect from the physical world. At the root of this belief lies a heretical misunderstanding of humankind's place in the world as old as Plato, as seductive in its mythic appeal as Gnosticism, as compelling as the Cartesian promise of Promethean power—and it has led to tragic results. We have misunderstood who we are, how we relate to our place within creation, and why our very existence assigns us a duty of moral alertness to the consequences of what we do. A civilization that believes itself to be separate from the world may pretend not to hear, but there is indeed a sound when a tree falls in the forest.

The richness and diversity of our religious tradition throughout history is a spiritual resource long ignored by people of faith, who are often afraid to open their minds to teachings first offered outside their own system of belief. But the emergence of a civilization in which knowledge moves freely and almost instantaneously throughout the world has led to an intense new interest in the different perspectives on life in other cultures and has spurred a renewed investigation of the wisdom distilled by all faiths. This panreligious perspective may prove especially important where our global civilization's responsibility for the earth is concerned. 56

Native American religions, for instance, offer a rich tapestry of ideas about our relationship to the earth. One of the most moving and frequently quoted explanations was attributed to Chief Seattle in 1855, when President Franklin Pierce stated that he would buy the land of Chief Seattle's tribe. The power of his response has survived numerous translations and retellings: 57

> How can you buy or sell the sky? The land? The idea is strange to us. If we do not own the freshness of the air and the sparkle of the water, how can you buy them? Every part of this earth is sacred to my people. Every shining pine needle, every sandy shore, every mist in the dark woods, every meadow, every humming insect. All are holy in the memory and experience of my people....
>
> If we sell you our land, remember that the air is precious to us, that the air shares its spirit with all the life it supports. The wind that gave our grandfather his first breath also received his last sigh. The wind also gives our children the spirit of life. So if we sell you our land, you must keep it apart and sacred, a place where man can go to taste the wind that is sweetened by the meadow flowers.
>
> Will you teach your children what we have taught our children? That the earth is our mother? What befalls the earth befalls all the sons of the earth.
>
> This we know: the earth does not belong to man, man belongs to the earth. All things are connected like the blood that unites us all. Man did not weave the web of life, he is merely a strand in it. Whatever he does to the web, he does to himself.
>
> One thing we know: Our God is also your God. The earth is precious to Him and to harm the earth is to heap contempt on its Creator.

A modern prayer of the Onondaga tribe in upstate New York offers an- 58
other beautiful expression of our essential connection to the earth:

> O Great Spirit, whose breath gives life to the world and whose voice is
> heard in the soft breeze … make us wise so that we may understand what
> you have taught us, help us learn the lessons you have hidden in every leaf
> and rock, make us always ready to come to you with clean hands and
> straight eyes, so when life fades, as the fading sunset, our spirits may come
> to you without shame.

The spiritual sense of our place in nature predates Native American cul- 59
tures; increasingly it can be traced to the origins of human civilization. A
growing number of anthropologists and archaeomythologists, such as
Marija Gimbutas and Riane Eisler, argue that the prevailing ideology of belief in prehistoric Europe and much of the world was based on the worship of a single earth goddess, who was assumed to be the fount of all life
and who radiated harmony among all living things. Much of the evidence
for the existence of this primitive religion comes from the many thousands
of artifacts uncovered in ceremonial sites. These sites are so widespread
that they seem to confirm the notion that a goddess religion was ubiquitous throughout much of the world until the antecedents of today's religions—most of which still have a distinctly masculine orientation—swept
out of India and the Near East, almost obliterating belief in the goddess.
The last vestige of organized goddess worship was eliminated by
Christianity as late as the fifteenth century in Lithuania.

The antiquity of the evidence and the elaborate and imaginative analy- 60
sis used to interpret the artifacts leave much room for skepticism about
our ability to know exactly what this belief system—or collection of reated beliefs—taught. Its best-documented tenet seems to have been a
reverence for the sacredness of the earth—and a belief in the need for
harmony among all living things; other aspects of the faith are less clear,
and it is probable that many barbaric practices accompanied the more be-
nign beliefs. Still, the archaelogical scholarship is impressive, and it seems
obvious that a better understanding of a religious heritage preceding our
own by so many thousands of years could offer us new insights into the
nature of the human experience.

Moreover, virtually all current world religions have much to say about 61
the relationship between humankind and the earth. Islam, for example,
offers familiar themes. The Prophet Mohammed said, "The world is green
and beautiful and God has appointed you His stewards over it." The central concepts of Islam taught by the Qu'ran—*tawheed* (unity), *khalifa*
(trusteeship), and *akhrah* (accountability)—also serve as the pillars of
the Islamic environmental ethic. The earth is the sacred creation of Allah,

and among Mohammed's many instructions about it is: "Whoever plants a tree and diligently looks after it until it matures and bears fruit is rewarded." The first Muslim caliph, Abu-Baker, drew upon the Qu'ran and the *hadith* (oral traditions of the Prophet) when he ordered his troops: "Do not cut down a tree, do not abuse a river, do not harm animals, and be always kind and humane to God's creation, even to your enemies."

A common thread in many religions is the sacred quality of water. 62 Christians are baptized in water, as a sign of purification. The Qu'ran declares that "we have created everything from water." In the *Lotus "Sutra,"* Buddha is presented metaphorically as a "rain cloud," covering, permeating, fertilizing, and enriching "all parched living beings, to free them from their misery to attain the joy of peace, joy of the present world and joy of Nirvana ... everywhere impartially without distinction of persons ... ever to all beings I preach the Law equally ... equally I rain the Law—rain untiringly."

The sacredness of water receives perhaps the greatest emphasis in 63 Hinduism. According to its teachings, the "waters of life" are believed to bring to humankind the life force itself. One modern Hindu environmentalist, Dr. Karen Singh, regularly cites the ancient Hindu dictum: "The earth is our mother, and we are all her children." And in the *Atharvaveda,* the prayer for peace emphasizes the links between humankind and all creation: "Supreme Lord, let there be peace in the sky and in the atmosphere, peace in the plant world and in the forests; let the cosmic powers be peaceful; let Brahma be peaceful; let there be undiluted and fulfilling peace everywhere."

Sikhism, the northern Indian monotheistic offshoot of Hinduism that 64 was founded around 1500, places a great deal of spiritual significance on the lessons we can learn directly from nature. Its founder, Guru Nanak, said, "Air is the Vital Force, Water the Progenitor, the Vast Earth the Mother of All: Day and Night are nurses, fondling all creation in their lap." According to the Sikh scripture, *Guru Granth Sahib,* human beings are composed of five elements of nature, which teach lessons and inspire stength in the formulation of our character: "Earth teaches us patience, love; Air teaches us mobility, liberty; Fire teaches us warmth, courage; Sky teaches us equality, broad-mindedness; Water teaches us purity, cleanliness."

One of the newest of the great universalist religions, Baha'i founded in 65 1863 in Persia by Mirza Husayn Ali, warns us not only to properly regard the relationship between humankind and nature but also the one between civilization and the environment. Perhaps because its guiding visions were formed during the period of accelerating industrialism, Baha'i seems to dwell on the spieitual implications of the great transformation to which it bore fresh witness: "We cannot segregate the human heart from the environment outside us and say that once one of these is reformed every-thing will be improved. Man is organic with the world. His inner life molds the environment and is itself deeply affected by it. The one acts upon the other and every abiding change in the life of man is the result of these mutual reactions." And, again, from the Baha'i sacred writings comes this: "Civilization, so often vaunted by the learned exponents of arts and sciences will, if allowed to overleap the bounds of moderation, bring great evil upon men."

This sensitivity to the changes wrought by civilization on the earth is also evident in new statements from the leaders of Western religions. Pope John Paul II, for example, in his message of December 8, 1989, on humankind's responsibility for the ecological crisis, said: "Faced with the widespread destruction of the environment, people everywhere are coming to understand that we cannot continue to use the goods of the earth as we have in the past ... a new *ecological awareness* is beginning to emerge which rather than being downplayed, ought to be encouraged to develop into concrete programs and initiatives." In concluding, the pope directly addressed his "brothers and sisters in the Catholic church, in order to remind them of their serious obligation to care for all of creation.... Respect for life and for the dignity of the human person extends also to the rest of creation, which is called to join man in praising God."   66

Many environmental theorists who think the Catholic church only long enough to complain bitterly about its opposition to birth control (which many Catholics, in fact, use) might be surprised to read the pope's powerful and penetrating analysis of the ecological crisis and recognize him as an ally: "Modern society will find no solution to the ecological problem unless it *takes a serious look at its lifestyle.* In many parts of the world, society is given to instant gratification and consumerism while remaining indifferent to the damage which these cause. As I have already stated, the seriousness of the ecological issue lays bare the depth of man's moral crisis."   67

The Judeo-Christian tradition has always presented a prophetic vision, from Joseph's warnings to Pharaoh about the seven lean years to John's jubilant promise in Revelations: "We will praise the Lamb, Triumphant, with *all* creatures." Many prophecies use the images of environmental destruction to warn of transgressions against God's will. For example, for those who believe in the literal truth of the Bible, it is hard to read about the predictions of hurricanes 50 percent stronger than the worst ones today, due to the accumulation of greenhouse gases that we have fostered, without recalling the prophecy of Hosea: "They have sown the wind, and they shall reap the whirlwind."   68

For some Christians, the prophetic vision of the apocalypse is used—   69 in my view, unforgivably—as an excuse for abdicating their responsibility to be good stewards of God's creation. Former Secretary of the Interior James Watt, who deserved his reputation as an anti-environmentalist, was once quoted as belittling concerns about environmental protection in part because it would all be destroyed by God in the apocalypse. Not only is this idea heretical in terms of Christian teachings, it is an appallingly self-fulfilling prophecy of doom. It is noteworthy that Watt did not see the need to forgo other obligations, however. He did not say, for example, that there was no point in conducting a bargain basement sale of grazing rights on federal rangelands to wealthy friends because the Four Horsemen are galloping this way.

Nevertheless, there is no doubt that many believers and nonbelievers   70
alike share a deep uneasiness about the future, sensing that our civilization may be running out of time. The religious ethic of stewardship is indeed harder to accept if one believes the world is in danger of being destroyed—by either God or humankind. This point was made by the Catholic theologian Teilhard de Chardin when he said, "The fate of mankind, as well as of religion, depends upon the emergence of a new faith in the future." Armed with such a faith, we might find it possible to resanctify the earth, identify it as God's creation, and accept our responsibility to protect and defend it. We might even begin to contemplate decisions based on long-term considerations, not short-term calculations.

And if we could find a way to understand our own connection to the   71
earth—all the earth—we might recognize the danger of destroying so many living species and disrupting the climate balance. James Lovelock, the originator of the Gaia hypothesis, maintains that the entire complex earth system behaves in a self-regulating manner characteristic of something alive, that it has managed to maintain critical components of the earth's life support systems in perfect balance over eons of time—until the unprecedented interference of modern civilization: "We now see that the air, the ocean and the soil are much more than a mere environment for life; they are a part of life itself. Thus the air is to life just as is the fur to a cat or the nest for a bird. Not living but something made by living things to protect against an otherwise hostile world. For life on earth, the air is our protection against the cold depths and fierce radiations of space."

Lovelock insists that this view of the relationship between life and the   72
nonliving elements of the earth system does not require a spiritual explanation; even so, it evokes a spiritual response in many of those who hear it. It cannot be accidental, one is tempted to conclude, that the percentage of salt in our bloodstreams is roughly the same as the percentage of salt in the oceans of the world. The long and intricate process by which evolution helped to shape the complex interrelationship of all living and

nonliving things may be explicable in purely scientific terms, but the simple fact of the living world and our place on it evokes awe, wonder, a sense of mystery—a spiritual response—when one reflects on its deeper meaning.

We are not used to seeing God in the world because we assume from the scientific and philosophical rules that govern us that the physical world is made up of inanimate matter whirling in accordance with mathematical laws and bearing no relation to life, much less ourselves. Why does it feel faintly heretical to a Christian to suppose that God is in us as human beings? Why do our children believe that the Kingdom of God is *up*, somewhere in the ethereal reaches of space, far removed from this planet? Are we still unconsciously following the direction of Plato's finger, looking for the sacred everywhere except in the real world? 73

It is my own belief that the image of God can be seen in every corner of creation, even in us, but only faintly. By gathering in the mind's eye all of creation, one can perceive the image of the Creator vividly. Indeed, my understanding of how God is manifest in the world can be best conveyed through the metaphor of the hologram. (Using a technological metaphor to make a spriritual point is not as odd as it may seem. The Bible often uses metaphors based on the technology of the time. For example, God scatters spiritual seeds on the barren land as well as the rich soil, some of them grow and some of them don't; the wheat must be separated from the tares; at the end of time men shall beat their swords into plowshares and their spears into pruning hooks.) When the light of a laser beam shines on a holographic plate, the image it carries is made visible in three dimensions as the light reflects off thousands of microscopic lines that make up a distinctive "resistance pattern" woven into the plastic film covering the glass plate—much the way a phonograph needle picks up music from the "resistance pattern" of tiny bumps in the grooves of a long-playing record. Each tiny portion of the hologram contains a tiny representation of the entire three-dimensional image, but only faintly. However, due to the novel and unusual optical principles on which holography is based, when one looks not at a small portion but at the entire hologram, these thousands of tiny, faint images come together in the eye of the beholder as a single large, vivid image. 74

Similarly, I believe that the image of the Creator, which sometimes seems so faint in the tiny corner of creation each of us beholds, is nonetheless present in its entirety—and present in us as well. If we are made in the image of God, perhaps it is the myriad slight strands from earth's web of life—woven so distinctively into our essence—that make up the "resistance pattern" that reflects the image of God, faintly. By experiencing nature in its fullest—our own and that of all creation—with 75 our senses and with our spiritual imagination, we can glimpse, "bright shining as the sun," an infinite image of God.

QUESTIONS FOR DISCUSSION AND WRITING

1.   Usually, the ability of human beings to adapt to change is seen as a positive thing, showing our resourcefulness, determination, and intelligence. Gore argues just the opposite. Why does Gore see this ability to adapt as one source of our present ecological crisis? What would he have us become instead of "resourceful"?

2.   How does Gore respond to the persistent "charge" that it is the Judeo-Christian tradition that began and continues to justify the domination of nature by civilization? Do you find his a convincing response?

3.   When *Earth in the Balance* was first published, he was accused by some critics of presenting an overly pessimistic picture of our present "ecological crisis" and an excessively apocalyptic view of the future. Based upon what you have now read of the book, and on your own view of our present environmental situation, how would you characterize Gore's views?

PAULA DiPERNA

*Paula DiPerna (b. 1949) is a freelance journalist who has written on environ-
mental and related health issues for major national newspapers and magazines.
DiPerna has also written and produced a number of television documentaries, including "Lilliput in Antarctica," about an expedition to Antarctica by children,
and "Outrage at Valdez," a documentary about the devastating Alaskan oil spill in
1991. DiPerna began her writing career after graduating from NYU, while she was
teaching in a New York City high school. Since then she has researched and written five books and numerous newspaper and magazine articles about environmental and related health issues. DiPerna's writing and her television films reflect
her international perspective on our present environmental problems; her research
has taken her from the rain forests of Brazil to the ice fields of Antarctica. DiPerna
also brings a strong feminist perspective to her examination of ecological concerns.
As "Truth vs. 'Facts'" attempts to illustrate, in most places in the world it is women
who most directly "feel the effects of dwindling resources and declining environmental quality." This basic connection with environmental problems, argues
DiPerna, means that women can also offer the most effective and the most lasting
solutions.*

Truth vs. "Facts"

It was 1984 and large snowflakes fell on Woburn, Massachusetts. De- 1
spite the cold, people gathered for the meeting of their group, For a
Cleaner Environment, the storefront throwing a glow into the snowy
evening. I was there to cover the story of Woburn, site of toxic waste
dumping, public wells contaminated with carcinogens, and a mysterious
grouping of leukemia cases among children.

It has been a haggle to convince my editor that what I saw as a fasci- 2
nating medical detective tale—did the contaminated drinking water cause
the leukemia cases?—was worthwhile. Now, there I was; the players
gathered, ripe for questioning. But the key person was missing: Anne
Anderson, the mother of one of the children who had died. After her son
was diagnosed with leukemia in 1972, well before Love Canal, and she became aware of other cases in her neighborhood, Anne Anderson began to
suspect the only common factor—the foul tapwater about which she and
her neighbors had been complaining for years. But the authorities insisted
the water was fine; her own husband, trying to dissuade her from keeping
a record of each new leukemia case, told her that "if this was unusual,

371

someone would know." But Anne Anderson remained undeterred, and in 1979, Woburn's toxic waste contamination broke into the news.

When we met the next morning, I sat notebook and pen at the ready. But mindful that she had lost a son, I prefaced my questions: "I know this may be painful to discuss, but I'd like to begin by asking you what made you suspect the water?" Anne interrupted, taking control. "You can't just jump into the facts like that. It is a long and complicated story and it took my Jimmy nine years to die."

My eyes burned with tears of embarrassment, and as I fought not to show them, I listened. She explained that she had missed the meeting the night before because it had been the third anniversary of Jimmy's death. She narrated a long history of trying to get her theory taken seriously. I began to realize that Woburn was not just about toxicology, or chemistry, or how many parts per million of carcinogenic substances were found in the water, or the criminal proceedings against the polluters, or any of the obvious reportorial aspects. The Woburn story eclipsed mere information. It was a human tragedy. Real children, real pain, real death.

There and then I altered my view of environmental issues. I saw that they are inseparable from ethics, indivisible from society. Proceeding from biology, agronomy, oceanography, hydrography, and other disciplines— yet more than their sum—environmentalism is a humanity, perhaps sometimes even more than a science.

Women understand this transcendent quality better than men, which is why women are uniquely suited to lead in environmental matters—not just lead the doing, but the thinking. Women process complexities and still focus on the undeniable fact: a healthy planet is not a luxury but a basic human necessity. In a way, environmentalism shouldn't even exist or be a specialty of any kind, but an "ism" without a name, so pervasive as to be virtually invisible. Anne Anderson did not think of herself as an environmentalist when her son fell ill. Yet she took on the most complicated environmental questions, motivated not only by deep love, but also by her commonsense belief that human beings should not be expected to drink contaminated water. Period.

As society hurtles through this decade, passion for environmental causes has never been higher (theoretically, at least). "Think green" evolved into "buy green" and for those affluent enough to exercise the option, "ecologically correct" behavior is in. But has this ground swell actually established a clean environment as a basic human right? Or have we created the *appearance* of protecting the earth?

Women, of course, know the difference, being experts at discerning substance from tokenism, real work from taking credit for it, the good buy from the bad.

Consider the challenges, against which governments have taken virtu-   9
ally no meaningful action.

Depletion of the ozone layer, which protects the earth and us from   10
harmful solar ultraviolet rays, seems under way. An ozone "hole" indisputably occurs seasonally over Antarctica, largely due to chlorofluorocarbons (CFCs) rising into the stratosphere, which shatter the ozone molecules. Lacking this filter, the sun becomes our enemy, the possible cause of increased skin cancers, immune system suppression, and the burning of the microscopic plants and animals that are the building blocks of the food chain, including plankton on the ocean surface.

Global climate change also looms, due to the buildup of certain gases   11
in the atmosphere, especially carbon dioxide. Much accumulation occurs because of the destruction of forest and grassland for farmland, causing organic matter to be oxidized. Thus, deforestation means not only loss of trees, but roughly one to three billion tons of carbon released per year, in addition to the approximately six billion tons attributable to the burning of fossil fuels.

Add to this, run-of-the-mill air pollution—sulfur dioxide, nitrogen ox-   12
ide, lead, and their numerous by-products—plus what are called toxic "trace" elements such as benzene and polychlorinated biphenyls (PCBs).

The water on which we depend for drinking, irrigation, and the like   13
can be polluted insidiously by chemicals and human waste. And in most countries, including the U.S., neither groundwater nor municipal water is routinely tested for chemical contamination (including pesticides). In the developing world, nearly one billion people have no access to safe water at all.

And despite the new consciousness, the world continues to lose 42 mil-   14
lion acres of tropical rain forest per year, and gain 14 million acres of desert. Diversity of species, the multitude of creatures and plants that account for the pyramid of life, is under siege as approximately 20,000 species become extinct each year.

The Persian Gulf War represented a hellish turning point. Roughly 600   15
oil wells were set ablaze by retreating Iraqi troops, following the deliberate and "incidental" wartime release of one to three million barrels of oil. The gulf provides food and a living to many in all the bordering states. Subsistence fishing suffered immediate losses and the shrimp industry was reportedly entirely eradicated.

I spoke with Munira Fakhro, an expert in women and development is-   16
sues, who had been at her Bahrain home in July. She reported, "There was black rain everywhere, affecting seafood, fish, so many things that I cannot name them." Fakhro was sure that "right now, the most important issue is damage caused to children. But everyone suffers from a

kind of virus from the chemicals in the air that affects their eyes and noses." In general, deadly pollutants can take their first toll on the female reproductive system, and in miscarriages, stillbirths, and congenital deformities. Yet she knew of no short- or long-term studies being initiated, or even whether the rate of miscarriages had risen. Concerning the impact of the inferno on health in the future, little data is being offered. As Fakhro says, "Maybe someone should be telling us about that."

Eco-warfare should be terrifying in itself, but especially in view of the 17 regular movement of toxic substances that could be the targets of ambush. All of which pales compared to the projected transport of plutonium to enable Japan and such countries as Belgium, France, Switzerland, and Germany to reprocess spent nuclear fuel for use in a new generation of nuclear reactors. Plutonium is the stuff of nuclear bombs, the most toxic substance we know. A single particle of plutonium inhaled can cause lung cancer.

The transition from fossil fuel to plutonium could mean nations would 18 then be dependent on an *inherently lethal substance* for energy—and by the late 1990s, about 400 shipments per year will take place by land, sea, and air, involving the movement of tons of plutonium.

So, despite growing awareness, dangerous trends persist, often the 19 subject of fruitless debate. Since most environmental impacts don't follow the traditional cause and effect pattern, there is room for "on the one hand, on the other" contention: CFCs do destroy the ozone layer, but not everyone will get cancer; it's true some climate models show increase in global temperature over time, but these could be "flukes"; fish stocks seem lower, but these could be "natural crashes" of the populations; since the fires in Kuwait are unprecedented, no one can accurately predict their impact. The flaming match can be shown to burn the finger, but disease—especially cancer—may appear much later than when the cause exerted its power, and often long after the causative agent can be found in the environment. The tobacco industry is the most shameless in exploiting this drawback.

Therefore, because clear-cut links between cause and effect are elu- 20 sive, remedies are evaded. Not to mention when information is deliberately covered up, of course, as chillingly described by Rosalie Bertell. But women bring to the discussion badly needed qualities—among them, a scalpel to cut away such evasions: women specialize in early warnings.

For example, few people knew that a woman second mate on the ill- 21 fated *Exxon Valdez,* Maureen Jones, was lookout on deck and first to notice that the tanker was traveling the wrong side of the flashing red buoy. Apparently, she twice warned the third mate, then at the helm. He ignored her, though heeding her warning could have prevented the accident entirely.

The causes of the accident were even deeper. Again, it was an all-too-   22
prescient woman—toxicologist and fisherwoman Frederika (Riki) Ott—
who enunciated them. In a speech the night before the grounding, she
had predicted what would happen, and why: "Given the high frequency
of tankers into Port Valdez, the increasing age and size of that tanker fleet,
and the inability to quickly contain and clean up an oil spill in the open
waters of Alaska, fishermen feel that we are playing a game of Russian
roulette. It's a question of when, not if...." Such women can be found
around the world, grasping and acting on connections that seem to elude
the men in charge.

In Tasmania, the southerly island state of Australia, a novice politician,   23
schoolteacher Christine Milne, won a seat in the state parliament in 1989.
She convincingly exposed the environmental shortcomings of a $1 billion
(Australian) paper plant. Her campaign proved that a cleaner paper mill
could still be cost-effective, halting the construction of an inferior facility
in Tasmania, and helping to raise the standard globally.

Milne received a Global 500 citation for achievement from the United   24
Nations Environment Programme. Only 11 other women (750 awards
have been made) have been similarly honored, including journalist
Barbara d'Achille of Peru, who died for her trouble. She had been a vanguard voice on environmental subjects in the region for about 18 years,
until she was stoned to death in 1989 by Shining Path guerrillas in the
highlands.

Wangari Maathai, winner this year of a Goldman Environmental Prize   25
among other awards, endured severe government criticism for her opposition to urban sprawl in Nairobi. Yet the Green Belt movement she began
in 1977, through which women mobilized in Kenya to combat desertification, catalyzed similar efforts throughout East Africa.

Last year I met Dagmar Werner, otherwise known as "Iguana Mama."   26
Trained in iguana biology, she is also a fervent interdisciplinarian.
Observing the decline of rain forests in the tropical Americas—to make
way for short-term slash-and-burn agriculture—Werner began to think
that iguanas could stem the trend. But the herbivorous iguanas, long a
prized food among the campesinos cutting down the trees, need the rain
forest habitat, and their number has declined dramatically. Werner reasoned that if there were enough iguanas to eat, campesinos would rather
hunt them than clear land to raise a few chickens or cows or low-paying
crops. They could also enter the cash economy by selling iguana skins instead of leather. As she explains her mission, "I work with campesinos all
the time and I know how few their economic choices are. Why shouldn't
they eat the meat that is part of their culture, especially if northern countries are always telling them not to cut down the trees?" She pioneered
the study of iguana reproduction in Panama, and when the U.S. invasion

plunged that country into turmoil, she packed her breeding population of iguanas into a van and drove to Costa Rica. Her Fundación Pro Iguana Verde is now installed there, underfunded but functional, a practical and innovative approach to a recalcitrant problem.

Sylvia Earle, a marine biologist renowned for her deepwater diving and for having made the first untethered walk on the ocean floor, is now the chief scientist at the U.S. National Oceanic and Atmospheric Administration. She advocates the establishment of large "ocean wilderness" areas stretching from the surface to the depths, including international waters, where human activities would be prohibited or strictly limited. These swaths would protect not only harvestable fish, but the waters themselves for their role in maintaining global climate and cleansing the earth. As Earl puts it, "Imagine if we tried today to set aside the large sanctuaries on land that we now enjoy." She also notes that "the two billion dollars Exxon spent at Prince William Sound did not bring the tides in twice a day." 27

Pressing exploration into service for the environment, mountaineer Ann Bancroft hopes to lead the first all-women team across Antarctica in 1992, to call attention to the environmental importance of the earth's last virtually pristine continent. (Though an agreement forged in July 1991 declared Antarctica off-limits to mining and minerals exploration for at least 50 years, tourism proceeds and accidents can happen. An Argentine vessel ran aground in 1989; the oil spill killed large numbers of seabirds and jeopardized scientific research into the effects of ozone depletion on marine organisms.) 28

Such women inspire us, and testify to the basic connections of women to environmental issues. 29

For one thing, women are in a position to know. Who more than women—who increasingly head families, and who provide and cook the world's food, gather the world's fuel, pump the world's water, nurse the world's sick children and carry them from camp to camp in famine —experience the effects of dwindling resources and declining environmental quality? 30

Filomina Chioma Steady, a social anthropologist from Sierra Leone who is serving as a special adviser on women to the United Nations Conference on Environment and Development (UNCED) to be held in Brazil in June 1992, observes: "Women are much more attuned to the idea of sustainability, the need for a steady, not short-term, supply of resources." Steady's role, in collaboration with the United Nations Development Fund for Women, is to ensure that gender issues become integral to the UNCED agenda. Former U.S. Congresswoman Bella Abzug, of the Women's Environment & Development Organization (WEDO), charges: "Women have been almost invisible in policy-making on environment and development issues. They're present in large numbers at the grass roots, but at 31 the top of most important nongovernmental organizations we find only male leadership."

For the past year, Abzug has been a senior adviser to Maurice Strong, secretary-general of the UNCED. The WEDO will sponsor a World Women's Congress for a Healthy Planet in Miami from November 8 to 12, to develop an action agenda to present in Brazil. One goal of Abzug and Steady is to convince each nation to send a delegation to the UNCED of at least 50 percent women.   32

In fact, little environmental progress can be achieved without women. For example, in Africa, at least 70 percent of agricultural work is performed by women, yet they have no say in what agricultural practices are adopted. And the need for women's involvement is nowhere more evident than in attempting to stem overpopulation. Without control over their reproductive destiny, empowerment, and fair access to education and income, women will continue, willingly and unwillingly, to bring children into the world the environment cannot support, rendering null the concept of sustainable development.   33

Some hold the view that the environment is a "women's issue" by virtue of women's "holistic" vision and nurturing tendencies—by now a cliché. But although biology and social conditioning cannot be ignored, I think women's affinity for environmental issues has more to do with the concept of *potential:* the environment, though modern living cloaks the relationship, is the giver of all human potential. Without water, air, natural resources, the diversity of nonhuman species, no human endeavor would be possible. Underpinning all human activity and enabling all human success, therefore, the environment is the true source of human possibility. Thus, women struggling to explore, define, reach, and prove potential, relate not just to the life-creating and life-sustaining aspects of nature, but to its life-*enhancing* role. For women, to protect the environment is to secure not only a minimum level of existence, but a fair quality standard of living.   34

Since such a concept embroils global economics, women are well positioned to be the architects of a new "eco-economics."   35

Political economist, goat farmer, and former member of parliament in New Zealand, Marilyn Waring pioneered this area in 1988 in her book, *If Women Counted,* demonstrating how the United Nations System of National Accounts and the world's accounting systems ignore the value of "nonproductive" work performed by women and by nature.   36

In fact, the paradox of our time, which trumpets a "free market," is that natural resources are worth no money in and of themselves. They convert money, i.e., marketability, only when used—then the cleanup operations and matériel are considered "productive"—but that use then generates environmental degradation and pollution. Furthermore, the notion that   37 raw materials are free demands debunking. That sufficient trees have been available has been a long-term subsidy to all the wood-using industries as, for example, has been the capacity of rivers and oceans to absorb manufacturing and municipal sludge. The environment has actually been the silent unpaid partner of all economic growth.

Traditional economic theory posits environmental protection and economic activity as mutually exclusive—but today the two may be on a collision course. Some problems, such as climate change and ozone depletion, have grown too large to ignore except at global peril. Moreover, as the Cold War ends, such concepts as "economic planning" and "subsidy" have become dirty words. Yet there can *be* no environmental management without planning, and the private sector will not take risks in still-fledgling industries, like household solar power, without subsidy. Therefore, in a global economy governed only by market forces, how can environmental protection find a viable form?

One promising innovation, though it has turned red ink into an asset rather than truly making new cash available to environmental programs, is the "debt-for-nature" swap. Conservation organizations have raised money to buy a portion of a nation's outstanding debt from commercial debt holders who, eager to realize some repayment, sell the debt at discounted rates. But the sale relieves the government of repaying the full principal amount, as long as it is made available in local currency exclusively for environmental projects.

Kathryn S. Fuller, the first woman president of the World Wildlife Fund and a lawyer and biologist by training, has been active in such landmark transactions in Ecuador, the Philippines, and elsewhere. Fuller has hope for such alternatives. "We are still tinkering on the margins of financing conservation," she notes, "and the first efforts were supposed to catalyze numbers of things and get people thinking about creative financing mechanisms. The question now is to shift to larger institutions."

In the end, the revamping of economics with the environment in mind will have to forge new paths between private and public, especially since the so-called planned economies offered little in environmental protection. On the contrary, dead air, water, and land seem of crisis proportion in Eastern Europe—but nowhere more dramatic than at Chernobyl in the USSR. Five years ago, the infamous reactor exploded. Today, 125,000 persons are at risk of dying from radiation-induced illnesses within five years, 1.5 to 2 million are at long-term risk, and even after entombment, the reactor remains unstable.

Women are eloquent witnesses, though few perhaps as unlikely as Olga Korbut, the Soviet gymnast who, at the age of 17, mesmerized the 1972 Olympic games with the sheer perfection of her forms. Having once epitomized good health and the excellence of the human body, Olga

Korbut fled her home in Minsk, only 180 miles from Chernobyl, fearing continued exposure.

She describes with lingering incredulity the innocence in which she and other citizens languished while living in the shadow of disaster. "For some time," she recounts, "nobody told us anything, and I went into the street without knowing what had happened." She remembers knowing women who were pregnant at the time, whose children were born with illnesses and birth defects, and adds, "Only now women know they are taking a risk in getting pregnant." Today, her health and that of her family are good, she says, "but in later time, who knows?" 43

Indeed. Unwilling to turn her back on the people she left behind, Korbut started the Olga Korbut Foundation at the Fred Hutchinson Cancer Research Center in Seattle, Washington, to raise money for Chernobyl victims, and to finance medical care for the hundreds of leukemic children. 44

Korbut joins the growing ranks of activist women in the Soviet Union, and when I asked her if this was because women were stronger, she simply answered, "I don't know. But what I do know is that for women, there is no exit. Woman is mother, and mother is always mother, and mothers are always stronger." 45

As the 1990s unfold, this strength, however defined and whatever the source, can be tapped to reexamine even the language that has dominated decisions affecting the environment. Women can remove the dialogue from the cycle of liberal versus conservative. Nowhere are these labels more inappropriately applied than in discussions of the environment, for though polluters may belittle "liberal environmentalists," what could be more liberal than irreverently dumping toxic sludge into streams, spewing acid into the rain, putting flame into forests? And what, after all, is more conservative than wanting to conserve the place where we live? 46

And if women have a single truly philosophical contribution to make, I believe it is to render the lack of traditional proof an irrelevant argument in environmental matters, as Anne Anderson did at Woburn. 47

For it may be that we will not have irrefutable evidence of such disturbances as global warming in time to address them. One can speak of a body of data, but each set has its detractor. The public, already skeptical of authority, shrinks from the cacophony into indifference and is inexcusably led to believe it is safe to do nothing "for now." 48

So the politician's statement that "all the evidence isn't in yet," is a perversion of science. Science is not the demonstration of fixed knowledge; it is only the quest, the ascent toward answers in aid of policy; it is not a justification for lack of action. 49

Fortunately, women can imagine the consequences of an act without having had to experience it. Physicist, feminist, and ecologist, Vandana Shiva of India contrasts this with what she has called "... a patriarchal re- 50 ductionism that values only the part of reality that can be exploited.... The rest of reality is ignored." Thus, the prospects of environmental consequences are minimized because those consequences may not be tangible or provable in the classic sense. Turning Shiva's "rest of reality" into reality itself is the critical task of what has come to be called "ecofeminism."

Women can play the crucial role in "nurturing" the public away from 51 expecting absolutes and toward redefining proof in Hippocratic terms— *in the absence of full knowledge, do no harm*. Under this banner, coupled with a rededication to the political process and campaigning for office, women could transform environmental policy.

The 1980s subversively denigrated the role of government, stimulating 52 a wave of privatization and deregulation, demeaning the notion of public good in favor of individual good. But true environmentalism requires the sense of public good, advanced by an imaginative, credible, even passionate government, especially given the unprecedented nature of international cooperation required to solve global problems.

It is no longer enough for environmentalists to remain in parallel rela- 53 tionship to power; however large the movement grows, a lobbying body is on the outside. Similarly, it is no longer sufficient for politicians to remain entrenched and distracted insiders.

Women are perhaps the only ones equipped to cross this gulf Mar- 54 shaling philosophy, strategy, experience, and a unique cross-cultural point of view, women can bridge local activism and global leadership, instating *potential environmental consequences as the gauge by which all policy is measured*. Ultimately, women cannot remain mere advocates for the environment but must reestablish the environment as the advocate of human survival.

The next goal may well be to make *all* parties green, even in the small- 55 est hamlets today reeling for lack of leadership on such problems as waste disposal, water treatment, and land use. This widespread political ignition could lead eventually to a new roster of women heads of government uniquely capable of setting new environmental priorities—women thinking globally and *acting* globally. Gro Harlem Bruntland, prime minister of Norway, was perhaps the first of this class, but even Margaret Thatcher was the most outspoken among her colleagues on global warming.

And true priority for environmental questions would be completely 56 consistent with redressing poverty and misery, for the poor are the first victims of environmental degradation and the least able to pay for medical care—and most of the poor are women and children.

Women and the environment is really about women and truth, and re- 57 defining politics as the use of truth for the public well-being. This means *truth as distinct from final "facts,"* truth being the best you can get when you thoughtfully weigh everything together. The environment is not a special interest, but the single common interest, and as such acquires unique political and moral force. In the hands of women, this force could be the light of the next century.

QUESTIONS FOR DISCUSSION AND WRITING

1. What does DiPerna believe that the example of Maureen Jones, the female crew member of the *Exxon Valdez,* tells us about the role of women in our current environmental situation? By contrast, how does DiPerna see the perspective of men (what she calls "patriarchal reductionism") contributing to the environment? Do her conclusions about the relative roles of men and women in the environment make sense to you?

2. What does DiPerna mean by the contention that women are "well positioned to be the architects of a new 'eco-economics'" (par. 35)? What exactly is this new economics? From what you can tell, how might it affect our daily lives? Is there anything in your experience that would support or contradict her assertion that women are specially positioned to design such a system?

BARRY LOPEZ

Barry Lopez (b. 1945) is one of the best-known and most respected of all American nature writers today. Born in New York State, Lopez grew up in California and now lives in western Oregon, near the McKenzie River. Lopez's many prizes and awards for nature writing include the Burroughs Award for Natural History and the American Book Award. Lopez's first three collections of essays— Desert Notes *(1976),* Giving Birth to Thunder *(1978), and* River Notes *(1979)— explore the contrasting concepts of nature in Western and non-Western cultures. In 1978 Lopez published* Of Wolves and Men, *a remarkable natural history of the wolf in which he contrasts the way that wolves have been understood in Native American cultures, in European myth, and in modern science. His most famous book,* Arctic Dreams *(1986) is a highly self-conscious exploration of that remote and fragile ecosystem. Lopez hopes to close the distance between himself and nature by experiencing the wilderness immediately, through his senses, rather than through the intellect. This concern about our isolation from nature also informs "Renegotiating the Contracts," first published in 1983. Here Lopez argues that, in the name of commerce and progress, we have broken our traditional "contracts" with nature, by which he means the sense of "mutual obligation and courtesy" held by peoples who live in daily contact with the land. "We will never find a way home," Lopez tells us, "until we find a way to look the caribou, the salmon, the lynx, and the white-throated sparrow in the face, without guile, with no plan of betrayal."*

Renegotiating the Contracts

In an essay in *Harper's* magazine several years ago, Lewis Lapham wrote that democracy was an experiment, a flawed enterprise that required continued human attention if it was going to serve us well. The philosophy behind our relationship with animals in the Western world is also flawed, and in need of continued attention.

To put this in the most basic terms, our relationships with wild animals were once contractual—principled agreements, established and maintained in a spirit of reciprocity and mythic in their pervasiveness. Among hunting peoples in general in the northern hemisphere, these agreements derived from a sense of mutual obligation and courtesy.

Over the past two decades, in particular, our contemporary relationships with wild animals have been energetically scrutinized by anthropologists, moral philosophers, and field biologists. A renewed interest in the mythologies and values of hunting peoples has caused us to question the moral basis for a continuation of hunting by industrialized cultures. Tests to determine the lethal dosages of consumer products and the corrosiveness of cosmetics in animal laboratories, the commercial harvest of infant harp seals, and research on cetacean brains have all provoked heated debate over animal rights. A proliferation of animal images in advertising, and their dominant presence in children's stories, have brought thinkers such as Paul Shepard to wonder how animals affect the very way we conceptualize.

We once thought of animals as not only sentient but as congruent with ourselves in a world beyond the world we can see, one structured by myth and moral obligation, and activated by spiritual power. The departure from the original conception was formalized in Cartesian dualism—the animal was a soulless entity with which people could not have a moral relationship—and in Ruskin's belief that to find anything but the profane and mechanistic in the natural world was to engage in a pathetic fallacy. Both these ideas seem short-sighted and to have not served us well.

4

Today, commerce raises perhaps the most strenuous objection to the interference of animals—their mere presence, their purported rights—in human activity. Wilderness areas the world over, the only places where animals are free of the social and economic schemes of men, are consistently violated for their wealth of timber, minerals, and hydrocarbons; and to fill zoos. Fundamentalist religions and reductionist science deny—or persist in regarding as "outdated"—the aboriginal aspects of our relationships with animals; and deny that animals themselves have any spiritual dimension.

5

If we have embarked on a shared path in reevaluating this situation as humanists and scientists, it has been to inquire how we are going to repair the original contracts. These agreements were abrogated during the agricultural, scientific, and industrial revolutions with a determined degradation of the value of animal life. Acts once indefensible became, over the centuries, only what was acceptable or expeditious. Such a reconsideration bears sharply on the fate of zoos and the future of animal experimentation, but it is also fundamentally important to us as creatures. Whatever wisdom we have shown in deriving a science of ecology, whatever insight we have gained from quantum mechanics into the importance of *relationships* (rather than the mere existence of *things*), urge us to consider these issues without calculation and passionately. We must examine a deep and long-lived insult.

6

I believe there are two failures to face. I speak with the view of someone who regards human beings as a Pleistocene species rather than a twentieth-century phenomenon; and who also believes that to set aside our relationships with wild animals as inconsequential is to undermine our regard for the other sex, other cultures, other universes. Animals exist

7

apart from us, and the balance here between self-esteem and a prejudice directed toward what is different is one of the most rarefied and baffling issues in anthropology. Our own direction as a culture has been to enhance self-esteem *and* to dismantle prejudice by eradicating ignorance. No culture, however, including our own, with its great admiration for compassion and the high value it places on a broad education, has erased prejudice. (No one for that matter has proved it a worthless aspect of cultural evolution and survival.) What is required—or our Western venture is for naught—is to rise above prejudice to a position of respectful regard toward everything that is different from ourselves and not innately evil.

The two ways we have broken with animals are clear and could easily   8
be the focus of our repair. One is that we have simply lost contact with them. Our notions of animal life are highly intellectualized, and no longer checked by daily contact with their environs. Our conceptions of them are not only bookish but stagnant, for, once discovered, we do not permit them to evolve as cultures. We allow them very little grace, enterprise, or individual variation. On the basis of even my own meager field experience—with wolves in Alaska, with mountain lion in Arizona, and with muskoxen, polar bear, and narwhal in the Canadian Arctic—this is a major blind spot in our efforts to erase ignorance. By predetermining categories of relevant information, by dismissing what cannot be easily quantified, by designing research to flatter the predilection of sponsors or defeat the political aims of a special interest group—field biologists have complained to me of both—we have produced distorted and incomplete images of animals.

We have created, further, mathematical models of ecosystems we only   9
superficially grasp and then set divisions of government to managing the lives of the affected animals on the basis of these abstractions. We come perilously close in this to the worst moments of our history, to events we regret most deeply: the subjugation of races, the violent persecution of minority beliefs, the waging of war. With animals, all that saves us here is Descartes' convenience. Of course, some believe him right and regard this as firm ethical ground. But we skirt such imperious condescension here, such hubris, that we cannot help but undermine our principles of behavior toward ourselves, toward each other.

Some doubt the validity or the pertinence of these themes. But I have   10
often heard, at grave and hopeful meetings, eloquent talk of the intellectual and social crises of our times—suppression of personality in a patriarchal society; the inhumane thrust of industry; the colonial designs of Russian or American foreign policy. With the change of only a word or two people could have been speaking of animals. The prejudices inform each other.

If the first failure is one of principle, where our attitudes toward animals   11 have become those of owners and our knowledge skewed because we no longer meet with them and rarely enter their landscapes, the second is a failure of imagination. We have largely lost our understanding of where in an adult life to fit the awe and mystery that animals excite. This sensibility is still maintained in some fashion, however, by many aboriginal peoples and I would suggest, again on the basis of my own short time with Eskimos, that to step beyond a superficial acquaintance with such people is to enter a realm of understanding where what has meant human survival for the past 40,000 years remains clear. Here the comprehension of fundamental human needs and their application—how to live a successful life—is revealed continuously in story, often in stories of human encounters with animals. These stories employ the prosaic to announce the profound, the profound to reveal the ineffable. They balance reassuringly the unfathomable and the concrete. In our age we prefer analysis, not awe; but historically, human beings have subsisted as much on the mystery and awe inspired by animals as they have on the actual flesh of the caribou or the salmon. They have actively sought them in the hunting experience and have preserved them in their oral literatures.

The cultivation of mystery and awe keeps the human capacity for metaphor alive. And a capacity for metaphor allows us to perceive several layers of meaning in a story about, say, a polar bear; to perceive animals not only as complex physiological organisms but as part of a coherent and shared landscape. 12

Our second failure with animals, then, has been to banish them from our minds, as though they were not capable of helping us with our predicaments, the myriad paradoxes of our existence. It is as though we had told the polar bear that his solitary life and the implacable hunger that makes him a persistent and resourceful hunter have no meaning for us. I believe this is a false sophistication of mind, and ultimately destructive. 13

A convenience of rational thought allows me to say there are but two places where our relationships with animals have been severed; audacity perhaps moves me to state that we must repair these breaks. I say so out of years of coming and going in a world inhabited largely by animals and aboriginal peoples, and out of repeated contact with human despair and loneliness in my own culture. What we do to animals troubles us—the horror of laboratory experiment, trophy shooting, factory farming; and our loss of contact with them leaves us mysteriously bereaved. If we could establish an atmosphere of respect in our relationships, simple awe for the complexities of animals' lives, I think we would feel revived as a species. And we would know more, deeply more, about what we are fighting for when we raise our voices against tyranny of any sort. 14

I am aware of having written here without reference to the incidents of day-to-day life by which most of us corroborate our beliefs. I think of several images. There is a group of sea ducks called scoters. They are dark, 15 thick-bodied birds. With the exception of the males, who have bright, oddly shaped bills, they are of undistinguished coloration. The casual spring visitor to Cape Cod or to Cape Flattery would very likely see a few, but we know little about them. Like the ribbon seal and the narwhal, we cannot easily find them again once they leave these accustomed meeting places. So they are not really known to us.

Taxonomists took years to finally differentiate the spotted seal *(Phoca* 16 *largha)* from the harbor seal *(Phoca vitulina)*. They distrusted the statements of Eskimos in the same Bering Sea region who had always separated the two seals on the basis of their ice-related behavior. Now the scientists speak like Yup'ik men about the matter.

A marine biologist, armed with a prestigious grant, went to Hawaii 17 to study a certain crab. The animal's behavior was so utterly different from what he had imagined it would be (from reading the literature) that his research proposal made no sense. To maintain his credibility he abandoned the experiment rather than restructure his conception of the animal.

One morning, walking through fresh snow, looking for mountain lion 18 tracks on the north rim of the Grand Canyon, a biologist with years of this behind him said to me suddenly, "It's not in the data." I looked at him. "It's not in the data," he reiterated. With his hands he made a motion to indicate his head, his chest. "It's here. What I know is here." We went on in silence. "But as a field biologist," I said, "you must offer data or—." "We are not biologists," he answered. "We are historians."

A final moment. In the Sea of Labrador one summer a sperm whale approached our ship head-on. I was standing in the bow with a retired Danish master mariner. The calm green sea broke over the whale's brow as he closed on us at ten or twelve knots. His approach was unwavering. I wondered out loud to my companion if they were aware on the bridge of our collision course. The whale surged past suddenly to port, crashing across our bow wave. I turned around—the mate shrugged from the superstructure several hundred feet away: who knows? The retired captain had not moved. He had not loosened the tenacious grip he had on the ship's rail. He slowly began to tell me a story about a convoy in the North Atlantic in 1942, the night they were torpedoed.

If we are to locate animals again at the complicated ethical and conceptual level of our ancestors, where they seem to have such a bearing on our state of mental health, we must decide what obligations and courtesies we will be bound by. The hunting contracts of our ancestors are no longer appropriate, just as their insight into natural history is no longer superior to our own at every point. These are to be new contracts. They must represent a new decorum, born of our aboriginal attachment to ancestral landscapes, our extraordinary learning, and the evolution of our culture from Altamira and Lascaux to the chambers of Washington, D.C. and the corridors of the Metropolitan Museum of Art.

Enormous as these steps are to contemplate, we seem in diverse ways to have firm hold of a beginning. The best of our books and films reflect a wider-than-Western, wider-than-purely-scientific, more-than-utilitarian view of animals. More philosophers are at work in a scholarly remodeling of Western philosophy in this area. And some people choose now to vacation among snow geese in northern California or among egrets and roseate spoonbills in Florida, as well as among the pyramids, or creations of the Medici.   21

However new agreements are drawn up, they must reflect as the old ones did an atmosphere of mutual regard, some latitude for mystery, and a sense of hope. As a European people we have taken great intellectual risks and made at various times penetrating insights—Leibnitz's calculus, Darwin's theory of natural selection, Heisenberg's uncertainty principle, Levi-Strauss's anthropology. We have in common with all other people in the world an understanding of how animals inform our intellectual, physical, aesthetic, and spiritual lives. From this reservoir of knowledge and sensitivity we could hope to forge a new covenant, fiercely honest, with other creatures.   22

In the time I have spent with native peoples in North America I have observed a deceptively simple event—how superstition, a slight, seemingly irrational prohibition, will be used to undercut arrogance in a young, headstrong hunter. To see it once is to be reminded forever that all life is a great gamble; wisdom is not simply erudition; and to behave in an irrational manner can, in fact, be life-enhancing. We tore up the animal contracts when the animals got in the way of our agriculture, our husbandry, and our science. We are now tearing up and rewriting our contracts with native peoples, because they block our political and industrial development. We cannot keep doing this. We will find ourselves with a false and miserable existence, a hollow probity, isolated far from our roots.   23

We will never find a way home until we find a way to look the caribou, the salmon, the lynx, and the white-throated sparrow in the face, without guile, with no plan of betrayal. We have to decide, again, after a long hiatus, how we are going to behave. We have to decide again to be impeccable in our dealings with the elements of our natural history.   24

QUESTIONS FOR DISCUSSION AND WRITING

1. Why did we tear up our "original contracts" (par. 6) with animals? On what qualities or actions was it based? How will the new "contract" Lopez would have us create with animals be similar to and/or different from that original? How will it be similar to and/or different from other "contracts" we establish in our lives?

2. What does Lopez have to say about the function and meaning of zoos in modern culture? Based upon what Lopez says, and upon inferences you draw from his essay, what would the "fate of zoos" (par. 6) be if we were to repair our "original contracts" with animals?

3. According to Lopez, in what sense (or senses) are we "isolated" from animals? What does Lopez mean when he says that this isolation leaves us "mysteriously bereaved" (par. 14), or when he ties our ability to locate animals again to "our state of mental health" (par. 20)?

JOHN MCPHEE

The author of more than twenty-five works of nonfiction, John McPhee (b. 1931) writes about topics ranging from basketball to oranges to geology. The common thread in these topics, as McPhee claims, is that "most of them originate when they strike an echo from my earlier experience." Whatever the topic, McPhee's writing is marked by the careful use of detail and extensive research. Through this detail he brings to life little-known people and worlds. The people in McPhee's books, driven by the desire to do something well, attend carefully to craft and work extremely hard. For whatever reason, they have a mission that gives meaning to all that they do. The places McPhee writes about are often worlds of great natural beauty, whether they be the pine barrens of central New Jersey or the wilds of Alaska.

The central character of Encounters with the Archdruid *(1971) is David Brower, the archdruid of the title. The onetime executive director of the Sierra Club, Brower helped build the club and then was forced out for his unwillingness to compromise on a variety of issues. The book describes Brower's encounters with three people, all of whom want to develop the wilderness in some way that Brower finds inappropriate. The excerpt given here is from the last encounter, that with Floyd E. Dominy, the U.S. commissioner of reclamation. The excerpt leaves out a long section that includes a discussion of Lake Powell, the lake the Monkey Wrench Gang would have emptied if they had succeeded in blowing up Glen Canyon Dam.*

From *Encounters with the Archdruid*

Floyd Elgin Dominy raises beef cattle in the Shenandoah Valley. Observed there, hand on a fence, his eyes surveying his pastures, he does not look particularly Virginian. Of middle height, thickset, somewhat bandy-legged, he appears to have been lifted off a horse with block and tackle. He wears bluejeans, a white-and-black striped shirt, and leather boots with heels two inches high. His belt buckle is silver and could not be covered over with a playing card. He wears a string tie that is secured with a piece of petrified dinosaur bone. On his head is a white Stetson. 1

Thirty-five years ago, Dominy was a county agent in the rangelands of northeastern Wyoming. He could not have come to his job there at a worse time. The Great Drought and the Great Depression had coincided, and the people of the county were destitute. They were not hungry—they could shoot antelope and deer—but they were destitute. Their livestock, with black tongues and protruding ribs, were dying because of lack of water. Dominy, as the agent not only of Campbell County but of the fed- 2 eral government, was empowered to pay eight dollars a head for these cattle—many thousands of them—that were all but decaying where they stood. He paid the eight dollars and shot the cattle.

Dominy was born on a farm in central Nebraska, and all through his youth his family and the families around them talked mainly of the vital weather. They lived close to the hundredth meridian, where, in a sense more fundamental than anything resulting from the events of United States history, the West begins. East of the hundredth meridian, there is enough rain to support agriculture, and west of it there generally is not. The Homestead Act of 1862, in all its promise, did not take into account this ineluctable fact. East of the hundredth meridian, homesteaders on their hundred and sixty acres of land were usually able to fulfill the dream that had been legislated for them. To the west, the odds against them were high. With local exceptions, there just was not enough water. The whole region between the hundredth meridian and the Rocky Mountains was at that time known as the Great American Desert. Still beyond the imagination were the ultramontane basins where almost no rain fell at all.

3

Growing up on a farm that had been homesteaded by his grandfather in the eighteen-seventies, Dominy often enough saw talent and energy going to waste under clear skies. The situation was marginal. In some years, more than twenty inches of rain would fall and harvests would be copious. In others, when the figure went below ten, the family lived with the lament that there was no money to buy clothes, or even sufficient food. These radical uncertainties were eventually removed by ground-water development, or reclamation—the storage of what water there was, for use in irrigation. When Dominy was eighteen years old, a big thing to do on a Sunday was to get into the Ford, which had a rumble seat, and go out and see the new dam. In his photo album he put pictures of reservoirs and irrigation projects. ("It was impressive to a dry-land farmer like me to see all that water going down a ditch toward a farm.") Eventually, he came to feel that there would be, in a sense, no West at all were it not for reclamation.

4

In Campbell County, Wyoming, the situation was not even marginal. This was high, dry country, suitable only for free-ranging livestock, not for farming. In the best of years, only about fourteen inches of rain might fall. "Streams ran water when the snow melted. Otherwise, the gulches were dry. It was the county with the most towns and the fewest people, the most rivers with the least water, and the most cows with the least milk in the world." It was, to the eye, a wide, expansive landscape with beguiling patterns of perspective. Its unending buttes, flat or nippled, were spaced out to the horizons like stone chessmen. Deer and antelope moved among them in herds, and on certain hilltops cairns marked the graves of men who had hunted buffalo. The herbage was so thin that forty acres of range

5

could reasonably support only one grazing cow. Nonetheless, the territory had been homesteaded, and the homesteaders simply had not received from the federal government enough land for enough cattle to give them financial equilibrium as ranchers, or from the sky enough water to give them a chance as farmers. They were going backward three steps for each two forward. Then the drought came.

"Nature is a pretty cruel animal. I watched the people there—I mean good folk, industrious, hardworking, frugal—compete with the rigors of nature against hopeless odds. They would ruin their health and still fail." Without waiting for approval from Cheyenne or Washington, the young county agent took it upon himself to overcome nature if the farmers and ranchers could not. He began up near Recluse, on the ranch of a family named Oedekoven, in a small bowl of land where an intermittent stream occasionally flowed. With a four-horse Fresno—an ancestral bulldozer— he moved earth and plugged the crease in the terrain where the water would ordinarily run out and disappear into the ground and the air. He built his little plug in the classic form of the earth-fill dam—a three-for-one slope on the water side and two-for-one the other way. More cattle died, but a pond slowly filled, storing water. The pond is still there, and so is Oedekoven, the rancher.

For two and a half years, Dominy lived with his wife and infant daugh- ter in a stone dugout about three miles outside Gillette, the county seat. For light they used a gasoline lantern. For heat and cooking they had a coal-burning stove. Dominy dug the coal himself out of a hillside. His wife washed clothes on a board. On winter mornings when the temperature was around forty below zero, he made a torch with a rag and a stick, soaked it in kerosene, lighted it, and put it under his car. When the car was warm enough to move, Dominy went off to tell ranchers and farmers about the Corn-Hog Program ("Henry Wallace slaughtering piglets to raise the price of ham"), the Wheat Program (acreage control), or how to build a dam. "Campbell County was my kingdom. When I was twenty- four years old, I was king of the God-damned county." He visited Soda Well, Wild Cat, Teckla, Turnercrest—single-family post offices widely spaced—or he followed the farmers and ranchers into the county seat of the county seat, Jew Jake's Saloon, where there was a poker game that never stopped and where the heads of moose, deer, elk, antelope, and bighorn sheep looked down on him and his subjects, feet on the rail at 9 A.M. Dominy had his first legitimate drink there. The old brass rail is gone—and so is Dominy—but the saloon looks just the same now, and the boys are still there at 9 A.M.

There was an orange scoria butte behind Dominy's place and an alfalfa field in front of it. Rattlesnakes by the clan came out of the butte in the spring, slithered around Dominy's house, and moved on into the alfalfa

6

7

8

for the summer. In September, the snakes headed back toward the butte. Tomatoes were ripe in Dominy's garden, and whenever he picked some he first took a hoe and cleared out the rattlesnakes under the vines. Ranchers got up at four in the morning and sometimes Dominy was outside honking his horn to wake them. He wanted them to come out and build dams—dams, dams, dams. "I had the whole county stirred up. We were moving! Stockpond dam and reservoir sites were supposed to be inspected first by Forest Service rangers, but who knows when they would have come? I took it upon myself to ignore these pettifogging minutiae." Changing the face of the range, he polka-dotted it with ponds. Dominy and the ranchers and farmers built a thousand dams in one year, and when they were finished there wasn't a thirsty cow from Jew Jake's Saloon to the Montana Border. "Christ, we did more in that county in one year than any other county in the country. That range program really put me on the national scene."

• • •

In the view of conversationalists, there is something special about dams, something—as conservation problems go—that is disproportionately and metaphysically sinister. The outermost circle of the Devil's world seems to be a moat filled mainly with DDT. Next to it is a moat of burning gasoline. Within that is a ring of pinheads each covered with a million people—and so on past phalanxed bulldozers and bicuspid chain saws into the absolute epicenter of Hell on earth, where stands a dam. The implications of the dam exceed its true level in the scale of environmental catastrophes. Conservationists who can hold themselves in reasonable check before new oil spills and fresh megalopolises mysteriously go insane at even the thought of a dam. The conservation movement is a mystical and religious force, and possibly the reaction to dams is so violent because rivers are the ultimate metaphors of existence, and dams destroy rivers. Humiliating nature, a dam is evil—placed and solid.   9

"I hate all dams, large and small," David Brower informs an audience.   10

A voice from the back of the room asks, "Why are you conservationists always against things?"   11

"If you are against something, you are for something," Brower answers. "If you are against a dam, you are for a river."   12

When Brower was a small boy in Berkeley, he used to build dams in Strawberry Creek, on the campus of the University of California, piling up stones in arcs convex to the current, backing up reservoir pools. Then he would kick the dams apart and watch the floods that returned Strawberry Creek to its free-flowing natural state. When Brower was born—in 1912 —there was in the Sierra Nevada a valley called Hetch Hetchy that paralleled in shape, size, and beauty the Valley of the Yosemite. The two val-   13 leys lay side by side. Both were in Yosemite National Park, which had been established in 1890. Yet within three decades—the National Park notwithstanding—the outlet of Hetch Hetchy was filled with a dam and the entire valley was deeply flooded. Brower was a boy when the dam was being built. He remembers spending his sixth birthday in the hills below Hetch Hetchy and hearing stories of the battle that had been fought over it, a battle that centered on the very definition of conservation. Should it mean preservation of wilderness or wise and varied use of land? John Muir, preservationist, founder of the young Sierra Club, had lost this bitter and, as it happened, final struggle of his life. It had been a battle that split the Sierra Club in two. Fifty-five years later, the Sierra Club would again divide within itself, and the outcome of the resulting battle would force the resignation of its executive director, David Brower, whose un-surprising countermove would be to form a new organization and name it for John Muir.

Not long after Brower's departure from the Sierra Club and his found-ing of the John Muir Institute, I went to Hetch Hetchy with him and walked along the narrow top of the dam, looking far down one side at the Tuolumne River, emerging like a hose jet from the tailrace, and in the other direction out across the clear blue surface of the reservoir, with its high granite sides—imagining the lost Yosemite below. The scene was bizarre and ironic, or so it seemed to me. Just a short distance across the peaks to the south of us was the Yosemite itself, filled to disaster with cars and people, tens of thousands of people, while here was the Yosemite's natural twin, filled with water. Things were so still at Hetch Hetchy that a wildcat walked insolently across the road near the dam and didn't even look around as he moved into the woods. And Brower—fifty-six years old and unshakably the most powerful voice in the conservation movement in his country—walked the quiet dam. "It was not needed when it was built, and it is not needed now," he said. "I would like to see it taken down, and watch the process of recovery." 14

During the years when Brower was developing as a conservation-ist, many of his most specific and dramatic personal accomplishments had to do with proposed dams. Down the tiers of the Western states, there are any number of excellent damsites that still contain free-flowing rivers be-cause of David Brower—most notably in the immense, arid watershed of the Colorado. Anyone interested, for whatever reason, in the study of water in the West will in the end concentrate on the Colorado, wildest of rivers, foaming, raging, rushing southward—erratic, headlong, incongru-ous in the desert. The Snake, the Salmon, the upper Hudson—all the other celebrated white torrents—are not in the conversation if the topic is the Colorado. This is still true, although recently (recently in the long span of things, actually within the past forty years) the Colorado has in places 15 been subdued. The country around it is so dry that Dominy's county in Wyoming is a rain forest by comparison. The states of the basin need water, and the Colorado is where the water is. The familiar story of contention for water rights in the Old West—Alan Ladd shooting it out with Jack Palance over some rivulet God knows where—has its mother narrative in the old and continuing story of rights to the waters of the Colorado. The central document is something called the Colorado River Compact, in which the basin is divided in two, at a point close to the Utah-Arizona line. The states of the Upper Basin are allowed to take so much per year. The Lower Basin gets approximately an equal share. And something gratuitous is passed on to Mexico. The Colorado lights and slakes Los Angeles. It irrigates Arizona. The odd thing about it is that all its writhings and foamings and spectacular rapids lead to nothing. The river rises in the Rockies, thunders through the canyons, and is so used by mankind that when it reaches the Gulf of California, fourteen hundred miles from its source, it literally trickles into the sea. The flow in the big river and in its major tributaries—the Green, the Yampa, the Escalante, the San Juan, the Little Colorado—is almost lyrically erratic, for the volume can vary as much as six hundred per cent from one year to the next. The way to control that, clearly enough, is storage, and this is accomplished under programs developed and administered by the federal Bureau of Reclamation. The Bureau of Reclamation, all but unknown in the American East, is the patron agency of the American West, dispenser of light, life, and water to thirty million people whose gardens would otherwise be dust. Most of the civil servants in the Bureau are Westerners—from the dry uplands as well as the deserts of the Great Basin. They have lived in the problem they are solving, and they have a deep sense of mission. There are many people in the Bureau of Reclamation—perhaps all nine thousand of them—who hope to see the Colorado River become a series of large pools, one stepped above another, from the Mexican border to the Rocky Mountains, with the headwaters of each succeeding lake lapping against the tailrace of a dam. The river and its tributaries have long since been thoroughly surveyed, and throughout the basic damsites of high quality and potentiality stand ready for river diversion, blast excavation, and concrete. Three of these sites are particularly notable here. One is near the juncture of the Green and the Yampa, close to the Utah-Colorado border. The two others are in northern Arizona—in the Grand Canyon. A fourth site would belong in this special list if it were still just a site, but a dam is actually there, is northernmost Arizona, in Glen Canyon. David Brower believes that the dam in Glen Canyon represents the greatest failure of his life. He cannot think of it without melancholy, for he sincerely believes that its very existence is his fault. He feels that if he had been more aware, if he had more adequately prepared himself for his own kind of mission, the dam would not be there. Its gates closed in 1963, and it began backing up water a hundred and eighty-six miles into Utah. The reservoir is called Lake Powell, and it covers country that Brower himself came to know too late. He made his only trips there—float trips on the river with his children—before the gates were closed but after the dam, which had been virtually unopposed, was under construction. Occasionally, in accompaniment to the talks he gives around the country, Brower shows an elegiac film about Glen Canyon, "the place no one knew." That was the trouble, he explains. No one knew what was there. Glen Canyon was one of the two or three remotest places in the United States—far from the nearest road, a hundred and twenty-five miles from the nearest railhead. The film records that the river canyon and its great trellis of side canyons was a deep and sometimes dark world of beauty, where small streams had cut gorges so profound and narrow that people walking in them were in cool twilight at noon, and where clear plunges of water dropped into pools surrounded with maidenhair fern in vaulted grottoes with names like Cathedral in the Desert, Mystery Canyon, Music Temple, Labyrinth Canyon. With all their blue-and-gold walls and darkly streaked water-drip tapestries, these places are now far below the surface of Lake Powell. "Few people knew about these canyons," Brower says quietly. "No one else will ever know what they were like."

The lost worlds of Utah notwithstanding, if conservationists were to   16 label their heroes in the way the English label their generals, David Brower would be known as Brower of the Colorado, Brower of the Grand Canyon. In the early nineteen-fifties, he fought his first major campaign—in his capacity as the first executive director of the Sierra Club—against the dam that the Bureau of Reclamation was about to build near the juncture of the Green and the Yampa. The reservoir would have backed water over large sections of Dinosaur National Monument. In the view of Brower, the Sierra Club, and conservationists generally, the integrity of the National Park system was at stake. The Dinosaur Battle, as it is called, was a milestone in the conservation movement. It was, to begin with, the greatest conservation struggle in half a century—actually, since the controversies that involved the damming of Hetch Hetchy and led to the debates that resulted in the creation, in 1916, of the National Park Service. The Dinosaur Battle is noted as the first time that all the scattered interests of modern conservation—sportsmen, ecologists, wilderness preservers, park advocates, and so forth—were drawn together in a common cause. Brower, more than anyone else, drew them together, fashioning the coalition, assembling witnesses. With a passing wave at the aesthetic argument, he went after the Bureau of Reclamation with facts and figures. He challenged the word of its engineers and geologists that the damsite was a sound one, he suggested that cliffs would dissolve and there would be a tremendous and cataclysmic dam failure there, and he went after the basic mathematics underlying the Bureau's proposals and uncovered embarrassing errors. All this was accompanied by flanking movements of intense publicity—paid advertisements, a film, a book—envisioning a National Monument of great scenic, scientific, and cultural value being covered with water. The Bureau protested that the conservationists were exaggerating—honing and bending the truth—but the Bureau protested without effect. Conservationists say that the Dinosaur victory was the birth of the modern conservation movement—the turning point at which conservation became something more than contour plowing. There is no dam at the confluence of the Green and the Yampa. Had it not been for David Brower, a dam would be there. A man in the public-relations office of the Bureau of Reclamation one day summed up the telling of the story by saying, "Dave won, hands down."

There are no victories in conservation, however. Brower feels that he   17
can win nothing. There is no dam at the Green and the Yampa now, but in 2020 there may be. "The Bureau of Reclamation engineers are like beavers," he says. "They can't stand the sight of running water." Below the Utah-Arizona border, in Marble Gorge, a part of the Grand Canyon, there is likewise no dam. The story is much the same. The Bureau of Reclamation had the dam built on paper, ready to go. A battle followed, and Brower won, hands down. In the Lower Granite Gorge, another part of the Grand Canyon, there is also no dam, and for the same reason. These Grand Canyon battles were the bitterest battles of all. The Bureau felt that Brower capitalized on literary hyperbole and the mystic name of the canyon. He implied, they said, that the dams were going to fill the Grand Canyon like an enormous bathtub, and that the view from the north rim to the south rim would soon consist of a flat expanse of water. Brower's famous advertising campaigns reached their most notable moment at this time. He placed full-page ads in *The New York Times* and the *San Francisco Chronicle,* among other places, under the huge headline "SHOULD WE ALSO FLOOD THE SISTINE CHAPEL SO TOURISTS CAN GET NEARER THE CEILING?" Telegrams flooded Congress, where the battle was decided. The Bureau cried foul, saying that it was intending to inundate only a fraction of one per cent of what Brower was suggesting. The Internal Revenue Service moved in and took away from the Sierra Club the tax-deductibility of funds contributed to it. Contributions to lobbying organizations are not tax-deductible, and the ads were construed as lobbying. The Sierra Club has never recovered its contributions-deductible status, but within the organization it is felt—by Brower's enemies as well as his friends— that the Grand Canyon was worth it. There are no dams in the Grand Canyon, and in the Bureau of Reclamation it is conceded that there will not be for at least two generations. The defeat of the high dams is frankly

credited, within the Bureau, to David Brower. "He licked us." "He had all the emotions on his side." "He did it singlehanded."

Popular assumptions to the contrary, no federal bureau is completely faceless—and, eyeball to eyeball with David Brower, there was a central and predominant figure on the other side of these fights, marshalling his own forces, battling in the rooms of Congress and in the canyon lands of the West for his profound and lifelong belief in the storage of water. This was the Bureau's leader—Floyd E. Dominy, United States Commissioner of Reclamation.

18

• • •

In the District of Columbia, in the labyrinthine fastnesses of the Department of the Interior, somewhere above Sport Fisheries and Wildlife and beyond the Office of Saline Water, there is a complex of corridors lined with murals of enormous dams. This is Reclamation, and these are its monuments: Flaming Gorge Dam, Hungry Horse Dam, Hoover Dam, Glen Canyon Dam, Friant Dam, Shasta Dam, Vallecito Dam, Grand Coulee Dam. I remember the day that I first saw these murals. In the moist and thermoelectric East, they seemed exotic, but hardly more so than the figure to whom the corridors led, the man in the innermost chamber of the maze. The white Stetson was on a table near the door. Behind a magisterial desk sat the Commissioner, smoking a big cigar. "Dominy," he said, shaking hands. "Sit down. I'm a public servant. I don't have any secrets from anybody."

19

He wore an ordinary Washington suit, but capital pallor was not in his face—a hawk's face, tanned and leathery. He had dark hair and broad shoulders, and he seemed a big man—bigger than his height and weight would indicate—and powerful but not forbidding. "Many people have said of me that I never meet a stranger," he said. "I like people. I like taxi-drivers and pimps. They have their purpose. I like Dave Brower, but I don't think he's the sanctified conservationist that so many people think he is. I think he's a selfish preservationist, for the few. Dave Brower hates my guts. Why? Because I've *got* guts. I've tangled with Dave Brower for many years."

20

On a shelf behind Dominy's desk, in the sort of central and eye-catching position that might be reserved for a shining trophy, was a scale model of a bulldozer. Facing each other from opposite walls were portraits of Richard M. Nixon and Hoover Dam. Nixon's jowls, in this milieu, seemed even more trapeziform than they usually do. They looked as if they, too, could stop a river. Seeing that my attention had been caught by these pictures, Dominy got up, crossed the room, and stood with reverence and devotion before the picture of Hoover Dam. He said, "When we built that, we—Americans—were the only people who had ever tried to

21

put a high dam in a big river." He said he remembered as if it were his birthday the exact date when he had first seen—as it was then called—Boulder Dam. He had taken a vacation from Campbell County, Wyoming, and driven, with his wife, into the Southwest, and on January 2, 1937, reached the Arizona-Nevada border and got his first view of the dam as he rounded a curve in the road descending toward the gorge of the Colorado. "There she was," he said, looking at the picture in his office. "The first major river plug in the world. Joseph of Egypt learned to store food against famine. So we in the West had learned to store water." He went on to say that he felt sure that—subconsciously, at least—the outline of his career had been formed at that moment. He had begun by building dams seven feet high, and he would one day build dams seven hundred feet high.

The rancher Fred Oedekoven, on whose place Dominy built his first 22 dam, is nearly eighty years old. A tall man, bent slightly forward, he lives in a peeled-log house on the land he homesteaded when he was twenty. I met him once, when I was in the county, and talked with him in the sitting room of his house. Two pictures hung on the walls. One was of Jesus Christ. The other was the familiar calendar scene of the beautiful lake in Jackson Hole, Wyoming, with the Grand Tetons rising in the background. Jackson Lake, as it is called, was built by the Bureau of Reclamation. "When Dominy come here, he took aholt," Oedekoven said. "I hated to see him go. They wanted him to go to Washington, D.C., to go on this water-facilities program, and I advised him to do it, for the advancement. He really clumb up in life."

Dominy had stayed up there as well, becoming the longest-running 23 commissioner in the Department of the Interior. Appointed by Eisenhower, he adapted so well to the indoor range that he was able to keep his position—always "at the pleasure of the President, without term of office"—through two Democratic Administrations, and now he was, in his words, "carrying the Nixon hod." He winked, sat down on the edge of his desk, and pronounced his absorbing code: "Never once have I made a decision against my will if it was mine to make." He had learned to plant creative ideas in senators' and congressmen's minds ("Based on your record, sir, we assume ... "), when to be a possum, and when to spring like a panther (" 'You get out of my office,' I said. The average bureaucrat would have been shaking, but I wasn't the least bit scared. No member of Congress is going to make me jump through hoops. I've never lost my cool in government work unless I thought it was to my advantage"). He had given crucial testimony against the proposed Rampart Dam, on the Yukon River, arguing that it was too much for Alaska's foreseeable needs; Rampart Dam would have flooded an area the size of Lake Erie, and Dominy's testimony defeated it. He had argued for federal—as opposed to private—power lines leading away from his big dams, thus irritating the special interests of senators and congressmen from several states. "I have been a controversial bastard for many years," he explained, lighting another cigar. Dominy knew his business, though, and he could run a budget of two hundred and forty-five million dollars as if he were driving a fast bus. He had cut down the Bureau's personnel from seventeen thousand to ten thousand. And he had built his stupendous dams. On the wall of his office there was also a picture of Dominy—a bold sketch depicting his head inside a mighty drop of water. It seemed more than coincidence that in an age of acronyms his very initials were FED.

Dominy switched on a projector and screened the rough cut of a movie 24 he had had prepared as an antidote to the Sierra Club's filmed elegy to the inundated canyons under Lake Powell. Dominy's film was called "Lake Powell, Jewel of the Colorado," and over an aerial shot of its blue fjords reaching into the red desert a narrator said, "Through rock and sand, canyon and cliff, through the towering formations of the sun-drenched desert, the waters of the Colorado River pause on their way to the sea." Water skiers cut wakes across the water.

"Too many people think of environment simply as untrammelled 25 nature," Dominy commented. "Preservation groups claim we destroyed this area because we made it accessible to man. Six hundred thousand people a year use that lake now."

The film showed a Navajo on horseback in a blazing-red silk shirt. "Into 26 his land came Lake Powell, which he has woven into his ancient ways," said the narrator.

"Right," said Dominy. "Now people can fish, swim, water-ski, sun- 27 bathe. Can't you imagine going in there with your family for a weekend, getting away from everybody? But Mr. Brower says we destroyed it."

"The canyon lay isolated, remote, and almost unknown to the outside 28 world," said the narrator, "until"—and at that moment a shot of the red walls of Glen Canyon came on the screen, and suddenly there was a great blast and the walls crumbled in nimbuses of dust. Ike had pressed a button. Bulldozers followed, and new roads, and fifty thousand trucks. Cut to dedication of dam, ten years later. "I am proud to dedicate such a significant and beautiful manmade resource," said Lady Bird Johnson. "I am proud that man is here."

Dominy blew smoke into the scene as Lady Bird dissolved. "The need 29 for films of this kind, for public information, is great, because of those who would have all forests and rivers remain pristine," he said. "People ignore facts and play on emotions."

There were more scenes of the blue, still water, lapping at high sand- 30 stone cliffs—panoramic vistas of the reservoir. An airplane now appeared over the lake—twin-engine, cargo. "Watch this," Dominy said. "Just watch this." What appeared to be a contrail paid out behind the plane—a long, cloudy sleeve that widened in the air. "Trout!" Dominy said. "Trout! Those are fingerling trout. That's how we put them in the lake."

Montages of shots showed the half-filled lateral canyons—Forgotten Canyon, Cascade Canyon, Reflection Canyon, Mystery Canyon—with people swimming in them, camping beside them, and singing around fires. "In this land, each man must find his own meanings," said the narrator. "Lake Powell, Jewel of the Colorado, offers the opportunity." 31

"Reclamation is the father of putting water to work for man—irrigation, hydropower, flood control, recreation," Dominy said as he turned on the lights. "Let's *use* our environment. Nature changes the environment every day of our lives—why shouldn't *we* change it? We're part of nature. Just to give you a for-instance, we're cloud-seeding the Rockies to increase the snowpack. We've built a tunnel under the Continental Divide to send water toward the Pacific that would have gone to the Atlantic. The challenge to man is to do and save what is good but to permit man to progress in civilization. Hydroelectric power doesn't pollute water and it doesn't pollute air. You don't get any pollution out of my dams. The unregulated Colorado was a son of a bitch. It wasn't any good. It was either in flood or in trickle. In addition to creating economic benefits with our dams, we regulate the river, and we have created the sort of river Dave Brower dreams about. Who are the best conservationists—doers or preservationists? I can't talk to preservationists. I can't talk to Brower, because he's so God-damned ridiculous. I can't even reason with the man. I once debated with him in Chicago, and he was shaking with fear. Once, after a hearing on the Hill, I accused him of garbling facts, and he said, 'Anything is fair in love and war.' For Christ's sake. After another hearing one time, I told him he didn't know what he was talking about, and said I wished I could show him, I wished he would come with me to the Grand Canyon someday, and he said, 'Well, save some of it, and maybe I will.' I had a steer out on my farm in the Shenandoah reminded me of Dave Brower. Two years running, we couldn't get him into the truck to go to market. He was an independent bastard that nobody could corral. That son of a bitch got into that truck, busted that chute, and away he went. So I just fattened him up and butchered him right there on the farm. I shot him right in the head and butchered him myself. That's the only way I could get rid of the bastard." 32

"Commissioner," I said, "if Dave Brower gets into a rubber raft going down the Colorado River, will you get in it, too?" 33

"Hell, yes," he said. "Hell, yes." 34

• • •

Mile 156. Already the talk is of Lava Falls, which lies twenty-four miles ahead but has acquired fresh prominence in the aftermath of Upset. 35

On the table of rated rapids—copies of which nearly everyone is at the moment studying—categories run from "Riffle" through "Heavy" to "Not Recommended." Upset was "Heavy" rapid, like Deubendorff. In the "Not Recommended" category there is only Lava Falls.

"Do you agree with that, Jerry?"   36

Sanderson grins with amusement, and speaks so slowly he seems wist-   37
ful. "It's the granddaddy of them all," he says. "There's a big drop, and a
lot of boulders, and several holes like the one at Upset. You have to look
the rapid over carefully, because the holes move."

In the stillness of a big eddy, the raft pauses under an overhanging cliff.   38
Lava Falls fades in the conversation. Twenty-four miles is a lot of country.
Through a cleft that reaches all the way down through the overhanging
cliff a clear green stream is flowing into the river. The cleft is so narrow
that the stream appears to be coming straight out of the sandstone.
Actually, it meanders within the cliff and is thus lost to view. The water is
so clear that it sends a pale-green shaft into the darker Colorado. The big
river may no longer be red with silt, but it carries enough to remain
opaque. In the small stream, the pebbles on the bottom are visible, mag-
nified, distinct. "Dive in," Brower suggests. "See where it goes."

Brower and I went into the stream and into the cliff. The current was   39
not powerful, coming through the rock, and the water was only four feet
deep. I swam, by choice—the water felt so good. It felt cool, but it must
have been about seventy-five degrees. It was cooler than the air. Within
the cliff was deep twilight, and the echoing sound of the moving water. A
bend to the right, a bend to the left, right, left—this stone labyrinth was a
crystal stream in it was moment enough, no matter where it ended, but
there lay beyond it a world that humbled the mind's eye. The walls
widened first into a cascaded gorge and then flared out to become the
ovate sides of a deep valley, into which the stream rose in tiers of pools
and waterfalls. Some of the falls were only two feet high, others four feet,
six feet. There were hundreds of them. The pools were as much as fifteen
feet deep, and the water in them was white where it plunged and foamed,
then blue in a wide circle around the plunge point, and pale green in the
outer peripheries. This was Havasu Canyon, the immemorial home of the
Havasupai, whose tribal name means "the people of the blue-green waters." We climbed from one pool to another, and swam across the pools,
and let the waterfalls beat down around our shoulders. Mile after mile, the
pools and waterfalls continued. The high walls of the valley were bright
red. Nothing grew on these dry and flaky slopes from the mesa rim down
about two-thirds of the way; then life began to show in isolated barrel cactus and prickly pear. The cacti thickened farther down, and below them
was riverine vegetation—green groves of oak and cottonwood, willows
and tamarisk, stands of cattail, tall grasses, moss, watercress, and maiden-

hair fern. The Havasupai have lived in this place for hundreds, possibly thousands, of years, and their population has remained stable. There are something like two hundred of them. They gather nuts on the canyon rim in winter and grow vegetables in the canyon in summer. They live about twelve miles up Havasu Creek from the Colorado. Moss covered the rocks around the blue-and-green pools. The moss on dry rock was soft and dense, and felt like broadloom underfoot. Moss also grew below the water's surface, where it was coated with travertine, and resembled coral. The stream was loaded with calcium, and this was the physical explanation of the great beauty of Havasu Canyon, for it was the travertine—crystalline calcium carbonate—that had both fashioned and secured the all but unending stairway of falls and pools. At the downstream lip of each plunge pool, calcium deposits had built up into natural dams, and these travertine dams were what kept Havasu Creek from running freely downhill. The dams were whitish tan, and so smooth and symmetrical that they might have been finished by a mason. They were two or three feet high. They sloped. Their crests were flat and smooth and with astonishing uniformity were about four inches thick from bank to bank. Brower looked up at the red canyon walls. He was sitting on the travertine, with one foot in a waterfall, and I was treading the green water below him. He said, "If Hualapai Dam had been built, or were ever built, this place where you are swimming would be at the bottom of a hundred feet of water." It was time to go back to the Colorado. I swam to the travertine dam at the foot of the pool, climbed up on it and dived into the pool below it, and swam across and dived again, and swam and dived—and so on for nearly two miles. Dominy was waiting below. "It's fabulous," he said. "I know every river canyon in the country, and this is the prettiest in the West."

• • •

Mile 171. Beside the minor rapids at Gateway Canyon, we stop, unload   40
the raft, and lay out our gear before settling down to drinks before dinner. Brower is just beyond earshot. Dominy asks me again, "What did Dave do during the war?"

I tell him all I happen to know—that Brower trained troops in climb-   41
ing techniques in West Virginia and Colorado, and that he later went with the 10th Mountain Division to Italy, where he won the Bronze Star.

Dominy contemplates the river. Brower goes to the water's edge and   42
dips his Sierra Club cup. He will add whiskey to the water. "Fast-moving water is a very satisfying sound," Dominy says to him. "There is nothing more soothing than the sound of running or falling water."

"The river talks to itself, Floyd. Those little whirls, the sucks and the   43
boils—they say things."

"I love to see white water, Dave. In all my trips through the West over   44 the years, I have found moving streams with steep drops to them the most scenic things of all."

Over the drinks, Brower tells him, "I will come out of this trip different   45
from when I came in. I am not in favor of dams, but I am in favor of Dominy. I can see what you have meant to the Bureau, and I am worried about what is going to happen there someday without you."

"No one will ever say that Dominy did not tell anyone and everyone   46
exactly what he thinks, Dave."

"I've never heard anything different, Floyd."   47

"And, I might say, I've never heard anything different about you."   48

"I needed this trip more than anyone else."   49

"You're God-damned right you did, with that white skin."   50

Dominy takes his next drink out of the Sierra Club cup. The bottle of   51
whiskey is nearly empty. Dominy goes far down into his briefcase and brings out another. It is Jim Beam. Dominy is fantastically loyal to Jim Beam. At his farm in Virginia a few weeks ago, he revived a sick calf by shooting it with a hypodermic syringe full of penicillin, condensed milk, and Jim Beam. Brower says he does not believe in penicillin.

"As a matter of fact, Dave Brower, I'll make a trip with you any time,   52
anywhere."

"Great," Brower mutters faintly.   53

"Up to this point, Dave, we've won a few and lost a few—each of us.   54
Each of us. Each of us. God damn it, everything Dave Brower does is O.K.—tonight. Dave, now that we've buried the hatchet, you've got to come out to my farm in the Shenandoah."

"Great."   55

To have a look at the map of the river, Dominy puts on Brower's   56
glasses. Brower's glasses are No. 22s off the counter of F. W. Woolworth in San Francisco. Dominy rolls the scroll back to the Upset Rapid.

"How come you didn't go through there, Dave?"   57

"I'm chicken."   58

"Are you going to go through Lava Falls?"   59

"No."   60

"No?"   61

"No, thank you. I'll walk."   62

Upstream from where we sit, we can see about a mile of straight river   63
between the high walls of the inner gorge, and downstream this corridor leads on to a bold stone portal. Dominy contemplates the scene. He says, "With Hualapai Dam, you'd really have a lake of water down this far."

"Yes. A hundred and sixty feet deep," notes Brower.   64

"It would be beautiful, and, like Lake Powell, it would be better for *all*   65
elements of society."

"There's another view, and I have it, and I suppose I'll die with it,   66

Floyd. Lake Powell is a drag strip for power boats. It's for people who won't do things except the easy way. The magic of Glen Canyon is dead. It has been vulgarized. Putting water in the Cathedral in the Desert was like urinating in the crypt of St. Peter's. I hope it never happens here."

"Look, Dave. I don't live in a God-damned apartment. I didn't grow up in a God-damned city. Don't give me the crap that you're the only man that understands these things. I'm a greater conservationist than you are, by far. I do things. I make things available to man. Unregulated, the Colorado River wouldn't be worth a good God damn to anybody. You conservationists are phony outdoorsmen. I'm sick and tired of a democracy that's run by a noisy minority. I'm fed up clear to my God-damned gullet. I had the guts to come out and fight you bastards. You're just a bunch of phonies and you'll stoop to any kind of God-damned argument. That's why I took my pictures. You were misleading the public about what would happen here. You gave the impression that the whole canyon was going to be inundated by the reservoir. Your weapon is emotion. You guys are just not very God-damned honorable in your fights." 67

"I had hoped things would not take this turn, Floyd, but you're wrong." 68

"Do you want to keep this country the way it is for a handful of people?" 69

"Yes, I do. Hualapai Dam is not a necessity. You don't even want the water." 70

"We mainly want the power head, but the dam would be part of the over-all storage project under the Colorado Compact." 71

"The Colorado Compact was not found on a tablet written on Mount Sinai. Hualapai Dam is not necessary, and neither was Glen Canyon. Glen Canyon Dam was built for the greater good of Los Angeles." 72

"You're too intelligent to believe that." 73

"You're too intelligent not to believe that." 74

"For Christ's sake, be objective, Dave. Be reasonable." 75

"Some of my colleagues make the error of trying to be reasonable, Floyd. Objectivity is the greatest threat to the United States today." 76

• • •

Mile 177. 9:45 A.M. The water is quite deep and serene here, backed up from the rapid. Lava Falls is two miles downstream, but we have long since entered its chamber of quiet. ¡ 77

"The calm before the storm," Brower says. 78

The walls of the canyon are black with lava—flows, cascades, and dikes of lava. Lava once poured into the canyon in this segment of the river. The river was here, much in its present form. It had long since excavated the canyon, for the volcanism occurred in relatively recent time. 79

Lava came up through the riverbed, out from the canyon walls, and even down over the rims. It sent the Colorado up in clouds. It hardened, and it formed a dam and backed water two hundred miles.

"If a lava flow were to occur in the Grand Canyon today, Brower and 80 the nature lovers would shout to high heaven that a great thing had happened," Dominy said, addressing everyone in the raft. "But if a man builds a dam to bring water and power to other men, it is called desecration. Am I right or wrong, Dave? Be honest."

"The lava dam of Quaternary time was eventually broken down by the 81 river. This is what the Colorado will do to the Dominy dams that are in it now or are ever built. It will wipe them out, recover its grade, and go on about its business. But by then our civilization and several others will be long gone."

We drift past an enormous black megalith standing in the river. For 82 eighty years, it was called the Niggerhead. It is the neck of a volcano, and it is now called Vulcan's Forge. We have a mile to go. Brower talks about the amazing size of the crystals on the canyon walls, the morning light in the canyon, the high palisades of columnar basalt. No one else says much of anything. All jokes have been cracked twice. We are just waiting, and the first thing we hear is the sound. It is a big, tympanic sound that increasingly fills the canyon. The water around us is dark-green glass. Five hundred yards. There it is. Lava Falls. It is, of course, a rapid, not a waterfall. There is no smooth lip. What we now see ahead of us at this distance appears to be a low whitewashed wall.

The raft touches the riverbank. Sanderson gets out to inspect the rapid, 83 and we go, too. We stand on a black ledge, in the roar of the torrent, and look at the water. It goes everywhere. From bank to bank, the river is filled with boulders, and the water smashes into them, sends up auroras of spray, curls thickly, and pounds straight down into bomb-crater holes. It eddies into pockets of lethal calm and it doubles back to hit itself. Its valleys are deeper and its hills are higher than in any other rapid in North America. The drop is prodigious—twenty-six feet in a hundred yards— but that is only half the story. Prospect Creek, rising black-walled like a coal chute across the river, has shoved enough rock in here to stop six rivers, and this has produced the preëminent rapid of the Colorado.

When Dominy stepped up on the ledge and into the immediacy of 84 LavaFalls, he shouted above the thunder, "Boy, that's a son of a bitch! Look at those *rocks!* See that hole over there? Jesus! Look at that one!"

Brower said, "Look at the way the water swirls. It's alive!" 85

The phys.-ed. teacher said, "Boy, that could tear the hell out of your 86 body."

Brower said, "Few come, but thousands drown." 87

Dominy said, "If I were Jerry, I'd go to the left and then try to move to 88 the right."

Lava protruded from the banks in jagged masses, particularly on the 89 right, and there was a boulder there that looked like an axe blade. Brower said, "I'd go in on the right and out on the left."

My own view was that the river would make all the decisions. I asked 90 Sanderson how he planned to approach what we saw there.

"There's only one way to do it," he said. "We go to the right." 91

The raft moved into the river slowly, and turned, and moved toward 92 the low white wall. A hundred yards. Seventy-five yards. Fifty yards. It seems odd, but I did not notice until just then that Brower was on the raft. He was, in fact, beside me. His legs were braced, his hands were tight on a safety rope, and his Sierra Club cup was hooked in his belt. The tendons in his neck were taut. His chin was up. His eyes looked straight down the river. From a shirt pocket Dominy withdrew a cigar. He lighted it and took a voluminous drag. We had remaining about fifteen seconds of calm water. He said, "I might bite an inch off the end, but I doubt it." Then we went into Lava Falls.

Water welled up like a cushion against the big boulder on the right, and 93 the raft went straight into it, but the pillow of crashing water was so thick that it acted on the raft like a great rubber fender between a wharf and a ship. We slid off the rock and to the left—into the craterscape. The raft bent like a V, flipped open, and shuddered forward. The little outboard— it represented all the choice we had—cavitated, and screamed in the air. Water rose up in tons through the bottom of the raft. It came in from the left, the right, and above. It felt great. It covered us, pounded us, lifted us, and heaved us scudding to the base of the rapid.

For a moment, we sat quietly in the calm, looking back. Then Brower 94 said, "The foot of Lava Falls would be two hundred and twenty-five feet beneath the surface of Lake Dominy."

Dominy said nothing. He just sat there, drawing on a wet, dead cigar. 95 Ten minutes later, however, in the dry and baking Arizona air, he struck a match and lighted the cigar again.

QUESTIONS FOR DISCUSSION AND WRITING

1. McPhee spends time carefully describing the formative influences on both Dominy and Brower. Dominy started his career helping ranchers control water with dams so they could survive in an arid place; Brower spent his sixth birthday in the Hetch Hetchy valley just before it was flooded and went on to fight successfully against a number of dams on the Colorado River. How much of the present positions of Dominy and Brower can be explained by these experiences, and how much can't?

2. Brower sees Dominy as a person who wants to destroy sacred places, like Havasu Canyon, and Dominy thinks Brower is an elitist who wants to keep most people from enjoying the wilderness. Lake Powell, which Dominy loves, now almost covers the Cathedral of the Desert, a canyon that was particularly beautiful, just as beautiful as Havasu Canyon. Yet, on the lake itself, thousands of people boat, picnic, explore, and enjoy nature in a way that would be impossible without the dam. If you could remove Glen Canyon Dam without harming anyone, would you do so?

3. If you were taking a trip in the wilderness, perhaps a raft trip down the Colorado, whom would you prefer for a companion, Dominy or Brower? With whom do you think you would get along better, and with whom would you have a better time? What is the relationship between your choice and your beliefs about preserving the wilderness?

CAROLYN MERCHANT

Carolyn Merchant (b. 1936) is professor of environmental history, philosophy, and ethics in the Department of Conservation and Resource Studies at the University of California, Berkeley. Merchant's first two books, The Death of Nature: Women, Ecology, and the Scientific Method *(1980) and* Ecological Revolutions: Nature, Gender, and Science *(1989), offer a radical rethinking of the way nature has been conceived in contemporary society. Both nature and women, Merchant contends, have been the subject of male domination, which means that the solutions to our ecological crisis cannot be separated from the struggle by women for social justice. In her most recent book,* Radical Ecology: The Search for a Livable World *(1990), Merchant outlines (and advocates for) what she calls the "new social vision" of radical ecological movements such as ecofeminism, ecowarriors, and Deep Ecology. Merchant argues that radical ecology in all its forms is a necessary response to the "crisis" in the industrialized world, a crisis whose roots are to be found in our most ancient and comfortable philosophical traditions. What interests Merchant is how these traditions have led us to see the destruction of nature as a logical and even necessary price of economic progress. As she prepares to argue that the "search for a livable world" will demand nothing less than an intellectual and economic revolution, Merchant opens her book with this uncompromising account of our current global ecological crisis.*

The Global Ecological Crisis

The world of the late twentieth century is experiencing a global ecological crisis, one that is both a product of past ecological and economic patterns and a challenge for the future. From Chernobyl radiation to the Gulf War oil spill; from tropical rainforest destruction to polar ozone holes; from alar in apples to toxics in water, the earth and all its life are in trouble. Industrial production accentuated by the global reproduction of population, has put stress on nature's capacity for the reproduction of life. Pollution and depletion are systematically interlinked on a scale not previously experienced on the planet.

As we approach the millennium of the twenty-first century, perceptions of planetary destruction and calls for the earth's renewal abound. Can planetary life sustain itself in the face of industrial assaults? How is the current environmental crisis in production manifested? How are the planet's

1

2

airs, waters, soils, and biota interconnected? How might life be restored to the planet? A new partnership between humans and nonhuman nature is needed.

During the past decade the dimensions of a global ecological crisis have become painfully visible. In January 1989, *Time* magazine's person of the year award went to "The Endangered Earth," graphically illustrated by sculptor Christo as a suffocating globe wrapped in plastic and bound with twine. With increasing public awareness of global problems, public concern has mounted. The Alaskan oil spill alerted millions to the tragic transformation of a pristine Alaskan shoreline surrounded by lush rainforest into black, motionless, silent beaches of dead birds, seals, sea otters, and contaminated waters devoid of sustenence for local fishers and their families. In June 1989, a *New York Times*/CBS poll found that an astonishing 80 percent of all Americans questioned overwhelmingly agreed with the statement: "Protecting the environment is so important that requirements and standards cannot be too high, and continuing environmental improvements must be made regardless of cost."

Air

Today the hot air of the "greenhouse gases" threatens atmospheric chemistry balances. As the amount of carbon dioxide and other gases in the atmosphere increases from the industrial processes and the burning of fossil fuels, global temperatures are predicted to rise from 3 to 10 degrees Fahrenheit over the next century. Perhaps the most widely-felt evidence of global warming was the intense hot weather experienced by Americans during the summer of 1988. "The greenhouse effect is already here and it will worsen," warned scientists and policy analysts at Congressional hearings held that summer. According to Senator Timothy Wirth, "The greenhouse effect is the most significant economic, political, environmental, and human problem facing the 21st century." Three countries, the United States (21 percent), the USSR (19 percent), and China (10 percent) together produce 50 percent of all carbon dioxide emissions. With the greenhouse effect, winters would become stormier, summers hotter and drier. Seas could rise one to three feet over the next half century; hurricanes would become more powerful as the oceans warm. Waterfront homes will be flooded, midwestern droughts will increase in severity, grain growing regions will move north, and whole forests and wild species will be lost. Although there is much debate over the timing of the effect, a series of measures to slow it have been recommended, such as stopping global deforestation, planting trees, conserving heating fuel, and shifting to alternative energy sources.

Ozone depletion is another global disruption caused by industrial   5
production. In 1985 scientists reported a hole in the ozone layer over the
Antarctic. As a result of worldwide concern, 24 countries meeting at
Montreal in 1987 agreed to reduce production of the prime culprit, chlorofluorocarbons (CFCs), by 35 percent by 1999. CFCs are used as refrigerator and air conditioner coolants, as primary components of styrofoam,
and as propellant gasses in spray cans (banned in the United States in the
1970s, but still used in other countries). Whenever we buy a hamburger
or a cup of coffee in a styrofoam container, whenever our automobile
air conditioner leaks, or we turn in an old refrigerator for a new one, we
are inadvertently contributing to upper atmosphere ozone depletion.
Alternatives to CFCs are now being sought, but much work needs to be
done by science, by Congress in regulating CFCs, and by all of us in
changing the habits of our everyday lives. These disruptions of the atmospheric balance of gases by industrial production are intimately connected to disruption of global waters.

Water

From high mountain lakes to wild rushing rivers, the waters of the   6
United States are threatened by acid rain. Beaches are inundated by solid
wastes; globules of oil float on the surface of even the remotest oceans.
Plastic wastes in the oceans are causing the deaths of upwards of 2 million
birds and 100,000 marine mammals a year. Dead and dying birds entangled in plastic six-pack rings appear on beaches every day. The plastic
rings will go on for another 450 years, outliving the generations they are
extinguishing. Seabirds, fish, turtles, and whales lunch on small plastic
pellets produced as wastes in the plastics industries. Diving birds and
mammals are entrapped in plastic drift nets 6 to 30 miles in length used
primarily by Japanese and other East Asian fishers. Seven hundred miles
of nets are lost each season in the Pacific ocean. When these nets escape
they go on trapping marine life until they sink under their own weight.
Global water pollution needs to be halted and water quality restored.

Soils

Soil erosion and pollution from insecticides with long lasting half-lives   7
are threatening croplands and ground water quality. In the United States
two billion tons of topsoil is being lost annually through wind and water
erosion, threatening one-third of our croplands. If allowed to continue
over the next fifty years, United States' grain production will sink to about
half of what it exported in 1980, affecting millions of people around the

world. In India, land has been used to feed people for over forty centuries, with only 5 to 10 percent of the surpluses leaving the local villages. According to conservationist Vandana Shiva, Green Revolution farming techniques have now replaced traditional methods, teaching Indian farmers "to forget about the hunger of the soil and the stomach and to go after their own hunger for profits." Soil conservation and sustainable agriculture based on the wisdom of traditional peoples need to be combined with many of the positive advances in twentieth-century agriculture.

Biota

Today, the reproduction of life itself is being aborted. in the words of 8 *Time* magazine, "the death of birth" poses another immense global threat to all nonhuman species. A National Science Foundation study predicts that a quarter of the earth's species of plants, animals, microbes, and fungi will become extinct over the next several years unless extraordinary measures are taken to protect the ecosystems in which they live. Only 1.4 million of the 5 to 10 million species of life in the world have ever been named. Increased efforts must be taken to identify them, understand their ecology, and to educate the public in the need for preservation. International agreements have been reached on halting some of the most visible threats. The United States and Europe have recently banned imports of ivory from the African elephant. Japan has reduced imports of some endangered species such as the Hawksbill Turtle used for exotic ornaments and wedding gifts. But changes in policies and practices may not be in time to preserve the lives of known endangered species, much less those not even identified.

Forests that absorb carbon dioxide and produce oxygen, linking air, 9 water, and biota in a unity, are disappearing at a rapid rate. Tropical forests, which cover 2.3 million square miles of the earth's surface, are disappearing at the rate of 100 acres a minute or more and the rate of destruction is increasing. If the destruction continues, it is predicted that little will be left by the year 2040. The United States imports enough timber from tropical rainforests each year to cover the state of West Virginia. In Central and Latin America, rainforests are being cut down to pasture cattle for the fast food industry. In Indonesia, 500,000 acres of rainforest have been converted to eucalyptus plantations to produce toilet paper for North America. Much of the rainforest being slashed in Malaysia is used by Japan to construct throwaway construction forms, boxes for shipping, and disposable chopsticks. In every inlet along the coasts of Papua New Guinea, Japanese ships anchor to receive timber, leaving behind slash as waste on beaches. Quoting Mahatma Gandhi at a June 1989 conference on "The Fate and Hope of the Earth" held in Managua, Nicaragua, Martin Khor of Indonesia admonished, "There are enough world resources for everyone's need, but not for everyone's greed."

In the United States, Pacific old-growth redwood and Douglas Fir   10 forests are threatened by logging for export to the Far East. Seventy percent of the total harvest of uncut logs are exported—enough for 37,000 jobs in the wood products industry. Through modernization over the past decade, labor-intensive lumber mills are being replaced by automation, reducing by one-third the number of jobs available. In the process, the Spotted Owl is threatened with extinction and loggers and millers with job losses. Trying to resolve complex problems such as these will require enormous sensitivity, as well as lifestyle changes on the part of northern hemisphere citizens.

Threats to the reproduction of nonhuman life are directly linked to   11 affects on human reproduction. Toxic chemicals range from factory emissions, smog, and radon in the air, to pesticides in the soil, to trichloroethylene in drinking water. According to environmentalist Barry Commoner, humans and other living things are being invaded by an immense number of toxic chemicals unknown to biological evolution. "An organic compound," he argues, "that does not occur in nature [is] one that has been rejected in the course of evolution as incompatible with living systems." Because of their toxicity, "they have a very high probability of interfering with living processes." Over the past thirty years the production of organic chemicals from petroleum has increased from about 75 billion pounds per year to over 350 billion. In 1986 concerns such as these led California citizens to pass Proposition 65, an anti-toxics initiative with a 63 percent vote. There are presently 242 chemicals on the state's list being examined for their risk of causing cancer or birth defects. Citizen actions, such as those being undertaken by the National Toxics Campaign, along with scientific research, are a vital part of the current effort to reduce toxics in the environment.

The global ecological crisis involves all levels of society—production,   12 reproduction, and worldviews—and differentially affects First, Second, and Third World peoples. The mixing and transferring of our planet's air, waters, soils, and biota that are publicized as global warming and ozone depletion are not solely the results of interacting physical, chemical, and biological systems. Such a scientific systems view ignores the linkages among processes of production, reproduction, consumption, depletion, and pollution that accompany human economies. Through commodity production and exchange, the rich soils, fossil fuels, minerals, and forests of the Third World end up in the First World as wastes in landfills and pollutants in rivers. Outlawed pesticides and toxic wastes from the First World make their way to the Third World for sale and disposal. When the price of oil rises in the Persian Gulf, First World consumers pay more at the pumps, but Third World tractors are idled and women walk an extra mile for cooking fuel. In First and Second World countries, production and consumption lead to overloaded ecological systems, while in Third World countries, resource extraction leads to exhausted and depleted lands. Economic development is uneven—centers of commerce and consumption toward which goods flow become "overdeveloped"; places on the periphery from which goods and resources flow remain "underdeveloped."

The relationships between ecology and production lead to the first 13 contradiction that constitutes the global ecological crisis. Human production systems put increasing stress on nonhuman nature through the biogeochemical cycles and energy exchanges that unify all ecological processes. As depletion and pollution accelerate, they exceed the resilience of nonhuman nature, severely undermining its capacity to recover from human-induced assaults. Systems of production, however, can be oriented toward basic subsistence, as they are in much of the Third World and indigenous cultures, or toward market exchange, as they are in First World capitalist economies and dependent Third World colonial economies. Different systems of production have different ecological impacts that result from historically different patterns of economic development.

Political Economy

The patterns of uneven development and their differential economic 14 and ecological effects are the products of a global market economy that has been emerging since the sixteenth century. The growth of a capitalist system in the European world was intimately connected to and dependent on a colonial system in the New World. As feudalism—based on the payment of goods and services to a lord by serfs bound to the land—broke down, a dynamic market system began to exploit both land and labor in more efficient ways. Mining and textile production were the first industries to be capitalized. Each expanded through the establishment of a company whose entrepreneurs pooled their wealth to take the risk of developing a mine, establishing a colony, or combining the operations of textile production under a single roof. The capitalists employed laborers who were paid in set wages from which they purchased their own food and clothing, rather than producing it from the land.

European capitalism expanded through the establishment of colonies 15 in the western and southern hemispheres that supplied both the natural resources and cheap labor that extracted them from the earth. The former hegemony of the Mediterranean world gave way to the new hegemony of the Atlantic. Triangular trading patterns established Europe as the center of manufactured goods, Africa as the source of slave labor, and the American colonies as the "inexhaustible" supply of natural resources. The oceans were charted, the new lands mapped, and the natural histories of the peoples, animals, plants, and minerals found there catalogued. European explorers and colonizers brought with them an ecological complex of diseases that devastated native peoples and livestock, crops, weeds, and varmints that invaded native lands. The colonies were maintained by force of arms, by economic dependency on trade items, by enslavement, and by religious ideologies as missionaries worked to supplant animistic religions with Judeo-Christian theologies.

Accumulation of economic surplus occurred as natural resources (or free raw materials) were extracted at minimum costs (minimum wages) and manufactured goods were sold at market value. This accumulation of economic surplus through mercantile expansion helped to fuel eighteenth and nineteenth century industrialization. Textiles and shoes, guns and ammunition, mechanized farming equipment, and standardized consumer products all depended on atomized replaceable parts and atomized replaceable laborers. Fewer people lived off the land by subsistence and more worked in cities fed by specialized market farmers. Since the period of Europe's industrial revolution (1750–1850) and North America's (1800–1900), no countries outside of those in the former Soviet bloc have been able to industrialize without economic assistance and dependency. 16

Today's global capitalist system is based on this same fundamental division between the industrialized or center economies of the First World and the underdeveloped or peripheral economies of the Third World. Unlike the industrialized nations the peripheral economies export low cost primary goods such as coffee, tobacco, sugar, jute, rubber, and minerals, and import luxury goods and military equipment for élite consumption. Mass consumer goods are produced through northern hemisphere capital (Western Europe, North America, and Japan) and southern hemisphere labor (Asia, Latin America, and Africa) for purchase by northern consumers and Third World élites. Instead of enslavement by force or theft of resources, neocolonialism uses economic investments and foreign aid programs to maintain economic hegemony. Today the cost of interest on debt equals or exceeds total export earnings. The poorer countries have become increasingly dependent on the industrialized countries. 17

While much of the development aid to the Third World is based on First World development patterns, this undifferentiated growth model is inadequate for breaking the Third World dependency cycle. Environmental problems in the Third World are rooted in poverty and hunger, population pressure on marginal lands, and unbalanced land distribution, while those 18 in the First World stem from industrial pollution, waste, conspicuous consumption, and planned obsolescence.

A major problem confronting the capitalist system is the inherent necessity for economic growth. Capitalists make money for further expansion by creating products that consumers will purchase. They do so by fabricating needs for more and fancier food, clothing, and homes, as well as producing luxury items such as better cars, television sets, video recorders, electric shavers, blenders, and microwave ovens. Why not stop the growth mania and focus on quality of life items that fulfill basic needs? If any given producer curtails growth, she or he will be bought out or forced out of business by a competitor. If all capitalists agree together to curtail growth, massive unemployment will occur in a system in which population continues to grow. [19]

Capitalism, however, is not isolated from government. Legislation, regulation, and citizen activism are powerful forces that can mitigate the effects of environmental pollution and improve environmental quality. Yet capitalism is historically subject to fluctuating cycles of inflation and recession and of output and unemployment. In periods of recession, concerns for environmental quality are overridden by attempts to increase productivity and employment. Governmental regulation may decline in the attempt to shore up the economic recovery. In relatively affluent periods, citizen demands for environmental quality tend to increase, as reflected in environmental movements and legal actions. Yet over time environmental quality may tend to lose ground, not returning to former levels during the peaks of relative affluence. Additionally, the environmental preferences and commitments of the political party in control of government agencies and legislatures during any given period may have positive or negative effects on the level of government regulation. All these factors are part of the structure of the social relations of the economic system of a given country and must be seen as interacting with the economy and adding to the complexity of environmental problems and their resolution. [20]

Environmental Problems in the Second World

The former Soviet Union and eastern European countries are experiencing environmental problems of a different character than those of the First and Third worlds. Former president Mikhail Gorbachev's policy of *glasnost,* or openness, revealed massive amounts of industrial pollution threatening air, water, and food qualities to such an extent that citizens have become increasingly alarmed about their own health. A gas-processing plant in the city of Astrakhan pumps a million tons of sul- [21]

phur into the atmosphere a year. Local people have been issued gas masks for emergency protection. In the industrial city of Nizhni Tagil, 700 miles east of Moscow, the smog is so thick that drivers turn on their headlights at noon. Throughout the commonwealth, vehicles use older engines that operate on gasoline with high lead content. In Arkhangelsk, workers contracted diseases that were traced to the Chernobyl nuclear disaster of 1986. Although animals grazing in the area of Chernobyl were "officially" killed to prevent radiation contamination, some of the meat was transferred to remote areas and mixed with other meat to make sausages, causing the illnesses. In the cotton-producing areas of central Asia, the Aral Sea has dried to form a dustbowl. A pulp processing factory on the shores of Lake Baikal, the largest, clear fresh-water lake in the world, has created a 23 mile wide polluted area and its smoke emissions have affected 770 square miles of surrounding wilderness.

In Poland, in an industrial area near Cracow, people retreat to a clinic   22
in an underground salt mine to breathe cleaner air when smog levels are especially high. High concentrations of toxic metals such as lead, mercury, and cadmium are found in the placentas of birthing women caused by sulphur dioxide and carbon monoxide in the air. Premature births and miscarriages result from low oxygen levels in fetuses stemming from chemical changes in the mother's blood. In agricultural areas, soil is contaminated by wind and water that spread the sulphur emissions from coal burning plants over large areas. In Czechoslovakia, 50 percent of the country's drinking water does not reach minimum standards, and in Prague people complain of continual headaches, asthma, and nausea from polluted air. In eastern Germany, cancer, lung, and heart disease rates are 15 to 20 percent higher than in Berlin.

Both the governments and citizens of Second World countries are tak-   23
ing action to curtail pollution. The former Soviet Union created a State Committee for the Protection of the Environment. Citizen groups have spearheaded conservation efforts and demonstrations against industrial polluters. Gorbachev, whose training was in agriculture, emerged as an outspoken world leader on environmental issues, and under his regime fines were levied and factories closed.

How do Second World environmental problems compare with those of   24
the First World? Do the capitalist and socialist systems have the same environmental problems? Do economic systems matter when it comes to questions of environmental deterioration? In searching for answers, it is important to recognize both differences of kind and differences of degree. Some observers have argued that because pollution is found in both types of economies, either the problem lies in industrialization or that capitalism's problems are less severe and more easily resolved. An example of this approach was presented by economist Marshall I. Goldman in his

1970 classic paper, "The Convergence of Environmental Disruption," whose subheading encapsulated his argument: "From Lake Erie to Lake Baikal, Los Angeles to Tbilisi, the debates and dilemmas are the same." By matching cases of environmental disruption in the two countries, he drew the conclusion that they were equally polluted. His convergence thesis was as follows:

> Most conservationalists and social critics are unaware that the U.S.S.R. has environmental disruption that is as extensive and severe as ours.... Yet before we can find a solution to the environmental disruption in our own country, it is necessary to explain why it is that a socialist or communist country like the U.S.S.R. finds itself abusing the environment in the same way, and to the same degree, that we abuse it.

The United States and the former Soviet republics are all committed to economic growth. The Soviet Union and eastern European countries achieved growth through an all-out effort to raise standards of living by means of industrialization and full employment. Central government planning was the decision-making method and bureaucrats were rewarded for gross productive output. The environment suffered the consequences. Yet an important distinction exists between environmental problems in the US and the former USSR. In the Soviet Union environmental disruption stemmed largely from the effects of industrial production rather than from consumption. Packaging, plastic products, cartons, disposable diapers, styrofoam containers, household products, spray cans, aluminum soft drink cans, paints, newspapers, paper products, and other accoutrements of a disposable consumer-oriented society that choke United States' landfills and pollute its soil, air, and water are not major environmental problems in the Second World. Twenty choices of cold cereals in gaudy boxes, fifteen types of frozen diet dinners with plastic microwaveable trays, and nineteen varieties of soft drinks in nineteen different colored aluminum cans do not line the shelves of Soviet stores. Heaps of rusting automobile bodies and mountains of used tires do not adorn Soviet landscapes. Corporations and advertizing agencies do not multiply products and needs in order to compete for consumers' cash. 25

Yes, environmental problems exist in both the capitalist and socialist systems, but the problems are not the same for both. There is no valid convergence argument based on qualitative examples and no valid quantitative formula for comparing the relative effects of environmental disruption between the two systems. A significant structural difference does exist, however. Economic growth is inherent in capitalism; it is not essential to socialism. Both systems have historically been committed to growth; both systems have experienced bureaucratic inefficiency, poor planning, ineffective regulation, and citizen protests. It is not yet clear how the Second 26

World will resolve its current economic and environmental crisis, or how much the push to adopt market economies in the new republics will exacerbate environmental problems. Perhaps new systems will emerge from the environmental crises in the three worlds. Perhaps these syntheses will deal with environmental problems in different ways. The environmental movements in the First, Second, and Third Worlds will play important roles in the outcomes.

Population

While the first contradiction of the global crisis emerges from the interaction between human production systems and nonhuman nature, the second contradiction arises from the interaction between production and reproduction. The impact of humans' biological reproduction on the environment is not direct, but mediated through a particular system of production. Social norms and ethical systems, as well as government policies concerning abortion, welfare, and employment, help to regulate the numbers of children born into a given society. Moreover, different modes of production support different numbers of people in particular ecological habitats. The second contradiction is thus between reproduction (both biological and social) and production. The ways in which population affects the environment must be considered within the context of biological and social reproduction and their interaction with production. 27

The world's population has been growing steadily during the modern era. In 1987 it reached 5 billion people and is predicted to surpass 6 billion by the year 2000. It could reach 10 to 15 billion before stabilizing sometime during the next century. Sheer numbers, however, tell only part of the story. Distribution of numbers, food, and wealth are integral to the total picture. William Keppler of the University of Alaska describes population distribution in terms of a global village: 28

> The present population of the world is approximately five billion people. If we could, at this very moment, shrink the earth population to a village of precisely 100 people, but all the existing human ratios remain the same, the world village would look like this:
>
> There would be 57 Asians, 21 Europeans, 14 western hemisphere people of both North and South America, and 8 Africans. Seventy would be non-white, 30 would be white, 70 would be non-Christian and 30 would be Christian. Fifty percent of the entire world's wealth would be in the hands of only 6 people and 5 of the 6 people would be citizens of the United States of America. Seventy percent of the population would be unable to read; 50

percent would suffer malnutrition; eight would live in substandard housing; and only one would have a university education.

When one considers our world from such an incredibly compressed perspective the need for both tolerance and understanding in a global way becomes glaringly apparent.

The population bomb, say biologists Paul and Ann Ehrlich, has now exploded. Ten thousand years ago, the world population was about five million people, but by 1650 the number had increased one hundred fold to 500 million, and by 1850 to about a billion. Since the mid-twentieth century world population has been growing by 1.7 to 2.1 percent a year, doubling about every forty years, with some nations, such as Kenya, doubling in half that time, and others, such as those in northern Europe, doubling at much slower rates. By 1990 the world growth rate had slowed from about 2.1 percent in the 1960s to about 1.8 percent in 1990, that is the doubling time increased from 33 to 39 years. Thus, at current rates, if the population reaches 6 billion in 2000, it will double to about 12 billion by 2040. The world would become a vast feedlot for the human species.

The Ehrlichs see all environmental problems as stemming from population: "Global warming, acid rain, depletion of the ozone layer, vulnerability to epidemics, and exhaustion of soils and groundwater are all ... related to population size.... We shouldn't delude ourselves: the population explosion will come to an end before very long. The only remaining question is whether it will be halted through the humane method of birth control, or by nature wiping out the surplus."

Questions of population size and control are extremely sensitive issues. They impinge on the most fundamental questions of human freedom. Freedom of how many children to bear and support, where to live, how goods and services should be distributed, a woman's right to abort a pregnancy, and the right of an unborn fetus to life. In rural China, an attempt to reduce population by a government policy of limiting families to one child resulted in the widespread abortion of female fetuses, brought about by an age-old agrarian preference for male labor. In India, Indira Gandhi's policy of pressuring sterilization of government employees after three offspring produced a backlash against its family planning program. In the United States, a woman's right to choose to abort a fetus versus the right of the fetus to life has become a major political issue in all elections, and in presidential appointments to the Supreme Court.

According to the Ehrlichs, reduced fertility depends on five factors: adequate nutrition, proper sanitation, basic health care, education of women, and equal rights for women. When women receive education they apply the results to preparing better meals, keeping cleaner, more sanitary homes, and improving the quality of life for their families. Education teaches them about family planning and contraception and affords them access to status other than through bearing and raising children. Men, on the other hand, use their education to obtain higher income producing jobs, raising their status, and decreasing the need for large families. These approaches, say the Ehrlichs, rather than overall development followed by the so-called demographic transition to lower birth rates, are the keys to population control.

While the interaction between population and the environment is certainly of critical concern, as are issues of women's opportunities and choices, an analysis that links all environmental problems to population growth and sees population control as the answer, say political ecologists, is too monolithic. To emphasize the impact of population on the land to the exclusion of economic development is to present a narrowly "Malthusian" perspective on the population question. In his 1798 *Essay on Population,* Thomas Malthus had argued that population tends to increase in a geometric series (2, 4, 8, 16, 64 …), whereas the food supply increased according to an arithmetic series (1, 2, 3, 4, 5, 6 …). Thus, even if the food supply could be doubled or tripled it could not keep pace with population growth. Environmental checks on population expansion, such as disease, famine, and warfare keep down the rate of increase. Rational checks such as those provided by education and foresight into the economic consequences of large families, induce birth limitation through abstinence, contraception, late marriage, and so on. Malthus argued that the educated upper-classes kept their populations down, whereas the poor reproduced at high rates. Social welfare simply encouraged them to maintain their low standard of living and their high rate of reproduction. Instead, incentives directed at individual self-interest should be provided, such as healthy work opportunities and agricultural improvement techniques.

But the analysis of this "population problem" can be approached from another direction—one rooted in political economy. Geographer David Harvey argues that population, resources, and the ideologies related to their use and control must be seen in connection with economic modes of production. The number of people that a given environment can support is related to the technologies and social relations that people use to turn nonhuman nature into resources for human use.

To function at an optimal level, capitalism requires a balance between the supply of labor and the demand for goods. If the labor supply (i.e. population) increases, wages fall. Then the workers do not have enough money to buy subsistence goods. More importantly, they do not have the money to purchase commodities about the subsistence level that the capitalists wish to sell—there is no effective demand for the capitalists' products. Thus for capitalism to expand by selling more goods, wages must be kept above the subsistence level. On the other hand, if there are too few

33

34

35

workers (i.e. a shrinking population), then wages will be too high and the capitalists will not reap sufficient profits to reinvest and expand production. For Malthus, the solution was to stimulate wants and tastes in the upper classes (landlords, state bureaucrats, etc.) thus creating fresh motives for industry. For others, such as nineteenth century economist David Ricardo, the problem could be solved by maintaining an equilibrium between capital and population, i.e. between supply and demand. Ricardo's rational, normative approach held that internal harmony within the system would allow a gradual expansion of capitalism.

A third approach is that of Karl Marx. Marx did not see a Malthusian 'population problem," but a poverty and exploitation problem. Marx replaced the inevitability of the Malthusian pressure of population on the land with an analysis of the historically specific relationship between the labor supply and employment within the capitalist mode of production. Instead of the Malthusian emphasis on "overpopulation," he developed the concept of a relative surplus population. For capitalism to function smoothly, there must be a "reserve army of labor." This consists of a small percentage (about 4–5 percent)—of, for example, unemployed males, immigrants, and women,—who can be hired when the workforce shrinks and laid off when the workforce expands. In this way the capitalist can regulate both wages and demand. 36

When capitalists keep wages above the subsistence level, workers can purchase enough goods to maintain a reasonable quality of life. Too many children become an economic liability, rather than an asset for producing agricultural subsistence or support for the parents in old age, keeping population growth low. If population grows too fast, however, capitalism is threatened by riots, strikes, and revolution. It thus walks a tightrope between capital, effective demand, and population. Inherent in capitalism and *essential* to its existence are abundance and scarcity, growth and natural resource depletion, and an economic division between capital and labor, i.e. between haves and have nots. 37

Marx envisaged a society in which poverty and misery would be replaced by a system that fulfilled all people's basic needs, not just the greed of the few. Whether one agrees or disagrees with Marxist goals, a Marxist perspective offers a critical stance from which to analyze other approaches. A Marxist approach is dynamic and relational. Neither population nor resources can be understood independently of their economic context. A given part of nature is a resource or not depending on its use in a particular system. Thus gold and oil were not resources to Native Americans, but became so for European immigrants to the Americas. 38

Environmentalist Barry Commoner approaches population as a problem related to standards of living. The demographic transition to lower population levels is characteristic of both the industrialized world and the 39 developing countries, but the two processes are different. As industrialization proceeded in Europe and North America, the standard of living rose and death rates declined from an average of 30 per thousand in 1850, to 24 per thousand in 1900, 16 per thousand in 1950, and 9 per thousand in 1985. Subsequently the birth rate also began to decline as fewer infants died, people lived longer, and the perceived need to bear additional children changed. The average birth rate began to decline after 1850 from 40 per thousand in 1850, to 32 per thousand in 1900, to 23 per thousand in 1950, and 14 per thousand in 1985. Overall population sizes grew during the nineteenth century, but the rate of increase slowly declined to the present rate of 0.4 percent.

In the developing countries the rate of decline has been slower. The average death rate was about 38 per thousand in 1850, 33 per thousand in 1900, 23 per thousand in 1950, and 10 per thousand in 1985. But the average birth rate has remained higher and declined much more slowly. It was 43 per thousand in 1925, 37 per thousand in 1950, and 30 per thousand in 1985. The rate of increase has slowed to about 1.7 percent a year. While death rates are about the same as those in the industrialized countries, birth rates are higher.

As the living standards improve and infant mortality declines, couples no longer need as many children to replace those who die. Instead of an economic asset to help support the parents in old age and to provide labor in agrarian communities, children become an economic liability. Costs of housing, clothing, food, travel, and a college education associated with a higher quality of life increase, providing incentives to keep family sizes smaller. Better health and childcare, better nutrition and education, steady employment, and old age security are the strongest incentives to reduction in family sizes. In addition, family planning education and safe birth control methods (as opposed to coercion and unsafe methods) provide added impetus to lowering birth rates.

In the developing countries the demographic transition has lagged because of the political and economic relationships between the center economies of the north and the peripheral economies of the south. Much of the wealth in Third World natural resources, which has been developed with northern capital and southern labor, has been removed from the southern countries. This wealth helps to fuel population decreases in the north while preventing the rise in living standards in the south that would tend to lower birth rates. The developing countries are also thwarted by enormous debts that further stall the demographic transition.

World food production is currently above the level needed to support its population and the food supply is growing faster than the population. Nevertheless, that food is not evenly distributed. Some nations, such as those in Africa, have large numbers of starving people while others, such as the United States, have large food surpluses. Not only improvements in sustainable agriculture, but a redistribution of food and resources is necessary to accelerate the demographic transition.

Commoner concludes his analysis with a recommendation: 44

> The world population crisis, which is the ultimate outcome of the exploitation of poor nations by rich ones, ought to be remedied by returning to the poor countries enough of the wealth taken from them to give their peoples both the reason and the resources voluntarily to limit their own fertility. In sum, I believe that if the root cause of the world population crisis is poverty, then to end it we must abolish poverty. And if the cause of poverty is the grossly unequal distribution of the world's wealth, then to end poverty, and with it the population crisis, we must redistribute that wealth, among nations and within them.

Steady State Economics

Ultimately growth oriented economies need to move toward a steady-state world economy, argues Herman Daly. While a rapid slowdown would disproportionately affect poor countries and peoples, a gradual transition to a no- or low-growth economy could help to bring about a sustainable and socially just world. A steady-state economy, Daly says, is "an economy with constant stocks of people and artifacts, maintained at some desired, sufficient levels by low rates of maintenance 'throughput.'" The throughput is the flow of matter and energy from nonhuman nature, through the human economy, and back to nature as pollution. A steady-state economy would use the lowest possible levels of materials and energy in the production phase and emit the least possible amount of pollution in the consumption phase. The total population and the total amount of capital and consumer goods would be constant. The economy could continue to develop, but need not grow. Culture, knowledge, ethics, and quality of life would continue to grow. Only physical materials would be constant. 45

While the rest of the biosphere lives off solar income, human beings, since the transition to an inorganic economy, have been living off non-renewable geological capital. This means that humans are no longer in equilibrium with the rest of nature, but are depleting and polluting it, overloading the natural cycles. All capital, according to twentieth-century mathematician A. J. Lotka, is a material extension of the human body. Clothing, houses, and bathtubs are extensions of the skin; food, drink, and cooking stoves of the digestive system; toilets and sewers of the elimination system; television and radio of the sensory organs; computers and books of the brain. 46

Services in the form of psychic satisfaction for humans come from increasing the numbers of artifacts and from the natural resources of the 47 ecosystem. Creating and maintaining the artifacts requires energy throughput which in turn depletes and pollutes the ecosystem. In terms of the laws of thermodynamics, the total amount of energy in the universe is constant (the first law), but the energy available for useful work is decreasing (the second law). The total entropy (the energy unavailable for work) tends toward a maximum and the universe as a whole moves from order to disorder. As the economy uses low-entropy raw materials, it transforms them into higher-entropy artifacts, and emits high-entropy waste. "The laws of thermodynamics," states Daly, "restrict all technologies, man's as well as nature's and apply to all economic systems whether capitalist, communist, socialist, or facist." While the economy and its artifacts achieve greater order, the ecosystem tends to greater disorder. At some point the ecosystem will be no longer able to provide the services required by the economy. These costs to nature, however, cannot be planned in ordered sequences as can economic costs.

Is a steady-state economy possible, and if so how? Can the world of the twenty-first century move toward a stable no- or low-growth economy as population growth slows and standards of living rise? To move toward a steady-state economy, depreciation of artifacts must be reduced. Planned obsolescence gives way to planned longevity. Cars, refrigerators and television sets are engineered to last. Obsession with growth is replaced by obsession with conservation. The goal of higher gross national product gives way to the repair of gross national pollution.   48

Conclusion

Ecology, economic production, and reproduction all interact in any given society. The global ecological crisis is a result of contradictions between systems of economic production and ecology and between reproduction and production. First, Second, and Third World political economies interact in ways that exacerbate many of the problems inherent in individual countries. The political economy of the First World is legitimated by a mechanistic worldview that has been dominant since the seventeenth century and an egocentric ethic that assumes that what is best for the individual is best for society as a whole.   49

QUESTIONS FOR DISCUSSION AND WRITING

1. In her often complex discussion of population as an environmental problem, how does Merchant explain the relationship between "production" and "reproduction"? How does wealth or "standard of living" affect

the levels of population growth? Given her p
tions does Merchant propose to control the
sion"? How are such solutions different from
being attempted?

2.   In Merchant's view, how will the transition
ics help to solve the persistent and perilous ec
in this chapter? Based upon what Mercha
longevity" and the "obsession with conservatic
the ways that American consumers would have
their expectations. Does such a solution seem

3.   As a Marxist thinker, Merchant is arguing for a view of environmental
problems that is quite different from that offered by other environmentalists, including many other radical environmentalists. As she discusses the
causes and solutions to our present environmental crisis, how careful is
Merchant to identify her own position? How does she characterize or label
her own views? Are there places where, in your view, Merchant's agenda
for change seems to go beyond what you think of as "environmental"
concerns?

P. J. O'ROURKE

en though we may not agree with the message behind some humor, often the humor itself allows us to understand a different perspective. The comedy of P. J. O'Rourke (b. 1947) can provide this service for people with leftist sympathies in general and, in "The Greenhouse Affect" (1990), for conservationists in particular. O'Rourke started his career writing for an underground newspaper that was against business, industry, and the war in Vietnam. After becoming disillusioned with the radical left wing, he turned to a job at the National Lampoon, *where he advanced to the position of editor in chief. His humorous books evolved from parodies of manners to discussions of why young people are natural Republicans in* Republican Party Reptile. *His recent works have been tremendously popular; they argue, always with a biting humor, that government is too big and needs to get out of the way of people's freedom.*

As with much of O'Rourke's work, "The Greenhouse Affect" works as a parody of people O'Rourke doesn't like. Here the target of the criticism is Earth Day and a mindless sort of ecological extremism. O'Rourke works his way from a distrust of all mass movements to the specific problems he sees in the ecological movement. In response to "parlor primitivism," O'Rourke hints at the hard reasoning that he believes is needed to overcome our ecological problems. Along the way, he makes a number of telling points, even for those who can't agree with much of what he says.

The Greenhouse Affect

If the great outdoors is so swell, how come the homeless aren't more fond of it? 1

There. I wanted to be the one to say a discouraging word about Earth Day—a lone voice *not* crying in the wilderness, thank you, but hollering in the rec room. 2

On April 22 [1990]—while everybody else was engaged in a great, smarmy fit of agreeing with himself about chlorofluorocarbons, while *tout le* rapidly-losing-plant-and-animal-species *monde* traded hugs of unanimity over plastic-milk-bottle recycling, while all of you praised one another to the ozone-depleted skies for your brave opposition to coastal flooding and every man Jack and woman Jill told child Jason how bad it is to put crude oil on baby seals—I was home in front of the VCR snacking high on the food chain. 3

But can any decent, caring resident of this planet possibly disagree with the goals and aspirations embodied in the celebration of Earth Day? No. 4

426

That's what bothers me. Mass movements are always a worry. There's   5
a whiff of the lynch mob or the lemming migration about any overlarge
gathering of like-thinking individuals, no matter how virtuous their cause.
Even a band of angels can turn ugly and start looting if enough angels are
hanging around unemployed and convinced that succubi own all the
liquor stores in heaven.

Whenever I'm in the middle of conformity, surrounded by oneness of   6
mind, with people oozing concurrence on every side, I get scared. And
when I find myself agreeing with everybody, I get really scared.

Sometimes it's worse when everybody's right than when everybody's   7
wrong. Everybody in fifteenth-century Spain was wrong about where
China is, and as a result, Columbus discovered Caribbean vacations. On
the other hand, everybody in fifteenth-century Spain was right about here-
sies: They're heretical. But that didn't make the Spanish Inquisition more
fun for the people who were burned at the stake.

A mass movement that's correct is especially dangerous when it's right   8
about a problem that needs fixing. Then all those masses in the mass
movement have to be called to action, and that call to action better be
exciting, or the masses will lose interest and wander off to play arcade
games. What's exciting? Monitoring the release into the atmosphere of
glycol ethers used in the manufacture of brake-fluid anti-icing additives?
No. But what about some violence, an enemy, someone to hate?

Mass movements need what Eric Hoffer—in *The True Believer,* his   9
book about the kind of creepy misfits who join mass movements—calls a
"unifying agent."

"Hatred is the most accessible and comprehensive of all unifying   10
agents," writes Hoffer. "Mass movements can rise and spread without belief in a God, but never without belief in a devil." Hoffer goes on to cite
historian F. A. Voigt's account of a Japanese mission sent to Berlin in 1932
to study the National Socialist movement. Voigt asked a member of the
mission what he thought. He replied, "It is magnificent. I wish we could
have something like it in Japan, only we can't, because we haven't got any
Jews."

The environmental movement has, I'm afraid, discovered a unifying   11
agent. I almost said "scapegoat," but scapegoats are probably an endangered species. Besides, all animals are innocent, noble, upright, honest
and fair in their dealings and have a great sense of humor. Anyway, the environmental movement has found its necessary enemy in the form of that
ubiquitous evil—already so familiar to Hollywood scriptwriters, pulp-
paperback authors, minority spokespersons, feminists, members of ACT
UP, the Christic Institute and Democratic candidates for president: Big
Business.

Now, you might think Big Business would be hard to define in this day   12
of leveraged finances and interlocking technologies. Not so. Big Business
is every kind of business except the kind from which the person who's
complaining draws his pay. Thus the rock-around-the-rain-forest crowd
imagines record companies are a cottage industry. The Sheen family considers movie conglomerates to be a part of the arts and crafts movement.
And Ralph Nader thinks the wholesale lobbying of Congress by huge tax-
exempt, public-interest advocacy groups is akin to working the family
farm.

This is why it's rarely an identifiable person (and, of course, never you   13
or me) who pollutes. It's a vague, sinister, faceless thing called industry.
The National Wildlife Federation's booklet on toxic-chemical releases
says, "Industry dumped more than 2.3 billion pounds of toxic chemicals
into or onto the land." What will "industry" do next? Visit us with a plague
of boils? Make off with our firstborn? Or maybe it will wreck the
Barcalounger. "Once-durable products like furniture are made to fall apart
quickly, requiring more frequent replacement," claims the press kit of
Inform, a New York–based environmental group that seems to be missing
a few sunflower seeds from its trail mix. But even a respectable old estab-
lishmentarian organization like the Sierra Club is not above giving a vil-
lainous and conspiratorial cast to those who disagree with its legislative
agenda. "For the past eight years, this country's major polluters and their
friends in the Reagan administration and Congress have impeded the
progress of bills introduced by congressional Clean Air advocates," says
the Sierra Club's 1989–90 conservation campaign press package. And here
at *Rolling Stone*—where we are so opposed to the profit motive that we
work for free, refuse to accept advertising and give the magazine away at
newsstands—writer Trip Gabriel, in his *Rolling Stone* 571 article "Coming
Back to Earth: A Look at Earth Day 1990," avers, "The yuppie belief in the
sanctity of material possessions, no matter what the cost in resource depletion, squared perfectly with the philosophy of the Reaganites—to exploit the nation's natural resources for the sake of business."

Sure, "business" and "industry" and "their friends in the Reagan admin-   14
istration and Congress" make swell targets. Nobody squirts sulfur dioxide
into the air as a hobby or tosses PCBs [polychlorinated biphenyls] into
rivers as an act of charity. Pollution occurs in the course of human enterprise. It is a by-product of people making things like a living, including
yours. If we desire, for ourselves and our progeny, a world that's not too
stinky and carcinogenic, we're going to need the technical expertise, en-
trepreneurial vigor and marketing genius of every business and industry.
And if you think pollution is the fault only of Reaganite yuppies wallow-
ing in capitalist greed, then go take a deep breath in Smolensk or a long
drink from the river Volga.

Sorry, but business and industry—trade and manufacturing—are in-   15
herent to civilization. Every human society, no matter how wholesomely
primitive, practices as much trade and manufacturing as it can figure out.
It is the fruits of trade and manufacturing that raise us from the wearying
muck of subsistence and give us the health, wealth, education, leisure and
warm, dry rooms with Xerox machines—all of which allow us to be the
ecology-conscious, selfless, splendid individuals we are.

Our ancestors were too busy wresting a living from nature to go on any   16
nature hikes. The first European ever known to have climbed a mountain
for the view was the poet Petrarch. That wasn't until the fourteenth century. And when Petrarch got to the top of Mont Ventoux, he opened a
copy of Saint Augustine's *Confessions* and was shamed by the passage
about men "who go to admire the high mountains and the immensity of
the oceans and the course of the heaven ... and neglect themselves."
Worship of nature may be ancient, but seeing nature as cuddlesome, hug-
a-bear and too cute for words is strictly a modern fashion.

The Luddite side of the environmental movement would have us de-   17
stroy or eschew technology—throw down the ladder by which we
climbed. Well, nuts (and berries and fiber) to you, you shrub huggers. It's
time we in the industrialized nations admitted what safe, comfortable and
fun-filled lives we lead. If we don't, we will cause irreparable harm to the
disadvantaged peoples of the world. They're going to laugh themselves to
death listening to us whine.

Contempt for material progress is not only funny but unfair. The aver-   18
age Juan, Chang or Mobutu out there in the parts of the world where every
day is Earth Day—or Dirt and Squalor Day anyhow—would like to have
a color television too. He'd also like some comfy Reeboks, a Nintendo
Power Glove and a Jeep Cherokee. And he means to get them. I wouldn't
care to be the skinny health-food nut waving a copy of *50 Simple Things
You Can Do to Save the Earth* who tries to stand in his way.

There was something else keeping me indoors on April 22 [1990].   19
Certain eco-doomsters are not only unreasonable in their attitude toward
business, they're unreasonable in their attitude toward reason. I can understand harboring mistrust of technology. I myself wouldn't be inclined
to wash my dog in toluene or picnic in the nude at Bhopal. But to deny
the validity of the scientific method is to resign your position as a sentient
being. You'd better go look for work as a lungwort plant or an Eastern
European Communist-party chairman.

For example, here we have the environmental movement screeching   20
like New Kids on the Block fans because President Bush asked for a bit
more scientific research on global warming before we cork everybody's
Honda, ban the use of underarm deodorants and replace all the coal fuel

in our electrical-generating plants with windmills. The greenhouse effect is a complex hypothesis. You can hate George Bush as much as you like and the thing won't get simpler. "The most dire predictions about global warming are being toned down by many experts," said a *Washington Post* story last January [1990]. And that same month the *New York Times* told me a new ice age was only a couple of thousand years away.

On the original Earth Day, in 1970—when the world was going to end   21
from overcrowding instead of overheating—the best-selling author of *The Population Bomb,* Dr. Paul Ehrlich, was making dire predictions as fast as his earnestly frowning mouth could move. Dr. Ehrlich predicted that America would have water rationing by 1974 and food rationing by 1980; that hepatitis and dysentery rates in the United States would increase by 500 percent due to population density; and that the oceans could be as dead as Lake Erie by 1979. Today Lake Erie is doing better than Perrier, and Dr. Ehrlich is still pounding sand down a rat hole.

Now, don't get me wrong: Even registered Republicans believe eco-   22
logical problems are real. Real solutions, however, will not be found through pop hysteria or the merchandising of panic. Genuine hard-got knowledge is required. The collegiate idealists who stuff the ranks of the environmental movement seem willing to do absolutely anything to save the biosphere except take science courses and learn something about it. In 1971, American universities awarded 4,390 doctorates in the physical sciences. After fifteen years of youthful fretting over the planet's future, the number was 3,551.

It wouldn't even be all that expensive to make the world clean and   23
prosperous. According to the September 1989 issue of *Scientific American,* which was devoted to scholarly articles about ecological issues, the cost of achieving sustainable and environmentally healthy worldwide economic development by the year 2000 would be about $729 billion. That's roughly fourteen dollars per person per year for ten years. To translate that into sandal-and-candle terms, $729 billion is less than three-quarters of what the world spends annually on armaments.

The Earth can be saved, but not by legislative fiat. Expecting President   24
Bush to cure global warming by sending a bill to Congress is to subscribe to that eternal fantasy of totalitarians and Democrats from Massachusetts: a law against bad weather.

Sometimes I wonder if the fans of eco-Armageddon even want the   25
world's problems to get better. Improved methods of toxic-chemical incineration, stack scrubbers for fossil fuel power plants, and sensible solid-waste management schemes lack melodramatic appeal. There's nothing apocalyptic about gasohol. And it's hard to picture a Byronic hero sorting his beer bottles by color at the recycling center. The beliefs of some envi-

ronmentalists seem to have little to do with the welfare of the globe or of its inhabitants and a lot to do with the parlor primitivism of the Romantic Movement.

There is this horrible idea, beginning with Jean Jacques Rousseau and still going strong in college classrooms, that natural man is naturally good. All we have to do is strip away the neuroses, repressions and Dial soap of modern society, and mankind will return to an Edenic state. Anybody who's ever met a toddler knows this is soy-protein baloney. Neolithic man was not a guy who always left his campsite cleaner than he found it. Ancient humans trashed half the map with indiscriminate use of fire for slash-and-burn agriculture and hunting drives. They caused desertification through overgrazing and firewood cutting in North Africa, the Middle East and China. And they were responsible for the extinction of mammoths, mastodons, cave bears, giant sloths, New World camels and horses and thousands of other species. Their record on women's issues and minority rights wasn't so hot either. You can return to nature, go back to leading the simple, fulfilling life of the hunter-gatherer if you want, but don't let me catch you poking around in my garbage cans for food.

Then there are the beasts-are-our-buddies types. I've got a brochure from the International Fund for Animal Welfare containing a section called "Highlights of IFAW's History," and I quote: "1978—Campaign to save iguanas from cruelty in Nicaraguan marketplaces—people sew animals' mouths shut."

1978 was the middle of the Nicaraguan civil war. This means that while the evil dirt sack Somoza was shooting it out with the idiot Marxist Sandinistas, the International Fund for Animal Welfare was flying somebody to besieged Managua to check on lizard lips.

The neo-hippie-dips, the sentimentality-crazed iguana anthropomorphizers, the Chicken Littles, the three-bong-hit William Blakes—thank God these people don't actually go outdoors much, or the environment would be even worse than it is already.

But ecology's fools don't upset me. It's the wise guys I'm leery of. Tyranny is implicit in the environmental movement. Although Earth Day participants are going to be surprised to hear themselves accused of fascist tendencies, dictatorship is the unspoken agenda of every morality-based political campaign. Check out Moslem fundamentalists or the right-to-lifers. Like abortion opponents and Iranian imams, the environmentalists have the right to tell the rest of us what to do because they are morally correct and we are not. Plus the tree squeezers care more, which makes them an elite—an aristocracy of mushiness. They know what's good for us even when we're too lazy or shortsighted to snip plastic six-pack collars so sea turtles won't strangle.

QUESTIONS FOR DISCUSSION AND WRITING

1. "Mass movements are always a worry," says O'Rourke (par. 5). What exactly are his worries about the "wise guys" (par. 30) in the environmental movement? As you think about what you have read and heard about modern environmentalism, do you share any of his concerns?

2. According to O'Rourke, mass movements always need a "unifying agent" (par. 9), and for the environmental movement this has been "Big Business" (par. 11). How does O'Rourke characterize what he calls "the scapegoating" of business and industry? Do you find his argument about the role of business in modern civilization convincing? Why or why not?

3. What does O'Rourke mean by his assertion "Tyranny is implicit in the environmental movement" (par. 30)? What, if any, evidence does he offer to illustrate and support this claim?

MICHAEL POLLAN

Michael Pollen was born in 1955 in the suburbs of Long Island, New York. After completing his master's degree at Columbia University (for which he wrote a thesis on Thoreau), Pollan went to work at Harper's Magazine, where he now serves as an editor at large. In 1991 Pollan published Second Nature: A Gardener's Education, *a collection of essays based upon his experiences as a landowner in rural Connecticut. What interests Pollan are the cultural symbols through which Americans have come to understand and live with nature. In "Why Mow?"— one of the more provocative essays from his book—Pollan examines America's preoccupation with the carefully manicured, weed-free lawn. In the neighborhoods of suburban America, lawns represent both social status and civic responsibility, Pollan argues, despite the fact that we poison ourselves with herbicides and pesticides to keep them green. In "The Idea of a Garden," also taken from his book, Pollan argues for what he calls a "garden ethic" to replace the traditional "wilderness ethic" that has so long defined our relationship with nature. In creating "wilderness preserves" in areas far from our everyday lives, Pollan argues, we isolate ourselves from nature. The typical backyard garden allows us a more local, less abstract relationship with nature.*

The Idea of a Garden

The biggest news to come out of my town in many years was the tornado, or tornadoes, that careened through here on July 10, 1989, a Monday. Shooting down the Housatonic River Valley from the Berkshires, it veered east over Coltsfoot Mountain and then, after smudging the sky a weird gray green, proceeded to pinball madly from hillside to hillside for about fifteen minutes before wheeling back up into the sky. This was part of the same storm that ripped open the bark of my ash tree. But the damage was much, much worse on the other side of town. Like a gigantic, skidding pencil eraser, the twister neatly erased whole patches of woods and roughly smeared many other ones, where it wiped out just the tops of the trees. Overnight, large parts of town were rendered unrecognizable. 1

One place where the eraser came down squarely was in the Cathedral Pines, a famous forest of old-growth white pine trees close to the center of town. A kind of local shrine, this forty-two-acre forest was one of the oldest stands of white pine in New England, the trees untouched since about 1800. To see it was to have some idea how the New World forest must have looked to the first settlers, and in 1985 the federal government 2

433

designated it a "national natural landmark." To enter Cathedral Pines on a hot summer day was like stepping out of the sun into a dim cathedral, the sunlight cooled and sweetened by the trillions of pine needles as it worked its way down to soft, sprung ground that had been unacquainted with blue sky for the better part of two centuries. The storm came through at about five in the evening, and it took only a few minutes of wind before pines more than one hundred fifty feet tall and as wide around as missiles lay jackstrawed on the ground like a fistful of pencils dropped from a great height. The wind was so thunderous that people in houses at the forest's edge did not know trees had fallen until they ventured outside after the storm had passed. The following morning, the sky now clear, was the first in more than a century to bring sunlight crashing down onto this particular patch of earth.

"It is a terrible mess," the first selectman told the newspapers; "a tragedy," said another Cornwall resident, voicing the deep sense of loss shared by many in town. But in the days that followed, the selectman and the rest of us learned that our responses, though understandable, were shortsighted, unscientific, and, worst of all, anthropocentric. "It may be a calamity to us," a state environmental official told a reporter from the *Hartford Courant,* but "to biology it is not a travesty. It is just a natural occurrence." The Nature Conservancy, which owns Cathedral Pines, issued a press release explaining that "Monday's storm was just another link in the continuous chain of events that is responsible for shaping and changing this forest." 3

It wasn't long before the rub of these two perspectives set off a controversy heated enough to find its way into the pages of *The New York Times.* The Nature Conservancy, in keeping with its mandate to maintain its lands in a "state of nature," indicated that it would leave Cathedral Pines alone, allowing the forest to take its "natural course," whatever that might be. To town officials and neighbors of the forest this was completely unacceptable. The downed trees, besides constituting an eyesore right at the edge of town, also posed a fire hazard. A few summers of drought, and the timber might go up in a blaze that would threaten several nearby homes and possibly even the town itself. Many people in Cornwall wanted Cathedral Pines cleared and replanted, so that at least the next generation might live to see some semblance of the old forest. A few others had the poor taste to point out the waste of more than a million board-feet of valuable timber, stupendous lengths of unblemished, knot-free pine. 4

The newspapers depicted it as a classic environmental battle, pitting the interests of man against nature, and in a way it was that. On one side were the environmental purists, who felt that *any* intervention by man in the disposition of this forest would be unnatural. "If you're going to clean it up," one purist declared in the local press, "you might as well put up 5 condos." On the other side stood the putative interests of man, variously expressed in the vocabulary of safety (the first hazard), economics (the waste lumber), and aesthetics (the "terrible mess").

Everybody enjoys a good local fight, but I have to say I soon found the whole thing depressing. This was indeed a classic environmental battle, in that it seemed to exemplify just about everything that's wrong with the way we approach problems of this kind these days. Both sides began to caricature each other's positions: the selectman's "terrible mess" line earned him ridicule for his anthropocentrism in the letters page of *The New York Times;* he in turn charged a Yale scientist who argued for non-interference with "living in an ivory tower."

But as far apart as the two sides seemed to stand, they actually shared more common ground than they realized. Both started from the premise that man and nature were irreconcilably opposed, and that the victory of one necessarily entailed the loss of the other. Both sides, in other words, accepted the premises of what we might call the "wilderness ethic," which is based on the assumption that the relationship of man and nature resembles a zero-sum game. This idea, widely held and yet largely unexamined, has set the terms of most environmental battles in this country since the very first important one: the fight over the building of the Hetch Hetchy Dam in 1907, which pitted John Muir against Gifford Pinchot, whom Muir used to call a "temple destroyer." Watching my little local debate unfold over the course of the summer, and grow progressively more shrill and sterile, I began to wonder if perhaps the wilderness ethic itself, for all that it has accomplished in this country over the past century, had now become part of the problem. I also began to wonder if it might be possible to formulate a different ethic to guide us in our dealings with nature, at least in some places some of the time, an ethic that would be based not on the idea of wilderness but on the idea of a garden.

Foresters who have examined sections of fallen trees in Cathedral Pines think that the oldest trees in the forest date from 1780 or so, which suggests that the site was probably logged by the first generation of settlers. The Cathedral Pines are not, then "virgin growth." The rings of felled trees also reveal a significant growth spurt in 1840, which probably indicates that loggers removed hardwood trees in that year, leaving the pines to grow without competition. In 1883, the Calhouns, an old Cornwall family whose property borders the forest, bought the land to protect the trees from the threat of logging; in 1967 they deeded it to the Nature Conservancy, stipulating that it be maintained in its natural state. Since then, and up until the tornado made its paths impassable, the forest has been a popular place for hiking and Sunday outings. Over the years, more than a few Cornwall residents have come to the forest to be married.

Cathedral Pines is not in any meaningful sense a wilderness. The nat-   9
ural history of the forest intersects at many points with the social history of
Cornwall. It is the product of early logging practices, which clear-cut the
land once and then cut it again, this time selectively, a hundred years later.
Other human factors almost certainly played a part in the forest's history;
we can safely assume that any fires in the area were extinguished before
they reached Cathedral Pines. (Though we don't ordinarily think of it in
these terms, fire suppression is one of the more significant effects that the
European has had on the American landscape.) Cathedral Pines, then, is
in some part a man-made landscape, and it could reasonably be argued
that to exclude man at this point in its history would constitute a break
with its past.

But both parties to the dispute chose to disregard the actual history of   10
Cathedral Pines, and instead to think of the forest as a wilderness in the
commonly accepted sense of that term: a pristine place untouched by
white men. Since the romantics, we've prized such places as refuges from
the messiness of the human estate, vantages from which we might tran-
scend the vagaries of that world and fix on what Thoreau called "higher
laws." Certainly an afternoon in Cathedral Pines fostered such feelings,
and its very name reflects the pantheism that lies behind them. Long before science coined the term *ecosystem* to describe it, we've had the sense
that nature undisturbed displays a miraculous order and balance, something the human world can only dream about. When man leaves it alone,
nature will tend toward a healthy and abiding state of equilibrium.
Wilderness, the purest expression of this natural law, stands out beyond
history.

These are powerful and in many ways wonderful ideas. The notion of   11
wilderness is a kind of taboo in our culture, in many cases acting as a
check on our inclination to dominate and spoil nature. It has inspired us
to set aside such spectacular places as Yellowstone and Yosemite. But
wilderness is also a profoundly alienating idea, for it drives a large wedge
between man and nature. Set against the foil of nature's timeless cycles,
human history appears linear and unpredictable, buffeted by time and
chance as it drives blindly into the future. Natural history, by comparison, obeys fixed and legible laws, ones that make the "laws" of human
history seem puny, second-rate things scarcely deserving of the label. We
have little idea what the future holds for the town of Cornwall, but
surely nature has a plan for Cathedral Pines; leave the forest alone and
that plan—which science knows by the name of "forest succession"—
will unfold inexorably, in strict accordance with natural law. A new climax
forest will emerge as nature works to restore her equilibrium—or at least
that's the idea.

The notion that nature has a plan for Cathedral Pines is a comforting one, and certainly it supplies a powerful argument for leaving the forest alone. Naturally I was curious to know what that plan was: what does nature do with an old pine forest blown down by a tornado? I consulted a few field guides and standard works of forest ecology hoping to find out.   12

According to the classical theory of forest succession, set out in the nineteenth century by, among others, Henry Thoreau, a pine forest that has been abruptly destroyed will usually be succeeded by hardwoods, typically oak. This is because squirrels commonly bury acorns in pine forests and neglect to retrieve many of them. The oaks sprout and, because shade doesn't greatly hinder young oaks, the seedlings frequently manage to survive beneath the dark canopy of a mature pine forest. Pine seedlings, on the other hand, require more sunlight than a mature pine forest admits; they won't sprout in shade. So by the time the pine forest comes down, the oak saplings will have had a head start in the race to dominate the new forest. Before any new pines have had a chance to sprout, the oaks will be well on their way to cornering the sunlight and inheriting the forest.   13

This is what I read, anyway, and I decided to ask around to confirm that Cathedral Pines was expected to behave as predicted. I spoke to a forest ecologist and an expert on the staff of the Nature Conservancy. They told me that the classical theory of pine-forest succession probably does describe the underlying tendency at work in Cathedral Pines. But it turns out that a lot can go, if not "wrong" exactly, then at least differently. For what if there are no oaks nearby? Squirrels will travel only so far in search of a hiding place for their acorns. Instead of oaks, there may be hickory nuts stashed all over Cathedral Pines. And then there's the composition of species planted by the forest's human neighbors to consider; one of these, possibly some exotic (that is, non-native), could conceivably race in and take over.   14

"It all depends," is the refrain I kept hearing as I tried to pin down nature's intentions for Cathedral Pines. Forest succession, it seems, is only a theory, a metaphor of our making, and almost as often as not nature makes a fool of it. The number of factors that will go into the determination of Cathedral Pines' future is almost beyond comprehension. Consider just this small sample of the things that could happen to alter irrevocably its future course: 15

A lightning storm—or a cigarette butt flicked from a passing car— ignites a fire next summer. Say it's a severe fire, hot enough to damage the fertility of the soil, thereby delaying recovery of the forest for decades. Or say it rains that night, making the fire a mild one, just hot enough to kill the oak saplings and allow the relatively fire-resistant pine seedlings to   16 flourish without competition. A new pine forest after all? Perhaps. But what if the population of deer happens to soar the following year? Their browsing would wipe out the young pines and create an opening for spruce, the taste of which deer happen not to like.

Or say there is no fire. Without one, it could take hundreds of years for   17
the downed pine trees to rot and return their nutrients to the soil. Trees grow poorly in the exhausted soil, but the seeds of brambles, which can lie dormant in the ground for fifty years, sprout and proliferate: we end up with a hundred years of brush. Or perhaps a breeze in, say, the summer of 1997 carries in seedpods from the Norway maple standing in a nearby front yard at the precise moment when conditions for their germination are perfect. Norway maple, you'll recall, is a European species, introduced here early in the nineteenth century and widely planted as a street tree. Should this exotic species happen to prevail, Cathedral Pines becomes one very odd-looking and awkwardly named wilderness area.

But the outcome could be much worse. Let's say the rains next spring   18
are unusually heavy, washing all the topsoil away (the forest stood on a steep hillside). Only exotic weed species can survive now, and one of these happens to be Japanese honeysuckle, a nineteenth-century import of such rampant habit that it can choke out the growth of all trees indefinitely. We end up with no forest at all.

Nobody, in other words, can say what will happen in Cathedral Pines.   19
And the reason is not that forest ecology is a young or imperfect science, but because *nature herself doesn't know what's going to happen here.* Nature has no grand design for this place. An incomprehensibly various and complex set of circumstances—some of human origin, but many not—will determine the future of Cathedral Pines. And whatever that future turns out to be, it would not unfold in precisely the same way twice. Nature may possess certain inherent tendencies, ones that theories such as forest succession can describe, but chance events can divert her course into an almost infinite number of different channels.

It's hard to square this fact with our strong sense that some kind of   20
quasi-divine order inheres in nature's workings. But science lately has been finding that contingency plays nearly as big a role in natural history as it does in human history. Forest ecologists today will acknowledge that succession theories are little more than comforting narratives we impose on a surprisingly unpredictable process; even so-called climax forests are sometimes superseded. (In many places in the northern United States today, mature stands of oak are inexplicably being invaded by maples—skunks at the climax garden party.) Many ecologists will now freely admit that even the concept of an ecosystem is only a metaphor, a human construct imposed upon a much more variable and precarious reality. An

ecosystem may be a useful concept, but no ecologist has ever succeeded in isolating one in nature. Nor is the process of evolution as logical or inexorable as we have thought. The current thinking in paleontology holds that the evolution of any given species, our own included, is not the necessary product of any natural laws, but rather the outcome of a concatenation of chance events—of "just history" in the words of Stephen Jay Gould. Add or remove any single happenstance—the asteroid fails to wipe out the dinosaurs; a little chordate worm called *Pikaia* succumbs in the Burgess extinction—and humankind never arrives.

Across several disciplines, in fact, scientists are coming to the conclusion that more "just history" is at work in nature than had previously been thought. Yet our metaphors still picture nature as logical, stable, and ahistorical—more like a watch than, say, an organism or a stock exchange, to name two metaphors that may well be more apt. Chance and contingency, it turns out, are everywhere in nature; she has no fixed goals, no unalterable pathways into the future, no inflexible rules that she herself can't bend or break at will. She is more like us (or we are more like her) than we ever imagined.   21

To learn this, for me at least, changes everything. I take it to be profoundly good news, though I can easily imagine how it might trouble some people. For many of us, nature is a last bastion of certainty; wilderness, as something beyond the reach of history and accident, is one of the last in our fast-dwindling supply of metaphysical absolutes, those comforting transcendental values by which we have traditionally taken our measure and set our sights. To take away predictable, divinely ordered nature is to pull up one of our last remaining anchors. We are liable to float away on the trackless sea of our own subjectivity.   22

But the discovery that time and chance hold sway even in nature can also be liberating. Because contingency is an invitation to participate in history. Human choice is unnatural only if nature is deterministic; human change is unnatural only if she is changeless in our absence. If the future of Cathedral Pines is up for grabs, if its history will always be the product of myriad chance events, then why shouldn't we also claim our place among all those deciding factors? For aren't we also one of nature's contingencies? And if our cigarette butts and Norway maples and acid rain are going to shape the future of this place, then why not also our hopes and desires?   23

Nature will condone an almost infinite number of possible futures for Cathedral Pines. Some would be better than others. True, what we would regard as "better" is probably not what the beetles would prefer. But nature herself has no strong preference. That doesn't mean she will countenance *any* outcome; she's already ruled out many possible futures   24 (tropical rain forest, desert, etc.) and, all things being equal, she'd proba-bly lean toward the oak. But all things aren't equal (her idea) and she is evidently happy to let the free play of numerous big and little contingen-cies settle the matter. To exclude from these human desire would be, at least in this place at this time, arbitrary, perverse and, yes, unnatural.

Establishing that we should have a vote in the disposition of Cathedral 25 Pines is much easier than figuring out how we should cast it. The discov-ery of contingency in nature would seem to fling open a Pandora's box. For if there's nothing fixed or inevitable about nature's course, what's to stop us from concluding that anything goes? It's a whole lot easier to assume that nature left to her own devices knows what's best for a place, to let ourselves be guided by the wilderness ethic.

And maybe that's what we should do. Just because the wilderness ethic 26 is based on a picture of nature that is probably more mythical than real doesn't necessarily mean we have to discard it. In the same way that the Declaration of Independence begins with the useful fiction that "all men are created equal," we could simply stipulate that Cathedral Pines *is* wilderness, and proceed on that assumption. The test of the wilderness ethic is not how truthful it is, but how useful it is in doing what we want to do—in protecting and improving the environment.

So how good a guide is the wilderness ethic in this particular case? 27 Certainly treating Cathedral Pines as a wilderness will keep us from build-ing condos there. When you don't trust yourself to do the right thing, it helps to have an authority as wise and experienced as nature to decide matters for you. But what if nature decides on Japanese honeysuckle— three hundred years of wall-to-wall brush? We would then have a forest not only that we don't like, but that isn't even a wilderness, since it was man who brought Japanese honeysuckle to Cornwall. At this point in his-tory, after humans have left their stamp on virtually every corner of the Earth, doing nothing is frequently a poor recipe for wilderness. In many cases it leads to a gradually deteriorating environment (as seems to be happening in Yellowstone), or to an environment shaped in large part by the acts and mistakes of previous human inhabitants.

If it's real wilderness we want in Cathedral Pines, and not merely an 28 imagined innocence, we will have to restore it. This is the paradox faced by the Nature Conservancy and most other advocates of wilderness: at this point in history, creating a landscape that bears no marks of human inter-vention will require a certain amount of human intervention. At a mini-mum it would entail weeding the exotic species from Cathedral Pines, and that is something the Nature Conservancy's strict adherence to the wilder-ness ethic will not permit.

But what if the Conservancy *was* willing to intervene just enough to   29
erase any evidence of man's presence? It would soon run up against
some difficult questions for which its ethic leaves it ill-prepared. For
what is the "real" state of nature in Cathedral Pines? Is it the way the forest looked before the settlers arrived? We could restore that condition
by removing all traces of European man. Yet isn't that a rather Eurocentric
(if not racist) notion of wilderness? We now know that the Indians were
not the ecological eunuchs we once thought. They too left their mark on
the land: fires set by Indians determined the composition of the New
England forests and probably created that "wilderness" we call the Great
Plains. For true untouched wilderness we have to go a lot further back
than 1640 or 1492. And if we want to restore the landscape to its pre-
Indian condition, then we're going to need a lot of heavy ice-making
equipment (not to mention a few woolly mammoths) to make it look right.

But even that would be arbitrary. In fact there is no single moment in   30
time that we can point to and say, *this* is the state of nature in Cathedral
Pines. Just since the last ice age alone, that "state of nature" has undergone
a thorough revolution every thousand years or so, as tree species forced
south by the glaciers migrated back north (a process that is still going on),
as the Indians arrived and set their fires, as the large mammals disappeared, as the climate fluctuated—as all the usual historical contingen-
cies came on and off the stage. For several thousand years after the ice
age, this part of Connecticut was a treeless tundra; is *that* the true state
of nature in Cathedral Pines? The inescapable fact is that, if we want wilderness here, we will have to choose *which* wilderness we want—an
idea that is inimical to the wilderness ethic. For wasn't the attraction of
wilderness precisely the fact that it relieved us of having to make
choices—wasn't nature going to decide, letting us off the hook of history
and anthropocentrism?

No such luck, it seems. "Wilderness" is not nearly as straightforward or   31
dependable a guide as we'd like to believe. If we do nothing, we may end
up with an impoverished weed patch of our own (indirect) creation,
which would hardly count as a victory for wilderness. And if we want to
restore Cathedral Pines to some earlier condition, we're forced into making the kinds of inevitably anthropocentric choices and distinctions we
turned to wilderness to escape. (Indeed, doing a decent job of wilderness
restoration would take all the technology and scientific know-how humans can muster.) Either way, there appears to be no escape from history,
not even in nature.

The reason that the wilderness ethic isn't very helpful in a place like   32
Cathedral Pines is that it's an absolutist ethic: man or nature, it says, pick

one. As soon as history or circumstance blurs that line, it gets us into trouble. There are times and places when man or nature is the right and necessary choice; back at Hetch Hetchy in 1907 that may well have been the case. But it seems to me that these days most of the environmental questions we face are more like the ambiguous ones posed by Cathedral Pines, and about these the wilderness ethic has less and less to say that is of much help.

The wilderness ethic doesn't tell us what to do when Yellowstone's 33 ecosystem begins to deteriorate, as a result not of our interference but of our neglect. When a species threatens to overwhelm and ruin a habitat because history happened to kill off the predator that once kept its population in check, the ethic is mute. It is confounded, too, when the only hope for the survival of another species is the manipulation of its natural habitat by man. It has nothing to say in all those places where development is desirable or unavoidable except: Don't do it. When we're forced to choose between a hydroelectric power plant and a nuclear one, it refuses to help. That's because the wilderness ethic can't make distinctions between one kind of intervention in nature and another—between weeding Cathedral Pines and developing a theme part there. "You might as well put up condos" is its classic answer to any plan for human intervention in nature.

"All or nothing," says the wilderness ethic, and in fact we've ended up 34 with a landscape in America that conforms to that injunction remarkably well. Thanks to exactly this kind of either/or thinking, Americans have done an admirable job of drawing lines around certain sacred areas (we did invent the wilderness area) and a terrible job of managing the rest of our land. The reason is not hard to find: the only environmental ethic we have has nothing useful to say about those areas outside the line. Once a landscape is no longer "virgin" it is typically written off as fallen, lost to nature, irredeemable. We hand it over to the jurisdiction of that other sacrosanct American ethic: laissez-faire economics. "You might as well put up condos." And so we do.

Indeed, the wilderness ethic and laissez-faire economics, antithetical as 35 they might at first appear, are really mirror images of one another. Each proposes a quasi-divine force—Nature, the Market—that, left to its own devices, somehow knows what's best for a place. Nature and the market are both self-regulating, guided by an invisible hand. Worshippers of either share a deep, Puritan distrust of man, taking it on faith that human tinkering with the natural or economic order can only pervert it. Neither will acknowledge that their respective divinities can also err: that nature produces the AIDS virus as well as the rose, that the same markets that produce stupendous wealth can also crash. (Actually, worshippers of the market are a bit more realistic than worshippers of nature: they long ago stopped relying on the free market to supply us with such necessities as food and shelter. Though they don't like to talk about it much, they accept the need for society to "garden" the market.)

Essentially, we have divided our country in two, between the kingdom 36 of wilderness, which rules about 8 percent of America's land, and the kingdom of the market, which rules the rest. Perhaps we should be grateful for secure borders. But what do those of us who care about nature do when we're on the market side, which is most of the time? How do we behave? What are our goals? We can't reasonably expect to change the borders, no matter how many power lines and dams Earth First! blows up. No, the wilderness ethic won't be of much help over here. Its politics are bound to be hopelessly romantic (consisting of impractical schemes to redraw the borders) or nihilistic. Faced with hard questions about how to confront global environmental problems such as the greenhouse effect or ozone depletion (problems that respect no borders), adherents of the wilderness ethic are apt to throw up their hands in despair and declare the "end of nature."

The only thing that's really in danger of ending is a romantic, pantheis- 37 tic idea of nature that we invented in the first place, one whose passing might well turn out to be a blessing in disguise. Useful as it has been in helping us protect the sacred 8 percent, it nevertheless has failed to prevent us from doing a great deal of damage to the remaining 92 percent. This old idea may have taught us how to worship nature, but it didn't tell us how to live with her. It told us more than we needed to know about virginity and rape, and almost nothing about marriage. The metaphor of divine nature can admit only two roles for man: as worshipper (the naturalist's role) or temple destroyer (the developer's). But that drama is all played out now. The temple's been destroyed—if it ever was a temple. Nature *is* dead, if by nature we mean something that stands apart from man and messy history. And now that it is, perhaps we can begin to write some new parts for ourselves, ones that will show us how to start out from here, not from some imagined state of innocence, and let us get down to the work at hand.

Thoreau and Muir and their descendants went to the wilderness and re- 38 turned with the makings of America's first environmental ethic. Today it still stands, though somewhat strained and tattered. What if now, instead of to the wilderness, we were to look to the garden for the makings of a new ethic? One that would not necessarily supplant the earlier one, but might give us something useful to say in those cases when it is silent or unhelpful?

It will take better thinkers than me to flesh out what such an ethic might 39 look like. But even my limited experience in the garden has persuaded me that the materials needed to construct it—the fresh metaphors about nature we need—may be found there. For the garden is a place with long experience of questions having to do with man in nature. Below are some provisional notes, based on my own experiences and the experiences of other gardeners I've met or read, on the kinds of answers the garden is apt to give.

1. An ethic based on the garden would give local answers. Unlike the wilderness idea, it would propose different solutions in different places and times. This strikes me as both a strength and a weakness. It's a weakness because a garden ethic will never speak as clearly or univocally as the wilderness ethic does. In a country as large and geographically various as this, it is probably inevitable that we will favor abstract landscape ideas—grids, lawns, monocultures, wildernesses—which can be applied across the board, even legislated nationally; such ideas have the power to simplify and unite. Yet isn't this power itself part of the problem? The health of a place generally suffers whenever we impose practices on it that are better suited to another place; a lawn in Virginia makes sense in a way that a lawn in Arizona does not.

So a garden ethic would begin with Alexander Pope's famous advice to landscape designers: "Consult the Genius of the Place in all." It's hard to imagine this slogan ever replacing Earth First!'s "No Compromise in Defense of Mother Earth" on American bumper stickers; nor should it, at least not everywhere. For Pope's dictum suggests that there are places whose "genius" will, if hearkened to, counsel "no compromise." Yet what is right for Yosemite is not necessarily right for Cathedral pines.

2. The gardener starts out from here. By that I mean, he accepts contingency, his own and nature's. He doesn't spend a lot of time worrying about whether he has a god-given right to change nature. It's enough for him to know that, for some historical or biological reason, humankind finds itself living in places (six of the seven continents) where it must substantially alter the environment in order to survive. If we had remained on African savanna things might be different. And if I lived in zone six I could probably grow good tomatoes without the use of plastic. The gardener learns to play the hand he's been dealt.

3. A garden ethic would be frankly anthropocentric. As I began to understand when I planted my roses and my maple tree, we know nature only through the screen of our metaphors; to see her plain is probably impossible. (And not necessarily desirable, as George Eliot once suggested: "If we could hear the squirrel's heartbeat, the sound of the grass growing, we should die of that roar." Without the editing of our perceptions, nature might prove unbearable.) Melville was describing all of nature

when he described the whiteness of the whale, its "dumb blankness, full of meaning." Even wilderness, in both its satanic and benevolent incarnations, is an historical, man-made idea. Every one of our various metaphors for nature—"wilderness," "ecosystem," "Gaia," "resource," "wasteland"— is already a kind of garden, an indissoluble mixture of our culture and whatever it is that's really out there. "Garden" may sound like a hopelessly anthropocentric concept, but it's probably one we can't get past.

The gardener doesn't waste much time on metaphysics—on figuring out what a "truer" perspective on nature (such as biocentrism or geocentrism) might look like. That's probably because he's noticed that most of the very long or wide perspectives we've recently been asked to adopt (including the one advanced by the Nature Conservancy in Cathedral Pines) are indifferent to our well-being and survival as a species. On this point he agrees with Wendell Berry—that "it is not natural to be disloyal to one's own kind." 44

4. That said, though, the gardener's conception of his self-interest is broad and enlightened. Anthropocentric as he may be, he recognizes that he is dependent for his health and survival on many other forms of life, so he is careful to take their interests into account in whatever he does. He is in fact a wilderness advocate of a certain kind. It is when he respects and nurtures the wilderness of his soil and his plants that his garden seems to flourish most. Wildness, he has found, resides not only out there, but right here: in his soil, in his plants, even in himself. Overcultivation tends to repress this quality, which experience tells him is necessary to health in all three realms. But wildness is more a quality than a place, and though humans can't manufacture it, they can nourish and husband it. That is precisely what I'm doing when I make compost and return it to the soil; it is what we could be doing in Cathedral Pines (and not necessarily by leaving the place alone). The gardener cultivates wildness, but he does so carefully and respectfully, in full recognition of its mystery. 45

5. The gardener tends not to be romantic about nature. What could be more natural than the storms and droughts and plagues that ruin his garden? Cruelty, aggression, suffering—these too are nature's offspring (and not, as Rousseau tried to convince us, culture's). Nature is probably a poor place to look for values. She was indifferent to humankind's arrival, and she is indifferent to our survival. 46

It's only in the last century or so that we seem to have forgotten this. Our romance of nature is a comparatively recent idea, the product of the industrial age's novel conceit that nature could be conquered, and probably also of the fact that few of us work with nature directly anymore. But should current weather forecasts prove to be accurate (a rapid, permanent warming trend accompanied by severe storms), our current romance will 47 look like a brief historical anomaly, a momentary lapse of judgment. Nature may once again turn dangerous and capricious and unconquerable. When this happens, we will quickly lose our crush on her.

Compared to the naturalist, the gardener never fell head over heels for nature. He's seen her ruin his plans too many times for that. The gardener has learned, perforce, to live with her ambiguities—that she is neither all good nor all bad, that she gives as well as takes away. Nature's apt to pull the rug out from under us at any time, to make a grim joke of our noblest intention. Perhaps this explains why garden writing tends to be comic, rather than lyrical or elegiac in the way that nature writing usually is: the gardener can never quite forget about the rug underfoot, the possibility of the offstage hook.

6. The gardener feels he has a legitimate quarrel with nature—with her weeds and storms and plagues, her rot and death. What's more, that quarrel has produced much of value, not only in his own time here (this garden, these fruits), but over the whole course of Western history. Civilization itself, as Freud and Frazer and many others have observed, is the product of that quarrel. But at the same time, the gardener appreciates that it would probably not be in his interest, or in nature's, to push his side of this argument too hard. Many points of contention that humankind thought it had won—DDT's victory over insects, say, or medicine's conquest of infectious disease—turned out to be Pyrrhic or illusory triumphs. Better to keep the quarrel going, the good gardener reasons, than to reach for outright victory, which is dangerous in the attempt and probably impossible anyway.

7. The gardener doesn't take it for granted that man's impact on nature will always be negative. Perhaps he's observed how his own garden has made this patch of land a better place, even by nature's own standards. His gardening has greatly increased the diversity and abundance of life in this place. Besides the many exotic species of plants he's introduced, the mammal, rodent, and insect populations have burgeoned, and his soil supports a much richer community of microbes than it did before.

Judged strictly by these standards, nature occasionally makes mistakes. The climax forest could certainly be considered one (a place where the number and variety of living things have declined to a crisis point) and evolution teems with others. At the same time, it should be acknowledged that man occasionally creates new ecosystems much richer than the ones they replaced, and not merely on the scale of a garden: think of the tallgrass prairies of the Midwest, England's hedgerow landscape, the countryside of the Ile de France, the patchwork of fields and forests in this part of New England. Most of us would be happy to call such places "nature," but that does not do them (or us) justice; they are really a kind of garden, a second nature.

The gardener doesn't feel that by virtue of the fact that he changes na-   52
ture he is somehow outside of it. He looks around and sees that human
hopes and desires are by now part and parcel of the landscape. The "environment" is not, and has never been, a neutral, fixed backdrop; it is in
fact alive, changing all the time in response to innumerable contingencies,
one of these being the presence within it of the gardener. And that presence is neither inherently good nor bad.

8. The gardener firmly believes it is possible to make distinctions   53
between kinds and degrees of human intervention in nature. Isn't the
difference between the Ile de France and Love Canal, or a pine forest
and a condo development, proof enough that the choice isn't really between "all or nothing"? The gardener doesn't doubt that it is possible to
discriminate; it is through experience in the garden that he develops this
faculty.

Because of his experience, the gardener is not likely to conclude from   54
the fact that some intervention in nature is unavoidable, therefore "anything goes." This is precisely where his skill and interest lie: in determin-
ing what does and does not go in a particular place. How much is too
much? What suits this land? How can we get what we want here while
nature goes about getting what she wants? He has no doubt that good
answers to these questions can be found.

9. The good gardener commonly borrows his methods, if not his goals,   55
from nature herself. For though nature doesn't seem to dictate in advance
what we can do in a place—we are free, in the same way evolution is,
to try something completely new—in the end she will let us know what
does and does not work. She is above all a pragmatist, and so is the successful gardener.

By studying nature's ways and means, the gardener can find answers to   56
the questions, What is apt to work? What avails here? This seems to hold
true at many levels of specificity. In one particular patch of my vegetable
garden—a low, damp area—I failed with every crop I planted until I
stopped to consider what nature grew in a similar area nearby: briars. So
I planted raspberries, which are of course a cultivated kind of briar, and
they have flourished. A trivial case, but it shows how attentiveness to nature can help us to attune our desires with her ways.

The imitation of nature is of course the principle underlying organic   57
gardening. Organic gardeners have learned to mimic nature's own methods of building fertility in the soil, controlling insect populations and
disease, recycling nutrients. But the practices we call "organic" are not
themselves "natural," any more than the bird call of a hunter is natural.
They are more like man-made analogues of natural processes. But they
seem to work. And they at least suggest a way to approach other problems—from a town's decision on what to do with a blown-down pine

forest, to society's choice among novel new technologies. In each case, there will be some alternatives that align our needs and desires with nature's ways more closely than others.

It does seem that we do best in nature when we imitate her—when we learn to think like running water, or a carrot, an aphid, a pine forest, or a compost pile. That's probably because nature, after almost four billion years of trial-and-error experience, has wider knowledge of what works in life. Surely we're better off learning how to draw on her experience than trying to repeat it, if only because we don't have that kind of time.   58

10. If nature is one necessary source of instruction for a garden ethic, culture is the other. Civilization may be part of our problem with respect to nature, but there will be no solution without it. As Wendell Berry has pointed out, it is culture, and certainly not nature, that teaches us to observe and remember, to learn from our mistakes, to share our experiences, and perhaps most important of all, to restrain ourselves. Nature does not teach its creatures to control their appetites except by the harshest of lessons—epidemics, mass death, extinctions. Nothing would be more natural than for humankind to burden the environment to the extent that it was rendered unfit for human life. Nature in that event would not be the loser, nor would it disturb her laws in the least—operating as it has always done, natural selection would unceremoniously do us in. Should this fate be averted, it will only be because our culture—*our* laws and metaphors, our science and technology, our ongoing conversation about nature and man's place in it—pointed us in the direction of a different future. Nature will not do this for us.   59

The gardener in nature is that most artificial of creatures, a civilized human being: in control of his appetites, solicitous of nature, self-conscious and responsible, mindful of the past and the future, and at ease with the fundamental ambiguity of his predicament—which is that though he lives in nature, he is no longer strictly *of* nature. Further, he knows that neither his success nor his failure in this place is ordained. Nature is apparently indifferent to his fate, and this leaves him free—indeed, obliges him—to make his own way here as best he can.   60

What would an ethic based on these ideas—based on the idea of the garden—advise us to do in Cathedral Pines? I don't know enough about the ecology of the place to say with certainty, but I think I have some sense of how we might proceed under its dispensation. We would start out, of course, by consulting "the Genius of the Place." This would tell us, among other things, that Cathedral Pines is not a wilderness, and so probably should not be treated as one. It is a cultural as well as a natural landscape, and to exclude the wishes of the townspeople from our plans for   61 the place would be false. To treat it now as wilderness is to impose an abstract and alien idea on it.

Consulting the genius of the place also means inquiring as to what nature will allow us to do here—what this "locale permits, and what [it] denies," as Virgil wrote in *The Georgics*. We know right off, for instance, that this plot of land can support a magnificent forest of white pines. Nature would not object if we decided to replant the pine forest. Indeed, this would be a perfectly reasonable, environmentally sound thing to do. 62

If we chose to go this route, we would be undertaking a fairly simple act of what is called "ecological restoration." This relatively new school of environmentalism has its roots in Aldo Leopold's pioneering efforts to recreate a tall-grass prairie on the grounds of the University of Wisconsin Arboretum in the 1930s. Leopold and his followers (who continue to maintain the restored prairie today) believed that it is not always enough to conserve the land—that sometimes it is desirable, and possible, for man to intervene in nature in order to improve it. Specifically, man should intervene to re-create damaged ecosystems: polluted rivers, clear-cut forests, vanished prairies, dead lakes. The restorationists also believe, and in this they remind me of the green thumb, that the best way to learn about nature's ways is by trying to imitate them. (In fact much of what we know about the role of fire in creating and sustaining prairies comes from their efforts.) But the most important contribution of the restorationists has been to set forth a positive, active role for man in nature—in their conception, as equal parts gardener and healer. It seems to me that the idea of ecological restoration is consistent with a garden ethic, and perhaps with the Hippocratic Oath as well. 63

From the work of the ecological restorationists, we now know that it is possible to skip and manipulate the stages of forest succession. They would probably advise us to burn the fallen timber—an act that, though not strictly speaking "natural," would serve as an effective analogue of the natural process by which a forest is regenerated. The fires we set would reinvigorate the soil (thereby enhancing *that* wilderness) and at the same time clear out the weed species, hardwood saplings, and brush. By doing all this, we will have imitated the conditions under which a white pine forest is born, and the pines might then return on their own. Or else—it makes little difference—we could plant them. At that point, our work would be done, and the pine forest could take care of itself. It would take many decades, but restoring the Cathedral Pines would strain neither our capabilities nor nature's sufferance. And in doing so, we would also be restoring the congenial relationship between man and nature that prevailed in this place before the storm and the subsequent controversy. That would be no small thing. 64

Nature would not preclude more novel solutions for Cathedral Pines— 65
other kinds of forest-gardens or even parks could probably flourish on this
site. But since the town has traditionally regarded Cathedral Pines as a
kind of local institution, one steeped in shared memories and historical
significance, I would argue that the genius of the place rules out doing
anything unprecedented here. The past is our best guide in this particular
case, and not only on questions of ecology.

But replanting the pine forest is not the only good option for Cathedral 66
Pines. There is another forest we might want to restore on this site, one
that is also in keeping with its history and its meaning to the town.

Before the storm, we used to come to Cathedral Pines and imagine that 67
this was how the New World forest looked to the first settlers. We now
know that the precolonial forest probably looked somewhat different—
for one thing, it was not exclusively pine. But it's conceivable that we
could restore Cathedral Pines to something closely resembling its actual
precolonial condition. By analyzing historical accounts, the rings of fallen
trees, and fossilized pollen grains buried in the soil, we could reconstruct
the variety and composition of species that flourished here in 1739, the
year when the colonists first settled near this place and formed the town
of Cornwall. We know that nature, having done so once before, would
probably permit us to have such a forest here. And, using some of the
more advanced techniques of ecological restoration, it is probably within
our competence to re-create a precolonial forest on this site.

We would do this not because we'd decided to be faithful to the "state 68
of nature" at Cathedral Pines, but very simply because the precolonial forest happens to mean a great deal to us. It is a touchstone in the history of
this town, not to mention this nation. A walk in a restored version of the
precolonial forest might recall us to our culture's first, fateful impressions
of America, to our thoughts on coming upon what Fitzgerald called the
"fresh green breast of the new world." In the contemplation of that scene
we might be moved to reconsider what happened next—to us, to the
Indians who once hunted here, to nature in this corner of America.

This is pretty much what I would have stood up and said if we'd had a 69
town meeting to decide what to do in Cathedral Pines. Certainly a town
meeting would have been a fitting way to decide the matter, nicely in
keeping with the genius of *this* place, a small town in New England. I can
easily imagine the speeches and the arguments. The people from the
Nature Conservancy would have made their plea for leaving the place
alone, for "letting nature take her course." Richard Dakin, the first selec-
man, and John Calhoun, the forest's nearest neighbor, would have warned
about the dangers of fire. And then we might have heard some other
points of view. I would have tried to make a pitch for restoration, talking about some of the ways we might "garden" the site. I can imagine

Ian Ingersoll, a gifted cabinetmaker in town, speaking with feeling about the waste of such rare timbers, and the prospect of sitting down to a Thanksgiving dinner at a table in which you could see rings formed at the time of the American Revolution. Maybe somebody else would have talked about how much she missed her Sunday afternoon walks in the forest, and how very sad the place looked now. A scientist from the Yale School of Forestry might have patiently tried to explain, as indeed one Yale scientist did in the press, why "It's just as pretty to me now as it was then."

This is the same fellow who said, "If you're going to clean it up, you might as well put up condos." I can't imagine anyone actually proposing that, or any other kind of development in Cathedral Pines. But if someone did, he would probably get shouted down. Because we have too much respect for this place; and besides, our sympathies and interests are a lot more complicated than the economists or environmentalists always seem to think. Sooner than a developer, we'd be likely to hear from somebody speaking on behalf of the forest's fauna—the species who have lost out in the storm (like the owls), but also the ones for whom doing nothing would be a boon (the beetles). And so the various interests of the animals would be taken into account, too; indeed, I expect that "nature"—all those different (and contradictory) points of view—would be well represented at this town meeting. Perhaps it is naïve of me to think so, but I'm confident that in the course of a public, democratic conversation about the disposition of Cathedral Pines, we would eventually arrive at a solution that would have at once pleased us and not offended nature.

But unfortunately that's not what happened. The future of Cathedral Pines was decided in a closed-door meeting at the Nature Conservancy in September, after a series of negotiations with the selectmen and the owners of adjacent property. The result was a compromise that seems to have pleased no one. The fallen trees will remain untouched—except for a fifty-foot swath clear-cut around the perimeter of the forest, a firebreak intended to appease the owners of a few nearby houses. The sole human interest taken into account in the decision was the worry about fire.

I drove up there one day in late fall to have a look around, to see what the truce between the Conservancy and the town had wrought. What a sad sight it is. Unwittingly, and in spite of the good intentions on both sides, the Conservancy and the selectmen have conspired to create a landscape that is a perfect symbol of our perverted relation to nature. The firebreak looks like nothing so much as a no-man's-land in a war zone, a forbidding expanse of blistered ground impounding what little remains of the Cathedral Pines. The landscape we've made here is grotesque. And yet it is the logical outcome of a confrontation between, on the one side, an abstract and mistaken concept of nature's interests and, on the other, a pinched and demeaning notion of our own interests. We should probably not be surprised that the result of such a confrontation is not a wilderness, or a garden, but a DMZ.

QUESTIONS FOR DISCUSSION AND WRITING

1.   According to Pollan, what is the "wilderness ethic," and why was it not a useful guide in the case of the Cathedral Pines? What result does he claim his "garden ethic" would have produced instead, and why would those results have been more satisfactory?

2.   As he considers the prospect of restoring the Cathedral Pines park, Pollan concludes, "The inescapable fact is that, if we want wilderness here, we will have to choose *which* wilderness we want" (par. 30). What does he mean by "which" wilderness, and why does he call this idea "inimical to the wilderness ethic" (par. 30)?

3.   What does Pollan mean by his declaration that "nature *is* dead" (par. 37)? Does he see this "death" as a necessarily bad thing? Why or why not? How is this death related to his claim that what we need is "fresh metaphors about nature" (par. 39)?

RIK SCARCE

Eco-Warriors *(1990) was the first book written by Rik Scarce (b. 1958), a jour-*
nalist and freelance writer who makes his home in Washington State. Scarce re-
ceived a master's degree in political futuristics from the University of Hawaii
and later served as an aide to a member of the California legislature. As the sub-
title to his book suggests, Scarce's goal is to help his readers understand why the
direct-action groups take such extreme measures: tree spiking, smashing testing
laboratories, sinking multi-million-dollar whaling ships. Although he tries to be
reasonably objective, Scarce is clearly sympathetic to what he calls the "front-line
warriors" in the war to "save the world from ourselves." For Scarce, it is impor-
tant to understand the history of radical groups like Sea Shepherds, the Animal
Liberation Front, and Earth First!, each of which began when disgruntled mem-
bers broke away from larger, more mainstream environmental organizations. As
Scarce explains, the philosophy of the ecowarriors is direct and simple: "No
compromise in defense of Mother Earth." On the book's back cover, Scarce says
he hopes to get behind the "media stereotypes and establishment fabrications" in
order to "humanize a movement fighting for the future of us all." In the chapter
from Eco-Warriors *presented here, Scarce presents the dramatic account of a raid*
by a team of Sea Shepherd saboteurs who sneak into Iceland in order to sink a fleet
of whaling ships before they can kill more whales in the North Atlantic.

Raid on Reykjavik

Rod Coronado watched in horror, tears streaming down his young   1
face, as the huge man strode to the side of a yelping, terrified harp seal
pup, knelt, and crushed its skull with one blow from his wooden club.
The man showed no emotion as he moved to another of the ivory-colored
baby seals and then another, striking ferociously each time. Then the
image on the television screen shifted to another man, this one being
dragged helplessly across the ice toward a nearby sealing ship. He had attached himself to a long cable that extended from the ship out over the
brilliant white ice; behind him freshly skinned pelts were pulled along
as well. Those images of the seals, the sealers, and of iconoclast Paul
Watson's attempt to stop the hunt, filmed during Watson's final days as a
Greenpeace activist, became a guiding star for the young Coronado's life.
"I immediately knew that that's what I had to do, those were the people
I wanted to work with and that was the avenue that I wanted to take,"
Coronado says. "It was no bullshit, just getting out there and doing what
had to be done."

That was 1979 when Coronado was twelve years old. He pursued his star, and within seven years his life grew to almost mythical proportions, his name and that of compatriot David Howitt written alongside Watson's in the list of legends of the environmental movement. 2

In fact, though, Coronado insists he is nothing more than an ordinary person unafraid of living out his dreams and taking risks for what he loves. Not long after the broadcast of the documentary on sealing, he saw news reports on the ramming of the pirate whaling ship *Sierra,* and his interest became focused on Watson's no-holds-barred fight for marine mammals. Coronado tracked down the Sea Shepherds and wrote to their leader. "It was funny because at that young age I wrote tons of letters to organizations," Coronado recalls. "I figured I would join all these groups. So I sent all these great twelve-year-old kid's totally naive letters to these people. The only personal reply I received was from Paul." The other organizations asked people to mark a box and send a check for the corresponding amount. In contrast, Coronado paraphrases the Sea Shepherd literature: "Send us money to buy fuel for our ship so we can go out and sabotage the bastards." And that is exactly what he did. In 1983 he mailed 200 hard-earned dollars to the Sea Shepherds to help purchase fuel for an expedition to stop those same sealers who had terrorized the harp seals on his television. 3

Like many other radical environmentalists, Coronado seems to have been born with ecological consciousness, the wilderness gene, a sense of connectedness, a higher level of compassion than most—*something* that catapults him over the Eco-Wall so early in life that he has no recollection of when or how it all began. Coronado's early interest in activism on behalf of animals bears this out and takes on a deeper, more ironic quality when juxtaposed with Watson's entre into radical environmentalism. As a young boy, Watson, too, took up the cause of those who could not speak for themselves; he wrote to Cleveland Amory, founder of the Fund for Animals, and asked how to get involved. Amory welcomed him without hesitation and later purchased Watson's first ship for him, the *Sea Shepherd,* which the renegade Watson used to hunt down and cripple the *Sierra.* 4

Watson would display the same sort of unswerving support for Coronado and Howitt as Amory bestowed on him. Somehow, it seemed that it was all meant to be. "One thing that I've believed in all along is synchronicity, that a lot of things weren't coincidence but were fate," Coronado says. "The time when I got out of high school to when I met Paul was a matter of only a few months, yet all through school I had wanted to do that. So, when I came back, a lot of my friends were actually shocked that I had achieved what I wanted to do, or at least part of it." It was, as Coronado says, as if he "didn't have a choice, that these things were just happening to me." 5

It was on a high school graduation trip to Vancouver, British Columbia, with his parents in 1984 that Coronado met Watson for the first time. Watson was not supposed to be there, but rather out on an action. Amazingly, and to Coronado's joy, it had been delayed. "I told him, 'I'm out of school. I want to work with you.' They were working on the Whaling Walls educational murals. He said, 'You can start now.' I saw my parents that night and packed my bags and said 'I'm off to work with the Sea Shepherds.'" Coronado's stunned mother and father bade him farewell.

When the *Sea Shepherd II* was returned to the Sea Shepherds by a Canadian court early the following year—it had been confiscated by the Canadian Navy during the harp seal campaign that Coronado had contributed to because of Watson's interference with the slaughter—he turned his energies to preparing the ship for its next voyage. After two years in mothballs the old cod boat was in rotten shape. Climbing aboard it for the first time was a decided disappointment, Coronado says glumly. "I spent three months in port aboard ship just trying to get the thing going again with no electricity, no heating, no hot water. It was hell. But we stuck it out." Then as now, the crew was all volunteer and paid nearly all of their own expenses. During those months Coronado was exposed to a rich mixture of idealism and practicality freely shared by the peace and environment activists who hung out with Watson. The Captain became the teenager's mentor, often advising Coronado in ways that benefitted the student and not the sage. Whenever Coronado's money ran out, he headed back home to work in his father's small steel materials firm, then returned to the ship.

With their vessel finally back in working order, the Sea Shepherds headed to the Atlantic that summer. On their way to protect pilot whales against the annual onslaught in the Faroe Islands, Watson issued an ultimatum during a *Sea Shepherd II* sojourn at Reykjavik, Iceland. The Sea Shepherds could not take action that summer, but he warned the Icelandic whalers that he expected compliance with the International Whaling Commission's (IWC) moratorium on whaling, scheduled to take effect the following January. "We told them that if they didn't [comply], we would come back and enforce the International Whaling Commission moratorium against them," Watson says.

Coronado took advantage of the stopover to wander down to the docks and check out the whaling fleet. He noticed that there was a twenty-four-hour patrol, but other than that only one guard was on duty with the four ships. "I thought, 'I bet if we weren't here there would only be that one guard on those four ships,'" Coronado recalls. "I just buried that in my mind. I thought, 'You could sabotage those boats.' That was that. I didn't think much more about it because of the Faroes."

Preparation

Nothing changed in the early months of 1986. Iceland continued to kill   10
whales, stating the kill was for scientific purposes and that it would abide
by the IWC's "research whaling" guidelines. Again Watson warned that he
was prepared to act, delivering his message with the *Sea Shepherd II*
parked in the Malmo, Sweden, harbor during the IWC's annual meeting
there. Research whaling was a sham, nothing but a cover for continued
commercial whaling despite the moratorium. With some of the hunted
species' populations dangerously low, there was no excuse for more
killing.

Then the Sea Shepherds waited for the United States to enforce amend-   11
ments recently passed by Congress to the International Fishery Conservation and Management Act. Watson explains, "These amendments
state that any nation that attempts to undermine the authority of the
International Whaling Commission will lose the right to sell fish products
in the U.S. and the right to fish in U.S. waters, which is the only teeth the
IWC had for enforcing its regulations." President Reagan "chose to discriminate on the application of the amendment," says Watson. He refused
to invoke sanctions against NATO ally Iceland, probably because he did
not want to risk losing the strategically important Keflavik Air Force Base.
In July the Reagan appointee-dominated U.S. Supreme Court declared the
amendments unconstitutional on a 5–4 vote. "And to add insult to injury,"
Watson says disgustedly, Reagan "turned a blind eye to Iceland's increased sale of whale meat to Japan in return for holding a summit with
Mr. Gorbachev in Reykjavik. So the price of that summit was an increased
number of whales being killed."

When Coronado heard of Iceland's intention to continue killing   12
whales, his mind immediately ran to the whaling ships lined up neatly in
Reykjavik's dark harbor. Following the Faroese campaign, he approached
David Howitt, a quiet spoken Brit and one of the *Sea Shepherd II* crew he
knew best. Coronado offered Howitt the chance to be constructive for nature through destruction of humans' killing tools, asking if he would like
to help sink the Icelandic whaling ships. Howitt quickly accepted. "It was
mutual," Howitt says. "He talked about the situation with me and I asked
for details about what was happening. We both felt that we ought to do
something together, and the plan grew out of talking with each other
about the possibility of bringing attention to it."

Howitt was a relative newcomer to the Sea Shepherds, having joined   13
them in March 1986 after some friends who were playing benefit concerts
for the group took him to see the ship in Plymouth. "At the time I was
looking for something more constructive to do in the way of environmental protection," Howitt says. A year older than Coronado, he had been

raised in St. Ives, a small coastal town in Cornwall, and had long felt a kinship with nature. "I trained as a natural history photographer.... And at the sight of the ship in Plymouth, I jumped at the chance to help put it to sea." Although he had no prior activistic experience of the sort he knew he was in for with the Sea Shepherds, he wanted to do more than take pictures. Howitt spent two months working on the *Sea Shepherd II* to make it seaworthy and then sailed as an engineer to the Faroes. "I was set to work in environmental protection in whatever way might be most effective," says Howitt. He adds, "After studying natural history you realize that the situation worldwide is getting pretty critical. I wanted to get involved in whatever way seemed most constructive."

Coronado and Howitt wasted little time in preparing for their expedition, one that would prove constructive for the whales but extremely destructive to the whaling industry. To fund the effort, the Californian found work refinishing furniture in London and Howitt went to Kent to pick hops. When they could, they researched Iceland's sordid whaling history, concentrating on its contemptuous attitude toward the IWC and its agreements with Japan for selling the meat. The conspirators also found that whaling was driven by anachronistic societal values wherein Icelanders clung to their ancient Viking heritage even as they enjoyed Western lifestyles and affluence. Whaling held little real significance for the average Icelander, although seventy percent of the population expressed support for the industry in public opinion polls. 14

The also learned that the Icelandic whaling operation was the exclusive province of Christian Lofsson, a rich businessman who owned a supermarket chain and had ties to the nation's political elite. The proceeds of the whale kill in 1986 amounted to $40,000 per animal, all coming from Japan. "Eighty whales," Coronado says. "It doesn't sound like a lot, but take eighty times $40,000 and you're talking about a huge profit for a month of work." 15

Neither Coronado nor Howitt doubted the legitimacy or the need for their plan of sabotage for one second. "We never had the qualms that a lot of people might think we had, or that people do have, in regards to the destruction of property and whether that is a line that you are ready to cross," Coronado says. From years of writing letters, passing out petitions, and attending demonstrations, as well as his familiarity with the failed efforts of those who had tried through non-destructive means to end the killing of whales, Coronado felt strongly that direct, decisive action was the only recourse. Driven by an innate love of all beings, Coronado and Howitt identified with the whales as one human might with another. They lived by—and were willing to risk death for—ecocentric principles. "For us, it was as simple as somebody who might stand in the line of fire to prevent somebody else from being killed," says 16

Coronado. "It was simple self-defense in the sense not of our self-defense, but of the defense of the animals that didn't have the power of self-defense, or that were so above us in terms of morality that they didn't have a sense of violence for the sake of violence. We had to deal with the humans because we were humans ourselves!"

When Coronado and Howitt told Watson of their plans, he agreed to speak for them if they could bring off the action; Coronado sensed some doubt in his mentor's voice. The only other people who knew of the plan were Coronado's sister in London and a British Sea Shepherd contact. The raiders arrived in Iceland on October 15, 1986. Coronado and Howitt spent "days and nights at the coffee shops across the way" from the docks where the four whaling ships tied up, watching and planning. They even hid in scrap yards around the Reykjavik harbor to note the comings and goings of the ships, the crew, and to gain whatever insight they could into the operation. "Before we went there, we didn't really know how much we would be able to do to draw attention to the illegal whaling," Howitt says. "We had talked about sinking a ship, about scuttling a ship, and ways of doing it. For instance, we researched the scuttling of *Sea Shepherd* and the elapsed time that it took. We thought about it, but we had no way of knowing if we could do that safely until we had gone through the reconnaissance and came up with the best plan." Early on in their stay they purchased a pair of bolt cutters and some heavy wrenches at a local hardware store in anticipation of their future needs. 17

Out of curiosity, Coronado and Howitt one afternoon hitchhiked up the coast about fifty miles to the whaling station where the carcasses were taken for butchering. "We heard they had tours there, so we went to go take a tour," says Coronado. "When we got there, no one was around. It was closed down for the year. So we just started walking around, and we realized there was a lot we could do there as well as damaging the ships." Following their self-guided tour, the whale processing center was added to their "little campaign." 18

After a couple of weeks, money got to be a little tight. Coronado landed a job through two Swedish women whom he and Howitt had met at the Salvation Army Hostel where they were staying. Coronado recalls it with a wry grin and a mixture of glee and revulsion: "There I was, the only dark-complexioned, non-Icelandic speaking vegetarian working at this Icelandic meat packing plant. And that didn't raise any suspicions!" 19

Had anyone bothered to ask, the queries would have been well-placed, for Coronado was not interested in the job for the money alone; he was searching for "Whale Meat Mountain." The Icelanders hid a huge and mysterious mound of whale meat somewhere, and a meat packing plant seemed a logical place for it. As part of their original plans, Coronado and Howitt wanted to find the mountain and ruin the meat. When they later 20 discovered the "mountain" at the whale processing station, it turned out to be the offal, bones, and non-sellable parts of carcasses that supposedly constituted 50.1 percent of the "usable meat" from Icelandic whale kills. A bare majority of the usable portions of the whales had to be kept in-country under the IWC's "scientific research" regulations. Iceland was clearly violating even those lenient restrictions.

Only nine days before the scheduled action date, Icelandic immigration   21 authorities found that Coronado was working without the necessary documents. This might not have been much of a concern except that his very presence in Iceland was a danger in itself. Coronado had been banned from the Faroe Islands, and all other Scandinavian nations as well, due to his arrest stemming from the confrontations with Faroe authorities earlier that year. No charges were ever filed, but the arrests made it impossible for him to obtain a special permit allowing him to work in the country. The discovery of his illegal work status would lead to an investigation which would bring his prior arrest to light. He would not only lose his job, but be expelled from the country as well, thereby ending the eco-warrior's mission. Fate, however, was on Coronado's side. In their background check the authorities somehow missed the arrest record. Coronado was out of a job but also out of jail and still in the country.

Just before Coronado had lost his job, Howitt had traveled north to in-   22 vestigate the booming Icelandic fur industry. He was looking for evidence to confirm his suspicions that Fin and Sei whale meat from the "research" whaling was being sent to fur firms, another violation of IWC regulations. Whale meat was probably a relatively inexpensive source of food for the animals, and the farms were a local market for the industry, so Howitt's theory had a certain logic to it. The best Howitt could do was find evidence that a number of pilot whales which had recently become stranded on shore had been killed and sent to the farms. But he could find no proof that meat from the whaling industry was used to feed the caged animals.

On Howitt's return, he and Coronado took two days off to rest and pre-   23 pare for their mission. After more reconnaissance came the fateful day. Coronado and Howitt mailed all of their research materials—notes, photographs, and a description of the action—to Sarah Hambly, the United Kingdom contact person for Sea Shepherd, then said their good-byes to friends at the hostel, telling them that they were going sight-seeing and would leave for home the next day.

Whaling on the Whaling Station

It was Saturday, November 8. Their agenda was set: first, they would   24 rent a car, then eat at Reykjavik's only vegetarian restaurant, trash the whaling station, sink the ships, and leave. After renting the car and checking in their luggage at the airport for an early morning flight the following day, Coronado and Howitt drove to the restaurant. They figured the odds were good that it would be their last meal outside of jail for some time, and they had been saving what little money they had for one final feast. When they arrived at the restaurant, however, it was closed. It was one of only two disappointments in an action that was rife with potential pitfalls.

They settled for buying some food at a grocery store and then drove   25
toward the whaling station, parking short of the processing center and eating their dinner while listening to the radio. When they tried to start the car, the battery was dead. There they sat, months of preparation and weeks of intensive reconnaissance behind them, plane tickets in hand, and, because they had listened to a radio powered by a weak battery, they were going nowhere. Or so it seemed. Coronado recalls with a smile, "Sure enough, here comes a van load of young Icelandic kids who probably lived in the adjoining town and probably worked at the whaling station. They were very friendly. They gave us a push and we got the car going. We said, 'Thanks a lot.'" The saboteurs changed clothes and parked in a quarry a mile south of the whaling station.

Coronado and Howitt slipped on day packs containing little more than   26
flashlights and the bolt cutters and wrenches they had purchased weeks earlier. The weather, which had been pleasant all day, turned nasty, and it was raining as they walked toward the whaling station. When they neared it, they noticed someone operating an excavator. "We immediately dropped to the ground," Coronado says. They lay on the grass for an hour, the storm now pouring over them. At about nine o'clock the worker finally left. Thoroughly soaked but eager to get on with their task, Coronado and Howitt circled beneath the mercury vapor lights bathing the huge facility to confirm that it was unguarded. Then, charged with adrenaline, they entered through an unlocked door, quickly located the main circuit box, and shut down the power. For the next four hours they methodically made their way by flashlight through the complex in a focused, intense rampage.

"In the corner of one warehouse we discovered this computer room,"   27
Coronado remembers. "They had all the machinery being run by computers in this small room, maybe eight by ten feet. The walls were nothing but computers, printout machines, and stuff. At first, I just grabbed a few little things and smashed them, because I was afraid of being electrocuted. David didn't care, apparently, 'cause he just went in there and started whacking everything. It was just like these movies you see with panels exploding and LEDs flashing." He laughs, then his countenance takes on a serious look. "I don't know. We were destroying something that we knew

was worth so much money. But at the same time it was such a good feel-ing because we knew it was costing the industry so much money."

The storm outside made for good cover as they smashed and bashed 28
from one room to another. Contrary to press reports, Coronado says they
never used sledge hammers. Two million dollars of damage was done
with brains, time, and comparatively lightweight tools. "At the time all we
had was a big crescent wrench and a pair of bolt cutters.... We did just as
much damage as a sledge hammer probably would have done. There
were eleven different rooms in the whaling station, and we tried to spend
as much time as possible to cover all of them. They had six huge
Caterpillar generators that they used to run the refrigeration units and
stuff. We spent at least an hour and a half, probably longer, methodically
taking them apart—bending valves, filling sumps with stuff, cutting
gauges. It was taking forever and we were getting all sweaty. We realized
that we could be there all night. A group of ten people could be there all
night sabotaging that stuff."

Outside they found the sterile trailer where the "research" was under- 29
taken. That the justification for this vast computerized world of cen-
trifuges, refrigeration, and electricity generation was for *research* became
all the more unbelievable when they broke into the small portable building. "They had a couple of microscopes and some whale tissue samples,"
Coronado says disgustedly. "It wasn't a laboratory.... It was on the fringe
of being a laboratory. They'd take a few samples to tell how old the
whales were, whether they were females, male, how long they were.
Basic statistics," a hush puppy to appease the pliant IWC.

At one point the saboteurs split up. Soon, Howitt discovered Whale 30
Meat Mountain stored in several massive refrigerators. He tried to maneu-
ver a fork lift to remove the "meat" and dump it down the slipway. When
that didn't work, Coronado and Howitt settled for wedging open the
freezer doors. "We cut off all the refrigeration, then we sabotaged all the
refrigeration units," Coronado says. "That was dangerous because we
starting cutting lines without knowing what they were for. Freon started
escaping and I started getting these visions of this environmental disaster
occurring in this beautiful fiord, so we just shut it down and left it like that.
We hoped to leave the meat like that long enough so that it would thaw
and they wouldn't be able to re-freeze the meat without damaging it. In
the end they claimed that it wasn't done at all." When Coronado heard
that, he urged that word be sent to the Japanese that the meat sold to them
might have become spoiled.

In the plant foreman's office the saboteurs found the "scientists' " note- 31
books and other records. They put them into their backpacks, then
smashed an array of radios used to communicate with the whaling boats.

"They had this stereo system for playing music for the employees while they were out cutting" up the whales, recalls Coronado. "We got this weird idea of leaving a tape of whale songs, or if somehow we could interfere while they were butchering and put on whale songs. It was just something we thought about. But we knew we couldn't do it, so we smashed that up, too." Before they returned to Reykjavik, they threw spare ship parts and flensing knives down the slipway and into the frigid water. And in their last act before leaving, the Sea Shepherds found gallon jugs of liquid in a laboratory and splashed their contents over desks and anything else they saw. The mysterious chemical smoked and foamed; it turned out to be cyanic acid, certain to etch deeply into whatever it touched.

Amazingly, neither of the whale warriors were ever scared during their   32
four-hour raid. "I don't remember any fear at all," Howitt says. "We had a lot of adrenaline flowing. Excited, I guess, is the word. We knew what we were doing, we were careful, methodical, and we felt we were doing a good job. We were alert—that's the adrenaline that keeps you alert. We were working pretty hard." Their determination and the elation at inflicting so much damage on the reviled industry drove them. Says Coronado, "We had made the promise that if the other got caught, *continue,* try to go forward and do the job.... Even if we get caught and jailed, we have to do what we can, even if it costs us our own freedom. We didn't put ourselves on any higher moral plane. We had decided to do this job." He adds, "Yes, we did that at a great risk. But to me it was a greater risk had we not accomplished it. I don't know how I would have felt if we had been nailed before we got into the whaling station or onto those ships. I would have felt like I had failed the whales."

Sinking Half the Fleet

Coronado and Howitt arrived back at Reykjavik at 1:30 on Sunday   33
morning, too early to sabotage the whaling ships unnoticed. They used the next hour or so to eat a bite and rest from the excitement at the whaling station. Composed, they pulled into the harbor parking lot. There was only one other car. Coronado and Howitt knew from their reconnaissance to expect only the night watchman to be around. The three seaworthy whaling ships—a fourth was in dry dock—were tied up side by side, and the watchman always spent the night on the nicer of the three, the one farthest from the dock. Masked by their common everyday wear for late fall in Iceland—balaklavas and hooded jacket—they dashed through the freezing night toward the lone whaler tied directly to the dock.

Coronado and Howitt knew that they would only be able to sink the   34
Hvalur 6 and the *Hvalur 7* because damaging the third ship would have

risked the guard's life and thereby violated the Sea Shepherds' code of non-violence. They wasted no time in getting to their task. "There was nobody around," says Coronado. "We timed it so that the tide was out enough so that the gunnel of the first ship was level with the docks. All we had to do was hop over. The engine room hatch was open. All the lights were on. Dave checked to see that no one was on board, just ran around the cabins." Then they went to work below decks of the 140-foot vessel.

Most ships' engines are cooled using salt water circulated by a pump. 35 A tightly sealed cover, called a "salt water cooling valve," can be opened in dry dock should the need arise to service the cooling system. Opening the vent when the ship is in the water, however, causes flooding and can sink a ship if the valve is not promptly closed. Coronado and Howitt lifted one after another of the heavy steel deck plates that made up the engine room's floor, searching beneath them for the manhole cover-sized valve. When they found it, they used the ship's tools to remove most of the bolts, then pried at the valve until water began seeping in. They tasted it: salty.

Together, the scuttlers moved on to the other ship without complete- 36 ly removing the first whaler's cooling valve; they feared that by doing so, the ship would sink before they could finish the job. The locked cabin door to the second ship was coaxed open with bolt cutters. After checking to see that no one else was aboard, they moved to the engine room and found the cooling system valve at the same location as on its twin ship. "We took off all the bolts but couldn't get the valve off," Coronado says. "So Dave ran to get a pry bar from the boat. I was sitting on the valve, and just as he was leaving all of a sudden, spshshsh, spshshshsh, water started squirting everywhere. I said, 'Dave, we'd better split. This thing's gonna go right now.' We pulled at the valve a little bit, then 'pop, pop' and water started gurgling all over the deck plates. Me and Dave got soaked, and we said, 'Shit, let's get outta here! This boat's gonna sink.'" They returned to the other ship and applied a pry bar to the valve with the same results. Mission accomplished, they threw their tools into the harbor and scampered to their car. Looking back, Howitt saw the boats listing. Half the Icelandic whaling fleet was harmlessly sinking to the harbor floor.

Trouble with the First Rule

Actually, their mission was not fully accomplished. The universally un- 37 derstood first rule of eco-defense, Don't Get Caught, had yet to test the young raiders. It didn't wait any longer. All day Coronado and Howitt had run on adrenaline and purpose. Nothing had deterred them, not missing their last meal or a battery sapped from playing the radio or even a misplaced but quickly found car key at the quarry parking site. Then fate threw them one final adrenaline rush. Coronado, who was driving, tells the story in a calm voice. "Not two minutes after we got into the car—where we had the record books, and I was wet from the knees down and I had grease all over me from the whaling station, plus we were wearing dark clothes—boom! A cop pulls me over. "I didn't even worry about it. I thought, 'They can't be *that* quick, they can't be that good.' When I rented the car I read about a bunch of their laws, and they said they were really strict about drunk driving. I thought, 'Just play it cool.' Sure enough, the policeman comes to the driver's side and asks me to get out of the car. He asked me to get in the back of his car. I had a stupid grin on my face, just tried to act as innocent as possible. I showed him my California driver's license, then he and his partner started speaking Icelandic. Then he asked, 'Have you been drinking any alcohol?' I said, 'Of course not. I don't drink.' He said, 'Okay. Have a nice trip,' and sent me on my way.

"David couldn't believe it! There they had me in the back seat of their car. You know those guys got yelled at when someone put the stories together!" Howitt had remained cool but felt fearful for the first time that night. "We didn't really think it was possible that we would be caught at that stage," says Howitt. 'An hour later—then it would have been a different story.... I was left in the passenger seat wondering whether to make a run for it but obviously knowing that we first had to check." During their reconnoitering, Coronado and Howitt hit many of the high spots in Iceland—docks, the whaling station, the meat processing plant, and a zoo outside of Reykjavik where captured orca ("killer") whales, harbor seals, and birds were held before being sold to marine parks or other facilities. The two thought they might be able to release a number of the animals before going to the airport. But they ran out of time—the scuttling operation took an hour and a half, and it was well after four in the morning by the time the police released Coronado. It was the only aspect of the ambitious mission that might be considered a "failure," and only the missed restaurant meal could rival it as a disappointment. 38

Once they had cleared customs at the airport, Coronado and Howitt learned that the poor weather conditions had forced a delay in their flight's departure, which was scheduled for 7:30. Anxious hours of waiting ensued. "Little did we know at the time but that they had discovered the ships," Coronado says. "They had sunk in thirty minutes." Watson had told them that the *Sea Shepherd,* which had been scuttled by opening its cooling valve, took about three hours to go down. "We thought 'Oh, we've got plenty of time,'" Coronado recalls. "But as it turns out, we didn't have plenty of time. The ships sunk right away. They discovered them right away, too. But the police dispatcher only sent one car to investigate because he didn't suspect sabotage. They knew about it 39 ore the flight left, but they didn't have the sense to

forty-five minute m and shut down the airport."

put out a gene witt escaped safely to Luxembourg, where Coronado   40

Coronado y in England. "I just said, 'Everything's been done just

called Sara wo went down and we got the station as well.' Then I

like we w called Paul Watson with the news. When the story got

hung u ped on it. Coronado says, "A reporter called Paul to see

out, t wanted to accept responsibility. Of course, if lightning

if S the Sea Shepherd agents were safely hidden in Europe.

ship, Paul would accept responsibility for it." Watson told

velandic authorities) believed us until they discovered the

on," says Coronado. "Then they thought we had done that

king the ships. They launched this big manhunt, looking for

r they thought that might be. Of course, we were long gone by

great because we hitchhiked from Luxembourg through Bel-   41
t on a ferry to Dover, got a bus from Dover to London, got off the
n London. We were going over to Plymouth to meet Sarah. I re-
mber going up to a kiosk where they had a bunch of newspapers. Of
course we went to look for our dirty work, and there, on the front pages,
was the headline, 'Saboteurs Scuttle Whaling Ships, Photo Page 6.' At that
point we didn't know whether they had possibly seen them and plugged
up the valves or what. We bought the papers and sure enough, there was
the photo of the two ships. Then we knew we had been effective. But it
didn't say a word about the whaling station." Coronado was amazed that
the authorities had not checked there, too, especially after the police
found that the ships were sunk through deliberate tampering. "They
didn't discover the whaling station until Monday morning," he says con-
temptuously. "They didn't even have enough sense to check it. It wasn't
discovered until people showed up for work."

In Plymouth, a network of safe houses was established to harbor   42
Coronado and Howitt. "I talked to Paul, and he felt the best thing was for
me to be in my own home country," Coronado says. "I flew to New York
and met him there." A press conference in Cleveland Armory's office
began a hectic several weeks of interviews and travelling for Coronado.
Meanwhile, Howitt flew to Greece to lay low and relax. Soon after the
action, Greenpeace announced a boycott against Icelandic fish products
that Coronado credits as the final blow to the tiny nation's whaling industry. Thus, for a time the "niches" of marine mammal organizations and
activists actually worked as a system, and they succeeded in focusing
intense pressure on Iceland in particular and on whaling in general.
However, Coronado noticed that it did not take long before every article

about the action "had at least one paragraph where Greenpeace separated itself from it and condemned it. But at the same time I think it was good because it showed that Greenpeace didn't support direct against whalers." Within Iceland, public opinion turned from several of the population in favor of whaling to sharply divided ent of months after the action. Sea Shepherd membership there grew of to 200, and one member founded the Whale Friends Society of Skarphedinsson, Sea Shepherd's leading advocate in Iceland, ha before nearly half of the nation's 20,000 teenagers and reports concerns are spreading to animal rights and ecology in general.

Looking back on it, Coronado and Howitt see that they star avalanche of publicity on whaling at a time that the whaling industry hoping to quietly go on about its deadly business. "A lot of people tho that the moratorium was in effect and that whaling was over," Corona says. "We showed that it was indeed continuing. The scientific and env ronmental communities started questioning why they were continuing t kill whales." All of the negative publicity placed the whaling industry on the defensive, making it appear guilty. In the public eye, Iceland was tried and convicted. Whale Meat Mountain was less mean than mess, and the "scientific research" whaling had only the most tenuous links to research. Although none of the documents that the Sea Shepherds absconded with were directly incriminating, oddities stood out. The sizes of many of the whales killed by the Icelanders were recorded as just over the legal minimum length established by the IWC. Without fail, females were always listed as "dry;" by regulation, lactating females are not supposed to be killed.

But the most damning evidence was that Iceland never charged 44 Coronado and Howitt, or anyone else, for the destruction of the whaling station and the ship scuttlings. "I wrote to Iceland *three times* demanding to know what charges were going to be laid," Paul Watson says, "and Iceland wouldn't answer my letters. In January of 1988 I flew to Reykjavik to demand that charges be laid, and they refused to lay charges.... What we proved through that campaign is that what we did was perfectly valid and legal." The whale processing facility eventually was repaired at enormous cost. The two sunken ships were raised from the bottom of Reykjavik harbor in unusable condition. They were eventually re-outfitted, but in 1989 Iceland discontinued its whaling operations until the International Whaling Commission could meet in 1990 to reconsider its moratorium on commercial whaling. Ultimately, "the commission refused to even consider a request from Iceland for an annual whaling quota of 200 minke whales." The ban on whaling worldwide remains in effect.

In the three and a half years since the attack, Howitt has spent nearly 45 all of his time aboard the *Sea Shepherd II* as its chief engineer. When not on board, he has travelled to Alaska and Morocco to help clean up the massive oil spills there. Coronado continued to sail with the Sea Shepherds, although he and partner Sue Rodriguez-Pastor decided to stop crewing with them in 1990. They established an environmental research and investigations service to expose ecologically damaging practices. Coronado is active in Earth First! and Animal Liberation causes as well. Following the Iceland action, the FBI visited him and has returned several times since with questions about everything from Animal Liberation activities to an alleged bomb planting at an Army recruiting center.

Perhaps more annoying than the FBI intrusions were the pitiful attempts by the American press after Iceland to decipher "what was so unique and strange about this kid that he would want to do this crazy thing," Coronado says. To the media "it wasn't a question of why did I do it, it was *what* made me do it." The honest answer to the former, "the whales," was never adequate. He adds, "I just want to tell people that they can do the same thing if they are committed enough, and if they believe in it enough. They should set their goals as high as they want and they can achieve them. Don't feel like there is only this one 'element' of people in the world who do these types of thing. It isn't that way. It's just that some people have reached a certain level and they just can't tolerate it any more." Once they have overcome the Eco-Wall within themselves they are "compelled to follow a higher law and to not follow the laws that are established by the power structure to protect themselves. Sometimes you have to not question whether it's right or wrong but how you're going to do it."

QUESTIONS FOR DISCUSSION AND WRITING

1. Coronado and Howitt report that they were careful not to violate the Sea Shepherd's "code of non-violence" (par. 34) as they prepared to sink the two whaling ships. Earlier that same night, the two men had methodically destroyed millions of dollars worth of machinery and computer equipment. What does this apparent contradiction say about how they define "non-violence"? How does their definition differ from your own?

2. The two saboteurs base their attack on the claim that Iceland was feigning research on whales in order to hunt whales for profit, a practice banned by international agreements. What evidence does Scarce report to support this contention? Does the evidence seem sufficient to Coronado and Howitt? To Scarce? Do you find the evidence convincing?

3. How would you characterize Rik Scarce's attitude toward Coronado and Howitt? Toward the actions they take? Toward the people and the industry that are the targets of the sabotage? As you consider your response, point to specific terms that Scarce uses to describe the two men, their actions, and the whalers.

ASSIGNMENT
SEQUENCES

Assignment Sequence One:
The Intrinsic Value of Nature

Readings: Maclean, from "A River Runs Through It"
Emerson, from *Nature*
Gore, "Environmentalism of the Spirit" from *Earth in the Balance*
Scarce, "Raid on Reykjavik" from *Eco-Warriors*
O'Rourke, "The Greenhouse Affect"

Assignment 1

Reading: From "A River Runs Through It"

Maclean describes in great detail the fly-fishing skill of his brother, Paul. We learn not only of Paul's grace but also of the way in which he has to think his way into the mind of the fish, almost into the mind of nature itself. But all this grace and effort are put in the service of an activity that is of value only to human beings. Fish are thought of simply as creatures to be out-thought and then hauled out of their natural element until the legal limit is reached. There is never any discussion of the importance of nature for its own sake.

Maclean and his father identify with Paul's skill and find meaning in it. Much of the emotional power of the story comes from the way in which this skill helps Maclean and his father make sense of Paul's death, or at least come to terms with it. It is clear in the story that the meaning of fly fishing is tied up with the discipline and skill invested in it. It has its rules and harsh demands that help shape experience. The concentration and focus provided by the discipline make it a powerful shaper of meaning. And this meaning is one that is driven by human needs—for example, the need for solace or ways to understand human relationships.

Describe some activity or skill in which you participate that demands something like the discipline needed for fly fishing. Don't try to make this activity stand for some sort of big meaning. Instead, pay attention to its texture, to its own particular demands, rules, and satisfactions. In other words, let a careful description of the activity say what you have to say. It might be something you do outdoors, perhaps skiing, canoeing, or hiking; or it might be something done inside, like playing an instrument or sewing a quilt. If you deal with an activity that takes place in the natural world,

471

discuss how nature affects the meaning you find in the activity. If the activity does not take place in a natural setting, discuss the role of the "natural" aspects of it—for example, the use of natural materials or physical skills. Try to show how the meaning of this activity is intertwined with your own needs and desires.

Assignment 2

Reading: From *Nature*

This is a difficult essay written by one of the most important figures in Nineteenth-Century American culture. A careful reading of it will help you think through one important notion of our rightful relationship with nature. Emerson himself tries to think through the difficult question of the relationship among human beings, nature, spirit, beauty, and human motivation. In doing this, he sometimes implies that nature is valuable because of what it offers human beings, from the mundane value of commodities to the way in which it motivates human actions. At other times he implies that nature has a certain value in and of itself because of the degree to which it is in contact with a higher power.

Write an essay in which you point out the various places where *Nature* either locates the value of nature in its utility for human beings or in some intrinsic quality of nature itself. How does Emerson reconcile these two positions? Or does he even try to do so? Which of the two positions do you find more convincing or important in your way of thinking? Think of this as an exploratory essay in which you don't have to tie up Emerson's work into a tidy little ball, but instead work to explore the richness of his thought.

Assignment 3

Readings: "Environmentalism of the Spirit" from *Earth in the Balance* and from *Nature*

If Emerson is somewhat ambiguous about whether or not nature has an intrinsic value, Gore is not. He feels that nature and humans are so intertwined that they can't be separated without disastrous consequences. This argument is based on the value of a spiritual wholeness that takes in all of life and all of the natural world. Gore quotes approvingly from James Lovelock's discussion of the Gaia hypothesis: "We now see that the air, the ocean and the soil are much more than a mere environment for life; they are a part of life itself. Thus the air is to life just as is the fur to a cat or the nest for a bird." Gore goes on to add a spiritual dimension to Lovelock's ideas: "It is my own belief that the image of God can be seen in every corner of creation, even in us, but only faintly." The opposite of the wholeness Gore advocates is alienation and mechanization, which lead to the destruction of others and to harm to ourselves. Do you endorse Gore's ideas? Does the idea of God's being present in every corner of creation make sense to you?

Write an essay in which you explain why you agree or disagree with Gore's ideas. In talking about the value of nature, you should go back to Emerson and ask yourself how he would feel about Gore's ideas. In his search for a sense of wholeness, Emerson has different ways of talking than do modern thinkers. What are they, and do you find them more or less understandable than those of Gore? You also might want to use examples from your own experience to expand your position.

Assignment 4

Reading: "Raid on Reykjavik" from *Eco-Warriors*

The story of Coronado and Howitt's raid on the whaling station and whaling ships of Reykjavik is told as a tale of high adventure with a strong moral purpose. The author claims that one of the proofs of their moral purpose is that Iceland never brought charges against the two. Yet it certainly is true that the ecotage caused a lot of damage, and even though the conspirators made an effort to be nonviolent, their run through the ships to make sure nobody was on board was done very quickly, and they well might have missed somebody who was asleep somewhere on the ship with disastrous results. In addition, even though the owner of the whaling business is portrayed as a rich man, the action certainly put a number of working-class Icelanders out of work.

Suppose that Coronado and Howitt had been caught and charged with destruction of property. And suppose that the prosecutor was asking for twenty years as a fit punishment for the two and that you were on the jury. What punishment, if any, do you think would be appropriate for Coronado and Howitt? Write a statement in which you recommend what you see as a fair decision in this trial. Your audience is other members of the jury, most of whom disagree with you.

Assignment 5

Reading: "The Greenhouse Affect"

Although it often seems that O'Rourke is more concerned with making a good joke than with considering an issue carefully, he does make a number of important points about the intrinsic value of nature in this essay. One of them has to do with the value of the material progress that is part of the lives of many Americans. As he says, "Contempt for material progress is not only funny but unfair. The average Juan, Chang or Mobutu out there in the parts of the world where every day is Earth Day—or Dirt and Squalor Day anyhow–would like to have a color television too. He'd also like some comfy Reeboks, a Nintendo Power Glove and a Jeep Cherokee." Leaving aside O'Rourke's use of names to reinforce a stereotype, the idea that most of the world would like to have our level of material progress does have some validity, as does the idea that much of the world lives closer to nature than we do. In the end, O'Rourke is claiming that the technology that separates us from nature is a good thing. In part, it is what makes us civilized and has led to the scientific advances of our time.

Describe what you believe is the appropriate level of technology for us to use at this point in history. The two extremes would be a life lived in a technologically advanced city such as New York, one in which nature seems very far away, and a life lived in the Third World. Keep in mind that even those people who live in the Third World have a great deal of technology, ranging from agricultural tools such as plows to wells and some form of building technology. You also might want to describe some sort of middle ground, or even a style of life that is unknown at this time—for example, a society that uses advanced electronics but not fossil fuels.

Assignment 6

Read back over all the pieces you have written in this assignment sequence. Are there contradictions in what you have written so far? If so, what are they, and what do you now want to say about them? Are these contradictions in some way inevitable, or should you try to find some way to make your ideas consistent? That is, do they make your thought richer and more complex, as may be true with Emerson's contradictions?

If you can find no contradictions in what you have written, you must have some unified position about the question of whether or not nature has an intrinsic value. Lay out that position as clearly as you can using the ideas you have generated in this sequence.

Assignment Sequence Two:
Reflecting upon Individual Encounters with Nature

Readings: Kerouac, "Alone on a Mountaintop"
Hawthorne, *The Scarlet Letter*
Alcosser, "Approaching August"
Thoreau, "Solitude" from *Walden*
Dillard, "Living Like Weasels"
Scarce, "Raid on Reykjavik" from *Eco-Warriors*

Assignment 1

Reading: "Alone on a Mountaintop"

As the selections in this book suggest, human encounters with the natural world are many and varied. Some are objective and scientific, some philosophical and abstract, some political and sociological. In many of the readings in this book, however, writers recall personal, immediate encounters with nature. In fact, in readings as diverse as those by Columbus, Audubon, Burroughs, and Bird, we see moments of great joy or recognition and moments of great confusion or even fear, as writers are overcome by the vastness or the strangeness of the wilderness. At the beginning of "Alone on a Mountaintop," for example, we see Kerouac's young hero overcome with self-doubt and fear as he spends a night alone in the wilderness.

Write an essay in which you recall a specific encounter you have had in nature, one that created some strong emotion in you. It may be a time when you were pushed to the edge of your physical or emotional endurance; it may be a time when you were frightened by a snake or bear; it may be a time when you found yourself suddenly alone in the middle of the night, listening to some wild creature tear through your food stash. Whatever incident you choose, take care to create the context of the encounter—where you were, exactly, why you were there, and with whom.

Assignment 2

Readings: From *The Scarlet Letter* and "Approaching August"

Once Kerouac's young hero settles down, he finds peace and self-healing in the wild forests of the Pacific Northwest. In fact, a common theme in many of the readings in this book is that nature can offer us refuge from the tensions of our daily lives. Many of the writers refer to particular moments of peacefulness or escape, and often these moments happen in a specific place—some riverbank or forest glen where they felt they had managed to get away and to find at least temporary solace. Two readings evoke such moments and places with particular power. In "A Flood of Sunshine" from *The Scarlett Letter*, Hawthorne allows Hester Prynne and Reverend Dimmesdale a brief escape in the forest. In other parts of the novel, the forest is a place of darkness and evil, but here the two lovers and their daughter are somehow consoled by the calm beauty of that secret place. As you reread this piece, notice how Hawthorne carefully creates a sense of physical place in order to show nature's effects on his troubled characters. In her short poem, Alcosser describes a place on the banks of the Bitterroot river where she goes to escape the busy life of "civilization" and to restore her spirits. There among the fish and flowers "all meanness is forgiven," Alcosser promises.

Write a descriptive essay in which you describe some special place in nature where you go to be alone or to escape the complications of daily life. It need not be a faraway place deep in the wilderness; in fact, it might be a small city park, a busy campground at a nearby lake, or a well-worn bike trail behind your house. As do Hawthorne and Alcosser, let the precise physical details help to create a strong sense of this place. Don't just tell us why a place is special; help us to see the place for ourselves.

Assignment 3

Readings: "Solitude" from *Walden* and "Living Like Weasels"

While some personal encounters with nature produce strong emotions or reactions, others evoke reflection and speculative thought. Most of the writers in this book are not philosophers, and yet we see scientists, essayists, naturalists, and even politicians so moved by their individual encounters with nature that they feel compelled to speculate about our larger place in the natural world.

For both Thoreau and Dillard, the moment of philosophical puzzlement or insight leapt out at them from a particular encounter with nature. Thoreau uses one "delicious evening" spent alone at Walden to speculate about the ideal relationship of civilization and the natural world. "Am I not partly leaves and vegetable mould myself?" he wonders. Startled by some weasels in the suburbs, Dillard begins to wonder if we might not be better off living like animals: "open to time and death painlessly, noticing everything, remembering nothing."

Write an essay in which you allow yourself to think some lofty thoughts about nature and our place in it. Obviously, "nature" is far too broad a topic to take on as a whole, so you may want to look at some of the specific questions asked by Thoreau: What should be the relationship of civilization and nature? From which of the two should we take our cues about living our lives? Or look to the kinds of questions asked by Dillard: What traits of animals would serve us well? What can animals teach us about how best to live our lives?

As do Thoreau and Dillard, see if you can ground your speculation in some particular experience in nature.

Assignment 4

Reading: "Raid on Reykjavik" from *Eco-Warriors*

Sometimes individual encounters with nature move people to take direct and even violent action. Some forms of direct action are quite modest and local—deciding to recycle or to join a neighborhood clean-up effort. Others involve global issues and extreme measures, as we see in Scarce's account of two ecowarriors who destroy valuable machinery and sink two expensive ships in order to protect whales.

Write an essay in which you discuss your own involvement with and your attitudes toward these various forms of direct action. Begin your essay by discussing your own local situation. What opportunities for action are available in your hometown or on your campus? What kinds of things can people try to accomplish? Do their efforts seem effective? Discuss your own participation in direct action, or your reasons for not participating. In the second part of the essay, present your views of the direct action taken by people like the ecowarriors. Look for places in Scarce's account where the ecowarriors attempt to justify their actions. Do you find their arguments compelling? In your view, should there be limits to our defense of "Mother Nature"?

Assignment 5

Read back through the essays you have written in this assignment sequence and choose the one you would most like to revise. You may choose the essay whose ideas most interest you; or the essay in which your views still seem vague or unsettled. It may be an essay in which you simply have more to say after having completed the rest of the sequence. Whichever essay you choose, use this revision as an opportunity to rethink and further develop your ideas.

Assignment Sequence Three:
The Influence of Nature

Readings: Momaday, from *The Way to Rainy Mountain*
Abbey, from *The Monkey Wrench Gang*
Callenbach, from *Ecotopia*
Thoreau, "Solitude" from *Walden*

Assignment 1

Reading: From *The Way to Rainy Mountain*

Using family stories, the legends of the Kiowas, and bits of history, Momaday describes a complex relationship between human beings and their environment. The Kiowas came to the Great Plains of America at a time that is within reach of recorded history, and they both adapted to the rigors of that place and shaped that place to meet their own needs and outlook. Within the plains they found a place of great freedom, openness, and beauty, but also a harsh place that made them strong in a number of ways. They found a certain harmony with nature for almost a hundred years, until the Europeans destroyed the buffalo and the Kiowa way of life.

Write an exploratory essay in which you consider the relationship between the Kiowas and the Great Plains. How did the plains shape the Kiowas, and how did the Kiowas shape the plains? You might want to consider the ways in which the various legends work within these relationships. What do the legends say about the Kiowa people, and how do the people use the legends to help make sense of their lives? And what does Momaday think has been lost with the passing of the Kiowa culture? There is a strong sense of nostalgia running through the essay. What good has passed from the earth, and what that is perhaps not so good?

Assignment 2

Reading: From *The Monkey Wrench Gang*

The characters in *The Monkey Wrench Gang*—Smith, Hayduke, Sarvis, and Abbzug—seem to be quite different from the Kiowas described in *The Way to Rainy Mountain*. Unlike the Native Americans, who live in a certain harmony with nature, Abbey's characters sometimes seem oblivious to the nature that surrounds them. In a section of the book not included in this reading, they toss beer cans by the side of the road, drink excessively, and feel obliged to end up "puking on innocent sand, befouling God's sweet earth." At least the men indulge in this sort of behavior. In the section excerpted here, the road-building machines are portrayed as living creatures, dinosaurs, that the gang takes great joy in destroying. The joy they feel is tied to the "considerable involuntary admiration" they have for the "controlled and directed superhuman force" of the machine-dinosaurs. The gang has a certain blood-lust for the hunt and the kill, a lust that is far different from the Native American conception of hunting as a necessary yet regrettable activity. In addition, Sarvis indulges in the violent destruction of an anthill. Although he rationalizes his anger, it seems clear that there are certain parts of nature he hates.

But there are similarities between the characters in *The Monkey Wrench Gang* and those in *The Way to Rainy Mountain*. Both works indulge in a certain nostalgia for the loss of pure nature, and both sets of characters value strength and what might be called ruthlessness. How do you account for the similarities and differences between the two works? Is there some sort of behavior that nature demands of human beings who live close to it, even people as widely separated in time and circumstances as the Kiowas and Abbey's characters? How much freedom do people have to shape their responses to nature?

Assignment 3

Reading: From *Ecotopia*

The relationship between human beings and nature in Ecotopia seems very different from that described in Abbey's book. The inhabitants of Ecotopia work hard to live in harmony with nature. In fact, everything they do, from eating to playing to working, is shaped by their desire to live ecologically. Even their political discussions are shaped by a desire to listen to everybody and not be controlled by a single voice. They believe that wisdom arises from this natural process, just as the earth, when left to itself with no controlling force from above, will bring itself into a productive and peaceful harmony.

But how realistic is this image of human life? Consider one aspect of life discussed in this excerpt, and describe how well your own experience bears out the value of the way of life described in Ecotopia. You might consider schooling, which in Ecotopia seems very informal and loose when compared with our institutions. Which method of education seems better to you? What are the advantages and disadvantages of each method? Or you might look at exercise and sports. Professional sports seem inconceivable in Ecotopia, yet in our culture they dictate much of how we conceive of exercise and how we spend our time.

Finally, step back from your comparison and speculate on whether or not the "natural" way of doing things really does seem better or worse. What can we take from nature and what should we not take?

Assignment 4

Readings: From *Ecotopia* and from *The Monkey Wrench Gang*

Ecotopia is a book written in the form of a report by William Weston, an inhabitant of the non-Ecotopian United States, for a newspaper. It consists of both formal stories written for the newspaper and informal diaries written for Weston's eyes alone. Although Weston has his doubts about Ecotopia before he gets there, doubts caused in part by the particular perspective he has known in the world he lives in, he slowly begins to see the value of the Ecotopian way of doing things. He begins to believe that it is possible to live a "natural" life that takes nothing from the earth that it does not give back, and that is sustainable forever, in theory. Part of the reason he is able to change his views is that he is a writer, a reporter who by profession has to be open to other perspectives.

Sarvis and Hayduke are another matter. In the first description of Hayduke in *The Monkey Wrench Gang*, in a section not in your reading, he is presented as a bum, "fiercely bearded, short, squat, malevolent, his motor vehicle loaded with dangerous weapons." In your reading he is profane, sexist, and single-minded. Sarvis is something of a philosopher and a poet. Although he seems to share many of the Ecotopian concerns, he also has a jaded, cynical, and violent air about him. It is hard to see him taking part in a free-form Ecotopian discussion.

Write a report on Ecotopia as it would be written by Sarvis or Hayduke, or another character in *The Monkey Wrench Gang*. Look closely at how the character is presented, and then try to show how that particular character's personality would interact with the people and institutions in Ecotopia. In this report, be sure to show how the character writing the report would view Ecotopia, given his or her attitude toward the shaping power of nature. You may write the report as a formal story for a newspaper, or as a private diary, or as both.

Assignment 5

Reading: "Solitude" from *Walden*

Although Thoreau's writing is difficult to read, in part because of its allusive nature and its tendency to circle around topics, it will repay the care put into it. In this section from *Walden,* it is clear that Thoreau values the solitude he finds in nature. He turns away from the company of other humans in order to make his life in the woods around Walden Pond. In order to help in your reading of this selection, make a list of the good influences Thoreau finds while living in the woods and of the destructive influences he sees in human society. Use the list to generalize about the value that Thoreau finds in nature. What does nature teach him? How are his life and his perceptions changed by nature? How would living in society detract from the valuable influences nature provides?

After you have generalized about the value Thoreau finds in nature, discuss the importance of these values in our modern society. Are they lessons we need to learn? Are we further from them than even the Nineteenth-Century society Thoreau avoided? Are they simply outdated and not appropriate for our lives? Is there some way we need to modify them in order to make them work for us?

Assignment 6

Write a position statement in which you lay out what you believe is your ideal relationship with nature. Be as honest as you can in this statement, discussing both what your relationship with nature really is and how you want to change it. Use the readings and previous writings in this assignment sequence as part of your statement. Use the ones you agree with to support your position, and show why you don't believe the ones with which you disagree. Has the nature you have experienced shaped you in some way as it has the Kiowas? Have you worked to live in harmony with nature, or, like Hayduke, have you tossed beer cans onto the highway in some way? Have you used nature to get away from the fragmentation of society as Thoreau does? Or do you find the positions taken by these writers idealistic and unworkable? Does it really make sense to turn to nature as a pattern for our ways of dealing with the world in a modern society that has seen the "end of nature"?

Assignment Sequence Four:
Constructing Nature Locally–The Campus as a Natural Landscape

Readings: Columbus, from the *Digest of Columbus's Log-Book on His First Voyage*
Jefferson, from *Notes on the State of Virginia*
Crèvecoeur, from *Letters from an American Farmer*
Pollan, "The Idea of a Garden"
Callenbach, from *Ecotopia*

Assignment 1

Readings: From the *Digest of Columbus's Log-Book on His First Voyage* and from *Notes on the State of Virginia*

One of the first things that travelers do is to provide those back home with clear descriptions of the landscape around them. Both Columbus and Jefferson take great care to survey objectively the key features of the terrain, its rivers and harbors, and its flora and fauna. Columbus finds himself in a completely strange land and so tries to compare what he sees to what he knew at home. At times, both writers tell their readers that they have no words for what they see or that they are unable to fully grasp its size or beauty. In places, these writers offer a judgment about what they see, but for the most part they stick to providing a detailed account of the natural terrain.

Write an essay in which you imagine you are an explorer surveying the natural landscape of your college campus. First, outline its overall character and shape. For example, my campus is a huge square surrounded on three sides by large fields of well-mowed grass, and on the fourth side by the university golf course. That done, point out its most famous and valued features. My campus has a long walkway lined with massive old oak trees; it is an area often used for public events and shows up in most brochures about our school. Note also how the landscape of your campus changes with the seasons.

Assignment 2

Reading: From *Letters from an American Farmer*

Assignment 1 asked you to write a more or less "objective" description of the natural landscape of your campus, noting but not commenting on its key features. As you reread Crèvecoeur's *Letters*, you will notice that he not only describes the natural landscape of rural America, he interprets it. Throughout the piece, Crèvecoeur offers his views about how the land both nurtures and reflects the character of the people who inhabit it. Crèvecouer clearly believes that the way people live with nature says a good deal about their principles and beliefs. Nicely kept, unpretentious farms reflect a simple, industrious people who live in harmony with nature.

Write an essay in which you "read" or interpret the natural landscape you have described in Assignment 1. If we were to walk around your campus, what would we conclude about how humans relate to and live with nature—harmony? conflict? confusion? Whenever possible, point to specific features of the landscape that help to illustrate your points. You may also want to consider how the natural landscape of your campus is used to represent your school in official brochures or promotional catalogs.

Assignment 3

Reading: "The Idea of a Garden"

As you reread Pollan's essay, notice how he connects a specific feature of his town's landscape to a wider view of nature. Pollan questions the decision to "return" the destroyed grove of trees to their "natural" state, in part because he believes we can never recover (or even know) what original "nature" would have been like. Pollan argues for other, more pragmatic uses for the land.

Write an essay in which you argue for some change in the natural environment of your campus. It could be ideas for improving or restoring the landscape by planting more trees, reducing the amount of concrete and asphalt, finding ways to stop people from wearing paths in the grass fields. It may also be matters of ecological policy that would, in your view, help to improve the environment of the campus: a ban on insecticides, a better recycling program to reduce litter, reducing auto traffic on campus. Conclude your essay with a discussion of how such changes happen on your campus. This may involve doing some research about what committees, offices, or administrators would be involved. Find out who would make the final decision and interview that person (or persons) in order to understand fully the process of bringing about changes to your campus.

Assignment 4

Readings: Old college brochures, yearbooks, or pictures of your campus

Obviously, the natural landscape you have described and interpreted has changed over time. Changes happen for various reasons. Some are pragmatic—as campuses grow, development is required; change also happens for aesthetic reasons—our changing tastes and perceptions of beauty influence everything from the layout of private gardens to our definitions of "wilderness." Finally, natural landscapes change for various "natural" reasons—fire, disease, drought, or cold.

Conduct some research in order to find out more about how (and why) your campus has changed over time. One good source will be old yearbooks or college catalogs, since they often have pictures of the campus's key natural features. You can also check with the admissions office or library, both of which might have archives of old pictures or paintings of the campus. If possible, look back at several historical periods—twenty years ago, fifty, one hundred. If your campus wasn't there one hundred years ago, how was the land being used? Once you have some information, write an essay in which you describe and discuss the most significant changes the natural landscape of your campus has undergone. In your view, what difference do the changes make? Have they improved or harmed the way people live with nature?

Assignment 5

Reading: From *Ecotopia*

In *Ecotopia*, Callenbach allows himself to imagine what it will be like to live in the future. He carefully reports on the social and cultural practices of the people he finds in Ecotopia, and he tries to explain how people live in a more ideal relationship with the natural world. For the final assignment of this sequence, write an essay (or a piece of speculative fiction) in which you imagine the future of your campus. First, decide how far into the future you want to look—fifty years? two hundred? five hundred? Then, let your imagination guide your look at how nature and civilization will coexist in that future. Be sure to use specific examples to let us see how the natural landscape of your campus will have changed, for better or for worse. In a sense, this essay is asking you to make some predictions about the ecological future not just of your campus but of our entire planet. Have fun with your campus of the future, but think hard about the implications of your predictions.

Assignment Sequence Five:
The Control of Nature

Readings: Jewett, "A White Heron"
Carson, from *Silent Spring*
Silko, "Landscape, History, and the Pueblo Imagination"
McPhee, from *Encounters with the Archdruid*

Assignment 1

Reading: From "A White Heron"

The young hunter in "A White Heron" wants to collect birds for his own use. As he puts it, the birds he collects are "stuffed and preserved, dozens and dozens of them." In preserving the birds, he has taken a bit of nature and killed it, and then has it for contemplation and study. Although he leaves most of the birds in their natural state, the control he exerts over the small part of nature in his collection shapes his relationship with the natural world, leaving him always on the lookout for rare and interesting birds. Sylvia, on the other hand, seems almost to become a part of nature and its rhythms. As her grandmother says of her, "There ain't a foot o' ground she don't know her way over, and the wild creatur's count her one o' themselves."

Which of these two, Sylvia or the hunter, do you feel has the most reasonable and satisfying relationship with nature? Keep in mind that the hunter doesn't want to control all of nature and that Sylvia certainly exerts some control over parts of nature. The hunter enjoys the time he spends outdoors, and he would probably want to preserve lots of wilderness. He is not a developer who wants to shape all of the natural world to human ends. And Sylvia tries to control the cow as well as other animals on the farm. In fact, the small farm itself, the site of Sylvia's happiness, is a part of nature turned to human ends. As you answer this question, be sure to keep in mind these qualifications.

Assignment 2

Reading: From *Silent Spring*

Carson argues not for a complete absence of control of nature but rather for a different kind of control. As she puts it, she wants "biological solutions, based on understanding of the living organisms they seek to control and of the whole fabric of life to which these organisms belong."

At another point she says that she advocates approaches with "a constant theme, the awareness that we are dealing with life—with living populations and all their pressures and counterpressures, their surges and recessions. Only by taking account of such life forces and by cautiously seeking to guide them into channels favorable to ourselves can we hope to achieve a reasonable accommodation between the insect hordes and ourselves."

Using Carson's distinction between the two types of control, analyze some living system that you know well. It might be a system that doesn't seek to control humans, such as a suburban lawn, a garden, or a forest used for timber, or it might be one that does involve humans, such as the family, school, military, or sports team. What sort of control seems to be in place in the system you look at: a control that takes into account life forces and seeks to guide them or one that controls absolutely with no room for accommodation? How well does this control seem to work? Why do some people attempt to gain absolute control? Are there situations in which an absolute control is necessary and others in which it is not?

Assignment 3

Reading: "Landscape, History, and the Pueblo Imagination"

"Landscape, History, and the Pueblo Imagination" is a complex essay that considers carefully the relationship between the Pueblo people and the natural world within which they live. The Pueblo people live in a harsh, dry land that makes survival difficult but that nourishes a deep spiritual and aesthetic sense. The connections the people feel with plants, animals, and inanimate features of the natural world help them survive and find beauty in the desert. Reread the essay carefully, looking for the connections that shape the Pueblo people's lives and make life possible in their dry land.

One issue to consider is the use the Pueblo people make of stories. What functions, both practical and spiritual, do their stories serve? In considering stories, also look carefully at the pictographs the people use and try to find connections between the stories and the pictographs. Another important issue is the people's attitude toward refuse. They waste nothing and look upon refuse not as some dirty, disgusting mass to be hidden or taken quickly away, but rather as a part of the cycle all living things go through. You also might take up the question of the individual as opposed to society. How does the attitude of the Pueblo people toward the nature of an individual's identity differ from ours?

Write your response as an exploratory essay in which you look for connections instead of trying to tie up all your ideas into a finished essay.

After you have explored the connections of the Pueblo people with the natural world, discuss the relationship between these connections and their attitude toward controlling the natural world.

Assignment 4

Readings: From *Silent Spring* and from "Landscape, History, and the Pueblo Imagination"

A recent thread on an electronic bulletin board having to do with gardening dealt with the difficulty of finding biological controls in the large home supply chains such as Wal-Mart, Home Depot, and Kmart. The thread was started by someone who was looking for a biological control mentioned by Carson in *Silent Spring, Bacillus thuringiensis*, or BT as it is known to gardeners. This person had to turn to a specialty store to find BT, and others on the bulletin board pointed out that the chains carry no biological controls. Instead they have rack after rack of chemical controls that many on the bulletin board feel are harmful to the environment.

Write a letter to the managers of these chains urging them to stock biological controls. Use the information provided by Carson in her selection for your evidence, and use the discussion of the proper relationship between humans and the natural world in "Landscape, History, and the Pueblo Imagination" to help suggest the advantages of not wiping out all the insect life on a crop when trying to stop the damage caused by a single species.

Assignment 5

Reading: From *Encounters with the Archdruid*

Dominy and Brower are diametrically opposed in their beliefs about what should be done with free-flowing rivers in the West. Dominy wants to dam them and control them so that human beings can make use of the power, water, and recreation they can provide. He wants as many people as possible to be able to enjoy the benefits controlled water can bring. On the other hand, Brower sees the beauty that is destroyed by dams and feels almost a spiritual loss when a river is impeded in its natural course. In spite of these differences, Dominy and Brower share a love of the outdoors and, in particular, of white-water rafting. In addition, they are alike in being hard fighters who are exceptionally stubborn in their beliefs.

Write a letter from Dominy to Brower, or from Brower to Dominy, trying to convince the recipient of the letter to change his mind about building Hualapai Dam. In the letter make use of the description of each man's past that McPhee provides to help you create the most compelling arguments. Given Dominy's history of building dams to help ranchers survive, what arguments might make him change his mind? And given Brower's long history of fighting against dams, what might make him soften his position? You also might make use of the similarities between the men to find some common ground for agreement.

Assignment 6

Read back through all you have written in this assignment sequence and all the readings you have done. What now seems to you to be the best attitude toward the control of nature? The two extremes are simply to let nature run its course or to control it absolutely. It would be difficult to sustain an argument for either extreme, but there are many intermediate positions. You might want to focus your essay by looking at some recent debate over control of the environment, perhaps the one over the wisdom of building levees to control floods or of controlling the harvesting of timber. Use the perspectives and ideas developed in this sequence to help you find a productive position.

ACKNOWLEDGMENTS

Edward Abbey. From *The Monkey Wrench Gang.* Copyright 1975 by Edward Abbey. Reprinted by permission of HarperCollins Publishers, Inc.

Sandra Alcosser. "Approaching August." From *Pushcart Anthology,* Volume 13, Number 134, 1988–89. Copyright 1988 Sandra Alcosser. Reprinted by permission of Sandra Alcosser.

Ernest Callenbach. "Car-Less Living in Ecotopia's New Towns," "Ecotopian Education's Surprises," "Ecotopian Television and Its Wares," and "The Unsporting Life of Ecotopia." From *Ecotopia.* Copyright 1975 by Ernest Callenbach. Used by permission of Bantam Books, a division of Bantam Doubleday Dell Publishing Group, Inc.

Rachel Carson. "The Other Road." From *Silent Spring.* Copyright 1962 by Rachel L. Carson. Copyright renewed 1990 by Roger Christie. Reprinted by permission of Houghton Mifflin Company. All rights reserved.

Bartolomé de Las Casas. From *The Devastation of the Indies: A Brief Account.* Copyright 1974 by The Continuum Publishing Company. Reprinted by permission of The Continuum Publishing Company.

Christopher Columbus. From *The Four Voyages of Christopher Columbus,* edited and translated by J. M. Cohen. Copyright J. M. Cohen, 1969. Reprinted by permission of Penguin Books Ltd.

Emily Dickinson. "The Brain—is wider than the Sky" and "There's a certain Slant of light." From *The Poems of Emily Dickinson,* edited by Thomas H. Johnson. Copyright 1951, 1955, 1979, 1983 by the President and Fellows of Harvard College. Reprinted by permission of Harvard University Press.

Annie Dillard. "Living Like Weasels." From *Teaching a Stone to Talk.* Copyright 1982 by Annie Dillard. Reprinted by permission of HarperCollins Publishers, Inc.

Paula DiPerna. "Truth vs. 'Facts'." From *Ms. Magazine* September/October 1991. Copyright 1991 by *Ms. Magazine.* Reprinted by permission of *Ms. Magazine.*

Gretel Ehrlich. "This Autumn Morning." From *Antaeus.* Reprinted in *The Best American Essays 1991.* Reprinted by permission of Gretel Ehrlich.

Dana Gioia. "Rough Country." From *The Gods of Winter.* Copyright by Dana Gioia. Reprinted by permission of Dana Gioia.

Al Gore. "Environmentalism of the Spirit." From *Earth in the Balance.* Copyright 1992 by Senator Al Gore. Reprinted by permission of Houghton Mifflin Company. All rights reserved.

Index of Authors and Titles